Urbanism in World Perspective:

A Reader

Urbanism in World Perspective:
A Reader

Edited by
Sylvia Fleis Fava

Brooklyn College of the City
University of New York

Thomas Y. Crowell Company

NEW YORK   ESTABLISHED 1834

Library of Congress Catalog Card Number: 68–24589

Manufactured in the United States of America

First Printing, May, 1968

Second Printing, November, 1968

To
Carol
Jeanne G.
Jeanne F.
Linda

The Urbanites of the Future

Preface

Teachers of urban sociology and related courses may be pardoned if they sometimes believe that emergence from the ethnocentric cocoon in studying the city is more a bane than a blessing. To their crisp analysis (and solution!) of the problems currently confronting American cities, they are now expected to add a reasoned evaluation of the historical and cross-cultural development of urbanism. All of this, of course, should be wrapped in a package of "real sociology," with a sharp eye toward the major theoretical concepts, classical and contemporary, which underlie the sociological study of the city.

This reader is a modest attempt to be helpful to teachers and students who are attempting to cope with the Niagara of material involved in the comparative study of urbanism. The task was undertaken in the belief that a broad comparative perspective is needed to understand and to plan wisely for the urban world which is almost upon us.

The reader is specifically designed for undergraduates to use with a minimum of classroom coverage. The selections have been chosen to cover both informational and analytical aspects of urbanism in other times, other places. Complex statistical treatments and hair-splitting theory have been avoided. The selections are integrated in a variety of ways: by reference to the Wirthian thesis which is discussed in virtually every course in the urban field, and which is especially worthy of comparative assessment; by introductions in the five major parts of the reader which relate the selections to one another and to major themes and questions; and by parallel organization with the text *Urban Society*, fifth edition by Gist and Fava. The instructor may, of course, ignore any or all of these devices and impose his own order on the individual readings, each of which is a meaningful entity in its own right. For example, many instructors may wish to introduce the comparative approach by assigning some of the selections from Part IV or Part V. Since the selections from Part IV are more social-psychological, they have a more immediate impact and are easier for most students to deal with than more purely sociological materials; the selections from Part V, concerned with urban problems, include vivid case materials which provide a helpful informational context.

The merit in any reader comes from the authors of the selections included, and I am happy to salute collectively those who are named individually in conjunction with their original or reprinted articles. Special thanks are due to Noel P. Gist and William E. Cole for their helpful comments on various versions of the table of contents, and to Leo P. Chall, editor of *Sociological Abstracts*, for use of the journal's archives. Correspondence or discussion with the following has also been useful at various points in the reader's career: Theodore Anderson, Eugene Arden, Robert Bell, Peter Berger, Herbert Blumer, Robert B. Campbell, David B. Carpenter, G. Franklin Edwards, Peter C. W. Gutkind, William J. Hanna, William F. Howton, Norman Jacobs, Howard B. Kaplan, J. J. Mangalam, Walter T. Martin, Paul Meadows, Albert McQueen, Ernest Mowrer, William Petersen, Chester Rapkin, Cara Richards, Morton Rubin, Harry Schwarzweller, William Sezak, William L. Rowe, Ivan Szclenyi, C. A. O. van Nieuwenhuijze, and Hilda Weiss. The staff of the college department of the Thomas Y. Crowell Company—especially Stuart Dorman, Tom Simpson, Herman Makler, and Batya Knapp—have been unfailing in patience, consideration, and professional expertise throughout the protracted gestation of this volume. At a critical juncture, Brooklyn College, through the Sociology Department and Dean Walter Mais, made it possible for me to continue work on the manuscript.

My greatest debt is to my husband, John L. Fava, whose wise counsel, encouragement, and good humor were indispensable.

All the errors—of omission and commission—in this volume rest, of course, on my shoulders.

Sylvia Fleis Fava

New York City
January, 1968

Contents

Part Two

Urban Ecological
Patterns Reviewed   145

Part Three

The Organization
of Urban Life 273

Part Four

**The Social Psychology
of Urban Life** 353

Part Five

Urban Housing
and Redevelopment 457

Urbanism in World Perspective:

A Reader

Part One

Urban Theory in Comparative View

It has become a truism to note the rapid urbanization of the world, welcoming or bemoaning this trend as one's vantage point may suggest. The world is in the midst of an unprecedented urban expansion which has spread to all but the most obscure or geographically inhospitable areas.

The task of urban sociology is to assess the meaning and social implications of world urbanization. The comparative approach to urban phenomena will be applied in this reader in an attempt to ascertain the underlying principles and major effects of urban development. It is particularly appropriate to apply the comparative view since so much data on cities have accumulated in the wake of widespread urbanization. The importance of comparative perspective is underlined by the fact that most urban sociological generalizations have been based on experience in industrialized Western societies.

The comparative method may be defined as the purposeful and rigorous study of the similarities and differences among a wide variety of units which are assumed to have at least one characteristic in common. The aim is to explain the causal relationships and interrelationships underlying the characteristic(s) which the units allegedly share. In this volume we will be concerned with investigating a range of communities all of which share the characteristic of being urban. Such an approach will help us to separate the causes and consequences of urban development from other related factors such as culture, industrialism, and social class.

There are many types of possible comparison in studying cities. One of the most obvious types is to compare cities in different societies, that is, cross-cultural comparison. A second type is to compare cities *within* a given society. The comparison may be among whole cities as units (for example, northern cities in the United States contrasted with southern cities) or among aspects of urban life within one given city (for example, central-city and suburban, upper-class and lower-class urban life, ethnic subareas). A third type is to compare cities of one period with those of another—historical comparison. Other kinds of comparison are also possible and several types of comparison may be combined. A number of types of comparison are exemplified by the selections in this reader, including the three major types noted.

There are pitfalls in the comparative method. If loosely applied it may lead to the accumulation of case studies whose main conclusion is that one city is "different" from another. Comparative studies are usually most successful if well focused and guided by theory. An important consideration is that the units being compared be clearly defined in terms of the characteristic(s) they are supposed to share—one man's "suburb" is often another man's "satellite city," and still another's "New Town."

Part I of this book is concerned with the broad significance of the comparative method for testing theory in the urban field, and is divided into three subsections. Section A presents the major dimensions of urban development to which the comparative method will be applied. Section B reviews Louis Wirth's classic formulations on "Urbanism as a Way of Life" in the light of comparative research, and Section C presents some typologies of cities which have resulted from comparative studies.

Although cities are growing rapidly all over the world, there are two distinct aspects to this phenomenon. In the advanced urban-industrial societies the trend is toward the metropolis—very large agglomerations of people and territory organized on the basis of a highly productive economy and sophisticated technology in transportation, communication, and distribution. The underdeveloped societies are characterized by the volume and rapidity of urban growth in conjunction with limited economic capacity and cultures which are often still traditional or disorganized by former colonial status. In Section A, the article by Charles N. Glaab and A. Theodore Brown describes the emergence of the metropolis in the United States while that by Noel P. Gist describes urban development in India, one of the most important underdeveloped nations. Kingsley Davis' article contrasts the dynamics of urban growth in the developed and underdeveloped nations.

Is the metropolis really different from the city? Why did the metropolis develop in the United States? What is the significance of this new urban form? These are some of the matters dealt with in Glaab and Brown's "The

Emergence of Metropolis." Metropolitan organization is more complex and its influence is more far-reaching than that of a city. The interdependent whole is mirrored physically in the specialized subareas of the metropolis—industrial "satellite cities," residential suburbs, ghettoization, commercial centers, and outlying subcenters—and the web of roads and telephone lines that keeps the far-flung parts functioning as a unit. The metropolis dominates a wide hinterland much larger than the municipal limits of the city whose name it usually bears. As Glaab and Brown note, city-country distinctions are virtually obsolete in a nation where the majority of inhabitants live in metropolitan areas. These areas are defined by the United States Census which has developed special criteria to measure the new shape of America. The specialization and decentralization, combined with coordination, which are the basic metropolitan hallmarks, rest on such foundations as automotive transport, mass merchandising, and mass communication.

Metropolitan development in the United States is a symptom of economic progress. Yet, as Glaab and Brown point out, one of its important consequences has been to increase residential segregation along racial and income lines. The core of the metropolis has become increasingly populated by Negroes, while middle-income whites have moved to the suburbs. This fact underlies many of the most pervasive and explosive problems of contemporary American life. In this, as in other ways, Americans have not yet "caught up" ideologically with metropolitan development.

India presents a vivid contrast to the United States and is representative of many underdeveloped nations undergoing rapid urban development. Gist, in "Urbanization in India," points out that more than ninety million Indians now live in cities; seven of these cities exceed a million in size. Yet the proportion of Indians living in cities is nevertheless small, only about 18 per cent in 1961, a result of the very large total population and the rapid increase in rural as well as urban population, due to the high birth rate. Unlike the United States where urban influences emanating from the metropolis have minimized rural-urban differences, such differences remain fundamental in India. Migrants often remain "villagers" even in large cities, mainly because of the difficulty of securing a stable livelihood. Commerce and industry are spread throughout the city in small units, rather than in assembly-line factories and department stores. This physical layout makes it apparent that Indian industrialism is still in an early stage. Although economic segregation exists in Indian cities it is not as pronounced as in American cities. Religion and caste are important bases of residential segregation and traditional family forms persist. In sum India presents an example of large-scale urban expansion in a nation which has neither a developed industrial base nor a Western-style social organization.

In "The Urbanization of the Human Population," Kingsley Davis makes a fundamental distinction between urbanization and city growth. Other authors in this volume may use the terms differently but Davis' conceptual distinction remains valid. Davis defines urbanization as "the proportion of the total population concentrated in urban settlements," and contrasts it with city growth which is simply the increase in the number of city people. Urbanization is related to the size of both urban and rural population, making it possible for *urbanization* to remain stationary while *cities* grow. For example, if the urban population grows but the rural population grows at the same or a higher rate the percentage of total population (urbanization) remains constant while the city population increases.

In the developed nations, according to Davis, increased urbanization resulted from rural to urban migration, stimulated and supported by technological improvements and by a low urban birth rate. As mechanization was applied both to agriculture and to industry, some rural population became "surplus," but was absorbed by expanding urban factories and related facilities. This process resulted in rapidly increasing urbanization but, as a higher and higher proportion of the total population lived in cities, the process of urbanization had in effect been completed, and the rate of increase in urbanization necessarily slowed down. Urbanization, says Davis, is a finite process and must end as the proportion of urbanization approaches 100 per cent.

In the underdeveloped nations the period of rapid increase in urbanization is just beginning, for these countries have low proportions of their total populations living in cities. Davis makes it clear that these nations are not repeating the urbanization process of the developed nations. Of major importance is the sheer volume of increase in numbers of urban dwellers in the underdeveloped areas (city growth), as distinguished from increase of the proportion of total population which is urban (urbanization). Cities as well as rural areas have high birth rates in the underdeveloped nations. In fact, the city population is increasing more because of its own natural increase (excess of births over deaths) than because of migration from rural areas to cities. Cities in the underdeveloped nations are, therefore, not absorbing a rural population which is too large for the land to support. Furthermore the cities are not even industrialized enough to provide jobs for the expanding population produced within the city. In the underdeveloped nations then, neither increased urbanization nor city growth are associated with higher standards of living as they were in the urban history of the developed nations.

Problems of city growth also occur in developed nations, but on a different basis than in the underdeveloped nations. In the developed nations advanced urbanization has been connected with a particular form of city —the metropolis—in which cities based on an intricate economic network spill over their boundaries and provide low residential densities for large numbers of people who work at nonagricultural jobs. The low densities of metropolitan living have often been related to "familism" and high birth rates. The result has been the seeming paradox of city growth while rates of urbanization remain steady in advanced industrial nations.

Davis concludes that the basic problem is not urbanization but the worldwide population explosion. In the underdeveloped areas it has resulted in unprecedented "runaway city growth" on a drastically inadequate economic foundation, while in the developed areas, population growth has begun to eat away at the amenities of life in large metropolitan areas.

As we turn to Section B it is appropriate that our review of urban theory should be centered on Louis Wirth's "Urbanism as a Way of Life." His article distilled much of the thinking of scholars of the city in his own generation and has provided a starting point for much work by scholars in the succeeding generation. Three articles are presented here to review Wirth's relation to the major dimensions of contemporary urban development. Thus, the article by Herbert J. Gans evaluates Wirth in the light of metropolitan growth in the industrial nations, especially the United States. William Bascom and Philip M. Hauser measure Wirth's thesis against the yardstick of Yoruba cities in Nigeria and the cities of the Indian subcontinent.

Wirth took as his central problem formulating a sociologically relevant definition of the city. After examining numerous criteria he concluded that "For sociological purposes a city may be defined as a relatively large, dense, and permanent settlement of socially heterogeneous individuals." Wirth's approach to urbanization is highlighted by contrasting it with Davis'. Davis deals with urbanization as a matter of physical residence and distinguishes between urbanization and city growth as different ways of measuring the distribution of city people. Wirth deals with urbanization as a matter of social process and characteristics. Therefore, Wirth distinguished between urbanization (he uses urbanism as a synonym) as a matter of physical residence and urbanization as a social phenomenon. For Wirth, social urbanization—urbanism as a way of life—was expected to be more pronounced in places that were physically urban, but was by no means restricted to such places. However, via the working of size, density, and heterogeneity, residential urbanism is usually associated with social urbanism.

What are the social consequences of size, density, and heterogeneity according to Wirth? Increases in size tend to produce dependence on a greater number of people, lesser dependence on particular persons; impersonal, transitory, segmental secondary contacts rather than primary contacts which are personal, lasting, and involve the whole person; more freedom from the personal and emotional control of intimate groups with the related emergence of anomie and social disorganization; association in a large number of groups, no total allegiance to a single group. Density reinforces the effects of size, particularly in differentiation and specialization, and produces spatial segregation—a "mosaic of social worlds" within the city. Heterogeneity puts a premium on superficial and standardized characteristics which are an aid in social identification and in handling large numbers of people. In sum, the social consequences of size, density, and heterogeneity affect the ecological structure of the city, the system of social organization, and the social psychology of urbanites. Hence urbanism as a way of life may be studied with emphasis on any one of these approaches. These approaches are covered in this volume in Parts, II, III, and IV, respectively.

"Urbanism and Suburbanism as Ways of Life; A Re-evaluation of Definitions" by Herbert J. Gans applies Wirth's concepts to the modern metropolis in the United States. Wirth's article was published in 1938 before many aspects of metropolitan life became evident. Much research has since been conducted on the "central city" of the metropolis and on its outlying parts, the residential and industrial suburbs. Gans contends that Wirth's formulation presents urbanism as *a* way of life when urbanism under metropolitan conditions is really *many* ways of life. Gans believes that Wirth was led to his position because his formulations derived from a comparison between urban-industrial and folk society; the social characteristics of urbanism were presented as characteristics of a total social system. Gans points instead to the important variations in ways of life *within* cities and suburbs as well as those *between* cities and suburbs. These variations, he suggests, are related to social class and the stage of the family cycle of the residents rather than to the size, density, and heterogeneity of their residential areas. In effect, Gans is stating that the life styles of social groups, such as the lower class or "young marrieds," will be similar regardless of city or suburban residence, although some adjustment will probably be made in the context of population size, density, and heterogeneity. It may be said that Gans has not rejected Wirth's thesis but has recast it in terms of the declining importance of residential location on social life in affluent, highly mobile societies.

How do the characteristics of "urbanism as a way of life" fare when reviewed in the light of non-Western cities? Bascom's "The Urban African and His World" examines the criteria of size, density, and heterogeneity in the Yoruba cities of western Nigeria. The Yoruba are a traditionally urban people, having lived in large cities for centuries before colonization by Europeans. Traditional Yoruba cities meet the criteria of urban size and density but, as Bascom points out, social heterogeneity is difficult to apply, suggesting a culture-bound quality in Wirth's choice of socially relevant urban traits. The social correlates of size and density in Yoruba cities include economic interdependence, secondary contacts, impersonal media of exchange, and a sense of urban sophistication. However, anomie and social disorganization are evident only among recent migrants to cities, especially to the "new" cities established over the last century or so by Europeans. In traditional Yoruba cities lineage and kin, far from being atrophied as Wirth's thesis holds, are an integral part of urban life and exert a stabilizing influence. Traditional Yoruba cities thus provide both confirmation and rejection of the social features of Wirth's urbanism as a way of life.

Similarly, Philip Hauser's impressionistic application of Wirth's thesis to Indian cities shows incomplete fulfillment of the social consequences expected on the basis of urban size, density, and heterogeneity. However, neither do large Indian cities fulfill all of Redfield's social traits of folk society. Hauser's main point is that Wirth's and Redfield's constructs have had "relatively blind acceptance . . . as generalizations based on research rather than as tools to be utilized in research."

No final appraisal can be given of Wirth's thesis at this time, nor perhaps at any time. The truth may lie in the changing sociological significance of size, density, and heterogeneity as they are filtered through new types of human settlement (the modern metropolis); stable non-Western, preindustrial cultures (traditional Yoruba cities); exploding cities in underdeveloped nations (contemporary Indian cities); or through other urban contexts.

Wirth's presentation of the urban way of life was, in effect, a typology, although he presented the nonurban way of life mainly by implication. Typology is a fruitful way of studying the city, both as a way of generalizing findings and as a tool for generating hypotheses for further research. In Section C we turn to several examples of the typological study of cities. Robert McC. Adams examines the earliest urban societies; Gideon Sjoberg searches for the characteristics differentiating preindustrial cities from industrial cities; and Leonard Reissman details the varied routes by which contemporary underdeveloped societies are emerging into the modern urban world. It is instructive to note the variety of disciplines and the range of data used in these studies, alerting us to the breadth of knowledge comparative study often requires. The studies presented here also concentrate on *process*, thus avoiding superficial "comparison" consisting of standing cities side by side and ticking off their similarities and differences. These studies ask not merely "what," but "why" and "how."

The origin of the city poses in the most fundamental way the question of the social causes and consequences of urban development. Adams examines this question in his study of the city in early Mesopotamia and prehispanic Mexico, the two generally accepted sites of the earliest, indigenous city development. For Mesopotamia the period covered is about 3900 B.C. to 2300 B.C.; for Mexico the period encompassing a broadly similar but independent transformation is from 100 B.C. to A.D. 1500. Early Mesopotamia included parts of present-day Iraq. Many of the early Mesopotamian cities such as Ur are mentioned frequently in the Bible. Mesopotamia and Mexico have undergone many changes since the early urban period described by Adams. Mesopotamia has been the site of numerous and shifting cultures and nations, while Aztec Mexico was invaded by the Spanish and was a colony until relatively recent times. The Aztec capital, called Tenochtitlán, now the site of Mexico City, is described in Norman S. Hayner's article (selection 12).

Adams' detailed review of the anthropological and archeological record indicates that despite the many differences between early Mesopotamia and prehispanic Mexico, both emerged into urban life as theocratic polities, then became militaristic polities, and finally developed into conquest states. In his analysis Adams focuses on the state (the "polity") because the organization of a society on the basis of the state is one major feature of the new integrating principles of urban society—"hierarchically organized on political and territorial lines rather than on kinship or other ascriptive groups and relationships." Changes in social organization are the fundamental "cause" of the origin of cities in that the allegiances and obligations subsumed under the state made it meaningful to concentrate the productivity of technological advances (domestication of plants and animals) toward maintaining a small group of non-food-producing specialists in densely settled communities (cities). Significantly, the earliest form urban states assumed in Mesopotamia and Mexico was the theocracy, the combination of religious and political authority. In addition to the state, Mesopotamia and Mexico both displayed another key feature of complex social organization as they evolved into urban societies. Social stratification and placement were increasingly on the basis of class rather than on the pre-urban basis of kinship. The tendency toward class stratification was heightened in both Mesopotamia and Mexico as their theocratic states became more and more militaristic, that is, as political-religious authority was replaced by political-military authority. Still later Mesopotamia and Mexico became empires, states based on "extended conquest, trade and tribute," which are sociologically significant because they involve intricate administration, bureaucracy, and many very different social groups. In Mesopotamia this was the Akkadian empire (Agade) and in Mexico the Aztec empire. Adams leaves his analysis at this juncture, having made the central points that cities emerged only with the development of a complex social order based on the state and class, and that the social order became even more complex as the state superseded religious authority and expanded its geographic base through military conquest. Adams' analysis is particularly important because it indicates that the crucial factor in the origin and maintenance of the two earliest, independently evolved urban societies was the "buildup" in social organization rather than in technology.

Gideon Sjoberg's "The Preindustrial City" approaches the question of what characteristics are urban by contrasting preindustrial cities with industrial cities. The preindustrial city emerges as a distinct type in Sjoberg's analysis.[1] In contrast to the industrial city, the preindustrial city has a small elite, a large lower class, and a very small middle class; formal education consists of rote learning of traditional precepts and is restricted to the elite,

---

[1] Sjoberg calls the total society of which the preindustrial city is a part "feudal." "Feudalism" is a broad term and this may pose problems. As it stands, Sjoberg's "feudalism" would include the societies of early Mesopotamia and prehispanic Mexico as well as many of those societies described by Reissman in the succeeding article. Very possibly the preindustrial city should be divided into subtypes, only some of which could properly be regarded as belonging to "feudal" society.

as is literacy; there is little social mobility and social class and economic position are strongly influenced by kinship. Thus, although the social organization of the preindustrial city is complex, it is also rigid, oriented toward traditional forms, and has a slow rate of social change. It might be said that the social organization is complex but the value system is homogeneous and exerts a conservative influence. In the industrial city both the social organization and the value system are highly differentiated.

Sjoberg suggests that "industrialization is a key variable accounting for the distinctions between preindustrial and industrial cities." Most contemporary underdeveloped countries have traditional preindustrial social organizations; the degree to which their social organizations alter prior to or in response to industrialization will be a test of economic and technological determinism.

Contemporary urban development is the focus of Leonard Reissman's "Urbanization: A Typology of Change." He presents an empirical typology of the extent to which societies currently manifest urbanism. According to Reissman, there are four ways in which a society may be urban. It may be demographically urban (urbanization in Davis' use of the term), economically urban (industrialization), politically urban (nationalism), or have an urban class structure (emergence of a middle class). Ranking the societies studied on these four indices results in four major types of urban development and several subtypes. Although Reissman calls the major types "stages"—"underdeveloped," "transitional," "urban transitional," and "metropolitan"—he makes clear that there is no necessary unfolding of a predetermined sequence in urban development. A society may stabilize at any point, more or less permanently. Furthermore he points out there is no one way by which countries become urban. Any of the four aspects of urbanization may lead in moving toward urbanization. Thus, a country may be more urban demographically or politically than it is industrially or more urban in class structure than in its demographic characteristics. Reissman's typology includes countries currently illustrating many diverse ways of becoming urban.

The construction of urban types based on such diverse urban forms as the earliest cities (Adams), preindustrial cities (Sjoberg), and a cross section of contemporary cities (Reissman) yields no final answers but does present some broad areas of agreement. All three analyses indicate that at any period the city milieu (and, to an undetermined extent, the society of which it is a part) differs socially from a nonurban milieu. The city is always based on a more complex social organization, but even the relatively few studies reported here make it clear that the content of that complexity is not universal or uniform. The three studies presented in Section C need only be compared with each other and with Wirth's presentation, which is essentially a description of the social organization of the American industrial city.

The selections in Section C also point to the vexing question of the relative potency of technology and social organization in influencing the course of urban life. It is insufficient to state that both are important and that they interact. Scanning the time period covered in the Adams, Sjoberg, and Reissman analyses it is possible to suggest that in the modern era the association of technology (industrialism) with a particular social organization (Western) may be stronger than in the past or, possibly, in the future. A successful "model" of urbanization, the industrial-Western organization, has been transmitted worldwide through rapid large-scale movement of people, goods, and ideas. Left to develop in isolation, there may very well be several potentially successful complex social organizations which could operate in conjunction with industrialism, but such variation may be sharply curtailed when industrialism develops in the context of established urban-industrial societies.

A | The Problem— New Dimensions of Urbanism

1 | The Emergence of Metropolis

CHARLES N. GLAAB and
A. THEODORE BROWN

Informing much of the late nineteenth-century examination of the problems and the prospects of the American city was the view that city and country represented distinct environments, opposed ways of life. This view would continue to influence the character of popular argument—especially in political debate—until at least the 1950's. But an occasional observer around the turn of the century recognized that the conception of city as one thing and country another—a conception which had such deep roots in western culture—could no longer be applied to American society. The city by this time had enormously extended its spatial area and its influence. There was often difficulty in physically distinguishing city from countryside, for the two often blended together in sprawling urban regions. The country no longer represented an independent community, since it was affected in hundreds of economic and social ways by the city. "The city has become the central feature in modern civilization and to an ever increasing extent the dominant one," wrote the municipal reformer Frederic C. Howe in 1906. "This rural civilization, whose making engaged mankind since the dawn of history, is passing away. The city has erased the landmarks of an earlier society. Man has entered on an urban age."

In a general way, Howe was describing an aspect of the phenomenon of "metropolitanism,"—the extension of the influence of the large city over

SOURCE: Charles N. Glaab and A. Theodore Brown, *A History of Urban America* (New York: The Macmillan Company, 1967), pp. 269–282, 285–289. Copyright © 1967 by The Macmillan Company. Reprinted by permission of the publisher.

11

enormous hinterland regions. A few years later, the phenomenon received more explicit demographic recognition in the statistics presented in the federal census of 1910. As early as 1880, the Census Bureau had provided data for the metropolitan district of New York and its suburbs. Aware of the inadequacy of the customary urban classifications (populations of 8,000, 4,000, and 2,500 had all been used), demographers now applied the statistical notion of the metropolitan district to the whole nation. Twenty-five metropolitan districts were identified ranging in size from New York (including Newark) with its 616,927 acres of land and 6,474,568 people to Portland with its 43,538 acres and 215,048 residents. Through this device it was possible to indicate the unity of such urban areas as the twin cities of Minnesota, the cities on San Francisco Bay, and the two Kansas Citys along the Missouri-Kansas border. Also evident was the importance of the clusters of suburban communities around the large eastern cities of New York, Boston, and Philadelphia. Through continued growth over the next half century, these cities and their suburbs would come to constitute a kind of continuous metropolitan region which may represent a new stage in urban organization—the megalopolis.[1]

The growth of the metropolis constitutes the central theme of twentieth-century American urban history. For the 1950 census, demographers devised a more sophisticated device than the metropolitan district to assess the importance of the rise of metropolitan regions. This was the Standard Metropolitan Area (renamed the Standard Metropolitan Statistical Area in 1960), which was defined as a whole county containing a central city of 50,000 or more, plus any adjacent counties that appeared to be integrated to the central city. For overall examination of twentieth-century metropolitan growth, it is perhaps most convenient to use the principal S.M.A.'s (those with 100,000 or more population at a given census), which the Census Bureau has "retrojected" to past census periods. But whatever measuring scheme is employed the trends are evident.

First, there was a great increase in the number of metropolitan areas and in the total population that lived in these areas. During the period from 1900 to 1950, the total United States population increased from 76.0 million to 150.7 million, while the number of principal S.M.A.'s increased from 82 to 147 and their total population from 24.1 million to 84.3 million. This represented a percentage change in the metropolitan population from 31.9 per cent of the nation's total to 56.0 per cent.

---

[1] The term "megalopolis" was devised by Jean Gottmann and is generally applied to an urban region that contains several metropolitan centers. An alternative term "conurbation" implies an urban region formed from the fusion of several earlier cities. It has more application in Europe than in the United States; the cities along the Ruhr River in Germany and the Amsterdam-Haarlem-Leiden-The Hague-Rotterdam-Utrecht complex in the Netherlands supply examples of this kind of urban development. The term "metropolis" acquired a different meaning in the twentieth century than it had historically.

Second, for the entire period the growth rate for the principal S.M.A.'s was substantially higher than for the country as a whole: 32.6 per cent as opposed to 21.0 per cent from 1900 to 1910, 25.2 per cent as opposed to 14.9 per cent from 1910 to 1920, 27.0 per cent as opposed to 16.1 per cent from 1920 to 1930, 8.3 per cent as opposed to 7.2 per cent from 1930 to 1940, and 21.8 per cent as opposed to 14.5 per cent from 1940 to 1950. For every decade in the period except 1900–10, when it was 15.0, the growth rate for nonmetropolitan areas of the country was substantially below 10 per cent.

Third, there has been a tendency for rapid growth to take place in the outlying areas of metropolitan centers at an accelerating rate. After 1920 metropolitan "rings" grew much faster than "central cities" themselves, by the 1940–1950 decade nearly two and a half times as fast (34.8 per cent as compared with 13.7 per cent). During the first decade of the century, metropolitan rings claimed only about one-sixth of the total United States population growth (15.7 per cent); in 1940–50 this figure had risen to nearly one-half (48.6 per cent).*

The metropolises of the twentieth century, whose growth constituted the most dramatic demographic development to be found in statistics of United States population, were much more than greatly enlarged traditional cities. Involved in the concept of the modern metropolis are complex changes in function and structure within the city and its suburban areas— decentralization of numerous activities, separation of areas of residence and work, and a high mobility over greatly extended spatial areas. Also involved are many relationships with other cities and areas outside the immediate limits of the urban region.[2] The sociologist R. D. McKenzie in his pioneer study of metropolitan communities in the early 1930's argued that these considerations were so striking that the huge city of the twentieth century

---

* The trends described by Glaab and Brown have continued since 1950. First, by 1965 the total United States population had reached 194 million, the number of metropolitan areas had reached 219, and their total population was 130 million. This represented about two-thirds of the population of the United States. Second, between 1960 and 1965 the metropolitan population increased by 9.3 per cent while the growth rate for the country as a whole was only 7.1 per cent, and the growth rate for nonmetropolitan areas of the United States was only 5.7 per cent. Third, the metropolitan "rings" grew by 14.5 per cent from 1960 to 1965 while the central cities of the metropolises grew by only 7.9 per cent.—Ed.

[2] The terminology relating to the metropolis is confusing. Some writers use the term "metropolitan community" to designate the area where population is integrated on a daily basis to the locale, that is, pretty much the commuting area of a metropolis; the term "metropolitan region" can then describe the larger area of more indirect influence. Employing the latter concept, it would be possible to divide the whole nation into a number of extended "metropolitan regions." But there is little consistency in the use of metropolitan nomenclature, and we have not attempted to be unduly precise here.

with its surrounding suburban towns and cities and its far-reaching economic relationships ought to be considered as "practically a new social and economic entity." A few years earlier N. S. B. Gras had examined the existence of a world-wide metropolitan community and the intricate relationship of world cities of various sizes within that community. "We may think of metropolitan economy as an organization of people having a large city as nucleus," Gras wrote. "Or we may put it this way, metropolitan economy is the organization of producers and consumers mutually dependent for goods and services, wherein their wants are supplied by a system of exchange concentrated in a large city which is the focus of local trade and the center through which normal economic relations with the outside are established and maintained."

"Just as villages remained when town economy prevailed," Gras continued, "so do towns remain when metropolitan economy comes into existence. Towns remain, but in economic subordination to the metropolis. They continue to play a part, but as tributaries to a larger center. A closer examination of these dependent towns would show different types performing different functions, but all subordinate."

Gras' conception of "metropolitan dominance"—the control of the huge city over vast surrounding areas—influenced much of the subsequent study of the metropolis. Yet, as Gras himself recognized, "dominance" alone supplied an insufficient explanation. Not only were outlying areas of the metropolis dependent upon the city, but the city in turn was dependent upon its hinterland. In fact, the whole series of relationships within a metropolitan area was so complex that the biological term of symbiosis was often employed to indicate their nature. The twentieth-century metropolis provided a new system of social and economic organization—a distinctive social configuration. As Leo F. Schnore observes, the metropolitan area cannot profitably be conceived of "as a simple two-part arrangement of center and ring, a large city with its adjacent territory. . . . The metropolitan community must be viewed—in organizational terms throughout—as a highly specialized mosaic of subareas tied together into a new functional unity. Moreover, it is to be viewed as a multinucleated territorial system. Within these broad areas, the large centers are marked by functional diversity, while the smaller places, many of them formerly independent cities in their own right, tend to be narrowly specialized. At the same time, however, the main centers are specialized in the coordinating functions of administration and control."

The rise of the metropolitan region is often associated with the introduction of the automobile. Up to a point this is accurate. Statistically, if all American cities are considered together, the great jump in suburban population occurred in the 1920's when the automobile became the main device of urban transportation. Nevertheless, it is clear that the process of population decentralization—a fundamental aspect of the rise of the metropolis— had begun for some cities and in some regions of the country in the latter part of the nineteenth century. Schnore, one of the few contemporary urban sociologists to undertake detailed historical analysis of urban demography, has provided an ingenious study of decentralization of population in ninety-nine metropolitan central cities that had a population of at least 100,000 at some point in their growth. His study, which takes into account annexations and the persistence through thirty-year periods of decentralizing patterns, indicates the early tendency of a number of individual cities to grow more rapidly in their peripheral areas than at their centers. New York began decentralizing as early as 1850. Nine other cities had begun to decentralize by 1900: another thirteen cities were added to the list during the first decade of the century. The process speeded up after 1920, of course, and fully sixty cities began to decentralize between 1920 and 1940. In short, suburbanization, although it greatly accelerated in the twentieth century, is a trend in American urban development that extends back at least a hundred years. In Philadelphia, to cite an extreme example, the population movement away from the center of the city was proportionally greater in the fifty years between 1860 and 1910 than in the half century between 1900 and 1950.

The basic economic institutions that enabled larger cities to develop highly specialized metropolitan functions within a network of varying sized towns and cities also had nineteenth-century origins. The techniques of modern merchandising—with their emphasis on trade over vast regions —were fully developed by the end of the century. In the 1860's, Marshall Field's in Chicago combined the features of a number of large stores in Paris and New York—a fixed price system, large display advertisements, and numerous special departments—to establish the modern department store. The Great American Tea Company was organized in 1864 in New York; five years later it became the Great Atlantic and Pacific Tea Company. It began to establish branches throughout the country and became one of the first major chain stores. Frank W. Woolworth opened his five-and-ten at Lancaster, Pennsylvania, in 1879, established branches at Harrisburg and Scranton, and within a decade owned stores in a number of localities. Modern advertising techniques, low-cost mass insurance, mail-order stores, centralized stock exchanges, and specialized banking were examples of other metropolitan activities that developed in the latter part of the century. Technological innovations in printing—new presses, Linotype machines, improved halftones—permitted city newspapers greatly to expand their circulations. This provided one of the most important means through which the influence of the metropolis was extended. In the early work of American urban sociologists, measurement of newspaper circulation provided a convenient way of estimating the range of metropolitan influence.

Another significant aspect of metropolitanism with nineteenth-century origins was industrial suburbanization—the growth of "satellite cities," as Graham Taylor termed them in one of the first investigations of manufacturing communities on the outskirts of large cities. Although this aspect of decentralization has not received as much attention as the creation of the residential "dormitory" suburbs, the suburbs of employment and production have been equally important in shaping the character of the modern metropolis. In the late nineteenth century, the substitution of electric power for steam in industry and improvements in transportation made it possible for manufacturers to move away from central cities, and they were encouraged to do so by a number of factors: the need for vast amounts of cheap land to build factories incorporating all stages of large-scale complex production, lower taxes, and freedom from regulation in regard to smoke and noise. . . .

. . . . .

The building of industrial towns and cities in the early part of the twentieth century reflected a general pattern of decentralization clearly indicated in statistics of manufacturing. A Census Bureau study of twelve of the thirteen largest "industrial districts" showed that from 1899 to 1904 the number of persons employed in industry in central cities increased by 14.9 per cent while in the outlying zones the number increased by 32.8 per cent. From 1904 to 1909 the increase in central cities was 22.5 per cent while in the surrounding zones it was 48.8 per cent. For the decade, the growth rate was over two times as great for the suburbs—97.7 per cent to 40.8 per cent. This trend toward industrial decentralization became even more pronounced with the general acceleration of suburbanization after 1920. In 1919 eleven central cities in the country's forty largest manufacturing counties still accounted for 85 per cent of the manufacturing workers; by 1937 this percentage had fallen to just under 60. The number of wage earners in the eleven central cities during the period declined from 2,045,789 to 1,808,692 while in the outlying areas of these cities the number increased from 365,403 to 1,218,465. In addition to the decentralization of manufacturing, many of the commercial functions of the nineteenth-century city showed a marked tendency to decentralization, again particularly after 1920.

Cheap electric power and the telephone were important in the decentralization of economic activities. Also important was the mobility of labor permitted by the trolleys and inter-urban railroads. But the most significant development stimulating rapid suburbanization was the automobile, and to a lesser extent, the motorized truck. In the early 1890's, mechanics in the United States and in Europe had put together workable automobiles. But until the turn of the century they were built on individual order and were largely a toy of the rich, with only 8,000 vehicles registered by 1900. During the next decade actual manufacturing began. By 1910 the number of motor vehicles had risen to 468,500, and in 1915 to 2,490,932. Then came the tremendous post-First World War expansion of the industry: motor vehicle registration jumped from 9,239,161 in 1920 to 19,940,724 in 1925 to 26,531,999 in 1930. In spite of the depression of the 1930's, the number of motor vehicles still increased by nearly a third during the decade, reaching a total of 32,035,424 registrations in 1940; by 1950 the number had grown to 48,566,984.

In addition to the obvious effects of increasing the mobility of workers and consumers and facilitating the movement of goods and materials in cities, the general use of motor vehicles also modified the spatial pattern of the metropolis. In the late nineteenth and early twentieth century, cities spread out along the lines of trolleys and inter-urban railroads. The suburbanized parts of the metropolis resembled tentacles extending from the central city in radial fashion. Highways, particularly in older and larger cities like Chicago and New York, first tended to follow the railroad lines. The new suburbs made possible by the automobile became part of the older pattern of growth. Gradually, however, as road building greatly expanded after the passage of the Federal Highway Act of 1916, the interstices of the metropolitan area began to be filled in. Complicated lateral movements of traffic became a defining characteristic of the metropolis. Newer cities, such as Los Angeles, that experienced great growth in the twentieth century, spread out along highways and did not develop the clearly defined central business districts of older cities. The transportation systems of older cities, even after the automobile came into general use, still tended to funnel traffic into the center, greatly intensifying the problem of congestion.

During the 1920's and early 1930's, engineers perfected and governments adopted the various devices that were part of a high speed system of motorized transportation—grade separation of highway from city street, traffic circle, divided dual highway, and synchronized stop lights. These techniques, along with new bridges such as the George Washington in New York and the Camden-Philadelphia, and an innovation such as the Holland Tunnel under the Hudson, permitted easier movement of automobile traffic through the huge, sprawling metropolitan region. But just as in past eras, the rush-hour, weekend, and holiday traffic jam was an all too familiar aspect of urban life.

The expanded economic opportunities created by the automobile stimulated an urban land boom that radically inflated property values in American cities. Particularly where automobile routes tended to follow older fixed forms of urban transportation, considerable expansion took place in central business districts. This expansion contributed to an optimism that caused property values to rise, and as Homer Hoyt has dryly observed, "In each successive land boom there is a speculative exaggeration of the trend of the period." In 1920, the total value of land in American cities of over 30,000 population—only about one-fifth of one per cent of all the land in the United States—was estimated at $25 billion; by 1926 this figure had doubled to $50 billion. During the same period the value of American farm land dropped from 55 to 37 billion dollars—a figure 33 per cent less than the value of land in cities above 30,000. Real estate on Manhattan

Island was assessed at over five billion dollars in 1930; this was more than the value of the farm land in 23 states in 1925. The corner of State and Madison in the heart of Chicago's Loop was leased during the decade at a rate of $50,000 a front foot, a rate equivalent to $21,789,000 an acre. One small holding at 1 Wall Street in New York City sold for $100,000 a front foot, a rate of nearly $44,000,000 an acre.

Inflation of downtown land values and the post-First World War prosperity of many sections of the economy stimulated the great era of skyscraper building in American cities. For twenty-five years after [William Le Baron] Jenney's initial efforts, architects experimented with the new building form; the Woolworth Tower of New York completed in 1913 established a standard style. Chicago's group of towers along the Chicago River built in the early 1920's differed little from the new "Woolworth Gothic" skyscrapers that sprang up in New York. Cleveland, Pittsburgh, San Francisco, and Kansas City developed the jagged skylines characteristic of the twentieth-century American city. By 1929, American cities had 377 skyscrapers of more than twenty stories in height, largely built without concern for the character of the surrounding urban space and without concern for the patterns of traffic created by the buildings. Even in the cities of the plains the skyscraper was as much demanded as on the tight plots of lower Manhattan Island. Many of the nation's tallest buildings were begun in 1928 and 1929 and only completed after the depression. The most famous skyscraper of all, the Empire State Building, was finished in 1930 and for many years was a white elephant in a city which during the depression had more than enough office space. Not until the late 1950's were the pressures of urban growth great enough to stimulate another era of skyscraper building.

· · · · ·

As cities went upward, they also went outward. The introduction of the automobile launched a great era of suburban building. The 1920's saw the complete emergence of modern residential suburbs and this was reflected in spectacular percentage growth rates during the decade for some of the more famous of them: Beverly Hills, 2485.0, Glendale, 363.5, Inglewood, 492.8, Huntington Park, 444.9 (suburbs of Los Angeles); Cleveland Heights, 234.4, Shaker Heights, 1000.4, Garfield Heights, 511.3 (suburbs of Cleveland); Grosse Pointe Park, 724.6, Ferndale, 689.9 (suburbs of Detroit); Webster Groves, 74.0, Maplewood, 70.3, Richmond Heights, 328.3 (suburbs of St. Louis); Elmwood Park, 716.7, Oak Park, 60.5, Park Ridge, 207.9 (suburbs of Chicago). Numerous new towns and villages appeared around large cities, as demonstrated in the incorporation statistics for the decade. Of the thirty-eight new incorporations in Illinois, twenty-six were located within the metropolitan regions of Chicago or St. Louis; of the thirty-three in Michigan, twenty-two were suburbs of Detroit, and of Ohio's fifty-five incorporations, twenty-nine were near Cleveland. Cities in the 2,500–10,000 bracket showed a rapid growth rate for the period, chiefly because so many of them were located on the fringes of metropolitan areas.

· · · · ·

In the twentieth century, expansion upward and outward modified the morphology of American cities. In addition the character of urban population and its distribution throughout the areas of the city also changed. The decade of 1900–1910 was the last in which foreign migration contributed substantially to the growth of American cities. In 1907, the high year for the decade, 1,285,349 immigrants arrived in the United States. With the outbreak of war in Europe, the number fell to 326,700 in 1915 and reached a low point of 110,618 in 1919 with European immigration constituting less than 25,000 of this total. Immigration revived in the early 1920's, reaching 805,228 in 1921, but the legislation establishing a quota system, passed in that year and revised in 1924, reduced annual immigration to around 300,000 in the years from 1925 to 1929. During the depression of the 1930's it dropped even more drastically and not until 1946 did the annual figure again rise above 100,000.

With immigration from abroad sharply restricted, cities grew largely through internal migration down to the 1940's when the birth rate of urban dwellers began to rise substantially. One of the most significant aspects of this rural-urban migration was the movement of southern Negroes to the cities of the East and Midwest and on a lesser magnitude to the cities of the South. From 1820 to 1910 the urbanization of the white population of the United States had always been at a more rapid rate than that of the Negro. But failures of the cotton crop in the south in 1915 and 1916 and the demand for industrial labor caused by the war reversed this pattern in the next decade, as the percentage of native white population classified as urban increased by 6 while that of Negroes increased by 6.7. The trend was intensified during the next decade, with the percentage of native white population classified as urban increasing by 4.9 while that of Negroes increased by 9.7. In 1910, 89 per cent of all Negroes lived south of the Mason-Dixon line; as a result of the migrations, by 1930 20 per cent of the Negro population lived in the Northeast and Middle West with 89 per cent of this group classified as urban. This was primarily a movement to the larger cities and it continued unabated during the years of depression. Between 1930 and 1940, for example, the Negro population of Chicago increased by more than 43,000, an increase of 18.7 per cent. During the whole period from 1900 to 1950 the percentage of Negroes outside the South increased from 10 per cent to 32 per cent and the percentage within cities rose from 17 to 48 per cent.

Urbanization of the Negro population modified the social patterns of larger cities. The older ethnic colonies had always contained a fair number of people not of the predominant group. In addition, these colonies had been relatively impermanent with one ethnic group succeeding another in a given area. The Negro colonies in northern cities were much more homogeneous, and, as time proved, much more permanent. Wards in New York and Chicago had percentages of Negro population that approached 95 by 1930. To a large extent cities within cities had been created. "Black Metropolis is the second largest Negro city in the world, only New York's Harlem exceeding it in size," wrote St. Clair Drake and Horace Cayton in their 1945 study of Negro life in Chicago. "It is a city within a city—a narrow tongue of land, seven miles in length and one and one-half miles in width where more than 300,000 Negroes are packed solidly. . . . Walk the streets of the Black Belt and you will find no difference in language to mark its people off from others in the city. Only the black and brown and olive and tan faces of Negro Americans seem to distinguish it from any other section of Midwest Metropolis. But beneath the surface are patterns of life and thought, attitudes and customs, which make Black Metropolis a unique and distinctive city within a city. Understand Chicago's Black Belt and you will understand the Black Belts of a dozen large American cities."

As Drake and Cayton's account so clearly indicated, the Negro ghetto intensified old urban problems. Racial segregation drastically limited the possibility of upward mobility by individual or group. The black metropolises of Chicago, New York, Cleveland, and Detroit were areas where few could benefit from the economic and cultural advantages of the city but where all the long-standing urban problems of crime, poverty, and disease existed in aggravated form.

The urban segregation of the Negro reflected a general tendency to increased economic and cultural segregation in the twentieth-century metropolis. The wealthier and more powerful members of the community steadily moved to the outer zones of the city and to the new suburban areas. A study of over 2,000 substantial Detroit families in the early 1930's demonstrated a striking deconcentration of that city's elite. In 1910 nearly 52 per cent of this group still lived within a three-mile radius of the main business center of Detroit, and only 9.7 per cent outside the municipal boundaries. By 1930 these percentages were nearly reversed with only 7.5 per cent of the substantial families near the business district and 50 per cent in suburban areas. Numerous studies of economic zones within cities and of spatial zones away from the center made by the urban sociologists of the 1920's and 1930's demonstrated clearly the cultural advantages and the greater stability of the outer regions of metropolitan centers. Crime, the need for public welfare, and infant mortality decreased radically in the outer areas and usually in direct proportion to the distance of the area from the center of the city. In the past, many had resented the city because its extremes of wealth and poverty seemed a denial of American equalitarian beliefs. In the twentieth-century metropolis these inequalities appeared more obvious, more rigidly confined, and more permanent.

The rise of the metropolis presented a whole new set of considerations to those concerned with ordering the urban environment. But despite the complexity of the twentieth-century supercity and its tremendous influence on society, much of the debate about the city in America was still conducted in terms of the old country-city polarity. The effort to restrict foreign immigration, the crusade for religious fundamentalism, the prohibition movement, and the election of 1928 were aspects of national history influenced by the traditional defense of the values of the country and the traditional attack on the values of the city. People could still accept at face value the famous photograph of President Calvin Coolidge seated on a hay wagon with rake in hand, his clothes spotless, while in the rear his assistants stand by an automobile waiting to whisk him back to the city. Writers of popular fiction in the twenties and thirties still employed the nineteenth-century imagery of the soulless city. To find "real values" one had to flee the city. "I have had to do many things, terrible things, things no decent man should have done," says a hero of a 1925 *Cosmopolitan* short story who finds peace in the wilderness. "Thank God that's all behind me now. Out here I can be a real person again." On a higher level, twelve southerners in their notable manifesto *I'll Take My Stand*, published in 1929, defended an idyllic rural life that probably never existed. "Back to the land," a position popularized by Ralph Borsodi who established a subsistence homestead outside New York City in 1920 and preached the virtues of the Thoreauvian way of life, became an organized movement that influenced federal policy during the depression of the thirties. Its disciples offered a classical Jeffersonian defense of the agrarian ideal. "The farms have always produced our great leaders in finance, industry and statesmanship," a witness testified before a House committee in the early 1930's. "The vast population must depart from the congested industrial centers and cities and once again become self-sustaining on our vast and fertile farms, pasture, and prairie lands. Herein lies the real hope for the bright destiny of America."

Despite the persistence of these old ideals, many thinkers and reformers abandoned the simple notion of country versus city and began to develop new conceptions of the social environment that emphasized the community, the neighborhood, the region. The old problems that had special urban dimensions—health, poverty, and the slum—had not disappeared, and housing the poor of the cities continued to be one of the principal concerns of urban reformers. But the complexity of the new metropolitan communities forced consideration of ways of reordering the whole urban environment. Proposals for new kinds of cities and for comprehensive plans that encompassed whole urban regions now became part of the discussion of the future of American cities. Writing in 1922, Lewis Mumford, who was to become one of the better known students of urban civilization, reflected the urgency of the new point of view: "Our metropolitan civilization is not a success. It is a different kind of wilderness . . . but the feral rather than the humane quality is dominant; it is still a wilderness. The cities of America must learn to remould our mechanical and financial regime; for if metropolitanism continues they are probably destined to fall by its weight."

2 | Urbanism in India

NOEL P. GIST

India is preponderantly a land of villagers. It is also a land of great and numerous cities. As in many other developing nations, city growth in the twentieth century has been rapid—more rapid, indeed, than in most of the industrialized countries during the same period.

In 1951, there were seventy-three cities having a population of one hundred thousand or over; by 1961, the number had increased to ninety-nine. In the United States, in 1960, there were 130 cities of metropolitan size. Seven Indian cities exceed a million inhabitants. These are Calcutta, Delhi, Bombay, Madras, Ahmedabad, Hyderabad, and Bangalore. Greater Calcutta, with nearly seven million population, ranks among the twenty largest metropolitan centers in the world. Over ninety million persons are urban residents.

City Growth Rates

There are numerous ancient cities in India today, but most of the large cities are fairly new, essentially creations of a foreign colonial power. These include particularly Calcutta, Bombay, Madras, Bangalore, and New Delhi, whose rise to greatness did not antedate the nineteenth century, though the initial founding dates were far earlier. These cities served as administrative centers for the British, or as *entrepôt* cities through which raw materials were shipped to Europe for processing and subsequently for redistribution to world markets. Some manufacturing occurred, primarily in textiles, but the basic functions of these centers were political and commercial.

During the nineteenth century and early years of the twentieth the rate of city growth in India was comparatively slow. But a combination of conditions in the middle decades of the present century resulted in unprecedented growth, especially of the larger cities. This growth rate apparently reached its peak in the 1941–51 decade, during which time the average population increase of all cities one hundred thousand or over was

SOURCE: This article has been especially prepared for this volume.

44 per cent, and for the ten largest cities 64 per cent. But in the following decade (1951–61) the rate of growth for all the cities of metropolitan size had dropped to 14 per cent.

These rates of growth for individual cities are interesting to note. In the 1941–51 decade numbers of cities doubled in population. Delhi had an increase of 107 per cent, Bangalore of 90 per cent, Hyderabad of 47 per cent. But in the succeeding decade the rate of growth dropped very sharply. Delhi's rate for the period was 63 per cent, Bangalore's 29 per cent, and Hyderabad's 15 per cent. Madras doubled its population in the 1941–51 period, but in the next decade the growth rate was only 22 per cent. This declining rate of growth, expressed percentagewise, is due in part to the large size of the base population. At any rate, the pattern of rapid growth followed by a moderate growth rate is similar to that of cities in the industrialized countries over the past century.

Paradoxically, the increase in the proportion of city dwellers in the total population of India has been slow. In the four decades preceding 1961 the proportion of urban population increased by only 6.4 per cent—from 11.4 per cent of the total in 1921 to 17.8 per cent in 1961. In numbers, however, the increase was very large—nearly seventy-eight million. The percentage increase in urban population contrasts rather sharply with the trend in the United States, where the proportion of persons living in urban centers increased from 51.2 per cent in 1920 to 69.9 per cent in 1960.[1] Stating the matter differently, whereas less than one in five persons in India live in an urban community at present, almost three-fourths of the American people are urban residents.

The comparatively slow rate of urbanization in India, when expressed as a percentage of the total population, is because the rural population is growing almost as rapidly as the urban population. Persistently high birth rates and declining death rates in the villages have resulted in an upsurge of the rural as well as the urban population. Although many of the "surplus" people produced in the rural areas do migrate to swell the numbers of urban residents, this migration is not sufficient to reduce the rural population or even to stabilize it. The imbalance of fertility and mortality in India, as indicated by a birth rate of 41 per thousand and a death rate of 16 per thousand in 1961, seems likely to last for an indefinite period, in which case the surplus rural population will continue to gravitate to the cities, possibly in increasing volume. The only measures that will slow down this outflow will be effective methods of reducing the birth rate.

City growth in India will likely continue indefinitely if for no other reason than that the pressures of population will force large numbers to

---

[1] These comparisons are not altogether valid because of differences in definition of "urban." In India a settlement is classified as urban if it has a population of 5,000 or over; in the United States the figure is 2,500. If the Indian dividing point were set at 2,500, the proportion of people classified as urban would be much greater.

forsake the land. Farms have been fragmented to such a degree that the small acreages are usually inadequate to support the growing number of people dependent upon the land for a livelihood. To improve their chances for a better standard of living, or even survival, many are almost literally pushed off the land and into the cities. Added to this major stream of urbanward migrants are the refugees, uprooted in neighboring countries and forced out by political pressures.

The technological agricultural revolution which occurred in the West and which drastically reduced the number of workers needed to operate the farms was a major factor in urban growth. But it occurred at a time when expansion of the urban economy was sufficient to absorb the migrants who were no longer needed on the land. Such a technological revolution in Indian agriculture would spell disaster for countless numbers of rural people since the urban economic institutions are not expanding sufficiently to provide gainful employment for them. Even under present conditions of inefficient cultivation the surplus rural population is not readily integrated into the urban economy.

It seems virtually assured that India's cities will account for an increasing proportion of the total population in the years ahead. But it is unlikely that within the present century the cities will contain as much as half the population of the country, and certainly not in the foreseeable future will they reach the proportions attained by the United States and Britain.

Migrants and Their Adjustments

The flow of population from villages to cities is determined in part by economic and other conditions in the receiving communities. The urban economy has not expanded rapidly enough to provide jobs for all employable migrants. Nor have these cities been able to provide adequate housing and other amenities for them. Yet the influx continues. Many of them gravitate to the already overcrowded slums or construct temporary shelters in open spaces or on the sidewalks. Hundreds of refugees arriving in Calcutta from East Pakistan constructed flimsy huts on the grounds of the railway station at the point of entry. In major cities there are thousands of "street sleepers" whose style of life is barely above the survival level. It is estimated that in Calcutta alone there are three hundred thousand people whose only homes are the city sidewalks. Even those who do live in houses or apartments commonly exist under crowded conditions. It is not surprising that outbreaks of virulent diseases such as cholera, smallpox, and plague occur fairly regularly.

In the course of time many of these migrants obtain some kind of employment and thus acquire an economic foothold enabling them to survive or even to gain some degree of security. But the job waiting list is formidable and the waiting period often a long one. Migrants who do not succeed may at least return to their native villages. For political refugees there may be no place to go.

In a real sense, many of these people are *in* the city but not an integral part of it. They are more closely identified with their sociocultural groupings and their native villages than with the urban community of their residence. These ethnocentric orientations and loyalties have considerable significance for public municipal policies. Indifference to municipal issues is generally the rule among most of the residents, unless such issues bear directly and clearly on their own lives.

Many of the recent arrivals, like the early immigrants in American cities, are primarily interested in earning some money and perhaps eventually returning to their native villages. Their earnings, beyond the requirements of living costs, are often sent "back home" to their own kinship group, with which they are strongly identified and for whose support they are morally obligated. This flow of wealth out of the cities into the villages creates problems of municipal management and maintenance since the cities are deprived of needed revenues. Many of these people are beyond the reach of the tax collector.

It should be pointed out, however, that many city people in India are longtime urban residents who are cosmopolitan in their outlook and style of life—persons who may be far removed in time and space from the villages of their ancestors. Many of these are identified with professional, business, or governmental pursuits; often they are well educated and financially secure. The Parsees are a case in point. Coming originally from Persia in the eighth century, the Parsees took up residence in cities, mainly in or near Bombay, but also to some extent in other large centers. Mostly they are well educated and relatively prosperous, occupied mainly in business and professional activities. They are true cosmopolites. So are the Jews and Armenians. There are also many Hindus and Muslims who have long traditions of urban residence and experience.

Selective Aspects of Migration

Migration to Indian cities is highly selective of age and sex. As in most other countries, the majority of urbanward migrants are young adults who are in, or just entering, the age period of highest economic productivity. In the matter of sex selection, however, adult males are drawn in grossly disproportionate numbers to the cities, especially the large cities having employment opportunities. In the 1941–51 decade, some 608,000 males over ten years of age migrated to Bombay, compared with 239,000 females. In other cities the differences were considerably less. Madras, for example, received 252,000 males and 235,000 females during the same period. In the age period between twenty and thirty the volume of male migrants is much greater than for females of comparable age.

If the male migrants are unmarried they may set out alone; if they are married, it is a common procedure for them to leave their families behind, sometimes permanently, but often temporarily until such time that they become established and are subsequently joined by their dependents. For those who leave their immediate families behind there is a social obligation for them to return periodically to their native villages. But even if they are accompanied by their wives and children they are likely to maintain strong attachments to their kinship group remaining in the village.

Women seldom migrate alone to cities; they usually accompany their families as dependents, or their husbands and their own children if they are married.

This selective migration has significant implications for the demographic structure of Indian cities. In most of the urban centers there is a preponderance of males, in contrast to American cities, which usually have more women than men. For the total urban population in the country, in 1951, 53 per cent were males. Cities vary considerably in their sex ratios. Almost two-thirds of Bombay's population (63 per cent) was male in 1951, but in Bangalore the figure was 53 per cent, and in Madras the proportions were tilted only slightly toward males. Grossly unequal sex ratios generally create problems of adjustment and behavior. Often the men live under crowded conditions unfavorable to physical or moral well-being. Since 1951, however, the trend has been toward an equal distribution of males and females in the urban population, although doubtless certain cities will continue to show an imbalance for some time.

Patterns of Segregation

Migrants to cities tend to settle in districts occupied by others similar in such attributes as economic status, cultural heritage, language, nationality, religion, or race. Indian cities are no exception. One of the strongest of these segregative tendencies stems from village, caste, and kinship ties. Migrants to Indian cities apparently find more security and satisfaction in settling near their kinsmen and former fellow villagers than in living among strangers. It has been said, with some truth, that Indian cities are made up of transplanted villages. This clustering tendency has helped to maintain and strengthen contacts between the migrant in the city and his kinsmen and friends remaining in the village.

Religion is a powerful force for segregation. Some city districts are occupied mainly by Muslims, others by Hindus, still others by different religious minorities. There are likewise areas in which the occupants are drawn mainly from particular castes. By the same token, people are distributed to a considerable extent on the basis of economic status. Hence the existence of slum areas and prestige residential districts which attract people according to their incomes and possessions. These economic boundaries often cut across social and cultural boundaries: destitute Muslims or

Hindus or Christians generally are residentially separate from their more affluent fellow religionists.

Social areas may, however, not be occupied entirely by people representing a particular language, religion, or caste. As noted above, economic forces often dictate the choice of an area of residence irrespective of the cultural or social attributes of the people who live there. Furthermore, many with cosmopolitan tastes and interests may have no aversion to living among those who differ in culture or religion. One of the major slum areas of Calcutta, for example, is occupied by Muslims, Anglo-Indians, and Indian-Christians, who often live as close neighbors even though they are separated by a wide social and religious gap. In the same city there are other districts, of a higher income level, which are occupied by families with widely divergent cultural backgrounds. Yet within any of these areas of mixed occupancy may be small homogeneous "pockets" whose residents are similar in some of the basic cultural attributes such as caste or language or religion.

Thus there are created in the cities many cultural and social worlds which serve as point of reference and identification for the people who live there. Aside from contacts in the work situation and marketplace, their lives are largely circumscribed by the limited social worlds in which they are firmly anchored. In many respects their situation is comparable to that of earlier Old World immigrants in American cities who re-created for themselves a social environment made up of people and institutions of their own kind. And like the Old World immigrants, they retain their loyalty and identification with their own cultural group and with the village communities which they have left behind.

Slum Huts and Mansions

Generally, poor people tend to live near other poor people, rich people near other rich people. Yet economic segregation in India is ordinarily not as pronounced as in American cities, partly because zoning restrictions in Indian cities are often nonexistent or not observed. It is not unusual to find a modern house wedged between two or more disreputable shacks, a cheek-by-jowl ecological arrangement of wealth and poverty. Nor are places of residence necessarily detached from places of work. Retail merchants or craftsmen often live, with their families, in residential quarters behind or above their shops. This intermingling of residence and commercial establishments, widespread as it may be, is by no means universal, however. In the larger cities particularly there are specialized commercial districts, especially the city's center, in which there are few residential structures.

Urban slums in India do not always conform to the locational characteristics of American slums. Generally the slums in Indian cities are located not in the immediate vicinity of the central business district but farther out, sometimes on the city's outskirts. Rural peoples moving to the cities often construct flimsy huts on vacant land, either within the city or beyond its boundaries, because no houses at a price they can afford are available. These settlements may be permanent or temporary, but in any case they do not have the amenities of modern urban life. In cities like Bombay or Calcutta thousands of in-migrants have constructed huts in available open spaces, and many of them have erected such shelters on the sidewalks of these cities.

On the other hand, the rich or well-to-do generally reside fairly near the commercial center of the city, or at points accessible to the major institutions. In Bangalore, for example, the elite are concentrated in a fairly small area well within the city's boundaries, not far from the central business district in a section known as High Ground. Bombay's fashionable apartment district is near the major commercial and municipal institutions, facing the bay on one side and a large park on the other.

Decentralization of Population

But there is also some tendency for the well-to-do to move outward, provided adequate transportation facilities are available. This trend has been encouraged by the increasing use of the private automobile and the taxicab and by electric or steam commuting trains. Around a few great cities such as Calcutta and Bombay there is developing a ring of suburban dormitory settlements whose residents commute daily by train to the central city. Some two hundred thousand suburban residents commute by train each day to Bombay, and an even greater number to Calcutta.

As cities expand peripherally the usual administrative procedure has been to annex the areas in which changes are occurring as a result of this expansion. Entire villages situated on the fringe may be annexed, and therefore become a part of the larger administrative city. Usually these villages retain their separate social and cultural identity, even though they have been swallowed up in the process of urban expansion. As in the United States, the fringe areas that are annexed represent varied forms of land occupancy. In a study of the fringe areas around Bombay, Delhi, Baroda, Madras, and Hyderabad, Ellefsen found, in addition to the older villages, makeshift housing by refugees or other in-migrants, public and private housing developments, scattered commercial or industrial establishments, and tracts of land devoted to agriculture.[2] With increasing distance from each of the preceding cities there was a decrease in the proportion of persons employed in nonagricultural occupations. That is, the closer to the city were the hinterland residents the more likely were they to be employed in the city's establishments, or in such nonagricultural occupations

---

[2] Richard A. Ellefsen, "City-Hinterland Relationships in India," in Roy Turner, ed., *India's Urban Future* (Berkeley: University of California Press, 1961), Chap. 5.

as operating small shops in the hinterlands. Similarly, the level of literacy declined rather sharply from the city to the more remote parts of the immediate hinterlands.

The metropolitan region as it is manifest in the United States is hardly comparable to the so-called metropolitan region in India. The American metropolitan region is generally larger in area than such a region in India, if we include as a part of the regional hinterland those areas more or less dominated economically and culturally by a central metropolis.[3] This difference undoubtedly exists in part because technological aspects of communication and transportation have not brought the remoter portions of the hinterlands so directly under the dominance of the central cities as in the United States.

Owing to the decentralization of metropolitan population in the United States, especially during the twentieth century, density in the central portions of the cities has usually been fairly low, and often it has declined. In Indian cities, on the other hand, internal pressures have not been relieved to any great extent by the peripheral movement of people. High densities in the central cities are, therefore, the rule. In some wards of Calcutta and Old Delhi there are as many as 400,000 persons per square mile, and in parts of Bombay the square-mile density exceeds 250,000. Even in smaller cities the density may exceed 100,000. In, or adjacent to, high-density areas may be residential districts that are sparsely occupied. New Delhi would be a case in point. Generally these are high-income districts that have been more or less systematically planned.

The Ecology of Commerce

The ecological and organizational patterns of institutions, economic or otherwise, differ considerably from the patterns characteristic of Western cities. For one thing, the small specialized retail shop is the predominant type of merchandising establishment. There are a few department stores in the major metropolises, but they are not comparable in size and variety of goods with the great merchandise marts in American or European cities. As might be expected, the Indian department store is located in or near the central business district, accessible to a high-income clientele. But scattered over the city, commonly intermingled with residential structures, are small retail shops catering mainly to a limited clientele from the immediate vicinity.

The planned shopping center which has figured so prominently in the expansion of American cities since World War II is seldom found in Indian cities. A conspicuous exception is Connaught Place (recently renamed India Chauk) in New Delhi, itself a planned city, the national capital. This circular shopping center, about a mile in circumference, and the hub of a

---

[3] *Ibid.*

major business district, was developed by the British nearly a half century ago as a part of the larger metropolitan plan. Radiating outward from the hub are numerous streets which for some distance are lined with various kinds of establishments—retail shops, cinemas, transportation offices, banks, embassies, hotels, and so on. The major shopping center of Old Delhi, Chandni Chauk, caters to quite a different clientele, mainly people in the middle or lower income groups. Thus there has developed in the twin cities a binuclear commercial pattern, in contrast to a polynuclear pattern in Bangalore, Poona, and Calcutta.

The bazaar or public market in an Indian city is the counterpart of the planned shopping center in an American city or even the Western-type department store. Usually located in a large building, sometimes covering a square block, and managed by the municipality, the various "departments" are actually small specialized shops whose proprietors rent space for their retail operations. One may find in the bazaar almost any kind of consumer goods—wearing apparel, cloth, house furnishings, kitchen utensils, food products, books and magazines, handicraft work, leather goods, jewelry, and the like. In major cities there are numerous bazaars, often a major one near the center and minor ones located in or near residential districts farther out.

In or near the centers of the great metropolitan communities are found the fashionable shops that specialize in relatively expensive goods in demand by Western residents or well-to-do Indians. The central business district of Calcutta, for example, includes the banking and insurance establishments, government buildings, travel agencies, luxury shops, and major hotels, a pattern somewhat similar to that of Bombay. But in smaller cities this concentration is less apparent.

Manufacturing, Cultural, and Historical Centers

Much of the manufacturing in India has been carried on in comparatively small industrial establishments, and these have been dispersed rather widely over the city landscape, with no sharp distinction between industrial and residential sections. This is especially true of small "cottage" industries in which the operations can be carried out in the households, or at least in adjacent structures.

But with the development of large-scale manufacturing, the location of industrial establishments has become a function of planning. Most of the mass-production factories established since World War II are now located near or beyond the city's boundaries, often in districts set aside for factories and ancillary enterprises. Two large factories, manufacturing airplanes and telephones, are located some five or six miles from the city boundary of Bangalore. Factories have sprung up on both sides of a major highway between New Delhi and Faridabad, a distance of some eighteen miles. Some of the older types of industries, however, such as jute or textile mills, may be found within the city, as in the case of Howrah, a major suburb of Calcutta. In some instances factories initially located at the edge of an expanding urban settlement have been "swallowed up" by the city in its push outward.

A few smaller cities have been selected as sites for major industrial developments. Among these are Jamshedpur, a steel manufacturing center in the state of West Bengal; Visakhapatnam, a shipbuilding center in Andra Pradesh; and Ranchi, in Bihar, destined to become, in the opinion of some, the "Pittsburgh" of India.

Other cities are cultural, educational, and historical centers. One of these is Agra, noted for the world-famous Taj Mahal. Others are Benares, famed as the fountainhead of Hinduism, and nearby Senarth, the birthplace of Buddhism. Benares, reputed to be the oldest "living" city in the world, is a mecca for tourists and for orthodox Hindus who make pilgrimages to the holy city in order to bathe in the sacred waters of the Ganges. Poona, near Bombay, is the seat of numerous colleges and universities, and Lucknow, east of Delhi, is an important educational center in a city having a rich historical background of Islamic culture. Among the numerous resort cities in the highlands are Oootacamund and Coonoor in Madras State, South India; Darjeeling in the foothills of the Himalayas; Nainital and Moosoorie in the state of Uttar Pradesh; and Srinigar in Kashmir.

City planning is by no means new in India. During the British administration extensive planning programs were carried out in several cities. These resulted in the development of spacious grounds for parks and public buildings. Perhaps the most spectacular plan undertaken by the British was the capital city of New Delhi, a project completed in the early years of the present century. Located adjacent to Old Delhi, an ancient city, New Delhi is a city characterized by spacious public and private buildings, wide boulevards, and attractive residential districts. Some impressive planning programs have also been undertaken in India since independence. The best known of these is Chandigarh, the new capital of Punjab State in the Northwest. This new city was completely planned, much of it by the distinguished French architect and planner Le Corbusier. Another planned city is Bhubaneswar, the new capital of Orissa State.

The Urban Impact

In considering the impact of the city on behavior and institutions one may view the influence both on city residents and those who live in rural communities. The picture is not altogether clear. For those who live in the city there are obviously many changes that must be made in order to effect an accommodation to urban life. Perhaps the most important are those pertaining to occupational behavior; another to consumer behavior. There is undoubtedly some "softening" of ethnocentric attitudes as individuals representing various ethnic, religious, caste, and language groups come into close contact with each other in the marketplace or the work situation. Taboos against inter-dining are often impractical in the city since it may be necessary for persons of different caste or religious affiliations to eat together in public dining places.

On the other hand, there is little evidence that urban influence has effectively changed the basic structure of the caste and family system. The taboos against intercaste or interfaith marriage remain strong. The author found in a survey in Bangalore of some 2,200 male household heads of the Hindu faith that only thirteen had married outside their own caste.[4] The joint family system has persisted in the city, even though its structure has sometimes been altered for the specific conditions of urban life. Such generalizations, however, must be tentative, since sufficient empirical evidence from many cities is not available at present.

That cities have had an impact on life in the villages there can be no doubt, but precisely the nature and extent of this impact is not altogether clear. Rural people who visit the city, or who work there temporarily and return to their village homes, do acquire some of the behavior patterns characteristic of urban life. More particularly, they acquire many material objects—factory-made artifacts which may have both utilitarian and symbolic prestige value for them. But the distance of the village to the city, the frequency and character of the contacts with urban people and situations are significant variables. Villages located within a short distance of a city are likely to be influenced much more than communities farther removed; and in India there are thousands of villages located remotely from any urban center.

Doubtless many of the changes in village life because of urban influence are superficial and of little significance to the basic structures of the major institutions. The family and caste system, as well as the economic and religious system, have probably remained much the same even though contacts with the outside world have multiplied with increased travel and more opportunities for contacts through the mass media.

3 | The Urbanization of the Human Population

KINGSLEY DAVIS

Urbanized societies, in which a majority of the people live crowded together in towns and cities, represent a new and fundamental step in man's social evolution. Although cities themselves first appeared some 5,500 years

---

[4] Noel P. Gist, "Caste Differentials in South India," *Social Forces*, 19:126-37 (April 1954).

SOURCE: *Scientific American*, September 1965, pp. 41-53. Copyright © 1965 by Scientific American. All rights reserved. Reprinted by permission of the publisher.

ago, they were small and surrounded by an overwhelming majority of rural people; moreover, they relapsed easily to village or small-town status. The urbanized societies of today, in contrast, not only have urban agglomerations of a size never before attained but also have a high proportion of their population concentrated in such agglomerations. In 1960, for example, nearly 52 million Americans lived in only 16 urbanized areas. Together these areas covered less land than one of the smaller counties (Cochise) of Arizona. According to one definition used by the U.S. Bureau of the Census, 96 million people—53 percent of the nation's population—were concentrated in 213 urbanized areas that together occupied only .7 percent of the nation's land. Another definition used by the bureau puts the urban population at about 70 percent. The large and dense agglomerations comprising the urban population involve a degree of human contact and of social complexity never before known. They exceed in size the communities of any other large animal; they suggest the behavior of communal insects rather than of mammals.

Neither the recency nor the speed of this evolutionary development is widely appreciated. Before 1850 no society could be described as predominantly urbanized, and by 1900 only one—Great Britain—could be so regarded. Today, only 65 years later, all industrial nations are highly urbanized, and in the world as a whole the process of urbanization is accelerating rapidly.

Some years ago my associates and I at Columbia University undertook to document the progress of urbanization by compiling data on the world's cities and the proportion of human beings living in them; in recent years the work has been continued in our center—International Population and Urban Research—at the University of California at Berkeley. The data obtained in these investigations . . . shows the historical trend in terms of one index of urbanization: the proportion of the population living in cities of 100,000 or larger. Statistics of this kind are only approximations of reality, but they are accurate enough to demonstrate how urbanization has accelerated. Between 1850 and 1950 the index changed at a much higher rate than from 1800 to 1850, but the rate of change from 1950 to 1960 was twice that of the preceding 50 years! If the pace of increase that obtained between 1950 and 1960 were to remain the same, by 1990 the fraction of the world's people living in cities of 100,000 or larger would be more than half. Using another index of urbanization—the proportion of the world's population living in urban places of all sizes—we found that by 1960 the figure had already reached 33 percent.

Clearly the world as a whole is not fully urbanized, but it soon will be. This change in human life is so recent that even the most urbanized countries still exhibit the rural origins of their institutions. Its full implications for man's organic and social evolution can only be surmised.

In discussing the trend—and its implications insofar as they can be perceived—I shall use the term "urbanization" in a particular way. It refers here to the proportion of the total population concentrated in urban settlements, or else to a rise in this proportion. A common mistake is to think of urbanization as simply the growth of cities. Since the total population is composed of both the urban population and the rural, however, the "proportion urban" is a function of both of them. Accordingly, cities can grow without any urbanization, provided that the rural population grows at an equal or a greater rate.

Historically, urbanization and the growth of cities have occurred together, which accounts for the confusion. As the reader will soon see, it is necessary to distinguish the two trends. In the most advanced countries today, for example, urban populations are still growing, but their proportion of the total population is tending to remain stable or to diminish. In other words, the process of urbanization—the switch from a spread-out pattern of human settlement to one of concentration in urban centers—is a change that has a beginning and an end, but the growth of cities has no inherent limit. Such growth could continue even after everyone was living in cities, through sheer excess of births over deaths.

The difference between a rural village and an urban community is of course one of degree; a precise operational distinction is somewhat arbitrary, and it varies from one nation to another. Since data are available for communities of various sizes, a dividing line can be chosen at will. One convenient index of urbanization, for example, is the proportion of people living in places of 100,000 or more. In the following analysis I shall depend on two indexes: the one just mentioned and the proportion of population classed as "urban" in the official statistics of each country. In practice the two indexes are highly correlated; therefore either one can be used as an index of urbanization.

Actually the hardest problem is not that of determining the "floor" of the urban category but of ascertaining the boundary of places that are clearly urban by any definition. How far east is the boundary of Los Angeles? Where along the Hooghly River does Calcutta leave off and the countryside begin? In the past the population of cities and towns has usually been given as the number of people living within the political boundaries. Thus the population of New York is frequently given as around eight million, this being the population of the city proper. The error in such a figure was not large before World War I, but since then, particularly in the advanced countries, urban populations have been spilling over the narrow political boundaries at a tremendous rate. In 1960 the New York-Northeastern New Jersey urbanized area, as delineated by the Bureau of the Census, had more than 14 million people. That delineation showed it to be the largest city in the world and nearly twice as large as New York City proper.

As a result of the outward spread of urbanites, counts made on the basis of political boundaries alone underestimate the city populations and exaggerate the rural. For this reason our office delineated the metropolitan areas of as many countries as possible for dates around 1950. These areas included the central, or political, cities and the zones around them that are receiving the spillover.

This reassessment raised the estimated proportion of the world's population in cities of 100,000 or larger from 15.1 percent to 16.7 percent. As of 1960 we have used wherever possible the "urban agglomeration" data now furnished to the United Nations by many countries. The U.S., for example, provides data for "urbanized areas," meaning cities of 50,000 or larger and the built-up agglomerations around them.

. . . My concern is with the degree of urbanization in whole societies. It is curious that thousands of years elapsed between the first appearance of small cities and the emergence of urbanized societies in the 19th century. It is also curious that the region where urbanized societies arose—northwestern Europe—was not the one that had given rise to the major cities of the past; on the contrary, it was a region where urbanization had been at an extremely low ebb. Indeed, the societies of northwestern Europe in medieval times were so rural that it is hard for modern minds to comprehend them. Perhaps it was the nonurban character of these societies that erased the parasitic nature of towns and eventually provided a new basis for a revolutionary degree of urbanization.

At any rate, two seemingly adverse conditions may have presaged the age to come: one the low productivity of medieval agriculture in both per-acre and per-man terms, the other the feudal social system. The first meant that towns could not prosper on the basis of local agriculture alone but had to trade and to manufacture something to trade. The second meant that they could not gain political dominance over their hinterlands and thus become warring city-states. Hence they specialized in commerce and manufacture and evolved local institutions suited to this role. Craftsmen were housed in the towns, because there the merchants could regulate quality and cost. Competition among towns stimulated specialization and technological innovation. The need for literacy, accounting skills and geographical knowledge caused the towns to invest in secular education.

Although the medieval towns remained small and never embraced more than a minor fraction of each region's population, the close connection between industry and commerce that they fostered, together with their emphasis on technique, set the stage for the ultimate breakthrough in urbanization. This breakthrough came only with the enormous growth in productivity caused by the use of inanimate energy and machinery. How difficult it was to achieve the transition is agonizingly apparent from statistics showing that even with the conquest of the New World the growth of urbanization during three postmedieval centuries in Europe was barely perceptible. I have assembled population estimates at two or more dates for

33 towns and cities in the 16th century, 46 in the 17th and 61 in the 18th. The average rate of growth during the three centuries was less than .6 percent per year. Estimates of the growth of Europe's population as a whole between 1650 and 1800 work out to slightly more than .4 percent. The advantage of the towns was evidently very slight. Taking only the cities of 100,000 or more inhabitants, one finds that in 1600 their combined population was 1.6 percent of the estimated population of Europe; in 1700, 1.9 percent, and in 1800, 2.2 percent. On the eve of the industrial revolution Europe was still an overwhelmingly agrarian region.

With industrialization, however, the transformation was striking. By 1801 nearly a tenth of the people of England and Wales were living in cities of 100,000 or larger. This proportion doubled in 40 years and doubled again in another 60 years. By 1900 Britain was an urbanized society. In general, the later each country became industrialized, the faster was its urbanization. The change from a population with 10 percent of its members in cities of 100,000 or larger to one in which 30 percent lived in such cities took about 79 years in England and Wales, 66 in the U.S., 48 in Germany, 36 in Japan and 26 in Australia. The close association between economic development and urbanization has persisted; . . . in 199 countries around 1960 the proportion of the population living in cities varied sharply with per capita income.

Clearly modern urbanization is best understood in terms of its connection with economic growth, and its implications are best perceived in its latest manifestations in advanced countries. What becomes apparent as one examines the trend in these countries is that urbanization is a finite process, a cycle through which nations go in their transition from agrarian to industrial society. The intensive urbanization of most of the advanced countries began within the past 100 years; in the underdeveloped countries it got under way more recently. In some of the advanced countries its end is now in sight. The fact that it will end, however, does not mean that either economic development or the growth of cities will necessarily end.

The typical cycle of urbanization can be represented by a curve in the shape of an attenuated S. Starting from the bottom of the S, the first bend tends to come early and to be followed by a long attenuation. In the United Kingdom, for instance, the swiftest rise in the proportion of people living in cities of 100,000 or larger occurred from 1811 to 1851. In the U.S. it occurred from 1820 to 1890, in Greece from 1879 to 1921. As the proportion climbs above 50 percent the curve begins to flatten out; it falters, or even declines, when the proportion urban has reached about 75 percent. In the United Kingdom, one of the world's most urban countries, the proportion was slightly higher in 1926 (78.7 percent) than in 1961 (78.3 percent).

At the end of the curve some ambiguity appears. As a society becomes advanced enough to be highly urbanized it can also afford considerable suburbanization and fringe development. In a sense the slowing down of urbanization is thus more apparent than real: an increasing proportion of urbanites simply live in the country and are classified as rural. Many countries now try to compensate for this ambiguity by enlarging the boundaries of urban places; they did so in numerous censuses taken around 1960. Whether in these cases the old classification of urban or the new one is erroneous depends on how one looks at it; at a very advanced stage the entire concept of urbanization becomes ambiguous.

The end of urbanization cannot be unraveled without going into the ways in which economic development governs urbanization. Here the first question is: Where do the urbanites come from? The possible answers are few: The proportion of people in cities can rise because rural settlements grow larger and are reclassified as towns or cities; because the excess of births over deaths is greater in the city than in the country, or because people move from the country to the city.

The first factor has usually had only slight influence. The second has apparently never been the case. Indeed, a chief obstacle to the growth of cities in the past has been their excessive mortality. London's water in the middle of the 19th century came mainly from wells and rivers that drained cesspools, graveyards and tidal areas. The city was regularly ravaged by cholera. Tables for 1841 show an expectation of life of about 36 years for London and 26 for Liverpool and Manchester, as compared to 41 for England and Wales as a whole. After 1850, mainly as a result of sanitary measures and some improvement in nutrition and housing, city health improved, but as late as the period 1901–1910 the death rate of the urban counties in England and Wales, as modified to make the age structure comparable, was 33 percent higher than the death rate of the rural counties. As Bernard Benjamin, a chief statistician of the British General Register Office, has remarked: "Living in the town involved not only a higher risk of epidemic and crowd diseases . . . but also a higher risk of degenerative disease—the harder wear and tear of factory employment and urban discomfort." By 1950, however, virtually the entire differential had been wiped out.

As for birth rates, during rapid urbanization in the past they were notably lower in cities than in rural areas. In fact, the gap tended to widen somewhat as urbanization proceeded in the latter half of the 19th century and the first quarter of the 20th. In 1800 urban women in the U.S. had 36 percent fewer children than rural women did; in 1840, 38 percent and in 1930, 41 percent. Thereafter the difference diminished.

With mortality in the cities higher and birth rates lower, and with reclassification a minor factor, the only real source for the growth in the proportion of people in urban areas during the industrial transition was rural-urban migration. This source had to be plentiful enough not only to overcome the substantial disadvantage of the cities in natural increase but also, above that, to furnish a big margin of growth in their populations. If, for example, the cities had a death rate a third higher and a birth rate a third lower than the rural rates (as was typical in the latter half of the 19th century), they would require each year perhaps 40 to 45 migrants from elsewhere per 1,000 of their population to maintain a growth rate of 3 percent per year. Such a rate of migration could easily be maintained as long as the rural portion of the population was large, but when this condition ceased to obtain, the maintenance of the same urban rate meant an increasing drain on the countryside.

Why did the rural-urban migration occur? The reason was that the rise in technological enhancement of human productivity, together with certain constant factors, rewarded urban concentration. One of the constant factors was that agriculture uses land as its prime instrument of production and hence spreads out people who are engaged in it, whereas manufacturing, commerce and services use land only as a site. Moreover, the demand for agricultural products is less elastic than the demand for services and manufactures. As productivity grows, services and manufactures can absorb more manpower by paying higher wages. Since nonagricultural activities can use land simply as a site, they can locate near one another (in towns and cities) and thus minimize the fraction of space inevitably involved in the division of labor. At the same time, as agricultural technology is improved, capital costs in farming rise and manpower becomes not only less needed but also economically more burdensome. A substantial portion of the agricultural population is therefore sufficiently disadvantaged, in relative terms, to be attracted by higher wages in other sectors.

In this light one sees why a large flow of people from farms to cities was generated in every country that passed through the industrial revolution. One also sees why, with an even higher proportion of people already in cities and with the inability of city people to replace themselves by reproduction, the drain eventually became so heavy that in many nations the rural population began to decline in absolute as well as relative terms. In Sweden it declined after 1920, in England and Wales after 1861, in Belgium after 1910.

Realizing that urbanization is transitional and finite, one comes on another fact—a fact that throws light on the circumstances in which urbanization comes to an end. A basic feature of the transition is the profound switch from agricultural to nonagricultural employment. This change is associated with urbanization but not identical with it. The difference emerges particularly in the later stages. Then the availability of automobiles, radios, motion pictures and electricity, as well as the reduction of the workweek and the workday, mitigate the disadvantages of living in the country. Concurrently the expanding size of cities makes them more difficult to live in. The population classed as "rural" is accordingly enlarged, both from cities and from true farms.

For these reasons the "rural" population in some industrial countries never did fall in absolute size. In all the industrial countries, however, the population dependent on agriculture—which the reader will recognize as a more functional definition of the nonurban population than mere rural residence—decreased in absolute as well as relative terms. In the U.S., for example, the net migration from farms totaled more than 27 million between 1920 and 1959 and thus averaged approximately 700,000 a year. As a result the farm population declined from 32.5 million in 1916 to 20.5 million in 1960, in spite of the large excess of births in farm families. In 1964, by a stricter American definition classifying as "farm families" only those families actually earning their living from agriculture, the farm population was down to 12.9 million. This number represented 6.8 percent of the nation's population; the comparable figure for 1880 was 44 percent. In Great Britain the number of males occupied in agriculture was at its peak, 1.8 million, in 1851; by 1961 it had fallen to .5 million.

In the later stages of the cycle, then, urbanization in the industrial countries tends to cease. Hence the connection between economic development and the growth of cities also ceases. The change is explained by two circumstances. First, there is no longer enough farm population to furnish a significant migration to the cities. (What can 12.9 million American farmers contribute to the growth of the 100 million people already in urbanized areas?) Second, the rural nonfarm population, nourished by refugees from the expanding cities, begins to increase as fast as the city population. The effort of census bureaus to count fringe residents as urban simply pushes the definition of "urban" away from the notion of dense settlement and in the direction of the term "nonfarm." As the urban population becomes more "rural," which is to say less densely settled, the advanced industrial peoples are for a time able to enjoy the amenities of urban life without the excessive crowding of the past.

Here, however, one again encounters the fact that a cessation of urbanization does not necessarily mean a cessation of city growth. An example is provided by New Zealand. Between 1945 and 1961 the proportion of New Zealand's population classed as urban—that is, the ratio between urban and rural residents—changed hardly at all (from 61.3 percent to 63.6 percent) but the urban population increased by 50 percent. In Japan between 1940 and 1950 urbanization actually decreased slightly, but the urban population increased by 13 percent.

The point to be kept in mind is that once urbanization ceases, city growth becomes a function of general population growth. Enough farm-to-city migration may still occur to redress the difference in natural increase. The reproductive rate of urbanites tends, however, to increase when they live at lower densities, and the reproductive rate of "urbanized" farmers tends to decrease; hence little migration is required to make the urban increase equal the national increase.

I now turn to the currently underdeveloped countries. With the advanced nations having slackened their rate of urbanization, it is the others—representing three-fourths of humanity—that are mainly responsible for the rapid urbanization now characterizing the world as a whole. In fact, between 1950 and 1960 the proportion of the population in cities of 100,000 or more rose about a third faster in the underdeveloped regions than in the developed ones. Among the underdeveloped regions the pace was slow in eastern and southern Europe, but in the rest of the underdeveloped world the proportion in cities rose twice as fast as it did in the industrialized countries, even though the latter countries in many cases broadened their definitions of urban places to include more suburban and fringe residents.

Because of the characteristic pattern of urbanization, the current rates of urbanization in underdeveloped countries could be expected to exceed those now existing in countries far advanced in the cycle. On discovering that this is the case one is tempted to say that the underdeveloped regions are now in the typical stage of urbanization associated with early economic development. This notion, however, is erroneous. In their urbanization the underdeveloped countries are definitely not repeating past history. Indeed, the best grasp of their present situation comes from analyzing how their course differs from the previous pattern of development.

The first thing to note is that today's underdeveloped countries are urbanizing not only more rapidly than the industrial nations are now but also more rapidly than the industrial nations did in the heyday of their urban growth. The difference, however, is not large. In 40 underdeveloped countries for which we have data in recent decades, the average gain in the proportion of the population urban was 20 percent per decade; in 16 industrial countries, during the decades of their most rapid urbanization (mainly in the 19th century), the average gain per decade was 15 percent.

This finding that urbanization is proceeding only a little faster in underdeveloped countries than it did historically in the advanced nations may be questioned by the reader. It seemingly belies the widespread impression that cities throughout the nonindustrial parts of the world are bursting with people. There is, however, no contradiction. One must recall the basic distinction between a change in the proportion of the population urban, which is a ratio, and the absolute growth of cities. The popular impression is correct: the cities in underdeveloped areas are growing at a disconcerting rate. They are far outstripping the city boom of the industrializing era in the 19th century. If they continue their recent rate of growth, they will double their population every 15 years.

In 34 underdeveloped countries for which we have data relating to the 1940's and 1950's, the average annual gain in the urban population was 4.5 percent. The figure is remarkably similar for the various regions: 4.7 percent in seven countries of Africa, 4.7 percent in 15 countries of Asia and 4.3 percent in 12 countries of Latin America. In contrast, in nine European countries during their period of fastest urban population growth (mostly in the latter half of the 19th century) the average gain per year was 2.1 percent. Even the frontier industrial countries—the U.S., Australia–New Zealand, Canada and Argentina—which received huge numbers of immigrants, had a smaller population growth in towns and cities: 4.2 percent per year. In Japan and the U.S.S.R. the rate was respectively 5.4 and 4.3 percent per year, but their economic growth began only recently.

How is it possible that the contrast in growth between today's underdeveloped countries and yesterday's industrializing countries is sharper with respect to the absolute urban population than with respect to the urban share of the total population? The answer lies in another profound difference between the two sets of countries—a difference in total population growth, rural as well as urban. Contemporary underdeveloped populations have been growing since 1940 more than twice as fast as industrialized populations, and their increase far exceeds the growth of the latter at the peak of their expansion. The only rivals in an earlier day were the frontier nations, which had the help of great streams of immigrants. Today the underdeveloped nations—already densely settled, tragically impoverished and with gloomy economic prospects—are multiplying their people by sheer biological increase at a rate that is unprecedented. It is this population boom that is overwhelmingly responsible for the rapid inflation of city populations in such countries. Contrary to popular opinion both inside and outside those countries, the main factor is not rural-urban migration.

This point can be demonstrated easily by a calculation that has the effect of eliminating the influence of general population growth on urban growth. The calculation involves assuming that the total population of a given country remained constant over a period of time but that the percentage urban changed as it did historically. In this manner one obtains the growth of the absolute urban population that would have occurred if rural-urban migration were the only factor affecting it. As an example, Costa Rica had in 1927 a total population of 471,500, of which 88,600, or 18.8 percent, was urban. By 1963 the country's total population was 1,325,200 and the urban population was 456,600, or 34.5 percent. If the total population had remained at 471,500 but the percentage urban had still risen from 18.8 to 34.5, the absolute urban population in 1963 would have been only 162,700. That is the growth that would have occurred in the urban population if rural-urban migration had been the only factor. In actuality the urban population rose to 456,600. In other words, only 20 percent of the rapid growth of Costa Rica's towns and cities was attributable to urbanization per se; 44 percent was attributable solely to the country's general population increase, the remainder to the joint operation of both factors. Similarly, in Mexico between 1940 and 1960, 50 percent of the urban population increase was attributable to national multiplication alone and only 22 percent to urbanization alone.

The past performance of the advanced countries presents a sharp contrast. In Switzerland between 1850 and 1888, when the proportion urban resembled that in Costa Rica recently, general population growth alone accounted for only 19 percent of the increase of town and city people, and rural-urban migration alone accounted for 69 percent. In France between

1846 and 1911 only 21 percent of the growth in the absolute urban population was due to general growth alone.

The conclusion to which this contrast points is that one anxiety of governments in the underdeveloped nations is misplaced. Impressed by the mushrooming in their cities of shantytowns filled with ragged peasants, they attribute the fantastically fast city growth to rural-urban migration. Actually this migration now does little more than make up for the small difference in the birth rate between city and countryside. In the history of the industrial nations, as we have seen, the sizable difference between urban and rural birth rates and death rates required that cities, if they were to grow, had to have an enormous influx of people from farms and villages. Today in the underdeveloped countries the towns and cities have only a slight disadvantage in fertility, and their old disadvantage in mortality not only has been wiped out but also in many cases has been reversed. During the 19th century the urbanizing nations were learning how to keep crowded populations in cities from dying like flies. Now the lesson has been learned, and it is being applied to cities even in countries just emerging from tribalism. In fact, a disproportionate share of public health funds goes into cities. As a result throughout the nonindustrial world people in cities are multiplying as never before, and rural-urban migration is playing a much lesser role.

The trends just described have an important implication for the rural population. Given the explosive overall population growth in underdeveloped countries, it follows that if the rural population is not to pile up on the land and reach an economically absurd density, a high rate of rural-urban migration must be maintained. Indeed, the exodus from rural areas should be higher than in the past. But this high rate of internal movement is not taking place, and there is some doubt that it could conceivably do so.

To elaborate I shall return to my earlier point that in the evolution of industrialized countries the rural citizenry often declined in absolute as well as relative terms. The rural population of France—26.8 million in 1846—was down to 20.8 million by 1926 and 17.2 million by 1962, notwithstanding a gain in the nation's total population during this period. Sweden's rural population dropped from 4.3 million in 1910 to 3.5 million in 1960. Since the category "rural" includes an increasing portion of urbanites living in fringe areas, the historical drop was more drastic and consistent specifically in the farm population. In the U.S., although the "rural" population never quite ceased to grow, the farm contingent began its long descent shortly after the turn of the century; today it is less than two-fifths of what it was in 1910.

This transformation is not occurring in contemporary underdeveloped countries. In spite of the enormous growth of their cities, their rural populations—and their more narrowly defined agricultural populations—are growing at a rate that in many cases exceeds the rise of even the urban population during the evolution of the now advanced countries. The poor countries thus confront a grave dilemma. If they do not substantially step up the exodus from rural areas, these areas will be swamped with underemployed farmers. If they do step up the exodus, the cities will grow at a disastrous rate.

The rapid growth of cities in the advanced countries, painful though it was, had the effect of solving a problem—the problem of the rural population. The growth of cities enabled agricultural holdings to be consolidated, allowed increased capitalization and in general resulted in greater efficiency. Now, however, the underdeveloped countries are experiencing an even more rapid urban growth—and are suffering from urban problems—but urbanization is not solving their rural ills.

A case in point is Venezuela. Its capital, Caracas, jumped from a population of 359,000 in 1941 to 1,507,000 in 1963; other Venezuelan towns and cities equaled or exceeded this growth. Is this rapid rise denuding the countryside of people? No, the Venezuelan farm population increased in the decade 1951–1961 by 11 percent. The only thing that declined was the amount of cultivated land. As a result the agricultural population density became worse. In 1950 there were some 64 males engaged in agriculture per square mile of cultivated land; in 1961 there were 78. (Compare this with 4.8 males occupied in agriculture per square mile of cultivated land in Canada, 6.8 in the U.S. and 15.6 in Argentina.) With each male occupied in agriculture there are of course dependents. Approximately 225 persons in Venezuela are trying to live from each square mile of cultivated land. Most of the growth of cities in Venezuela is attributable to overall population growth. If the general population had not grown at all, and internal migration had been large enough to produce the actual shift in the proportion in cities, the increase in urban population would have been only 28 percent of what it was and the rural population would have been reduced by 57 percent.

The story of Venezuela is being repeated virtually everywhere in the underdeveloped world. It is not only Caracas that has thousands of squatters living in self-constructed junk houses on land that does not belong to them. By whatever name they are called, the squatters are to be found in all major cities in the poorer countries. They live in broad gullies beneath the main plain in San Salvador and on the hillsides of Rio de Janeiro and Bogotá. They tend to occupy with implacable determination parks, school grounds and vacant lots. Amman, the capital of Jordan, grew from 12,000 in 1958 to 247,000 in 1961. A good part of it is slums, and urban amenities are lacking most of the time for most of the people. Greater Baghdad now has an estimated 850,000 people; its slums, like those in many other underdeveloped countries, are in two zones—the central part of the city and the outlying areas. Here are the *sarifa* areas, characterized by self-built reed huts; these areas account for about 45 percent of the housing in the entire city and are devoid of amenities, including even latrines. In addition to such urban problems, all the countries struggling for higher living levels find their rural population growing too and piling up on already crowded land.

I have characterized urbanization as a transformation that, unlike economic development, is finally accomplished and comes to an end. At the 1950–1960 rate the term "urbanized world" will be applicable well before the end of the century. One should scarcely expect, however, that mankind will complete its urbanization without major complications. One sign of trouble ahead turns on the distinction I made at the start between urbanization and city growth per se. Around the globe today city growth is disproportionate to urbanization. The discrepancy is paradoxical in the industrial nations and worse than paradoxical in the nonindustrial.

It is in this respect that the nonindustrial nations, which still make up the great majority of nations, are far from repeating past history. In the 19th and early 20th centuries the growth of cities arose from and contributed to economic advancement. Cities took surplus manpower from the countryside and put it to work producing goods and services that in turn helped to modernize agriculture. But today in underdeveloped countries, as in present-day advanced nations, city growth has become increasingly unhinged from economic development and hence from rural-urban migration. It derives in greater degree from overall population growth, and this growth in nonindustrial lands has become unprecedented because of modern health techniques combined with high birth rates.

The speed of world population growth is twice what it was before 1940, and the swiftest increase has shifted from the advanced to the backward nations. In the latter countries, consequently, it is virtually impossible to create city services fast enough to take care of the huge, never ending cohorts of babies and peasants swelling the urban masses. It is even harder to expand agricultural land and capital fast enough to accommodate the enormous natural increase on farms. The problem is not urbanization, not rural-urban migration, but human multiplication. It is a problem that is new in both its scale and its setting, and runaway city growth is only one of its painful expressions.

As long as the human population expands, cities will expand too, regardless of whether urbanization increases or declines. This means that some individual cities will reach a size that will make 19th-century metropolises look like small towns. If the New York urbanized area should continue to grow only as fast as the nation's population (according to medium projections of the latter by the Bureau of the Census), it would reach 21 million by 1985 and 30 million by 2010. I have calculated that if India's population should grow as the U.N. projections indicate it will, the largest city in India in the year 2000 will have between 36 and 66 million inhabitants.

What is the implication of such giant agglomerations for human density? In 1950 the New York–Northeastern New Jersey urbanized area had an average density of 9,810 persons per square mile. With 30 million people in the year 2010, the density would be 24,000 per square mile. Although this level is exceeded now in parts of New York City (which averages about

25,000 per square mile) and many other cities, it is a high density to be spread over such a big area; it would cover, remember, the suburban areas to which people moved to escape high density. Actually, however, the density of the New York urbanized region is dropping, not increasing, as the population grows. The reason is that the territory covered by the urban agglomeration is growing faster than the population: it grew by 51 percent from 1950 to 1960, whereas the population rose by 15 percent.

If, then, one projects the rise in population and the rise in territory for the New York urbanized region, one finds the density problem solved. It is not solved for long, though, because New York is not the only city in the region that is expanding. So are Philadelphia, Trenton, Hartford, New Haven and so on. By 1960 a huge stretch of territory about 600 miles long and 30 to 100 miles wide along the Eastern seaboard contained some 37 million people. (I am speaking of a longer section of the seaboard than the Boston-to-Washington conurbation referred to by some other authors.) Since the whole area is becoming one big polynucleated city, its population cannot long expand without a rise in density. Thus persistent human multiplication promises to frustrate the ceaseless search for space—for ample residential lots, wide-open suburban school grounds, sprawling shopping centers, one-floor factories, broad freeways.

How people feel about giant agglomerations is best indicated by their headlong effort to escape them. The bigger the city, the higher the cost of space; yet, the more the level of living rises, the more people are willing to pay for low-density living. Nevertheless, as urbanized areas expand and collide, it seems probable that life in low-density surroundings will become too dear for the great majority.

One can of course imagine that cities may cease to grow and may even shrink in size while the population in general continues to multiply. Even this dream, however, would not permanently solve the problem of space. It would eventually obliterate the distinction between urban and rural, but at the expense of the rural.

It seems plain that the only way to stop urban crowding and to solve most of the urban problems besetting both the developed and the underdeveloped nations is to reduce the overall rate of population growth. Policies designed to do this have as yet little intelligence and power behind them. Urban planners continue to treat population growth as something to be planned for, not something to be itself planned. Any talk about applying brakes to city growth is therefore purely speculative, overshadowed as it is by the reality of uncontrolled population increase.

B | Perspectives on Urbanism as a Way of Life

4 | Urbanism as a Way of Life

LOUIS WIRTH

. . . The city and the country may be regarded as two poles in reference to one or the other of which all human settlements tend to arrange themselves. In viewing urban-industrial and rural-folk society as ideal types of communities, we may obtain a perspective for the analysis of the basic models of human association as they appear in contemporary civilization.

A Sociological Definition of the City

Despite the preponderant significance of the city in our civilization, however, our knowledge of the nature of urbanism and the process of urbanization is meager. Many attempts have indeed been made to isolate the distinguishing characteristics of urban life. Geographers, historians, economists, and political scientists have incorporated the points of view of their respective disciplines into diverse definitions of the city. While in no sense intended to supersede these, the formulation of a sociological approach to the city may incidentally serve to call attention to the interrelations between them by emphasizing the peculiar characteristics of the city as a particular form of human association. A sociologically significant definition of the city seeks to select those elements of urbanism which mark it as a distinctive mode of human group life.

The characterization of a community as urban on the basis of size alone is obviously arbitrary. It is difficult to defend the present census definition which designates a community of 2,500 and above as urban and all others as

SOURCE: *American Journal of Sociology*, XLIV (July 1938), 3-24. Reprinted by permission of the University of Chicago Press. Copyright © 1938 by the University of Chicago.

rural. The situation would be the same if the criterion were 4,000, 8,000, 10,000, 25,000, or 100,000 population, for although in the latter case we might feel that we were more nearly dealing with an urban aggregate than would be the case in communities of lesser size, no definition of urbanism can hope to be completely satisfying as long as numbers are regarded as the sole criterion. Moreover, it is not difficult to demonstrate that communities of less than the arbitrarily set number of inhabitants lying within the range of influence of metropolitan centers have greater claim to recognition as urban communities than do larger ones leading a more isolated existence in a predominantly rural area. Finally, it should be recognized that census definitions are unduly influenced by the fact that the city, statistically speaking, is always an administrative concept in that the corporate limits play a decisive role in delineating the urban area. Nowhere is this more clearly apparent than in the concentrations of population on the peripheries of great metropolitan centers which cross arbitrary administrative boundaries of city, county, state, and nation.

As long as we identify urbanism with the physical entity of the city, viewing it merely as rigidly delimited in space, and proceed as if urban attributes abruptly ceased to be manifested beyond an arbitrary boundary line, we are not likely to arrive at any adequate conception of urbanism as a mode of life. The technological developments in transportation and communication which virtually mark a new epoch in human history have accentuated the role of cities as dominant elements in our civilization and have enormously extended the urban mode of living beyond the confines of the city itself. The dominance of the city, especially of the great city, may be regarded as a consequence of the concentration in cities of industrial and commercial, financial and administrative facilities and activities, transportation and communication lines, and cultural and recreational equipment such as the press, radio stations, theaters, libraries, museums, concert halls, operas, hospitals, higher educational institutions, research and publishing centers, professional organizations, and religious and welfare institutions. Were it not for the attraction and suggestions that the city exerts through these instrumentalities upon the rural population, the differences between the rural and the urban modes of life would be even greater than they are. Urbanization no longer denotes merely the process by which persons are attracted to a place called the city and incorporated into its system of life. It refers also to that cumulative accentuation of the characteristics distinctive of the mode of life which is associated with the growth of cities, and finally to the changes in the direction of modes of life recognized as urban which are apparent among people, wherever they may be, who have come under the spell of the influences which the city exerts by virtue of the power of its institutions and personalities operating through the means of communication and transportation.

The shortcomings which attach to number of inhabitants as a criterion of urbanism apply for the most part to density of population as well.

Whether we accept the density of 10,000 persons per square mile as Mark Jefferson [1] proposed, or 1,000, which Willcox [2] preferred to regard as the criterion of urban settlements, it is clear that unless density is correlated with significant social characteristics it can furnish only an arbitrary basis for differentiating urban from rural communities. Since our census enumerates the night rather than the day population of an area, the locale of the most intensive urban life—the city center—generally has low population density, and the industrial and commercial areas of the city, which contain the most characteristic economic activities underlying urban society, would scarcely anywhere be truly urban if density were literally interpreted as a mark of urbanism. Nevertheless, the fact that the urban community is distinguished by a large aggregation and relatively dense concentration of population can scarcely be left out of account in a definition of the city. But these criteria must be seen as relative to the general cultural context in which cities arise and exist and are sociologically relevant only in so far as they operate as conditioning factors in social life.

The same criticisms apply to such criteria as the occupation of the inhabitants, the existence of certain physical facilities, institutions, and forms of political organization. The question is not whether cities in our civilization or in others do exhibit these distinctive traits, but how potent they are in molding the character of social life into its specifically urban form. Nor in formulating a fertile definition can we afford to overlook the great variations between cities. By means of a typology of cities based upon size, location, age, and function, such as we have undertaken to establish in our recent report to the National Resources Committee,[3] we have found it feasible to array and classify urban communities ranging from struggling small towns to thriving world-metropolitan centers; from isolated trading-centers in the midst of agricultural regions to thriving world-ports and commercial and industrial conurbations. Such differences as these appear crucial because the social characteristics and influences of these different "cities" vary widely.

A serviceable definition of urbanism should not only denote the essential characteristics which all cities—at least those in our culture—have in common, but should lend itself to the discovery of their variations. An industrial city will differ significantly in social respects from a commercial, mining, fishing, resort, university, and capital city. A one-industry city will present different sets of social characteristics from a multi-industry city, as will an industrially balanced from an imbalanced city, a suburb from a satellite, a residential suburb from an industrial suburb, a city within a metropolitan region from one lying outside, an old city from a new one, a southern city

---

[1] "The Anthropogeography of Some Great Cities," *Bull. American Geographical Society*, XLI (1909), 537–66.

[2] Walter F. Willcox, "A Definition of 'City' in Terms of Density," in E. W. Burgess, *The Urban Community* (Chicago, 1926), p. 119.

[3] *Our Cities: Their Role in the National Economy* (Washington: Government Printing Office, 1937), p. 8.

from a New England, a middle-western from a Pacific Coast city, a growing from a stable and from a dying city.

A sociological definition must obviously be inclusive enough to comprise whatever essential characteristics these different types of cities have in common as social entities, but it obviously cannot be so detailed as to take account of all the variations implicit in the manifold classes sketched above. Presumably some of the characteristics of cities are more significant in conditioning the nature of urban life than others, and we may expect the outstanding features of the urban-social scene to vary in accordance with size, density, and differences in the functional type of cities. Moreover, we may infer that rural life will bear the imprint of urbanism in the measure that through contact and communication it comes under the influence of cities. It may contribute to the clarity of the statements that follow to repeat that while the locus of urbanism as a mode of life is, of course, to be found characteristically in places which fulfil the requirements we shall set up as a definition of the city, urbanism is not confined to such localities but is manifest in varying degrees wherever the influences of the city reach.

While urbanism, or that complex of traits which makes up the characteristic mode of life in cities, and urbanization, which denotes the development and extensions of these factors, are thus not exclusively found in settlements which are cities in the physical and demographic sense, they do, nevertheless, find their most pronounced expression in such areas, especially in metropolitan cities. In formulating a definition of the city it is necessary to exercise caution in order to avoid identifying urbanism as a way of life with any specific locally or historically conditioned cultural influences which, while they may significantly affect the specific character of the community, are not the essential determinants of its character as a city.

It is particularly important to call attention to the danger of confusing urbanism with industrialism and modern capitalism. The rise of cities in the modern world is undoubtedly not independent of the emergence of modern power-driven machine technology, mass production, and capitalistic enterprise. But different as the cities of earlier epochs may have been by virtue of their development in a preindustrial and precapitalistic order from the great cities of today, they were, nevertheless, cities.

For sociological purposes a city may be defined as a relatively large, dense, and permanent settlement of socially heterogeneous individuals. On the basis of the postulates which this minimal definition suggests, a theory of urbanism may be formulated in the light of existing knowledge concerning social groups.

A Theory of Urbanism

In the rich literature on the city we look in vain for a theory of urbanism presenting in a systematic fashion the available knowledge concerning the city as a social entity. We do indeed have excellent formulations of theories on such special problems as the growth of the city viewed as a historical trend and as a recurrent process,[4] and we have a wealth of literature presenting insights of sociological relevance and empirical studies offering detailed information on a variety of particular aspects of urban life. But despite the multiplication of research and textbooks on the city, we do not as yet have a comprehensive body of compendent hypotheses which may be derived from a set of postulates implicitly contained in a sociological definition of the city, and from our general sociological knowledge which may be substantiated through empirical research. The closest approximations to a systematic theory of urbanism that we have are to be found in a penetrating essay, "Die Stadt," by Max Weber,[5] and a memorable paper by Robert E. Park on "The City: Suggestions for the Investigation of Human Behavior in the Urban Environment." [6] But even these excellent contributions are far from constituting an ordered and coherent framework of theory upon which research might profitably proceed.

In the pages that follow we shall seek to set forth a limited number of identifying characteristics of the city. Given these characteristics we shall then indicate what consequences or further characteristics follow from them in the light of general sociological theory and empirical research. We hope in this manner to arrive at the essential propositions comprising a theory of urbanism. Some of these propositions can be supported by a considerable body of already available research materials; others may be accepted as hypotheses for which a certain amount of presumptive evidence exists, but for which more ample and exact verification would be required. At least such a procedure will, it is hoped, show what in the way of systematic knowledge of the city we now have and what are the crucial and fruitful hypotheses for future research.

The central problem of the sociologist of the city is to discover the forms of social action and organization that typically emerge in relatively permanent, compact settlements of large numbers of heterogeneous individuals. We must also infer that urbanism will assume its most characteristic and extreme form in the measure in which the conditions with which it is congruent are present. Thus the larger, the more densely populated, and the more heterogeneous a community, the more accentuated the characteristics associated with urbanism will be. It should be recognized, however, that in the social world institutions and practices may be accepted and continued for reasons other than those that originally brought them into existence, and that accordingly the urban mode of life may be perpetuated under conditions quite foreign to those necessary for its origin.

Some justification may be in order for the choice of the principal terms

---

[4] See Robert E. Park, Ernest W. Burgess, *et al., The City* (Chicago, 1925), esp. chaps. ii and iii; Werner Sombart, "Städtische Siedlung, Stadt," *Handwörterbuch der Soziologie,* ed. Alfred Vierkandt (Stuttgart, 1931).

[5] *Wirtschaft und Gesellschaft* (Tübingen, 1925), Part II, chap. viii, pp. 514–601.

[6] Park, Burgess, *et al., op. cit.,* chap. i.

comprising our definition of the city. The attempt has been made to make it as inclusive and at the same time as denotative as possible without loading it with unnecessary assumptions. To say that large numbers are necessary to constitute a city means, of course, large numbers in relation to a restricted area or high density of settlement. There are, nevertheless, good reasons for treating large numbers and density as separate factors, since each may be connected with significantly different social consequences. Similarly the need for adding heterogeneity to numbers of population as a necessary and distinct criterion of urbanism might be questioned, since we should expect the range of differences to increase with numbers. In defense, it may be said that the city shows a kind and degree of heterogeneity of population which cannot be wholly accounted for by the law of large numbers or adequately represented by means of a normal distribution curve. Since the population of the city does not reproduce itself, it must recruit its migrants from other cities, the countryside, and—in this country until recently—from other countries. The city has thus historically been the melting-pot of races, peoples, and cultures, and a most favorable breeding-ground of new biological and cultural hybrids. It has not only tolerated but rewarded individual differences. It has brought together people from the ends of the earth *because* they are different and thus useful to one another, rather than because they are homogeneous and like-minded.[7]

There are a number of sociological propositions concerning the relationship between (*a*) numbers of population, (*b*) density of settlement, (*c*) heterogeneity of inhabitants and group life, which can be formulated on the basis of observation and research.

Size of the Population Aggregate

Ever since Aristotle's *Politics*,[8] it has been recognized that increasing the number of inhabitants in a settlement beyond a certain limit will affect the relationships between them and the character of the city. Large numbers involve, as has been pointed out, a greater range of individual variation.

---

[7] The justification for including the term "permanent" in the definition may appear necessary. Our failure to give an extensive justification for this qualifying mark of the urban rests on the obvious fact that unless human settlements take a fairly permanent root in a locality the characteristics of urban life cannot arise, and conversely the living together of large numbers of heterogeneous individuals under dense conditions is not possible without the development of a more or less technological structure.

[8] See esp. vii. 4. 4–14. Translated by B. Jowett, from which the following may be quoted:

"To the size of states there is a limit, as there is to other things, plants, animals, implements; for none of these retain their natural power when they are too large or too small, but they either wholly lose their nature, or are spoiled. . . . [A] state when composed of too few is not as a state ought to be, self-

Furthermore, the greater the number of individuals participating in a process of interaction, the greater is the *potential* differentiation between them. The personal traits, the occupations, the cultural life, and the ideas of the members of an urban community may, therefore, be expected to range between more widely separated poles than those of rural inhabitants.

That such variations should give rise to the spatial segregation of individuals according to color, ethnic heritage, economic and social status, tastes and preferences, may readily be inferred. The bonds of kinship, of neighborliness, and the sentiments arising out of living together for generations under a common folk tradition are likely to be absent or, at best, relatively weak in an aggregate the members of which have such diverse origins and backgrounds. Under such circumstances competition and formal control mechanisms furnish the substitutes for the bonds of solidarity that are relied upon to hold a folk society together.

Increase in the number of inhabitants of a community beyond a few hundred is bound to limit the possibility of each member of the community knowing all the others personally. Max Weber, in recognizing the social significance of this fact, pointed out that from a sociological point of view large numbers of inhabitants and density of settlement mean that the personal mutual acquaintanceship between the inhabitants which ordinarily inheres in a neighborhood is lacking.[9] The increase in numbers thus involves a changed character of the social relationships. As Simmel points out:

[If] the unceasing external contact of numbers of persons in the city should be met by the same number of inner reactions as in the small town, in which one knows almost every person he meets and to each of whom he has a positive

---

sufficing; when of too many, though self-sufficing in all mere necessaries, it is a nation and not a state, being almost incapable of constitutional government. For who can be the general of such a vast multitude, or who the herald, unless he have the voice of a Stentor?

"A state then only begins to exist when it has attained a population sufficient for a good life in the political community: it may indeed somewhat exceed this number. But, as I was saying, there must be a limit. What should be the limit will be easily ascertained by experience. For both governors and governed have duties to perform; the special functions of a governor are to command and to judge. But if the citizens of a state are to judge and to distribute offices according to merit, then they must know each other's characters; where they do not possess this knowledge, both the election to officers and the decision of lawsuits will go wrong. When the population is very large they are manifestly settled at haphazard, which clearly ought not to be. Besides, in an overpopulous state foreigners and metics will readily acquire the rights of citizens, for who will find them out? Clearly, then, the best limit of the population of a state is the largest number which suffices for the purposes of life, and can be taken in at a single view. Enough concerning the size of a city."

[9] *Op. cit.*, p. 514.

relationship, one would be completely atomized internally and would fall into an unthinkable mental condition.[10]

The multiplication of persons in a state of interaction under conditions which make their contact as full personalities impossible produces that segmentalization of human relationships which has sometimes been seized upon by students of the mental life of the cities as an explanation for the "schizoid" character of urban personality. This is not to say that the urban inhabitants have fewer acquaintances than rural inhabitants, for the reverse may actually be true; it means rather that in relation to the number of people whom they see and with whom they rub elbows in the course of daily life, they know a smaller proportion, and of these they have less intensive knowledge.

Characteristically, urbanites meet one another in highly segmental roles. They are, to be sure, dependent upon more people for the satisfactions of their life-needs than are rural people and thus are associated with a greater number of organized groups, but they are less dependent upon particular persons, and their dependence upon others is confined to a highly fractionalized aspect of the other's round of activity. This is essentially what is meant by saying that the city is characterized by secondary rather than primary contacts. The contacts of the city may indeed be face to face, but they are nevertheless impersonal, superficial, transitory, and segmental. The reserve, the indifference, and the blasé outlook which urbanites manifest in their relationships may thus be regarded as devices for immunizing themselves against the personal claims and expectations of others.

The superficiality, the anonymity, and the transitory character of urban-social relations make intelligible, also, the sophistication and the rationality generally ascribed to city-dwellers. Our acquaintances tend to stand in a relationship of utility to us in the sense that the role which each one plays in our life is overwhelmingly regarded as a means for the achievement of our own ends. Whereas, therefore, the individual gains, on the one hand, a certain degree of emancipation or freedom from the personal and emotional controls of intimate groups, he loses, on the other hand, the spontaneous self-expression, the morale, and the sense of participation that comes with living in an integrated society. This constitutes essentially the state of *anomie* or the social void to which Durkheim alludes in attempting to account for the various forms of social disorganization in technological society.

The segmental character and utilitarian accent of interpersonal relations in the city find their institutional expression in the proliferation of specialized tasks which we see in their most developed form in the professions. The operations of the pecuniary nexus leads to predatory relationships,

---

[10] Georg Simmel, "Die Grossstädte und das Geistesleben," *Die Grossstadt*, ed. Theodor Petermann (Dresden, 1903), pp. 187–206.

which tend to obstruct the efficient functioning of the social order unless checked by professional codes and occupational etiquette. The premium put upon utility and efficiency suggests the adaptability of the corporate device for the organization of enterprises in which individuals can engage only in groups. The advantage that the corporation has over the individual entrepreneur and the partnership in the urban-industrial world derives not only from the possibility it affords of centralizing the resources of thousands of individuals or from the legal privilege of limited liability and perpetual succession, but from the fact that the corporation has no soul.

The specialization of individuals, particularly in their occupations, can proceed only, as Adam Smith pointed out, upon the basis of an enlarged market, which in turn accentuates the division of labor. This enlarged market is only in part supplied by the city's hinterland; in large measure it is found among the large numbers that the city itself contains. The dominance of the city over the surrounding hinterland becomes explicable in terms of the division of labor which urban life occasions and promotes. The extreme degree of interdependence and the unstable equilibrium of urban life are closely associated with the division of labor and the specialization of occupations. This interdependence and instability is increased by the tendency of each city to specialize in those functions in which it has the greatest advantage.

In a community composed of a larger number of individuals than can know one another intimately and can be assembled in one spot, it becomes necessary to communicate through indirect mediums and to articulate individual interests by a process of delegation. Typically in the city, interests are made effective through representation. The individual counts for little, but the voice of the representative is heard with a deference roughly proportional to the numbers for whom he speaks.

While this characterization of urbanism, in so far as it derives from large numbers, does not by any means exhaust the sociological inferences that might be drawn from our knowledge of the relationship of the size of a group to the characteristic behavior of the members, for the sake of brevity the assertions made may serve to exemplify the sort of propositions that might be developed.

Density

As in the case of numbers, so in the case of concentration in limited space certain consequences of relevance in sociological analysis of the city emerge. Of these only a few can be indicated.

As Darwin pointed out for flora and fauna and as Durkheim [11] noted in the case of human societies, an increase in numbers when area is held con-

---

[11] E. Durkheim, *De la division du travail social* (Paris, 1932), p. 248.

stant (i.e., an increase in density) tends to produce differentiation and specialization, since only in this way can the area support increased numbers. Density thus reinforces the effect of numbers in diversifying men and their activities and in increasing the complexity of the social structure.

On the subjective side, as Simmel has suggested, the close physical contact of numerous individuals necessarily produces a shift in the mediums through which we orient ourselves to the urban milieu, especially to our fellow-men. Typically, our physical contacts are close but our social contacts are distant. The urban world puts a premium on visual recognition. We see the uniform which denotes the role of the functionaries and are oblivious to the personal eccentricities that are hidden behind the uniform. We tend to acquire and develop a sensitivity to a world of artefacts and become progressively farther removed from the world of nature.

We are exposed to glaring contrasts between splendor and squalor, between riches and poverty, intelligence and ignorance, order and chaos. The competition for space is great, so that each area generally tends to be put to the use which yields the greatest economic return. Place of work tends to become dissociated from place of residence, for the proximity of industrial and commercial establishments makes an area both economically and socially undesirable for residential purposes.

Density, land values, rentals, accessibility, healthfulness, prestige, aesthetic consideration, absence of nuisances such as noise, smoke, and dirt determine the desirability of various areas of the city as places of settlement for different sections of the population. Place and nature of work, income, racial and ethnic characteristics, social status, custom, habit, taste, preference, and prejudice are among the significant factors in accordance with which the urban population is selected and distributed into more or less distinct settlements. Diverse population elements inhabiting a compact settlement thus tend to become segregated from one another in the degree in which their requirements and modes of life are incompatible with one another and in the measure in which they are antagonistic to one another. Similarly, persons of homogeneous status and needs unwittingly drift into, consciously select, or are forced by circumstances into, the same area. The different parts of the city thus acquire specialized functions. The city consequently tends to resemble a mosaic of social worlds in which the transition from one to the other is abrupt. The juxtaposition of divergent personalities and modes of life tends to produce a relativistic perspective and a sense of toleration of differences which may be regarded as prerequisites for rationality and which lead toward the secularization of life.[12]

---

[12] The extent to which the segregation of the population into distinct ecological and cultural areas and the resulting social attitude of tolerance, rationality, and secular mentality are functions of density as distinguished from heterogeneity is difficult to determine. Most likely we are dealing here with phenomena which are consequences of the simultaneous operation of both factors.

The close living together and working together of individuals who have no sentimental and emotional ties foster a spirit of competition, aggrandizement, and mutual exploitation. To counteract irresponsibility and potential disorder, formal controls tend to be resorted to. Without rigid adherence to predictable routines a large compact society would scarcely be able to maintain itself. The clock and the traffic signal are symbolic of the basis of our social order in the urban world. Frequent close physical contact, coupled with great social distance, accentuates the reserve of unattached individuals toward one another and, unless compensated for by other opportunities for response, gives rise to loneliness. The necessary frequent movement of great numbers of individuals in a congested habitat gives occasion to friction and irritation. Nervous tensions which derive from such personal frustrations are accentuated by the rapid tempo and the complicated technology under which life in dense areas must be lived.

Heterogeneity

The social interaction among such a variety of personality types in the urban milieu tends to break down the rigidity of caste lines and to complicate the class structure, and thus induces a more ramified and differentiated framework of social stratification than is found in more integrated societies. The heightened mobility of the individual, which brings him within the range of stimulation by a great number of diverse individuals and subjects him to fluctuating status in the differentiated social groups that compose the social structure of the city, tends toward the acceptance of instability and insecurity in the world at large as a norm. This fact helps to account, too, for the sophistication and cosmopolitanism of the urbanite. No single group has the undivided allegiance of the individual. The groups with which he is affiliated do not lend themselves readily to a simple hierarchical arrangement. By virtue of his different interests arising out of different aspects of social life, the individual acquires membership in widely divergent groups, each of which functions only with reference to a single segment of his personality. Nor do these groups easily permit of a concentric arrangement so that the narrower ones fall within the circumference of the more inclusive ones, as is more likely to be the case in the rural community or in primitive societies. Rather the groups with which the person typically is affiliated are tangential to each other or intersect in highly variable fashion.

Partly as a result of the physical footlooseness of the population and partly as a result of their social mobility, the turnover in group membership generally is rapid. Place of residence, place and character of employment, income and interests fluctuate, and the task of holding organizations together and maintaining and promoting intimate and lasting acquaintanceship between the members is difficult. This applies strikingly to the local areas within the city into which persons become segregated more by virtue of differences in race, language, income, and social status, than through choice or positive attraction to people like themselves. Overwhelmingly the city-dweller is not a home-owner, and since a transitory habitat does not generate binding traditions and sentiments, only rarely is he truly a neighbor. There is little opportunity for the individual to obtain a conception of the city as a whole or to survey his place in the total scheme. Consequently he finds it difficult to determine what is to his own "best interests" and to decide between the issues and leaders presented to him by the agencies of mass suggestion. Individuals who are thus detached from the organized bodies which integrate society comprise the fluid masses that make collective behavior in the urban community so unpredictable and hence so problematical.

Although the city, through the recruitment of variant types to perform its diverse tasks and the accentuation of their uniqueness through competition and the premium upon eccentricity, novelty, efficient performance, and inventiveness, produces a highly differentiated population, it also exercises a leveling influence. Wherever large numbers of differently constituted individuals congregate, the process of depersonalization also enters. This leveling tendency inheres in part in the economic basis of the city. The development of large cities, at least in the modern age, was largely dependent upon the concentrative force of steam. The rise of the factory made possible mass production for an impersonal market. The fullest exploitation of the possibilities of the division of labor and mass production, however, is possible only with standardization of processes and products. A money economy goes hand in hand with such a system of production. Progressively as cities have developed upon a background of this system of production, the pecuniary nexus which implies the purchasability of services and things has displaced personal relations as the basis of association. Individuality under these circumstances must be replaced by categories. When large numbers have to make common use of facilities and institutions, an arrangement must be made to adjust the facilities and institutions to the needs of the average person rather than to those of particular individuals. The services of the public utilities, of the recreational, educational, and cultural institutions must be adjusted to mass requirements. Similarly, the cultural institutions, such as the schools, the movies, the radio, and the newspapers, by virtue of their mass clientele, must necessarily operate as leveling influences. The political process as it appears in urban life could not be understood without taking account of the mass appeals made through modern propaganda techniques. If the individual would participate at all in the social, political, and economic life of the city, he must subordinate some of his individuality to the demands of the larger community and in that measure immerse himself in mass movements.

The Relation Between a Theory
of Urbanism and Sociological Research

By means of a body of theory such as that illustratively sketched above, the complicated and many-sided phenomena of urbanism may be analyzed in terms of a limited number of basic categories. The sociological approach to the city thus acquires an essential unity and coherence enabling the empirical investigator not merely to focus more distinctly upon the problems and processes that properly fall in his province but also to treat his subject matter in a more integrated and systematic fashion. A few typical findings of empirical research in the field of urbanism, with special reference to the United States, may be indicated to substantiate the theoretical propositions set forth in the preceding pages, and some of the crucial problems for further study may be outlined.

On the basis of the three variables, number, density of settlement, and degree of heterogeneity, of the urban population, it appears possible to explain the characteristics of urban life and to account for the differences between cities of various sizes and types.

Urbanism as a characteristic mode of life may be approached empirically from three interrelated perspectives: (1) as a physical structure comprising a population base, a technology, and an ecological order; (2) as a system of social organization involving a characteristic social structure, a series of social institutions, and a typical pattern of social relationships; and (3) as a set of attitudes and ideas, and a constellation of personalities engaging in typical forms of collective behavior and subject to characteristic mechanisms of social control.

Urbanism in Ecological Perspective

Since in the case of physical structure and ecological processes we are able to operate with fairly objective indices, it becomes possible to arrive at quite precise and generally quantitative results. The dominance of the city over its hinterland becomes explicable through the functional characteristics of the city which derive in large measure from the effect of numbers and density. Many of the technical facilities and the skills and organizations to which urban life gives rise can grow and prosper only in cities where the demand is sufficiently great. The nature and scope of the services rendered by these organizations and institutions and the advantage which they enjoy over the less developed facilities of smaller towns enhances the dominance of the city and the dependence of ever wider regions upon the central metropolis.

The urban-population composition shows the operation of selective and differentiating factors. Cities contain a larger proportion of persons in the prime of life than rural areas which contain more old and very young people. In this, as in so many other respects, the larger the city the more this specific characteristic of urbanism is apparent. With the exception of the largest cities, which have attracted the bulk of the foreign-born males, and a few other special types of cities, women predominate numerically over men. The heterogeneity of the urban population is further indicated along racial and ethnic lines. The foreign born and their children constitute nearly two-thirds of all the inhabitants of cities of one million and over. Their proportion in the urban population declines as the size of the city decreases, until in the rural areas they comprise only about one-sixth of the total population. The larger cities similarly have attracted more Negroes and other racial groups than have the smaller communities. Considering that age, sex, race, and ethnic origin are associated with other factors such as occupation and interest, it becomes clear that one major characteristic of the urban-dweller is his dissimilarity from his fellows. Never before have such large masses of people of diverse traits as we find in our cities been thrown together into such close physical contact as in the great cities of America. Cities generally, and American cities in particular, comprise a motley of peoples and cultures, of highly differentiated modes of life between which there often is only the faintest communication, the greatest indifference and the broadest tolerance, occasionally bitter strife, but always the sharpest contrast.

The failure of the urban population to reproduce itself appears to be a biological consequence of a combination of factors in the complex of urban life, and the decline in the birth-rate generally may be regarded as one of the most significant signs of the urbanization of the Western world. While the proportion of deaths in cities is slightly greater than in the country, the outstanding difference between the failure of present-day cities to maintain their population and that of cities of the past is that in former times it was due to the exceedingly high death-rates in cities, whereas today, since cities have become more livable from a health standpoint, it is due to low birth-rates. These biological characteristics of the urban population are significant sociologically, not merely because they reflect the urban mode of existence but also because they condition the growth and future dominance of cities and their basic social organization. Since cities are the consumers rather than the producers of men, the value of human life and the social estimation of the personality will not be unaffected by the balance between births and deaths. The pattern of land use, of land values, rentals, and ownership, the nature and functioning of the physical structures, of housing, of transportation and communication facilities, of public utilities —these and many other phases of the physical mechanism of the city are not isolated phenomena unrelated to the city as a social entity, but are affected by and affect the urban mode of life.

Urbanism as a Form of Social Organization

The distinctive features of the urban mode of life have often been described sociologically as consisting of the substitution of secondary for primary contacts, the weakening of bonds of kinship, and the declining social significance of the family, the disappearance of the neighborhood, and the undermining of the traditional basis of social solidarity. All these phenomena can be substantially verified through objective indices. Thus, for instance, the low and declining urban-reproduction rates suggest that the city is not conducive to the traditional type of family life, including the rearing of children and the maintenance of the home as the locus of a whole round of vital activities. The transfer of industrial, educational, and recreational activities to specialized institutions outside the home has deprived the family of some of its most characteristic historical functions. In cities mothers are more likely to be employed, lodgers are more frequently part of the household, marriage tends to be postponed, and the proportion of single and unattached people is greater. Families are smaller and more frequently without children than in the country. The family as a unit of social life is emancipated from the larger kinship group characteristic of the country, and the individual members pursue their own diverging interests in their vocational, educational, religious, recreational, and political life.

Such functions as the maintenance of health, the methods of alleviating the hardships associated with personal and social insecurity, the provisions for education, recreation, and cultural advancement have given rise to highly specialized institutions on a community-wide, statewide, or even national basis. The same factors which have brought about greater personal insecurity also underlie the wider contrasts between individuals to be found in the urban world. While the city has broken down the rigid caste lines of preindustrial society, it has sharpened and differentiated income and status groups. Generally, a larger proportion of the adult-urban population is gainfully employed than is the case with the adult-rural population. The white-collar class, comprising those employed in trade, in clerical, and in professional work, are proportionately more numerous in large cities and in metropolitan centers and in smaller towns than in the country.

On the whole, the city discourages an economic life in which the individual in time of crisis has a basis of subsistence to fall back upon, and it discourages self-employment. While incomes of city people are on the average higher than those of country people, the cost of living seems to be higher in the larger cities. Home ownership involves greater burdens and is rarer. Rents are higher and absorb a large proportion of the income. Although the urban-dweller has the benefit of many communal services, he spends a large proportion of his income for such items as recreation and advancement and a smaller proportion for food. What the communal services do not furnish the urbanite must purchase, and there is virtually no human need which has remained unexploited by commercialism. Catering to thrills and furnishing means of escape from drudgery, monotony, and routine thus become one of the major functions of urban recreation, which at its best furnishes means for creative self-expression and spontaneous group association, but which more typically in the urban world results in passive spectatorism on the one hand, or sensational record-smashing feats on the other.

Being reduced to a stage of virtual impotence as an individual, the urbanite is bound to exert himself by joining with others of similar interest into organized groups to obtain his ends. This results in the enormous multiplication of voluntary organizations directed toward as great a variety of objectives as there are human needs and interests. While on the one hand the traditional ties of human association are weakened, urban existence involves a much greater degree of interdependence between man and man and a more complicated, fragile, and volatile form of mutual interrelations over many phases of which the individual as such can exert scarcely any control. Frequently there is only the most tenuous relationship between the economic position or other basic factors that determine the individual's existence in the urban world and the voluntary groups with which he is affiliated. While in a primitive and in a rural society it is generally possible to predict on the basis of a few known factors who will belong to what and who will associate with whom in almost every relationship of life, in the city we can only project the general pattern of group formation and affiliation, and this pattern will display many incongruities and contradictions.

Urban Personality and Collective Behavior

It is largely through the activities of the voluntary groups, be their objectives economic, political, educational, religious, recreational, or cultural, that the urbanite expresses and develops his personality, acquires status, and is able to carry on the round of activities that constitute his life-career. It may easily be inferred, however, that the organizational framework which these highly differentiated functions call into being does not of itself insure the consistency and integrity of the personalities whose interests it enlists. Personal disorganization, mental breakdown, suicide, delinquency, crime, corruption, and disorder might be expected under these circumstances to be more prevalent in the urban than in the rural community. This has been confirmed in so far as comparable indices are available; but the mechanisms underlying these phenomena require further analysis.

Since for most group purposes it is impossible in the city to appeal individually to the large number of discrete and differentiated individuals, and since it is only through the organizations to which men belong that their interests and resources can be enlisted for a collective cause, it may be inferred that social control in the city should typically proceed through formally organized groups. It follows, too, that the masses of men in the city are subject to manipulation by symbols and stereotypes managed by individuals working from afar or operating invisibly behind the scenes through their control of the instruments of communication. Self-government either in the economic, the political, or the cultural realm is under these circumstances reduced to a mere figure of speech or, at best, is subject to the unstable equilibrium of pressure groups. In view of the ineffectiveness of actual kinship ties we create fictional kinship groups. In the face of the disappearance of the territorial unit as a basis of social solidarity we create interest units. Meanwhile the city as a community resolves itself into a series of tenuous segmental relationships superimposed upon a territorial base with a definite center but without a definite periphery and upon a division of labor which far transcends the immediate locality and is world-wide in scope. The larger the number of persons in a state of interaction with one another the lower is the level of communication and the greater is the tendency for communication to proceed on an elementary level, i.e., on the basis of those things which are assumed to be common or to be of interest to all.

It is obviously, therefore, to the emerging trends in the communication system and to the production and distribution technology that has come into existence with modern civilization that we must look for the symptoms which will indicate the probable future development of urbanism as a mode of social life. The direction of the ongoing changes in urbanism will for good or ill transform not only the city but the world. Some of the more basic of these factors and processes and the possibilities of their direction and control invite further detailed study.

It is only insofar as the sociologist has a clear conception of the city as a social entity and a workable theory of urbanism that he can hope to develop a unified body of reliable knowledge, which what passes as "urban sociology" is certainly not at the present time. By taking his point of departure from a theory of urbanism such as that sketched in the foregoing pages to be elaborated, tested, and revised in the light of further analysis and empirical research, it is to be hoped that the criteria of relevance and validity of factual data can be determined. The miscellaneous assortment of disconnected information which has hitherto found its way into sociological treatises on the city may thus be sifted and incorporated into a coherent body of knowledge. Incidentally, only by means of some such theory will the sociologists escape the futile practice of voicing in the name of sociological science a variety of often unsupportable judgments concerning such problems as poverty, housing, city-planning, sanitation, municipal administration, policing, marketing, transportation, and other technical issues. While the sociologist cannot solve any of these practical problems

—at least not by himself—he may, if he discovers his proper function, have an important contribution to make to their comprehension and solution. The prospects for doing this are brightest through a general, theoretical, rather than through an *ad hoc* approach.

5 | Urbanism and Suburbanism as Ways of Life: A Re-evaluation of Definitions

HERBERT J. GANS

The contemporary sociological conception of cities and of urban life is based largely on the work of the Chicago School, and its summary statement in Louis Wirth's essay "Urbanism as a Way of Life" (40).* In that paper, Wirth developed a "minimum sociological definition of the city" as "a relatively large, dense and permanent settlement of socially heterogeneous individuals." (40, p. 50) From these prerequisites, he then deduced the major outlines of the urban way of life. As he saw it, number, density, and heterogeneity created a social structure in which primary-group relationships were inevitably replaced by secondary contacts that were impersonal, segmental, superficial, transitory, and often predatory in nature. As a result, the city dweller became anonymous, isolated, secular, relativistic, rational, and sophisticated. In order to function in the urban society, he was forced to combine with others to organize corporations, voluntary associations, representative forms of government, and the impersonal mass media of communications (40, pp. 54–60). These replaced the primary groups and the integrated way of life found in rural and other pre-industrial settlements.

Wirth's paper has become a classic in urban sociology, and most texts have followed his definition and description faithfully (5). In recent years, however, a considerable number of studies and essays have questioned his formulations (1, 5, 13, 15, 17, 19, 20, 23, 24, 27, 28, 30, 35, 38, 41).[1] In ad-

---

* I am indebted to Richard Dewey, John Dyckman, David Riesman, Melvin Webber, and Harold Wilensky for helpful comments on earlier drafts of this essay.

[1] I shall not attempt to summarize these studies, for this task has already been performed by Dewey (5), Reiss (23), Wilensky (38), and others.

SOURCE: Arnold Rose, ed., *Human Behavior and Social Processes* (Boston: Houghton Mifflin Company, 1962), pp. 625–648. Reprinted by permission of the publisher.

dition, a number of changes have taken place in cities since the article was published in 1938, notably the exodus of white residents to low- and medium-priced houses in the suburbs, and the decentralization of industry. The evidence from these studies and the changes in American cities suggest that Wirth's statement must be revised.

There is yet another, and more important reason for such a revision. Despite its title and intent, Wirth's paper deals with urban-industrial society, rather than with the city. This is evident from his approach. Like other urban sociologists, Wirth based his analysis on a comparison of settlement types, but unlike his colleagues, who pursued urban-rural comparisons, Wirth contrasted the city to the folk society. Thus, he compared settlement types of pre-industrial and industrial society. This allowed him to include in his theory of urbanism the entire range of modern institutions which are not found in the folk society, even though many such groups (e.g., voluntary associations) are by no means exclusively urban. Moreover, Wirth's conception of the city dweller as depersonalized, atomized, and susceptible to mass movements suggests that his paper is based on, and contributes to, the theory of the mass society.

Many of Wirth's conclusions may be relevant to the understanding of ways of life in modern society. However, since the theory argues that all of society is now urban, *his analysis does not distinguish ways of life in the city from those in other settlements within modern society.* In Wirth's time, the comparison of urban and pre-urban settlement types was still fruitful, but today, the primary task for urban (or community) sociology seems to me to be the analysis of the similarities and differences between contemporary settlement types.

This paper is an attempt at such an analysis; it limits itself to distinguishing ways of life in the modern city and the modern suburb. A re-analysis of Wirth's conclusions from this perspective suggests that his characterization of the urban way of life applies only—and not too accurately —to the residents of the inner city. The remaining city dwellers, as well as most suburbanites, pursue a different way of life, which I shall call "quasi-primary." This proposition raises some doubt about the mutual exclusiveness of the concepts of city and suburb and leads to a yet broader question: whether settlement concepts and other ecological concepts are useful for explaining ways of life.

The Inner City

Wirth argued that number, density, and heterogeneity had two social consequences which explain the major features of urban life. On the one hand, the crowding of diverse types of people into a small area led to the segregation of homogeneous types of people into separate neighborhoods (40, p. 56). On the other hand, the lack of physical distance between city dwellers resulted in social contact between them, which broke down existing social and cultural patterns and encouraged assimilation as well as acculturation—the melting pot effect (40, p. 52). Wirth implied that the melting pot effect was far more powerful than the tendency toward segregation and concluded that, sooner or later, the pressures engendered by the dominant social, economic, and political institutions of the city would destroy the remaining pockets of primary-group relationships (40, pp. 60–62). Eventually, the social system of the city would resemble Tönnies' *Gesellschaft*—a way of life which Wirth considered undesirable.

Because Wirth had come to see the city as the prototype of mass society, and because he examined the city from the distant vantage point of the folk society—from the wrong end of the telescope, so to speak—his view of urban life is not surprising. In addition, Wirth found support for his theory in the empirical work of his Chicago colleagues. As Greer and Kube (19, p. 112) and Wilensky (38, p. 121) have pointed out, the Chicago sociologists conducted their most intensive studies in the inner city.[2] At that time, these were slums recently invaded by new waves of European immigrants and rooming house and skid row districts, as well as the habitat of Bohemians and well-to-do Gold Coast apartment dwellers. Wirth himself studied the Maxwell Street Ghetto, an inner-city Jewish neighborhood then being dispersed by the acculturation and mobility of its inhabitants (39). Some of the characteristics of urbanism which Wirth stressed in his essay abounded in these areas.

Wirth's diagnosis of the city as *Gesellschaft* must be questioned on three counts. First, the conclusions derived from a study of the inner city cannot be generalized to the entire urban area. Second, there is as yet not enough evidence to prove—nor, admittedly, to deny—that number, density, and heterogeneity result in the social consequences which Wirth proposed. Finally, even if the causal relationship could be verified, it can be shown that a significant proportion of the city's inhabitants were, and are, isolated from these consequences by social structures and cultural patterns which they either brought to the city, or developed by living in it. Wirth conceived the urban population as consisting of heterogeneous individuals, torn from past social systems, unable to develop new ones, and therefore prey to social anarchy in the city. While it is true that a not insignificant proportion of the inner city population was, and still is, made up of unattached individuals (26), Wirth's formulation ignores the fact that this population consists mainly of relatively homogeneous groups, with social and cultural moorings that shield it fairly effectively from the suggested conse-

---

[2] By the *inner city*, I mean the transient residential areas, the Gold Coasts and the slums that generally surround the central business district, although in some communities they may continue for miles beyond that district. The *outer city* includes the stable residential areas that house the working- and middle-class tenant and owner. The *suburbs* I conceive as the latest and most modern ring of the outer city, distinguished from it only by yet lower densities, and by the often irrelevant fact of the ring's location outside the city limits.

quences of number, density, and heterogeneity. This applies even more to the residents of the outer city, who constitute a majority of the total city population.

The social and cultural moorings of the inner city population are best described by a brief analysis of the five types of inner city residents. These are:

1. the "cosmopolites";
2. the unmarried or childless;
3. the "ethnic villagers";
4. the "deprived"; and
5. the "trapped" and downward mobile.

The "cosmopolites" include students, artists, writers, musicians, and entertainers, as well as other intellectuals and professionals. They live in the city in order to be near the special "cultural" facilities that can only be located near the center of the city. Many cosmopolites are unmarried or childless. Others rear children in the city, especially if they have the income to afford the aid of servants and governesses. The less affluent ones may move to the suburbs to raise their children, continuing to live as cosmopolites under considerable handicaps, especially in the lower-middle-class suburbs. Many of the very rich and powerful are also cosmopolites, although they are likely to have at least two residences, one of which is suburban or exurban.

The unmarried or childless must be divided into two subtypes, depending on the permanence or transience of their status. The temporarily unmarried or childless live in the inner city for only a limited time. Young adults may team up to rent an apartment away from their parents and close to job or entertainment opportunities. When they marry, they may move first to an apartment in a transient neighborhood, but if they can afford to do so, they leave for the outer city or the suburbs with the arrival of the first or second child. The permanently unmarried may stay in the inner city for the remainder of their lives, their housing depending on their income.

The "ethnic villagers" are ethnic groups which are found in such inner city neighborhoods as New York's Lower East Side, living in some ways as they did when they were peasants in European or Puerto Rican villages (15). Although they reside in the city, they isolate themselves from significant contact with most city facilities, aside from work places. Their way of life differs sharply from Wirth's urbanism in its emphasis on kinship and the primary group, the lack of anonymity and secondary-group contacts, the weakness of formal organizations, and the suspicion of anything and anyone outside their neighborhood.

The first two types live in the inner city by choice; the third is there partly because of necessity, partly because of tradition. The final two types are in the inner city because they have no other choice. One is the "deprived" population: the very poor; the emotionally disturbed or otherwise handicapped; broken families; and, most important, the non-white population. These urban dwellers must take the dilapidated housing and blighted neighborhoods to which the housing market relegates them, although among them are some for whom the slum is a hiding place, or a temporary stop-over to save money for a house in the outer city or the suburbs (27).

The "trapped" are the people who stay behind when a neighborhood is invaded by non-residential land uses or lower-status immigrants, because they cannot afford to move, or are otherwise bound to their present location (27).[3] The "downward mobiles" are a related type; they may have started life in a higher class position, but have been forced down in the socioeconomic hierarchy and in the quality of their accommodations. Many of them are old people, living out their existence on small pensions.

These five types all live in dense and heterogeneous surroundings, yet they have such diverse ways of life that it is hard to see how density and heterogeneity could exert a common influence. Moreover, all but the last two types are isolated or detached from their neighborhood and thus from the social consequences which Wirth described.

When people who live together have social ties based on criteria other than mere common occupancy, they can set up social barriers regardless of the physical closeness or the heterogeneity of their neighbors. The ethnic villagers are the best illustration. While a number of ethnic groups are usually found living together in the same neighborhood, they are able to *isolate* themselves from each other through a variety of social devices. Wirth himself recognized this when he wrote that "two groups can occupy a given area without losing their separate identity because each side is permitted to live its own inner life and each somehow fears or idealizes the other." (39, p. 283) Although it is true that the children in these areas were often oblivious to the social barriers set up by their parents, at least until adolescence, it is doubtful whether their acculturation can be traced to the melting pot effect as much as to the pervasive influence of the American culture that flowed into these areas from the outside.[4]

The cosmopolites, the unmarried, and the childless are *detached* from neighborhood life. The cosmopolites possess a distinct subculture which causes them to be disinterested in all but the most superficial contacts with their neighbors, somewhat like the ethnic villagers. The unmarried and childless are detached from neighborhood because of their life-cycle

---

[3] The trapped are not very visible, but I suspect that they are a significant element in what Raymond Vernon has described as the "gray areas" of the city (32).

[4] If the melting pot has resulted from propinquity and high density, one would have expected second-generation Italians, Irish, Jews, Greeks, Slavs, etc., to have developed a single "pan-ethnic culture," consisting of a synthesis of the cultural patterns of the propinquitous national groups.

stage, which frees them from the routine family responsibilities that entail some relationship to the local area. In their choice of residence, the two types are therefore not concerned about their neighbors, or the availability and quality of local community facilities. Even the well-to-do can choose expensive apartments in or near poor neighborhoods, because if they have children, they are sent to special schools and summer camps which effectively isolate them from neighbors. In addition, both types, but especially the childless and unmarried, are transient. Therefore, they tend to live in areas marked by high population turnover, where their own mobility and that of their neighbors creates a universal detachment from the neighborhood.[5]

The deprived and the trapped do seem to be affected by some of the consequences of number, density, and heterogeneity. The deprived population suffers considerably from overcrowding, but this is a consequence of low income, racial discrimination, and other handicaps, and cannot be considered an inevitable result of the ecological make-up of the city.[6] Because the deprived have no residential choice, they are also forced to live amid neighbors not of their own choosing, with ways of life different and even contradictory to their own. If familial defenses against the neighborhood climate are weak, as is the case among broken families and downward mobile people, parents may lose their children to the culture of "the street." The trapped are the unhappy people who remain behind when their more advantaged neighbors move on; they must endure the heterogeneity which results from neighborhood change.

Wirth's description of the urban way of life fits best the transient areas of the inner city. Such areas are typically heterogeneous in population, partly because they are inhabited by transient types who do not require homogeneous neighbors or by deprived people who have no choice, or may themselves be quite mobile. Under conditions of transience and heterogeneity, people interact only in terms of the segmental roles necessary for obtaining local services. Their social relationships thus display anonymity, impersonality, and superficiality.[7]

---

[5] The corporation transients (36, 38), who provide a new source of residential instability to the suburb, differ from city transients. Since they are raising families, they want to integrate themselves into neighborhood life, and are usually able to do so, mainly because they tend to move into similar types of communities wherever they go.

[6] The negative social consequences of overcrowding are a result of high room and floor density, not of the land coverage of population density which Wirth discussed. Park Avenue residents live under conditions of high land density, but do not seem to suffer visibly from overcrowding.

[7] Whether or not these social phenomena have the psychological consequences Wirth suggested depends on the people who live in the area. Those who are detached from the neighborhood by choice are probably immune, but those who depend on the neighborhood for their social relationships—the unattached individuals, for example—may suffer greatly from loneliness.

The social features of Wirth's concept of urbanism seem therefore to be a result of residential instability, rather than of number, density, or heterogeneity. In fact, heterogeneity is itself an effect of residential instability, resulting when the influx of transients causes landlords and realtors to stop acting as gatekeepers—that is, wardens of neighborhood homogeneity.[8] Residential instability is found in all types of settlements, and, presumably, its social consequences are everywhere similar. These consequences cannot therefore be identified with the ways of life of the city.

The Outer City and the Suburbs

The second effect which Wirth ascribed to number, density, and heterogeneity was the segregation of homogeneous people into distinct neighborhoods [9] on the basis of "place and nature of work, income, racial and ethnic characteristics, social status, custom, habit, taste, preference and prejudice" (40, p. 56). This description fits the residential districts of the *outer city*.[10] Although these districts contain the majority of the city's inhabitants, Wirth went into little detail about them. He made it clear, however, that the socio-psychological aspects of urbanism were prevalent there as well (40, p. 56).

Because existing neighborhood studies deal primarily with the exotic sections of the inner city, very little is known about the more typical residential neighborhoods of the outer city. However, it is evident that the way of life in these areas bears little resemblance to Wirth's urbanism. Both the studies which question Wirth's formulation and my own observations suggest that the common element in the ways of life of these neighborhoods is best described as *quasi-primary*. I use this term to characterize relationships between neighbors. Whatever the intensity or frequency of these relationships, the interaction is more intimate than a secondary contact, but more guarded than a primary one.[11]

There are actually few secondary relationships, because of the isolation of residential neighborhoods from economic institutions and work places.

---

[8] Needless to say, residential instability must ultimately be traced back to the fact that, as Wirth pointed out, the city and its economy attract transient—and, depending on the sources of outmigration, heterogeneous—people. However, this is a characteristic of urban-industrial society, not of the city specifically.

[9] By neighborhoods or residential districts I mean areas demarcated from others by distinctive physical boundaries or by social characteristics, some of which may be perceived only by the residents. However, these areas are not necessarily socially self-sufficient or culturally distinctive.

[10] For the definition of *outer city*, see Footnote 2.

[11] Because neighborly relations are not quite primary, and not quite secondary, they can also become *pseudo-primary*; that is, secondary ones disguised with false affect to make them appear primary. Critics have often described suburban life in this fashion, although the actual prevalence of pseudo-primary relationships has not been studied systematically in cities or suburbs.

Even shopkeepers, store managers, and other local functionaries who live in the area are treated as acquaintances or friends, unless they are of a vastly different social status or are forced by their corporate employers to treat their customers as economic units (30). Voluntary associations attract only a minority of the population. Moreover, much of the organizational activity is of a sociable nature, and it is often difficult to accomplish the association's "business" because of the members' preference for sociability. Thus, it would appear that interactions in organizations, or between neighbors generally, do not fit the secondary-relationship model of urban life. As anyone who has lived in these neighborhoods knows, there is little anonymity, impersonality or privacy.[12] In fact, American cities have sometimes been described as collections of small towns.[13] There is some truth to this description, especially if the city is compared to the actual small town, rather than to the romantic construct of anti-urban critics (33).

Postwar suburbia represents the most contemporary version of the quasi-primary way of life. Owing to increases in real income and the encouragement of home ownership provided by the FHA, families in the lower-middle class and upper working class can now live in modern single-family homes in low-density subdivisions, an opportunity previously available only to the upper and upper-middle classes (34).

The popular literature describes the new suburbs as communities in which conformity, homogeneity, and other-direction are unusually rampant (4, 32). The implication is that the move from city to suburb initiates a new way of life which causes considerable behavior and personality change in previous urbanites. A preliminary analysis of data which I am now collecting in Levittown, New Jersey, suggests, however, that the move from the city to this predominantly lower-middle-class suburb does not result in any major behavioral changes for most people. Moreover, the changes which do occur reflect the move from the social isolation of a transient city or suburban apartment building to the quasi-primary life of a neighborhood of single-family homes. Also, many of the people whose life has changed reported that the changes were intended. They existed as aspirations before the move, or as reasons for it. In other words, the suburb itself creates few changes in ways of life. Similar conclusions have been reported by Berger in his excellent study of a working-class population newly moved to a suburban subdivision (4).

---

[12] These neighborhoods cannot, however, be considered as urban folk societies. People go out of the area for many of their friendships, and their allegiance to the neighborhood is neither intense nor all-encompassing. Janowitz has aptly described the relationship between resident and neighborhood as one of "limited liability." (20, Chapter 7)

[13] Were I not arguing that ecological concepts cannot double as sociological ones, this way of life might best be described as small-townish.

A Comparison of City and Suburb

If urban and suburban areas are similar in that the way of life in both is quasi-primary, and if urban residents who move out to the suburbs do not undergo any significant changes in behavior, it would be fair to argue that the differences in ways of life between the two types of settlements have been overestimated. Yet the fact remains that a variety of physical and demographic differences exist between the city and the suburb. However, upon closer examination, many of these differences turn out to be either spurious or of little significance for the way of life of the inhabitants (34).[14]

The differences between the residential areas of cities and suburbs which have been cited most frequently are:

1. Suburbs are more likely to be dormitories.
2. They are further away from the work and play facilities of the central business districts.
3. They are newer and more modern than city residential areas and are designed for the automobile rather than for pedestrian and mass-transit forms of movement.
4. They are built up with single-family rather than multi-family structures and are therefore less dense.
5. Their populations are more homogeneous.
6. Their populations differ demographically: they are younger; more of them are married; they have higher incomes; and they hold proportionately more white collar jobs (8, p. 131). '

Most urban neighborhoods are as much dormitories as the suburbs. Only in a few older inner city areas are factories and offices still located in the middle of residential blocks, and even here many of the employees do not live in the neighborhood.

The fact that the suburbs are farther from the central business district is often true only in terms of distance, not travel time. Moreover, most people make relatively little use of downtown facilities, other than work places (12, 21). The downtown stores seem to hold their greatest attraction for the upper-middle class (21, pp. 91–92); the same is probably true of typically urban entertainment facilities. Teen-agers and young adults may take their dates to first-run movie theaters, but the museums, concert halls, and lecture rooms attract mainly upper-middle-class ticket-buyers, many of them suburban.[15]

The suburban reliance on the train and the automobile has given rise to

---

[14] They may, of course, be significant for the welfare of the total metropolitan area.

[15] A 1958 study of New York theater-goers showed a median income of close to $10,000 and 35 per cent were reported as living in the suburbs (10).

an imaginative folklore about the consequences of commuting on alcohol consumption, sex life, and parental duties. Many of these conclusions are, however, drawn from selected high-income suburbs and exurbs, and reflect job tensions in such hectic occupations as advertising and show business more than the effects of residence (29). It is true that the upper-middle-class housewife must become a chauffeur in order to expose her children to the proper educational facilities, but such differences as walking to the corner drug store and driving to its suburban equivalent seem to me of little emotional, social, or cultural import.[16] In addition, the continuing shrinkage in the number of mass-transit users suggests that even in the city many younger people are now living a wholly auto-based way of life.

The fact that suburbs are smaller is primarily a function of political boundaries drawn long before the communities were suburban. This affects the kinds of political issues which develop and provides somewhat greater opportunity for citizen participation. Even so, in the suburbs as in the city, the minority who participate are the professional politicians, the economically concerned businessmen, lawyers and salesmen, and the ideologically motivated middle- and upper-middle-class people with better than average education.

The social consequences of differences in density and house type also seem overrated. Single-family houses on quiet streets facilitate the supervision of children; this is one reason why middle-class women who want to keep an eye on their children move to the suburbs. House type also has some effects on relationships between neighbors, insofar as there are more opportunities for visual contact between adjacent homeowners than between people on different floors of an apartment house. However, if occupants' characteristics are also held constant, the differences in actual social contact are less marked. Homogeneity of residents turns out to be more important as a determinant of sociability than proximity. If the population is heterogeneous, there is little social contact between neighbors, either on apartment-house floors or in single-family-house blocks; if people are homogeneous, there is likely to be considerable social contact in both house types. One need only contrast the apartment house located in a transient, heterogeneous neighborhood and exactly the same structure in a neighborhood occupied by a single ethnic group. The former is a lonely, anonymous building; the latter, a bustling micro-society. I have observed similar patterns in suburban areas: on blocks where people are homogeneous, they socialize; where they are heterogeneous, they do little more than exchange polite greetings (16).

Suburbs are usually described as being more homogeneous in house type than the city, but if they are compared to the outer city, the differences are small. Most inhabitants of the outer city, other than well-to-do homeowners, live on blocks of uniform structures as well—for example, the end-

---

[16] I am thinking here of adults; teen-agers do suffer from the lack of informal meeting places within walking or bicycling distance.

less streets of rowhouses in Philadelphia and Baltimore or of two-story duplexes and six-flat apartment houses in Chicago. They differ from the new suburbs only in that they were erected through more primitive methods of mass production. Suburbs are of course more predominantly areas of owner-occupied single homes, though in the outer districts of most American cities homeownership is also extremely high.

Demographically, suburbs as a whole are clearly more homogeneous than cities as a whole, though probably not more so than outer cities. However, people do not live in cities or suburbs as a whole, but in specific neighborhoods. An analysis of ways of life would require a determination of the degree of population homogeneity within the boundaries of areas defined as neighborhoods by residents' social contacts. Such an analysis would no doubt indicate that many neighborhoods in the city as well as the suburbs are homogeneous. Neighborhood homogeneity is actually a result of factors having little or nothing to do with the house type, density, or location of the area relative to the city limits. Brand new neighborhoods are more homogeneous than older ones, because they have not yet experienced resident turnover, which frequently results in population heterogeneity. Neighborhoods of low- and medium-priced housing are usually less homogeneous than those with expensive dwellings because they attract families who have reached the peak of occupational and residential mobility, as well as young families who are just starting their climb and will eventually move to neighborhoods of higher status. The latter, being accessible only to high-income people, are therefore more homogeneous with respect to other resident characteristics as well. Moreover, such areas have the economic and political power to slow down or prevent invasion. Finally, neighborhoods located in the path of ethnic or religious group movement are likely to be extremely homogeneous.

The demographic differences between cities and suburbs cannot be questioned, especially since the suburbs have attracted a large number of middle-class child-rearing families. The differences are, however, much reduced if suburbs are compared only to the outer city. In addition, a detailed comparison of suburban and outer city residential areas would show that neighborhoods with the same kinds of people can be found in the city as well as the suburbs. Once again, the age of the area and the cost of housing are more important determinants of demographic characteristics than the location of the area with respect to the city limits.

Characteristics, Social Organization, and Ecology

The preceding sections of the paper may be summarized in three propositions:

1. As concerns ways of life, the inner city must be distinguished from the outer city and the suburbs; and the latter two exhibit a way of life bearing little resemblance to Wirth's urbanism.

2. Even in the inner city, ways of life resemble Wirth's description only to a limited extent. Moreover, economic condition, cultural characteristics, life-cycle stage, and residential instability explain ways of life more satisfactorily than number, density, or heterogeneity.
3. Physical and other differences between city and suburb are often spurious or without much meaning for ways of life.

These propositions suggest that the concepts urban and suburban are neither mutually exclusive, nor especially relevant for understanding ways of life. They—and number, density, and heterogeneity as well—are ecological concepts which describe human adaptation to the environment. However, they are not sufficient to explain social phenomena, because these phenomena cannot be understood solely as the consequences of ecological processes. Therefore, other explanations must be considered.

Ecological explanations of social life are most applicable if the subjects under study lack the ability to *make choices*, be they plants, animals, or human beings. Thus, if there is a housing shortage, people will live almost anywhere, and under extreme conditions of no choice, as in a disaster, married and single, old and young, middle and working class, stable and transient will be found side by side in whatever accommodations are available. At that time, their ways of life represent an almost direct adaptation to the environment. If the supply of housing and of neighborhoods is such that alternatives are available, however, people will make choices, and if the housing market is responsive, they can even make and satisfy explicit *demands*.

Choices and demands do not develop independently or at random; they are functions of the roles people play in the social system. These can best be understood in terms of the *characteristics* of the people involved; that is, characteristics can be used as indices to choices and demands made in the roles that constitute ways of life. Although many characteristics affect the choices and demands people make with respect to housing and neighborhoods, the most important ones seem to be *class*—in all its economic, social and cultural ramifications—and *life-cycle stage*.[17] If people have an opportunity to choose, these two characteristics will go far in explaining the kinds of housing and neighborhoods they will occupy and the ways of life they will try to establish within them.

Many of the previous assertions about ways of life in cities and suburbs can be analyzed in terms of class and life-cycle characteristics. Thus, in the inner city, the unmarried and childless live as they do, detached from neighborhood, because of their life-cycle stage; the cosmopolites, because of a combination of life-cycle stage and a distinctive but class based subculture. The way of life of the deprived and trapped can be explained by low socio-economic level and related handicaps. The quasi-primary way of

---

[17] These must be defined in dynamic terms. Thus, class includes also the process of social mobility, stage in the life-cycle, and the processes of socialization and aging.

life is associated with the family stage of the life-cycle, and the norms of child-rearing and parental role found in the upper working class, the lower-middle class, and the non-cosmopolite portions of the upper-middle and upper classes.

The attributes of the so-called suburban way of life can also be understood largely in terms of these characteristics. The new suburbia is nothing more than a highly visible showcase for the ways of life of young, upper-working-class and lower-middle-class people. Ktsanes and Reissman have aptly described it as "new homes for old values" (22). Much of the descriptive and critical writing about suburbia assumes that as long as the new suburbanites lived in the city, they behaved like upper-middle-class cosmopolites and that suburban living has mysteriously transformed them (7; 14, pp. 154–162; 25; 36). The critics fail to see that the behavior and personality patterns ascribed to suburbia are in reality those of class and age (6). These patterns could have been found among the new suburbanites when they still lived in the city and could now be observed among their peers who still reside there—if the latter were as visible to critics and researchers as are the suburbanites.

Needless to say, the concept of "characteristics" cannot explain all aspects of ways of life, either among urban or suburban residents. Some aspects must be explained by concepts of social organization that are independent of characteristics. For example, some features of the quasi-primary way of life are independent of class and age, because they evolve from the roles and situations created by joint and adjacent occupancy of land and dwellings. Likewise, residential instability is a universal process which has a number of invariate consequences. In each case, however, the way in which people react varies with their characteristics. So it is with ecological processes. Thus, there are undoubtedly differences between ways of life in urban and suburban settlements which remain after behavior patterns based on residents' characteristics have been analyzed, and which must therefore be attributed to features of the settlement (11).

Characteristics do not explain the causes of behavior; rather, they are clues to socially created and culturally defined roles, choices, and demands. A causal analysis must trace them back to the larger social, economic, and political systems which determine the situations in which roles are played and the cultural content of choices and demands, as well as the opportunities for their achievement.[18] These systems determine income distributions, educational and occupational opportunities, and in turn, fertility patterns, child-rearing methods, as well as the entire range of consumer behavior. Thus, a complete analysis of the way of life of the deprived residents of the inner city cannot stop by indicating the influence of low income, lack of education, or family instability. These must be related to

---

[18] This formulation may answer some of Duncan and Schnore's objections to socio-psychological and cultural explanations of community ways of life (9).

such conditions as the urban economy's "need" for low-wage workers, and the housing market practices which restrict residential choice. The urban economy is in turn shaped by national economic and social systems, as well as by local and regional ecological processes. Some phenomena can be explained exclusively by reference to these ecological processes. However, it must also be recognized that as man gains greater control over the natural environment, he has been able to free himself from many of the determining and limiting effects of that environment. Thus, changes in local transportation technology, the ability of industries to be footloose, and the relative affluence of American society have given ever larger numbers of people increasing amounts of residential choice. The greater the amount of choice available, the more important does the concept of characteristics become in understanding behavior.

Consequently, the study of ways of life in communities must begin with an analysis of characteristics. If characteristics are dealt with first and held constant, we may be able to discover which behavior patterns can be attributed to features of the settlement and its natural environment.[19] Only then will it be possible to discover to what extent city and suburb are independent—rather than dependent or intervening—variables in the explanation of ways of life.

This kind of analysis might help to reconcile the ecological point of view with the behavioral and cultural one, and possibly put an end to the conflict between conceptual positions which insist on one explanation or the other (9). Both explanations have some relevance, and future research and theory must clarify the role of each in the analysis of ways of life in various types of settlement (6, p. xxii). Another important rationale for this approach is its usefulness for applied sociology—for example, city planning. The planner can recommend changes in the spatial and physical arrangements of the city. Frequently, he seeks to achieve social goals or to change social conditions through physical solutions. He has been attracted to ecological explanations because these relate behavior to phenomena which he can affect. For example, most planners tend to agree with Wirth's formulations, because they stress number and density, over which the planner has some control. If the undesirable social conditions of the inner city could be traced to these two factors, the planner could propose large-scale clearance projects which would reduce the size of the urban population, and lower residential densities. Experience with public housing projects

---

[19] The ecologically oriented researchers who developed the Shevsky-Bell social area analysis scale have worked on the assumption that "social differences between the populations of urban neighborhoods can conveniently be summarized into differences of economic level, family characteristics and ethnicity." (3, p. 26) However, they have equated "urbanization" with a concept of life-cycle stage by using family characteristics to define the index of urbanization (3, 18, 19). In fact, Bell has identified suburbanism with familism (2).

has, however, made it apparent that low densities, new buildings, or modern site plans do not eliminate anti-social or self-destructive behavior. The analysis of characteristics will call attention to the fact that this behavior is lodged in the deprivations of low socio-economic status and racial discrimination, and that it can be changed only through the removal of these deprivations. Conversely, if such an analysis suggests residues of behavior that can be attributed to ecological processes or physical aspects of housing and neighborhood, the planner can recommend physical changes that can really affect behavior.

A Re-evaluation of Definitions

The argument presented here has implications for the sociological definition of the city. Such a definition relates ways of life to environmental features of the city qua settlement type. But if ways of life do not coincide with settlement types, and if these ways are functions of class and life-cycle stage rather than of the ecological attributes of the settlement, a sociological definition of the city cannot be formulated.[20] Concepts such as city and suburb allow us to distinguish settlement types from each other physically and demographically, but the ecological processes and conditions which they synthesize have no direct or invariate consequences for ways of life. The sociologist cannot, therefore, speak of an urban or suburban way of life.

Conclusion

Many of the descriptive statements made here are as time-bound as Wirth's.[21] Twenty years ago, Wirth concluded that some form of urbanism would eventually predominate in all settlement types. He was, however, writing during a time of immigrant acculturation and at the end of a serious depression, an era of minimal choice. Today, it is apparent that high-density, heterogeneous surroundings are for most people a temporary place of residence; other than for the Park Avenue or Grenwich Village cosmopolites, they are a result of necessity rather than choice. As soon as they can afford to do so, most Americans head for the single-family house and

---

[20] Because of the distinctiveness of the ways of life found in the inner city, some writers propose definitions that refer only to these ways, ignoring those found in the outer city. For example, popular writers sometimes identify "urban" with "urbanity," i.e., "cosmopolitanism." However, such a definition ignores the other ways of life found in the inner city. Moreover, I have tried to show that these ways have few common elements, and that the ecological features of the inner city have little or no influence in shaping them.

[21] Even more than Wirth's they are based on data and impressions gathered in the large Eastern and Midwestern cities of the United States.

the quasi-primary way of life of the low-density neighborhood, in the outer city or the suburbs.[22]

Changes in the national economy and in government housing policy can affect many of the variables that make up housing supply and demand. For example, urban sprawl may eventually outdistance the ability of present and proposed transportation systems to move workers into the city; further industrial decentralization can forestall it and alter the entire relationship between work and residence. The expansion of present urban renewal activities can perhaps lure a significant number of cosmopolites back from the surburbs, while a drastic ·change in renewal policy might begin to ameliorate the housing conditions of the deprived population. A serious depression could once again make America a nation of doubled-up tenants.

These events will affect housing supply and residential choice; they will frustrate but not suppress demands for the quasi-primary way of life. However, changes in the national economy, society, and culture can affect people's characteristics—family size, educational level, and various other concomitants of life-cycle stage and class. These in turn will stimulate changes in demands and choices. The rising number of college graduates, for example, is likely to increase the cosmopolite ranks. This might in turn create a new set of city dwellers, although it will probably do no more than encourage the development of cosmopolite facilities in some suburban areas.

The current revival of interest in urban sociology and in community studies, as well as the sociologist's increasing curiosity about city planning, suggest that data may soon be available to formulate a more adequate theory of the relationship between settlements and the ways of life within them. The speculations presented in this paper are intended to raise questions; they can only be answered by more systematic data collection and theorizing.

References

1. AXELROD, MORRIS. "Urban Structure and Social Participation," American Sociological Review, Vol. 21 (February 1956), pp. 13–18.

2. BELL, WENDELL. "Social Choice, Life Styles and Suburban Residence," in William M. Dobriner (ed.), The Suburban Community. New York: G. P. Putnam's Sons, 1958, pp. 225–247.

3. BELL, WENDELL, and MARYANNE T. FORCE. "Urban Neighborhood

---

[22] Personal discussions with European planners and sociologists suggest that many European apartment dwellers have similar preferences, although economic conditions, high building costs, and the scarcity of land make it impossible for them to achieve their desires.

Types and Participation in Formal Associations," *American Sociological Review*, Vol. 21 (February 1956), pp. 25–34.

4. BERGER, BENNETT. *Working Class Suburb: A Study of Auto Workers in Suburbia*. Berkeley, Calif.: University of California Press, 1960.

5. DEWEY, RICHARD. "The Rural-Urban Continuum: Real but Relatively Unimportant," *American Journal of Sociology*, Vol. 66 (July 1960), pp. 60–66.

6. DOBRINER, WILLIAM M. "Introduction: Theory and Research in the Sociology of the Suburbs," in William M. Dobriner (ed.), *The Suburban Community*. New York: G. P. Putnam's Sons, 1958, pp. xiii-xxviii.

7. DUHL, LEONARD J. "Mental Health and Community Planning," in *Planning 1955*. Chicago: American Society of Planning Officials, 1956, pp. 31–39.

8. DUNCAN, OTIS DUDLEY, and ALBERT J. REISS, JR. *Social Characteristics of Rural and Urban Communities, 1950*. New York: John Wiley & Sons, 1956.

9. DUNCAN, OTIS DUDLEY, and LEO F. SCHNORE. "Cultural, Behavioral and Ecological Perspectives in the Study of Social Organization," *American Journal of Sociology*, Vol. 65 (September 1959), pp. 132–155.

10. ENDERS, JOHN. *Profile of the Theater Market*. New York: Playbill, undated and unpaged.

11. FAVA, SYLVIA FLEIS. "Contrasts in Neighboring: New York City and a Suburban Community," in William M. Dobriner (ed.), *The Suburban Community*. New York: G. P. Putnam's Sons, 1958, pp. 122–131.

12. FOLEY, DONALD L. "The Use of Local Facilities in a Metropolis," in Paul Hatt and Albert J. Reiss, Jr. (eds.), *Cities and Society*. Glencoe, Ill.: The Free Press, 1957, pp. 237–247.

13. FORM, WILLIAM H., *et al.* "The Compatibility of Alternative Approaches to the Delimitation of Urban Sub-areas," *American Sociological Review*, Vol. 19 (August 1954), pp. 434–440.

14. FROMM, ERICH. *The Sane Society*. New York: Rinehart & Co., Inc., 1955.

15. GANS, HERBERT J. *The Urban Villagers: A Study of the Second Generation Italians in the West End of Boston*. Boston: Center for Community Studies, December 1959 (mimeographed).

16. GANS, HERBERT J. "Planning and Social Life: An Evaluation of Friendship and Neighbor Relations in Suburban Communities," *Journal of the American Institute of Planners*, Vol. 27 (May 1961), pp. 134–140.

17. GREER, SCOTT. "Urbanism Reconsidered: A Comparative Study of Local Areas in a Metropolis," *American Sociological Review*, Vol. 21 (February 1956), pp. 19–25.

18. GREER, SCOTT. "The Social Structure and Political Process of Suburbia," *American Sociological Review*, Vol. 25 (August 1960), pp. 514–526.

19. GREER, SCOTT, and ELLA KUBE. "Urbanism and Social Structure: A

Los Angeles Study," in Marvin B. Sussman (ed.), *Community Structure and Analysis*. New York: Thomas Y. Crowell Company, 1959, pp. 93–112.

20. JANOWITZ, MORRIS. *The Community Press in an Urban Setting*. Glencoe, Ill.: The Free Press, 1952.

21. JONASSEN, CHRISTEN T. *The Shopping Center Versus Downtown*. Columbus, Ohio: Bureau of Business Research, Ohio State University, 1955.

22. KTSANES, THOMAS, and LEONARD REISSMAN. "Suburbia: New Homes for Old Values," *Social Problems*, Vol. 7 (Winter 1959–60), pp. 187–194.

23. REISS, ALBERT J., JR. "An Analysis of Urban Phenomena," in Robert M. Fisher (ed.), *The Metropolis in Modern Life*. Garden City, N.Y.: Doubleday & Company, Inc., 1955, pp. 41–49.

24. REISS, ALBERT J., JR. "Rural-Urban and Status Differences in Interpersonal Contacts," *American Journal of Sociology*, Vol. 65 (September 1959), pp. 182–195.

25. RIESMAN, DAVID. "The Suburban Sadness," in William M. Dobriner (ed.), *The Suburban Community*. New York: G. P. Putnam's Sons, 1958, pp. 375–408.

26. ROSE, ARNOLD M. "Living Arrangements of Unattached Persons," *American Sociological Review*, Vol. 12 (August 1947), pp. 429–435.

27. SEELEY, JOHN R. "The Slum: Its Nature, Use and Users," *Journal of the American Institute of Planners*, Vol. 25 (February 1959), pp. 7–14.

28. SMITH, JOEL, WILLIAM FORM, and GREGORY STONE. "Local Intimacy in a Middle-Sized City," *American Journal of Sociology*, Vol. 60 (November 1954), pp. 276–284.

29. SPECTORSKY, A. C. *The Exurbanites*. Philadelphia: J. B. Lippincott Co., 1955.

30. STONE, GREGORY P. "City Shoppers and Urban Identification: Observations on the Social Psychology of City Life," *American Journal of Sociology*, Vol. 60 (July 1954), pp. 36–45.

31. STRAUSS, ANSELM. "The Changing Imagery of American City and Suburb," *Sociological Quarterly*, Vol. 1 (January 1960), pp. 15–24.

32. VERNON, RAYMOND. *The Changing Economic Function of the Central City*. New York: Committee on Economic Development, Supplementary Paper No. 1, January 1959.

33. VIDICH, ARTHUR J., and JOSEPH BENSMAN. *Small Town in Mass Society: Class, Power and Religion in a Rural Community*. Princeton, N.J.: Princeton University Press, 1958.

34. WATTELL, HAROLD. "Levittown: A Suburban Community," in William M. Dobriner (ed.), *The Suburban Community*. New York: G. P. Putnam's Sons, 1958, pp. 287–313.

35. WHYTE, WILLIAM F. *Street Corner Society*. Chicago: The University of Chicago Press, 1955.

36. WHYTE, WILLIAM H., JR. *The Organization Man*. New York: Simon & Schuster, 1956.

37. WILENSKY, HAROLD L. "Life Cycle, Work, Situation and Participation in Formal Associations," in Robert W. Kleemeier, *et al.* (eds.), *Aging and Leisure: Research Perspectives on the Meaningful Use of Time.* New York: Oxford University Press, 1961, Chapter 8.

38. WILENSKY, HAROLD L., and CHARLES LEBEAUX. *Industrial Society and Social Welfare.* New York: Russell Sage Foundation, 1958.

39. WIRTH, LOUIS. *The Ghetto.* Chicago: The University of Chicago Press, 1928.

40. WIRTH, LOUIS. "Urbanism as a Way of Life," *American Journal of Sociology,* Vol. 44 (July 1938), pp. 1–24. Reprinted in Paul Hatt and Albert J. Reiss, Jr. (eds.), *Cities and Society.* Glencoe, Ill.: The Free Press, 1957, pp. 46–64. [All page references are to this reprinting of the article.]

41. YOUNG, MICHAEL, and PETER WILLMOTT. *Family and Kinship in East London.* London: Routledge & Kegan Paul, Ltd., 1957.

6 | The Urban African and His World

WILLIAM BASCOM

By millions, Africans have been moving from rural areas into cities. . . . Some of these cities are . . . new, but West Africa had cities before the advent of Europeans, some dating back at least a thousand years. . . .

. . . . .

There are, then, two kinds of African cities, the old and the new, both of which are rapidly expanding. And there are two kinds of urban Africans, those who have moved to the cities from rural areas, and those who were born and raised in the city, who have married and raised their families in the city, who will live their lives, and will die and be buried there with their ancestors. The "urban worlds" of these two kinds of urban Africans are quite different. . . .

. . . . .

In an important article on Africa, [J. C.] Mitchell has pointed out the danger of confusing the demographic sense of urbanization with its sociological sense. The demographic sense has to do with residence in a large city, and the sociological sense has to do with its effect on the individual's behavior, as for example, the *anomie,* or sense of loneliness and isolation

SOURCE: *Cahiers D'Études Africaines,* 1963, pp. 163, 164, 170–183. Reprinted by permission of the author and publisher.

associated with life in the large cities of Europe and America, which urban sociologists, following Durkheim, have stressed. Mitchell emphasizes the danger of assuming that if a man is urbanized in a demographic sense, he is also urbanized in the sociological sense. It is all too easy to assume that the longer a man has been in town, the more severe is his state of *anomie*.

In fact, as Mitchell has pointed out, there is some evidence that *anomie* is most severe among those who have only recently come to the city, and that those who have lived there for longer periods accept certain standards of behavior and conform to them. *Anomie* seems to be not the product of urban conditions of life in Africa, per se, but rather a form of "cultural shock" such as even anthropologists experience when first moving into a different culture, with a new set of rules and standards.

Mitchell's conclusion is borne out by research among the traditional cities of the Yoruba in the Western Region of Nigeria, but before turning to them let us look more closely at a demographic and a sociological definition of the city. For this we will take a study which, though recent, is already a classic, because of the influence it has had on urban studies in Africa and elsewhere. This is *Urbanism as a Way of Life* by Louis Wirth, a sociologist who was a contemporary of Robert Redfield at the University of Chicago, and whose definition of the city relates to Redfield's folk-urban continuum. Wirth's description of the sociological aspects of the urban way of life was based mainly on his studies of American cities, but it provides a useful background against which to compare life in both the newer cities of Africa and the traditional Yoruba cities.

Wirth defines a city for sociological purposes as "a relatively large, dense, and permanent settlement of socially heterogeneous individuals." The first three criteria are clearly demographic; and are qualified by the word "relative". Different countries take populations of over 2,000, 2,500, or 5,000 as a basis for classifying communities as cities for census purposes, and densities of 1,000 and 10,000 per [square] mile have been proposed by Wilcox and by Jefferson as a criterion of urban settlement. But as Wirth points out, whatever figure is taken for size or density it must be an arbitrary one, and the same is true for the number of years which constitute permanence.

Wirth's definition has been widely accepted, but it has proved difficult to apply cross-culturally because of the factor of "social heterogeneity". Because this factor was not clearly defined it has proved difficult, in Africa for example, to distinguish between social heterogeneity and homogeneity. Probably the difficulty also lies in the fact that however it is defined, social heterogeneity is a sociological result of urbanization under certain circumstances, rather than a feature essential or even pertinent to a demographic definition of the city.

The shortcomings of the criterion of social heterogeneity are suggested by the equivocal positions taken by those who have attempted to apply it to traditional African communities. In his study of a Yoruba city in Nigeria, William Schwab concludes that "if Oshogbo was viewed on the level of form, it was an urban community; if viewed in terms of social organization and process, it was folk." In an earlier study, Horace Miner described Timbuctoo as "a primitive city" and its inhabitants as a "city-folk". Yet he concluded that "Timbuctoo is a city. It has a stable population of over six thousand persons, living in a community roughly a square mile in area, and patterning their lives after three distinct cultural heritages. The size, density and heterogeneity of the city are all evident." Timbuctoo, of course, was known as an important center of trade and learning long before European contact.

Miner, who studied at the University of Chicago at the time of Wirth and Redfield, commented on "the lack of any concise benchmark from which to appraise the degree of homogeneity." He admittedly rests his case for heterogeneity on the cultural diversity of the three distinct ethnic groups which inhabit Timbuctoo, the Songhai people, the Tuareg, and the Arabs. Yet neither he nor Wirth suggests that ethnic diversity is essential to a definition of the city. American and European cities, and many of the new cities of Africa, include peoples of different racial, linguistic, and cultural backgrounds, but this can be regarded as a secondary feature of urbanization, and a basis for distinguishing two types of cities, which I have called cosmopolitan and non-cosmopolitan.

Compared to Timbuctoo's 6,000 inhabitants, over half of the 5,000,000 Yoruba in Nigeria live in cities over 5,000. Over thirty percent live in cities of over 40,000, of which six are larger than 100,000 including Ibadan, the largest Negro city in Africa, with a population today of over half a million.

In 1952 the Yoruba had an index of urbanization (as developed by Davis and Casis) of 39.3. This falls below Great Britain with 65.9, Germany with 46.1, and only slightly below the United States with 42.3; but it exceeds that of Canada with 34.3, France with 31.2, Sweden with 28.7, Greece with 25.2, and Poland with 17.4. The Yoruba are the most urban of all African people of any considerable size, and their urban way of life is traditional.

Official figures on population density of Yoruba cities are lacking except for Lagos, where they are given as 25,000 per square mile in 1901, 50,000 in 1921, 58,000 in 1931, and 87,000 in 1950. In 1950 the three wards of Lagos Island had densities of 67,000, 111,000 and 141,000 per square mile. [James] Grant gives an area of nine square miles for Ibadan with an estimated 500,000 inhabitants in 1960, or 55,555 per square mile. It has been possible to calculate approximate densities for three other cities as of 1931, giving 5,720 for Abeokuta, 13,914 for Oyo, and 43,372 for Ogbomosho. These figures compare with 24,697 per square mile for New York City, 15,850 and 15,743 for Chicago and Philadelphia and 5,451 for Los Angeles in 1960, the four largest cities in the United States.

Because of the high ratio of inhabitants per room and per square foot and the compactness of the traditional housing, the size of older Yoruba cities is easily underestimated by visitors. Abeokuta, for example, appears much larger than Ogbomosho, which is actually eight times as dense and half again as large.

Yoruba cities are large, and even the traditional ones are dense. Their permanence over the past 100 years is documented by the estimates of Bowen of about 1856, of Delany and Campbell in 1860, of Moloney in 1890, and in the census reports of 1911, 1921, 1931, and 1952. Bowen gave no estimates of the population of Ife, Ilesha, or Oshogbo, but he mentions that the countries of Ife, Ilesha, Igbomina, and Efon-Alaiye had not yet been visited by missionaries, adding "we are assured that there are many large towns in that region."

Yoruba territory was first penetrated in 1825 by the expedition of Clapperton and Lander, who travelled inland west of the large cities of today. They estimated the size of some of the cities they visited, including eight to ten thousand for Ijana, five to six thousand for Assula, upwards of 10,000 for Assoudo, ten to fifteen thousand for Duffo, and upwards of 7,000 for Chiado. No estimate is given for the "large and populous town" of Shaki, although they were told that its chief had two thousand wives. Beyond Shaki lay Kooso which "at least contains twenty thousand people." At this point Lander wrote, "the further we penetrated into the country, the more dense we found the population to be, and civilization became at every step more apparent. Large towns at the distance of only a few miles from each other, we were informed, lay on all sides of us." Yet of the remaining Yoruba towns visited, estimates are given only for Adja with four thousand, Ateepa with six thousand, Leobadda with six or seven thousand, and Tshow with four thousand.

Of all these towns, only Ijana and Shaki can be identified today. Presumably all the rest were destroyed or abandoned during the wars of the last century. Bowen, the first American missionary in Nigeria, who travelled through much of Yoruba country in 1849–56, wrote:

I have counted the sites of eighteen desolated towns within a distance of sixty miles between Badagry and Abbeokuta—the legitimate result of the slave trade. The whole of Yoruba country is full of depopulated towns, some of which were even larger than Abbeokuta is at present. Of all the places visited by the Landers, only Ishakki (Shaki), Igboho, Ikishi (Kishi) and a few villages remain. Ijenna (Ijana) was destroyed only a few weeks after my arrival in the country. Other and still larger towns in the same region have lately fallen. At one of these Oke-Oddan, the Dahomy army killed and captured 20,000 people, on which occasion the king presented Domingo, the Brazilian slaver, with 600 slaves. The whole number of people destroyed in this section of the country, within the last fifty years, can be not less than five hundred thousand.

Clapperton and Lander went on to visit Old Oyo, and by comparing their statements about it and other Nigerian cities like Kano, we can judge that it was at least 20,000 and perhaps 40,000. One can also judge that they felt that Ilorin, Igboho and perhaps Kishi, which still exist today, exceeded 20,000. Clapperton described Old Oyo as surrounded by a dry moat and a mud wall about twenty feet high. The wall was oval in shape, "about four miles in diameter one way and six miles the other", fifteen miles in circumference, and entered by ten gates. Following another visit by Richard Lander and his brother John in 1830, Old Oyo was evacuated about 1839, after a defeat by Ilorin, and was reestablished farther south at the present site of Oyo, today a city of 72,000 and traditional in character. Recent archaeological investigations at the site of Old Oyo suggest that it was inhabited by a large, dense population.

From reports from Dahomey to the west, which was explored earlier, we know that Old Oyo intervened in the affairs of this powerful state at least since 1724. For a century from about 1729 Old Oyo received gifts and tribute from Dahomey until about 1827, when Oyo was deeply involved with the wars with Ilorin, and King Gezo of Dahomey seized his opportunity to end the payment of annual tribute.

Ijebu-Ode near the coast, which had a population of 28,000 in 1952, appears on a Portuguese map of about 1500 and is described as "a very large city called Geebu, surrounded by a moat" by Pacheco Pereira, writing in 1507–1508. From 1500 onwards, Ijebu-Ode or 'Jebu is mentioned repeatedly in the literature or shown on maps, at least six times in the seventeenth century, four times in the eighteenth century, and four times in the nineteenth century before it was visited by Hinderer and Irving in 1854. Recent investigations at Ijebu-Ode have discovered an enormous earth rampart, 80 miles long, enclosing an area of 400 square miles, which surrounds the city at distances from about 5 to 15 miles. It is formed by a bank which is still 15 to 20 feet high and 50 feet wide at the base, and a ditch 20 to 25 feet deep and 40 feet wide, which together create a wall 40 feet high.

Even earlier, before the discovery of America, when Portuguese explorers of Nigeria first reached Benin in 1485, they brought back in 1486 to the King of Portugal an ambassador from the King of Benin, which was itself an important city of considerable size. From him they learned of Ogané, "the most powerful monarch in these parts." Spurred on to their exploration of the African coast by the belief that Ogané was Prester John, they passed the Cape of Good Hope in 1487 and reached India by sea in 1498. Recent studies in Benin make it almost certain that Ogané was the Oni or King of the Yoruba city of Ife, whose successor became the first Governor of the Western Region of independent Nigeria. Yoruba and Benin traditions agree that the ruling dynasty of Benin originally came from Ife, and archaeological discoveries at Ife, today a city of over 110,000, indicate that it was far more important as a center of elaborate ritual and art in earlier times.

The evidence is incomplete, because Yoruba territory remained *terra incognita* for centuries after Benin to the east and Dahomey to the west had been explored. Nevertheless it is clear that the Yoruba have cities which are relatively large, dense, and permanent, and that urbanism as a traditional feature of the Yoruba way of life cannot be explained in terms of industrialization, acculturation, or the development of colonial administrative headquarters, ports, and mining centers.

Acculturative factors have affected the traditional Yoruba cities in the past century, but urbanism as a way of life clearly antedated the earliest European contact, and is clearly not an outgrowth of European acculturation. Urbanization is related to acculturation, as Ralph Beals has said. Urbanization is a process which involves an adjustment to the new urban setting, and the adoption of new standards and forms of life; but urbanism as a way of life is distinct from acculturation, and it existed among the Yoruba before the first penetration of their area by Europeans.

Ibadan and Abeokuta are not old cities, having been founded in the first half of the last century by refugees from the wars with Ilorin, and Ilorin was only a small village before these wars began. Ibadan and Abeokuta differ from the ancient Yoruba cities in house types and other features but, clearly, neither they nor Ilorin are in the category of the new cities of Africa. Oyo is far more traditional, even though it moved to a new site in the same period. Of all the large Yoruba cities, only Lagos, which is the capital of Nigeria and its principal port and railhead, is a new African city. The site of Lagos had long been known as the entrance to the lagoon from which it is named, and as a small village which numbered only 5,000 at the end of the eighteenth century.

Of all major Yoruba cities, only Lagos is ethnically heterogeneous and in this sense cosmopolitan, yet in 1950 its population was still seventy-three percent Yoruba. Ilorin, which is neither ancient nor one of Africa's modern cities, is eighty-four percent Yoruba although it has been ruled by Fulani from the north for more than a century and is now included in the Northern Region of Nigeria. All other major cities range from over ninety-four to over ninety-nine percent Yoruba according to the census, though in many cases the only published official figures include outlying rural areas.

With the end of the slave wars of the last century, Hausa from the North, Ibo and Jekri from the East, and other peoples have settled in Yoruba cities, but in relatively small numbers except for Lagos. Even in the present century the European population of the twelve largest Yoruba cities was negligible compared with South, East, and North Africa. In 1931 the non-native population, which includes Europeans, numbered only 1,443 for Lagos, the capital, 226 for Ibadan, and 159 for the remaining ten major cities combined. The wars of the last century flooded some cities with refugees from others which were evacuated or destroyed, including those from different Yoruba kingdoms and subcultures; but even on this level of subcultural variation we may assume that in earlier times Yoruba cities were ethnically homogenous, and that non-Yoruba probably consisted mainly of slaves and transient traders.

How did these traditional cities exist without industrialization, which caused the development of urban life in Europe and America? The real base of the Yoruba economy was, and still is, farming; but farming is not an exclusively rural occupation. Many farmers are city dwellers who would regard American suburbia as a curious inversion of their way of life. They are commuters, not from the suburbs to their places of work in the city, but from their city homes to the belt of farms which surrounds each city.

Nearly all Yoruba engage in farming, but the production of many other goods is specialized. Weaving, dyeing, ironworking, brass-casting, wood-carving, ivory-carving, calabash-carving, beadworking, leatherworking, and pottery, as well as drumming, divining, the compounding of charms and medicines, and certain other activities are crafts whose techniques are known only to a small group of specialists, and often protected as trade secrets through supernatural sanctions. These specialists, who are organized into guilds, may engage in farming, but they supply other members of the community with their goods and services.

Farming, specialization and trade were the three cornerstones on which the Yoruba economy rested. Intercommunity and intertribal trade was in the hands of specialists in earlier times, either the King's wives or male traders, though this was ended when British control was established and they were replaced by European trading firms. Local retail trade has remained primarily in the hands of women, who tend to specialize in yams, corn, chickens, cloth or other commodities, and who, like the craftsmen, are organized into guilds.

The size and importance of Yoruba markets, visited by many tens of thousands in the large cities, impress the visitor today as they did the early explorers. Trade does not involve a simple exchange of goods between the producer and consumer, as in the Pacific for example, but was carried on by middlemen whose role and motivations are similar to those in our own society. In the simplest case a trader buys from a producer and sells at a higher price for a monetary profit; but in some cases the goods are sold and resold through a chain of middlemen with so many links that it becomes difficult to distinguish wholesaler from retailer. Before European contact the Yoruba had money in the form of cowrie shells, a pecuniary society, large markets, and true middlemen.

Yoruba cities were of course nonindustrial, and lacked the degree of specialization based upon the machine. Yet Wirth himself specifically excludes industrialism as an essential feature of urbanism, although it accounted for the development of cities in Europe and America.

It is particularly important to call attention to the danger of confusing urbanism with industrialism and modern capitalism. The rise of cities in the modern world is undoubtedly not independent of the emergence of modern power-driven machine technology, mass production, and capitalistic enterprise. But different as the cities of earlier epochs may have been by virtue of their development in a preindustrial and precapitalistic order from the great cities of today, they were, nevertheless, cities.

Yet among the Yoruba the craft form of specialization made each individual economically dependent upon the society as a whole. The weaver depended upon the blacksmith for tools and upon the farmer, the hunter, and the trader for food. The blacksmith depended upon others for food and upon the weaver for clothes. The farmer depended upon the hunter for his meat, the smith for his hoe and cutlass, and the weaver for his clothing. Each of these, moreover, had to rely upon the herbalist, the priest, the chief, the drummer, the potter, the woodcarver, and other specialists for goods and services which they could not provide for themselves. Specialization, even on this level, resulted in an economic interdependence of all members of the city, a factor which I consider as extremely significant.

In Yoruba cities today one can buy a can of food, a machette, or a piece of cloth from Europe, Japan, or India, but food from the local farms is still for sale and the craftsmen are still producing at their looms and smithies, and competing effectively with imported goods from the factories of the world.

Wirth emphasizes economic interdependence as a result of the size of cities.

The specialization of individuals, particularly in their occupations, can proceed only, as Adam Smith pointed out, upon the basis of an enlarged market, which in turn accentuates the division of labor. This enlarged market is only in part supplied by the city's hinterland; in large measure it is found among the large numbers that the city itself contains. The dominance of the city over the surrounding hinterland becomes explicable in terms of the division of labor which urban life occasions and promotes. The extreme degree of interdependence and instability is increased by the tendency of each city to specialize in those functions in which it has the greatest advantage.

This statement fits Yoruba cities which produce primarily for their own inhabitants, while Oyo and Iseyin, for example, export weaving and iron goods to other Yoruba cities. Yet local or regional specialization is the basis of inter-tribal trade in many parts of the world where cities are lacking. To cite only one example, it is found in the islands of the Pacific where the people of the interior specialize in the production of agricultural foods which they export to the coast in exchange for fish and other products of the sea, but where cities, money, and true middlemen are lacking. The important feature here is that a city, even though nonindustrial as among the Yoruba, finds its market mainly within its own boundaries. The degree of specialization, even though limited to the craft level, makes individuals economically interdependent and provides a basis for the development of larger, denser, and more stable communities. One might also postulate that these results may give rise to the need for some broader forms of political control, which formally unite neighboring kinship groupings into larger communities, but this remains an unsupported hypothesis.

Yoruba cities were heterogeneous only in terms of craft specialization, social stratification, and socio-political segmentation. The city is divided into clearly defined "quarters" or wards, sub-quarters or political precincts, and lineages. In Ife the heads of each patrilineage constituted the precinct council, with one of their number serving as precinct chief. Precinct chiefs formed the ward council, which again was headed by one of its members. The five ward chiefs and three other city chiefs whose titles were "owned" by certain lineages represented the interests of the townspeople, and with eight palace chiefs from the King's retinue, served as the King's council and chief tribunal of the capital of the kingdom. The King, or Oba, whose position was hereditary within the related lineages of the royal clan, was responsible for the affairs of the capital city and of the outlying towns and villages within his kingdom.

Wirth cites the delegation of individual interests to representatives as another feature of urban life which derives from its size:

In a community composed of a larger number of individuals than can know one another intimately and can be assembled in one spot, it becomes necessary to communicate through indirect mediums and to articulate individual interests by a process of delegation. Typically, in the city, interests are made effective through representation. The individual counts for little, but the voice of the representative is heard with a deference roughly proportional to the numbers for whom he speaks.

This clearly is the case in Yoruba cities, where an individual makes his interests known to the head of his family, and through him to the head of his lineage, the head of his precinct, the head of his ward, the town chiefs, the King's council, and ultimately to the King. However deference is based on the social status of his lineage, as well as its size. Within the lineage, individual relationships were dependent on such factors as seniority, sex, wealth, personal qualities and status as slave, pawn, or free, but between lineages individual relationships were defined by the relative status of the lineages. The individual counted for little, except as a member of the lineage. In Ife social stratification involves nine social strata of which five, comprising perhaps ninety-five percent of the population, were ascribed or attributed on the basis of lineage affiliation. The four highest strata were primarily achieved, but often within specific lineages or clans.

Wirth says "the contacts of the city may indeed be face to face, but they are nevertheless impersonal, superficial, transitory, and segmental." All these characteristics are exemplified in Yoruba market transactions, where the principle of *caveat emptor* is as well established as in Timbuctoo. As in our own urban centers, one may have regular customers with whom relations are not transitory or superficial, but one must also deal with casual customers of whom one must always beware in either buying or selling.

Wirth emphasizes that urbanism refers to a distinctive mode of life, and this is evident among the Yoruba in clothing, food, habits, manners and attitudes. City dwellers ridicule the unsophisticated "bush" people, and their attitudes toward the non-urban Yoruba, as expressed in conversation and proverbs, closely parallel our concepts of the "rube" or the "hick." The attitudes of the rural Yoruba toward the city dweller also seem to resemble those in our society.

Yoruba cities are secondary in the sociological sense, as Wirth says, while the lineages are primary. Wirth dismisses the factor of political organization as an unsatisfactory criterion of urbanism. Yet it is the presence of a formalized government which exercises authority over neighboring primary groups, such as lineages, and incorporates them into larger secondary groupings like the city, town, or village. And it is this factor which distinguishes the Yoruba, who are urban, from the Ibo of Nigeria's Eastern Region, who had no cities until recently, despite their larger numbers and higher population densities.

Some Yoruba cities, such as Oyo, Ife, Ilesha, Ijebu-Ode, Ondo and Ketu served as capitals and centers of whole kingdoms and in this sense can be considered as metropolitan. They maintained regular communications with the outlying cities, towns, and villages through representatives stationed in them, collected taxes through them, and tried serious crimes which were reserved to the court of the King. Other large cities, such as Iseyin, Ogbomosho, and more recently Ibadan, had formalized city governments but were ruled by a town Chief (*Bale*) under the authority of the King (*Oba*). These cities were not capitals, but they served as centers of trade and warfare. From them the goods and services of specialists reached the smaller towns and villages. This was also true of the capitals, which served not only as centers of warfare and trade, but also of political authority, religion, and arts and crafts.

Here, however, the parallels end. *Anomie* is not apparent, except among those who have recently come to the cities from rural areas. Since the residential unit is the lineage, which involves reciprocal social and economic obligations, the city dweller need not feel lonely and insecure. Yoruba society is pecuniary and highly competitive, and economic failure can lead to frustration, aggression, or suicide, but not to starvation because one can count on the support of his lineage. And one can count on it for social as well as economic support. Lineages were differentiated in status, but these statuses were stable.

Wirth says:

> The bonds of kinship, of neighborliness, and sentiments arising out of living together for generations under a common folk tradition are likely to be absent or, at best, relatively weak in an aggregate the members of which have such diverse origins and backgrounds. Under such circumstances competition and formal control mechanisms furnish the substitutes for the bonds of solidarity that are relied upon to hold a folk society together.

In Yoruba cities, formal control mechanisms were not developed as substitutes for those of kinship, but rather as mechanisms of political control on a secondary, supra-kinship level, transcending the primary groups such as lineages. Yoruba cities clearly lack the diversity of origins and backgrounds of other cities, and kinship bonds were not weakened either by urban life or political control on a higher level by city governments. The lineage, rather, was the basis of Yoruba political structure, both urban and rural. A small village might contain only one or a few lineages, but the social and political structure of Yoruba cities were founded on the lineage. The many lineages of the cities were united as a community by the superior authority of city government. To the extent that lineage and other kinship bonds have been weakened among the Yoruba, this has been the result of acculturation, rather than of urbanism as a way of life. And more recent studies of American cities have revealed a greater strength of ties of kinship and neighborhood than were realized by sociologists at the time when Wirth wrote.

In earlier publications on this subject, I suggested that either economic interdependence or centralized political organization, or both, might be substituted for the criterion of social heterogeneity, as a basis for a definition of cities which might be more meaningful cross-culturally. I still regard these factors as important and as less subjective and no more arbitrary than the factor of social heterogeneity and as less likely to be the results of urbanization in certain cases, than prerequisites for the development of cities.

Now, however, I am inclined to go even farther than Mitchell suggested, and to recommend that cities should be defined strictly in terms of demographic factors: relative size, density, and permanence. There will still be room for argument about how large, how dense, and how permanent communities must be to be accepted as cities, but the range of disagreement does not seem large, and should eventually be narrowed. There can be little question that the Yoruba had cities as defined in demographic terms, and once this definition is accepted we can proceed to examine the social, economic, political and other cultural features of urban life in the hope of being able to distinguish its consequences from causes of its development.

Defined demographically, urbanism as a way of life and urbanization as the process of urban growth may have a cause-or-effect relationship with cultural and social factors, such as acculturation, Europeanization, detribalization, cosmopolitanism, and other types of social heterogeneity, with the economic or technological factors of specialization and industrialization, and with political factors such as city government. All of these factors should be considered separately to determine whether they are necessary to city growth or are the results of urban life, and whether they pertain to all cities.

Wirth explicitly distinguished urbanism from industrialism; [Ellen] Hellman's study shows that both urbanization and Europeanization are distinct from detribalization; and while [Ralph] Beals maintains that acculturation is related to urbanization as a process, I have tried to show that it differs from urbanism as a way of life. The Yoruba, who were urban before their country was even explored by Europeans, show that urbanism as a way of life differs from urbanization, Europeanization, acculturation, detribalization, industrialization, and ethnic heterogeneity, though there was social heterogeneity in terms of craft specialization, social stratification, and socio-political segmentation.

A comparison of the ancient cities of Africa, as illustrated by the traditional Yoruba cities, with the more modern cities which have developed as a result of direct European contact, reveals some significant differences which may shed some light on the future of the urban Africans.

In the traditional cities most of the inhabitants are born and raised, marry and raise their children, live with their families throughout most of their lives, and die and are buried within the city and their own lineage. Statistical data are lacking, but my guess would be that this held for over ninety percent of the population of the major traditional Yoruba cities until only twenty years ago, and that it is probably not much different even today. This is in very marked contrast to the newer cities of South and East Africa where a high proportion of the African inhabitants have come to the city only very recently, where they are only temporary urban residents, and where they hope to return to their homes before they die.

In Africa's traditional cities, husbands lived together with their wives, their children, and their lineages most of their lives in an urban environment. Ties with the family and lineage were not broken by urban life, nor even temporarily suspended. The authority of the family, lineage, and the chiefdom were maintained according to traditional standards. Traditional forms of discipline were maintained in the cities through the family and lineage, and through the town chiefs and the Kings of the independent Yoruba states. As a result illegitimacy, juvenile delinquency, and crime were surprisingly low, in comparison with the newer African cities and with cities of America and Western Europe.

In newer African cities urbanization involves separation from the lineage and family and has resulted in the weakening of the family as an institution, with the increase of extra-marital relations, and of illegitimate children raised in poor home surroundings with inadequate care and discipline, and the development of juvenile delinquency. As families and lineages are re-established in the new cities and populations stabilize, one may expect illegitimacy, juvenile delinquency and crime to decline, if one can judge from the pattern of urbanism in the traditional African cities.

Yet even the traditional Yoruba cities are being affected by the outside influences which have changed Africa so rapidly during the present century. Newcomers from the farms and villages face problems similar in many ways to those of the new cities, and both the new and old urban residents must adapt to the changes resulting from European acculturation.

The strength of Yoruba religion, and its sanctions of behavior have also been undermined by missions, both Christian and Moslem, and by schools and government. Old beliefs have been destroyed for some, without having been replaced by new sanctions or internalized controls, though the number of such individuals is probably smaller than is to be found in Europe and America. The authority of Yoruba chiefs and Kings was weakened during the period of colonial administration, but they have retained the respect of the large majority of the people. The major question here is where they will fit in the political structure of Nigeria as an independent nation.

Western concepts of individual salvation and individual responsibility, which have been taught by the missions and by the schools, have been undermining the traditional respect for the elders, lineage responsibilities, and the strength of lineage controls. The Yoruba are eager for schooling, and grateful to the missions for their role in providing it. Schooling has been a major source of social change, and has added to mobility, as those who leave school often seek suitable employment in other towns and cities where they are separated from their lineages. Industrialization, which has been taking place at a surprising rate in Nigeria since 1956, will further contribute to mobility from the farms and villages to the towns and cities, and to urban growth.

It is easy to predict that urbanization will continue at a rapid rate in Africa for some time, but it is difficult to go much farther. I would suggest that although African cultural features will be retained, probably to a greater degree than many are willing to admit, the new and old cities of Africa will tend to approximate each other and the cities of Europe and America in their sociological characteristics. The evidence from New York, Detroit, Chicago, Havana, and other cities in the Americas indicates the adaptability of descendants of Africans to Westernized urban life, and their preference for it.

7 | Application of the Ideal-Type Constructs to the Metropolis in the Economically Less-Advanced Areas

PHILIP M. HAUSER

As a preliminary to the type of research and analysis by means of which the ideal-type constructs, both the folk-urban and the urban-rural dichotomizations, could be subjected to the test of empirical research, there

SOURCE: Philip M. Hauser and Leo F. Schnore, eds., *The Study of Urbanization* (New York: John Wiley & Sons, Inc., 1965), pp. 511–514. Reprinted by permission of the publishers.

follows a detailed listing of the characteristics of the urban social order as set forth by Wirth, in relation to the characteristics of the urban society, that is, size, density, and heterogeneity, respectively. For each of these items, a judgment is indicated in column 2 on whether the characteristic is, in fact, observable in the urban society in Asian cities in which the writer has lived (primarily Rangoon, but including Bangkok, Djakarta, and Calcutta).

Urban Condition	Expected Characteristic	Actual Characteristic (Presence of characteristic in urban areas of less developed countries)
Size	1. Atomization (Simmel)	No
	2. Schizoid character	No
	3. Segmental roles	Some
	4. Secondary contacts	Some
	5. Superficiality	Some
	6. Anonymity	Some
	7. Sophistication	No
	8. Rationality	No
	9. Loses spontaneous self-expression	Mainly no
	10. Utilitarian contact	Some
	11. Pecuniary nexus	Some
	12. Interdependence—specialization	Some, but very limited
	13. Mass media of communication	Mainly no
Density	1. Differentiation and specialization	Mainly no
	2. Shift in media through which we orient ourselves to urban milieu and fellow man, that is the emphasis on vision world of artifacts, etc. (Simmel)	Very little
	3. Place of work separated from place of residence	Some, but limited
	4. Glaring contrasts Poverty and riches Squalor and splendor Ignorance and intelligence	Some
	5. Patterning of city ecologically— the Burgess hypothesis	Yes and no
	6. Secularization of life	No
	7. Competition, aggrandizement, and mutual exploitation	Yes and no
	8. Clock and traffic signals as symbols	No

Urban Condition	Expected Characteristic	Actual Characteristic (Presence of characteristic in urban areas of less developed countries)
	9. Loneliness	Yes and no
	10. Friction, irritation, frustration	Some
Heterogeneity	1. Breaks caste lines, complicating class structure	No
	2. Instability and insecurity of individual	Yes and no
	3. Sophistication and cosmopolitanism	Mainly no
	4. No single group has undivided allegiance	No
	5. Turnover in group membership rapid	Mainly no
	6. Personality segments corresponding to group memberships	Mainly no
	7. Place of residence, employment, income, interests fluctuate	Mainly no
	8. Not a home owner	No
	9. Mass behavior fluid and unpredictable	No
	10. Depersonalization	Yes and no
	11. Money economy	Yes and no
	12. Mass media communication operate as leveling influences	Mainly no

If we turn next to a consideration of the characteristics of folk society set forth by Redfield, and look for their presence or absence in the large urban area in the economically less-advanced areas in the world, a similar table may be prepared.

Expected Characteristic	Actual Characteristic (Presence in urban areas in less developed countries)
Social unit is:	
1. Small	Yes
2. Isolated social world	Yes and no
3. Nonliterate order	Yes
4. Homogeneous groups	Yes
5. Strong group solidarity	Yes
6. Simple technology	Yes
7. Simple division of labor	Yes

8. Economically independent	Yes and no
9. "Culture"—the organization of conventional understanding	Yes
10. Behavior strongly patterned conventional	Yes and no
11. Status	Yes
12. No systematic knowledge	Yes
13. Behavior personal	Yes
14. Society familial	Yes and no
15. Society sacred	Yes
16. Mentality personal and emotional	Yes
17. No market	Yes and no

It is hardly necessary to reiterate that the responses indicating the "actual" in relation to the "expected" are not responses grounded in empirical research. *They are based largely on the limited experience and impressions of the writer.* They are not presented, therefore, as definitive answers to the questions raised, but rather as approximations or hypotheses that merit further investigation for their validation or rejection.

Concluding Observation

The folk-urban and the urban-rural dichotomies may be regarded as ideal-type constructs which are the products of Western writers. These ideal-type constructs have not been used in accordance with Weber's injunctions on the use of ideal-type constructs. Even in the literature of social science as well as that in general education, there has been a relatively blind acceptance of the ideal-type constructs as generalizations based on research rather than as tools to be utilized in research. Investigators have been more impressed with their findings of conformance than motivated to look for deviations from the constructs. Moreover, fundamental logical errors have been committed in the utilization of these constructs in the drawing of diachronic conclusion from synchronic observations. That is, the concepts have also been used in a neo-evolutionary way on the assumption that the "folk" and the "urban" actually represented different stages in the development of societies.

There is evidence, by no means conclusive as yet, that both parts of these dichotomies represent confounded variables and, in fact, complex systems of variables which have yet to be unscrambled. The dichotomizations perhaps represent all too hasty efforts to synthesize and integrate what little knowledge has been acquired in empirical research. The widespread acceptance of these ideal-type constructs as generalizations, without benefit of adequate research, well illustrates the dangers of catchy neologisms which often get confused with knowledge. In some respects, these ideal-type constructs represent an admixture of nineteenth-century speculative efforts to achieve global generalization, and twentieth-century concern with the integration of knowledge for general education purposes, as a result of which integration is often achieved of that which is not yet known.

It is hoped that the materials which have been presented will help to highlight the need for next steps in the evaluation of these ideal-type constructs. Obviously, what is necessary are well-designed empirical researches in which deviations from the constructs are noted in greater detail and with greater precision than are now available. Such research would better illuminate the nature of diverse social orders and, in the process, perhaps lead to the construction of ideal typology more useful than that which is now available as prolegomena to empirically based generalizations.

C | Types of Cities

8 | The Evolution of Urban Society: Early Mesopotamia and Prehispanic Mexico

ROBERT McC. ADAMS

This volume is concerned with the presentation and analysis of regularities in our two best-documented examples of early, independent urban societies [early Mesopotamia and prehispanic Mexico]. It seeks to provide as systematic a comparison as the data permits of institutional forms and trends of growth that are to be found in both of them. Emphasizing basic similarities in structure rather than the many acknowledged formal features by which each culture is rendered distinguishable from all others, it seeks to demonstrate that both the societies in question can usefully be regarded as variants of a single processual pattern.

. . . . .

There is no need to dwell at length on definitions of the entities with which this study deals. The major characteristics of early states have been repeatedly described, and in any case I am more concerned with the *process* of their growth than with a detailed discussion of their characteristics. There is no more adequate term evoking this process than that introduced by V. Gordon Childe, the "Urban Revolution." Among its important advantages are that it places stress on the transformative character of the change, that it suggests at least relative rapidity, and that it specifies a restricted, urban locus within which the process was concentrated.

Yet it must be admitted that there are potential distortions involved in the use of the term as well as advantages, quite apart from the specific attributes Childe attaches to it. The more common usage of the word "revolution," for example, implies aspects of conscious struggle. Possibly

SOURCE: Robert McC. Adams, *The Evolution of Urban Society: Early Mesopotamia and Prehistoric Mexico* (Chicago: Aldine Publishing Co., 1966). Reprinted by permission of the author and publisher.

there were overtones of consciousness about certain stages or aspects of the Urban Revolution, although the issue is unsettled. Any implication that such was generally the case, however, is certainly false. Again, the term perhaps implies a uniform emphasis on the growth of the city as the core of the process. At least as a form of settlement, however, urbanism seems to have been much less important to the emergence of the state, and even to the development of civilization in the broadest sense, than social stratification and the institutionalization of political authority.

Still a further possible drawback is that uncritical use of the term may invoke an implicit, and therefore dangerous, assumption of the unity of all urban phenomena. This is at best a proposition that applies at so gross a level as to be hardly more than trivial, and yet it sometimes has served to divert attention toward misleading analogies with other cultural settings sharing only the fact of settlement in dense, "urban" clusters rather than toward the empirical investigation of the phenomena in hand. In short, the purpose of this study emphatically is not to generalize about the nature of cities but rather to discuss the processes by which, at least in some cases, they seem first to have come into existence. And as will become apparent, the achievement of these first steps in urban growth leads to a distinctive constellation of features that cannot be regarded simply as progressively approximating contemporary urbanism more and more closely.

In balance, the insights engendered by the term seem to outweigh its drawbacks. But the characteristics with which Childe sought to describe and associate it are less satisfactory. His criteria were the following: (1) increase in settlement size toward "urban" proportions; (2) centralized accumulation of capital resulting from the imposition of tribute or taxation; (3) monumental public works; (4) the invention of writing; (5) advances toward exact and predictive sciences; (6) the appearance and growth of long-distance trade in luxuries; (7) the emergence of a class-stratified society; (8) the freeing of a part of the population from subsistence tasks for full-time craft specialization; (9) the substitution of a politically organized society based on territorial principles, the state, for one based on kin ties; and (10) the appearance of naturalistic—or perhaps better, representational—art.

One objection to such a listing is that it gives us a mixed bag of characteristics. Some, like monumental architecture, can be unequivocally documented from archeological evidence but also are known to have been associated occasionally with noncivilized peoples. Others, like exact and predictive sciences, are largely matters of interpretation from evidence that is at best fragmentary and ambiguous. And still others, if not most of Childe's criteria, obviously must have emerged through a gradual, cumulative process not easily permitting distinctions in kind to be kept apart from those merely in degree. Moreover, these characteristics differ radically from one another in their importance as causes, or even as indices, of the Urban Revolution as a whole. The significance of the reappearance of representational art—indeed, its initial appearance, insofar as it deals with the human figure—for example, is at least not immediately apparent.

.   .   .   .   .

The term "Urban Revolution" implies a focus on ordered, systematic *processes* of change through time. Hence the identifying characteristics of the Urban Revolution need to be more than loosely associated features (no matter how conveniently recognizable), whose functional role is merely assumed and which are defined in terms of simple presence or absence. Usefully to speak of an Urban Revolution, we must describe a functionally related core of institutions as they interacted and evolved through time. From this viewpoint, the characteristics Childe adduces can be divided into a group of primary variables, on the one hand, and a larger group of secondary, dependent variables, on the other. And it clearly was Childe's view that the primary motivating forces for the transformation lay in the rise of new technological and subsistence patterns. The accumulative growth of technology and the increasing availability of food surpluses as deployable capital, he argued, were the central causative agencies underlying the Urban Revolution.

. . . I believe that the available evidence supports the conclusion that the transformation at the core of the Urban Revolution lay in the realm of social organization. And, while the onset of the transformation obviously cannot be understood apart from its cultural and ecological context, it seems to have been primarily changes in social institutions that precipitated changes in technology, subsistence, and other aspects of the wider cultural realm, such as religion, rather than vice versa.

.   .   .   .   .

The term "state" . . . is useful for this discussion in that it centers on the political order, one of our major subjects of inquiry. For all the acrimonious debate about the essential features of state societies, they may reasonably be defined as hierarchically organized on political and territorial lines rather than on kinship or other ascriptive groups and relationships. Internally, at least, even primitive states tended to monopolize the use of force for the preservation of order, while externally they exercised a degree of sovereignty. Like the state itself, these root characteristics emerged at varying rates during the course of the Urban Revolution. While our recognition of them is often rendered dubious and never precise by the nature of the data, they clearly serve to distinguish a new, qualitatively more complex and extensive, mode of social integration.

.   .   .   .   .

Subsistence and Settlement

It is a truism that complex, civilized societies depend upon a subsistence base that is sufficiently intensive and reliable to permit sedentary, nucleated

Comparative Chronologies for Early Mesopotamia and Prehispanic Central Mexico

MESOPOTAMIAN ALLUVIUM				CENTRAL MEXICO		
	B.C.			A.D.		
Dynasty of Agade	2300–	CONQUEST STATES		–1500		
						IV
	2500–			–1300	Aztec	III
Early Dynastic III		MILITARISTIC POLITIES				II
	2700–			–1100		I
II						
I					Coyotlatelco	
	2900–			–900		
d						
	3100–			–700	Metepec	
c		THEOCRATIC POLITIES				
Protoliterate					Xolalpan	
	3300–			–500		
b					Tlamimilolpa	
a	3500–			–300		
					Miccaotli	
Warka				–100		
	3700–				Tzacualli	
Late Ubaid				A.D.		
				B.C.	Patlachique	
	3900–			–100		
					Cuicuilco	

settlements, a circumstance that under most circumstances, and certainly in the long run, has implied agriculture.

*   *   *   *   *

The domestication of cereals immensely expanded the environmental range within which these crops were an effective subsistence source, and it surely also increased substantially the size and reliability of yields in relation both to labor input and to available land. As the numbers and range of sheep and goats also expanded following their domestication, an assured supply of milk and meat products came to overlap the expanding ranges of distribution of the cereals, further establishing the superiority of agriculture. It was upon this basis, although with such important later additions as cattle, pigs, donkeys, and the domesticated date palm, that early Mesopotamian civilization met its underlying subsistence needs.

In Mesoamerica, the pattern was somewhat different. The wild progenitors of the great New World triad of food plants, especially maize but also beans and squash, required a much longer period of selective breeding before they became sufficient, as domesticates, to replace a wide spectrum of hunted and gathered products. Fully sedentary village life accordingly began much later than in the Old World, perhaps even as late as the middle of the first millennium B.C., although the earliest incipient cultivation extends back into at least the seventh millennium.

. . . . .

For purposes of understanding the Urban Revolution, however, differences in the onset of food production between the Old and the New World are of little consequence, except insofar as they reflect cumulative differences in subsistence potentialities. What matters are the underlying similarities in the conditions precipitating the Food-Producing Revolution, as well as in the major changes of which it was constituted. For these, it now seems clear, identify the Food-Producing Revolution not merely as the predecessor and prerequisite for the Urban Revolution but as a type of transformation profoundly different from the latter.

. . . . .

What were the essential features of agriculture, not only as a mode of subsistence but as a set of social problems and activities, which seem to have influenced the course of the Urban Revolution? We may begin with certain very general consequences of food production that tend to be common to all its manifestations, and then turn subsequently to those whose effects may have been at least partly different in Mesopotamia and in Mesoamerica.

Increased yields, in relation to labor input, have already been mentioned. An essential feature of virtually every agricultural regime is that its demands upon the farmer are discontinuous through the year and, moreover, are generally phased fairly uniformly for the population of an entire region. This provides a basis not merely for a substantially greater aggregate of leisure time than most hunting-collecting societies can achieve but also for its organized disposition as labor not directly tied to the satisfaction of the immediate subsistence requirements of the primary producers and their families—and hence for the control and manipulation of labor as a form of capital.

. . . . .

Next we may consider the nature of agricultural "surpluses" insofar as they may have been a precondition for the Urban Revolution in Mesopotamia and Mesoamerica. That agricultural producers can, to a degree quite unprecedented among hunters and collectors, be induced or compelled to provide a surplus above their own subsistence needs for socially defined ends is little more than a truism. But does the exploitation of a given environment by a given agricultural technology, implying a potential level of productivity from which actual consumption can be subtracted to define the surplus available for reallocation, actually help to engender the ideologies and institutional contexts that are required to mobilize that surplus? Is there an inherent tendency for agriculturalists to advance in productivity toward the highest potential level consistent with their technology, that is, to maximize their production above subsistence needs and so to precipitate the growth of new patterns of appropriation and consumption involving elites freed from responsibilities for food production? Gordon Childe, although never dealing with these issues directly, appears to have thought so. Karl Polanyi and his collaborators have argued persuasively to the contrary, noting that actual agricultural surpluses are always defined and mobilized in a particular institutional setting and that it is precisely the growth of the collective symbols and institutions of the primitive states that can explain the conversion of peasant leisure into foodstuffs in urban storehouses.

A useful and somewhat different approach to the problem of interpreting the significance of agricultural surpluses has recently been suggested by Martin Orans. . . . Briefly, he focuses criticism on the conception of surplus as it is applied at the level of the individual producer. What really matters, he argues, is not the margin between per capita production and consumption, which implies improving "efficiency" as the major factor in change and which is inherently incalculable from the usual archeological-historical data. At least from the viewpoint of understanding sociocultural change, the crucial variable, instead, is the *gross* amount of deployable wealth or "surplus."

· · · · ·

Calculated as gross amounts of deployable wealth rather than per capita ones, the significance of surpluses changes from an implied independent factor of change to a component in an interdependent network of cause and effect. Extensions of territorial control, new forms of political superordination, and a multiplicity of technological advances all may have had as much effect on the size of the surplus as improvements in immediate agricultural "efficiency," while the deployment of the surplus, however it was formed, obviously had important reciprocal effects on these other factors. Further to emphasize the interdependency of surpluses with a host of political, economic, and technological institutions, it may be noted that agriculture received organizational inputs from some of the institutions that emerged during the course of the Urban Revolution . . . , suggesting that surpluses can be isolated from the processes constituting the Urban Revolution as a whole only in the sense that they may serve as convenient indices for it. In reality, they and the institutions promoting and disposing of them were inextricably intertwined to form its substance.

· · · · ·

. . . The subsistence patterns of late fourth and early third millennium B.C. Mesopotamia involve specialized groups of producers whose relations were characteristically mediated by the dominant urban institutions, including the palace and the temple. Although a quantitative summary has not yet been attempted . . . the general outline of the system conforms strikingly well to the "redistributive" model that Polanyi and his collaborators have sketched; moreover, there are at least hints in the available data that the actual flow of goods and services was large in relation to the total available supply of such goods and services. Surely we see here, as was adumbrated earlier, not merely a complex pattern of subsistence but one in which the interdependence of its component features played a material part in shaping the institutions by which we identify the Urban Revolution itself.

The Mesoamerican pattern was different in important ways and yet generically similar. There were densely settled enclaves where conditions were favorable for continuous or intensive agriculture with the indigenous crops and technology, separated from one another by extremely rugged areas, permitting, at best, marginal settlement. Differences in rainfall, in soils, and, above all, in elevation, profoundly affected the complex of cultivable crops upon which depended not only trade in luxuries but also some commodities closely linked with subsistence. . . .

This regional contrast, and the prevailing symbiosis that it encouraged, constituted an "ecological mosaic," as it has been called, of strikingly different and yet interdependent zones of specialization. The pattern as a whole was similar to Mesopotamia in its high degree of internal differentiation, and, as in Mesopotamia, it is not unreasonable to suppose that some of the most advanced and characteristic institutions of Mesoamerican society were centrally involved, and may even have had their origins, in mediating the relationships and interchanges between the specialized components.

. . . . .

A further general similarity between Mesopotamian and Mesoamerican subsistence patterns, again accompanied by regionally variable forms whose differences are also significant for our purposes, is an increasing intensity of land use. Best known among the patterns of ecological modification to which this refers is the introduction of irrigation, and there seems little reason to doubt that it was generally accompanied by at least a relative increase in the productivity of lands under cultivation. But in one sense the term "intensity" is perhaps a misleading one. It implies a special emphasis upon labor-intensive techniques of agriculture in which the productivity of a fixed, limited amount of agricultural land rises in direct proportion to a spiraling labor input. . . .

A better way of characterizing these modified patterns of land use, at least in terms of the changes in social organization they may have brought about, involves not their productivity in relation to land area or labor input but their unstabilizing effect upon communal systems of land tenure and the consequent inducement they provide to the growth of social stratification. Irrigation systems, for example, are capital investments that enhance the productivity of the tracts and groups they serve but not others. Given inadequacies in water supply (whether arising from a limited average supply in relation to land, from year-to-year fluctuations, or from lack of congruence between maximum stream flow and the growing season), the usual condition in both Mesopotamia and Mesoamerica, such systems represent relatively permanent improvements, which restrict or distort uniformity of access to the primary productive resources of the community and which tend to concentrate the potentialities for the production of a surplus of deployable wealth in the hands of a limited social segment. Depending on local circumstances, such potentialities may be reckoned in terms of rights to land or to water, but the effect is the same in either case. They stimulate the concentration of hereditable, alienable wealth in productive resources, and hence also the emergence of a class society.

· · · · ·

Although the evidence is admittedly inconclusive, there are suggestions of a significant, if partial, contrast between Mesopotamia and central Mexico. In the former, . . . leveling devices involving the redistribution of corporately held lands apparently were absent, while, on the other hand, there was vigorous buying and selling not merely among royally appointed officeholders but among small agricultural producers, applying, according to Igor Diakonoff's estimate, to "at least 40 to 50 per cent of the lands, with about two thirds of the population" of the important city-state of Lagash at the end of Early Dynastic times. In central Mexico, on the other hand, the institutions of sale were poorly developed and largely limited to the nobility, while the bulk of the population enjoyed only a portion of the usufruct (minus tribute and labor service) of corporately owned, rigorously entailed land. In the Mesopotamian instance, a contribution to the growth of social stratification from local differentia in subsistence seems assured. In Mesoamerica, on the contrary, the growth of social stratification seems to have been pre-eminently a politically induced process associated with royal largesse in the distribution of lands and tribute. . . .

· · · · ·

Kin and Class

Almost by definition, the growth of social complexity has been accompanied by social stratification. If the term "class" is used to describe objectively differentiated degrees of access to the means of production of the society without any necessary implications of sharply reduced mobility, class consciousness, or overt interclass struggle, the early states characteristically were class societies. Hence perhaps the central task in a comparative essay is to consider parallelisms both in emergent class structures and in the sequence of changes by which they were brought about.

. . . . .

[In early Mesopotamia] clearly, there were groupings of nuclear families into ascriptive units organized at least in part along lines of descent. Such groups in some (and perhaps in most) cases corporately held title to agricultural lands. They also played a role in the organization of the crafts, of corvée labor called up by the state for certain purposes, and probably of the army. Such widely manifested functions suggest that lineage groupings had not become merely vestigial by late Early Dynastic and Akkadian times but, instead, were still both powerful and important. . . .

Turning to central Mexico, we find ramifying organizations based on both kinship and residence that were essentially similar to what has been traced in Mesopotamia. Given the nature of our sources in this case, there is no difficulty in establishing at least the basic structure and activities of the more inclusive units, the so-called "calpullis." . . .

. . . . .

. . . While debate continues over the precise nature of the calpullis, the trend of all more recent research supports the conclusion that they were localized endogamous lineages that under most circumstances maintained their own lands and temples and that, particularly in urbanized, politically organized communities, also exercised a variety of other functions. Even the Spaniards were not entirely consistent in their translation of the word. Usually they spoke of calpullis as "barrios" or quarters, emphasizing the aspect of these groups as zones of contiguous residence. But on other occasions they spoke of them as "lineages" and defined their leaders as "elder kinsmen." In fact, Zurita, one of the most penetrating of early Spanish observers, often translates the term by both words together. In any event, officers were chosen by election from the group, although generally from the same family.

. . . . .

Thus we find that traditional, localized groupings, composed of related nuclear families, were the elementary units upon which the states of Early Dynastic Mesopotamia and late prehispanic central Mexico were erected. These units in both cases seem to have taken the form of "conical clans," in which the degree of relationship to a real or fictive common ancestor served as a basis for internal tendencies toward stratification. Probably they were of high antiquity, considerably antedating the onset of civilized life by any definition, and there seems no reason to question Paul Kirchoff's assertion that they represented "the *condition sine qua non*" for the formation of complex, flexible hierarchies of economic and social differentiation that characterized the growth of the state itself. At the same time, however, they survived the superimposition of new political relationships for a considerable time, retaining loyalties and forms of internal organization that were rooted in kin relationships, while adapting to the needs of the state through the elaboration of a new series of specialized functions. Among the specialized functions, three in particular may be mentioned: (1) serving as units for military training and service; (2) providing a corporate framework for the development, employment, and retention of the skills and attitudes of specialized craftsmanship; and (3) serving as units of labor management for state projects and services.

Turning from cohesive bonds based on real or fictive kin affiliations within social segments, we must consider the growth of differentiated, hierarchical principles or organization affecting the society at large. What is our evidence for the development of social stratification? What forms did it take in our respective areas? Can we identify a common structure of stratification beneath the welter of divergent local features? Of course, this problem is complicated by the fact that we are dealing with relatively "primitive," undifferentiated systems in which social stratification did not develop as an autonomous, distinctive feature but was "embedded" in multifunctional institutions embracing political and religious components as well. . . .

To begin with early Mesopotamia, the available evidence takes a succession of forms which influence the interpretations that can be made of it. In the late Ubaid period, apparently the "take-off" point for the Urban Revolution, it consists almost exclusively of reports from excavations in cemeteries, . . .

In the late Ubaid period significant differentiation in grave wealth was almost entirely absent. . . . In the Warka and Protoliterate periods greater variation begins to be apparent. . . . By late Early Dynastic times there is much fuller and less ambiguous evidence to suggest the existence of . . . a system [of class distinctions].

· · · · ·

. . . In early Mesopotamia, I believe we can trace the emergence of a fully developed class society by no later than the end of the Early Dynastic period. Its origins, prior to the appearance of cuneiform documents, can be followed only indirectly, in the gradual emergence of a difference between richly furnished tombs, on the one hand, and the much more numerous graves of a relatively impoverished peasantry, on the other. Subsequently, however, we can establish the internal gradations within this society more and more clearly from written sources. The system of stratification was, of course, closely articulated with systems of political and military powers and prerogatives, but those relationships . . . [will be considered later]. Here our major concern is the economic basis of stratification, particularly as defined in terms of degrees of servitude and access to land.

Standing at the pinnacle of Mesopotamian society were small numbers of princely families who seem to have been vigorously extending their control of land by purchase during the later Early Dynastic and Akkadian periods. . . .

. . . Ruling families in Mesopotamia seem to have headed semi-integrated manorial estates that varied greatly in size. Their labor force, dependent in varying degrees on the distribution of rations, allotments of land, and other forms of clientage, also included a small but significant proportion of persons employed under repressive, closely controlled conditions of outright slavery. Yet, in spite of the proliferation and increasing importance of these class-oriented forms of organization, there still existed kin-based communities both outside and within the manorial establishments, and, while such communities were declining in the relative amount of land under their corporate control, it is likely that they still had very large areas at their disposal.

This was, in short, a complex, changing amalgam of older forms of social organization and new ones. But it is important to remember that the older, kin-based institutions were not merely pushed aside by patron-client relationships, to decay slowly along the neglected margins of the latter. As in the case of the continuing role of kin ties in the administration of army and labor service, clientage, and the crafts, the older forms at least at times were readapted and retained as important structural features. . . .

. . . The prehispanic Mexican system of social stratification can be much more briefly treated than can that of the early Sumerians. . . .

· · · · ·

. . . At the apex of the Aztec social pyramid stood the polygynous royal household, its line of divinely descended Tlatoanis marrying daughters of the leading chieftains of the realm to produce in time a largely endogamous nobility sharply differentiated from the rest of the population in wealth, education, diet, dress, and other prerogatives. While these pillis, or members of the nobility, comprised the upper echelons of the political and military administration, they were lords, as Zurita says, "by virtue not of dominion or command, but of lineage." Large numbers of them—600, according to Cortés, as well as their servants and followers—were constantly in attendance upon the royal court, where they were maintained with support from the state treasury.

In addition to an impressive flow of tribute from subjugated towns, . . . there were great estates at the king's disposal comparable to those in early Mesopotamia. Apparently a distinction was recognized between patrimonial lands, which belonged privately to the king as a result of inheritance or conquest, and entailed lands set aside for the maintenance of administrative personnel and other specific purposes. . . .

Private lands were also held by the nobility. In some cases they were apparently subject to various forms of entail, and they reverted to the crown in the event of the death of an owner without heirs. However, they were subject to sale, and the produce from them could be appropriated by their noble owners without the deduction of a share as royal tribute.

The source of all such private lands, it should be observed, was the successful conquest of neighboring territories. . . .

In addition to an aristocracy of lineage there was an aristocracy of service, made up in the main of commoners who had distinguished themselves in warfare. . . . Also of an intermediate status, . . . were corporate groups of merchants. Since they were engaged exclusively in long-distance trade, largely on behalf of the ruler and the nobility, they were closely involved in the expansion of the Aztec state. . . .

Below these groups a large part (in most regions the major part) of the population was grouped in calpullis, as we have seen earlier—localized clans or lineages that were highly stratified internally, that held corporate title to agricultural lands, and that also served as a basis for the organization of many of the crafts and professions. There seems to have been a minimum of twenty calpullis, and probably there were several times that number, with recognized territories in Tenochtitlán at the time of the Spanish Conquest, and there is some evidence that the calpullis were ranked among themselves from highest to lowest.

As the persistence of vertically oriented (i.e., stratified) kin-based social groupings across the growing horizontal barrier between nobles and commoners implies, this was a society embarked upon fundamental change and hence not easily summarized in terms of unifying organizational principles. . . .

Below the "plebeian" population of macehuales organized in calpullis stood the mayeques, who cultivated the private lands of the nobility and who (like the client populations on Mesopotamian agricultural estates) have been likened to serfs on medieval fiefs. . . .

. . . . .

Slaves constituted a bottom stratum in the society, and, as in early Mesopotamia, their absolute number was seemingly not large. . . .

. . . . .

From the viewpoint of stratification, it is not too much to describe early Mesopotamia and central Mexico as slightly variant patterns of a single, fundamental course of development in which corporate kin groups, originally preponderating in the control of land, were gradually supplemented by the growth of private estates in the hands of urban elites. And, while such corporate kin groups still remained active and viable in many respects at the termination points in our two sequences, it is only fair to conclude that they had by then become encapsulated in a stratified pattern of social organization that was rigidly divided along class lines.

Parish and Polity

The restructuring of stratified clans along class lines has a vital but indirect relation to the growth of the state. Older, vertically oriented, solidary forms of organization were replaced by more functionally specified, authoritarian, and all-encompassing horizontal ones that were better adapted to the administrative requirements of increasingly large and complex societies. In some respects the older forms may have provided a model that the newer ones needed only to readapt and systematize; such was the case in connection with the extension of the traditional labor and tribute system from within the calpullis to meet the needs of the emergent Aztec state. But an analysis of the state, and of the class system on which it was based, nevertheless are more than complementary approaches to the same unified reality. Their paths of development obviously intertwined and reinforced one another, but in important respects each followed laws of its own. . . .

The first to appear were the priests—or, at any rate, an elite whose claims to leadership were primarily validated in religious terms. Shrines and small temples surely long antedate the beginnings of our chronological chart. In fact, for the New World at least, Gordon Willey has argued that they may be as old as the establishment of settled village life. But, as the precincts of specialists somehow chosen to lead or represent the community in worship, there is little basis at present for assuming that they antedate the Middle Formative period in Mesoamerica and the Ubaid period in Mesopotamia.

.   .   .   .   .

. . . Hence the probability of a primarily religious focus to social life at the outset of the Urban Revolution, while often somewhat naïvely exaggerated, appears to be the decidedly most reasonable reconstruction of the available evidence.

Why should this have been so? Part of the answer may lie with the necessity for providing an intelligible moral framework of organization for society as it increased cumulatively in scale and complexity. . . .

Although it is hardly possible to elucidate all the specific factors at work in Mesopotamia and Mesoamerica, our earlier discussion of underlying subsistence patterns in the two areas at least suggests what some of the most important of the factors are likely to have been. In the first place, there is substantial evidence from both areas of ecological instability, which has repeatedly been reflected in drouths, famines, floods, and similar disasters. At a magicoreligious level, it is thus no surprise to find that the earliest conceptions of deity to crystallize were those associated with the assurance of fertility and the annual regeneration of crops and livestock.

.   .   .   .   .

Powerless as man might be before the major disasters, the emphasis on the building of temples and the formation of priesthoods undoubtedly also reflects a more "rational," economic aspect. In the absence of widely extended political controls, offerings brought to a sanctuary in aggregate would have constituted a larger reserve than otherwise could be attained, a reserve transcending the environmental limitations of its parent community and reflecting the advantages of complementarity to be derived from establishing a network of permanently related communities in adjacent ecological zones.

For reasons already suggested, Mesopotamia met this challenge in one way and central Mexico in another. In the former, the temple developed not only as a sanctuary but also as a redistributive center and a focus of managerial activity. In the latter, attention was turned outward, overcoming great distances, as well as the absence of long navigable waterways and draft animals, with an astonishing hyperdevelopment of interregional exchange or "trade." In neither case is it necessary to argue that the socioeconomic importance of the function fully "explains" the enormous growth of temples as architectural complexes and as consumers of a major share of the available surplus in the form of subsistence goods and luxury products. Their socioeconomic contribution at one time might be shown (but only in the complex, reified calculations of an external observer) to have been very nearly equivalent to their consumption, or again it may not. All that I would insist on is that their genesis is likely to have involved elements of a direct economic contribution by the temples to the well-being of their communities, as well as a perhaps more clearly perceived and deeply felt religious one.

Let us consider the character of temple activities and organization somewhat more fully for our two respective areas, both as it existed soon after the outset of the Urban Revolution and as it began to change toward the end of the era of Theocratic Polities, the Urban Revolution's first phase.

In Mesopotamian temples we can trace a broad trend toward both an increase in size and an increasing differentiation in function. . . .

Less can be said with respect to the overall organization of temples, and of the theocratic elite that presumably was identified with them, in central Mexico during the "Classic" period than in Protoliterate Mesopotamia. . . .

. . . . .

As in Protoliterate Mesopotamia, the conclusion seems relatively certain that political and religious systems of authority were largely undifferentiated at Teotihuacán. Throughout the occupation of the site the major building activity was on structures of a preponderantly ceremonial character, and both the lavish production of ritual goods and the general preoccupation with religious themes tend to confirm the impression that political leadership was predominantly theocratic in orientation. Nevertheless, the sheer size of Teotihuacán, and of the still unknown but presumably large supporting territory under its influence or control, strongly suggests that the prestige of the city as a focus of voluntary pilgrimage and offerings must have been increasingly supplemented by superordinate controls of a more strongly politicomilitary nature.

. . . . .

Thus a further axis of comparison between Mesoamerican sites like Teotihuacán and their homotaxial equivalents in Mesopotamia involves internal trends leading to systematic change rather than static characterization. In both cases the key development was an apparently gradual rise in the power and influence of militaristic groups, closely accompanied by the transformation of a solidary social organization composed of ascriptive segments into a hierarchical, increasingly autocratic one. The rate of this change, to be sure, was not the same; the designation of the period within which Teotihuacán falls as "Classic" properly implies a substantial, independent aesthetic achievement as well as considerable duration, while its Protoliterate counterpart in Mesopotamia emphasizes instead a more transitory stage in a developmental sequence. But the essentials of the trend, culminating in the rise to power of politically fragmented Toltec groups, on the one hand, and in the increasingly sanguinary internecine warfare of Early Dynastic Sumerian city-states, on the other hand, were the same in each case.

. . . . .

As the foregoing account has hinted at several points, the emergence of the political and economic organs of the state cannot be understood exclusively as a series of internal processes within even the largest urban communities. Both the perils and the rewards of militarism lay beyond the immediately adjoining, more or less permanently attached and dependent, territories. The increasing concentration of political authority in dynastic institutions at the expense of older communal and religious bodies obviously took place in a setting in which both the perils and the rewards of militaristic contention were fully and deeply understood. Successful conquest brought political prestige in its wake, not uniformly enriching the community but, instead, increasing the stratification within it and permitting the consolidation of an independent power base by forces whose initial role had merely been that of leading elements in a common enterprise. In these and many other ways, the consolidation of the institutional structures of the newly developed urban polities must be seen as an internal adjustment to a steadily widening and sharpening context of intercommunity, and even interregional, hostilities.

Hence, having dealt with internal political developments, we must turn to their complementary external manifestations. Unprecedented patterns of extended territorial control were to be found in Mesopotamia as a product of the Akkadian conquests and in the Aztec realm on the eve of its rapid destruction by the Spaniards. The term "empire" is not an entirely suitable one for these patterns in either area; it implies a degree and durability of economic consolidation, as well as of administrative control, for which there is no convincing evidence. Many features we tend to associate with empires apparently were missing or at best very poorly developed, such as royal encouragement of a free peasantry with loyalties directed toward its authority; a mobile, achievement-oriented bureaucracy; policies directed toward the breaking-up of ascriptive landholding units; and the establishment of professional military units whose fortunes were directly linked with those of the state itself. Yet the fact of great territorial extension, and of the taking at least of some preliminary steps toward empire formation, is undeniable. A consideration of the nature and extent of these steps in the two areas will provide a broader basis for the comparison between them.

· · · · ·

If we contrast the Akkadian and Aztec imperial systems at a more general level, the essential character of both as trade-and-tribute systems, with only limited tendencies toward centralized administration, stands out immediately. The differences that have been noted seem to imply a somewhat greater degree of direct control on the part of the Akkadians, which in reality may be no more than an artifact of differently oriented and inadequate sources. Given the considerably more integrated character of the great palace, temple and private estates controlling much more of the land in Mesopotamia than the equivalent holdings of the nobility in Mexico, it would not be surprising if there were a somewhat greater involvement of the Mesopotamian state in an economic managerial role. The techniques and even the records were at hand, after all; they only needed to be centrally applied. Yet as the Aztec disbursement of royal stores and construction of aqueducts and irrigation systems in response to famine shows, the Mexican state upon occasion also did undertake productive economic investment, rather than merely consume a portion of the tribute its predatory activities had brought and redistribute the rest to its followers. If there is a difference at all, in other words, it is surely not one of kind but only one of degree.

· · · · ·

Conclusion

In what must always be a process of selection and emphasis from among many details, valid and accurate for some purposes and not for others, the main purpose of this essay has been to suggest that two territorially extensive, complex, long-lived, innovative, characteristically "civilized" societies were *fundamentally* similar, which is not meant to imply that there is a one-for-one correspondence in all their parts—even in broadly conceived function, let alone in formal details. But the similarities are sufficiently close and numerous to suggest that in this and similar cases it is genuinely useful, that is, productive of insights at the level of understanding the individual historical sequence, to proceed at times from a generalizing, comparative stance rather than exclusively from a contrastive and compartmentalizing one.

. . . . .

. . . It is interesting to note that approximately the same correlation of homotaxial phases seems to hold between the Mesopotamian and Mexican sequences. The rough equivalence of Teotihuacán and Protoliterate Uruk with respect to stylistic virtuosity and monumentality of architecture has already been referred to. Since both reflect an all-embracing intensity of religious styles and an apparently unquestioned ascendancy of theocratic leadership, they also serve as starting points of equivalent sequences of change along the axis of social differentiation. Moreover, the appearance of the first formally represented traces of militarism in late Protoliterate times and toward the end of Teotihuacán, as well as the bifurcation between religious and political institutions toward the end of the occupation of Tula and during the Early Dynastic period, corroborates the main lines of the correlation set forward in . . . [the chart, page 101] and followed throughout this essay. Finally, the very close and detailed similarities in the organization of the Akkadian and Aztec realms of extended conquest, trade, and tribute seem to confirm the postulated equivalence of the terminal points of our sequences.

. . . . .

There are . . . differences as well as similarities in the course of development followed in the two areas, and the objective of systematic comparison would not be advanced by ignoring the former and overstressing the latter. We have dealt, to be sure, with independently recurring examples of a single, fundamental, cause-and-effect sequence. Each example, however, involved not the reenactment of a predetermined pattern but a continuing interplay of complex, locally distinctive forces whose specific forms and effects cannot be fully abstracted from their immediate geographical and historical contexts. . . .

. . . How may we succinctly describe the differences between two alternative pathways leading from a common origin among village agriculturalists to a common end in urban states and primitive imperial systems? The foregoing analysis suggests that among the crucially distinctive features of early Mesopotamian civilization were its relatively more compact area and settlement pattern and correspondingly more unified culture; its prevailing ability to dissolve the ethnic identifications of immigrants and to foster urban loyalties instead; the striking continuity of occupation and tradition in all its major cultural centers; its precocious innovativeness in the crafts and hence its rapidly, cumulatively advancing technology; and its emphasis on the development of administrative and redistributive institutions concerned with economic management. In central Mexico, on the other hand, smaller, more widely dispersed valley enclaves were the characteristic units of settlement; the basic continuities were found more often in self-conscious, periodically mobile ethnic groups than in urban centers; technology remained essentially static over long periods; and there was more emphasis on market integration than on vertically organized redistributive networks.

What seems overwhelmingly most important about these differences is how small they bulk, even in aggregate, when considered against the mass of similarities in form and process. In short, the parallels in the Mesopotamian and Mexican "careers to statehood," in the forms that institutions ultimately assumed as well as in the processes leading to them, suggest that both instances are most significantly characterized by a common core of regularly occurring features. We discover anew that social behavior conforms not merely to laws but to a limited number of such laws, which perhaps has always been taken for granted in the case of cultural subsystems (e.g., kinship) and among "primitives" (e.g., hunting bands). Not merely as an abstract article of faith but as a valid starting point for detailed, empirical analysis, it applies equally well to some of the most complex and creative of human societies.

9 | The Preindustrial City

GIDEON SJOBERG

In the past few decades social scientists have been conducting field studies in a number of relatively non-Westernized cities. Their recently acquired knowledge of North Africa and various parts of Asia, combined with what was already learned, clearly indicates that these cities are not like typical cities of the United States and other highly industrialized areas but are much more like those of medieval Europe. Such communities are termed herein "preindustrial," for they have arisen without stimulus from that form of production which we associate with the European industrial revolution.

Recently Foster, in a most informative article, took cognizance of the preindustrial city.[1] His primary emphasis was upon the peasantry (which he calls "folk"); but he recognized this to be part of a broader social structure which includes the preindustrial city. He noted certain similarities between the peasantry and the city's lower class. Likewise the present author sought to analyze the total society of which the peasantry and the

---

[1] George M. Foster, "What Is Folk Culture?" *American Anthropologist*, LV (1953), 159–73.

SOURCE: *American Journal of Sociology*, LX (March 1955), 438–445. Reprinted by permission of the University of Chicago Press. Copyright © 1955 by the University of Chicago.

preindustrial city are integral parts.[2] For want of a better term this was called "feudal." Like Redfield's folk (or "primitive") society, the feudal order is highly stable and sacred; in contrast, however, it has a complex social organization. It is characterized by highly developed state and educational and/or religious institutions and by a rigid class structure.

Thus far no one has analyzed the preindustrial city per se, especially as it differs from the industrial-urban community, although Weber, Tönnies, and a few others perceived differences between the two. Yet such a survey is needed for the understanding of urban development in so-called underdeveloped countries and, for that matter, in parts of Europe. Such is the goal of this paper. The typological analysis should also serve as a guide to future research.

Ecological Organization

Preindustrial cities depend for their existence upon food and raw materials obtained from without; for this reason they are marketing centers. And they serve as centers for handicraft manufacturing. In addition, they fulfil important political, religious, and educational functions. Some cities have become specialized; for example, Benares in India and Karbala in Iraq are best known as religious communities, and Peiping in China as a locus for political and educational activities.

The proportion of urbanites relative to the peasant population is small, in some societies about 10 per cent, even though a few preindustrial cities have attained populations of 100,000 or more. Growth has been by slow accretion. These characteristics are due to the nonindustrial nature of the total social order. The amount of surplus food available to support an urban population has been limited by the unmechanized agriculture, transportation facilities utilizing primarily human or animal power, and inefficient methods of food preservation and storage.

The internal arrangement of the preindustrial city, in the nature of the case, is closely related to the city's economic and social structure.[3] Most

---

[2] Gideon Sjoberg, "Folk and 'Feudal' Societies," *American Journal of Sociology*, LVIII (1952), 231–39.

[3] Sociologists have devoted almost no attention to the ecology of preindustrial centers. However, works of other social scientists do provide some valuable preliminary data. See, e.g., Marcel Clerget, *Le Caire: Étude de géographie urbaine el d'histoire économique* (2 vols.; Cairo: E. & R. Schindler, 1934); Robert E. Dickinson, *The West European City* (London: Routledge & Kegan Paul, 1951); Roger Le Tourneau, *Fès: Avant le protectorat* (Casablanca: Société Marocaine de Librairie et d'Édition, 1949); Edward W. Lane, *Cairo Fifty Years Ago* (London: John Murray, 1896); J. Sauvaget, *Alep* (Paris: Librairie Orientaliste Paul Geuthner, 1941); J. Weulersse, "Antioche: Essai de géographie urbaine," *Bulletin d'études orientales*, IV (1934), 27–79; Jean Kennedy, *Here Is India* (New York: Charles Scribner's Sons, 1945); and relevant articles in American geographical journals.

streets are mere passageways for people and for animals used in transport. Buildings are low and crowded together. The congested conditions, combined with limited scientific knowledge, have fostered serious sanitation problems.

More significant is the rigid social segregation which typically has led to the formation of "quarters" or "wards." In some cities (e.g., Fez, Morocco, and Aleppo, Syria) these were sealed off from each other by walls, whose gates were locked at night. The quarters reflect the sharp local social divisions. Thus ethnic groups live in special sections. And the occupational groupings, some being at the same time ethnic in character, typically reside apart from one another. Often a special street or sector of the city is occupied almost exclusively by members of a particular trade; cities in such divergent cultures as medieval Europe and modern Afghanistan contain streets with names like "street of the goldsmiths." Lower-class and especially "outcaste" groups live on the city's periphery, at a distance from the primary centers of activity. Social segregation, the limited transportation facilities, the modicum of residential mobility, and the cramped living quarters have encouraged the development of well-defined neighborhoods which are almost primary groups.

Despite rigid segregation the evidence suggests no real specialization of land use such as is functionally necessary in industrial-urban communities. In medieval Europe and in other areas city dwellings often serve as workshops, and religious structures are used as schools or marketing centers.[4]

Finally, the "business district" does not hold the position of dominance that it enjoys in the industrial-urban community. Thus, in the Middle East the principal mosque, or in medieval Europe the cathedral, is usually the focal point of community life. The center of Peiping is the Forbidden City.

Economic Organization

The economy of the preindustrial city diverges sharply from that of the modern industrial center. The prime difference is the absence in the former of industrialism which may be defined as the system of production in which *inanimate* sources of power are used to multiply human effort. Preindustrial cities depend for the production of goods and services upon *animate* (human or animal) sources of energy—applied either directly or indirectly through such mechanical devices as hammers, pulleys, and wheels. The industrial-urban community, on the other hand, employs inanimate generators of power such as electricity and steam which greatly enhance the productive capacity of urbanites. This basically new form of energy production, one which requires for its development and survival a

---

[4] Dickinson, *op. cit.*, p. 27; O. H. K. Spate, *India and Pakistan* (London: Methuen & Co., 1954), p. 183.

special kind of institutional complex, effects striking changes in the ecological, economic, and social organization of cities in which it has become
dominant.

Other facets of the economy of the preindustrial city are associated with
its particular system of production. There is little fragmentation or specialization of work. The handicraftsman participates in nearly every phase of
the manufacture of an article, often carrying out the work in his own home
or in a small shop near by and, within the limits of certain guild and community regulations, maintaining direct control over conditions of work and
methods of production.

In industrial cities, on the other hand, the complex division of labor requires a specialized managerial group, often extra-community in character,
whose primary function is to direct and control others. And for the supervision and co-ordination of the activities of workers, a "factory system" has
been developed, something typically lacking in preindustrial cities. (Occasionally centralized production is found in preindustrial cities—e.g., where
the state organized slaves for large-scale construction projects.) Most commercial activities, also, are conducted in preindustrial cities by individuals
without a highly formalized organization; for example, the craftsman has
frequently been responsible for the marketing of his own products. With a
few exceptions, the preindustrial community cannot support a large group
of middlemen.

The various occupations are organized into what have been termed
"guilds." [5] These strive to encompass all, except the elite, who are gainfully employed in some economic activity. Guilds have existed for merchants and handicraft workers (e.g., goldsmiths and weavers) as well as for
servants, entertainers, and even beggars and thieves. Typically the guilds
operate only within the local community, and there are no large-scale economic organizations such as those in industrial cities which link their members to their fellows in other communities.

Guild membership and apprenticeship are prerequisites to the practice
of almost any occupation, a circumstance obviously leading to monopoliza-
tion. To a degree these organizations regulate the work of their members
and the price of their products and services. And the guilds recruit workers

---

[5] For a discussion of guilds and other facets of the preindustrial city's economy
see, e.g., J. S. Burgess, *The Guilds of Peking* (New York: Columbia University
Press, 1928); Edward T. Williams, *China, Yesterday and Today* (5th ed.; New
York: Thomas Y. Crowell Co., 1932); T'ai-ch'u Liao, "The Apprentices in
Chengtu during and after the War," *Yenching Journal of Social Studies*, IV
(1948), 90–106; H. A. R. Gibb and Harold Bowen, *Islamic Society and the
West* (London: Oxford University Press, 1950), Vol. I, Part I, chap. vi; Le
Tourneau, *op. cit.*; Clerget, *op. cit.*; James W. Thompson and Edgar N. John-
son, *An Introduction to Medieval Europe* (New York: W. W. Norton Co.,
1937), chap. xx; Sylvia L. Thrupp, "Medieval Guilds Reconsidered," *Journal of
Economic History*, II (1942), 164–73.

into specific occupations, typically selecting them according to such particularistic criteria as kinship rather than universalistic standards.

The guilds are integrated with still other elements of the city's social structure. They perform certain religious functions; for example, in medieval European, Chinese, and Middle Eastern cities each guild had its "patron saint" and held periodic festivals in his honor. And, by assisting members in time of trouble, the guilds serve as social security agencies.

The economic structure of the preindustrial city functions with little rationality, judged by industrial-urban standards. This is shown in the general nonstandardization of manufacturing methods as well as in the products and is even more evident in marketing. In preindustrial cities throughout the world a fixed price is rare; buyer and seller settle their bargain by haggling. (Of course, there are limits above which customers will not buy and below which merchants will not sell.) Often business is conducted in a leisurely manner, money not being the only desired end.

Furthermore, the sorting of goods according to size, weight, and quality is not common. Typical is the adulteration and spoilage of produce. And weights and measures are not standardized: variations exist not only between one city and the next but also within communities, for often different guilds employ their own systems. Within a single city there may be different kinds of currency, which, with the poorly developed accounting and credit systems, signalize a modicum of rationality in the whole of economic action in preindustrial cities.[6]

The economic system of the preindustrial city, based as it has been upon animate sources of power, articulates with a characteristic class structure and family, religious, educational, and governmental systems.

Of the class structure, the most striking component is a literate elite controlling and depending for its existence upon the mass of the populace, even in the traditional cities of India with their caste system. The elite is composed of individuals holding positions in the governmental, religious, and/or educational institutions of the larger society, although at times groups such as large absentee landlords have belonged to it. At the opposite pole are the masses, comprising such groups as handicraft workers whose goods and services are produced primarily for the elite's benefit.[7] Between

---

[6] For an extreme example of unstandardized currency cf. Robert Coltman, Jr., *The Chinese* (Philadelphia: F. A. Davis, 1891), p. 52. In some traditional societies (e.g., China) the state has sought to standardize economic action in the city by setting up standard systems of currency and/or weights and measures; these efforts, however, generally proved ineffective. Inconsistent policies in taxation, too, hinder the development of a "rational" economy.

[7] The status of the true merchant in the preindustrial city, ideally, has been low; in medieval Europe and China many merchants were considered "outcastes." However, in some preindustrial cities a few wealthy merchants have acquired considerable power even though their role has not been highly valued. Even then most of their prestige has come through participation in religious, governmental, or educational activities, which have been highly valued (see, e.g.,

the elite and the lower class is a rather sharp schism, but in both groups there are gradations in rank. The members of the elite belong to the "correct" families and enjoy power, property, and certain highly valued personal attributes. Their position, moreover, is legitimized by sacred writings.

Social mobility in this city is minimal; the only real threat to the elite comes from the outside—not from the city's lower classes. And a middle class—so typical of industrial-urban communities, where it can be considered the "dominant" class—is not known in the preindustrial city. The system of production in the larger society provides goods, including food, and services in sufficient amounts to support only a small group of leisured individuals; under these conditions an urban middle class, a semileisured group, cannot arise. Nor are a middle class and extensive social mobility essential to the maintenance of the economic system.

Significant is the role of the marginal or "outcaste" groups (e.g., the Eta of Japan), which are not an integral part of the dominant social system. Typically they rank lower than the urban lower class, performing tasks considered especially degrading, such as burying the dead. Slaves, beggars, and the like are outcastes in most preindustrial cities. Even such groups as professional entertainers and itinerant merchants are often viewed as outcastes, for their rovings expose them to "foreign" ideas from which the dominant social group seeks to isolate itself. Actually many outcaste groups, including some of those mentioned above, are ethnic groups, a fact which further intensifies their isolation. (A few, like the Jews in the predominantly Muslim cities of North Africa, have their own small literate religious elite which, however, enjoys no significant political power in the city as a whole.)

An assumption of many urban sociologists is that a small, unstable kinship group, notably the conjugal unit, is a necessary correlate of city life. But this premise does not hold for preindustrial cities.[8] At times sociologists and anthropologists, when generalizing about various traditional so-

---

Ping-ti Ho, "The Salt Merchants of Yang-Shou: A Study of Commercial Capitalism in Eighteenth-Century China," *Harvard Journal of Asiatic Studies*, XVII [1954], 130–68).

[8] For materials on the kinship system and age and sex differentiation see, e.g., Le Tourneau, *op. cit.*; Edward W. Lane, *The Manners and Customs of the Modern Egyptians* (3d ed.; New York: E. P. Dutton Co., 1923); C. Snouck Hurgronje, *Mekka in the Latter Part of the Nineteenth Century*, trans. J. H. Monahan (London: Luzac, 1931); Horace Miner, *The Primitive City of Timbuctoo* (Princeton: Princeton University Press, 1953); Alice M. Bacon, *Japanese Girls and Women* (rev. ed.; Boston: Houghton Mifflin Co., 1902); J. S. Burgess, "Community Organization in China," *Far Eastern Survey*, XIV (1945), 371–73; Morton H. Fried, *Fabric of Chinese Society* (New York: Frederick A. Praeger, 1953); Francis L. K. Hsu, *Under the Ancestors' Shadow* (New York: Columbia University Press, 1948); Cornelius Osgood, *The Koreans and Their Culture* (New York: Ronald Press, 1951), chap. viii; Jukichi Inouye, *Home Life in Tokyo* (2nd ed.; Tokyo: Tokyo Printing Co., 1911).

cieties, have imputed to peasants typically urban kinship patterns. Actually, in these societies the ideal forms of kinship and family life are most closely approximated by members of the urban literate elite, who are best able to fulfil the exacting requirements of the sacred writings. Kinship and the ability to perpetuate one's lineage are accorded marked prestige in preindustrial cities. Children, especially sons, are highly valued, and polygamy or concubinage or adoption help to assure the attainment of large families. The pre-eminence of kinship is apparent even in those preindustrial cities where divorce is permitted. Thus, among the urban Muslims or urban Chinese divorce is not an index of disorganization; here, conjugal ties are loose and distinctly subordinate to the bonds of kinship, and each member of a dissolved conjugal unit typically is absorbed by his kin group. Marriage, a prerequisite to adult status in the preindustrial city, is entered upon at an early age and is arranged between families rather than romantically by individuals.

The kinship and familial organization displays some rigid patterns of sex and age differentiation whose universality in preindustrial cities has generally been overlooked. A woman, especially of the upper class, ideally performs few significant functions outside the home. She is clearly subordinate to males, especially her father or husband. Recent evidence indicates that this is true even for such a city as Lhasa, Tibet, where women supposedly have had high status.[9] The isolation of women from public life has in some cases been extreme. In nineteenth-century Seoul, Korea, "respectable" women appeared on the streets only during certain hours of the night when men were supposed to stay at home.[10] Those women in preindustrial cities who evade some of the stricter requirements are members of certain marginal groups (e.g., entertainers) or of the lower class. The role of the urban lower-class woman typically resembles that of the peasant rather than the urban upper-class woman. Industrialization, by creating demands and opportunities for their employment outside the home, is causing significant changes in the status of women as well as in the whole of the kinship system in urban areas.

A formalized system of age grading is an effective mechanism of social control in preindustrial cities. Among siblings the eldest son is privileged. And children and youth are subordinate to parents and other adults. This, combined with early marriage, inhibits the development of a "youth culture." On the other hand, older persons hold considerable power and prestige, a fact contributing to the slow pace of change.

As noted above, kinship is functionally integrated with social class. It also reinforces and is reinforced by the economic organization: the occupations, through the guilds, select their members primarily on the basis of kinship,

---

[9] Tsung-Lien Shen and Shen-Chi Liu, *Tibet and the Tibetans* (Stanford: Stanford University Press, 1953), pp. 143–44.
[10] Osgood, *op. cit.*, p. 146.

and much of the work is carried on in the home or immediate vicinity. Such conditions are not functional to the requirements of a highly industrialized society.

The kinship system in the preindustrial city also articulates with a special kind of religious system, whose formal organization reaches fullest development among members of the literate elite.[11] The city is the seat of the key religious functionaries whose actions set standards for the rest of society. The urban lower class, like the peasantry, does not possess the education or the means to maintain all the exacting norms prescribed by the sacred writings. Yet the religious system influences the city's entire social structure. (Typically, within the preindustrial city one religion is dominant; however, certain minority groups adhere to their own beliefs.) Unlike the situation in industrial cities, religious activity is not separate from other social action but permeates family, economic, governmental, and other activities. Daily life is pervaded with religious significance. Especially important are periodic public festivals and ceremonies like Ramadan in Muslim cities. Even distinctly ethnic outcaste groups can through their own religious festivals maintain solidarity.

Magic, too, is interwoven with economic, familial, and other social activities. Divination is commonly employed for determining the "correct" action on critical occasions; for example, in traditional Japanese and Chinese cities, the selection of marriage partners. And nonscientific procedures are widely employed to treat illness among all elements of the population of the preindustrial city.

Formal education typically is restricted to the male elite, its purpose being to train individuals for positions in the governmental, educational, or religious hierarchies. The economy of preindustrial cities does not require mass literacy, nor, in fact, does the system of production provide the leisure so necessary for the acquisition of formal education. Considerable time is needed merely to learn the written language, which often is quite different from that spoken. The teacher occupies a position of honor, primarily because of the prestige of all learning and especially of knowledge of the sacred literature, and learning is traditional and characteristically based upon sacred writings.[12] Students are expected to memorize rather than

[11] For information on various aspects of religious behavior see, e.g., Le Tourneau, *op. cit.*; Miner, *op. cit.*; Lane, *Manners and Customs*; Hurgronje, *op. cit.*; André Chouraqui, *Les Juifs d'Afrique du Nord* (Paris: Presses Universitaires de France, 1952); Justus Doolittle, *Social Life of the Chinese* (London: Sampson Low, 1868); John K. Shryock, *The Temples of Anking and Their Cults* (Paris: Privately printed, 1931); Derk Bodde (ed.), *Annual Customs and Festivals in Peking* (Peiping: Henri Vetch, 1936); Edwin Benson, *Life in a Medieval City* (New York: Macmillan Co., 1920); Hsu, *op. cit.*

[12] Le Tourneau, *op. cit.*, Part VI; Lane, *Manners and Customs*, chap. ii; Charles Bell, *The People of Tibet* (Oxford: Claredon Press, 1928), chap. xix; O. Olufsen, *The Emir of Bokhara and His Country* (London: William Heinemann, 1911), chap. ix; Doolittle, *op. cit.*

evaluate and initiate, even in institutions of higher learning.

Since preindustrial cities have no agencies of mass communication, they are relatively isolated from one another. Moreover, the masses within a city are isolated from the elite. The former must rely upon verbal communication, which is formalized in special groups such as storytellers or their counterparts. Through verse and song these transmit upper-class tradition to nonliterate individuals.

The formal government of the preindustrial city is the province of the elite and is closely integrated with the educational and religious systems. It performs two principal functions: exacting tribute from the city's masses to support the activities of the elite and maintaining law and order through a "police force" (at times a branch of the army) and a court system. The police force exists primarily for the control of "outsiders," and the courts support custom and the rule of the sacred literature, a code of enacted legislation typically being absent.

In actual practice little reliance is placed upon formal machinery for regulating social life.[13] Much more significant are the informal controls exerted by the kinship, guild, and religious systems, and here, of course, personal standing is decisive. Status distinctions are visibly correlated with personal attributes, chiefly speech, dress, and personal mannerisms which proclaim ethnic group, occupation, age, sex, and social class. In nineteenth-century Seoul, not only did the upper-class mode of dress differ considerably from that of the masses, but speech varied according to social class, the verb forms and pronouns depending upon whether the speaker ranked higher or lower or was the equal of the person being addressed.[14] Obviously, then, escape from one's role is difficult, even in the street crowds. The individual is ever conscious of his specific rights and duties. All these things conserve the social order in the preindustrial city despite its heterogeneity.

Conclusions

Throughout this paper there is the assumption that certain structural elements are universal for all urban centers. This study's hypothesis is that their form in the preindustrial city is fundamentally distinct from that in the industrial-urban community. A considerable body of data not only from medieval Europe, which is somewhat atypical,[15] but from a variety of

---

13 Carleton Coon, *Caravan: The Story of the Middle East* (New York: Henry Holt & Co., 1951), p. 259; George W. Gilmore, *Korea from Its Capital* (Philadelphia: Presbyterian Board of Publication, 1892), pp. 51–52.

14 Osgood, *op. cit.*, chap. viii; Gilmore, *op. cit.*, chap. iv.

15 Henri Pirenne, in *Medieval Cities* (Princeton: Princeton University Press, 1925), and others have noted that European cities grew up in opposition to and were separate from the greater society. But this thesis has been overstated for medieval Europe. Most preindustrial cities are integral parts of broader social structures.

cultures supports this point of view. Emphasis has been upon the static features of preindustrial city life. But even those preindustrial cities which have undergone considerable change approach the ideal type. For one thing, social change is of such a nature that it is not usually perceived by the general populace.

Most cities of the preindustrial type have been located in Europe or Asia. Even though Athens and Rome and the large commercial centers of Europe prior to the industrial revolution displayed certain unique features, they fit the preindustrial type quite well.[16] And many traditional Latin-American cities are quite like it, although deviations exist, for, excluding pre-Columbian cities, these were affected to some degree by the industrial revolution soon after their establishment.

It is postulated that industrialization is a key variable accounting for the distinctions between preindustrial and industrial cities. The type of social structure required to develop and maintain a form of production utilizing inanimate sources of power is quite unlike that in the preindustrial city.[17] At the very least, extensive industrialization requires a rational, centralized, extra-community economic organization in which recruitment is based more upon universalism than on particularism, a class system which stresses achievement rather than ascription, a small and flexible kinship system, a system of mass education which emphasizes universalistic rather than particularistic criteria, and mass communication. Modification in any one of these elements affects the others and induces changes in other systems such as those of religion and social control as well. Industrialization, moreover, not only requires a special kind of social structure within the urban community but provides the means necessary for its establishment.

Anthropologists and sociologists will in the future devote increased attention to the study of cities throughout the world. They must therefore recognize that the particular kind of social structure found in cities in the United States is not typical of all societies. Miner's recent study of Timbuctoo,[18] which contains much excellent data, points to the need for recognition of the preindustrial city. His emphasis upon the folk-urban continuum diverted him from an equally significant problem: How does Timbuctoo differ from modern industrial cities in its ecological, economic,

---

[16] Some of these cities made extensive use of water power, which possibly fostered deviations from the type.

[17] For a discussion of the institutional prerequisites of industrialization see, e.g., Bert F. Hoselitz, "Social Structure and Economic Growth," *Economia Internazionale*, VI (1953), 52–77, and Marion J. Levy, "Some Sources of the Vulnerability of the Structures of Relatively Non-industrialized Societies to Those of Highly Industrialized Societies," in Bert F. Hoselitz (ed.), *The Progress of Underdeveloped Areas* (Chicago: University of Chicago Press, 1952), pp. 114 ff.

[18] *Op. cit.*

and social structure? Society there seems even more sacred and organized than Miner admits.[19] For example, he used divorce as an index of disorganization, but in Muslim society divorce within certain rules is justified by the sacred literature. The studies of Hsu and Fried would have considerably more significance had the authors perceived the generality of their findings. And, once the general structure of the preindustrial city is understood, the specific cultural deviations become more meaningful.

Beals notes the importance of the city as a center of acculturation.[20] But an understanding of this process is impossible without some knowledge of the preindustrial city's social structure. Although industrialization is clearly advancing throughout most of the world, the social structure of preindustrial civilizations is conservative, often resisting the introduction of numerous industrial forms. Certainly many cities of Europe (e.g., in France or Spain) are not so fully industrialized as some presume; a number of preindustrial patterns remain. The persistence of preindustrial elements is also evident in cities of North Africa and many parts of Asia; for example, in India and Japan,[21] even though great social change is currently taking place. And the Latin-American city of Merida, which Redfield studied, had many preindustrial traits.[22] A conscious awareness of the ecological, economic, and social structure of the preindustrial city should do much to further the development of comparative urban community studies.

---

[19] This point seems to have been perceived also by Asael T. Hansen in his review of Horace Miner's "The Primitive City of Timbuctoo," *American Journal of Sociology*, LIX (1954), 501–2.

[20] Ralph L. Beals, "Urbanism, Urbanization and Acculturation," *American Anthropologist*, LIII (1951), 1–10.

[21] See, e.g., D. R. Gadgil, *Poona: A Socio-economic Survey* (Poona: Gokhale Institute of Politics and Economics, 1952), Part II; N. V. Sovani, *Social Survey of Kolhapur City* (Poona: Gokhale Institute of Politics and Economics, 1951), Vol. II; Noel P. Gist, "Caste Differentials in South India," *American Sociological Review*, XIX (1954), 126–37; John Campbell Pelzel, "Social Stratification in Japanese Urban Economic Life" (unpublished Ph.D. dissertation, Harvard University, Department of Social Relations, 1950).

[22] Robert Redfield, *The Folk Culture of Yucatan* (Chicago: University of Chicago Press, 1941).

10 | Urbanization: A Typology of Change

LEONARD REISSMAN

Urbanization is not a determined revolutionary change by which an undeveloped society moves in a unilinear direction toward transformation into a fully urbanized society. Alternatives among which societies must choose are constantly open. Some societies, apparently, initiate the process with industrial development and move on from there. Others are dominated first by the growth of cities, tending to delay the creation of a broader middle class base or industrial development. Still others begin with the creation of nationalistic ideologies and then seek to move toward industrial and urban development. Each choice carries its own consequences and the developmental choices at any given time impart to a society a set of accompanying characteristics. It is within that context that cities can be viewed as "parasitic" or "generative," for example, in line with the distinction that Hoselitz has drawn between cities that have a favorable or unfavorable impact upon the economic growth of a country.

Urbanization is not a process that requires a society to go through the full cycle of change and to become, say, massively metropolitan. For reasons which we poorly understand as yet, some societies stop short, are retarded so to speak, at one or another stage. Hence, some do not go on to full metropolitan expansion even though they have attained all the other features of an urban industrial society. Doubtless there are reasons in each case to explain why some countries stop where they do and others continue to the next stage in the development process, but there is as yet no general explanation of them. Let me now describe the several types in general terms, recognizing that there may be particular exceptions to some of those general comments.

Stage I
a. Underdeveloped Societies

The underdeveloped societies, of course, are those that have made no move toward, among other things, urban change. They are identified as

SOURCE: Leonard Reissman, *The Urban Process* (New York: The Macmillan Company, 1964), pp. 212–235, 236. Reprinted with permission of The Macmillan Company. Copyright © The Free Press of Glencoe, a Division of the Macmillan Company 1964.

those countries that rank in the lowest quartiles on all four indices.* Generally, these are the newly independent countries of Africa and of Southeast Asia, countries that have recently gained their independence from colonial status and that for the first time in the modern era have a measure of control over their own development.

Societies in this stage are largely traditionalistic, agricultural, and rural. This is not to say they are homogeneous; they are far from it. They are often split by differences in tribal, religious, and linguistic origins that are an integral part of their complexion. The fight for political independence is at one and the same time a prerequisite for national development and an internal power struggle between competing elite factions within the society. The struggle frequently appears as a negative nationalism; that is, a search for internal unity through attack on the outside colonial power as everyone's villain. Independence, once achieved (and sometimes even before), can threaten such unity as may have been established by the strife from subsequent attempts to gain power by the several contending elite leaders and their supporting factions. Another burden is thereby added to the already heavy load that must be carried in the course of change.

The cities within these countries are usually former colonial administrative and economic centers. They served principally as centers for colonial authority, places from which the economic and political affairs of the colony could be directed. Given these purposes, such cities, for the most part, were segregated from the surrounding region where the bulk of the native population lived, as well as segregated within, housing two societies: the colonial, administrative elite and the native population. After independence, these cities in underdeveloped countries become the locales for native administration and control. They remain socially isolated areas for the most part, and they are not part of the social perceptions held by most of the population. They do serve, however, as effective symbols of independence, material reminders of victory over the colonizing elites, and foci for the development of nationalistic appeals.

---

* In this study the four indices of transformation to an urban society are (1) *urbanism:* percentage of total population in cities 100,000 and over; (2) *industrialism:* per cent of national domestic product from manufacturing; (3) *middle-class:* per capita national income; (4) *nationalism:* per cent literate in population fifteen years and older. Forty-five countries were ranked on each of the four indices and each distribution divided into quartiles. A four-stage typology of urban change was constructed by grouping countries according to their ranking on the four indices. Countries whose rank was in the lowest quartile on all four indices were the least advanced in urbanism (Stage I), and countries whose rank was in the highest quartile on all four indices were the most advanced in urbanisms (Stage IV). (In case of disparity in quartile ranks on the indices, a country was located in one of the four Stages on the basis of its lowest rank in any index.) The Stages were further subdivided in terms of the sequence of development that countries seemed to be following in their movement toward urbanism.—Ed.

The majority, though, is still at a tribal or primitive level of social organization. Mainly uneducated and illiterate, although the extent varies from country to country depending upon the policies of the colonizers, the native population is still far outside the modern era. Its loyalties are local, centering around kin, tribe, village, and language. The attitudes necessary for modernization have yet to be developed; the newer loyalties to the nation have yet to be forged. For the few who are educated and politically wise, the city provides a center for future aspirations. They are the members of the new elite who provide the impetus for independence and change. It is in the city they have been nurtured and through which their activities will be funneled. For the next period, at any rate, their future is united with their nation's future; their aspirations must become broadly held national aspirations.

Stage I
b. Nationalizing Societies

One direction in which a country can move as a first step in development is nationalism. This may be a negative nationalism, sharply focused on the outsider but serving the useful purpose of unifying the opposing elements within, behind a common cause. The experiences of many societies that have attained independence in the postwar decades bear out the generalization. However, the new nations are not the only ones that have pursued this line of development. El Salvador and Turkey also symbolize this type. What is common to them is the early emergence of a middle class and an emphasis upon nationalism. Countries of this type have not made any especially significant gains in either urban or industrial growth. It is this condition that puts them in the category of Stage I nationalizing societies.

The development of nationalism in such societies is accompanied by the emergence of a middle class elite, which is small, educated, and likely to consist of professionals, usually lawyers, the military leadership, and small landholders. No economic basis exists as yet for a sizable white-collar group; this comes later, along with industrial growth. The nationalizing countries have yet to start a sustained industrial development, so they remain predominately rural. The middle class elite provides the only personnel available at the moment to champion the ideology of nationalism.

Fortunately, Lerner gives us an excellent portrait of this nationalizing role of the middle class in Turkey. Although Turkey ranks highest in modernization of the six middle-eastern countries that Lerner and his colleagues studied, it is still very near the beginning of its development, compared with advanced nations. The creative minority that Lerner calls the "moderns" constitute about ten per cent of the population, by his criteria. They are the guiding middle class elite who shape Turkey's future. They are urban, educated, young, and fill the higher income and occupational categories. They are cosmopolitan, well-read, informed, and unlike the tradition-minded Turks, they see where they want development to move, and are committed to its success. Clearly, on the success of this nationalizing middle class elite will depend where Turkey and similar countries move next in the development process.

Cities play an important role for countries of this type. Although they contain a minority of the population, the cities are the residence of the elites, and it is from the city that the power of the elite will emanate. The city serves as the center, as the locale for elite contacts with one another and with the world. The elite is not isolated and it rightly recognizes its need to know about the world outside. In fact, it may be better attuned to the world outside than to the country of its origin. As one of the respondents in Lerner's study of Turkey explained "I want to know what is happening. I want to get different opinions on it, and get a clear and unbiased idea. I want to find out where the world is heading."

Stage I
c. *Industrializing Societies*

Some societies begin their development with industrial growth rather than with the middle class or nationalistic moves of the preceding type. The last two features are not entirely absent, relative to other facets of development, but the major effort seems to be behind industrialization. In other words, change begins primarily in the economic sector, with a lesser emphasis upon change in class structure or political ideologies. These are relative differences, of course, because it must be assumed that a middle class elite of sufficient strength and a nationalistic ideology of some force already exists to move the country toward industrial development. Certainly, this seems to be an accurate characterization of India, which is one of the countries in this category. For all of the change in the last decade or so the caste system in India has not been seriously modified as far as the bulk of the population is concerned, and the Indian middle class is still in a minority. Yet, the pressure toward industrialization has been great during that same period.

The important single feature of this type, then, is the push toward industrial development. The major emphasis upon industrialism best characterizes the usual sequence of development as it is most often described: Industrial ventures are seen as the take-off point from which underdeveloped countries move into the urbanizing process. In some measure the character of an industrial take-off today probably is a function of the type of economic assistance that is received. Technical and economic assistance programs for the underdeveloped countries tend to be based on the assumption that the effort to expand an industrial potential is the quickest way to induce a viable economy, which is especially important where the country has strategic political significance internationally. Any other approach takes more time because it depends so much upon inculcating a new set of attitudes in a large part of the population, be they attitudes toward education, new farming techniques and implements, or work disciplines. Attitudes necessary for effective industrialization are also new, to be sure, but they require less subtlety and individual discretion than others; industrial work routines can be group-taught, they can be minutely specified and efficiently supervised. I suspect, too, that Western countries as contributors to development understand the priority of industrial development in the light of their own histories more easily than they do other facets of the process. The West sees its own development as having been primarily due to industrialization and only followed by the other features we have come to link to the process.

One advantage of beginning with industrial development is its minimizing of some of the problems attending change, especially those associated with urban imbalance. Not that industrialization is an easy social transformation under any circumstances. But in relative terms, keeping the bulk of the population out of the cities until industrial development has reached the point where it can employ a significantly large labor force undoubtedly can ease several urban problems, including housing, unemployment, and living standards. The large cities in India, for example, suffer from the characteristic problems of cities in underdeveloped countries, but this affects only some six per cent of the total population. One is properly impressed by the several massive urban concentrations in India, by the million-plus cities of Bombay, Calcutta, Delhi, and Madras. Yet these are relatively small proportions of a population that is estimated to exceed 400 million persons. Any significant increase in that urban population before sufficient industrial growth to provide it with employment could only exacerbate the misery, perhaps bringing disaster. The countries that emphasize industrialization first have the likely advantage of inducting relatively small proportions of the population into the vortex of urban change at any one time. The other features of change can come soon enough, as history has shown. If the goal is industrial urbanization, the priority of industrial growth seems soundest, if it can be achieved.

Stage I
d. Urbanizing Societies

A final variation by which underdeveloped societies begin the process of change is the increasing of their urban centers. As noted before, the priority of urban growth is relative, for countries cannot urbanize without some alteration in the other indices of change. Of the five societies that fit in this type, Egypt, Guatemala, Peru, Southern Rhodesia, and Korea, only Korea indicated urban growth unaccompanied by similar changes in the other variables of development. This would suggest that at the initial stage of development, urban expansion depends upon some support from either a developing middle class or, less frequently, from industry. The validity of this conclusion is supported by Pye's analysis of the cities of Southeast Asia, where "the basis of the city has been commercial and administrative activities."

The outstanding characteristic of this type is that urban growth takes place before a *comparable* industrial growth. It is worth quoting Pye again on Southeast Asia because his conclusions are so applicable to countries elsewhere.

It is extremely significant that the rapid growth of all the cities in the area occurred with almost no encouragement from industrial development. . . . In Southeast Asia people are being attracted to the cities with the expectation that they will be able to find a way of life and a standard of living that are dependent on industrial development. Also, of course, people are being pushed toward the cities because of the bankruptcy of the peasant economy under the pressures of population growth and commercialization.

Herein lies the tragedy. Urban growth under such conditions means that the economy is generally unable to support those who have come or have been pushed into the city. Whether they have been pushed by rural poverty or pulled to the city for positive reasons, the result is the overcrowding of these cities to the point that they cannot provide for the populations they contain. The cities are the unprepared recipients of a stream of population from the land which reaches the city without either the skills or the opportunities for employment.

The conditions of urban imbalance at the earliest stage of development make the process of change more severe, more destructive, and more painful than it would likely be at a later stage. Consider Egypt, with a population in 1947 of almost 19 million, of whom almost 20 per cent lived in the seven largest cities. At this time, 80 per cent of the population was illiterate and had a per capita income of about $100, and only 10 per cent of Egypt's national product came from manufacturing activities. Urban expansion under such conditions could only be the path to the greatest misery for the greatest number.

The countries that find themselves in this condition, where urban growth has progressed faster than industrial and middle class growth, are generally in a worse position than even the completely underdeveloped nations. In the latter case, at least, the great bulk of the population is still rural, and still rooted to the past and to tradition, for whatever security can be gained from that attachment. I do not mean to glorify tradition for its own sake or to romanticize the land; but, in this case, they are the lesser evils. Rural poverty is no more palatable than urban poverty, but the last can be worse because the individual has fewer community resources available to him in the city than he had in the village. The people in the cities of

Stage I urbanizing societies, perhaps, do not have much choice between rural poverty and urban misery, but having chosen to migrate to the city they suffer most of the disadvantages of trying to exist in an alien environment.

Stage II
a. Transitional Societies

Societies at this level have moved ahead on all four of the development indices. They are still quite a way from urban industrial status, but they have already taken more than the first, faltering steps in the process toward it. Mexico, Brazil, and Nicaragua typify the countries that belong in this category. There are, of course, differences between them, aside from those similarities here emphasized. Brazil is twice as populous as Mexico and, of course, their histories differ. Yet they compare on the measures used here. In both, about 15 per cent of the population resides in cities of 100,000 or more; about half of the population of each is literate; about 18 per cent of the net domestic product of each is contributed by manufacturing; and approximately the same per capita income, a little over $100, is characteristic of both countries.

The mark of these societies is the balance that exists between the several facets of development. Compared with other countries, their urban growth is more or less in line with industrial growth, with the size of the middle class, and with their nationalistic potential. Development could stop here, although the usual assumption is that it will continue. It is more likely that these Stage II societies are transitional and ready to change further, or, at least, such countries seem to be greatly and publicly concerned about not stopping at this point. This has been the case for Brazil, for example, which has not been able to pick up its development beyond this stage, as yet, and which seems to worry a good deal about its progress. The question that emerges is: Which direction is to be followed in the next step of development? As can be seen from those societies that have moved just beyond this stage, there are critical problems ahead, their nature depending upon the direction of change that is next taken. These are the same alternatives and reflections, once removed, that had to be faced by the underdeveloped societies at Stage I.

I do not wish to leave the impression that these are stable societies because they have attained a plateau of balance. The pressures toward succeeding changes are already formed within these transitional societies. It is to be expected, therefore, that internal tensions must accompany the complex decisions of where and how these societies are to move. The presence of a larger, more coherent, and politically oriented middle class than was found in the underdeveloped societies means that this class will engender a greater pressure toward development favorable to their aspirations. At the same time, the presence of a relatively stable urban population of some size means that other political voices aside from the middle class are heard, notably that of an urban proletariat much less docile than the new urban migrants in the underdeveloped countries. For example, in Mexico, the professionals, managers, and white-collar workers comprise some 15 per cent of the total male labor force, and we can assume that most of them are urban and middle class. At the other end of the occupational hierarchy, however, are those employed in transportation, crafts, and services, comprising about 25 per cent of the labor force. They, too, are predominately urban but working class. The middle class, therefore, has no political monopoly but must contend with other classes. In Brazil, similar proportions obtain: about 12 per cent engaged in the professions, managerial, or white-collar occupations, and some 20 per cent engaged in the laboring occupations. It would seem to follow that class conflict is an inherent part of the urban political scene.

Cities within transitional societies are the locales in which future change is decided and begun. Here are concentrated the greater part of the educated middle class as well as the organized urban proletariat. From the political dynamics inherent in that confrontation, the decisions will most likely be forged. Though the middle class seeks a stable situation for future development, the population at large has not yet benefited from industrial gains. Urban slums are the most evident symbols of the failure of these societies to spread the benefits of whatever development has taken place. Though industrial production has increased beyond that of the Stage I societies, income disparities are a source of dissatisfaction. Compare, for example, the per capita national product of Brazil ($230) and Mexico ($220) with such societies of Stage I as Guatemala ($160) and Egypt ($120). With more wealth to distribute, the transitional countries have not solved the problems attendant to industrial urban development, as evidenced by the low living standards in the cities for those at the bottom of the economic scale—but then, neither have the more developed countries. The pressure for change, therefore, is relieved little, if at all, for these transitional societies.

Stage II
b. Industrializing Societies

One direction that can be followed by transitional societies, as was true for underdeveloped societies at an earlier stage, is to increase the tempo of industrial development over that of the other components. Today, of course, the origins of this movement are more complex than simply the wish or the desire to industrialize. The two societies in this category are both older—Greece and Portugal. The new nations are not yet at this stage, nor are the countries of Latin America. It is altogether likely that this type of Stage II industrialization is a more valid category for the past than for the future of developing societies. In the case of Greece and Portugal, we have countries that are more probably fixed at this stage of development than poised to move further ahead in that process. These are generally rural countries that have never caught up with the pace of urbanization set by England, Germany, or Italy. Nor does it seem likely that they will.

They are not highly industrialized countries, and by contemporary standards are decidedly rural and agricultural. Yet, if Greece and Portugal are disregarded for the moment and we consider instead the theoretical implications alone, this stage ideally represents one alternative in the development process. Industrialization has increased beyond the level of most transitional societies, and for developing societies this phase could represent an effective goal.

It is possible to consider this stage as one that was attained by Western countries in the course of their development. Urban development in the West followed industrial growth. Indeed the problem in Western cities was more often that of a shortage than of a surfeit of industrial labor. London in 1801, for example, was the only city in England and Wales with a population over 100,000, containing 11 per cent of the total population, approximately the same proportion as that for Greece and Portugal in 1950 (12.7 per cent). These societies, in other words, were not highly industrialized nor did they have large urban populations, but instead, were still moving toward that goal.

There is another parallel that can be drawn between Stage II industrializing societies today and Western countries a century and a half or so ago, if we assume that their levels of literacy and the size of the middle class were comparable to those of the countries that belong in this category today. From what we can tell, the power of nationalism was well developed in Great Britain and in the United States at the beginning of the last century, as was the cohesiveness of the emerging middle class, which lends credence to the similarity between past and present developments.

The main feature of this type is the emphasis on industrial growth rather than on urban growth. For whatever reason, rural areas still, and perhaps for almost the last time in this development process, remain able to hold their own, to dominate the scene. The agricultural village is still the residence for most of the population, apparently with sufficient vitality, either economically or by the force of tradition, to restrain a significant urban migration. More than half of the labor force in these countries, for example, is still engaged in agriculture. Urbanization under these circumstances appears more in balance with other facets of growth. On the basis of this type, it would seem that planning should maintain rural traditions and rural economies as a means of preventing the problems that could otherwise come from too rapid urban growth at this stage.

Stage II
c. Unbalanced Urban Societies

Not all transitional societies are as fortunate. The societies in this category have moved from the point of balanced transition toward urban growth at a faster pace than economic growth. The two societies representative of this direction of development are Colombia and Panama. Panama has also evidenced advances in the middle class and nationalism indices; even so, for Panama the imbalance between urban and economic growth is the critical characteristic. Certainly for Panama, the involvement of the U.S. in the Canal Zone makes a difference.

The consequences of the imbalance between urban and industrial growth should be similar to those for Stage I urbanizing societies. The consequences are even more serious for a country like Colombia, where no comparable advance has taken place either in the expansion of the middle class or in nationalism. There is an explosive form of urban expansion with little or no support for change in other sectors of the process. The cities in this type of society are especially vulnerable to the stresses of change because they haven't an economic base sufficient to sustain them, nor do they have a significant middle class that might provide stability in this period. This would be more true for Columbia than Panama. Of course, should industrial growth begin, as has been happening since 1950 in Cali, Colombia, then the imbalance and its effects might be alleviated. However, rapid industrial growth is not enough without the simultaneous growth of a more responsible middle class committed to the nation. The situation of imbalance engenders inadequate housing, minimal living standards, chronic unemployment, and urban discontent. In the case of Colombia, the effects of *la violencia* (marauding bands raiding and murdering) in the rural areas endanger the situation even more, by hampering the growth of a responsible middle class.

Societies of this type are still in their transitional period. In their development and in the accompanying stress, both political and economic, there prevail the effects of an urban population that is larger than it should be. City growth is more a symptom of weakness in the political and economic spheres of the nation than it is a positive indication of development. The relative absence of the middle class is further evidence of that weakness. It implies that urban migration occurs because of unsatisfactory conditions in the rural areas rather than as a consequence of urban attractiveness, as a growing middle class might suggest.

Stage III
a. Urban Transitional Societies

Societies at this stage have achieved a new level of balance in all four sectors of the industrial urban process. What is more, they are now urban societies, possibly on the way to the final stage of metropolitan growth. None of the countries that were studied fits this category, but the type is logically possible, and other countries might well be included here in the future.

Societies of this type would be similar to those described as Stage II transitional, but here would be distinguished by further development; urban growth, industrial growth, the emergence of the middle class, and the hold of nationalism would be well advanced. I would think that this urban transitional stage might represent a second plateau through which Western societies moved in the course of their development, around the middle of the last century in Britain and after the Civil War in the United States.

Insofar as reconstruction of the process is possible in terms of the dimensions considered here, there does seem to be a plausible basis for this interpretation. Around the middle of the nineteenth century, England had about a third of its population residing in cities of 50,000 or more and London had reached a population of about 2 million. These are high densities even by present standards, but relative to England's subsequent growth, that stage would resemble what is here defined as an urban transitional one. In the United States around 1870, about one third of the population was classified as urban, and the labor force was almost equally divided between farm and nonfarm workers.

Societies in the urban transitional phase are significantly urbanized and seem to be on the very edge of another chain of developments within a short time. These societies are still the kind, however, that can be described as Great Britain was in 1851 in its census of that year.

One of the moral effects of the increase of the people is an increase of their mental activity, as the aggregation in towns brings them oftener into combination and collision. The population of the towns is not so completely separated in England, as it is in some other countries, from the population of the surrounding country: for the walls, gates, and castles which were destroyed in the civil wars have never been rebuilt; and the population has outgrown the ancient limits; while stone lines of demarcation have never been drawn around the new centres of population. . . . The freeman in some of the towns enjoyed anciently exclusive privileges of trading; . . . and by the great measure of Municipal Reform (1835) every town has been thrown open to settlers from every quarter. At the same time, too, that the populations of the towns and of the country have become so equally balanced in number . . . the union between them has become, by the circumstances that has led to the increase of the towns, more intimate than it was before; for they are now connected together by innumerable relationships, as well as by the associations of trade . . . a large proportion of the population in the market towns, the county-towns, the manufacturing towns, and the metropolis, was born in the country; and that, in England, town and country are bound together not only by the intercourse of commerce and the interchange of intelligence, but by a thousand ties of blood and affection.

Cities in this phase grow, but they grow primarily as a result of immigration rather than of the natural increase of the urban population itself. This condition prevailed in American cities, for example, well into the twentieth century, and was the basis of a major complaint that rural romantics levied against urban society. In fact, the advantages of urban life described above for England in 1851 were not often encountered in other writings in England or the United States during the time. It must be recalled that it was this kind of urban existence that had driven Ebenezer Howard to expound plans for the garden city. This era in urban growth was not idyllic for most urban residents. For the wealthy, for the successful entrepreneurs, the city was a place to be enjoyably lived in; for others, the city manifested many of the evils that Howard and others usually ascribed to it.

In considering the future, it seems likely that developing societies will pass through an urban transitional stage more or less of this kind. However, given our knowledge of urban failures in the past, it is certainly not inevitable these newer societies reiterate the West's experience fully. Whether they will be able to avoid it is a question that will have to be answered in the future.

Stage III
b. Rural Balanced Societies

Rural societies at this stage are more influenced by urban developments than were the peasant and village societies at earlier stages. For all societies at this third stage are relatively advanced and heavily, though not predominately, urbanized. About 20 per cent of the population lives in large cities, which is a relatively high proportion. The characteristic urban feature of these societies is that there is a small population concentration in a few very large cities. Instead, there are more evenly dispersed, smaller, urban concentrations. Norway, for example, defines half of its population as urban but it is dispersed in some twelve relatively small cities. Ireland, too, has more than one quarter of its population living in eight cities of 20,000 persons or more, and only 18 per cent living in Dublin, the only city of more than 100,000 in Ireland.

Agriculture plays an important role in the economy of these rural, balanced societies, but it shares its economic importance with industrial facilities and is no longer entirely dominant. In terms of per capita income and of literacy these societies are on a level with the most developed metropolitan societies. They differ both in the relative absence of industry and in the lack of overly dense urban concentrations. These cities are more manageable than metropolitan concentrations because the countryside has remained viable and economically important. The pressures for urban migration are not as constant as they have become for the dense metropolitan societies.

Beginning with societies in this third stage of development, there is the possibility that urban development will stop instead of continuing on to an expanding metropolitan level. Such would seem to be true for Norway and Ireland. Once a certain urban level is reached, there are alternative directions that Stage III societies can pursue, such as the enlargement of the middle class and the stabilization of national ideology. This is accompanied by raising educational levels, as by raising the material standard of living for more persons in the society. These societies, however, remain essentially rural in character. Their cities are major industrial and commercial centers, separated but not isolated from the rural hinterland because urban attitudes and values are spread by means of the mass media and other socializing channels. We find in these rural balanced societies, then, a possible end point for development. Such societies can achieve a balance between agriculture and industry, between the rural and the urban.

Stage III
c. Urban Industrial Societies

Societies in this category, as typified by Italy, Hungary, and Poland, have continued their industrial expansion after having attained a reasonably high urban concentration. Urban concentration is below the high level attained by the fully metropolitan societies; about one quarter of the population lives in the large cities, which may number a dozen or more. Agriculture continues to play a significant role, but industrial growth has continued as well.

The striking feature of these societies is the fact that urban growth has reached a plateau and has not greatly increased, in spite of continued industrialization. Hungary, for example, had only increased from 30 per cent urban in 1900 to 34 per cent in 1949, a gain of 5 per cent during the fifty years. In that respect the urban industrial societies are similar to the rural balanced ones just described. The major difference between them is that the former have continued their industrial expansion. In fact, the level of industrial development is equal to that attained by the most industrialized nations. Poland, for example, ranked first on the industrialization index with 47 per cent of the net domestic product contributed by manufacturing. Hungary followed next with 46 per cent. Yet, this advance apparently has been at the cost of other aspects of development. Middle class growth has been stabilized at a much lower level than industrialization. In spite of its relatively high industrial output, Poland in 1950 still had 5 to 10 per cent illiteracy and a per capita income of $300. Similar statistics have been obtained for Italy and Hungary as well. (Italy, of course, after 1950 would no longer belong in this category.)

What we find, in effect, are industrial societies that have as yet failed to distribute the advantages of development throughout the population as evenly as they might. Middle class standards are not widespread. Not that these standards are an unmixed blessing, but they do indicate a certain measure of material affluence, an advance in such things as health, nutrition, and education, that I presume is a desirable goal. Rural areas are more economically depressed here than in the societies of the preceding type. Urban problems are due less to an unmanageable density and much more to the failure of middle class growth to keep pace. Through maldistribution due to centralized control, or for other reasons, industrial expansion has exacerbated class differences within the city, as well as between the city and the countryside. Urban poverty, therefore, is more likely to be the dominant problem that cities have to contend with, rather than clogged transportation or similar problems characteristic of the more affluent metropolitan societies.

Stage III
d. Industrial Balanced Societies

The major difference between societies of this and the preceding type is that in these societies there has been commensurate development in living standards, nationalism, middle class growth, and industrial growth. Here, then, is found a more balanced variant of the urban industrial societies just described.

The countries that fit this category are France and Canada, both of which are urbanized, industrialized, and at the same time have a wider dispersal of middle class standards throughout the population than had the preceding type. France, for example, has more than half of its population classified as urban, but with only some 17 per cent living in twenty-four of its larger cities. Yet the rate of urban growth has not been startling, for France increased its urban population by only 10 per cent in the fifty years after 1900. In Canada, less than one-quarter of the population resided in its ten largest cities in 1950. At the same time, industrial development has been generally on a par with that of the most highly industrialized nations.

The cities in these societies are clearly cosmopolitan cities, but they are not as densely occupied as the cities in the fully metropolitan societies. A strong middle class exists, but the middle class is no longer the revolutionary elite seeking to change the power structure, as is the case in the developing nations. In these societies at the stage of industrial balance, middle class attitudes and values have been filtered down to other classes and become as dominant as urban values. Educational attainments are generally high, as are the levels of per capita income. By this point in development, if not earlier, the initiating middle class of an earlier phase has already won its battles and has succeeded in reaching its objectives of development.

Further urban growth is likely to take place as the population increases, although lower birth rates and lower death rates are characteristic demographic features of these societies because of the spread of urban and middle class values. What has tended to stabilize the urban growth potential in these societies is a widespread system of small landholding that has tended to be hereditary, thereby keeping a significant proportion of the population on the land. In France, for instance, a third of the population is engaged in agriculture, a proportion that is twice that found in the United States. As long as that tradition, which makes migration to the city unlikely, is maintained, and there is no reason for it to change sharply, and as long as urban natural increase is low, then *explosive* urban growth is not likely to occur. The circumstances of Algerian immigration into France during 1962 must be considered as exceptional. Cities will grow, but not overnight. They are also likely to spread out, as is already evident in both France and Canada, through suburbanization. That expansion has resulted from the raised living standards of a significant part of the population, coupled with the middle class aspirations for home ownership or, at the least, better housing than can be found in the older parts of the city. The French suburb, the *banlieue*, apparently has been increasing since the end of the war. Such movement outward from the city's center can be seen as a consequence of better living standards and the generally greater concern given to the appurtenances of status and prestige in an industrial urban society.

Stage IV
a. Unbalanced Metropolitan Societies

With this type we reach the first of two kinds of metropolitan societies. The distinguishing feature of this unbalanced form is a metropolitan growth that has outrun all the other facets of growth that we have been discussing. Chile and Argentina, the two countries that belong in this category, have urban concentrations that are comparable with anything found in other metropolitan countries. This is especially true for Argentina, where almost two-thirds of the population live in cities, with over one-third concentrated in the fifteen largest cities in the country. Moreover, the history of its urban development has matched that of the United States and, if anything, has been more rapid. For example, before 1900, Argentina's urban population comprised 37 per cent of the total population, compared with 40 per cent in the United States. By 1914, Argentina's urban population had reached 53 per cent, while in the United States for the closest comparable year it was only 46 per cent. By 1947, Argentina was 63 per cent urban while it took the United States until 1950 to reach a comparable proportion.

Yet, with this rapid urban expansion, the unbalanced metropolitan societies have not been able to maintain comparable growth rates for other aspects of development. The middle class, for example, has not developed as rapidly as has metropolitan concentration. Illiteracy is still about 14 per cent in Argentina and almost 20 per cent in Chile. Per capita income in Argentina in 1950 was $346, and in Chile, a low $188, compared with the higher levels found in all other metropolitan countries and even in some less urbanized countries, such as Norway. These figures symbolize an inadequate middle class base and consequently an inadequate dispersion of middle class views, which usually provide political and economic stability.

In large measure the failure to expand more evenly in these areas can be traced to inadequate industrial development. About one-third of the working population is still engaged in agriculture, which is a much higher proportion than in comparable metropolitan countries.

The result of this unbalanced situation is burgeoning cities with neither sufficient industrial support nor class stability. Cities in this type of society are marked ecologically by the segregation of those who are economically comfortable from those who are economically deprived, which in turn contributes to the presence of slums and similar urban inadequacies. Economic problems plague societies at this stage; there is a generally high and constant proportion of unemployment in the cities, as well as a marked inequality of incomes. Such societies are under chronic political stress created by the demands of a large urban proletariat and the chronically unemployed, seeking to increase their benefits, clashing with the demands of a significant middle class segment seeking to hold on to what it has.

Urban redevelopment is difficult under such circumstances, first, because of the large populations that are involved, and second, because of the chronic financial problems that leave little room for supposedly unprofitable civic or welfare activities. The only hope for amelioration under such circumstances would seem to be an industrial growth that is rapid enough to exceed population growth, especially in the cities. Anything less means that the imbalance continues for these societies and they become unwilling heirs to all of the consequent difficulties of metropolitanism.

Stage IV
b. Metropolitan Societies

This type includes the remaining societies that are in or near the first quartile ranks on all four indices. In other words, these are the developed, metropolitan societies that have attained the final stage of industrial, urban development that we have thus far experienced. A description of this type applies to such countries as the United States and Great Britain.

I have also included in this type Denmark, Austria, West Germany, and Israel, even though each of them ranks in the second quartile on one index other than urban status. Denmark is less industrialized than the other countries in this category; Austria and Germany have somewhat lower per capita income levels; and Israel has a somewhat lower level of literacy. But since these differences are not considered as crucial for societies at this point, these four countries have been grouped along with Great Britain, the United States, and the Netherlands.

There is little need to describe the urban characteristics of these societies. . . . All that needs to be said here is that they represent the presently known limit of urbanization. The features of these metropolitan societies probably are less the consequences of an actual imbalance between urban and industrial development and more those of a failure to foresee the effects of continued urban expansion beyond the city to the metropolis. Generally, these countries have the economic means to redevelop and to maintain their metropolitan centers, but they have been late in acting and reluctant in changing traditional conceptions of political administration that no longer apply to the actual situation.

Hence, in both the United States and England a current metropolitan problem is to redefine the traditional limits of urban administration and responsibility in order to reflect the realities of metropolitan existence. The urban boundaries and their administrative units stemming from an earlier era have continued even though urban society no longer corresponds to those definitions. In both countries, steps have been taken, over much opposition, to bring metropolitan administration into being. Such administrative reorganization is not a solution for all metropolitan problems, but it would appear to be a step in the direction of placing those problems in a more relevant perspective for constructive discussion and action. Clearly, relying upon traditional *urban* solutions for what are essentially *metropolitan* problems is like using witchcraft to provide directions for building a space missile. The difficulties in realizing that a metropolitan approach is basically necessary indicate how far we must come, to plan for effective redevelopment. What good is any solution that cannot be put into effect at the metropolitan level? The power constellations that stand in the way of metropolitan reorganization are great, be it the opposition of the Labour dominated London County Council or the powerful, conservative county and city officials in American metropolitan regions.

Residual Societies

Of the forty-five societies that were used to construct this typology, six have not been included in any category because each represents a special type: Finland, Bulgaria, Japan, New Zealand, the Union of South Africa, and Paraguay. . . . Each country has widely discrepant and idiosyncratic features.

For example, Japan ranked in the first quartile on urban status and on nationalism, but in the second quartile on industrial status and in the third quartile on the middle class index. This is undoubtedly a temporary classification for Japan, reflecting its status in 1950 and not at present. Industrialization was, of course, restricted by the postwar occupation and by the war itself. Japan's restricted middle class similarly was a consequence of the war, as well as of the generally depressed wages that prevailed in Japan around 1950. Indications at present are that wages since have increased significantly, as has Japan's industrial production. It seems likely, therefore, that Japan should be included among the Stage IV metropolitan societies, on the basis of current statistics.

Apartheid makes South Africa a unique case. The strict, repressive, legal segregation in South African cities creates, in reality, a dual urban society that appears nowhere else to a like extent. Comparisons of national statistics with other countries therefore are not really justified. Hence, the native population accounts for the low rank of South Africa on the nationalism index. Admittedly, this is an insensitive measure of nationalism in South Africa, where there are two opposing and bitterly militant nationalisms, the one a legacy of the Boers, the other an emerging nationalism among native Africans. (African nationalism, it should be noted, has made no headway, so that perhaps the index is not so insensitive.) Similarly, the relatively higher rank of South Africa on the middle class index obviously has excluded most of the native population, and reflects only the minority white population. These difficulties stem from the biracial division of South African society that has been made rigid in the cities where Africans are housed within strictly segregated boundaries and kept under tight surveillance and control. Native Africans, for example, can live in the city only with the permission of the authorities, and even then under an enforced provision that requires them to be employed by the same employer for a period of time, in a kind of occupational immobility that harks back to feudalism.

Bulgaria was excluded because it had a unique pattern, ranking lowest on the urban index, but in the second quartile on the remaining three indices. This too, then, is a variant pattern that does not easily fit in with any other type. New Zealand is an urban society on all counts except for industrialism, and has not been included in the general discussion. It might be classed with Denmark, whose characteristics it generally shares on these four indices. Finland is under-urbanized relative to the other three indices. It is a special case that does not fit the typology easily. The same must be said for Paraguay, a country which strikes me as being the least understood of all Latin American countries.

Conclusion

... The aim of finding a theory to explain the industrial city and its development ... cannot be said to have been completely achieved .... What has occupied us, however, was the preparatory task of rephrasing and reorienting our perspectives on urban society in such a way as to increase the probability of constructing a systematic and valid theory of the industrial city. It was to that end that the typological description of this chapter was directed.

.   .   .   .   .

The typology has shown too that the conception of cities in terms of size alone, or solely as social responses to industrial needs, is a tendency that has misled our best efforts in the past. Of course, both conceptions are somewhat valid, and to that extent they have been incorporated into the typology. However, size and industry are not inevitable concomitants of urbanization. Size, for one thing, must be shown to have sociological consequences, in the manner that was used here. Moreover, industrialization is not always the critical variable involved in development, as was illustrated in several types that moved in directions other than industrial growth. When urbanism and industrialism do occur simultaneously, and they frequently do, it is not enough to simply think of them as synonyms for one another, as is usually done. Each plays a special role in the process of development; each makes its own special contribution to the shape and content of the city.

It might be asked: Where do we go from here? The next step that is called for is detailed analysis of cities themselves, but one that is made within the framework of the typology. For this, there is already at hand a large and important literature, but the information available must be sifted for recognition of the fact that cities do not exist apart from the societies in which they are located. The statement is obvious but has too frequently been disregarded. We must now describe and compare cities drawn from the range of societies at different stages in their development. The aim of that analysis would be to compare institutional structures and the prevalence and content of a whole range of urban attitudes, major political and economic values, and distinctive ecological features. If there is any theoretical potential in the typology, and I am convinced that there is, it should appear in the differences between cities at different points in the development process and in the characteristics just mentioned. There is no doubt that such differences exist, but the need is to determine the framework within which those differences systematically appear.

Part Two

Urban Ecological Patterns Reviewed

Wirth pointed out human ecology as one of the three major ways of conceptualizing urban phenomena, the other approaches being social organization and social psychology. In Part II we turn to human ecology, which is concerned with the interrelationships among man, society, and the urban environment. In Section A Janet Abu-Lughod provides an overview of several important aspects of human ecology, while Section B describes the physical and social patterning of past and present preindustrial cities. Changes in the form and the sustaining social and economic systems in cities in the United States are described in Section C.

"Social ecology is the study of the form, distribution, and organization of people in physical and social space." This is the definition of human ecology formulated by Janet Abu-Lughod in "The City Is Dead—Long Live the City: Some Thoughts on Urbanity." She applies Wirth's criteria of size, density, and heterogeneity as ecological measurements to preindustrial, industrial, and post-industrial cities, indicating that the three types of cities represent significantly different physical and social networks. In the post-industrial city (the metropolitan region) the criteria of size, density, and heterogeneity are, in fact, no longer adequate measures of ecological relationships, because with rapid, far-flung communication physical space is no longer an index to social space. The "classical" view of human ecology has also changed as social ecologists examined cities in other cul-

145

tures and found that the patterns of distribution and relationships did not necessarily follow those of American industrial cities. Even within American society accumulating studies of American suburbs have shown that the ecological impact of size, density, and heterogeneity is screened through cultural variables. The implications of the revision in ecological thought are important not only in updating theory but in the practical application of human ecology. Urban planners must become aware that manipulation of size, density, and heterogeneity is not sufficient to effect desired social changes.

In Section B we turn to more detailed examinations of ecological patterns in a variety of cities which have preindustrial histories. These include Mexico City, Bangalore, Peking, and several of the older European cities— London, Paris, Vienna, and Stockholm. These cities present many points of ecological contrast to industrial cities but also differ among themselves, thus raising several questions on the relationship of ecological patterns to the social and technological base on which they rest.

The long history of Mexico City, summarized in four periods by Norman S. Hayner in "Mexico City: Its Growth and Configuration," includes three preindustrial phases. In the first period (1345–1521) as Tenochtilán, capital of the Aztec empire, a totally different but very large city (500,000) existed on the site of Mexico City. (For a discussion of prehispanic Mexico see Adams, selection 8.) The Spanish colonial period (1521–1821) began with the invasion of the Aztecs by the conquistadors under Cortés and established many lasting ecological features of Mexico City. The years 1821– 1920 were a period of French influence in architecture and town planning. Since 1920 the influence has been primarily from the United States and it is in this fourth period that industry has also become important in Mexico City. Present-day Mexico City, which has a population of almost five million and is still growing very rapidly, is a fusion of preindustrial and industrial ecological patterns. The patterns established under the Spanish were themselves a fusion of preindustrial and colonial forces. Thus, the major buildings for trade, administration, and ritual (especially religion), which are the main functions performed by preindustrial cities, are concentrated in Mexico City in a central plaza area on the model of Spanish cities. Similarly the gulf between the elite and the lower-class masses is wide in preindustrial cities but was heightened in Mexico City by the fact that the elite were of a totally different culture and were conquerors. The elite settled around the central plaza, just as the nobility and upper classes settled in the center of medieval Spanish and other European cities. There was after all no manufacturing and associated dirt and fumes, while the poor transportation of the preindustrial era put a premium on living close to the center where the functions in which the elite played a large part took place. As a result there was a distinct ecological pattern to preindustrial Mexico City in which high-status residences concentrated at the city center and low-status residences on the city's outskirts. This is the reverse of the pattern in United States cities where high status residences are concentrated in the suburbs. Recent decades of extensive city growth, more rapid transportation, and industrialism have altered the high-status, plaza-centered core of Mexico City. A deteriorated "zone of transition" has developed near the city center and high-status suburban residential districts have emerged in the southwest. These changes are in the direction of the "model" of United States industrial cities, but the differences in historical development are still very apparent.

Bangalore, India, is like Mexico City in showing major ecological patterns laid down by preindustrial and colonial forces, as described by Noel P. Gist in "The Ecology of Bangalore, India: An East-West Comparison." However, the precolonial city was not destroyed by the British as the conquistadors destroyed the Aztec city on the site of Mexico City. One result is that Bangalore exhibits more of a "dual" structure. The British and other foreigners settled mainly in the Cantonment section of Bangalore which, until the independence of India in 1947, was administered separately from the rest of Bangalore. The differences between the Cantonment and the rest of Bangalore are not all-or-none and probably never were. Yet the more British quality of the Cantonment area is still evident today: lower residential density; higher concentration of Christian and Anglo-Indian populations; luxury goods and some Western-style shops, including a department store; the effects of planning are also visible. On the whole Bangalore displays a preindustrial ecological pattern. Various major installations—retail stores, banks, hotels, and governmental facilities—are scattered throughout the city, rather than concentrated in a central business district. Furthermore, each of the areas of Bangalore has its own "mix" of these installations, lending each area its own distinctiveness. This aspect of Bangalore is reminiscent of Janet Abu-Lughod's description of the "cells" of the preindustrial city. Residential segregation in Bangalore shows some resemblance to Mexico City and to most preindustrial cities, namely in the tendency for low socioeconomic groups to live on the outskirts of the city while higher groups are more centralized. The recent expansion of governmental functions in Bangalore has led, as Gist has noted in subsequent visits, to many large residences being taken over for governmental purposes. These houses are concentrated in those areas where the affluent live.[1] Bangalore also illustrates the importance of cultural factors in ecological segregation, for caste lines are commonly maintained in residence. The lower castes, particularly the untouchables, tend to locate in the outlying sections of Bangalore.

Hans Koningsberger's "Peking" gives us a glimpse of a city few Westerners and fewer Americans have seen in recent years. The preindustrial features of Peking are evident in his description of contemporary Peking as "a very loose grid, stuffed as it were with dozens of villages," and in the

---

[1] Personal communication from Noel P. Gist, 1967.

centrality of Tien An Men Square, once the gateway to the administrative and ritual centers of the Imperial "City" and the Forbidden "City." The conquest and colonialism of Peking's history are manifest in the traces not of dual but of multiple structure—the Tartar (Manchu) walled enclosure, the Chinese walled enclosure, and Legation Quarter, the area formerly inhabited by Westerners. Contemporary Peking is of special ecological interest because industrialism is taking place in the context of cultural isolation and large-scale governmental control. From other accounts we know that industrial plants are being built on the outskirts of Peking, as they are in most cities with an already established preindustrial core. The ecological impact of cultural isolation is in the nature of the case a long-term question, although Koningsberger gives some insight into it. The impact of government control is already evident—tearing down the "feudal" city walls, moving embassies to selected locations, construction of broad avenues for status rather than traffic. Ideology and governmental control are ecological forces elsewhere than in Peking. Yet perhaps we shall see them assume greater impact there than elsewhere.

Thus far we have examined the ecology of the preindustrial city as it has been filtered through colonialism. In Europe, however, we find preindustrial cities unaffected by colonialism in recent centuries and being transformed by industrial technology and new forms of social organization as indigenous inventions. Francis L. Hauser's "Ecological Patterns of European Cities" describes both the preindustrial and contemporary ecology of London, Paris, Vienna, and Stockholm. Of the four cities, London displays the least carry-over from the preindustrial past because London's layout was altered in the rebuilding after the great fire of 1650. Although London, Paris, Vienna, and Stockholm differ greatly from one another there were two aspects of the industrial "revolution" to which they all had to make ecological adjustments—housing for the expanding middle classes and sites for industry itself. The dynamics of the response varied, but in each case there was a tendency for middle- and upper-class groups to live near the center and for low-status groups and industry to locate at the periphery. The inertia of major preindustrial facilities in the city center, the pull of tradition, and deliberate planning, all played a part in this distribution. It contrasts with the pattern in cities established in the United States during industrialization in which low-status groups concentrate at the center and a gradual upgrading of social status in residential districts occurs as distance from the center increases. As Hauser points out, neither London, Paris, Vienna, nor Stockholm exhibit a concentric distribution; they come closer to the sector model, but even this seems forced in describing them. One factor inhibiting concentric and sector patterning is the remnant of preindustrial "quarters" such as the Left Bank university area of Paris.

In comparing the ecological patterns of these contemporary European cities with those of the United States two final points are suggested by the data in Hauser's description. The European cities show a larger proportion of apartment housing. This is a heritage from the preindustrial period when space in the protected, walled city was at a premium and may now have become a matter of custom and preference. The role of government in London, Paris, Vienna, and Stockholm as they underwent industrial expansion is much greater than in United States cities at a comparable period. The process is most apparent in Stockholm, where much land is publicly owned and leased to private developers for specific purposes, but it is also apparent in Baron Haussmann's wholesale redesign of Paris in the 1870's, in Crown influence on construction of the Regent Park complex in London, and in the large-scale housing developments in Vienna. The government's role in urban planning continues strong in European cities, as indicated by Jack Long (selection 45) and John C. Bollens and Henry J. Schmandt (selection 48).

In the United States urban-industrial development began with a clean slate, so to speak. American cities received most of their shape and form under the impact of industrialism. American social organization also was relatively less encumbered by tradition as it combined many cultural strands against the backdrop of expanding geographical and technological horizons. The ecology of United States cities presents then an instance of relatively "pure" impact of industrial technology and modern Western culture. Part C presents the ecological evolution of the American city. Homer Hoyt evaluates the classical model of the ecological structure of United States cities, a model derived from these cities at the height of their growth and industrial expansion. Norman J. Johnston describes the urban form of pre-Civil War Philadelphia before the full flood of industrialism, while Edgar M. Hoover and Raymond Vernon describe the structure of a city after the impact of industrialism has matured—the contemporary New York metropolitan region. Richard Austin Smith's description of Los Angeles presents a view of another form of contemporary United States metropolis. Finally two specific aspects of metropolitan development are examined in detail: Frank and Dorrian Sweetser illuminate the nature of American suburbs by contrasting Boston's suburban housing with that of Helsinki, Finland; Karl and Alma Taeuber describe the segregation of Negroes in metropolitan cores.

Homer Hoyt's "Recent Distortions of the Classical Models of Urban Structure" provides a base line for study of the ecology of United States cities. The concentric and sector models have been standard descriptions since they were introduced in the 1920's and 1930's and as broad generalizations they were accurate enough. However, it now appears that these generalizations were time-bound. They described American cities whose ecological dynamics were founded on rapid growth of industry and population and on rail and trolley transport, resulting in highly centralized cities whose core areas experienced blight as industrial and commercial uses expanded and whose higher socioeconomic residential districts steadily moved farther out before the noise, dirt, and congestion. As Hoyt points out, the technological and social base of American urbanization has changed, as evidenced in automobile transportation and in increased income. One might say that the classical models of United States ecological structure applied to these cities as they were industrializing. The models became distorted once the process of industrialization had been thoroughly established and matured. An over-all term for this industrial maturation, and associated social changes, is metropolitanization. A general view of metropolitan development in the United States is presented in Glaab and Brown, selection 1.

The major ecological effect of metropolitan development is the diminishing emphasis on centralization. Using Chicago as his major example, Hoyt shows that the Central Business District has lost many of its functions to outlying areas such as shopping centers and campus-style office complexes. Similarly light and heavy industry have been decentralizing, and the suburban residential boom has been a major feature of the American landscape in recent decades. Significantly, as Hoyt notes, suburbs are coming to include many apartment houses and a wider spectrum of socioeconomic groups so that the residential, high-status character of American suburbs is not as apparent as it was formerly. Other land uses and classes are decentralizing, too. Extensive decentralization is likely to be limited to the United States for some time. Hoyt notes that in other countries such factors as low rates of auto ownership, public ownership or control of land, and lack of mortgage money inhibit large-scale decentralization.

Against the base line of Hoyt's classical model of the centralized, industrializing city, we may measure the ecological pattern of United States cities before major and rapid industrialization. Such a study is available in Norman J. Johnston's "The Caste and Class of the Urban Form of Historic Philadelphia." Using records of white and Negro Protestant churches, he mapped the residential location of members by denomination, social class, and race for 1811, 1838, and 1856. The results demonstrate that the physical ecological order mirrors the social order. Although members of the several denominations concentrated in different residential districts, members of denominations of similar class levels tended to share residential districts. In addition to social class, racial segregation was a major factor in residential distribution. Within the Negro areas there was only incipient differentiation by social class. It seems apparent that class and race are fundamental criteria in residential location in American cities. One important contrast to present-day location by social class is portrayed in Johnston's study. In 1811, "the fashionable upper class residential area of . . . Philadelphia . . . is south of Market Street and running east-west on either side of Independence Hall. . . . This area is within easy distance of the centers of commerce and government for the community leaders who direct them." In this period the central residential location of high status groups in Philadelphia is reminiscent of the preindustrial European city. By 1856 the first signs of change are apparent—some addresses for high status groups are located in an outlying area. This supports our contention that the association of central residential location with low status came to be characteristic of American cities during their rapid industrializing phase.

Against the base line of Hoyt's classical models we may also move forward and measure the ecological patterns of American cities after the rapid, industrializing phase. Hoover and Vernon's description of New York and Smith's description of Los Angeles present the largest and the second largest metropolitan communities in the United States. In 1960 the almost seven thousand square mile area of the New York metropolis spread over parts of three states and included about sixteen million people; the Los Angeles metropolitan area covered almost five thousand square miles and had more than six and a half million inhabitants. This in itself is a vivid illustration of the decline of centralization as an organizing principle in the metropolis. Yet there are significant differences between the New York and Los Angeles metropolises. New York had its major growth during the industrializing, centralizing phase of American urbanization, while Los Angeles had its major growth in very recent decades under the full impact of the automobile, automation, affluence, leisure, and familism. Los Angeles is much more a multinucleated, perhaps even nonnucleated, metropolis than New York. The distribution of communities in the New York metropolis, meshed as they are in a many-faceted network of dominance, subdominance, and interdependence, nevertheless still shows major reference to the core area; in Los Angeles this is much less so. Just as existing preindustrial patterns in historic European and other cities inhibited and altered the ecological impact of industrialism so, too, the impact of mature industrialism on the form of American cities will be inhibited and altered by the extent of established centralized patterns. The practical importance of the distinction between more and less centralized metropolises lies in whether either type has a competitive advantage in maintaining a viable economic base and in providing an attractive environment for modern urban life.

The characteristics of the United States metropolis may also be highlighted by comparison with those produced by other cultures, as is done in Frank and Dorrian Sweetser's "Social Class and Single-Family Housing: Helsinki and Boston." The study finds that in both Helsinki and Boston single-family housing is located mainly on the periphery. However, in Helsinki as a whole there is proportionately less single-family housing and it is inhabited mainly by blue-collar workers and tends to be of lower quality than apartment housing. This finding is in accord with the ecology of other European cities. The Sweetser study is especially noteworthy for its planning implications and for its methodology. Detached suburban housing in Helsinki is mainly a result of inclusion within the city limits of preexisting rural housing. The high quality suburban apartment housing, however, resulted from careful, over-all planning of residences and ancillary facilities for an expanding population. In American cities major planning efforts are directed toward deterioration and congestion at the urban core rather than toward planned expansion of suburbs. Other factors than planning are involved in making the apartment-house suburbs of Helsinki so much more attractive than apartment-house living in American cities. As the Sweetsers point out, the former come in a "package" including low rates of automobile ownership, shops within walking distance, and reliance on public transportation for commuting to work. Nevertheless Finnish experience suggests that planning is in itself a powerful tool.

The methods used by the Sweetsers to analyze the ecology of Helsinki and Boston are an instance of the "new ecology" noted by Janet Abu-Lughod. The methods derive from social area analysis and involve a technically sophisticated statistical approach capable of describing the complex patterns of the metropolis. Only a small portion of the Sweetsers' study, which included factor analysis, is presented in this reader. The Sweetsers' analysis of Helsinki and Boston indicated that several factors (familism, social class ethnicity, and culture) were operating independently to produce the ecological distributions observed. Put another way, this means that in the metropolis, the ecological effects of size, density, and heterogeneity vary in terms of familism, social class, ethnicity, and culture. The combination of characteristics produces a pattern which may be superficially concentric, particularly in "older" metropolises like Boston, whose dynamics have less and less reference to radiation from the core. Social area analysis frees ecology from spatial determinism, in keeping with the physical mobility of metropolitan life, and focuses instead on nonspatial characteristics (familism, social class, ethnicity) which have been found to influence residential location. Although not a social area analysis in the strict sense, the Hoover and Vernon description of the New York metropolitan region may be explained in these terms. It is probably not coincidental that social area analysis was first developed and applied in Los Angeles.

The metropolis has brought not only a new ecological structure to cities in the United States but a whole host of problems, such as governmental coordination, taxation and public finance, obsolete core areas, air pollution, and preservation of open space. Of all the ecological features of the metropolis one is of overriding importance—the increasing segregation of large Negro populations in central city areas. In "Negroes in Cities," Karl and Alma Taeuber describe some dimensions of metropolitan racial segregation. Their study, which measured residential segregation by race on a block-by-block basis in 207 large (over 50,000 population) United States cities in 1940, 1950, and 1960, shows that racial segregation is uniformly high and increasing, although the history of northern and southern cities has given them somewhat different racial patterning. Residential racial segregation is deeply rooted in American society. Johnston's description of pre-Civil War Philadelphia showed a high degree of segregation even though most of the Negroes there were not slaves. Metropolitan development has made racial segregation highly visible and brought the problems of low-income Negroes in particular to the forefront of public attention. The movement of white middle-income families to suburban areas has left the central cores of metropolitan areas increasingly inhabited by Negroes, many at the poverty level, who have migrated to cities in the wake of declining manpower needs on mechanized farms. The Taeubers point to a complex set of causes of residential segregation: discrimination, relative degree of Negro and white population growth in metropolitan areas, tightness or looseness of the housing market, general economic conditions, availability of open land for building, and regional customs. These may operate in various degrees in conjunction with one another to produce the variations in observed segregation between northern and southern cities or between the decades 1940–50 and 1950–60.

The Taeubers' empirical study is valuable because it illustrates once again that human ecological explanations are not reducible to economics and technology but are also concerned with attitudes and socially determined behavior. They show that "economic factors . . . cannot account for more than a small portion of observed levels of racial residential segregation. Regardless of their economic status, Negroes rarely live in 'white' residential areas, while whites, no matter how poor, rarely live in 'Negro' residential areas." More important than theory, however, is the fact that the Taeubers' national survey documents and alerts us to the extent of segregation, and makes it possible to discern points of leverage to exert effective pressure for change. The Taeubers point to several broad forces which may alter Negro segregative patterns, particularly that "an increasing number of Negro migrants to cities are coming from other cities rather than farms; they are of higher average educational and occupational status than the resident Negro population in the cities to which they move." However, given the extent of segregation and the noneconomic forces supporting it, as well as its ramifying effects on our national life, concerted action also is called for on the basis of the Taeubers' analysis. Only if there is a systematic effort by government, industry, religious, civic, educational, and other leadership groups will underlying processes promoting residential integration prevail over those which are perpetuating patterns of segregation and discrimination.

A | Overview

11 | The City Is Dead—Long Live the City: Some Thoughts on Urbanity

JANET ABU-LUGHOD

Social ecology is the branch of sociology most closely identified with the study of American cities and is the field with perhaps the greatest relevance to city planners. It traces the reciprocal relationships between people and their social organization on the one hand, and their physical environment on the other hand, focusing especially upon the phenomena of spatial distribution, size, density, composition of population, topography, and patterns of movement and exchange. A briefer definition would be: social ecology is the study of the form, distribution, and organization of people in physical and social space.

Planners are familiar with the pioneering ideas of such social ecologists as Louis Wirth, Ernest Burgess, and Robert Park who reported on the structure of the American city in the 1920's and 1930's. Taking their cues from the causality assumptions of these early ecologists, city planners have sometimes attempted to cure social ills or bring about desired social consequences by manipulating the spatial and physical variables over which they have the greatest control, namely: size, density, and patterns of occupancy. But when anticipated social results fail to materialize, planners feel frustrated and, indeed, cheated by social science (37, 38, 41, 43). Recently, however, social ecologists have been developing a fuller if more complicated understanding of the relationship between environmental factors and social life than that propounded by members of the early Chicago school. An un-

SOURCE: This article is based upon a paper prepared in partial performance of Contract No. PH 86–66–120, with the National Center for Urban and Industrial Health, U. S. Public Health Service. Reprinted by permission. A summary, prepared by Allen Blackman, appeared in the *American Behavioral Scientist*, X (September 1966), 3–5. A more complete version of this article will appear in a forthcoming volume edited by John Dyckman and Allan Blackman.

derstanding of these new notions in ecology should help city planners to be both more realistic and more effective.

Our review of some of these ideas is divided into three parts. First, we review the real changes that have taken place in the nature and form of our cities and show how these changes have dictated a new conception of urban life. Second, we review the revisions in ecological thinking and research that have resulted both from the objective changes in our cities and from growing theoretical sophistication. And finally, we present in very summary form a few sample findings from recent studies to illustrate the complexity of the ecological variables which planners must take into account if they would create physical environments that promote social welfare.

The Changing City
The Medieval and Preindustrial City [1]

The earliest cities were usually enclosed spaces with walls separating townsmen from the countryside. Defense, commerce, and religious ritual were the chief functions of this type of city, even though some inhabitants were engaged in agriculture. Internally, the community was subdivided into component cells, often on the basis of common occupation or trade, religious sect or persuasion, or even common origin or culture. Within the medieval city and especially *within* each cell, the relationships among inhabitants were *primary*, in the sense that people maintained face-to-face contacts with one another in a variety of different yet interlocking social relationships. The area in which citizens had social relations was almost never different from the area in which they had physical contacts. Given this congruence, the legitimate ecological measures for the preindustrial city were numbers of people, area, and simple density. While this type of city, with its circumscribed horizons and limited contacts, has virtually disappeared in the West, residuals still persist over the rest of the globe and *all* large cities, even in the United States, still contain some cells with a unity similar to that of the medieval town.

The Industrial City [2]

By the nineteenth century the development of new technologies and widening national economies doomed the European medieval city to extinction. The industrial city came into existence, created by increased concentrations of people in urban centers as well as by the development of

---

[1] See references 4, 16, 17, and 21.
[2] See references 11, 18, 23, and 57.

extensive cultures which all cities within a nation shared. Industrial urbanity heightened the urban-rural contrast but also allowed the influence of city culture to extend into the hinterlands. Under these new conditions, the relevant ecological measures became population size and density, the rate of growth, and the radii of urban services to the hinterlands. The latter were roughly determined by the means and axes of transportation. Within the industrial city, despite the efforts of numerous migrant groups to develop unified protective cells, a new kind of heterogeneity came into being. Primary cells could be maintained only rarely, because physical and social mobility changed membership, because the cells came to serve relatively unimportant functions, and because they no longer received support and sanction from the legal structure. While the primary relationships continued to prevail in the weakened cells, *secondary* relationships developed in the wider city, where people frequently knew one another and had physical contact only in specialized types of situations. The concepts which sociologists such as Simmel and Wirth developed to describe the urbanity of the industrial city (23, based largely on Simmel) are still largely relevant both to conditions in the rapidly growing metropolitan centers of newly industrializing nations and to those that prevail in certain parts of Western cities, such as "ports of entry," non-family zones and areas with high rates of residential turnover (57,58).

The Post-Industrial City [3]

The type of city we now find developing in America is quite different from those which existed in earlier eras. The emerging form of American urbanism is characterized by the development of *urban regions*, rather than by single cities and their supportive hinterlands. Within the nation, people are concentrating in a limited number of regions, while within these regions decentralization is taking place, thus reducing the densities at which people must live. It will be recalled that the critical distinction in the medieval city was between town dwellers and those who lived outside the walls. In the industrial city the important distinction was between urban (including those within the urban zone of influence) and rural folk. Today, in the post-industrial city, the basic cleavage lies between life within the evolving systems of cities and life in those increasingly rare and declining settlements outside the urban network. Post-industrial cities are defined functionally by a *communication system* much broader in scope and extent than the daily transportation network that defined the borders of the industrial city. Furthermore, the primary and secondary relationships previously known have been supplemented in this new city by *tertiary* relations

---

[3] See references 2, 3, 4, 5, 6, 7, 8, 13, 14, 19, 20, and 22.

—that is, interactions in which the parties have no necessary physical contact and in which the exchange is limited to impersonal functions or acts. The stock market, in which the buyer and seller interact with only the most indirect contact, is an example of a tertiary relationship, as is a programmed recorded announcement that conveys a message. It is obvious that to comprehend the nature of this new form of urbanism and urbanity, ecological measures more sophisticated than those hitherto employed will be needed.

The Changing Views of Social Ecology
Classical Ecology

Classical ecology stemmed from an understanding of the Occidental industrial city, and was for some time crippled by this myopic viewpoint. Furthermore, it took a rather simple-minded approach to causality, tending to view ecological factors, such as building type, site plan, and community size, as independent variables or causes which had predictable effects on the quality of social life. The early ecologists, following the principles of the classical economists, viewed the impersonal competition for land as the *deus ex machina* by which spatial patterns in cities were determined. Furthermore, they were optimistically in search of *universal* city forms and ideal spatial organizations which they thought might underlie all cities, regardless of cultural differences.

The inadequacy of classical ecology was demonstrated in a variety of studies. Burgess' zonal model of city form was challenged by Hoyt's sector model. Land use distribution was found to be determined not only by land values and impersonal competition but also by law, sentiment, politics, and private preferences (29,31,34,35,36,39). Many ecological patterns, each differing from the ideal proposed by the Chicago ecologists, were discovered as more cities were studied. Not only did physical structures vary but even the social consequences of similar structures were found to be far from uniform. The classical ecologists had believed that the weakening of primary and kinship ties, the growth of anonymity, the proliferation of voluntary associations and secondary relations, etc., which they had observed were the direct and inevitable consequences of increases in size, density, and heterogeneity. Later ecologists demonstrated how grossly oversimplified this view had been. On the one hand, it could be shown that within American cities, for example, class, occupation, ethnic identity, life cycle stage, and other social characteristics of residents intervened to moderate and ameliorate the development of a cold and unfeeling urban environment. The importance of kinship affiliations, even in the city, was rediscovered. Nor, upon closer examination, was it found that urban areas had a monopoly over these human problems. Within cities there existed urban villagers who lived essentially "rural" social existences, while some small "nonurban" places contained populations with a highly urbane style of life (3,8,12,14,56,58,59,60). Furthermore, urban sociologists began to turn their attention to the large, densely settled, and heterogeneous cities of the East, and what they found made their heads (and generalizations) reel. These communities, although equal in size, density, and heterogeneity to many American and European cities, exhibited few of the expected characteristics. Cellular organization prevented the development of "urban" anonymity, and the larger community was elaborately crossed by extensive primary and potent kinship networks (9,10,16,21). Wirth's early generalizations (23) came to be qualified. Within each culture or subculture, differences in size, density, and degree of heterogeneity might create variations in social behavior, but the effects of these ecological variables could not be predicted unerringly from one culture to another. Two cities of different size *within* the same society might be quite diverse (15), but both would be more alike socially than two cities of the same size which existed in very different societies.

The New Ecology

Along with the ecologists of the old school, the new school accepts the basic assumption that ecological factors have an effect upon resulting spatial arrangements and upon the social behavior carried on within them. This intimate connection between physical and social space remains unquestioned (31,32,45). However, the present ecologists see the factors of space, numbers, growth rates, density, population composition, etc., as contributing to ecological forms and social relations *only after* being continuously filtered through the social structure, the value systems, the technology, and the economy. Ecology, then, is shaped and modified by social and economic conditions, and these, in turn, are altered by ecological parameters. There are complex interrelationships among these diverse elements (26,27,28,30,33,34,35,36,39,40).

The new ecologists have, to a large degree, abandoned the search for universal rules and patterns applicable to all cities. They accept a more specific reference for their research and are attempting at most to generalize gradually to subtypes of cities (9,11,16). This change in focus is not dissimilar to the rejection of universal systems that has been taking place in related fields of psychology and economics.

In addition, the ecological measures that were appropriate for studying medieval and industrial cities have been deemed inadequate when applied to the post-industrial region (7). Size, for example, has become increasingly difficult to measure, as the boundaries of the new urban regions multiply and diverge. Functional boundaries, as contrasted with legal or even physical ones, are related to the particular aspect of the regional system under study. Thus, there may be political boundaries, a variety of economic boundaries, auto commuting boundaries, airplane transit boundaries, television boundaries, etc. *Scale* has been advocated as a substitute for size. Scale measures the *extent* of a given network of relationships, not the number of participants (8,12,13,22). According to this new view, metropolitanization represents an increase in scale, even when the component units do not change in size; they are simply more widely linked.

The concept of density has also required a redefinition to make it applicable to the regional urbanism that has been developing. Historically, *material* density, i.e., the ratio of people to land, has been an excellent index to *dynamic* density, i.e., the rate at which individuals interact (4,28, 42). The congruence between these two measures, however, has been breaking apart, as interactions of many types are freed from the requirements of physical proximity. Especially since the proliferation of tertiary interactions which by their very nature do not require physical contact, people may interact with one another at rates far exceeding those that could be tolerated in older urban forms. No adequate measure of this dynamic density of interactions has yet been developed, much less accepted, although several writers have recently advocated some measurement based upon "bits of information" (1,6,13,19,22).

Even the idea of heterogeneity has required revised conceptualization. Under older urban conditions, heterogeneity arose primarily from sources *outside* the city and, in fact, was continuously sustained and reinforced by migrations from nonurban areas. But as foreign immigration to American cities declined, and as rural areas became increasingly urban in culture if not physical appearance, there was a reduction in the amount of externally generated heterogeneity within urban regions. This did not, however, lead to homogeneity. Rather, within the new urban social structure, an elaborate internal process of subdivision and differentiation has occurred which has promoted a new type of heterogeneity. The measures of the older type focused upon place of birth, background, and language. These are becoming increasingly irrelevant to the new heterogeneity which manifests itself chiefly in different life styles. These variations, while largely a function of class and occupation, are also affected by many other social variables, such as age, family type, education, and subarea of residence (12,51,52). New measures, such as those developed through social area analysis (to be discussed below), are needed.

Some Examples of Social Ecology Findings

Just as the large city centers of the United States provided the grounds for early ecological generalizations, so suburbia has now become the area of research which has yielded some of our more recent insights into the relationship between ecological parameters and social behavior. This research has demonstrated clearly how a number of critical social and economic variables intervene between ecological "cause" and social "effect." These findings in turn have stimulated revisions in ecological theory. Some of them may be summarized as follows:

The rapid development of social intimacy in suburbia, which many had assumed to be the result of smaller community size, was found only during the pioneering stage of settlement and was associated more with "problems" than with ecology, older established suburbs, regardless of their size, were found to be generally unreceptive to invading families (54,60).

Superficial neighborliness and energetic participation in community voluntary and service associations, also thought to result from the small scale of the suburban setting, were found to be confined almost exclusively to middle-class suburbs; working-class residents of suburbia tended to retain their kinship ties and to shun associationalism (53,55).

The life cycle and one's degree of involvement with urban occupational roles were found to be critical determinants of behavior, even more influential than the type of community in which one lives. Thus, retirement communities differ radically from suburbs containing concentrations of families with young children (55). Suburbs with a balance of ages and family types are quite different from suburbs with a concentration of the old or of the young (40).

Dormitory suburbs exhibit a different life style than do diversified satellite communities, regardless of size (55). And, even within the same town, commuters live a life distinct from that of non-commuters.

Not only suburbia but the more familiar urban lower-class subcommunities in the heart of our largest cities began to yield additional revisions, once they were reexamined in the light of new questions. For example, such communities were studied in London (59) and Boston (56); each failed to support the stereotypes of "urbanism as a way of life." Both urban lower-class subcommunities were characterized by residential stability, extensive kinship networks, and a closely guarded "frontier" sustained not by walls but by a suspicion of outsiders. The highly structured nature of these subcommunities was found to provide a defense against the potentially anomic influences of "urbanity." Class, family, and exclusiveness were important components of this defense. Even more interesting was the finding that when families from the urban London "slum" were relocated to a housing project in a suburban setting, their intimate social relationships decreased significantly and anonymous secondary relationships increased (59). Obviously, more than ecological factors were operative.

Social Area Analysis

Social area analysis is one of the more promising approaches to urban ecology that developed because of a growing dissatisfaction with earlier conceptualizations (44,45,46,47,50,51,52). It begins by rejecting both the simple-minded causality of unidirectionalism and the notion that the spatial pattern of any city is more than an abstraction dependent upon the types of measures employed by an investigator to "discover" it. It posits that in American cities today, at least three different types of measures are required to comprehend ecological organization, namely: measures of class or prestige; measures of family type or stage in the family cycle; and measures of ethnicity and race. Factor analysis of census tract data from American cities has tended to substantiate the hypothesis that these three "dimensions" of differentiation are indeed somewhat independent of one another, and that each dimension yields its own fairly typical geographic pattern, with class tending to be organized sectorally but family types tending to be disturbed zonally (24,25). Application of this new approach thus far has been chiefly in selecting urban subareas in which to investigate the interrelationship between social characteristics and neighborhood interaction patterns and attitudes (45,47). While these studies have generally ignored the traditional ecological variables, there appears to be no reason why this statistical technique could not be used to study the effects of ecological variables as well. By controlling socioeconomic level, family cycle stage, and ethnicity through the matching of subsample areas, the residual effects (upon social behavior) of house type, density, mobility, and other ecological variables could be traced. This would permit social area analysis to make an important contribution in continuing a legitimate line of ecological inquiry thus far pursued by social psychologists (26,27,33,38,40,41).

Other Ecological "Schools"

Recently there has been a resurgence of the classical ecological approach, but with a far more sophisticated set of variables and with a less deterministic view of the manner in which ecological factors affect social behavior. The work of the Duncans and such neoclassical ecologists as Hawley and Schnore exemplifies this promising revision (29,30,31,42,48,49).

In addition, although studies of optimum city size have continued, these too have become less deterministic. It is now recognized that no one city size can optimize all social goals, and that even separate optima can change with technology and values. These studies attempt to discover what city size can best provide a particular set of community facilities, services, and organizations, maximizing efficiency and variety while minimizing congestion and social disorganization. Since the public's ideas of efficiency and of desirable community services are constantly changing, the optimum city size must also change. The present consensus, based upon current values, focuses upon an ideal community size of between 250,000 and 500,000 (2), but the social consequences of this ecological parameter have not yet been studied. Furthermore, as the concept of scale is increasingly substituted for size, new types of investigations into urban optima may become necessary.

Some Implications

The major implication of current thought in social ecology is that there is no one "city type," no one form of "urbanity." There are varieties of urban experience which owe their differences to the way subgroups of the population choose from the urban environment the relationships in which they participate. Common residence in the same physical territory with the same place name, same size, and same density does not imply common psychic or social exposure to the same set of environmental stimuli. The three city types described earlier continue to coexist in the American urban community and the behavior of any given individual or group will depend in part on the extent to which they live in each type of city. The recently arrived Spanish-speaking aged Puerto Rican woman who joins an ethnic cell in New York City and lives almost exclusively a preindustrial existence is one extreme of American urban life. At the opposite extreme is the unencumbered freewheeling executive who lives with almost no fixed physical anchor and whose secondary and tertiary relationships, which may span the continent, far outnumber his primary contacts.

The manipulation of physical space does have effects on social behavior, but the effects will vary according to the presence of various nonphysical variables. The effects on our aged Puerto Rican woman will differ from the effects on our freewheeling executive. Since the variables which the planner can manipulate are ecological, the discovery of the indeterminate effects of these variables may be discouraging. Planners must learn to accept their limited potency. This is not the counsel of despair; rather it is first wisdom to know what is possible.

Bibliography

General works dealing with urban types—preindustrial, industrial, and post-industrial

1. BESHERS, JAMES. *Urban Social Structure.* New York: The Free Press, 1962.

2. BLUMENFELD, HANS. "The Urban Pattern," in the issue devoted to *Urban Revival: Goals and Standards, Annals of the American Academy of Political and Social Science* (March 1964), pp. 74–83.

3. DEWEY, RICHARD. "The Rural-Urban Continuum: Real but Relatively Unimportant," *American Journal of Sociology* (July 1960), pp. 60–66.

4. DURKHEIM, EMILE. *The Division of Labor in Society.* Translated by George Simpson. Book II, Ch. 2 and 3. New York: MacMillan Company, 1933.

5. ELAZAR, DANIEL J. "Are We a Nation of Cities?" *The Public Interest* (Summer 1966), pp. 42–58.

6. FRIEDMANN, JOHN, and ALONSO, WILLIAM (eds.). *Regional Development and Planning.* Cambridge: M.I.T. Press, 1964.

7. GOTTMANN, JEAN. *Megalopolis.* Cambridge: M.I.T. Press, 1961.

8. GREER, SCOTT. *The Emerging City: Myth and Reality.* New York: The Free Press, 1962.

9. HAUSER, P., and SCHNORE, L. (eds.). *The Study of Urbanization.* New York: John Wiley & Sons, 1965.

10. HAUSER, PHILIP (ed.). *Urbanization in Asia and the Far East.* Calcutta: UNESCO, 1957.

11. LAMPARD, ERIC. "The History of Cities in the Economically Advanced Areas," *Economic Development and Cultural Change* (January 1955), pp. 81–136.

12. McELRATH, DENNIS. "Urban Differentiation: Problems and Prospects," *Law and Contemporary Problems* (Winter 1965), pp. 103–110.

13. MEIER, RICHARD. A Communications Theory of Urban Growth. Cambridge: M.I.T. Press, 1962.

14. REISSMAN, LEONARD. *The Urban Process.* New York: The Free Press, 1964.

15. SCHNORE, LEO. "Some Correlates of Urban Size: A Replication," *American Journal of Sociology* (September 1963), pp. 185–193.

16. SJOBERG, GIDEON. *The Preindustrial City: Past and Present.* New York: Glencoe Free Press, 1960.

17. SMITH, PAGE. *As a City Upon a Hill.* New York: Knopf, 1966.

18. TONNIES, FERDINAND. *Community and Society.* Edited and translated by Charles Loomis. East Lansing: Michigan State University Press, 1957.

19. WEBBER, MELVIN M. "The Urban Place and the Nonplace Urban Realm," *Explorations into Urban Structure,* Webber *et al.* Philadelphia: University of Pennsylvania Press, 1964.

20. WARNER, SAM (ed.). *Planning for a Nation of Cities.* Cambridge: M.I.T. Press, 1966.

21. WEBER, MAX. *The City.* Translated by Don Martindale and Gertrud Neuwirth. New York: Collier Books, 1962 (reprint.)

22. WINGO, L. (ed.). *Cities and Space.* Baltimore: The Johns Hopkins Press, 1963.

23. WIRTH, LOUIS. "Urbanism as a Way of Life," *American Journal of Sociology* (July 1938). Reprinted in *Cities and Society.* Edited by Hatt and Reiss, Jr. New York: Glencoe Free Press, 1957.

Ecology and its social effects

24. ANDERSON, THEODORE, and EGELAND, JANICE. "Spatial Aspects of Social Area Analysis," *American Sociological Review* (June 1961), pp. 392–398.

25. BLUMENFELD, HANS. "On the Concentric Circle Theory of Urban Growth," *Land Economics* (May 1949), pp. 209–212.

26. CAPLOW, THEODORE, and FOREMAN, R. "Neighborhood Interaction in a Homogeneous Community," *American Sociological Review* (1950), pp. 357–366.

27. DEUTSCH, MORTON, and COLLINS, M. *Interracial Housing.* Minneapolis: University of Minnesota Press, 1951.

28. DUHL, LEONARD (ed.). *The Urban Condition.* New York: Basic Books, 1963.

29. DUNCAN, BEVERLY, SABAGH, GEORGE, and VAN ARSDOL, MAURICE, JR. "Patterns of City Growth," *American Journal of Sociology* (January 1962), pp. 418–429.

30. DUNCAN, OTIS D. "From Social System to Ecosystem," *Sociological Inquiry,* 31 No. 2 (1961), pp. 140–149.

31. DUNCAN, OTIS D. and BEVERLY. "Residential Distribution and Occupational Stratification," *American Journal of Sociology* (March 1955), pp. 493–503.

32. FELDMAN, ARNOLD, and TILLY, CHARLES. "The Interaction of Social and Physical Space," *American Sociological Review* (December 1960), pp. 877–884.

33. FESTINGER, LEON, SCHACHTER, S., and BACK, K. *Social Pressures in Informal Groups.* New York: Harper Brothers, 1950.

34. FIREY, WALTER. *Land Use in Central Boston.* Cambridge: Harvard University Press, 1947.

35. FIREY, WALTER. "Sentiment and Symbolism as Ecological Variables," *American Sociological Review* (April 1945), pp. 140–148.

36. FORM, WILLIAM. "The Place of Social Structure in the Determination of Land Use: Some Implications for a Theory of Urban Ecology," *Social Forces* (May 1954), pp. 317–323.

37. GANS, HERBERT. "Planning and Social Life," *Journal of the American Institute of Planners* (May 1961), pp. 134–140.

38. GUTMAN, ROBERT. "Site Planning and Social Behavior," *The Journal of Social Issues,* 22 (October 1966), pp. 103–115.

39. HAUSER, FRANCIS L. "The Ecological Pattern of Four European Cities and Two Theories of Urban Expansion," *Journal of the American Institute of Planners* (Summer 1951), pp. 111–129.

40. MERTON, ROBERT. "The Social Psychology of Housing," in *Current Trends in Social Psychology,* edited by W. Dennis. Pittsburgh: University of Pittsburgh Press, 1947.

41. ROSOW, I. "The Social Effects of the Physical Environment," *Journal of the American Institute of Planners* (May 1961), pp. 127–133.

42. SCHNORE, LEO. "Social Morphology and Human Ecology," *American Journal of Sociology* (May 1958), pp. 620–634.

43. WALLACE, ANTHONY. *Housing and Social Structure,* Philadelphia Housing Authority, 1952.

Social area analysis

44. ANDERSON, THEODORE, and BEAN, LEE. "The Shevky-Bell Social Areas: Confirmation of Results and a Reinterpretation," *Social Forces* (December 1961), pp. 119–124.

45. BELL, W. "Urban Neighborhoods and Individual Behavior," *Problems of Youth*. Edited by Muzafer and Caroline Sherif. Chicago: Aldine Press, 1965.

46. BELL, W. "Social Areas: Typology of Urban Neighborhoods," in *Community Structure and Analysis*. Edited by Marvin Sussman. New York: Thomas Y. Crowell, 1959.

47. BELL, W. "The Utility of the Shevky Typology for the Design of Urban-Suburban Area Field Studies," *Journal of Social Psychology* (February 1958), pp. 71–83.

48. DUNCAN, O. D. "Review of *Social Area Analysis* by E. Shevky and W. Bell," *American Journal of Sociology* (July 1955), pp. 84–85. See also the rejoinder by W. Bell in the same volume, pp. 260–261.

49. HAWLEY, AMOS, and DUNCAN, OTIS D. "Social Area Analysis: A Critical Appraisal," *Land Economics* (November 1957), pp. 337–343.

50. ORLEANS, PETER. "Robert Park and Social Area Analysis: A Convergence of Traditions in Urban Sociology," *Urban Affairs Quarterly* (June 1966).

51. SHEVKY, ESHREF, and BELL, WENDELL. *Social Area Analysis: Theory, Illustrative Application and Computational Procedures*. Stanford: Stanford University Press, Stanford University Series in Sociology, No. 1, 1955.

52. SHEVKY, ESHREF, and WILLIAMS, MARILYN. *The Social Areas of Los Angeles: Analysis and Typology*. Los Angeles and Berkeley: University of California Press, 1949.

Behavior Studies in the contemporary city

53. BERGER, BENNETT. *Working Class Suburb*. Berkeley and Los Angeles: University of California Press, 1960.

54. DOBRINER, WILLIAM. *Class in Suburbia*. Englewood Cliffs, N.J.: Prentice-Hall, 1963.

55. FOOTE, NELSON, et. al. *Housing Choices and Housing Constraints*. New York: McGraw-Hill, 1960.

56. GANS, HERBERT. *The Urban Villagers*. New York: The Free Press, 1962.

57. GANS, HERBERT. "Urbanism and Suburbanism as Ways of Life: A Reevaluation of Definitions," *Human Behavior and Social Processes*. Edited by Arnold Rose. Boston: Houghton Mifflin Company, 1962.

58. ROSSI, PETER. *Why Families Move*. New York: The Free Press, 1955.

59. YOUNG, MICHAEL, and WILLMOTT, PETER. *Family and Kinship in East London*. London: Routledge and Kegan Paul, 1957.

60. GANS, HERBERT. *The Levittowners*. New York: The Free Press, 1967.

B | Ecology of the Preindustrial City — Old and New

12 | Mexico City: Its Growth and Configuration, 1345–1960

NORMAN S. HAYNER

For almost six hundred years Mexico City grew slowly. Most of that time residential desirability declined with distance from the central plaza. But in recent years under the influence of rapid growth in population, many new industries, and some improvement in the means of transportation, the metropolis seems to be shifting toward a basic structure similar to that of large cities north of the Border. Yet it retains certain important differences.

Anglo-American cities usually develop their worst slums in a zone just outside the central business district. As business expands outward, land values for commercial purposes rise, but homes deteriorate and rents go down. Better residential areas are most frequently located a considerable distance from the center. Until recent decades, Latin American cities have grown very slowly over a long period of time. In a city that is not growing there is naturally no "zone in transition." The central business district is not expanding into surrounding residential areas. Where this is true it is more desirable to have a home within easy walking distance of the central square. Less favored sites for homes tend to be farther away, and the least desirable on the outskirts. Ordinarily the band plays for a *serenata* in the plaza two evenings a week. For smaller cities like Oaxaca or Querétaro, this public square is still the social center. But Mexico City today shows an interesting shift from this older pattern.

Since 1900, when its population was only 345,000, the capital's central business district has expanded outward, creating a "horseshoe" of high-land-value slums immediately to the north and east (see map, p. 167). Then too,

SOURCE: Norman S. Hayner in collaboration with Una Middleton Hayner, *New Patterns in Old Mexico* (New Haven, Conn.: College and University Press, 1966), pp. 51–64 and Map V.

one of its best residential areas (the Pedregal Gardens) is located a full ten miles southwest of the Zócalo. In spite of these facts, its tendency to develop a circle of low-land-value slums on the outer edge of the metropolitan area has persisted for more than 440 years. In this respect it is similar to other large Latin American cities but different from the larger cities north of the Border. A 1957 United Nations *Report on the World Social Situation*

Mexico City—Homes of Intellectuals and the Poor

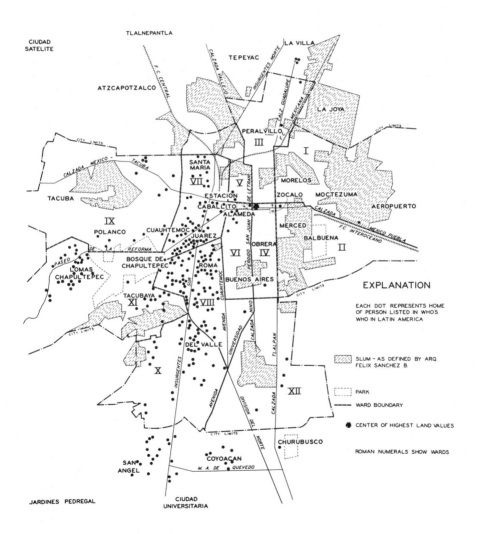

concludes that in Latin American cities "peripheral slums are frequently displaced and pushed farther out by the expansion of the city proper."

Aztec Settlement to Modern Metropolis

To understand the present configuration of Mexico's capital, it is helpful to think in terms of four major periods in its development. First there was the ancient Aztec city of Tenochtitlán (1345–1521). Then came the Spanish-colonial city (1521–1821) founded by Hernán Cortés and his followers. With independence came a century of French influence (1821–1920). The present city combines a rich heritage from the past with an increasing infiltration of ideas from the United States.

Most archeologists agree that Tenochtitlán was founded about 1345 on islands in the salt sea of Texcoco. The name "México" was at that time used for the high valley in which Tenochtitlán was located. In the beginning, this Aztec settlement was a small village of reed huts with thatched roofs. By 1398 the earliest stone houses were built. When Cortés first saw Tenochtitlán and adjoining Tlaltelolco (1519), it was reputedly a city of more than five hundred thousand people, perhaps larger than any other in the world. It had narrow canals as in Venice and three main avenues two spear-lengths in width. The pink stone dwellings of the nobles included courtyards with fountains, birds, and flowers. An aqueduct brought fresh water to the Aztec capital. Since these structures were almost completely destroyed by the conquistadors, few vestiges of the ancient city remain.

. . . [The early growth of Mexico City may be understood as follows.] The central area, a block roughly one mile on each side, is the section planned for occupation by the Spaniards in 1521, but actually not used until 1524. During the period when the city streets were being reconstructed in the form of a grid, the seat of government, the home of Cortés, and that of his captain, Alvarado, were in Coyoacán, a suburb just south of the present city limits. It is significant that even at this early date the native population was largely accommodated outside the limits of the Spanish city, their humble huts "scattered without order—as is the ancient custom among them."

During the next three centuries Mexico City grew slowly from perhaps thirty thousand, after the destruction of Tenochtitlán, to more than one hundred thousand. At the beginning of the nineteenth century it was again the largest city in the Western Hemisphere. A century later the capital had grown to more than three hundred thousand; by 1921, at the end of the revolution, its population had passed the six hundred thousand mark, finally exceeding the size Tenochtitlán is alleged to have reached four centuries earlier.

. . . Growth during these four centuries has been primarily westward. During this long period the area occupied by dwellings expanded only one-half mile to the south and about a mile east and north, but three and one-half miles to the west. Until 1903 further expansion eastward was blocked by Lake Texcoco. At that time this lake was partially drained by a gigantic canal and tunnel project, but the establishment of new residential neighborhoods to the east was still discouraged by the alkaline character of the reclaimed soil. During the major portion of these four centuries, the least desirable areas for residence were those beyond an easy walking distance from the Zócalo and the Alameda.

Throughout the colonial stage in its development, Spanish influence was of course dominant. The official language, the Roman Catholic church, the burros, the siesta, the patio, paintings, public administration, were all heritages from Spain. Buildings in the older part of the city, whether governmental, ecclesiastical, educational, or residential, are still predominantly Spanish in architecture.

The oldest official panorama map of Mexico City, dated 1737, shows the largest and best residences in the center, the smallest and poorest on the periphery. Cortés had ordered the Indians to move out of the center and had divided up the more desirable section among his retainers. The house used by Cortés himself is still to be seen near the Zócalo. Canals came as far as the Zócalo from the east and almost connected with the oldest plaza in the Americas from the west.

After Mexico gained its political independence from Spain in 1821, Spanish cultural patterns continued to be important. Of the other European nations, probably the dominant influence through the next century came from France. During this period, French was the preferred foreign language in the schools. Up to the 1950's, it still was in Oaxaca's Institute of Arts and Sciences. It was not until after the Revolution of 1910–21 that English came to lead other foreign languages in the metropolis. Maximilian, emperor of Mexico from 1863 to 1867, designed a Boulevarde Imperiale patterned after the Champs-Elysées of Paris. This magnificent avenue—later renamed the Paseo de la Reforma—extends as a fourteen-lane, tree-lined boulevard from the equestrian statue of Charles IV of Spain* about two miles southwest to Diana the Huntress at the entrance to Chapultepec Park. In the Díaz regime (1876–1910) many pretentious *palacios* were constructed along the Reforma. It is significant that the two older *colonias* (neighborhoods) north of the Reforma, Santa María (1869) and San Rafael (1891), are predominantly Spanish in architecture, whereas in the newer colonias south of the Reforma, Juárez (1902) and Roma (1906), the homes are distinctly French in style—many recently replaced, however, by modern commercial and residential buildings.

Before the Spaniards came the capital city was Indian; during the next four centuries it was predominantly Latin; recently it has bee. moving toward a fusion of these two elements supplemented by a growing influx of ideas and artifacts from the United States. Since the opening of the

---

* A statue affectionately referred to as the Caballito (Little Horse).

México-Laredo Highway (1932), followed by construction of three other highways from Mexico City to the Border, increasing streams of American tourists have poured into the capital. World War II accentuated the flow. Many travelers, who could not visit Europe, turned to Mexico. By 1960 the tourist trade was generating 23 per cent of Mexico's foreign exchange earnings. At the same time, *norteamericanos* not only had invested a billion dollars in Mexico's expanding industries but also had provided much of the technical know-how for their development.

The impact of this North American influence may be seen both in the business center and in the newer colonias to the south and southwest. Many of the office buildings of the central business district and along the Reforma are now as modern as those in large cities north of the Rio Grande. In fact, Mexican engineers have recently overcome the handicap imposed by the spongy lake bottom on which the city is built. As a result, by 1961 many skyscrapers of more than ten stories had been completed and numerous others were under construction. Beginning with the 44-story Latin American Tower just south of the center of highest land values, these tall buildings tend to form a row extending west along Juárez and southwest along the Reforma. Such a development spells centralization.

Another influence from the United States and an index to decentralization of services, combined with centralization in control, is to be seen in the well-organized *supermercados* located in better residential districts, such as the Lomas, Polanco, Anzures, Condesa, Roma, and Del Valle. These supermarkets sell a wide variety of both Mexican and foreign groceries. As in similar institutions north of the Rio Grande, prices are marked for every item, carts are available to carry purchases, and everything is checked over and paid for on departure. In the spring of 1961 the Mexico City supermarkets celebrated their fifteenth anniversary. None of the supermarkets, however, had parking lots for automobiles. In fact, at that time the writer saw no automobile-oriented shopping center of the type that has developed in the United States.

Externally, the city's upper-class residential district, the Lomas de Chapultepec, is very similar to certain sections of Los Angeles. All houses in the area must have gardens extending around the outside in repudiation of the patio of the Spanish-style home.

There is another way in which the Mexican capital can be compared with Los Angeles, and that is in its recent growth. In 1930 the population of Mexico City was over a million and that of the Federal District (comparable from a legal standpoint to the District of Columbia in the United States) about 1,250,000. By 1960 the city had almost reached 3,750,000, and the Federal District was approaching five million. In the period 1930–60 the population of the Republic doubled; that of the capital tripled; that of the Federal District quadrupled. The Mexico City "metropolitan area" as determined by International Urban Research had a population of 2,960,120 in 1950 and 4,816,393 in 1960—an increase of 63 per cent. This growth rate is faster than the 54 per cent increase for the Los Angeles-Long Beach metropolitan area during that decade and almost as rapid as the estimated 67 per cent increase for the metropolitan area of São Paulo, Brazil.

Heavy in-migration to the capital, and to cities like Guadalajara (with 734,346 persons in 1960) and Monterrey (601,085), has been stimulated by such factors as the persistent low real incomes among peasants, and industrial developments fostered by the government's policy of "Mexico for the Mexicans." Up to 1926, for example, all makes of cars were imported. Beginning in that year automobile companies willing to assemble their cars in Mexico were favored. By 1961 importation of expensive cars, such as Cadillacs, was stopped while corporations willing to use a large proportion of parts manufactured in Mexico were encouraged. It is probable that eventually all new cars purchased by Mexicans will be manufactured within the Republic.

Along with the growth in Mexico City's population, there have been improvements in transportation, but nothing comparable to the subways or commuter trains of New York or Chicago. This fact has prevented the star-shaped spread of the metropolis along lines of fast transit. But wherever burgeoning cities are found, transportation has difficulty in keeping up. Two-fifths of the passenger automobiles of Mexico are registered in the Federal District—three times its quota in proportion to population, but still only one privately owned car registered as of 1958 for every 36 individuals (1960). During the past decade improvements have been made in the highways leading into the metropolis and in arterials within and around the city. With the exception of jitneys which operate along major avenues for a flat one-peso charge per person and the slightly more expensive taxis, the use of passenger automobiles is largely limited to the middle and upper classes. For the masses, transportation is by streetcar or, increasingly, by the clumsy, crowded "ubiquitous bus." And the buses, which do seem to go everywhere, are neither rapid nor dependable.

The expansion of the city, at first largely to the south and southwest and more recently in all directions, has pulled the business district westward along the Avenida Juarez and southwest along the Reforma. The old French-style houses in the northern part of Colonia Juarez and the "palaces" along the northeastern end of the Reforma have been replaced by hotels, apartment houses, governmental and commercial establishments including automobile agencies. Apartments have increased greatly in number. In 1941 the huge Arch of the Revolution, on an extension westward of the Avenida Juarez, stood alone among vacant lots; now it is surrounded by apartment and office buildings. The area near the Caballito . . . is perhaps the clearest example of the process so common in North American cities in which a neighborhood of individual homes is "invaded" by apartments or commercial enterprises. Old buildings in this area have, in fact, been sold for the value of the land.

A similar process of invasion and succession has been taking place during the past two decades along Avenida de los Insurgentes south of the Reforma. The success of Sears Roebuck de México in Colonia Roma, the congestion and parking difficulties for a major department store still located near the Zócalo, and the fact that most of its upper- and middle-class clients lived to the southwest, encouraged the Palacio de Hierro to establish a large branch a few blocks west of Roma. Changes such as these have resulted in sharp increases in land values in the areas invaded.

As is true to a greater or lesser extent for many capitals in progressing countries, and demonstrably so for Latin America, the metropolitan area of Mexico City had in 1960 six times the population of the metro area for the next largest Mexican city, Guadalajara. From this standpoint the capital ranked ninth in a list of 39 such areas having an estimated population of over one million in 1955 and may, therefore, be described as a "primate city." This growing metropolis is the dominant center of the political, business, and intellectual life of the Republic. Here is the largest center of manufacturing, the focus for transportation facilities, the financial hub of the Republic, and here are the managerial headquarters for many enterprises. It attracts leading professionals from all the states and territories. In the words of Hubert Herring, it "devours the leadership of the country. Every politician, doctor, and lawyer nurses the ambition to live in the capital—draining the states of their leadership."

Data on personages listed in *Who's Who in Latin America* indicate the extent to which this was true in 1946. The occupations represented most often among these *intelectuales*, in order of frequency, were: lawyer, engineer, writer, physician, army officer, businessman, professor, painter, newspaperman, and banker. Although only 148, or 18 per cent, of the 808 listed for the whole of Mexico were born in the Federal District, 672 or 82 per cent lived there, a ratio of two to nine. It is assumed that the ratio between the number of distinguished persons born in a given state and the number who live there provides a rough measure of the relative drawing power of the Federal District as compared with the state. This ratio was twenty-one to one for Oaxaca and eight to one for Puebla; but two to one for Jalisco where Guadalajara is located and four to three for Nuevo León, where Monterrey is the capital.

The distribution of Mexico City and local newspapers serves also as a rough measure of the extent to which the metropolis actually dominates the social and economic life of the country. Where the number of Mexico City papers drops below that of local papers it may be assumed that the capital has ceased to be dominant. If this index is adequate, the capital's social and economic pre-eminence is felt most on the Central Mesa with a substantial share of the western part of this great plateau controlled by Guadalajara.

In addition to the natural attraction which the metropolis offers, even to people from Guadalajara, there is the insecurity created by the governmental policy of expropriation of agricultural lands. In 1937 under President

Lázaro Cárdenas this reached the peak of five million hectares (about twelve and a half million acres). Whatever one's personal opinion on this fundamental question, it has produced an insecurity among landowning classes that has caused many to migrate to the city.

Palaces and Slums

The best available index to the ecological structure of the metropolis proved to be land-value gradients. Estimated commercial land values for 1943 and 1948 . . . were based on actual sales, offers, or demands. A map prepared by Professor Edmundo Flores of the National University, using what are presented as "approximate commercial values" for 1958, shows a similar pattern with the most notable increases along the Reforma. The center of highest values is occupied by the Guardiola Building on San Juan de Letrán between Cinco de Mayo and Madero avenues. Values decline slightly as one moves east from this building to the Zócalo. Westward on Avenida Juárez and southwestward along the Reforma, values remain high as far as the intersection with Avenida Insurgentes. They are slightly lower from Insurgentes to Chapultepec Park. In general, values drop as one moves north or south from this Zócalo-Caballito-Chapultepec Park axis with the longest continuation of high values south along Insurgentes. The center of population in Mexico City gradually shifted from the Zócalo southwest so that by 1940 it reached La Garita at the intersection of Bucareli and Avenida Chapultepec (southeast corner of Ward VII). A panorama of the city as it was in 1856 shows this intersection three or four blocks beyond the built-up portions.

As the city grew, factors determining the southwestward movement of the middle and upper classes included: the more fertile soil, higher elevations, and greater scenic beauty to the southwest; railroad yards little more than a mile to the north and northwest of the center (moved three miles northwest in 1958); city sewers that flow eastward and then, without covers, northward on a natural gradient; and prevailing winds from the northeast which, just before the rainy season starts, stir up alkaline dust storms from the dried-up bottom of Lake Texcoco northeast of the capital. This shift of people, together with the fact that the streets are wider, has helped to make Avenida Juárez and the Reforma more important than Avenida Madero, long the stronghold of real estate values.

Two phenomena seem to be correlated roughly with socioeconomic status in the metropolis. For one of these, the sex ratio, the correlation is negative; for the other, the number of distinguished persons, the correlation is positive. As the number of men per one hundred women decreases, the socioeconomic status of an area, within certain limits, increases. Two wards (*cuarteles*) with high average financial standing had in 1940 a sex ratio of 68.5 males to 100 females (76.5 in 1960). These wards (VII and VIII) include the prosperous colonias north and south of the Reforma. The ratio for the city as a whole was 83.3 (88.4 in 1960). In the three poorest wards (I, II, and IX), which include the Morelos, Merced, and Tacuba neighborhoods, the percentage stood at 90.6 (95.3 in 1960). This difference seems to be due to the larger number of women servants in the wealthier districts. Interestingly enough, when one studies the very wealthy Lomas, the sex ratio rises again. Chauffeurs and gardners have been added to the servant group. The fact that between 1940 and 1960 the sex ratio increased 1.6 times as much in the rich wards (8.0) as for the city as a whole (5.1) suggests that the higher wages offered by factories make it more difficult now to retain female help in the homes.

In contrast to large Anglo-American cities like Chicago, this Mexican city contains no area of homeless men. Women and children share with men life in the worst slums. This is probably best explained in terms of family mores. Women put up with more in Mexico.

The spots on [the] map . . . show the "homes" of distinguished persons as revealed by the above-mentioned study of *Who's Who in Latin America*. Cases where only office addresses were given are not included on the map. It will be noted that Colonia Juárez, the Lomas, and Del Valle, with about thirty personages each, have the largest number in *Who's Who*. San Angel, Roma, Hipodromo (west of Roma), and Cuauhtémoc came next with about fifteen each. The low number in Polanco (3) and Nueva Anzures (4) is to be accounted for by the newness of these colonias and the predominance of the *nouveaux riches*. The north-south avenue, which is named Guerrero on the north and Cuauhtémoc on the south, divides the land area occupied by dwellings and the population of the metropolitan area approximately in half, and yet there were only 22 spots east of this line as against 225 west. In fact, using the same line as [the] eastern boundary and an imaginary extension westward of Avenida Juárez as [the] northern, the southwest sector of the metropolitan area contained 202, or more than four-fifths, of these distinguished persons.

An interesting housing map prepared by the National Urban Mortgage Bank showed for 1932 the exact distribution of various types of housing in Mexico City. *Vecindades* and other types of homes for workers were most frequently present in the congested areas of "Old Mexico" north, east, and south of the Zócalo (Morelos, La Merced, Obrera), whereas west of the north-south line of Guerrero-Cuauhtémoc mentioned above there was a preponderance of residencias and very few vecindades. In 1947 the National Urban Mortgage Bank continued its studies of Mexico City's housing problem with an investigation by architect Felix Sánchez B. The slum areas on [the] map . . . are based on this report. One-fifth of the land area of the city (1946) was covered by these slum zones, and one-fourth of the estimated population—about half a million persons—lived in them. One hundred and thirty thousand individuals lived in dwellings whose destruction was recommended.

As was mentioned earlier, when the boundary of the Spanish city was established in 1521 the huts of the Indians were built outside. Architect Sánchez points out that this hodgepodge of jacales outside the Spanish city was the beginning of the present high-land-value slums. Areas of greatest density of population—from 1,000 to 2,500 persons to the acre—and some of the worst present-day slums form a "horseshoe" around the north and east sides of "México Viejo," the older, central part of the city.

Northeast of the Merced district is the neighborhood called Moctezuma studied by the author in 1948. Here in 1961 the pressures from the expanding city could be seen. An earlier population of manual laborers (*obreros*) had been replaced by white-collar workers (*empleados*) who could pay higher rents. This increase in rentals, however, has made it necessary for many newly married couples to live in the home of the husband's father. Schools that operated two shifts in 1948 had four in 1961.

One answer to these problems is the construction now in process (1963), on the northern edge of the inner "horseshoe," of the largest housing project in Latin America. This project extends from Insurgentes Norte on the west to a proposed prolongation of the Reforma on the east—about one and a half miles. It will average three-eighths of a mile in width. Extensions northward of Guerrero and of San Juan de Letrán will divide it into three semi-independent units. Here, eventually, in buildings that are two, three, and seven stories high, ninety thousand people will be housed. Markets, playgrounds, and schools will be included. Apartments will range in size from one to four bedrooms and will rent for 12 to 40 dollars per month. They are planned for workers who earn from 32 to 96 dollars monthly. The construction is being financed by the same government-supported institution that has been making some of the housing studies—the National Urban Mortgage Bank. The location was made available by the moving of railroad freight yards (nationally owned) three miles to the northwest. It gets its hyphenated name, Nonoalco-Tlaltelolco, from two ancient communities that once occupied the site. A nine-level pyramid discovered here convinces archeologists that Tlatelolco (*sic*) was at least four hundred years older than Tenochtitlán.

At some distance outside the "horseshoe" Sánchez found a broken circle of low-land-value slums. These slums seem to develop in vacant areas between or peripheral to established communities. Such clusters may be initiated by so-called "parachutists," squatters who just "fall" into these open spaces. In the beginning at least, these aggregations of makeshift huts and substandard houses lack transportation, lighting, water, and sewage disposal. Eventually such services tend to come in and the shantytown achieves the status of a "proletarian community."

If for the Federal District data on recorded offenders against the law consistently covered the geographical distribution of their homes rather than merely the place where the crime was committed, probably they would fail to show the same degree of concentration in a transitional belt near the center as in North American cities. In addition to the outer circle of slum zones outlined on [the] map . . . smaller slums are often to be found near the best residential neighborhoods. In some instances these have been started by a few jacales where poorly paid quarry workers and their families lived.

About three-fourths of Sánchez' half million slum dwellers lived east of the Guerrero-Cuauhtémoc line. These poverty-stricken people were for the most part crowded into the older, more congested sections or into the new proletarian additions to the east and northeast. In "Old Mexico" every sidewalk and every entrance to the numerous vecindades seem to be teeming with humanity. Due perhaps to better facilities than in the spot that is called home, eating and even sleeping on the street are commonplace. The other one-fourth of the city's slum dwellers lived in the Tacubaya, Tacuba, and Pro-hogar (north of Santa María) zones. But between Tacubaya and Tacuba the magnificent residences of the Lomas rival anything in Hollywood.

Comparison of air photos of the metropolis and its vicinity for 1936 and 1959 plus field observations of 1941 and 1961 indicate a large increase in homes for workers in the area north of Morelos outside the city limits, in the flat lands northeast of La Villa extending into the State of Mexico, and in the industrial suburbs of Atzcapotzalco and Tlalnepantla to the northwest. New proletarian colonias have sprung up to the east along the Puebla highway and to the southeast in the Ixtapalapa delegation. A 1958 report on *Colonias Proletarias* locates three hundred such areas and concludes that by the end of 1955 they covered 30 per cent of the land area of the city. These neighborhoods make an almost complete circle around the outer part of the city with a two-mile break on the west and another two-mile break on the south. There is also an increase in homes, some of them palatial, in new subdivisions west and southwest of the city's legal boundaries.

Between 1940 and 1950 the tier of delegations in the Federal District immediately outside the political city grew four times as rapidly as the city itself, and from 1950 to 1960 eight times as rapidly. The remaining delegations in the Federal District, farther from the city, grew in the earlier decade a little less rapidly than the political city but between 1950 and 1960 2.4 times as fast. Actually, the four central wards of Mexico City declined 4.6 per cent between 1950 and 1960. This decrease at the center is, of course, to be found in other large cities. In other words, the Mexico City metropolitan region is growing most rapidly on the fringe of its built-up area and not in spatially independent suburban towns.

. . . . .

In conclusion, the following observations have been emphasized: (1) the slow and more recently the rapid growth of Mexico City; (2) the shift in basic configuration from the plaza-centered structure of the older Mexican cities toward certain characteristics similar to Anglo-American urbanized areas, including a "zone in transition"; and (3) certain differences between

Mexico City and the latter. The absence of an area of homeless men, and of better-class residential suburbs with matricentric families, the tendency for low-land-value slums to form a zone on the periphery, and the greater tendency to be the political, business, and intellectual center for an entire country are features of the Mexican capital which differ sharply from the ecological patterns presented by larger cities north of the Border. Reflecting as they do distinctive aspects of modern Latin American family and community life, these structural differences are apparently characteristic also of most of the larger urban aggregations south of Mexico.

13 | The Ecology of Bangalore, India: An East-West Comparison

NOEL P. GIST

Ecological research in American cities has revealed rather striking uniformities of ecological patterning, sufficient at least for certain tentative theories concerning urban ecology. It would be a fallacy, however, to assume that these theories are necessarily applicable to societies that differ strikingly from the United States in history, stage of technological development, socio-economic organization, and cultural interests.

Observations made in a few Latin American cities, for example, reveal ecological patterns quite different from those characteristic of many American cities.[1] The classical urban pattern in these cities may be summarized as follows: high-status and high-income residents live near a central plaza, which is the social and institutional heart of the community; low-status and low-income residents locate near the periphery; economic establishments tend to be dispersed throughout the city, rather than highly centralized; and suburban growth from residential decentralization is limited.

Ecological segregation in one form or another appears to be almost universal, but the particular form in which such segregation occurs is highly variable, and changes in segregative patterns are affected by broad ideological, political, economic, and technological changes. Probably all communities

---

[1] See Theodore Caplow, "The Social Ecology of Guatemala City," *Social Forces*, 28 (December 1949), pp. 113–33.

SOURCE: *Social Forces*, XXXV, 4 (May 1957), 356–359, 361, 363–365. Reprinted by permission of the publisher.

approaching urban status also manifest some form of centralization of institutional functions. Such centralization usually reflects developments in communication, transportation, and economic organization, especially the growth of large bureaucratic structures. But it should not be assumed that western forms of centralization have necessarily occurred in technologically and economically underdeveloped countries.

Bangalore, Its History and Growth

With these observations in mind, we shall examine the ecological structure of Bangalore, the capital city of Mysore State, South India. As the largest metropolis in Mysore State and the seventh largest city in India, Bangalore has well over three-fourths of a million inhabitants. In recent years its growth has been rapid; during the 1941–51 decade the population almost doubled. Industrialization is proceeding at a rapid pace, and mechanized mass transportation is replacing some of the older forms.

From 1809 to the late 1940's the city was divided into two separate administrative units: Bangalore City on the west side, which was independently administered, and the Civil and Military Station (Cantonment), under British jurisdiction. With the merger of the two divisions after India's independence, the larger municipality assumed integrated administrative functions as the Bangalore Municipal Corporation.

Until the second decade of the present century the growth of Bangalore Municipality was comparatively slow, and the number of inhabitants was less than the number in the Cantonment. By 1921, however, the two administrative divisions were about equal in size (118,000 each). Thereafter the Municipality outdistanced the Cantonment in population growth. In the 1941 census the Municipality had a population of a quarter of a million compared with about 160,000 for the Cantonment. There is no doubt that the spatial arrangement of institutions and people was greatly influenced by this dual administrative organization and the presence of British military and civil personnel.

Since the terrain upon which Bangalore is located is comparatively level, without any sharp topographic contrasts to limit seriously or restrict the character of land usage, the ecological structure must therefore be interpreted mainly in terms of *social* factors that have operated to give the city its distinctive patterning. These factors have never functioned in a competitively laissez faire environment; in recent times, at least, planning procedures have been systematically applied with the result that the city's ecology has been considerably affected. Large parks in the central part of the city, mainly in the Cantonment, are patently products of municipal planning.

But the scope and degree of planning have, nevertheless, been limited. Certainly there is no rigidly planned economy, nor have tight restrictions been imposed specifying the location of economic establishments. Presumably most establishments related directly to the economy have been relatively free to compete for favorable sites and to locate without much interference from the government.

The rapid growth of Bangalore in recent decades has had the effect of increasing the over-all density of population, especially in the old Municipality. In 1941, before the merger, the Municipality had nearly 19,000 persons per square mile as compared with a density of about 12,000 persons in the Cantonment. Between 1901 and 1941, the metropolitan area increased by 35 percent (from 9.8 to 13.2 square miles), but the population increased by 258 percent and the density by 164 percent. This rapid growth of population without a corresponding increase in occupied area has greatly accentuated the piling up of people in the metropolis. Actual increase in density has been considerable for all sections, but the range in density for different areas has been even more impressive. In 1941, the most sparsely settled section (which included a fashionable residential center and the palace grounds) was 6,485 persons per square mile, but in the most densely settled area the corresponding density figure was 135,311, or twenty times as great.

The Ecology of Business

Bangalore has a major retail and wholesale district, near the largest municipal market (Central Market), in the old Municipality, but the area has limited resemblance to the central business district of an American city. Central Market itself is a commercial nucleus, a center of buying and selling, mainly of articles for household or personal consumption. Within the vicinity of the Market are streets lined with shops specializing in such merchandise as silk, cotton, and leather goods; silverware, hardware, and musical instruments; drugs, jewelry, and household furnishings; supplies, books, and hemp products. In the district are also numerous small boarding and lodging hotels, pawnbrokers' establishments, lawyers' offices, and offices of various merchants' associations. Shops carrying the same type of merchandise tend to cluster together, creating small districts or sectors more or less specialized in character. One may find, for example, clusters of shops dealing with silverware or brassware or other clusters of shops selling bicycles or drugs.

This district is by no means limited exclusively to retail merchandising. As in American cities wholesale establishments are located conveniently near the retailers. Some of the retail and wholesale merchants receive certain kinds of merchandise directly from small-scale manufacturing enterprises located in the same area. On side streets, for instance, are weavers and ribbon manufacturers who supply nearby retail shops with finished articles. Certain merchants, notably dealers in indigenous drugs and silverware, perform dual functions of manufacturer and distributor, fabricating and selling commodities in the same building.

A wholesale district is located about one-fourth mile to the west of Central Market, on a major arterial thoroughfare and not far from the southwestern boundary of the city. Wholesaling activity here is confined mainly to agricultural products such as grain, vegetables, ginger, garlic, and fruits, which are piled on the sides of streets or under shelters, to be disposed of to retailers. Even in this area open-air retail vendors operate sidewalk businesses alongside the wholesalers. Hence there is no clear-cut areal differentiation based on the nature of distributive functions.

Nearly a mile north of Central Market, beyond the perimeter of the shopping district, is a "big business" street (Kempe Gowda Road) on which are concentrated banking and insurance firms, film distributing companies, offices of out-of-town newspaper correspondents, a large transportation firm, and the Bangalore Chamber of Commerce. Within a distance of about two or three blocks on this street are seven large motion picture houses, the largest concentration of theaters in the city.

About a half mile south of Central Market, and likewise beyond the major shopping district, is another area devoted mainly to banking and the financing and management of cooperatives. In this district there is a variety of cooperative institutions, including several cooperative banks, a land mortgage bank, a grain merchant's cooperative society, a house-building society, and government departments dealing with various cooperative enterprises.

Some two miles northeast of Central Market, in the Cantonment, are two important business areas. One of these, strung along the south side of Mahatma Gandhi Road for a distance of three or four blocks, and including portions of two intersecting streets, specializes mainly in luxury goods and services. Here are offices of airlines, movie theaters, photographers' establishments, expensive jewelry stores, a department store, a large artcraft shop, book stores, radio and automobile sales houses, apparel shops, and pharmacies.

The other area, a few blocks north of Gandhi Road, is adjacent to Russell Market, which is similar to, but smaller than, Central Market. The main shopping avenue in this area is Commercial Street, three blocks long, where almost everything, ranging from luxury items to household necessities, may be purchased. Many of the shops in this district are operated by Muslims, for the district itself is next to the principal Muslim residential section.

Ecological theory based on American studies has emphasized the importance of large-scale organizations, particularly business and industrial chains, in the centralization of functions in the central business district. Large corporate enterprises are commonly "headquartered" in the American central business zone although operations may be widely scattered. Furthermore, the department store has been an important feature of the central business district of the large or medium-sized city in the United States.

Most business in Bangalore is conducted in small shops. The chain-store type of merchandising organization has never developed to any extent, although a few enterprises, such as a small department store, a book store, and several banks, are links in regional chains of fairly small dimensions. Perhaps the nearest approach to the department store carrying products for mass consumption is the municipal market, dealing mainly in fruits, vegetables, flowers, hardware, inexpensive clothing, baskets and the like. But in the market place the stalls are privately managed. The nature of business is therefore not such as to foster the growth of complex bureaucracies so characteristic of the American metropolis. Hence the centralized office building housing an army of bureaucratic functionaries, including clerical staffs to do paper work, is almost nonexistent.

The distribution of banking and insurance in Bangalore differs considerably from the prevailing patterns in large American cities. In this country banking and insurance tend to be rather highly centralized. There is decentralization, to be sure, but outlying banking institutions are commonly branch banks whose parent establishments are in the central business area. This also is the prevailing pattern for insurance, although there seems to be a trend toward decentralization.

In Bangalore, there are four principal clusters of large banks, with a few banking houses located somewhat apart from these clusters. None of these major banks is in the heart of the major business district, although there are numerous small-scale money-lending establishments in the area. One cluster of major banks is about a half mile north of Central Market; another about a mile south of the Market; a third in the Gandhi Road shopping area; and a fourth in the retail district near Russell Market. The Imperial Bank of India, for example, is located two or three blocks south of Gandhi Road, in a spacious setting on the edge of an attractive residential district. Another, a comparatively small bank, British-owned, is located on the second floor of a building opposite the municipal offices, about a mile east of Central Market.

The distribution of hotels likewise represents a departure from the highly centralized pattern characteristic of American cities. There are numerous small hotels in the major business district and near the central railroad station, but the luxury hotels are some distance from concentrations of business or transportation facilities. For these hotels spacious and attractive surroundings appear to be more important considerations than proximity to business activities. No doubt attractiveness of location is important because many hotel residents are permanent or semipermanent guests rather than transients. The West End Hotel, Bangalore's well known hostelry, is located at least a mile and a half from Central Market, and almost as far from the railway station, in a spacious semirural setting. The British apparently liked it this way.

The foregoing observations concerning the ecological patterning of business enterprises point up to two facts relating to intercultural comparisons: First, ecological centralization of business is much more marked in the average American city than in Bangalore. Second, commercial areas of comparable size in an American city tend to be strikingly similar in their institutional characteristics, whereas each of the areas in Bangalore, described here briefly, is more or less specialized and therefore somewhat distinctive. This distinctiveness, born of specialization, is in part the result of Bangalore's political and military history. But the distinctiveness of business areas also reflects the differential buying power and cultural interests of the population. For example, British personnel resided mainly in the Cantonment, and the luxury goods enterprises in this area, especially those on Gandhi Road, were largely maintained by them.

The Ecology of Industry

Although Bangalore is in the emergent stage of large-scale industrialization, much of the industrial output is still from small, independent industries, many of the cottage type. The smaller industries are widely scattered, mainly over the western part of the city, some of them near the railroad yards. As noted earlier, within the major business district, or in its vicinity, considerable manufacturing is carried on as an adjunct to the wholesale and retail establishments in the area. Indeed, manufacturing and selling is sometimes combined under one roof. A number of machine shops, including those with lathes and grinding equipment, have sprung up in the vicinity of Binney Mills, a large British-owned textile factory employing some seven thousand workers and located a short distance west of the principal business district. In this area also are builders and repairers of bullock carts and wheels, transportation vehicles used by wholesale dealers who are located close by. About a mile southeast of Central Market is the bamboo bazaar, and near it a slaughter house and a number of welding, forging, and weaving establishments.

But the larger industries tend to be rather highly decentralized. The extent to which decentralization of manufacturing has occurred depends on the kind and size of the particular industry. Three major textile mills are located near the western periphery of the city; a large tobacco factory is situated on the northeastern edge. Others similarly located with reference to the peripheral settlement area include a porcelain factory, a lamp works, and a brick and tile works, all on the west side. The major exception to this ecological pattern is the government soap factory, located in the central area occupied by public buildings.

Recent industrial developments are even more decentralized in location. Plants manufacturing airplanes and telephones are located five or six miles east of the municipal boundaries, and a factory producing electrical equipment is even farther removed on the west side. Henceforth all large-scale manufacturing will be located in a peripheral zone reserved by the Improvement Trust Board for industrial development.

Ecology of Public Institutions

In American cities most public buildings are usually located in or near the central business zone. Most of the public buildings in Bangalore are some distance from the main centers of commercial activity. The municipal building (city hall), for example, is located on Narasimharaja Square, about a mile east of Central Market. Nearby is Town Hall (city auditorium). The main post office, the telephone and telegraph office, and the central police station are a mile and a half northeast of Central Market. Each of these organizations, of course, has suboffices in other sections of the city. The public library is in the center of Cubbon Park, at least a mile from a business district.

Most of the city's major hospitals, on the other hand, are concentrated in a medical center on the south side of Market Square, within hailing distance of Central Market. This appears to be the reverse of the pattern in American cities, where hospitals tend to be decentralized, or at least distributed rather widely over a metropolitan area. Clinics and dispensaries in Bangalore, however, are rather widely scattered, and there are a few hospitals removed from the major medical center.

The location of public and semipublic institutions definitely indicates the role of municipal planning, especially in the Cantonment. A number of institutions are located within, or at the edge of, spacious Cubbon Park; these include the university, the city YMCA, Occupational Institute, the state government secretariat, and several cultural institutions. A mile or two south of Central Market, beyond the hospital area, is another cluster of cultural, religious, and educational institutions. Farther on, in Basavangudi, is the Indian Institute of Culture, a well known intellectual center. Some institutions are removed from the city: Far to the northwest, beyond the municipal boundaries, is the Indian Institute of Science; to the southeast, also beyond the city, is a large mental hospital. Several agricultural experiment institutions are also located on the fringe.

Whether or not this planning represents the most efficient use of public institutions it is difficult to say. In some instances, such as the case of a public library set in the center of a large park, it apparently does not.

Residential Segregation

Urban ecologists have taken account of the tendency of people to select residential sites in cities on the basis of racial, cultural, religious, or ethnic preferences or prejudices, to choose residential locations that are symbolic of wealth, power, or social prestige, or to gravitate to low-income and low-prestige areas whose costs of occupancy are within the limits of their purchasing power. Ecological literature concerning American cities contains abundant examples of such segregative tendencies.

These tendencies are exhibited in Bangalore, as in western cities, except that caste preference or prejudice forms an additional basis for residential segregation. The importance of any of these factors depends, in the main, upon the values attached to them by particular individuals or families, although low purchasing power may override actual social preference in the selection of a residential location.

Viewing the ecological patterning of Bangalore in perspective, one may discern "natural areas" that are occupied predominantly or exclusively by members of a particular caste or religion and areas in which there is a mixed occupancy of people with different social affiliations and backgrounds. These segregative tendencies probably reflect the strength of communal sentiment, but they may also reflect prejudices against particular groups, especially low-caste or religious groups. By and large, the segregative tendency is probably stronger among the uneducated than among families on the higher income and educational levels where caste or religious interests and loyalties, if they exist, become secondary or even unimportant factors in selection of a residential site.

Data are not available to indicate the residential locations of all Hindu castes, of which there are upwards of a hundred in the city. Even where a number of castes are considered collectively—"depressed" or "scheduled" castes, for example—the broader categories conceal segregative tendencies of particular castes. Residential locations of "depressed" castes in the city therefore do not tell us anything much about the locations of, say, the Adikarnataka, Korama, and Koracha castes. But since the various depressed or untouchable castes have a social position and style of life that are fairly comparable, we are able to secure some idea of their ecological position in the community. . . . It is clear that the depressed castes manifest a tendency toward segregation, with some areas having more than half the residents in this class of castes. No doubt within these larger areas would be smaller areas in which occupancy by particular depressed castes would approach 100 percent.

It is interesting to note . . . that areas of highest occupancy by depressed castes are on or near the city's outskirts. This is the reverse of the situation in the United States, where the major "depressed caste"—Negro —lives mainly in the deteriorated sections of the inner zones of cities. Undoubtedly there is more pronounced segregation of American Negroes than of depressed castes in Bangalore. Only five districts in Bangalore had no low-caste residents, but most of the white residential areas in American cities are occupied exclusively by Caucasians.

Members of the Brahmin caste, at the other extreme of the social hierarchy, show similar segregative tendencies. This is evidenced by the fact that fourteen census districts have less than 1 percent Brahmin residents, whereas in four districts more than half the inhabitants are Brahmins. There is a strong tendency for the Brahmins to concentrate in the western part of the city in the original Bangalore municipality. In general, areas occupied heavily by Brahmins are attractive residential districts, among the most attractive in the city. But not all Brahmins live in fashionable districts, whatever may be their position in the social hierarchy. Some of them, in fact, live in physically deteriorated houses under conditions of congestion.

Of the religious minorities in Bangalore none is perhaps as tightly segregated as the Muslim "community." There are four important Muslim concentrations, most of which represent extreme congestion. Segregation of religious groups, however, involves something more than mere religious differences; it is segregation based on a whole complex of beliefs and behavior patterns that differentiate Muslims, Hindus, Christians, Parsees, and other groups one from the other.

Europeans, Indian Christians, and Anglo-Indians are heavily concentrated in the Cantonment. Europeans by virtue of their comparatively superior incomes tend to live in areas of high-quality houses, or at expensive clubs and hotels. Indian Christians are widely distributed according to their purchasing power, the affluent living in areas having superior housing accommodations.

Anglo-Indians show a marked tendency to develop their own community life and therefore to reside in areas occupied by others of the same racial mixture. Most of them are concentrated in the southeastern portion of the Cantonment in districts locally known as Richmond Town, Langford Town, and Austin Town. As a culturally marginal group which, in the past, chose to be identified with Britain rather than with India, but whose members were often socially unacceptable to both British and Indians, the Anglo-Indians developed a "birds of a feather" consciousness which was manifest in residential segregation. To what extent they actually preferred to live apart it is difficult to say, but since they were *persona non grata* to the British and to many Indians as well, particularly Hindus and Muslims, spatial isolation was a logical outcome of their social isolation.

The Slum

The familiar ecological picture of an American slum is a zone centering around, or adjacent to, the central business district, with perhaps radial extensions of deteriorated areas along transportation routes or waterways, or around manufacturing establishments. Ecological theory has interpreted the American slum as an "area in transition," the result in part of a continuous process of invasion and succession by population, industry, and business. This invasion is most spectacular in expanding cities where competition for favorable locations is intense. The unstable character of the area is reflected in physical deterioration and, commonly, social disorganization. For the most part it is the city's low rent area, and for this reason tends to be the port of entry for impoverished in-migrants.

Bangalore presents no such picture. The central business district around

Central Market has never experienced an areal expansion comparable to the pattern so common in American cities. Consequently there has been no significant ecological invasion by business of adjacent residential districts; hence no "zone of transition." Until the past thirty years or so the population and economy grew slowly. Only in recent years has rapid economic expansion occurred, and it has been mainly industrialization. Although the residential areas surrounding the central business district and the more important secondary business centers are characterized by high density and by various manifestations of social and personal disorganization, they are by no means the areas of poorest housing, nor are they occupied by the lowest income groups.

The most conspicuous slums, at least in the physical sense, are located elsewhere, some of them on or near the periphery of Bangalore. Unoccupied fringe areas are often settled by in-migrants who cannot afford to pay rents charged in the inner zones, even if they could find housing accommodations, which is not always the case. Furthermore, by settling on the periphery they may retain their communal solidarity if there is a considerable migration of persons representing a particular caste. It is therefore easier and cheaper for them to erect mud huts on the fringe than to find rental housing in areas already occupied. There are several such areas, all of them located outside the immediate vicinity of the business districts. Some of these settlements have been surrounded by the expanding city but continue to exist at points intermediate between the outer fringe and the central zones of the city. This pattern of outlying slums appears to resemble more closely the ecological configuration of Latin American cities than of cities in the United States.

Upper-Class and Middle-Class Districts

The residential areas of highest prestige are not on the outskirts, as is usually the case in American cities, but are somewhat centrally located. Probably the most fashionable district in the city is on or near High Ground, a slightly elevated area in the northwest sector, about two miles north of the central business district but well within the city. Just south of High Ground, north of the "big business" district on Kempe Gowda Road, is another high-income residential area, presumably somewhat less fashionable than the High Ground district. Still another, Basavangudi, is about a mile south of Central Market. Many of the homes in these areas are spacious and luxurious. Most of the middle-class residential districts are well within the city limits.

Residential Decentralization

Suburban developments beyond the settled portions of Bangalore simply do not exist. Wealthy or well-to-do families have shown little inclination to shift to fringe areas. No doubt inadequate transportation in the past tended to discourage residential location very far from the center of activities, but even with modern transportation facilities available—automobiles and buses—there is still little evidence that Bangalore residents are interested in suburbia as a way of life. Since residence in certain areas within the city (High Ground, for example) is a symbol of prestige, high status families presumably prefer to be identified with residential localities that support or enhance their own claims to status. Certainly the suburban mode of living does not have the popular appeal it enjoys in the United States.

Nor have workers shown any marked tendency to develop industrial suburbs adjacent to the outlying manufacturing establishments. Even Hindustan Aircraft and the Indian Telephone Industries, located five or six miles beyond the city's boundaries, have not become the nuclei of satellite factory towns. The thousands of workers who are employed in these industries reside in Bangalore and commute by bus, work train, or bicycle. These industries are relatively new, however, and it may be that in time they will act as a magnet for suburban developments of workingmen's homes. At any rate, the absence of any marked pattern of suburbanization gives the city a compactness that is not characteristic of most American metropolises.

This is not to say that fringe residential developments are completely absent. Public housing programs, mainly for working-class or lower-white-collar families, are located on or near the city's edge. Housing construction under private auspices likewise tends to assume this pattern—extensions of the outer edges of metropolitan settlement rather than the development of detached satellite communities. Basavangudi, a new upper-class district on the south side of the city, is a case in point.

Conclusions

The present ecological structure of Bangalore bears the heavy imprint of the city's historical past. That past was characterized by limited industrialization, slow economic growth, divided political authority, and extensive planning, especially in the Cantonment. Today there is an upsurge of industrialism. Bangalore is the industrial boom town of South India. A planned economy is in prospect, both for the city and the nation as a whole. There will undoubtedly be continued population growth, and rapid growth at that.

What effect, if any, will these changes or others have on the basic ecological structure of the city? Will industrialization, along with developments in trade, transportation, and communication, evolve a pattern similar to the western configuration? Will communal segregation (caste and religion) decline in the wake of measures taken to strengthen political and economic democracy? Only a self-assured prophet would attempt to provide specific answers to these questions.

A possible clue to future ecological changes may be found in Latin American cities. Dotson,[2] Caplow,[3] and Hayner[4] observed a tendency for the classical pattern to change under the impact of technology and North American or European value systems. The most industrialized metropolis of Latin America, Mexico City, has exhibited rather striking changes in the direction of ecological configurations similar to those of cities in the United States or western Europe. It is possible, then, that the impact of industrial technology, large-scale economic organization, modern transportation, and western status values will bring about similar changes in the ecological structure of Bangalore.

There is reason to believe that industry will become increasingly decentralized and that industrial districts will eventually emerge. In fact, the Improvement Trust Board has already delineated several fringe districts for new industrial developments, and all of these areas are well beyond the borders of the city. What is not so clear are possible trends in the ecology of business. Fundamental changes in the organization of trade, such as the growth of large-scale chain enterprises, would likely make for greater centralization of controls and hence stimulate the growth of a central business area. But such changes will likely come slowly. For a long time Bangalore will be a city of small shops.

Nor is it clear what the trend will be in patterns of residential segregation. The removal of caste barriers penalizing the untouchables or scheduled castes, together with a general improvement in their economic position, may make it possible for them, as well as other minority groups, to achieve a more favorable ecological location. But the ties of caste, family, and religion are strong, and existing ecological patterns so deeply imbedded in custom, that changes will probably come slowly for most of the groups. Possibly the most effective force making for re-distribution of the various caste, ethnic, or religious groups will be slum clearance and public housing programs in which occupants will be selected on the basis of need rather than social or cultural attributes.

The foregoing observations demonstrate clearly a fundamental problem of ecological theory as well as of sociological theory in general. It is the hazards involved in developing theories of society based upon observed data from a single society or culture area. Generalizations derived from a single culture tend to give American sociology a rather narrow provincialism which seriously limits its usefulness outside our national boundaries.

---

[2] Floyd Dotson and Lillian Ota Dotson, "Ecological Trends in the City of Guadalajara, Mexico," *Social Forces*, 32 (May 1954), pp. 367–74.

[3] Caplow, *op. cit.*

[4] Norman S. Hayner, "Mexico City: Its Growth and Configuration," *American Journal of Sociology*, 50 (January 1945), pp. 295–304.

14 | Peking

HANS KONINGSBERGER

The summers of Peking are as vile as those in New York; and in Peking, too, people tell each other, "It's not the heat, it's the humidity." Indeed, both cities lie at the eastern edge of a continent and both are at about forty degrees northern latitude. Those forty-latitude city summers are so very much worse than the real tropics, of course, because the houses and life in general cannot be adapted to the heat: in Peking as in New York the winters are grey, cold, icy and sleety. But both towns have a marvelous Indian summer with a limitless blue sky and nostalgic, heartbreaking sunsets.

And that is about where the similarities end. No two places could be farther apart in all senses of those words; and no two societies right now seem more different than China and the United States. . . .

Peking is in its seventeenth year as capital of a communistic China and, say, in its one thousand and first year as capital of Imperial China—both called, and both considered, by their inhabitants *Zung Ghuo*, the Central Country, or Middle Kingdom as it used to be translated into English.

. . . . .

Do not visualize Peking as a new Metropolis, a sinister Orwellian capital of seven hundred million souls, nor as an oriental Moscow filled with gingerbread government offices in the style Stalin admired, nor as an enlarged American Chinatown with political slogans instead of advertisements and thin waistlines instead of bulging ones. Some of Peking, its poorest streets, are like Djakarta on Java, at least during the hot months; apart from that, it isn't reminiscent of any other capital. Peking rarely gives the feeling of a big city, although it has seven million people within its boundaries. The wide avenues, the new buildings, and the old gates, temples, and palaces are but a very loose grid, stuffed as it were with dozens of villages. These are Asian villages in that their inhabitants pursue a good deal of their activities in the street or in sight of the street; they dine, have their hair cut, wash their babies, buy and sell, on the sidewalks. They are very un-Asian in being clean, without smells, without beggars, and even without flies.

. . . . .

Peking . . . is very much in flux. Centuries seem to march through it as once did the camel caravans from Mongolia. The Forbidden City, being restored, looks again more or less as Marco Polo found it in Khan-Balik, but schoolchildren with red Pioneer scarves now play hopscotch where Kublai Khan used to play with his Thousand Women. Old men still sing in falsetto voices and do calisthenics at dawn on Coal Hill. Factories belch smoke. Cadres deliver Brave New World lectures to deputees from Sinkiang and Tibet. In an alleyway, an old, old woman in a sarong, her shriveled breasts bare, cooks her supper of rice and vegetables in an iron pot on a charcoal fire. Little boys have card games at tables in front of their houses, or in the evening under a street light right in the middle of the road; men play checkers in the shadow of the old gate towers. The famous city walls are being torn down and have almost gone. A silversmith painstakingly boards up his shop window with numbered planks. Swallows circle through the sky in patterns as if posing for a bamboo paper print. Cicadas sing in the trees and crickets in little reed cages hanging against doorposts. Neon advertisements blink from rooftops. Hungarian- and Chinese-made buses dash through the streets.

And, riding in one of these, just after nightfall, with a threat of rain in the air, standing hemmed in by people going home and too preoccupied to stare much, the lights of shops and lampposts streaking by, and a conductress with a tired smile counting out your change, you may of a sudden feel that Peking is soon going to be a big city like any other, that its strangenesses should be enjoyed while they last, because one day it will be as sophisticated, incoherent, slick and hard as New York.

Walls, typically, used to be the most striking feature of Peking. The town has the contour of two boxes lying against each other, like this:

The square box was called the Tartar Town and the oblong one the Chinese Town. Within the square box was another walled box, the Imperial City, and within that still another one, the Forbidden City. All those walls had the very real function of preventing the populace from going where they pleased; through the centuries, China has been at war with itself. After the Manchus had captured Peking in 1644 and established their dynasty, the Tartar Town became the exclusive residence for them and their Chinese collaborators. But even when the last emperor had been overthrown in 1911, the Forbidden City remained forbidden; and by that time the Western nations had added another out-of-bounds spot, Legation Quarter, which almost stopped up the gap left between the southern wall of the Imperial City and the northern wall of the Chinese Town. Part of that wall looked down upon Legation Quarter, and here Western troops patrolled and Western ladies and gentlemen strolled evenings and Sundays after church. Unlike Shanghai Park, the promenade was open to dogs, but like that park, closed to Chinamen.

Until 1949, the gates in the outer city wall were closed at eight in the evening in summer, and in winter at twilight; Peking was the last big town in the world to fit its days in such a medieval frame. It had reason to do so, for life was as insecure as in the worst time of the empire. By then Peking (the name means "Northern Capital") had been rechristened by Chiang Kai-shek into Peiping which is "Northern Peace," and the capital had been moved to Nanking. In 1949, when the Communist government took the town, they made it the capital once more and gave it back its name Peking. . . .

The beautiful gate towers of Peking have been left standing, with their double and triple roofs curving upward at the points—exactly as once the tents of the Golden Horde did. A few stretches of wall are left, too; the city has spread beyond them in housing developments, factories, schools, and student dormitories. Chinese archaeologists regret it; one predicted that in one or two generations everyone will mourn those vanished walls, including party officials who, in his words, "could not in time overcome their prejudices." But the same has happened from Paris to Samarkand; it is not difficult to see how the tearing down of medieval walls ("feudal walls," they would say in China) must provide post-revolution city planners with an almost sensual pleasure. The Forbidden City is now the Palace Museum, and Legation Quarter, probably the sorest spot of all to local sensitivities, is just some city blocks like any others. Its main street is still called "Legation Street" by the few Westerners in Peking, and a letter with that address will reach is destination. It is pretty and shady, and it again houses a number of diplomatic posts: the Rumanians, the Indians, the Burmese, and the East Germans . . . . The only original Western mission left in the street is that of the Dutch, who have a cluster of charming houses, in old Dutch East Indies fashion, around a lawn with shade trees and even a swimming pool, the one diplomatic pool in town and thus a social center of gravity. . . . The Dutch are on notice to pack up, as though the Chinese government feels nervous as long as any of the masters from the old days remains in his traditional spot. They may have to move—like the English and the French before them—to one of the new buildings put up for foreigners far from the center of town, air-conditioned, shadeless horrors in New Jersey neo-suburban style. The one-time American embassy, next to the Dutch, is now used as a guest house for foreign V.I.P.'s—it usually stands empty, with a lonely gardener squatting amidst the well-kept lawns, smoking or feeding his chickens. . . .

. . . . . .

In the simple symmetry of Peking's avenues, Tien An Men Square forms the focal point. Here indeed is monumentality suiting a capital. *Men* means gate, and Tien An Men is the Gate of Heavenly Peace. It closes off the north side of the square named after it, and makes the background to all those photographs of May Day parades and October 1 celebrations; it has the hierarchical and hieratic role filled by Lenin's tomb against the Kremlin wall in Moscow, and here one may expect that Mao Tse-tung will be buried one day. Tien An Men dates back to the Ming emperors of the late Middle Ages and its red brick walls have a marvelous patina; on each side, somewhat jarring wooden boards with inscriptions read: "Long Live the Chinese People's Republic!" and "Long Live the Unity of the Peoples of the World!" (The Western exclamation mark has been incorporated in the list of Chinese characters.) Tours of the Imperial City begin at Tien An Men. . . .

The east and west sides of the square are taken up by two new buildings, the Museum of Chinese History and the Great Hall of the People—both, as visitors are told repeatedly, put up in only ten months. They look alike, and have long, low façades with columns and pseudo-pillars in light stone—the kind of architecture American congressmen like too. Looking south, Tien An Men faces the great axial road through Chien Men, once the gate of the Tartar Town. There is a little park here with benches which serves on summer evenings as a lovers' lane. Chien Men is one of the classical Peking beauty spots and as such has to be savored at a specific time: when the full moon stands directly above the gate. The Marco Polo Bridge, to name another one, must be seen under a waning moon, and the imperial stone informing the traveler so still stands. Topping the axial road through Chien Men is Changan Avenue, a boulevard which has eight or ten car lanes and seems even wider than it is because of an absence of cars to fill all those lanes. There is very little motor traffic in Chinese towns; the vastness of Tien An Men Square and its boulevards is softened only by clusters of pedestrians almost lost within that stone desert. Its unrelieved emptiness actually makes it one of the depressing sights in Peking, which of course does not stop proud officials from bringing visitors here rather than to the bustle of other districts. Only on a summer's night does the square achieve a new mood, when hundreds of families come to it for their fresh air, and, sitting or lying in Chinese fashion on straw mats wherever they want to, mitigate the harshness of the lack of human scale in this project. Changan Avenue (The name means "Perpetual Peace") has a street-light system of Parisian brightness; the difference is that to save electricity it is used only at certain hours and on certain occasions—for instance when a foreign statesman is guest at a banquet in the Great Hall of the People. It is soothing to walk in the square once all those big lights have been extinguished; there is a vague glimmer left then of lamps here and there, and maybe of the moon, points of light from cigarets, soft voices of people, and, rarely, the sound of a truck. Peking becomes very still at night.

Tien An Men was the gate through which the emperor left the Imperial City for the yearly sacrifices to Heaven and Earth which alone preserved the harmony of man and nature, and from here all his edicts were issued. A visitor needs to wrap himself in such historical and literary reminiscences to be properly impressed by the Imperial City which has in common with some other famous sights of the world that by itself—if one dares admit it —it is rather disappointing. It must have presented an overwhelming spectacle in the days when it was filled with the thousands of officials, servants, concubines, and soldiers of the Imperial household. Now, empty but for the Eternal Tourists—here, too, with cameras—it does not come to life any more, and its ever-repeated architectural pattern becomes, sacrilegious as it may sound, just boring.

Temples and palaces as remembrances from a dead past, the monumental thoroughfares and the teeming narrow side streets, the throngs of pedestrians in all kinds of getups and speaking a dozen dialects (many newly in from the countryside), the scarcity of wheeled traffic, all give Peking a touch of Europe—of an Italian town, perhaps, in the sixteenth century. Fitting within that era is the role foreigners play: there are many emissaries from faraway countries, but little contact, no mass travel across the frontiers. Especially in this respect, Peking must look once more as it did three hundred years ago. . . .

15 | Ecological Patterns of European Cities

FRANCIS L. HAUSER

Theories which try to explain the physical order of urban societies—i.e., the way in which the use of land is organized into patterns—admit of exceptions. In this paper a few European cities are used to demonstrate deviations from the concentric-ring and sector theories. The sample consists of London, Paris, Vienna, and Stockholm.

London

In size and importance London is the only rival of New York. There are actually three Londons. Greater London is the sociological entity. It embraces a territory which in 1938 had a population of 8,655,000. The political entity called London is somewhat smaller; its official name is the Administrative County of London. It is a federal system of originally independent

SOURCE: T. Lynn Smith and C. A. McMahan (eds.), *The Sociology of Urban Life: A Textbook with Readings* (New York: Dryden Press, 1951), pp. 370–388. Reprinted with the permission of the publisher, the author, and the editors.

cities, called boroughs. In 1938 London's population was 4,028,000. London surrounds the City of London, the ancient city core from which the metropolis grew. The City today makes up one half of what may be called the central office district. Its residential population is, as in the case of Chicago's Loop district and New York's Wall Street district, negligible. In 1938 it had less than 10,000 inhabitants. The City of London, however, contains the sites of work of a considerable fraction of the gainfully employed of London and Greater London.

London is bisected by the river Thames, the main topographic factor which helped create the city. The City of London existed in Roman times; it grew around a ford over the river near London Bridge. The ford was the focus from which a series of roads radiated into the countryside. Neither the Roman camp nor the medieval city which succeeded it have been of lasting influence upon the ecology of London. The metropolitan greatness of today is the result of economic and social developments which began in the middle of the seventeenth century, in the mercantile era. During this period the old city was destroyed by fire, and it was rebuilt in the spirit and technology of the time. Between 1650 and 1800 London expanded toward the west, southwest, northwest, and east. A governmental office center, Westminster, sprang up to the west of the old commercial city, around the royal palace and the houses of Parliament. Four residential districts, housing the new wealthy middle class, political officeholders, and the nobility, developed between 1650 and 1814; they were Bloomsbury and the Marylebone section near Regent Park, both in the northwest, and Belgravia and Mayfair, adjacent to Westminster and extending to the west and southwest. Until 1939 three of these, Mayfair, Belgravia, and the Regent Park section, remained the most exclusive residential areas. The fourth, Bloomsbury, became the university district of London during the interwar period of 1918–1938. Today it is a middle-class residential area with some buildings that are used by non-profit organizations, some hotels, and some boardinghouses accommodating students.

The old residential districts constituted a core about which new middle-class residential sections developed. To a certain extent the old elite districts expanded into the new middle-class districts, but on the whole the most fashionable areas remained within the same geographical boundaries.

Homer Hoyt, in the study in which he developed the sector theory,[1] found that the most fashionable residential areas in American cities have a tendency to shift from central locations toward the periphery. Homer Hoyt's sample consists of cities which grew rapidly during the period 1900–1936 in terms both of area and of population, but London's growth during the same period was also one of dynamic intensity. The stability of the fashionable areas therefore cannot be explained by stagnation.

---

[1] *The Structure and Growth of Residential Neighborhoods in American Cities,* Washington: Federal Housing Administration, 1939.

Many of the old eighteenth-century houses are still in use; others have given way to newer ones. Originally, large single-family mansions prevailed in all four residential areas. In Mayfair, and to a smaller extent in the other areas, modern apartment houses had all but replaced single-family houses by 1938. The intrusion of apartments did not, however, mean a decline in the social desirability of the traditionally fashionable neighborhoods, nor did it bring an influx of groups that were economically less powerful.

In other aspects the locational pattern of London's upper-class residential areas seems to support the sector theory. Such districts radiate from given points or sections of the business districts. The western part of the government section (Westminster) and the northwestern corner of the financial center are areas from which the residential sections grew. Another support of the sector theory is found in the relationship between rapid avenues of transportation and the site of high-rent residential areas. All the traditionally exclusive sections and most of the middle-income areas in their vicinity developed either along or in proximity to arteries of main traffic.

According to the sector theory, retail establishments, such as department stores and specialty stores, tend to concentrate in a street or district of their own which is located between the central business district and the residential section, and retail areas develop along rapid lines of traffic as do residential districts. London's retail establishments do not conform. They develop in small areas, usually public squares, along main traffic arteries and come to form narrow ribbons along main roads. The more expensive and the largest department stores, as well as the most luxurious specialty shops, form bands which partly envelop one of the old fashionable areas (Mayfair) and extend along some of the main avenues which serve as boundaries for Belgravia and the newer upper-middle-class district, South Kensington.

Whereas London's land-use pattern seems to deviate only in certain respects from patterns asserted as typical by the sector theory, the land-use pattern of the concentric-circle theory is wholly inapplicable. This becomes clear when we consider the location of low-rent residential areas and of industrial sections.

According to the concentric-ring theory, light industry and the slums intermingle. Lofts and overcrowded tenements form a zone about the wholesale district, which in turn surrounds the retail section. The latter is presented as a ring around the central office district. In London the tenement districts for low-income groups, often constituting slums, are intermingled with light- as well as heavy-industry areas. They also enclose bands of retail establishments as substantial as the ones in the fashionable sections. On a map this combination of industrial, retail, and low-rent residential areas looks like a huge pair of pincers closing in on the better residential portions of London. The only generalization which can be made, and that one must be made with qualifications, is that the residential quarters of low-income groups extend in an easterly direction and the middle- and high-income groups tend to live in neighborhoods extending to the west.

The locations of industrial and low-rent residential areas extend eastward to the periphery of Greater London. Light and heavy industry, as well as low-rent residential areas, actually surround what is called the West End. Middle-income residential sections have developed south of the Thames near the periphery and in the outlying sections of London and Greater London to the north and west. None of these, however, has replaced the upper- and middle-class areas of the West End.

What factors operated to create the puzzle pattern of the West End and the East End?

1. The historical stages of economic and technological developments provide some of the answers.

2. London as a whole is not a planned city, like Washington, D.C., but the old residential areas of Bloomsbury, Mayfair, Belgravia, and the Regent Park section are the products of city planning.

3. The combination of political and economic functions, both of which are concentrated in the adjoining central-core sections of Westminster and the City, may have contributed much to the geographical stability of the West End.

London's path to metropolitan greatness parallels roughly the economic development of England from a country at the edge of Europe, rich in agricultural products which it exported to the more prosperous Lowlands, to France, and to Germany, into a center of overseas trade and then into an industrial workshop and investment center manufacturing and exporting a great many industrial products.

Roughly, three great periods of development can be distinguished, all affecting London's land-use pattern. The first extends from 1650 to 1800 and may be called the mercantilist stage; the second, from 1800 to 1890, spans the period of the English industrial revolution and the time when England was the predominant industrial producer of the world; and the third, from 1890 to the present, was a period of adjustment to changes in technology and to shifts in political power at home and abroad.

The mercantilist period increased the number of wealthy families which could make London their home. It was a time when public power was increasing in terms of manpower and economic strength. London attracted a larger number of government employees, political leaders, and professional men. To this number were added successful adventurers and rich refugees from the then war-ravaged continent of Europe. The former could make fortunes in colonial enterprise; the latter brought money, machinery, and skills to England from Germany and the Low Countries and helped to develop Britain's mining resources—alum, tin, ore and coal. In order to succeed, the adventurer and the foreign capitalist had to obtain monopolistic privileges from the government. Consequently they had to work hand in glove with political leaders. Residence near the seat of power (Westminster) was one of the prerequisites of success.

The defeat of the Stuarts did away with regulations which prevented the large-scale enclosure of rural lands. The disintegration of the old institutional pattern of agricultural production coincided with the development of scientific methods of farming and with a growing specialization in sheep breeding for the purpose of wool production. The enclosure movement also created a large underemployed labor force in the countryside. The increase in the production of wool, combined with the importation of machinery, skills, and capital from abroad, provided a basis for processing wool instead of exporting it in its raw stage. The unemployed and underemployed agricultural laborers were set to work in a system generally known as cottage industry. This system, a rather exploitative one with respect to labor, created a group of wealthy middlemen who were the organizers of production, dealers in the finished product, and financiers. These groups formed the bulk of what became the middle classes. They were numerous enough during the latter half of the eighteenth century to constitute an element of wealth and power worthy of the attention of the traditional ruling classes—the large landowners.

In London the wool manufacturers, the trader-adventurers in overseas goods, the bankers, the growing number of professional men, and the politicians constituted a group which could afford to pay high rentals for housing. The Crown and some of the old aristocratic families owned large tracts of land in Westminster, Bloomsbury, Belgravia, and what later became the Regent Park section. These tracts of land were originally used for rural purposes. Crown and feudal landowners decided during the mercantilist period to retain ownership but to rent the tracts to large-scale builders who would improve them with single-family homes. The developers, who thus transformed rural land into urban land, would hold long-term leases extending over hundreds of years. They were entitled to sublease the houses they would build to prospective occupants, and such leases would also extend over long periods.

The success of such improvements in the four old fashionable areas was due to a series of factors. One of the most potent was that speculative builders, as well as the architects they employed, had an extremely clear perception of the cultural needs and ambitions of the group who were to be their customers. They provided an adaptation to urban usage of the country house, which was and has remained the ideal of the English upper and middle classes. Houses were built around open squares of various sizes. Individual structures contained enough room to serve the needs of large families with many servants. Stables for carriage horses were built in the rear. Materials were traditional and the design quiet and unobtrusive. The rising middle class put a premium on all these features.

Another factor which made for the lasting success of these developments was the policy of landowners. Belgravia, Mayfair, and the Regent Park section of Marylebone are adjacent to huge public parks. The Crown, which owned large tracts of land in these sections, deliberately refrained from leasing these to developers because the proximity of public parks would operate to enhance and later to stabilize land values. In one instance (Regent Park) the park was created with a view to ensuring the success of the contemplated residential development.

A third factor was the large-scale character of the improvement. The earliest transformations of rural land to urban use were relatively modest in scale. They involved land on Westminster's boundaries and consisted of isolated squares enclosing a tree-studded area. These squares, among them Soho Square and Leicester Square, have lost their exclusive residential character. Soho Square is now within the restaurant and quaint-shop section which is wedged in between Mayfair and the business district. Leicester Square is the movie center in a narrow entertainment area between the office district, Mayfair, and Belgravia.

The more comprehensive developments of the later years of the mercantilist era indicate a deliberate attempt to plan the location of residential sections in connection with the location of shopping centers and with main roads leading into the office district. Thus the architect who designed the plan for Regent Park and for the residential development in its vicinity also planned the layout and house designs on two main roads connecting the district with Westminster. One of these, Regent Street, was planned as a shopping section—or, rather, a shopping band. Today it is one of the main department-store and specialty-shop areas of London.

The development of the West End and of the office districts, Westminster and the City, had by 1850 reached a stage of development which had utilized almost all the land. A pattern had been created which did not allow for much change unless one of the two major functions of London, trade and government, were to decline. In the City practically all land had been taken for financial and wholesale establishments; and in Westminster the best land had been allocated to government buildings, offices, clubs, and exclusive retail stores. However, the middle classes increased in numbers, and there was a need for expansion. This took place in the traditional directions, west, southwest, and northwest. The West End, however, never extended to the western, southwestern, or northwestern boundary lines of London. The main reason for the stop in territorial expansion is tied up with the coming of the railroads and canal building. The railroad terminals are located at the rim of the West End in such a way that a line connecting the terminals would practically coincide with the boundaries of the West End. The roads were surface lines and they depended upon coal. Consequently, the vicinity of the tracts was undesirable for high-rent housing. On the other hand, the railroads attracted industrial establishments, which formed clusters to the rear of the terminals. The canal which connects the peripheral north and northwest with the Thames exercised a similar attraction for industrial establishments. Because of the location of industry and railroads, the areas were closed to housing for the upper and middle classes, but they did have an attraction for low-income housing similar to that of the parks and broad avenues in the West End for housing for the elite and near elite.

The Thames River has also been a factor in determining the ecological structure of London. The city's economic bases have been and continue to be trade, transportation, and finance. London is an entrepôt city. When England entered the second stage of capitalism (industrialization through the use of coal, iron ore, and railroad transportation), its heavy industrial establishments were built near mineral and coal deposits. English cities such as Birmingham and Manchester came closer, therefore, in their ecological pattern to American cities such as Pittsburgh and Chicago than to London, already set in its ways. However, the particular formation of the British coastline made London the number one collecting point and shipping center for all of Great Britain's industrial products and the point of entry for a major part of the imported raw materials. Consequently, land along the Thames River was more and more in demand for docks, warehouses, railroad sidings, and industrial establishments which process goods on sites located where a break in transportation occurs. The banks of the river were in demand as far as seagoing vessels could navigate. With the growth of Britain's industrial potential, less and less space was available on the banks because demand increased apace. The banks of the river therefore developed a "hinterland" of warehouses and light industrial establishments intermingled with houses for the labor force of the dock and warehouse area.

The expansion of the dock and working-class sections to the west was checked by the navigability of the river. On the other hand, industrial establishments which could use barges for transportation found it theoretically desirable to move on upstream. On the south bank of the Thames they actually did this; on the north bank expansion was checked because the central office district—the City—blocked the way.

By 1870 the ecological pattern of the East End was set. The pincerlike shape of this other half of London needs just a few additional words of explanation. The wants and needs of the working class were met by the development of retail districts in ribbonlike bands along main avenues of traffic similar to developments in the West End. In one instance the needs of the East End population created a district that combined retail establishments, light industry, and residences and received unity only from the ethnic character of the inhabitants. Whitechapel, adjacent to the City in downstream direction, is populated largely by the descendants of Jewish immigrants from eastern Europe. The more successful families have been moving away from the district to medium-income areas which are partly within the old West End, partly in a newer area to the north of the most westerly tip of the East End pincers, but enough have had to remain to permit the district to retain its character.

The working-class population of the East End was housed in structures which were built during the period of industrialization. Landownership was on a large scale, as in the West End. However, restraints and precautions to keep density low and the quality of structures high were absent. The municipal government of London in its 1945 analysis of the city calls attention to the absence of large public parks in the East End. Houses were built on smaller lots. The layout was in rows facing narrow streets rather than in polygons and rectangles facing squares of greenery. On the whole, single-family houses prevailed over tenements. London's working-class districts have been called horizontal slums.

Since the turn of the century the national government as well as the London County Council—the government of the Administrative County of London—have been engaged in slum clearance and city-planning schemes on an ever increasing scale. If the present plan is executed, the slums of the East End will give way to houses adjusted to the needs and habits of the English worker. The drab muddle of homes and workshops will give way to segregation of industrial and residential uses. A series of new public parks will bring to the East End some of the health standards which contributed so much to the geographic indestructibility of the old West End sections. London of the past has presented to students of urban societies a twofold lesson: how to build for residential stability and how to create slums and to flee them by migrating to the periphery.

The success of London's stable elite and middle-class areas consisted largely in the ability of landowners and developers to analyze the cultural needs and tastes of future occupants. On the other hand, housing for the working classes, prior to the current reform movement, showed a complete lack of this skill on the part of developers and builders. Working-class houses were replicas of middle-class houses, minus the amenities, the quality of structure, the public parks and private gardens, the lack of noise and smoke, and the provisions for privacy which are characteristic of the West End.

In closing, the interwar development of London's ecology should be mentioned. Partly through the aggregate demand for goods and services represented by a huge metropolis and partly through a shift toward protective tariffs in 1931, light industries began to migrate to London on a larger scale than ever before. On the other hand, industries already there underwent technological changes of production which required more space than had been used or could be acquired in the traditional neighborhoods. These developments resulted in a migration of industrial establishments to sites along the main highways and railroads in the area of Greater London and beyond into the countryside. Residential builders followed up with housing projects for industrial workers. The narrow bandlike developments have been christened "ribbon developments" by English city planners. Public policy takes a pessimistic view of the ribbon developments. Housing quality is considered low; good agricultural land was lost by taking the sites for housing and industrial production. Consequently, national as well as municipal governments within the metropolitan areas are now discouraging this recent change in the ecological pattern of the three Londons.

Paris

On a map Paris looks almost elliptic. Like London it consists of a larger sociological and a smaller municipal entity. The former had almost three million inhabitants before World War II, the latter more than one million. The sociological entity is roughly conterminous with the Préfecture de la Seine, a political subdivision in a way comparable to a county. In population Paris thus seems to correspond to Chicago and Cook County.

Paris, too, is bisected by a river. However, the economic significance of the Thames for London is not matched by the Seine. Paris owes its economic basis primarily to public policy. It is in this sense much more a planned city than London.

Among the institutional factors which had an enduring effect upon the land-use pattern of Paris was the military organization of France. Paris was a fortress, the key point in a system of strongholds which covered the entire north of France. It was a natural stronghold in Roman and in early medieval days. Then the city was built on an island in the Seine. It remained a fortress until after the First World War. In the interim old fortification rings gave way to new ones embracing more and more territory as the city grew. However, the walled fortifications affected the city's ecological structure by producing a limitation of space within its confines which left indelible marks upon the city plan. During the eighteenth century Paris grew in population as well as in economic significance. This was largely the result of a policy of deliberate promotion of craft- and artisan-based production by the government. Through governmental planning Paris received a virtual monopoly in the production of commodities. Establishment of independent business was facilitated there while it was impeded by laws and guild restrictions in other cities. Paris, consequently, attracted migrants. Its territory hemmed in by the military zone, the city became overcrowded and began to expand by spilling out into adjoining communities.

A hundred years before the Revolution, which put an end to this type of economic planning, the absolute monarchy had divided all of France into zones. These resembled concentric rings, with Paris and a surrounding area several miles deep constituting the inner core of the system. The purpose of zoning was to allocate nonagricultural production to the various zones, generally by following the principle that in outlying zones such production should be curtailed and that the more central the zone the more it would be permitted to increase the quantity and variety of its production. Since Paris and a number of neighboring communities were in the innermost circle, enterprising Parisians could avail themselves of a large labor force but did not necessarily have to carry on production within the city limits. Certain stages of production could be farmed out to suburban communities. The result was a twofold growth of population, within the city and in the suburbs. The suburbs became the homes of lower-income groups, the small masters who depended for work upon the orders of a Paris entrepreneur. The journeymen, who would have to remain in this status, settled predominantly in suburban communities.

On the other hand, Paris proper attracted more and more residents before the Revolution. The rise of France to continental predominance, which took place as a result of the imperialist policy of the absolute monarchy, attracted people—including many foreigners—who were similar in composition to the groups which settled in London during the corresponding era of mercantilism.

The industrial revolution came to France about fifty years later than to England. When it set in, there was already a pattern in existence which would, in the absence of countermeasures, determine the sites of industrial establishments and of the districts housing the working class. These sites would be concentrated either in independent suburban communities or in former suburbs which had become peripheral parts of the city as the fortifications were extended. These, however, were not the only potential slum areas. Paris and the metropolitan area around it contain heavy as well as light industries. The latter, especially the women's-wear industry and the many luxury lines affiliated with it, retained much of the craftlike character of preindustrial times and could therefore be located in crowded old buildings. Industrial activities could be carried on in the central districts and the working class could, to some extent, be housed there.

Paris, too, has its East End and West End, but this segregation of residential sections came about by a deliberate attempt to use some of the experience of London by adjusting English methods to the culture of France. This deliberate attempt was made during the dictatorial regime of Napoleon III in the eighteen sixties. The attempt was made by the prefect of the Départment de la Seine (the Greater Paris unit), Baron Haussmann. Haussmann determined the boundaries of the West End as they are today, or rather he gave direction to the expansion of Parisian high-rent residential quarters and expensive retail districts.

To understand the effect of Haussmann's policies and plans one should review the previous stages of urban growth which constituted the base from which he proceeded. The oldest part of the city is an island in the Seine called La Cité. It still contains some very good residential sections and it is also to some extent an administrative center. Paris grew in two directions. To the north medieval guildsmen built their houses, which were combinations of workshop and home; and to the south the University of Paris, one of the four oldest in Europe, had its site. Around the university grew a community with the peculiar population of the ancient Continental university town. It consisted largely of unmarried males and prostitutes. The students came from all parts of Europe. This partly alien population was, by the nature of things, transient. It attracted a group of people whose business it would be to keep house for the students and to feed them. All these elements created the atmosphere and peculiar mixture of rooming houses, inns, and pawnshops which are typical of what, after a term first coined in Paris, is called a Latin Quarter. Because the population of the Latin Quarter consisted largely of unmarried persons, the population growth in the sector to the south of the Cité was relatively small and slow. The contrary was true of the northern sector, inhabited by families of craftsmen and merchants, their servants, and their employees.

The northern sector became more and more congested, because the growing population there had its expansion blocked by the fortifications and by the government's increasing use of the land within the fortified ring. Residential palaces of the Crown and administrative buildings began to form a government section similar to that of London. At the time of Napoleon I it covered more acreage than the old Cité. The government center extended downstream along the banks of the Seine. Napoleon I, during the first years of the nineteenth century, promoted the establishment of a residential section for the elite. It consisted of a street (the rue Rivoli) along the northerly part of the Seine embankment.

The rue Rivoli contained certain characteristic features which influenced Haussmann and affected the later development of the city. The section was a combination residential and retail center. The buildings were apartment houses with expensive shops on the first floor. Structures were built flush with the street, and arcades served as sidewalks and protected shoppers against the rain.

The apartment-house organization of living and the arcade were adaptations of building techniques of medieval cities to more modern needs. The arcade is a feature of many European cities which have retained the medieval structures of their past. The apartment house is in essence the product of the lack of space produced by walled fortifications, a customary feature of medieval urban societies, and the habit that guild masters had of maintaining their homes and workshops in the same building. In Paris, as well as in some other cities, the number of stories in the houses gradually increased and the ground floors no longer were necessarily used as a combination of workshop and salesroom by the people who lived in the upper stories. Finally, even ownership of structures was so divided that one could own physical parts of a building and buy and sell these independently of other part owners. Usually the independently transferable unit within such a structure was a floor. In Paris and most other cities of the Continent, ownership of floors gave way to lease arrangements. Since it was legally possible, however, for several stories of a house to be under separate ownership, this device was occasionally used in Paris as recently as 1920–1930.

Fifty years after the construction of the rue Rivoli, Haussmann found a pattern of housing and shopping which had become the customary expression of French middle-class culture. He also had a geographic nucleus with which to work if he desired to create middle- and upper-income districts on a larger scale. On the other hand, he was faced with a number of problems. These were in part created by technological and cultural changes, in part the result of resentment against the politics of the dictatorial regime of Napoleon III.

Industrialization came to France about 1840, at a time when the steamboat and the railroad were coming into economic play. French finance used railroad transportation quite consciously as a prime mover in the industrialization process. The pattern of railroad lines would—this much was clear to all concerned—decide the future of cities. The large banking firms of these days, the Rothschilds and the Pereires, worked in intimate contact with Napoleon III. Both Napoleons had reinstituted the pre-Revolutionary policy of promoting the centralization of production and government, which favored the growth of Paris and, with a few exceptions in the extreme south of the country, restricted the growth of all the other cities of France. The economic aspect of Haussmann's task, therefore, was to adjust the ecological structure of Paris to the technological requirements of a new era.

Between 1789 and 1848 France had gone through three full-fledged revolutions and an equal number of successful coups d'état. All these upheavals had begun in Paris, and in all cases the outcomes had been decided in Paris. There was widespread resentment against Napoleon III among the middle classes, especially among professional groups and intellectuals.

The French industrial revolution had to reckon with a working class which was poorly organized but far less docile and helpless than its English counterpart had been during the corresponding stages of English industrialization. Violent overthrow of governments had occurred through revolts in Paris in which the working class provided the bulk of revolutionary manpower, while the dissatisfied groups of the middle class provided the leadership. The narrow, winding streets of the city had proved of advantage to the revolutionaries and their technique of street fighting was well adapted to the intricacies of the city they knew so well. For reasons of reliability, government forces—both the regular army and the police—were recruited from rural areas, and they did not know Paris well. But the greatest handicap of the government was that it could not successfully employ artillery and infantry rifles against the rebels. Such military armament required clear vistas and broad expanses of level terrain. Paris was not built that way.

Haussmann solved the economic as well as the political problem by dividing Paris into a West End and an East End. He was quite conscious that this meant one city for the rich and powerful, another for the poor. For the new, modern Paris that he set out to create, he borrowed the device of parks from the West End of London. In this case, however, he displayed consideration for the well-being of the working class, as the modern dictatorial regimes of the Mussolinis and the Peróns have done. Haussmann solved the problem of riots and the problem of traffic jointly by cutting a series of long, broad streets through the city with utter disregard for the old street pattern. By means of the government's power to grant or withhold licenses for railroad construction and operation, he determined the sites of terminals and the location of tracts within the limits of Paris and of the Préfecture de la Seine. Finally, his street-widening plans were combined with a scheme of surrounding public buildings by open spaces or street areas to such an extent that attackers would be detected when they were still at a considerable distance from their targets and could be kept at bay with the help of the weapons of the regular army or police.

Haussmann's park system consisted mainly of two peripheral areas, one in the west and another in the east. The western one had previously been connected with the government center by a broad avenue which cut across open fields to reach the square which today is the famous Étoile, with the Arch of Triumph in its center. Haussmann developed a whole series of broad, straight avenues radiating from the Etoile through open country until they reached either the built-up areas of the city or the belt of fortifications. The purpose of this street plan connecting the most desirable residential parts of Paris with the peripheral park area to the west was to provide space for future expansion of the residential districts for the ruling classes. Haussmann did substantially the same for the working-class district of the east. Here broad avenues were cut through congested ancient quarters and, radiating from a square near the peripheral eastern park area, another set of avenues was built which connected with built-up sections to the west or directed expansion toward the southeastern part of the periphery.

Haussmann's street planning bears some resemblance to the sector theory. The latter's assertion is that high-rent residential areas start at a given point of origin, the exclusive retail district, the office district, or the old traditional residential district, and expand in fan shape along main traffic arteries which lead toward the periphery. Over the years the fashionable residential districts of Paris actually took shapes which are in rough conformity with the sector theory. Although this development may not be credited to Haussmann in its entirety, he had a decisive influence in its initiation. He foresaw a need for expansion. He decided that this expansion should begin at the western edge of the government district because this area would be the cultural center of the groups living in the West End and because the western boundaries of the district were close to vacant land extending to the periphery and beyond. By laying out the avenues which radiated from the Etoile, Haussmann linked the sector emanating from the government center with an already existing residential section to the north of it. He tried to cut both areas off from the East End residential quarter by building one broad street, running from north to south, which started at the eastern railroad terminal and actually divided the city into halves. Previously, for political reasons, he had extended the rue Rivoli to the east in such a way that Paris had been all but divided into a north and south portion. The resulting northwesterly quadrant was intended as a West End. Actually the city did grow in the direction which Haussmann tried to impose upon it. The middle portion of the north-south axis became the retail, business, hotel, and amusement district. During the twentieth century the more expensive retail stores began to push outward and formed another bandshaped retail district along the Champs-Élysées, one of the avenues leading from the Étoile to the government section.

Haussmann could not have accomplished the goals of his social engineering, the division between West and East End, by street building alone. What additional methods did he use? The answer is that he employed the government's power to regulate industrial pursuits. On one hand, Haussmann compelled entrepreneurs engaged in meat packing and the large-scale processing and marketing of foodstuffs to centralize their activities, to use public slaughterhouses and markets. On the other hand, Haussmann selected the sites for such functions. Those that would involve noise, smoke, and obnoxious smells were all relegated to the East End.

The unimpeded expansion of the West End was due largely to the location of railroad terminals. None of these was permitted to penetrate the northwestern quadrant of the city, whereas terminals were located in the other three segments. This gave an incentive to industries to locate plants along the tracks in the East End.

To a considerable degree Haussmann accepted already existing trends and concentrated upon controlling them. One should overestimate neither his rather undemocratic way of promoting a classbound urban society nor his often-displayed consideration for the welfare of all classes. To understand the shortcomings of Haussmann's pattern-setting endeavors, one has to look once more to the character of the economic controls which the regime employed. The street-building program was executed by using the government's power of eminent domain. This meant that government—in some instances that of the city, in others that of the nation—paid for the land and improvements taken from private owners. Under French law more land than was actually needed for public improvements could be so acquired. Hausmann used this power to obtain for the government the lots fronting the new avenues and squares, and he then sold them to private real-estate developers. As a condition of sale he imposed upon the purchaser obligations and restrictions which would make the buildings uniform in architectural style, in height, and in character. (Most of the residential buildings were to be apartment houses.) This control over new structures did not extend, however, to the internal arrangement of rooms, the access to light and air, sanitary facilities, or the number of people who could inhabit dwelling units of a given size. In brief, housing was not within the scope of Haussmann's planning.

Haussmann's work provided more light and air, as well as a change from old to new construction, along the broad traffic arteries which he created. Houses and streets back of these were not affected. Old slums therefore remained, and new ones could spring up as a result of overcrowding along new roads. This helps to explain the character and location of the slum areas in

Paris. They are of three kinds. The largest are in the outer districts of the East End and on its periphery. Smaller ones are found in or near the center, at a distance from main traffic arteries; often they consist of very old houses. French housing reformers have called these "islands of ill health," because they coincide roughly with areas in which the ratio of tuberculosis tends to be the highest. Most of these are to the east of the north-south axis which Haussmann created. The third group cannot be delimited by area at all. It is the result of the allotment of space within the older apartment houses. In Haussmann's time and after 1870, rows of apartment houses were built along the broad boulevards or avenues which he had cut through the built-up portions of Paris. Within each of these, some apartments, especially those between the ground and top floors, were spacious and well appointed. Attics and top floors, the rear parts of the structures, street levels, and basements were, however, often divided into very small rooms, devoid of light and deficient in ventilation. At first these were used as servants' quarters by the wealthy occupants of the front quarters. Later they were rented to lower-income groups.

The life span of European apartment houses is much longer than that of their American counterparts. Many of the nineteenth-century apartment structures of Paris are still in use. They represent a situation which could perhaps be called the back-yard slum. Its closest American approximations are the alley dwellings to the rear of good residential buildings in Washington, D.C.

Paris slums are not necessarily identical with working-class sections. The central and back-yard slums may house people who belong to the lower-income brackets of the middle class, transients, the large group of unsuccessful intellectuals, and, last but not least, prostitutes. However, until the interim between the two world wars the families of the manual workers lived, practically without exception, in areas and structures which we identify as slums.

Paris has made comparatively little progress in building decent houses for its lower-income groups and manual workers. Efforts made in this direction will not greatly change the ecological pattern of the city. New housing, all of which consists of tall apartments, has gone up on the land which had been used as a fortification belt prior to 1920. The consequence of this development will be to anchor industrial and working-class districts more firmly in an outer peripheral zone.

Vienna

Just as London's park- and square-centered West End inspired Haussmann's plans for Paris, so, in turn, did his policy of adjusting old communities to technological change and his methods of giving direction to expansion inspire other municipalities.

The development of the ecological structure of Vienna is a good example of the interpenetration of ideas and forms of urban life. This city rose to prominence much later than Paris or London. It was relatively insignificant in terms of population and economic importance until well into the eighteenth century. Before 1700 its international importance consisted in its character as an outpost against the iron curtain of former ages represented by the borders of the Turkish empire, then only thirty miles to the east of Vienna. The city consisted originally of a walled-in medieval core to the southwest of the Danube. The river played a part in the development of the city, greater in importance, perhaps, than that played by the Seine in the development of Paris, but much less important than that played by the Thames in the development of London. The old city is located on the bank of an arm of the Danube which was later made into a canal.

Vienna grew by merging with suburbs which had increased in population between 1700 and 1867. The suburban communities retained many aspects of their original character, such as civic centers and a degree of self-government. Some of these communities still embrace large areas of woods and game preserves—among them one consisting of primeval forest—and some agricultural lands. Vienna first merged with nine suburban communities which were grouped around it in roughly circular form. Later another circle of suburban communities was added, consisting of ten formerly independent little cities; finally, another suburb was added to the merger list, this one located on the north bank of the Danube. Contemporary Vienna is thus made up of twenty-one districts.

Three distinct periods of growth shaped the ecology of the city. The first covers the years between 1700 and 1814. It was one in which the city grew from its relatively insignificant position into a major capital and trade center, ranking eighth in size among cities of the Western world. The second crucial period covers the years 1867–1914. This was one of industrialization and rapid expansion as well as population increase, and at its end the city had slightly over two million inhabitants. Finally, the period between 1918 and 1933 is of importance. During this short era the city lost in economic potential, and its population declined by about two hundred thousand. However, during this same period the municipality inaugurated an extensive rehousing and slum-clearance program which, along with the more comprehensive and better-integrated schemes of Amsterdam and Stockholm, has exercised a strong influence upon urban land policies in England and America.

Prior to the first period of growth, a diagram of land uses within the old city would have indicated a division of the land among government, a monastery, the university, and craft-based production. Residences were not segregated from these to any degree. The intermingling of residential and nonresidential uses within one building was more than a holdover from the medieval guild era; it was an evolving pattern of combining land uses. The gist of this pattern—common in France, Italy, southern Germany, Austria, and other countries in the Danube Basin—consisted in the concentration of groups in different sections of the city, usually around a main center of common interest. Within the section residential and economic functions would be performed, with only as much segregation between the two as seemed necessary. Consequently, the elite residential section in Vienna, prior to the first period of expansion, coincided with the government section, the Latin Quarter was in the vicinity of the university, and middle-class people and craftsmen took over the remainder of the city.

After 1700, Vienna grew largely because it gained a huge trade area to the east. This was the result of conquest by the Hapsburg dynasty of the entire Danube Basin, which the Turks had overrun several centuries before. The result of Turkish rule in Danube countries—especially in Hungary—was depopulation and a stupendous decline of agricultural production. To rehabilitate the newly acquired provinces the Hapsburgs initiated an immigration program, recruiting settlers from Germany. They also rewarded successful generals with large land grants and attracted capitalists who would develop the natural resources of the Basin. The wars with Turkey led to an improvement in trade relations between the two countries, which had been restricted to a minimum when the Turkish Empire was strong enough to constitute a threat to Austria. These economic policies and programs coming in the wake of war made Vienna into a focal point in much the same way as colonial conquest and discoveries had made London into one of the centers of the Western world. The city grew in two ways. It became a commercial center and it increased its importance as a governmental center.

The ecological consequences of all this for Vienna was expansion into the suburbs in two directions. Hapsburg rule had been extremely intolerant toward groups professing a religion other than Catholicism. Changes took place only very gradually. The conquest of the Danube Basin brought one of these. Vienna had been a forbidden city to Jews. Together with Armenians and Greeks, they had become the main trading and business class within the Turkish Empire. Since trade relations with Turkey were to be promoted, the Hapsburgs permitted Jews who were citizens of Turkey to settle in one of the communities adjacent to Vienna. The area allotted them was within a suburban community, located on an island formed by the main body of the Danube and the arm which touched Vienna. This suburban district became a center of trade, especially for the marketing and shipment of agricultural commodities. Later, once the anti-Semitic tendencies of the government had given way to a more liberal attitude, portions of the area became the equivalent of the London Whitechapel district. With its growing political importance the walled-in city became short of space. More and more wealthy landowners, politicians, and aristocrats from the far-flung provinces of the Hapsburg Empire settled in Vienna. Moreover, the Catholic character of the dynasty made the capital the main refuge for those who had been expelled from Protestant countries, and after the French Revolution a large number of French royalists came to Vienna. All these groups sought residence near the seats of power. However, within city limits there was no room for good housing. The Crown and some of the leading aristocrats began to build spacious summer residences surrounded by large parks. These were located outside the city limits, near suburban communities. Two of these summer residences were located near the main highways, to the south and southeast. Around these summer residences— today public parks and museums—and within the suburban cities, residential quarters of the elite began to develop. These residential districts maintained their upper-class nature through all subsequent stages of development. After 1870 they began to house all the embassies and legations; and, in addition to the town houses of the wealthiest landowners, the most fashionable apartment dwellings were built in this sector.

The industrial revolution gained momentum in Austria after 1870. Its effect upon Vienna was to create one city out of the old inner core and the suburban communities, which had developed so that they actually constituted a sociological entity, a Greater Vienna. However, the ecological structure which was the consequence of industrialization was the product of planning in the Haussmann style, with all its good and most of its bad features.

The difference between Haussmann's programs for the adjustment of Paris and the Viennese policies was that the latter operated mainly through scrapping the outmoded fortifications around the old inner core city and through creating a system of railroad terminals and intracity railroad lines which was in its way unique.

The fortification belt covered a landed area which was deep enough to permit the construction of two almost parallel streets of great width. These streets were almost circular. On a diagram they constitute two concentric perimeters with the ends connected by an almost straight line—representing a street along the embankment of the arm of the Danube. Between the two circular streets was an area about two to three city blocks in depth. Between the inner limits of the inner perimeter street (the Ring) and the houses of the old city there also remained space, varying in depth from one to two city blocks. The government sold part of this land to private builders and real-estate investors, who erected tall apartment houses on the sites; but a considerable portion of the area that was not needed for street purposes was used for the creation of three public parks and the erection of a series of public buildings, among them a new city hall, a new building for the national legislature, and a new university building. The number of streets connecting the two perimeter traffic arteries was purposely kept small. Moreover, these connecting streets were made narrow. This was done in order to direct heavy commercial traffic along the outer perimeter street (a purpose which was also pursued by means of city ordinances) and to reserve the inner perimeter street for passenger and other light vehicles.

The improvement of the land formerly used for fortifications had, on the whole, a fourfold effect upon Vienna's land-use pattern. Apartment houses along and between the two perimeter streets became the habitat of the upper-income groups of the middle class. This group of prominent business leaders, bankers, and industrialists and their associates in the professions grew in number after 1860. The inner core city was gradually being rebuilt with medium-income apartment houses intermingled with office buildings. Four shopping streets came into being which constituted, along with a band on the Ring, the more expensive retail district.

The perimeter streets also affected the land-use pattern of the inner tier of formerly independent suburbs. The University of Vienna had been moved from its old location in the inner city to the Ring. Between 1870 and 1914 the university increased greatly in importance. It became one of the great international schools of higher learning. The original building became too small to house the research laboratories of the medical faculty and new buildings went up in the adjoining two of the former suburbs. The proximity of campus buildings operated as an incentive for students, medical practitioners, teachers, and other groups of the intelligentsia to establish residences and offices, as well as meeting places, in these suburbs. A Latin Quarter thus came into being which had the shape of a triangular sector with the main university building as its starting point. Park areas were added to the already existing ones in the two fashionable suburbs. This operated as an incentive to increase building activities there. Between the fashionable sector and the Latin Quarter there were three suburbs. Within these, craft-based production and light industry had developed during the first half of the nineteenth century. A broad street leading from the outer perimeter street toward the periphery became a retail center for medium- and low-priced goods. Most of the larger department stores selected sites within this district.

While the utilization of the land within the old fortification belt determined the ecological pattern of the inner core city and of the nine suburbs immediately adjacent to it, the location of railroad terminals and of intra-city railroad tracks determined the ecological structure of the outer tier of formerly independent suburbs. In essence the railroad system operated to surround Vienna almost entirely with a ring of industrial sites and working-class districts. Only two gaps were left in this proletarian ring. They are located to the northwest adjoining the foothills of the Alps and are wild-life preserves.

The location of railroad tracks and terminals took place in two stages. The first consisted in the construction of lines and terminals connecting the city with the network of the continent; the second stage consisted in the building of an intra-urban system, in essence the connecting of all terminals with one another by an elevated line almost circular in shape. With two exceptions terminals serving overland routes were located on the inner rims of the outer tier of suburbs, so that tracks and sidings for industrial purposes penetrated deeply into the outer suburbs. The division line between the outer and inner tiers of suburbs was a third broad perimeter street, which was appropriately named "the Belt." About 1900 an elevated line was built in the center of the Belt, connecting all railroad terminals and constituting the nucleus of a system of rapid transit.

The location of the railroad lines, the terminals, and their interconnections attracted industrial establishments to the outer tier of suburbs. As in Paris and London this brought about the construction of low-rent residences, mostly of the apartment-house type. Their quality was similar to that of the houses in the East End of Paris. The residential quarters of most of the industrialized suburbs were built as slums but not all of the outer-tier suburbs became working-class districts. As mentioned above, there were gaps in the Viennese slum ring.

Generally speaking, heavy industrial establishments concentrated in the suburb beyond the Danube (the last to be merged with the city), on the riverward portions of the island between the main river and the canal, and in the outer tier of suburbs on the southeast. Light industry was scattered over the outer suburbs with the exception of those bordering upon the foothills of the Alps. As in Paris, poor housing conditions were not restricted to working-class districts. The lower parts of the middle class, as well as a congeries of in-between groups, such as unsuccessful intellectuals and artists, were equally slum-ridden. Their quarters were often in groups of neglected old houses in central sections of the city. Most of the slums, however, were at or near the periphery.

The last decisive stage in the ecological development of Vienna is of broader significance, and not merely because of the great improvement in the housing conditions of the working class. The real significance consists in the lesson learned through the process of trial and error. Until about 1900, housing for the working class, as well as for the lower middle class, had consisted of cheap imitations of the facilities of the well-to-do. There was no analysis of the life, the needs, or the particular habits of families which could not afford servants and could not carry on a division of labor whereby the husband worked for a living while the wife took care of the household. The result was slums, either because houses were built in complete disregard of the needs of their occupants or because houses built for groups with entirely different living standards were made over into dwellings for the poor.

Around the turn of the century a reform movement got under way in England which advocated the decentralization of large cities and the construction of new communities with the plants and the homes for industrial workers and middle-income families in the countryside. This new-town movement exercised a strong influence in America, as well as on the Continent. In Vienna the first result of this foreign influence was not the building of houses for low-income groups but the erection of expensive single-family houses for the upper middle class in peripheral areas not a part of the slum ring. The switch from the traditional apartment house to single-family dwellings in a garden setting was the result of the same blending of cultural influences which, on the other hand, brought the apartment house to Mayfair and to the lake front of Chicago. On the Continent it created an antitenement movement; and the first Viennese attempts at improving housing for the working class consisted in the construction of single-family homes surrounded by gardens. These houses were built with public subsidies by semipublic corporations, such as cooperatives, on land on the periphery of the city. Construction was large scale, and individual projects meant the creation of entire communities.

This program of low-rent housing came in response to a shortage created by the First World War. Impetus came from the ambitions of the working class, which, through the medium of the Socialist Party, ruled Vienna from the end of the First World War to 1934. However, the garden communities proved to be ill fitted to the needs of the working class. They were too far from places of work and too much of a burden for the housewife. In 1923 the municipality began to take control of the housing program. It built apartment houses, not single-family homes. However, these were different from the old tenements. Individual dwelling units were small but they were grouped together in structures which covered extensive areas. The apartments contained collective household facilities designed to reduce the burden of housework for wives who worked outside the home. Kindergartens, libraries, and shops were blended into the apartment-house framework. Moreover, all the larger developments were built around areas of vacant land, shutting such open spaces off completely from the public streets. These open areas were made into gardens—proletarian opposite numbers of the upper-middle-class squares of London's old West End—in which children could play unattended yet safe from traffic hazards.

Stockholm

Although the structures of the three cities which we have been discussing have been influenced by public policies, the land-use patterns of these cities were, during formative periods, shaped largely by private initiative.

Stockholm, on the other hand, is representative of a group of European cities which originally developed a pattern of land use as the result of public policies. The results achieved in shaping the ecological structure are due largely to ownership of large tracts of land by the local government.

Sweden, today one of the few wealthy countries besides the United States, was late to industrialize. We are inclined to think of this process as one brought about by the revolutionary techniques which utilized coal as a source of energy, and we overlook the fact that there are many stages in the process, many industrial revolutions. The development of hydraulic power and its transmission over great distances were prerequisites for the industrialization of Sweden. Previously, the country had been compelled to export its ores and its timber—its two main resources—in relatively unprocessed form.

Stockholm's population increased greatly between 1870 and 1900. This growth created a high density of population in the city. Traditionally, houses and apartment-dwelling units covered little space and, among the lower-income groups, often consisted of only one room. The reasons for this cultural trait may have been the scarcity of fuel relative to the high consumption ratio made necessary by the long, severe winters. Industrialization did not gain full momentum until, around the turn of the century, hydraulic power could be used increasingly in industrial processes, such as the manufacture of machine tools, armaments, and chemicals. However, the migration to cities during the last decades of the nineteenth century and the consequent overcrowding were signals of worse things to come.

On the assumption of an increase in migration, laws were passed in 1904 which authorized the city of Stockholm to buy land outside its limits and improved or unimproved real estate within them. This land-buying policy was pursued consistently until the city owned an area of land outside city limits which was greater than that within.

The city's original policy was to use the suburban land reserve for housing low-income groups, mainly manual workers, and as sites for industrial establishments. On the whole, the city actually used the land in three ways. It leased large tracts to building cooperatives and to industrial firms which would erect housing facilities for their workers near the plants. It leased individual lots to prospective homeowners and to private investors. Finally, the city itself built low-rent houses. A number of economic factors reduced the participation of private investors, and today the main builders and owners of housing around the old city core are the municipality and a few very large and financially powerful cooperatives.

The ownership of land by the local government was used as a tool to control the layout, style, density, and price of the buildings. The city never sold any land; it leased it for long periods, usually sixty years. The land policy of Stockholm in its attempts to control expansion may, therefore, be compared to the policy of the Crown and of large aristocratic landowners in London at the time the residential sections of Bloomsbury, Mayfair, and Regent Park were initiated. Then the problem with which landowners and builders were confronted was to provide adequate housing for a new class—wealthy business and professional groups. There is another parallel between London of the seventeenth and the early eighteenth century and Stockholm on the threshold of the twentieth. The organization of industrial workers and the revolutionary character of the labor movement continuously increased in momentum in all industrialized countries of Europe during the second half of the nineteenth century. Sweden's conservative party saw the country entering belatedly into the process of industrialization, and it tried to prevent some of the hardships which might cause social strife. On the other hand, the organization of the labor movement in Sweden came under way apace with industrialization and not, as elsewhere, subsequently. The result of this interplay of social and political forces was the creation of forms of urban life and housing designed to meet the cultural and biological needs of industrial workers.

Since 1904 the land policy of Stockholm has undergone changes in many important details. In their analysis of the needs and preferred forms of life of the growing working class, Stockholm's policy makers at first tried to achieve a housing scheme which would stand midway between urban and rural ecology. The trend of thought was that the industrial revolution in England and other countries had been a severe shock to the manual workers who had migrated to the city. The disintegration of standards and traditional ways of rural life, sociologists felt, had caused much of the social strife which accompanied the European labor movements. Consequently, the preferred form of housing consisted at first in single-family homes with ample garden spaces. In a number of cases the garden space was large enough to permit some truck farming and even a little animal husbandry. Another attempt at cushioning the shock of a change from agricultural to industrial labor, from rural to urban forms of life, was the promotion of homogeneity. New housing was to be built not piecemeal but on a large scale. The city was to grow not by adding block to block but by building entire new communities. Another consequence of this analysis was that the city was more willing to lease land to developers who proposed a scheme which would group together in one community families of one age group, single persons of one sex, manual workers of one factory, or families from one particular province of Sweden. This policy has gradually been changed. Today apartment houses are favored. Large-scale community building is the rule, but only because it has proved itself superior to piecemeal construction in respect to housing and recreation. Homogeneity is being discouraged in every new development.

Why did the policy of Stockholm planners change in its sociological content? The answer is that the economic development of Sweden took a course completely different from that of Britain, France, and Germany. Industrialization was based upon a completely different technology. The political structure of the country was already a democratic one when industrialization began. Because of the difference in political structure, the distribution of incomes which resulted from the increase in national income owing to industrialization tended to be much more even and equalitarian than it had been during the half century of industrialization in England, France, and Germany. The speed of industrialization was more rapid because technological "know-how" was greater. Consequently, the stage when industry needs a very large number of white-collar employees who are paid relatively high wages was reached sooner than in countries which had been industrialized earlier. Because the main power source of Swedish industry was electricity, not steam from coal, the railroad lines and terminals did not have the same effect upon the land-use pattern as in London, Vienna, or Paris. They represented a force of attraction for industry but did not repel high-rent residences. Finally, the facilities for the transmission of electric energy operated in Sweden as a deterrent to urban growth rather than as a stimulus. Expansion of its main cities was not as dramatic as had been anticipated, because industrial plants could be built in small rural market towns, thus avoiding the dislocation of labor forces.

The effect of Sweden's industrial revolution upon the ecological structure of Stockholm was to create a class structure in no way like the pattern of few rich opposed by many poor, which is the sociological stand-by of Marxists. The social stratification in the urban society of Sweden's capital seems to be the result rather of cultural differences which in turn are the product of education and professional activities. The differences of culture between white-collar and manual workers grew until, by 1937, the tastes and habits of the two groups differed considerably. Thus, because they wanted to be near cultural centers such as theaters and concert halls, white-collar workers seemed to prefer apartments to single-family homes and central locations to peripheral ones. Manual workers seemed more satisfied with the house-and-garden plan of living.

Taking a cue from the concentric-circle theory of urban expansion, one may divide Stockholm into three concentric zones. The central core contains offices, retail stores, theaters, museums, public buildings, and relics of the medieval city which are inhabited by various groups. The middle zone consists largely of apartment houses and is in general the habitat of medium-income and well-to-do groups. The outer zone consists mostly of single-family homes with gardens; some of the gardens are so large that they are used for subsistence farming. Besides residences the outer zone contains industrial establishments. The population of this zone consists primarily of factory workers. To reverse trends which would make these patterns more accentuated and ossified seems to be one of the main objectives of Stockholm's present land policy.

It is beyond the scope of this article to evaluate the deviations from the sector and concentric-ring theories in London, Paris, Vienna, and Stockholm with a view to determining the accuracy of these theories for American cities. However, the analysis of urban societies which developed under conditions similar to those in America and within the orbit of the same civilization indicates some limitations of the applicability of both theories.

Neither theory has taken into consideration the effect of public policies upon city structures. Both the sector and the concentric-ring theories assume that land-use patterns are the result of the free play of economic forces. Such a degree of *laissez faire* has never existed in America, or anywhere else.

If we compare the applicability of the two theories to European communities we will find that the concentric-ring theory almost never, the sector theory sometimes, seems to apply. But if we look more closely we may become a bit doubtful about basing any theory about the working of a social organism upon surface symptoms such as land use instead of upon an analysis of social forces and their reaction to technological change.

C | Evolution of the Ecology of United States Cities

16 | Recent Distortions of the Classical Models of Urban Structure

HOMER HOYT

Since the general patterns of city structure were described by Burgess in 1925 [1] and 1929 [2] and by myself in 1939 [3] there has been a tremendous growth of urban population, not only in the United States, but throughout the world. To what extent has this factor of growth changed the form or shape of urban communities?

While the Burgess concentric circle theory was based on a study of Chicago—a city on a flat prairie, cut off on the east by Lake Michigan—and patterns of growth in other cities would be influenced by their unique topography, his formulation had a widespread application to American cities of 1929. Burgess made a brilliant and vivid contribution to urban sociology and urban geography which inspired the present writer as well as the sociologists and geographers who made subsequent studies of city patterns.

---

[1] R. E. Park and E. W. Burgess, *The City* (Chicago, Illinois: University of Chicago Press, 1925), pp. 47–62.

[2] E. W. Burgess, "Urban Areas," in *Chicago: An Experiment in Social Science Research*, T. V. Smith and L. D. White (editors) (Chicago, Illinois: University of Chicago Press, 1929), pp. 114–123.

[3] Homer Hoyt, *The Structure and Growth of Residential Neighborhoods in American Cities* (Washington, D.C.: Federal Housing Administration, 1939).

SOURCE: *Land Economics*, XL (May 1964), 199–212. Copyright, The Regents of the University of Wisconsin. Reprinted by permission of the publisher.

In the era of the Greek cities in the fifth century B.C. a city was considered an artistic creation which should maintain its static form without change. To take care of population growth, the Greeks sent out colonies, like swarms of bees, to found new cities on the ideal model. Plato said that the ideal city should not contain over 5,000 inhabitants although he himself was the product of an Athens with a 250,000 population. In the Middle Ages most continental European cities were surrounded by walls and many, like Milan, Italy, preserved an unaltered form for hundreds of years.

In the United States, however, there has been a tremendous growth of metropolitan areas since 1930. The number of large urban concentrations with a population of a million or more has increased from 10 to 22. The population in the 140 metropolitan districts was 57,602,865 in 1930, of which 40,343,422 were in central cities and 17,259,423 were outside these cities. In 1940 in these 140 metropolitan districts the population was 62,965,773 of which 42,796,170 were in central cities and 20,169,603 were outside these cities.[4] After World War II, in the rapidly growing decade from 1950 to 1960, the population of 216 Standard Metropolitan Areas grew from 91,568,113 to 115,796,265. Most of the growth in the past census decade was in the suburbs, but central city population grew from 52,648,185 to 58,441,995, a gain of only 11 percent, while the population outside central cities increased from 38,919,928 to 57,354,270, a rise of 47.4 percent.[5] The population in the central areas of 12 of the largest American metropolitan regions actually declined in this decade from 22,694,799 to 21,843,214, a loss of 3.8 percent.[6] The population loss in the central cores of these cities was much greater, since some central cities still had room for new growth within the outer edges of their boundaries. There was also a displacement of white population by non-white population. From 1930 to 1950 the non-white population in 168 SMA's increased from 4,913,703 to 8,250,210.[7] The chief gain was in the central cities where the non-white 1960 the non-white population in central cities increased to 10,030,314. The population rose from 3,624,504 in 1930 to 6,411,158 in 1950. From 1950 to non-white population in SMA's outside central cities was only 2,720,513 in 1960. On the other hand while 43,142,399 white persons lived in central cities of SMA's in 1960, 49,081,533 white persons lived in SMA's outside the central cities. While the central city population in these 12 SMA's was

---

[4] United States Census of Population 1940, Vol. I, Table 18, p. 61.

[5] United States Department of Commerce, Bureau of the Census, Standard Metropolitan Areas in the United States as defined October 18, 1963, Series P-23, No. 10, December 5, 1963. (Newark, New Jersey, is included in New York Metropolitan Area).

[6] Baltimore, Boston, Chicago, Cincinnati, Cleveland, Detroit, Minneapolis-St. Paul, New York, Philadelphia, St. Louis, San Francisco-Oakland and Washington, D.C.

[7] United States Census of Population, 1930, 1940, 1950.

declining, population outside the central cities rose from 13,076,711 in 1950 to 20,534,833 in 1960, a gain of 57 percent.

In 1960 the population of the areas outside the central cities in these 12 great metropolitan areas almost equalled the population in the central areas and by 1964 the population in the areas outside the central cities has certainly surpassed the number in the central city.

While the cities of 50,000 population and over have been growing at a rapid rate in the past decade, the smaller cities with less than 50,000 population have been increasing in numbers at a slower pace, or from 27.4 million in 1950 to 29.4 million in 1960.[8] The smaller cities thus would be enabled to maintain their static form with the growth element chiefly affecting the larger metropolitan areas as a result of the shift in population growth from the center to the suburbs and a change in the racial composition of many central cities.

Not merely population growth, but a rise in per capita national income from $757 in 1940 to $2,500 in 1963, with a greater proportionate increase in the middle class incomes, an increase in the number of private passenger automobiles from 22,793,000 in 1933 to 70 million in 1963, and the building of expressways connecting cities and belt highways around cities, were all dynamic factors changing the shape and form of cities since the description of city patterns in 1925 and 1939. Let us examine the different concentric circles or zones or sectors described in the books over a quarter of a century ago and see how the principles then enunciated have been changed by the growth factors.

The Central Business District: Financial and Office Zone and the Retail Shopping Zone

In 1929 Burgess wrote: "Zone I: The Central Business District. At the center of the city as the focus of its commercial, social and civic life is situated in the Central Business District. The heart of this district is the downtown retail district with its department stores, its smart shops, its office buildings, its clubs, its banks, its hotels, its theatres, its museums, and its headquarters of economic, social, civic and political life." [9] Burgess thus accurately described the central business district of Chicago and most large American cities as of the date he was writing (1929), a description which would hold true in the main to the end of World War II. Since 1946, extraordinary changes in the American economy have occurred which have had a pronounced effect on the structure of the downtown business districts of American cities.

---

[8] Harold M. Mayer, "Economic Prospects for the Smaller City," *Public Management*, August 1963.
[9] Ernest W. Burgess, "Urban Areas," *op. cit.*

Burgess had noted in 1929 the existence of local business centers, or satellite "loops" in the zone of better residences: "The typical constellation of business and recreation areas includes a bank, one or more United Cigar stores, a drug store, a high class restaurant, an automobile display row, and a so-called 'wonder' motion picture theatre." [10] I also had noted, in 1939, the extensions of stringlike commercial developments beyond the central business districts, and the rise of satellite business centers: "Again, satellite business centers have developed independently beyond the central business district, or on the city's periphery. These are usually located at or near suburban railway stations, elevated or subway stations, intersecting points between radical and crosstown street car lines, or intersecting points of main automobile highways." [11]

In 1964, the central retail district, with its large department stores still remains the largest shopping district in its metropolitan area, and all the outlying business districts at street car intersections, subway or suburban railway stations are still operating, but their dominating position has been greatly weakened by the construction, since 1946, of an estimated 8,300 planned shopping districts, with free automobile parking, in the suburbs or on the periphery of the central city mass. The tremendous growth of the suburban population, which moved to areas beyond mass transit lines, facilitated by the universal ownership of the automobile, and decline in the numbers and relative incomes of the central city population, invited and made possible this new development in retail shopping.

The regional shopping center—with major department stores, variety, apparel and local convenience stores, practically duplicating the stores in the downtown retail area and built on large tracts of land entirely away from street cars, subways, elevated or railroad stations—was virtually unknown prior to World War II. The first of these centers, Country Club Plaza in Kansas City, had been established in 1925 and there were a few others with department stores and a number of neighborhood centers on commercial streets, with parking areas in front of the stores, but the wave of the future was not discerned by planners or land economists before 1946.

There are many types of these new planned centers; the regional center on 50 to 100 acres of land with at least one major department store; the community center on 20 to 30 acres of land with a junior department store as the leading tenant; and the neighborhood center with a supermarket, drug store and local convenience shops on 5 to 10 acres of land. But the type having the greatest impact on the downtown stores is the regional center which directly competes with downtown in the sale of general merchandise.

General merchandise stores, that is, department and variety stores, had long been the dominating magnets and attractions of the central retail

---

[10] *Ibid.*
[11] Hoyt, *op. cit.* p. 20.

areas. In this field the CBD stores had almost a monopoly in most cities prior to 1920 and even held a dominating position after the establishment of some outlying department stores at street car intersections or subway stations in Chicago and New York. There had been for years neighborhood grocery stores, drug stores and even small apparel and dry goods stores and some variety stores outside of the central business district but the department store sales of the CBD's were probably 90 percent or more of the total department store volume of the entire metropolitan area.

In 1958 the central general merchandise stores, chiefly department stores, in the largest cities of a million population and over, had a lower sales volume than the aggregate of the sales of department stores in all the shopping centers outside of the CBD, or $3.6 billion compared to $5.65 billion. There were 125 regional shopping centers in 1958 but many more have been completed since that date and the 1963 United States Retail Census of Shopping Districts will undoubtedly show a still greater increase in the department store sales outside of the CBD.

In 94 metropolitan areas with a population of 100,000 and over and total population of 91,937,103 in 1960, dollar sales outside the CBD's had increased by 53.8 percent, but in the CBD's only 3.4 percent. There was an actual decline in general merchandise sales from 1954 to 1958 in the CBD's of Los Angeles, Chicago, Philadelphia, Detroit, Boston, St. Louis, Washington, D.C., Cleveland, Baltimore, Milwaukee and Kansas City.

These new planned shopping districts, with their ample parking areas, cover more ground than the combined areas of the CBD's in all American cities. I have calculated that there were 30,460 acres or 47.5 square miles in the central business districts of the standard metropolitan areas in the United States in 1960, compared with 33,600 acres or 52.5 square miles in all types of new planned centers.[12] Since 1960, however, many new planned centers have been built and there are now probably 150 regional shopping centers. In 1964 the ground area occupied by these centers, as well as that of the many new discount houses with large parking areas, has considerably increased the space occupied by shopping centers as compared with 1960.

In contrast to the tremendous growth of the planned shopping districts, there has been very limited building of new retail stores in downtown areas; the notable exceptions being Midtown Plaza in Rochester, New York; the redevelopment of the business center of New Haven, Connecticut, with new department stores, offices and garages, connected by a new highway to the existing expressway; the location of new Sears Roebuck and Dayton department stores in central St. Paul; and the erection of garages for department stores in other cities.

---

[12] Homer Hoyt, "Changing Patterns of Land Values," *Land Economics*, May 1960, p. 115.

Office Buildings

Office building expansion, unlike retail stores, bears no direct relation to population growth but depends entirely upon the extent to which a city becomes an international or regional office management or financial center. Generalization therefore cannot be made about office buildings which would apply to all cities since the number of square feet of office space per capita in the metropolitan area varies from 2.2 square feet in San Diego to 7.5 square feet in Chicago, 16 square feet in New York and 25 square feet in Midland, Texas.

New York City has become the outstanding headquarters center of the United States, with an estimated 171,300,000 square feet of office space. It has had a tremendous growth since 1946, with 55 million square feet added since World War II. The trend has been uptown, away from downtown Wall Street to Park Avenue, 42nd Street and Third Avenue near Grand Central Station. The world's greatest concentration of office buildings is in the Grand Central and Plaza districts of New York City. From 1947 to 1962 inclusive, there was a total increase of 50,632,000 square feet of rentable office area in Manhattan, of which 33,839,000 square feet, or 66.8 percent, was in the Grand Central and Plaza areas. In the same period, in the lower Manhattan area, or the combined financial, city hall and insurance districts, 10,935,000 square feet or 21.6 percent of the total were constructed. A partial reversal of the uptown trend in Manhattan will result from the proposed building of the World Trade Center with 10 million square feet of office space, in twin towers 1350 feet high, on the Lower West Side. This development, by the Port of New York Authority, will be started in 1965 and is scheduled for completion by 1970.[13]

In Washington, D.C., there is approximately 16 million square feet of office space. An estimated 11 million square feet have been built since 1946, of which 9 million square feet are in the area west of 15th Street, in the direction of the high grade residential growth.

The location of new office buildings in central city areas has been determined in part by the slum or blighted areas, with old buildings which could be cleared away, such as in the Golden Triangle of Pittsburgh or Penn Center in Philadelphia, or location in air rights over railroad tracks as the Merchandise Mart and Prudential buildings in Chicago, the Pan Am Building and other buildings on Park Avenue in New York and the Prudential Building in Boston. The ability to secure land at a relatively low cost on West Wacker Drive in Chicago caused insurance companies to build there.

---

[13] *The New York Times,* January 19, 1964.

Sometimes these new office districts are not at the center of transportation. In Los Angeles new office building has moved away from the central business districts toward the high grade residential areas. From 1948 to 1960 15,500,000 square feet of office floor space was constructed in Los Angeles, of which only 1,500,000 square feet was built in the 400-acre area of the central business district, although 1,000,000 square feet were erected in the southwesterly and western fringe areas of the central business district.[14] This decentralization is in marked contrast to the concentration of offices in New York City.

There has also been a tendency for large office buildings of insurance companies, which conduct a self-sufficient operation not dependent on contact with other agencies, to locate on large tracts of land several miles from the center of the city as the Prudential regional office buildings in Houston and Minneapolis in 1951, and the Connecticut General Insurance Company in Hartford. Office centers are also developing around some of the regional shopping centers, as at Northland in Detroit, Ward Parkway in Kansas City and Lenox Square in Atlanta.

In Houston more than 6 million square feet of new office space has been added to downtown areas in the past three years, the growth proceeding westerly in the direction of the high income areas. While the main office building district of most cities is still within the confines of the central area, the office center is not fixed but is moving in the direction of high income areas, as in New York City, Washington, D.C., Los Angeles and Houston. This conforms to the statement I made in 1939.[15]

A tall office building that looms in the sky as a beacon or landmark has been built in many cities of moderate size by banks, oil companies or insurance companies for the sake of prestige, regardless of cost or rental demand. In many cities of growing population few new office buildings have been erected. Thus, generalizations can no longer be made about office building locations which will apply to all cities in the United States.

Hotels and Motels

There is a concentration of hotels near each other in large cities so that they can accommodate conventions but central hotels have declined in importance because of the new motels and motor hotels (with parking) on the periphery of the central business district or on the outskirts of the city. This rapid growth in both intown motels and those on the periphery is a use not anticipated in 1939.

---

[14] *Los Angeles Centropolis 1980, Economic Survey,* Los Angeles Central City Committee and Los Angeles City Planning Department, December 12, 1960, p. 19.

[15] Hoyt, *Structure and Growth, op. cit.,* p. 108.

Apartments in Central Areas

There is a trend to the building of new apartments in or near central business districts, such as the Marina Towers in Chicago, the apartments in redeveloped areas in Southwest Washington, D.C., and as proposed for the Bunker Hill redevelopment in downtown Los Angeles. Hence the statement by Burgess that: "Beyond the workingmen's homes lies the residential district, a zone in which the better grade of apartments and single family residences predominate" must be qualified now, as it was in 1939, when I pointed to the Gold Coast of Chicago and Park Avenue in New York City.[16]

Thus, in view of the shifting of uses in the central business districts, the overall decline in the predominance of central retail areas, the rapid growth of office centers in a few cities compared to a static situation in others, the emergence of redeveloped areas, and intown motels, the former descriptions of patterns in American cities must be revised to conform to the realities of 1964.

The Wholesale and Light Manufacturing Zone

Burgess described the zone next to the central business district as: "Clinging close to the skirts of the retail district lies the wholesale and light manufacturing zone. Scattered through this zone and surrounding it, old dilapidated buildings form the homes of the lower working classes, hoboes and disreputable characters. Here the slums are harbored. Cheap second-hand stores are numerous, and low-priced 'men only' moving picture and burlesque shows flourish." [17] This is a vivid description of West Madison Street and South State Street in Chicago in the 1920's. Since that time the wholesale function has greatly declined and with the direct sale by manufacturers to merchants the 4-million-square-foot Merchandise Mart, across the Chicago River north of the Loop, absorbed most of the functions formerly performed by wholesalers. The intermixture of slums and old dilapidated buildings with light industry is being cleared away in redevelopment projects and the West Side Industrial District in Chicago has been created immediately west of the Loop on cleared land.

Light manufacturing, in the garment industry particularly, still clings close to the retail and financial center in New York City because the garment industry depends on fashion and the entertainment of out-of-town buyers.

---

[16] *Ibid.*, p. 23.

[17] Ernest M. Fisher, *Advanced Principles of Real Estate Practice* (New York: The Macmillan Co., 1930), p. 126, citing R. E. Park and E. W. Burgess, *The City, op. cit.*, Ch. II.

Other light manufacturing industries have tended to move away from the center of the city to the suburbs where they can secure ample land areas for one-story plants, storage, and parking for their employees' cars. These new modern plants, in park-like surroundings, which emit no loud noise or offensive odors, are not objectionable even in middle-class residential areas, and workers can avoid city traffic in driving to their place of employment, or they can live nearby.

The Factory or Heavy Industrial District

In 1929 Burgess placed the wholesale district in Zone I, the central business district, and described Zone II as the zone in transition, which included the factory district in its inner belt as follows:

Zone II: The Zone in Transition. Surrounding the Central Business District are areas of residential deterioration caused by the encroaching of business and industry from Zone I. This may therefore be called the Zone in Transition, with a factory district for its inner belt and an outer ring of retrogressing neighborhoods, of first-settlement immigrant colonies, of roominghouse districts, of homeless-men areas, of resorts of gambling, bootlegging, sexual vice, and of breeding-places of crime. In this area of physical deterioration and social disorganization our studies show the greatest concentration of cases of poverty, bad housing, juvenile delinquency, family disintegration, physical and mental disease. As families and individuals prosper, they escape from this area into Zone III beyond, leaving behind as marooned a residuum of the defeated, leaderless, and helpless.[18]

In 1939 I pointed out tendencies of heavy industries to move away from close-in locations in the "transition zone."[19] Since that time heavy manufacturing has tended more and more to seek suburban locations or rural areas, as nearly all workers now come in their own automobiles and for the most part live in the suburban areas themselves. Factory location in slum areas is not now desired for the clerks and factory workers no longer live there. All of the reasons I cited in 1939 for industries moving to suburban areas apply with greater force in 1964.

In regard to residential uses, this zone in transition was defined as the slum and blighted area of Chicago in 1943[20] and under the slum clearance and redevelopment laws which enabled federal authorities to acquire by condemnation properties in blighted areas, it has been extensively cleared and rebuilt with modern apartments, both private and public. The remnants of this area which have not been cleared away still retain the characteristics Burgess described in 1929, and the problems of juvenile delinquency

[18] Burgess, "Urban Areas," *op. cit.*
[19] Hoyt, *op. cit.* p. 20.
[20] Chicago Plan Commission, *Master Plan of Residential Land Use of Chicago*, Homer Hoyt, Director of Research, 1943, Fig. 89, p. 68.

and overcrowding have been accentuated in the last 35 years by the immigration of low income Negro families to Chicago as well as to other northern cities.

Zone of Workingmen's Homes

Encircling the zone of transition, now the slum and blighted area, is Zone III, described by Burgess as follows:

Zone III: The Zone of Independent Workingmen's Homes. This third broad urban ring in Chicago, as well as in other northern industrial cities, is largely constituted by neighborhoods of second immigrant settlement. Its residents are those who desire to live near but not too close to their work. In Chicago, it is a housing area neither of tenements, apartments, nor of single dwellings; its boundaries have been roughly determined by the plotting of the two-flat dwelling, generally of frame construction, with the owner living on the lower floor with a tenant on the other.[21]

The buildings in this zone, now 35 years older than when Burgess wrote in 1929, were in general classified in the Master Plan of Residential Land Use of Chicago as "conservation." [22] This area is not yet a slum but next in order of priority to be cleared away. In some blocks older structures can be razed and the newer ones rehabilitated. A large proportion of its former occupants, white families with children of school age, have moved to the suburbs and it is now occupied mainly by single white persons, older white families or by Negro families in all age groups.

In some cases these older close-in residential sections may be rehabilitated and become fashionable, as in the Georgetown area of Washington, D.C., Rittenhouse Square in Philadelphia and the Near North Side of Chicago; and this is an exception to be noted to Burgess' theory.

Better Residential Area

Zone IV: The Zone of Better Residences. Extending beyond the neighborhoods of second immigrant settlements, we come to the Zone of Better Residences in which the great middle-class of native-born Americans live, small business men, professional people, clerks, and salesmen. Once communities of single homes, they are becoming, in Chicago, apartment-house and residential-hotel areas.[23]

This zone was classified in the Master Plan of Residential Land Use of Chicago in 1943 as "stable," indicating that the residences were still of sound construction and had many remaining years of useful life. As the second im-

---

[21] Burgess, "Urban Areas," *op. cit.*
[22] Chicago Plan Commission, *op. cit.*
[23] Burgess, "Urban Areas," *op. cit.*

migrant settlers, now indistinguishable from the native-born population, once moved from Zone III into this area, so now many of the former residents of this area have moved mainly from this area into the new areas near the periphery of the city, or into the suburbs. Some of the areas vacated by them are now occupied by the non-white population.

The Commuters Zone

Burgess described the commuters zone as follows:

Zone V: The Commuters Zone. Out beyond the areas of better residence is a ring of encircling small cities, towns, and hamlets, which, taken together, constitute the Commuters Zone. These are also, in the main, dormitory sub-urbs, because the majority of men residing there spend the day at work in the Loop (Central Business District), returning only for the night.[24]

Burgess thus took into account in his fifth zone the existence of suburban towns. However, he refers to them as a "ring" implying that they formed a circular belt around Chicago. However, at the time Burgess wrote in 1929, there was no circle of towns around Chicago but a pattern of settlement along the railroads with six great bands of suburban settlement radiating out from the central mass of Chicago like spokes of a wheel and with large vacant areas in between.[25] Chicago's early growth had taken the form first of starfish extensions of settlement along the principal highways and street car lines.[26] By 1929 the vacant areas in the city between these prongs had been filled in with homes so that there were then in fact belts or concentric circles of settled areas within the City of Chicago. At that time, however, the suburban area of Chicago conformed to the axial pattern of growth with the highest income sector located on one of the six radial bands—the North Shore, along Lake Michigan. There were other high income areas in the other bands of growth but no continuous belt of high income areas around Chicago. Since 1929 the vacant areas between these radial extensions of settlement along suburban railroads have been filled in largely with homes of middle income residents. Many of the new planned shopping districts are now located in between these bands of original settlement along railroads, where large vacant tracts could be secured.

Beyond his five zones, Burgess later identified two additional zones lying beyond the built-up area of the city: "The sixth zone is constituted by the agricultural districts lying within the circle of commutation . . . The seventh zone is the hinterland of the metropolis." [27]

---

[24] *Ibid.*

[25] Chicago Plan Commission, *op. cit.*, frontispiece, p. 2.

[26] *Ibid.*, Fig. 3, p. 22.

[27] E. W. Burgess, "The New Community and Its Future," *Annals of the American Academy of Political and Social Science*, Vol. 149, May 1930, pp. 161, 162.

Richard M. Hurd, in his classic *Principles of City Land Values*,[28] had as early as 1903 developed the central and axial principles of city growth; yet to many persons, before Burgess formulated his theory many years later, cities appeared to be a chaotic mixture of structures with no law governing their growth. Burgess, with acute powers of observation and without all of the great body of census and planning data that has been made available since he wrote, made a remarkable formulation of principles that were governing American city growth in 1929 and he related these principles to the basic facts of human society. Since 1929, however, not only have the vast detailed city data of the United States censuses been made available for study and analysis, but dynamic changes have occurred in our economy which have had a profound influence on the structure of our cities. Since 1929 over 10 million new houses have been constructed on the suburban fringes of American cities, beyond the old central mass, in areas made available for residential occupancy by the increase in the number of private passenger automobiles in the United States from 8 million in 1920 to 66 million in 1964, and the highways subsequently built to accommodate them.

Apartment buildings, once confined to locations along subways, elevated lines or near suburban railroad stations, are now springing up in the suburbs, far from mass transit. Many families without children of school age desire the convenience of an apartment, involving no work of mowing lawns, painting and repairing, and with the comforts of air-conditioning and often a community swimming pool. Complete communities are now being developed in the suburbs, with a mixture of single family homes, town houses and apartments, and with their own churches, schools, shopping centers and light industries, some even with a golf course and bridle paths, of which the 7,000-acre Reston development near the Dulles Airport in the Washington, D.C., area is an outstanding example. Thus the dynamic changes of the past quarter century make it necessary to review concepts developed from studies of American cities in 1925 and 1939.

The Sector Theory

One concept needs to be examined again—the sector theory of residential development. In 1939 I formulated the sector theory which was to the effect that the high income areas of cities were in one or more sectors of the city, and not, as Burgess seemed to imply when he said: "beyond the workingmen's homes lies the residential district, a zone in which the better grade of apartment houses and single family residences predominate."

In a study of 64 American cities, block by block, based on the federal government's Work Project Administration's basic surveys of 1934, and

---

[28] Richard M. Hurd, *Principles of City Land Values* (1st edition 1903, republished by *The Record and Guide*, New York, New York, 1924).

studies of a number of large metropolitan areas, I prepared maps showing that high rent areas were located in one or more sectors of the city, and did not form a circle completely around it. Has this changed since 1939? In a survey of the entire Washington, D.C., metropolitan area in 1954 it was found that the main concentration of high-income families was in the District area west of Rock Creek Park, continuing into the Bethesda area of Montgomery County, Maryland. There were other scattered high income clusters in the Washington area. In surveys of other metropolitan areas it was discovered that the main concentration of high income families is on the north side of Dallis, the west and southwest sides of Houston, northward along the Lake Shore of Chicago, the south side of Kansas City, in the Beverly Hills area of Los Angeles, on the south side of Tulsa, the north side of Oklahoma City, the west side of Philadelphia, and the southwest side of Minneapolis. In the New York metropolitan area there are a number of nodules of high income in Westchester County, Nassau County, Bergen and Essex Counties in New Jersey, but the predominant movement was northward and eastward.

In a trip to Latin American cities in the summer of 1963 I found that the finest single family homes and apartments in Guatemala City, Bogota, Lima, La Paz, Quito, Santiago, Buenos Aires, Montevideo, Rio de Janeiro, Sao Paulo and Caracas were located on one side of the city only.[29]

The automobile and the resultant belt highways encircling American cities have opened up large regions beyond existing settled areas, and future high grade residential growth will probably not be confined entirely to rigidly defined sectors. As a result of the greater flexibility in urban growth patterns resulting from these radial expressways and belt highways, some higher income communities are being developed beyond low income sectors but these communities usually do not enjoy as high a social rating as new neighborhoods located in the high income sector.

Changes in Population Growth in Metropolitan Areas Outside the United States

Since the rate of population growth, particularly of the great cities of one million population and over, is a most important element in changing city structure, let us examine these differential rates of growth.[30] There has, in fact, been a wide variation in the rate of population growth in the great metropolitan areas throughout the world since 1940. In England, in London

---

[29] "The Residential and Retail Patterns of Leading Latin American Cities," *Land Economics*, November 1963.

[30] Homer Hoyt, *World Urbanization—Expanding Population in a Shrinking World*, Urban Land Institute Technical Bulletin 43, Washington, D.C., April 1962. See also "The Growth of Cities from 1800 to 1960 and Forecasts to Year 2000," *Land Economics*, May 1963, pp. 167–173.

and the other large metropolitan areas, the population has remained stationary; on the Continent of Europe outside of Russia, the growth rate of the great metropolitan areas has slowed down to 20 percent in the decade from 1950 to 1960. In Russia, eight of the largest older metropolitan areas increased in population only 15 percent from 1939 to 1962 but in this period many entirely new cities were built and other smaller cities grew in size until Russia now has 176 metropolitan areas with a population of 100,000 or more. China has had a great urban surge since . . . 1950 and reports a gain of 91 percent in the population of 18 great metropolitan areas as a result of its enforced industrialization process. This was reportedly carried too far and city dwellers had to be ordered back to the farms to raise food. Japan's five largest metropolitan area concentrations increased in numbers by 41 percent from 1951 to 1961. Fast suburban trains carry workers to and from downtown places of employment. In India, Delhi and New Delhi have more than doubled in population from 1951 to 1961 as a result of greatly expanded government and manufacturing activity. Other great Indian cities have grown rapidly, with 300,000 or more sleeping in the streets of Calcutta. In Australia, Sydney and Melbourne increased by 32 percent from 1951 to 1961. In Egypt, Cairo has gained 155 percent in numbers since 1940 as a result of being the chief headquarters of the Arab world. African cities like Nairobi and Leopoldville have gained rapidly. In Latin America, the urban population has exploded, with eight of its largest metropolitan areas gaining 166 percent from 1940 to 1962. The Sao Paulo metropolitan area, jumping from 1,380,000 to 4,374,000, gained 217 percent. Mexico City shot up from 1,754,000 to 4,666,000, a rise of 166 percent, in the same period of time.

Changes in Structure of Cities Outside the United States

While there are some similarities in the patterns of urban growth in the United States and foreign cities, as for example, in the sector theory, there are also some marked differences, as a result of the following five factors:

(1) Ownership of Automobiles

The chief factor in enabling city populations to spread out, to develop vast areas of single family homes on wide lots far from main transit facilities, to develop so many new shopping centers and so many dispersed factories, has been the almost universal ownership of the private automobile. Only the United States, New Zealand, Australia and Canada, which have developed city patterns similar to ours, had a high ratio of auto ownership to population in 1955, or from 181 per 1,000 in Canada and 183 in

Australia to 339 per 1,000 in the United States.[31] Northern European nations had from 58 to 111 cars per thousand of population but most Asiatic and African nations and most of the South American countries had less than 15 cars per 1,000 population. Argentina and Uruguay had 32 cars per 1,000 population in 1955.

The number of automobiles in northwestern Europe has shown marked gains recently: in West Germany from 1955 to 1963 the rate increased from 58 to 122 per 1,000 persons; in the United Kingdom for the same period the rate increased from 92 to 120 per 1,000 persons; and for the same period in Belgium the rate increased from 60 to 106 per 1,000 persons.

Obviously, in most of the world the urban population must depend upon buses or bicycles and live in apartments which can be economically served by subways, street cars or buses. Hence the great expansion into rural areas can take place only when there are suburban railroads as in Buenos Aires, Rio de Janeiro, Delhi and Tokyo, or subways as in London, Moscow, Tokyo, Madrid, Barcelona and Paris. Poor families live in central areas on steep mountainsides in Rio de Janeiro and Caracas, in shacks built by themselves; they live in blocks of tenements in central Hong Kong; sleep on the streets in downtown Calcutta, and build mud huts in central Nairobi.

(2) Private Ownership of Property

The pattern of American cities is the result of private ownership of property, which cannot be taken by condemnation except for a public use or in a blighted area and for which compensation must be paid when appropriated. There is now almost universal zoning control which regulates types of use, density of use and height of buildings; but these controls, first adopted in New York in 1916, had no effect upon early city growth and they have been modified or changed thousands of times. Otherwise it would not have been possible to develop the 8,300 new shopping centers nearly all of which required zoning in depth rather than strip zoning, nor could thousands of apartment buildings have been constructed in suburban areas.

Consequently, it is impossible to preserve green areas and open spaces without paying for the right. While the public cannot prevent the private owner from building on his land, zoning ordinances in some communities requiring one to five acres of land for each house have practically limited the utilization to occupancy by wealthy families because the high cost of sewer and water lines and street pavements in such low density areas virtually prevents building of houses for middle-or low-income family occupancy. Urban sprawl, or the filling in of all vacant areas, has been the bane of planners who would like to restore the early star-shaped pattern.

---

[31] Morton Ginsburg *Atlas of Economic Development* (Chicago, Illinois: University of Chicago Press, 1961), p. 74.

Where the State owns all of the land, as in Russia, or controls it rigidly, as in Finland, dense apartment clusters can be built along subway lines and the areas in between kept vacant.

(3) Central Area Attractions

The central retail areas of foreign cities have not deteriorated as a result of outlying shopping center competition for there are few such centers because very few people own cars. Crowds throng the shops on Florida Street in Buenos Aires and Union Street in Lima, which are closed to automobile traffic in shopping hours. Galerias, an elaborate expansion of the arcade, often extending up to five or six levels, have recently been built in downtown Santiago, Sao Paulo and Rio de Janeiro. Rotterdam has its new central retail area; Cologne its shopping street, a pedestrian thoroughfare. In these foreign cities, residents find the downtown area the chief attraction. The parks of Tokyo, London, Paris, Buenos Aires and Rio de Janeiro are downtown; so are the palaces and government offices, the great cathedrals, the museums, theatres, restaurants and night life of many foreign cities. The Forum and Colosseum in Rome, the Acropolis in Athens, Notre Dame in Paris, Westminster Abbey and the Tower of London are all in or near central areas.[32]

One change is occurring which is altering the skyline of many foreign cities—the advent of the tall office building. Formerly, cities outside the United States prized their uniform skyline broken only by the spire of a great cathedral or an Eiffel Tower. But now tall office buildings loom above London and Milan; they are planned for Paris. Caracas has its 30-story Twin Towers; Rio de Janeiro a new 35-story office building, El Centro; Mexico City its 32-story office building; and Sao Paulo has a great concentration of tall buildings in its downtown area.

(4) Stability of the Currency

The great building boom in the United States has been financed on money borrowed from banks and insurance companies. Despite gradual inflation, most people have confidence in the American dollar. The volume of mortgage credit for building in 1 to 4 family units increased from $17.4 billion in 1940 to $182.4 billion in December 1963. Shopping centers are financed on the basis of guaranteed leases by national chain store tenants which afford sufficient funds to construct the center. In nations

---

[32] Homer Hoyt, "The Structure and Growth of American Cities Contrasted With the Structure of European and Asiatic Cities," *Urban Land,* Urban Land Institute, Washington, D.C., September 1959.

like Brazil, however, where the interest rates are 3 to 5 percent a month and the cruzeiro has dropped from 384 to 1300 to the dollar in a year's time, it is impossible to secure long term loans. New buildings can be effected only by paying all cash as the work proceeds. An inflation of any marked extent in the United States would drastically curtail the supply of mortgage funds available for new building.

(5) Redevelopment Laws

The federal government in 1952 was authorized by Congress to pay two-thirds of the difference between the cost of acquiring sites in blighted areas and the re-sale price for new development. This has made possible the clearing and rebuilding of central areas which could not be done without both the power of condemnation and the write-down of the difference between the acquisition cost and the re-use value.

The principles of city growth and structure, formulated on the basis of experience in cities in the United States prior to 1930, are thus subject to modification not only as a result of dynamic changes in the United States in the last few decades but these principles, originating here, are subject to further revisions when it is sought to apply them to foreign cities.

17 | The Caste and Class of the Urban Form of Historic Philadelphia

NORMAN J. JOHNSTON

The devices of the social survey are familiar ones in planning methodology, especially those that have followed the monumental precedent established by the Lynds with their 1929 *Middletown*. A whole literature subsequently emerged in the tradition, the Middletowns of the 20s and 30s giving way to the Yankee Cities, Jonesvilles, and Organization Man's suburbias of the 40s and 50s. Can the processes of analysis demonstrated by such studies be set in reverse, trained not upon the nature of the contemporary community but instead on its historic predecessor? This paper makes an effort to do so.

SOURCE: *Journal of the American Institute of Planners*, XXXII (November 1966), 334–350. Reprinted by permission of the author and publisher.

The format is Philadelphia in the first half of the nineteenth century; this is the city which J. C. Wild recorded in four panoramic drawings of the late 1830s [1] which show, block by block, the closed ranks of row houses and public buildings, giving form to the orderly pattern determined by Thomas Holmes' plan of 1682. Trees that still generously shaded the interior residential yards broke what was otherwise an almost uniform line of building heights. Not quite uniform, for a series of cupolas and steeples acted as visual accents across the line of the city's horizon: Carpenters' Hall, Strickland's Merchants' Exchange, the Pennsylvania Hospital, and, notably, Philadelphia's State House (today's Independence Hall).

Of greater visual impact in number, though, was the punctuation provided by the city's churches: to the north the tall pointed steeple of St. Augustine's and the heavy turret of Zion; westward, the towers of St. John's, St. Stephen's, and the Fifth Presbyterian Church; to the south the cupola of the First Presbyterian Church facing Washington Square; and the east, of course, refined by Christ Church's elegant spire. Wild's view of Philadelphia was no exception in its sense of their pattern; for years the early drawings of the city had affirmed their presence in the urban prospect whose flavor would both aesthetically and literally have become all the flatter for their absence.

From such drawings we have evidence of the forms of architecture and urbanism of the Philadelphia of that day; but what of the society they housed? Are these the houses and streets of the Philadelphia gentleman and his peers; or working class neighborhoods; or areas of no set social pattern at all, reflecting only indifference to class in a city where all share indiscriminately its residential spaces and institutions? Lithographs and maps leave such questions unanswered; yet for an understanding of Philadelphia in the first half of the nineteenth century, this surface needs penetrating. The city's organization is only in part its blocks and streets and the architecture facing them. For the sense of another kind of organization, a social and spatial one, an ecology of social class, I propose turning again to Philadelphia's churches.

Social Class and Religion

The traditional trappings of the American dream have always included an assumption of the classlessness out of which the institutions of the nation were shaped and as a consequence class stratification was institutionally uncoded. Nevertheless, a kind of class structure emerged peculiar in this period to America: a non-formal social ranking system and the establishment of the citizen's position within it, ease of the individual's mobility within that system, and a certain refinement required in distinguishing the hallmarks of each class. The process has usually become visible through such devices as club memberships, schools attended, occupations, amounts

---

[1] J. C. Wild, *Views of Philadelphia*, 1st ed. (Philadelphia: NP, 1838).

of inherited wealth and income, race or ethnic origins—all are part of a puzzle of indices that have served as raw material for many studies.[2]

In this system the role the Protestant churches have been shown to play has been impressively documented. Kurt Mayer is explicit in defining our contemporary denomination-class status: "Individual Protestant churches tend to be class churches and each denomination, while it usually included members from several social levels, is apt to be closely associated with one particular class." [3]

This is a study then of pre-Civil War Philadelphia in terms of the degree of its class structure as expressed in certain of its churches' members and their spatial segregation. The approach is based on the hypotheses that there is a class bias in the period's Protestant churches in Philadelphia and that the location of their members by denomination will reveal this bias as well as class ranking by residential area.

The Scheme in Philadelphia

From the tone of literary sources if not from the detachment of systematic studies and records one senses a stratification system for Protestant churches in early Philadelphia.[4] Their status system with certain exceptions appears similar to the national scaling of the Princeton study [5] of our own time with the Episcopalians and Presbyterians at the high end of the scale, the Baptists and Methodists somewhere below them, and the Negro counterparts all sharing the bottommost limits of status, having none at all in the white social and class system. Though Scharf and Wescott's treatment of the denominations is not precisely contemporaneous with the period of

---

[2] Noel P. Gist and L. A. Halbert, *Urban Sociology*, 4th ed. (New York: Thomas Y. Crowell Co., 1956), p. 299. Gist and Halbert define a social class as "a relatively permanent division of society or a community in which aggregates of individuals are marked off by considerations of status, style of life, and power." A number of pioneering studies have been made toward understanding of such class structuring in American culture, all seeking to show how the classless American community through a complex system of symbols assigns its members to their position in its ranks. *Middletown* (1929) and *Middletown in Transition* (1937) of the Lynds, *Democracy in Jonesville* by Warner et al. (1948), and Hollingshead's *Elmtown's Youth* (1949) are in this group.

[3] Kurt B. Mayer, *Class and Society* (New York: Random House, 1955), p. 44.

[4] This study is confining its efforts to the Baptist, Episcopalian, Methodist, and Presbyterian denominations. Not only were all four active in Philadelphia during the study period, but they also had Negro counterparts. The Quakers, Unitarians, and Lutherans had no significant membership among Negroes, and the Congregationalists and evangelical sects of our own day were late arrivals in Philadelphia.

[5] The study was done by the Office of Public Opinion Research of Princeton University and is reported on in detail by Liston Pope in his "Religion and the Class Structure," *Annals of the American Academy of Political and Social Science*, 256 (March, 1948), pp. 84–91.

study, they can for the moment give some substance to this ranking inference. For both the Presbyterian and Episcopalian churches they note the prominence, social status, and wealth of their members. "The Protestant Episcopal church in Philadelphia has always comprised a large number of persons of wealth and prominent social position," or, writing of the First Presbyterian Church, "some of the most distinguished men of our city worshipped within its walls," and "one of the most influential churches . . . ." For the Baptists they have no comments on membership status. They dispose of the Methodists with the statement that "though the congregations were weak, some noted men occasionally attend"; but they acknowledged that the Methodists were late-comers to the field and that their denominational rivals had been occupying the territory some one hundred years before their arrival.[6]

There is no uncertainty about the location in the class hierarchy of the Negroes of Philadelphia and their churches—at the bottom. From the earliest days of the nation up to about 1800 it was apparently not unusual for white Philadelphia congregations to treat Negroes with relative equanimity. But by the 1830s this had changed to increased tension between the two races marked by routine acts of cruelty and brutality against Negroes, particularly by the "lower and rougher classes of whites," and a series of race riots in the city during the period from 1834 to 1849. Turner suggests the reason for this change in attitude was largely due to Abolitionism which seems to have reached crusading proportions during these years.[7] This managed to stir up racial antagonism which was only latent in the earlier period of what passed for racial harmony. Editorializing on the causes behind the race riots, *Hazard's Register* writes that in part their excesses came about "because Negro churches, owing to their noise and disorder, had come to be regarded as a nuisance in the neighborhood."[8] (Their existence in the first place, though, was largely due to the gradual exclusion policy of white congregations.) In 1810, at a time when there were forty white churches, there were four Negro churches in the city: two Methodist, one Episcopalian, and one Baptist. By 1852, Negro churches numbered fifteen, including Presbyterian, Baptist, Episcopalian, and Methodist denominations.

As a basis for analysis, certain representative churches have been selected, including those which, through some circumstances (usually a first-founded status), have a mutually shared high prestige within their denominational groups [see map 1]:

---

[6] J. Thomas Scharf and Thompson Westcott, *History of Philadelphia*, Vol. II (Philadelphia: L. H. Everts & Co., 1884), pp. 1262–1365 and 1394–1402.
[7] Edward R. Turner, *The Negro in Pennsylvania* (Washington: American History Assoc., 1911), p. 160.
[8] Samuel Hazard, ed., *Hazard's Register of Philadelphia*, XIV (September 15, 1834), 200–203.

MAP 1. Location of Study Churches

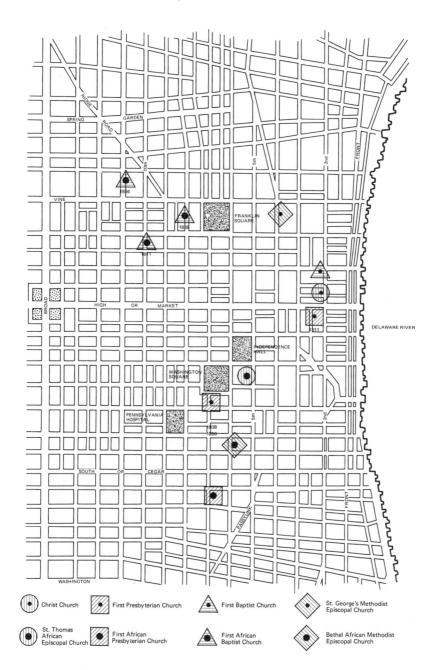

Christ Church	First Presbyterian Church	First Baptist Church	St. George's Methodist Episcopal Church
St. Thomas African Episcopal Church	First African Presbyterian Church	First African Baptist Church	Bethel African Methodist Episcopal Church

White Churches

Christ Church (Episcopal). Founded 1695, this prestigious church is closely identified with the Colonial and Revolutionary periods in Philadelphia and national history. Its present building was built over the period 1724–1755. In its churchyard are the graves of many early Americans of importance (for example Benjamin Franklin, Robert Morris, and several Continental Army generals).

First Presbyterian Church. Founded 1698. At the opening of the nineteenth century, the congregation was meeting in a new building completed in 1794. In 1821, it moved to a Washington Square location. "The new church building was the largest and finest yet erected in the city." It has since disappeared.

First Baptist Church. Founded 1698. It is no longer at its old center city site, though still serving a center city congregation.

St. George's Methodist Episcopal Church. Founded 1767. It is the world's oldest Methodist church building in continuous service since 1769. "A rough board floor was put down on the east end of the church, while the other half was an earthen floor. The seats were rough, and the pulpit was simply a square box." This building, much remodeled from its humbler days, is still in service.

Negro Churches

None of these buildings stand today:

St. Thomas African Episcopal Church. Founded 1794. Both St. Thomas' and Bethel were Negro offshoots of St. George's. However, Absalom Jones, St. Thomas' founder, chose to break not only with St. George's but with Methodism as well and so affiliated with the Episcopalians.

First African Presbyterian Church. Founded 1804. William Catto, its minister in 1855, states its founding was "not due to ill treatment" but rather so there might be a church "subject to colored organization and government but without separation from fellow Presbyterians." [9] Its first minister was a former Negro slave, John Glouster. It was the first Negro Presbyterian church in the United States.

First African Baptist Church. Founded in 1809 by thirteen former members of the First Baptist Church of Philadelphia.

Bethel African Methodist Episcopal Church. Founded 1794. Its

---

[9] William T. Catto, *A Centenary Discourse* (Philadelphia: Joseph M. Wilson, 1857), pp. 18–19.

founder, Richard Allen, withdrew in protest over St. George's forcing of Negro members of its congregation to the gallery by white members. The mother church of African Methodist Episcopalians, it today has branches throughout the nation and abroad.

Occupational Status

The coincidence of history, time, and circumstances force a far more abbreviated technique for class analysis, of course, than was at the disposal of social scientists such as the Lynds or Warner. But even Warner, for all the accoutrements of the Yankee City study, acknowledged a high correlation between one aspect of an individual's role and his class position—his occupation; and others confirm that, given no opportunity for greater depth of research, occupation is the one best index of social class. Since records contemporary to the period have been found that include occupational information, their use and analysis are the basis for this study's class inferences in evaluating its hypotheses.[10]

Any use of occupations for population ranking requires ranking of the occupations first. One such study was made for the Research Division of the *Chicago Tribune* by the sociologist Bevade McCall whose purpose was to establish "prestige order" of jobs in the Chicago area. Its conclusions resulted in a simple grouping running from 1 through 7 with the lowest number being the category of greatest prestige.[11] Warner's scale for occupational rating as used in *Democracy in Jonesville* has more elegance, but the stratifying end is the same for either system, Warner's having the grace of implying more precision.[12]

The use of scaling devices for nineteenth-century Philadelphia is not a simple transliteration of the twentieth-century model to the preceding century's scene, primarily because of two complications involving occupations themselves. Where in the model are, say, a shallopman or mantua maker, occupations no longer practiced by those labels in our economic world—if at all? And what was the attitude of the Philadelphian of that period toward either of these or any of the other occupations in terms of

---

[10] All city directories include occupation as part of the information for each name listed. In addition, the 1811 directory asterisked all Negroes listed. The Abolition Society's census data for 1838 and 1856 gave detailed information on the occupations of Negroes. The existence of these manuscripts determined the 1838 and 1856 cut-off dates used in the study, material that was not otherwise available. The 1838 census also gave Negro church membership by specific church, but no denomination or church was indicated in the 1856 census.

[11] Typical first rank jobs: architect, top executive, federal judge, Bishop; seventh rank: hod carrier, janitor, dishwasher, laborer.

[12] Warner *et al.*, *Democracy in Jonesville* (New York: Harper and Brothers, 1949).

prestige? The problem is partly one of identification—a shallopman was a boatman on a large boat or dinghy; a mantua maker was a dressmaker—but their location within the ranking model is more illusive. The approach used here includes research on contemporary wage scales and a subjective assignment; for example, the knowledge that seamen are paid more than mariners is a hint in deciding the relative status of each.

The rating scale set up for present purposes is based on scoring of status running from 7 (highest status of individual's occupation gets highest score) to 1 within six general occupational groupings: Proprietary and Official, Mercantile and Industrial, Clerks and Kindred, Skilled Workers, Semi-skilled Workers, and Unskilled Workers. Once this scale and its sub-categories had been set up, scoring for church members by occupation could proceed.[13] [The score for each church is] . . . the average total occupational status score for all members listed in the city directory for the year indicated.

Upper class status of their members is clearly scored by both the First Presbyterians and Christ Church for each of the sampling years; though there is a jockeying for top spot between them, their scores are almost the same, separated by only fractions of percentage points. Below the average are the First Baptists, clearly the middle class church of its day. In light of the Princeton study and other suggestions that the Methodists in our own time occupy this middle class position and the Baptists a lower class one, is this a Philadelphia variation of the norm or a change in national status over time between the relative positions of these two denominations? For well below the Baptists from 1811 to 1865 is St. George's, almost half way between the Baptists and the all-Negro average at survey year. The Methodists in the Philadelphia of that period are the lower class church.

The lack of suitable records for Negro church memberships makes it impossible to give the detail to status scoring that was possible among the white congregations. However, a gross score for Negroes can be calculated for 1811 and 1856 since the 1811 city directory included an indication of race as well as occupation, and the Pennsylvania Abolitionist Society's Negro census of 1856 recorded names which were then used as a basis for 1856 directory listings and occupations. Happily, the Society's census for 1838 included detailed church membership data, so for that year only, specific scoring analysis can be made for Negroes. Within the narrow confines of their caste position it shows close relative status between the scoring by Negro denominations and their white counterparts. Both white and Negro Episcopalian and Presbyterian groups lie bunched together well above their

---

[13] The scaling system of 7 through 1 admittedly makes detailed value judgments about relative status. However, no more should be read into the scoring than its use for placing occupations and denominations by *relative* rank, though the temptation to arrive at decimal point differentiation will not be resisted by me.

respective all-church summary scores. And lying below the all-church score are the Negro Baptists and Bethel Methodists, again in a similar relationship between the two as were their white counterparts.[14] Though the Negro churches do not represent as wide a total scoring spread as the white churches, their relative positions are essentially the same as those of their white brethren. The only variation is between the Episcopalian and Presbyterian congregations, and in both racial groups the differences in ranking are so slight as to be negligible.

Thus, on the basis of occupation as an index of social class, there is a clear bias among the Protestant churches of pre-Civil War Philadelphia as reflected in the status prestige of their members, as follows:

Upper Class: Christ Church
                        First Presbyterian Church
Middle Class: First Baptist Church
Lower Class: St. George's Methodist Episcopal Church
   Low Caste: (All Negro churches, but ranked as indicated)
      Upper Class: St. Thomas African Episcopal Church
                           First African Presbyterian Church
      Middle Class: First African Baptist Church
      Lower Class: Bethel African Methodist Episcopal Church

Analysis of Residential Locations

Having determined this class ranking by denominations, does the residential location of their members reveal a similar ranking of neighborhoods? The balance of this study is concerned with such an analysis and consequent interpretation. Mapping techniques were the same for each of the cut-off dates of 1811, 1838, and 1856. Spot maps recorded residential location pattern by denomination as well as significant areal linkages that suggested a more than chance proximity (three or more member families living within the distance of a Philadelphia city block of each other). From these maps generalized linkage areas summarized significant groupings of all denominations for both races and for each cut-off date [see Map 2]. Finally, based on the linkage area maps, inferences were made as to structuring of residential areas by social class and were subsequently translated into a mapped interpretation. The balance of this paper describes and explains these inferences and their mapping.

---

[14] The similarity is a striking one. By a simple ratio calculation the distance by which the white Episcopalian and Presbyterian scores are above the white summary score is proportionally almost exactly the same as the Negro Episcopalian and Presbyterian scores are above their all-church score. The same proportional relationship shows up in the distances in both racial groups between their Baptist and Methodist churches.

MAP 2. Generalized Linkage Areas: Spatial Analysis, 1811

|||| Christ Church   \\\\ St. George

/// First Presbyterian   ▓ Negro enclave

≡ First Baptist

MAP 3. Generalized Class Ecology: Spatial Analysis, 1811

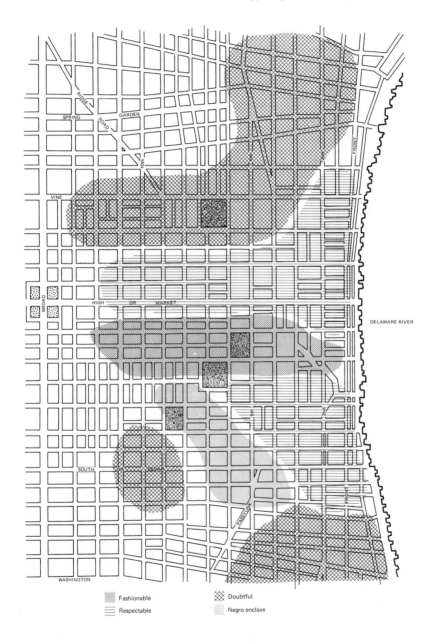

Fashionable   Doubtful

Respectable   Negro enclave

Spatial Analysis, 1811

An abruptly sharp ecological isolation of the two races in terms of residential areas is the first impression gained from the 1811 maps. The mapping of generalized linkage areas tends to exaggerate this pattern, but there still can be little question that residential segregation between the races was a pattern of Philadelphia very early in the nineteenth century.

The two upper class white denominations dominate residential neighborhoods west of Fourth and on either side of Market Street, close to the activity center on the Delaware but not too close. Waterfront sections are shared by all denominations with a marked tendency for St. George's people to locate to the north of Market, possibly from the desire to be well away from the caste ghetto. On the basis of linkage areas among white congregations, the Presbyterians are most likely to be found sharing residential space with Episcopalians and are found sharing that space with Methodists only when the other two denominations are present in significant numbers. Episcopalians and Baptists are sometimes found together, but the former are, like the Presbyterians, similarly isolated from the Methodists except when the other denominations are there. Baptists, however, share residential neighborhoods alone with Methodists or are in an enclave of their own.

.   .   .   .   .

The spatial pattern of the denominational groups in 1811 supports the inference that there is a clear class ranking of residential areas. Map 3 represents an interpretation of these conclusions of class ecology. The fashionable upper class residential area of the Philadelphia of that date is south of Market Street and running east-west on either side of Independence Hall. As suggested above, this area is within easy distance of the centers of commerce and government for the community leaders who direct them. Generalized linkage areas show this section is almost entirely dominated by Episcopalians and Presbyterians. (Only four Baptists and one St. George membership were recorded on the spot map.) Granting the status orientation of these denominations, the nucleation here of Episcopalians and Presbyterians appears beyond explanation as coincidence.

Paralleling Market Street and spreading northward along the river front is a residential section whose class character is more modest than those of its neighbors immediately to the south—middle class and respectable. An area of similar class level lies to the south of the fashionable district and along the river, but its westward extension is cut off by the Negro ghetto. In both these sections denominational distribution includes almost equal numbers of Episcopalians, Presbyterians, and Baptists with the latter having strongest linkage patterns along the river north of Market Street. The "respectable" district to the south includes a scattering of these three denominations, with the Baptists represented in significant numbers. Curiously, while no Methodists from St. George's are found in this latter district, there are a number of Negro residents recorded. This may be evidence of an ecological invasion still in process by middle class white families into an area previously held by Negroes who are now being displaced into their enclave to the west.

Except for some nucleation of Methodists around Market Street at the river front, St. George's members are almost entirely confined to areas peripheral to the fashionable and respectable districts just described. The inference here is that this then indicates these residential sections are of "doubtful" social status. Map 3 gives their general definition. There is some sharing of space by the Methodists with other denominations in these outlying sections, but where it occurs it is with Baptists or Episcopalians or a scattering of Negroes.

Spatial Analysis, 1838

The essential separation of the two races in 1811 still persists 27 years later. However, the ecological forces of invasion and succession, only hinted at by the 1811 mapping, emerge more clearly in 1838. The coincidence of significant Negro residential location in an area south of Market Street along the river, a locality otherwise clearly middle class in composition in 1811, enabled us to make the tentative inference of invasion by whites. This can now be supported by the clear evidence of Negro displacement away from there. Now that this area has been successfully annexed for white residential purposes, another one appears involved in the same process, that to the west of Washington Square where linkages of white residents, predominantly Presbyterian, are in apparent competition with their Negro neighbors. But other than such zones of transition, the spatial caste system persists and has been reinforced by time. The Negroes have been pushed south and west under pressure from the whites who are retiring before the increased space demands for central city commercial uses. Where this move to the west and south is largely dominated by the white Presbyterians and Episcopalians, the move northward is a Baptist and Methodist operation.

Among white congregations, Episcopalians during this period appear to share space again predominantly with Presbyterians, though there is a tendency for Episcopalian nucleation along the Delaware just north of Vine Street, coinciding with the Baptist move into that section. The Presbyterians again live in the same areas in association only with Episcopalians except for a minor grouping in a Baptist neighborhood in the southeast part of the city and their transition zone west of Washington Square. While there are signs of competition from the Negroes and Episcopalians, the northern part of the city is still essentially a Baptist–Methodist stronghold.

In contrast to the class distribution possible in the white world, the distribution pattern of Negroes . . . is one of layer upon layer, indicating the density of population and absence of much choice of symbols of class differences within the caste in terms of spatial segregation. There seem to be centers shared by all denominations with some circumferential zone patterns outward from the center, the Methodists as lowest class being farthest afield. In this respect their spatial patterns resemble those of the whites: nearness to the center is more desirable than the inconvenience of distance. A curious vacuum separates the major Negro enclave from the transition sector west of Washington Square.

Class ecology in 1838 . . . shows that the fashionable area is still predominantly south of Market Street with an anchor in the area east of Washington Square and extending west and somewhat northward into space that in 1811 appeared unable to support the pretensions of a fashionable address. In return, much of the formerly upper class area east of the civic center (Independence Hall) has now been claimed by residents of no more than respectable attainments, uniting into one middle class oriented district all those residential parts of center city along the river. The center of the city is moving west. Areas of doubtful residential prestige remain essentially unchanged to the north and with some succession into formerly middle class districts in the south or into areas not previously settled in the southeast. The tight Negro enclave has itself established succession to the west and by growth and fission formed a satellite enclave to the north. This latter hints at another instance of ecological process, though the 1838 spot maps did not themselves indicate just what was at work.

Spatial Analysis, 1856

The pincer movement of warfare may be an appropriate analogy for what shows up [in maps for 1856]. The development in those residential sections south of Market is to the west and south completing encirclement of the caste ghetto. The latter appears to be shrinking into a tigher total space within which more people are being crowded with the whites continuing their invasion and succession processes in the conflict zone that . . . in 1838 . . . was undisputably Negro. Now the Presbyterians, with only nominal help from Episcopalians, have challenged this with a sweep through that area we referred to as a vacuum in 1838, . . .

The white Episcopalians and Presbyterians also seem to have assumed complete control of residential areas south of Market except where the Negroes had preceded them (and as the processes just analyzed suggest, even Negro hold on parts of their ghetto seems insecure). North of Market Street there is a wider range of denominational representation, with Episcopalians, Baptists, and Methodists being present. Now Presbyterians usually either share space with Episcopalians, or are busy invading Negro neighborhoods, or live among themselves. Episcopalians seem to live comfortably with both Baptists and Methodists as a denominational trio but not separately with either. If the Baptists or Methodists decide to form any monogamous association it is with each other rather than with either of the upper class denominations.

Class ecology . . . shows fashionable addresses still anchored to Washington Square but moving south and west toward what can be expected to become a consolidated triangular block defined approximately by Independence Hall, Pennsylvania Hospital, and Broad Street a few blocks below its junction with Market. Respectable middle class neighborhoods almost entirely surround this upper class zone except where the Negroes block it to the south. They [respectable white middle class neighborhoods] have resumed domination of Market Street which has acted as a route for a marked advance up Broad Street and eastward around the Vine Street section which still remains in the pall of doubtful distinction. There is also a marked move west of Broad Street, particularly among the Baptists, and for the first time in the research, residential addresses for a number of Episcopalians were indicated as Germantown, an early Philadelphia satellite community; spatial moves are to be taken with larger leaps in the years ahead.

Summary

In summarizing the implications of these ecological patterns, the grouping of the white denominations where mixing occurs is especially telling. Of the two upper class churches, Presbyterian and Episcopalian, the former's members in all three time periods either tend to live separately or share space with the latter. (Invasion patterns are only transitory deviations from this norm.) Their residential patterns also continue the tightest sense of community, showing an interesting disinclination to move far afield from their home base south of Market Street and east of Broad. When the break comes, as it will after the Civil War, they will make it over a ring of middle class development to land in the Rittenhouse Square area, well to the west.

Closer attention to the denomination members as people may help to explain this segregation. Initial listing of Episcopalians by occupation showed a much broader representation than was so for the Presbyterians. This was no doubt influenced by the origins of Episcopalianism itself, closer to the roots of Roman Catholicism, a break from the mother church for political gain rather than reasons of doctrine and initially maintaining the same class universality of membership as that denomination. The nature of Episcopalianism in this country and its associations with England had resulted, then, in the inclusion in Philadelphia of persons of notably high status within a membership filtering down through the class structure, though not so far as to include any of the lowest status group. The Presbyterians on the other hand, a true Protestant denomination with its origins in Calvinist doctrine and its accent on work, success, and material reward, not only tended to discourage lowest class members but probably even repelled them. The Presbyterian membership's occupational profile read that way, a homogeneous and business-oriented block of respectability. Perhaps here lay its success and its insecurity, a conservatism of outlook in which no chances were taken. The Philadelphia Presbyterian achieved position through ambition and hard work, lived correctly, associated with the right people, and *had a proper address*. It was the prosperous upper status merchant who made the First Presbyterian Church of Philadelphia what we have seen it to be, secure in its hold on the best neighborhood and hesitant to brave residential unknowns beyond its hard core. The Episcopalians on the other hand were less restrained in choice of residential locations. Where they allied themselves with the Presbyterians, as they so often did, they reinforced the high status of that neighborhood. Where they found themselves in association with the Methodists and Baptists, it evidenced the breadth of the congregation's social base (or perhaps the security its members felt in their position). But this breadth did not ever appear wide enough to share space significantly with the lower class Methodists alone; it was always either with or in close proximity to the middle class Baptists or not at all. These Baptists, by the nature of their position in the hierarchy, could be found on both sides of the status fence, but through the years included in this study they were increasingly unlikely to either be off by themselves or in the same constellation with the Methodists. The Methodists were farthest removed from the upper class Presbyterians, both in terms of class status and physical distance. As they tended to move north, the Presbyterians moved south and west. The fringe was lower class oriented.

It is a curious coincidence of spatial segregation and competition that the Philadelphia Presbyterian should either be associated with the Episcopalian or with the Negroes. Of course the latter relationship is, as has been indicated, one of process rather than rapport, a sharing of space for purposes of exclusion, not association. This study appears to substantiate the fact that the incidence of Negro retainers and their families sharing the same neighborhood with the upper class families they served must have been rare. . . .

An aspect of early Philadelphia ecology that has markedly changed in our own times is the relationship of fashionable address to center city. The convenience of close proximity to the concentration of governmental, commercial, and industrial life was an apparent influence in early times making a close-in address a desirable one. The competitive advantages of the upper status residents insured them these locations and relegated the lower status groups to marginal areas peripheral to the more desirable center. This appears true even for the distribution of Negro residences within the 1838 enclave. Within its limited confines the enclave represented a complex of all denominations, but it was the lower class Negro Methodist who lived on its fringes.

In time this pattern will be reversed. By 1865, as has been noted, Episcopalian addresses were recorded for Germantown. The railroad, street car, and automobile would accelerate this pace to flood proportions by the 1950s, threatening for the future a center city of the economically, socially, and racially underprivileged. But such present processes are one hundred years distant from the time of this study when both convenience and choice maintained the desirability of a central city residential neighborhood.

Conclusion

This, then, has been an analysis of the social structure of an early nineteenth-century city, approached through certain prominent institutions which housed it and flavored its urban form. Philadelphia's churches of that day were indeed ranked by a prestige hierarchy, and the neighborhoods in which their members lived reflected that ranking in class spatial segregation. With this kind of understanding the earlier two dimensional simplicity of the Wild drawings of the 1830 scene can be read with a new and revealing perspective. Philadelphia begins to be seen for what it was —a city of considerable architectural charm, the steady rhythm of its row houses disciplined by the framework of the city's plan, and accented by an impressive range of public buildings. As ensemble it manifested the institutions, attainments, ambitions, and passions of the people who occupied it: pride and prejudice held within a pecking order of caste and class.

18 | The New York Metropolitan Region's Community Types

EDGAR M. HOOVER and
RAYMOND VERNON

Having considered the effect upon residence choice of the three critical factors—job types, income level, and children—we can now trace their combined effects in determining "who lives where" in the Region.*

* For this study the New York Metropolitan Region was defined as a 22-county area, including parts of New York State, New Jersey, and Connecticut. Manhattan and the four other most highly developed counties are designated the Core. The Inner Ring comprises the seven counties immediately surrounding the Core and is the next most highly developed section. The Outer Ring consists of the remaining counties and is the section with the lowest development.—Ed.

SOURCE: Edgar M. Hoover and Raymond Vernon, *Anatomy of a Metropolis* (Cambridge: Harvard University Press, 1959), pp. 181–182. Copyright 1959 by the Regional Plan Association, Inc.

The inner part of the Core—Manhattan and parts of adjacent counties —is peopled mainly by two contrasting types of household. First, there is a preponderant mass of bottom-income unskilled manual and service workers, including most of the Region's members of "disadvantaged" recent in-migrant groups. They are there because of the supply of obsolete, dilapidated, and highly compressed housing; because their jobs are mainly in Manhattan and nearby heavy-industry zones, and the subway affords cheap access; because they are excluded from most Inner Ring suburbs by social counter-pressures as well as by lack of rock-bottom housing; and because they find some community solidarity and better job opportunity within the focal cluster and its huge and variegated labor market. The other conspicuous element in the inner Core (far smaller, and mainly confined to certain sections of Manhattan) consists of wealthy and mainly childless people in the professional and executive categories, who value quick access to their Manhattan jobs and also the many avocational attractions of the Region's center, and who have been able to afford the high costs of luxury-apartment redevelopment.

A little farther out, in the outer parts of the Core and the most urban-ized parts of the Inner Ring, the population is predominantly lower-mid-dle in income, with both extremes under-represented. The housing here is somewhat less old and more spacious than in the inner Core and includes some relatively new apartments. Occupationally, these communities consist mainly of lower white-collar commuters to Manhattan and semiskilled in-dustrial workers employed in the Inner Ring and Core.

Going farther out in the Inner Ring, there is a gradual rise in income level and improvement in the newness and quality of housing, with the single-family house becoming predominant. The proportion of skilled in-dustrial workers relative to semiskilled and unskilled rises, with a similar upward shift in the status of the white-collar groups, and a rising propor-tion of households with children. Interspersed in the pattern are the older, zoning-protected, upper-class suburbs populated largely by Manhattan-em-ployed professional and executive workers.

Still farther out (in the outer parts of the Inner Ring and some of the inner edges of the Outer Ring) is a zone of active new construction, almost entirely in single-family houses on fairly ample lots. These suburbs house primarily upper-income people with children who want space and can afford new housing. A considerable proportion, by the time we reach this zone, work in the Inner Ring rather than the Core. Here are interspersed, too, some rather low-income communities (largely old industrial cities and towns), populated by unskilled manual and service workers with suburban jobs and, predominantly, with children.

Finally, in the more outlying parts of the Region we find a few exclusive exurbs where high-income families with children have accepted remoteness from Manhattan in order to get space, privacy, and neighborhood homoge-neity. Most other people living that far out, however, work nearby in the outer suburbs; and economic and other links with the Region's center become more and more tenuous as we approach the largely arbitrary outer boundary.

19 | Los Angeles, Prototype of Supercity

RICHARD AUSTIN SMITH

Ever since the first figures of the 1960 Census began to appear, the great cities of the East have been turning, with some of Balboa's "wild surmise," to discern what a whole new ocean of people has been doing to Los Angeles. To be sure, a simple superfluity of people was not enough in itself to make Los Angeles a cynosure of eastern interest—New York has been drowning in humanity for years, and Chicago is still America's second-biggest city, albeit by so narrow a margin that a busload of newcomers may next month put L.A. in that slot. The attraction Los Angeles holds for eastern metropoles is rather that of a rapidly unfolding pattern for megalopolis. L.A.'s population has shot up by 2,375,000 within a ten-year period, an influx of humanity almost massive enough to people present-day Boston. Borne upward by the greatest westward migration in U.S. history, the growth of Los Angeles has eclipsed that of every other metropole in the nation—double metropolitan Chicago's, more than New York's and San Francisco's put together. This one American city has accounted for 10 percent of the population increase in the sum total of our metropolitan areas, and now, with 6,740,000 people, its sheer size has given it the grandeur of a city-state; indeed it is bigger than all save seven of the states of the Union.

Under such circumstances, Los Angeles provides a scaled-down, speeded-up version of the process of urbanization that is even now engulfing the fewer and fewer islands of darkness in the vast sea of light that stretches from Philadelphia to Boston. L.A. in the grip of smog is no longer a special situation, but one impending for every city of size. L.A. struggling to handle more than three million automobiles—80 percent of those employed in the area drive to work—is now regarded as providing a preview of traffic jams that, in a few years, might stretch a hundred miles along the Atlantic seaboard. L.A.'s long—and successful—battle to provide adequate water is no longer viewed as something apart from common experience, the consequence of 50 percent of a state's population being concentrated in a

SOURCE: *Fortune*, March 1965, pp. 99–101, 200. Reprinted by permission of the publisher.

region that contains only 2 percent of its water resources; the dry hand of shortage has steadily tightened on eastern throats as population rises and the water table falls.

What gives Los Angeles added interest is the tremendous amount of territory it covers and the unexampled heterogeneity of its components. Here is no simple city set in a symmetrical matrix of suburbs, but a metropolitan area, covering far and away the largest acreage of any of the 216 listed in the U.S. Census. It begins at the northeastern border of Los Angeles County and ends some seventy miles to the south, thrust part way through neighboring Orange County. Roughly in the center of the Los Angeles metropolitan area—4,842 square miles of sun-drenched mountains, plains, valleys, and beaches—is the city of Los Angeles itself.

The city proper, 458 square miles in its own right, is an amalgam of sixty-four place-name communities—most of them absorbed between 1910 and 1927 as the city pushed ever outward, trading its precious water for territorial rights. Surrounding the city limits are seventy-five satellite cities ranging in size from Long Beach (population: 369,000) to the City of Industry (746). Because the oldest and sturdiest of these—Pasadena, Santa Monica, Burbank, Culver City, Beverly Hills, etc.—survived only by resisting Los Angeles' encroachment (and annexing a little territory of their own), they form something of an encircling ring of militantly independent communities. To these have been added a whole new crop of small cities, strung along the new freeways like trees along a river, their way to incorporation made easy by a state constitution that permits incorporation of any unincorporated area on petition of 500 citizens.

Untypical as this evolution has been by eastern standards, it has lately come to have a certain fascination. A new shape for urban agglomerations is in the making and Los Angeles may ultimately establish the pattern for it. Here is an obvious proving ground for metropolitan, even regional, government. It is perhaps no more than justice that Los Angeles, so long derided as "twenty-four suburbs in search of a city," may now be emerging as a forerunner of the urban world of tomorrow. Yet what can be learned from L.A. today, as it struggles with the problems of size and change, regression and trail blazing, may well determine whether some sociologist of the Nineties will be deprecating the metropoles of the *East* as "a half-dozen cities in search of a supercity."

The Struggle for the Center

Somewhat ironically, just at the time Los Angeles is attracting attention as a nascent supercity of the future, a group of influential citizens is trying to make it over in conformance with the "classic city" patterns of the past. The idea, promulgated in a series of "Centropolis" studies, was that every great city of the nation had a downtown core or center and L.A. would have to have one too. According to the reports, the central area, which had once held "a virtual monopoly on all major activities in Los Angeles," would have to be rejuvenated because "the future growth and prosperity of Los Angeles and the surrounding metropolitan region depend very largely upon the economic health and physical attraction of the central area." A sizable amount of new construction had already gone up since the first Centropolis study was published in 1960—Welton Becket's lovely new Music Center, the bulk of a civic center, second in size only to that of the nation's capital, new additions to a group of banking headquarters, the Wilshire Metropolitan Medical Center, to mention a few. This past December the Los Angeles Central City Committee released its master plan: "a bold program," according to the Los Angeles *Times*, "to make its Central City one of the world's great centers for commerce, finance, and culture." The over-all space target for the downtown core: 18,137,000 net square feet of new construction.

The size of this target, building 1.7 times as much square footage in the next fifteen years as was built in the 1954–63 decade, suggests a major marshaling of civic effort. And certainly some downtown businessmen believe the magnitude of the problem merits such effort. Retail sales, once 75 percent of those in the metropolitan area, have declined to 18.2 percent in thirty years' time, as new shopping centers proliferated outside the central-city area; the majority of new buildings have been erected elsewhere. As banker Robert Gordon, president of the Downtown Businessmen's Association, a prime backer of Centropolis, recently put it: "The only way we can preserve the property values is to keep the central city. We have seen building rentals go down from $6 a square foot to $2.75 a square foot. I could take you around downtown and show you buildings that are only 10 to 15 percent occupied. There is too much money invested in downtown to let it rot." Rot, of course, is a word calculated to give the average American the shivers, but the real question appears to be, what price so grand a re-establishment of downtown hegemony? Should all this effort be channeled into trying to reestablish a "central core"?

The average Angeleno would probably answer in the negative. Downtown stands as a firmly established center of such old-line business activities as banking, insurance, finance, oil, and publishing, and is where 160,000 people have jobs. It contains such essentials as the courts, the main offices of city and county government, the Stock Exchange. But nobody "loves" downtown, and to the average citizen it is just 4,000 acres of parking lots, an abundance of bad restaurants, a paucity of good hotels. Downtown is something he and 380,000 other freeway drivers—68 percent of those coming into the area—are pleased to hurtle by every day without stopping. The Angeleno's loyalty is to his suburb, where he can obtain most of the amenities of life, and anyway it would take him twice as long to drive downtown in search of entertainment as to cover the same distance on the city's periphery. Many thoughtful observers like Ruben Mettler, president of TRW Space Technology Laboratories, believe it's too late for the establishment of a core city: geography would lick a central system.

James Gillies, professor of urban land economics at U.C.L.A.'s graduate school of business administration, reports similar skepticism. "I live in Encino, out in the San Fernando Valley but still within the city limits," he remarked recently. "Ninety percent of the people there enjoy all the advantages of life in a big city but identify with suburban Encino. They have no interest in the redevelopment of downtown. They see no need for any great rejuvenation. The slums are not a problem. Nor are they convinced of the central-city concept. The big developments in L.A. have been outside central-city planning." Fritz Burns, one of L.A.'s biggest builders, regards the natural trend as "away from the downtown core. It is in the interest of the downtown area to preserve itself, and that is justifiable, but I see no great reason to spend the taxpayers' money building up the central core. To try to revitalize the downtown area when the natural expression of public taste and preference is for other areas becomes a losing battle. Writing-down land values for some prospective buildings may reduce the trend away from the downtown core, but no such inducement can reverse it."

The truth of the matter would seem to be that if the promoters of the central core were to ask the general citizenry what kind of city they wanted it would probably look very much like the city they've got. Metropolitan Los Angeles is made up of a number of cores whose very existence indicates that the bulk of its citizens neither need nor want to be tied to downtown for employment, culture, social activities, and the good life. Wilshire Boulevard is one such core, a "linear" downtown, whose seventeen miles now include the new Los Angeles County Museum of Art, most of L.A.'s smart shops, plus impressive concentrations of high-rise apartments and skyscraper offices, the newest of which represent defections from the central city. The University of California at Los Angeles, ably directed by Chancellor Franklin Murphy, provides the cultural center of another core; U.C.L.A. runs full blast with 24,000 regular students, 19,000 more taking extension courses, and no school night goes by that it doesn't offer a choice of one or more concerts, lectures, plays, musicales. The million people in the San Fernando Valley, where the population shot up 250 percent between 1950 and 1960, are now numerous enough to be considered a core; one of its shopping centers is a virtual downtown itself with four department-store branches, and its airfield ranks fourth after Chicago's O'Hare, L.A.'s International, and Long Beach. Alcoa's Century City, a complex of office buildings and shopping centers just west of Beverly Hills, will no doubt become a core upon completion, for this "city within a city" was designed to have a self-contained residential population of 12,000 plus a working population of 20,000. And the Los Angeles International Airport, twelve miles southwest of City Hall as the crow flies, must also be counted an incipient core, one already on the rise with tall new office buildings and hotels; more will come when completion of the San Diego freeway brings new areas within reach of this "air harbor."

On a smaller scale there is the contra-center pull of the innumerable urban concentrations either within the city limits or spilling over into the surrounding county. These are served by decentralized civic government (thirteen separate centers), decentralized banking (over 500 offices or branches), decentralized retailing (nearly 140 branch stores, part of forty-one regional shopping centers with anywhere from fifty to a hundred stores), decentralized journalism (212 newspapers operate in L.A. County). But self-oriented as the citizens of these communities are, when they do leave their own areas for downtown they are far more likely to be attracted by the older incorporated cities on L.A.'s border than by a rejuvenated central core. Beverly Hills offers the best hotels, intellectual excitement, the art galleries along La Cienega Boulevard, "restaurant row," and some of the loveliest houses on the West Coast. Santa Monica has its own symphony, the broad beaches of the Pacific, a good newspaper, a complex of aerospace and "think" factories with one of the nation's greatest concentration of people holding scientific degrees. Pasadena has Caltech, the Rose Bowl, a symphony, and the world-renowned Huntington Library and Art Gallery.

The key problem of the city is not the downtown area, but learning how to live with movement. Here is a metropolis whose real shape has been dictated by the automobile and the limitless appetite of its citizens for outdoor living. Everyone has moved about as if personally pursued by haunting memories of winter immobility and the dreary row houses of the sunless East. As Reuben Lovret, of the city planning staff, shrewdly observed: "The prophets of the future show that if you have complete dependence on the automobile it can lead to nothing but change. As long as you are oriented toward the automobile, any location is subject to reorganization or redevelopment according to how the driver can exert pressure —for shopping centers or apartment houses. As long as unbridled fluidity exists, there can be no permanent pattern." Under such conditions of perpetual motion, what is needed is not the mystical pull of brick and mortar newly erected in a central core but government with speed to match that of the automobile and the scope to embrace the whole changing region: Los Angeles County, the city, and the seventy-five satellite municipalities. Cybernetics, the science of communication and control, could supply the speed and *metropolitan* government the framework.

20 | Social Class and Single-Family Housing: Helsinki and Boston

FRANK L. SWEETSER and DORRIAN APPLE SWEETSER

Single-family homes are so common—and so much preferred—in the United States that it comes as a distinct surprise to an American to find that in Helsinki, the capital of a modern and fairly prosperous European nation, there are not very many separate, one- or two-family houses, and most of those which exist are located in the less desirable residential areas. In this paper we describe first the contrast between the detached family housing in Helsinki and that in a typical American metropolis, Boston, and discuss some of the reasons for the difference. Next we discuss in general terms the relation between the amount of land which a city devotes to such detached housing and the ecological distribution of shops, places of work, transportation facilities, and parks and other green areas. Important ecological concepts used in this paper are residential segregation by social class, competition for land use, and the effect of values on land use. Since not many Americans have visited Finland, or are familiar with its history, we begin with a brief overview of Finland's geographic location and a few words about its culture and its past.

Helsinki, the capital of Finland, is a city of half a million people located on the Gulf of Finland, which is an arm of the Baltic Sea. Finland is roughly rectangular in shape, several hundred miles wide and about 750 miles long, with the long axis running north and south. It is bounded on the east by the Soviet Union, on the north by a narrow strip of Norway which separates it from the Arctic Ocean, and on the west by a portion of Sweden, then by the Gulf of Bothnia and the Baltic Sea. Finland is the most northerly nation in the world but has a much milder climate than land in similar latitudes elsewhere, such as Alaska. The climate in Helsinki is like that of Portland, Maine.

Finland was part of Sweden for hundreds of years; became a semiautonomous Grand Duchy of Russia in 1809, as a result of the political up-

SOURCE: This paper is a revision, prepared especially for this volume, of an article entitled "Omakotiasutus Helsingissa ja Bostonissa" ("Single-Family Housing in Helsinki and Boston") and published in *Asuntoreformi* (*Housing Reform*), No. 2, 1965. Copyright 1966 Frank L. and Dorrian A. Sweetser. Reprinted by permission of the authors and publishers.

heavals in Scandinavia that were a consequence of the Napoleonic Wars; and gained its independence from Russia by a revolution in 1917. In recent years, Finland's chief problem in foreign policy has been to preserve its independence without antagonizing its powerful neighbor to the east, the Soviet Union. The Finns successfully fought off efforts by the Russians to occupy their country during World War II, but were forced to cede valuable territory and pay heavy reparations to the Soviet Union for having been at war with them.

The culture and social institutions of Finland are very much like those of the other Scandinavian countries. The chief exception to this cultural similarity is the Finnish language, which is totally unlike any Germanic, Romance, or Slavic tongue. The country is officially bilingual; about 8 percent of the inhabitants speak Swedish as their mother tongue. Many towns and cities have both Finnish and Swedish names, which accounts for the fact that Helsinki (the Finnish name) is sometimes shown on maps as Helsingfors (the Swedish name).

Helsinki had its beginning in the sixteenth century as a small trading village on a little river. Later, when the river silted up and ships were larger, the center of the city was moved a few miles south to a fine harbor on a peninsula which extends southward into the Gulf of Finland. After the move, the city prospered as population grew, and its territory was extended westward, northward and eastward, until it now occupies a fan-shaped area, including the entire peninsula and a number of adjacent islands.

Impressionistically, Helsinki looks like many other Northern European cities, though with rather more attractive architecture. In the downtown, there are some handsome, three- and four-story eighteenth-century stone buildings, two famous churches, streets paved with granite blocks, many bus and trolley lines and not as many cars as in an American city, some large department stores and many small shops, and numerous modern buildings, though no skyscrapers. In summer people make more recreational use of open areas in the downtown than they do in American cities: strolling, sitting in the sun, lingering at outdoor cafe tables with a newspaper and a cup of coffee.

Moving out into the suburbs, the American visitor is struck by the prevalence of multiple-unit housing and small shops and offices. Within walking distance in residential areas, one is almost certain to find a branch office of a bank, a small grocery store, a laundry and dry cleaning shop, a florist (etiquette requires a gift of a few flowers on many occasions), a shoe-repair shop, a paper and tobacco shop, and a bread and milk store, as well as a *baari* or snack shop.

The visitor's impression of the prevalence of multiple-unit housing is borne out by a special tabulation of 1960 Finnish Census data prepared for the senior author's Helsinki Ecology Project. In 1960, only 9.7 per cent of all dwellings in Helsinki were one- or two-family, separate structures. The great majority of Helsinki residents live in apartment houses or in row houses. In contrast, in metropolitan Boston in 1960, according to figures from the senior author's Metropolitan Boston Ecology Project, 65.4 per cent of all dwelling units were one- or two-family detached houses. In the average residential area in the Boston suburbs, 68.9 per cent of the dwelling units were single-family homes. Even the housing in the urban core in

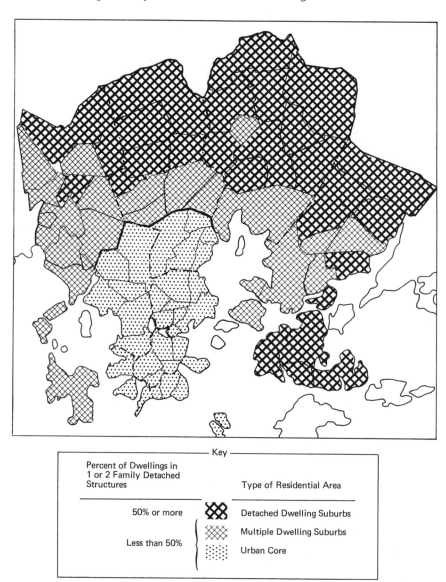

Key

Percent of Dwellings in
1 or 2 Family Detached
Structures

Type of Residential Area

50% or more   Detached Dwelling Suburbs

Multiple Dwelling Suburbs

Less than 50%

Urban Core

FIGURE 1.   Detached and Multiple Dwelling Areas in Helsinki, Finland, 1960

metropolitan Boston, where more apartment houses are to be found, had three and a half times the per cent of detached one-family homes to be found in Helsinki as a whole (16.3 per cent as compared with 4.6 per cent).

What kind of people live in the areas of Helsinki which have a large amount of detached housing? Are these areas of higher socioeconomic status, as would be the case in an American city? To answer this question, it is necessary to look at neighborhoods rather than at individuals, because census data for both Helsinki and Boston come in packages for small areas, so to speak; census tracts in metropolitan Boston, and "statistical areas" in Helsinki.

The statistical areas in Helsinki with half or more of their dwelling units located in one- or two-family houses lie on the outer edge of the city, to the north and east. This can be seen in Figure 1, which shows the per cent of detached housing in each of the statistical areas of Helsinki and also the boundary between the urban core and the suburbs.

In the Helsinki Social Ecology Project, the statistical areas of Helsinki were reduced in number to seventy, because some areas with very small populations were combined with a neighboring area. Twenty-two of these seventy statistical areas, all in the suburbs, have half or more of their dwelling units in detached one- or two-family houses. These twenty-two areas are referred to in this paper as "detached dwelling areas." Table 1 gives some figures on population and housing characteristics for these detached dwelling areas, for the other suburban areas, for the urban core, and for Helsinki as a whole. As can be seen in Table 1, the detached dwelling areas have a more familistic population than the urban core, a characteristic which they share with the other suburban areas. The detached dwelling areas differ from the other suburban areas, and from the urban core as well, in having more substandard dwelling units and a largely working-class population.

For contrast, we present similar data on metropolitan Boston in Table 2. The information in Table 2 was taken from special tabulations of 1960 census tract data prepared for the Metropolitan Boston Social Ecology Project. In this project, metropolitan Boston was divided into six ecological zones, beginning with zone 1 in the downtown Boston area and moving outward to a sixth zone in the outer suburbs. The "urban core" mentioned in Table 2 consists of zones 1 through 3; the "suburbs" are zones 4, 5, and 6.

In Table 2, unlike Table 1, the areas are not further classified on the basis of the amount of detached housing. Such a division, while it shows something important about the social ecology of Helsinki, would not make sense in metropolitan Boston, because the amount of detached housing is rather uniformly high in the suburbs, with the exception of census tracts in some of the satellite cities and urban towns of the metropolitan fringe.

Comparing Tables 1 and 2, some similarities and some differences are

TABLE 1.   Unweighted Means of Selected Characteristics of Statistical Areas in Subdivisions of Helsinki in 1960

Characteristics	Urban core (n = 28)	Detached dwelling areas (n = 22)	Other suburban areas (n = 20)	Total (n = 70)
Per cent of dwelling units which are one- or two-family houses	2	70	16	28*
Index of housing defects (per cent lacking flush toilet plus per cent lacking central heat, divided by 2)	19	60	24	34
Per cent of employed population in blue-collar occupations	37	56	37	43
Per cent of population aged 25 or over who have passed student examination to qualify for admission to a university	12	5	15	11
Fertility ratio †	322	449	474	405
Per cent of population which is non-family (living alone or in institutions)	10	5	6	7
Per cent of population aged 6-13	11	13	13	12

* Note that this figure is much larger than the 9.7 per cent of dwelling units of this kind reported previously for the city as a whole. The smaller figure is a weighted mean, which takes into account the differences between areas in the total number of dwelling units in them. The weighted mean is smaller than the unweighted mean because areas with more detached housing tend to have fewer dwelling units than other areas. Unweighted means are given in this table (and in Table 2) because the emphasis in the tables is on characteristics of areas, not of the city as a whole.

† Because of the great excess of females in the Helsinki population, which would have artificially lowered the fertility ratio, it was calculated as the number of children under 5 per 1,000 *males* in the ages 20–49, times 1,000.

evident. In both metropolitan Boston and Helsinki, there are more married couples and children in the suburbs than in the urban core. In Helsinki, those suburban areas with much detached housing have on the average much defective housing and a predominantly blue-collar population. In Boston, on the other hand, housing defects are more common in the urban core than in the suburbs, and there is on the average a slight preponderance of blue-collar workers in the census tracts comprising the urban core.

Tables 1 and 2 provide a broad picture of large subdivisions of the two cities. But for more precise information about the differences between

TABLE 2. Unweighted Means of Selected Characteristics of Census Tracts in the Urban Core (Zones 1–3) and the Suburbs (Zones 4–6) in Metropolitan Boston in 1960

Characteristics	Urban core (n = 216)	Suburbs (n = 225)	Total (n = 441)
Per cent of dwelling units which are one-family houses	16	68	43
Index of housing defects (per cent of dwellings lacking plumbing amenities, central heat, or both)	49	27	38
Per cent of employed population in blue-collar occupations	41	36	38
Per cent of population aged 25 or over who are college graduates	8	12	10
Fertility ratio*	476	565	522
Per cent of population which is non-family (living alone or in institutions)	15	7	11
Per cent of population aged 6-13	12	15	14

* Number of children under 5 per 1,000 women aged 15–44, times 1,000.

small areas with differing amounts of detached housing, it is necessary to make use of a statistical measure called Pearson's coefficient of correlation. This coefficient of correlation can have values ranging from 1.00 through 0.00 to -1.00. If for a set of small areas the correlation coefficient between the amount of detached housing and another variable is positive and of appreciable size, this means that areas with much detached housing tend to have high values on the other variable, and areas with little detached housing tend to have low values on the other variable. Or, if the correlation coefficient is negative and of appreciable size, it means that areas with much detached housing tend to have low values on the other variable, and those with little detached housing tend to have high values on the other variable. If the correlation coefficient is somewhere close to .00, this means that the amount of detached housing in a small area does not show any tendency to be related to the other variable.

For judging the size of correlation coefficients in these data, we suggest the following rule of thumb: coefficients in the range from -.20 through .00 to .20 mean there is no correlation; those in the .20's, whether plus or minus, show a slight correlation; those in the .30's and .40's, whether positive or negative, indicate a moderate amount of correlation, and those which are plus or minus .50 or more indicate a large amount of correlation.

Table 3 gives the coefficients of correlation between the amount of detached housing in small areas in each city and certain other population and housing characteristics. These correlation coefficients show in a precise way the similarities and differences in the two cities with respect to detached housing in small areas. In both cities, a familistic population in small areas is on the whole moderately correlated with the amount of detached housing, while the per cent of blue-collar workers and of housing defects is related to the amount of detached housing in markedly different ways in the two cities.

It is not surprising to find a familistic population in Helsinki's detached dwelling areas, since this is a characteristic they share with other suburban areas of Helsinki, and in Helsinki, as in American cities, couples with children tend to live in the suburbs, while couples without children and the unmarried tend to live in the urban core. The puzzling question, to an American, is why detached dwellings, substandard housing, and a working-class population area are associated in Helsinki.

The answer to this question has two parts. One has to do with the recent history of the areas in the city with numerous detached dwellings. The other part of the answer has to do with recent housing construction in Helsinki.

TABLE 3. Correlation Between the Amount of Detached Housing in Small Areas of Helsinki and of Boston in 1960 and Selected Population and Other Characteristics

Characteristics	Correlation with detached housing*	
	Helsinki (n = 70)	Boston (n = 441)
Index of housing defects	.72	−.48
Per cent of employed population in blue-collar occupations	.64	−.32
Per cent of population aged 25 or over who are highly educated †	−.50	.40
Fertility ratio	.35	.40
Per cent of population which is non-family (living alone or in institutions)	−.41	−.38
Per cent of population aged 6-13	.25	.57

* "Detached housing" is single-family houses in Boston, one- or two-family housing in Helsinki.

† "Highly educated" means college graduates in Boston; those who passed student examination for admission to a university in Helsinki.

Most of the city areas with half or more of their homes consisting of detached dwellings, and with a predominance of substandard housing, were brought within the city limits by an expansion of these limits in 1946. As a rule, the housing we are concerned with was already in existence at that time. Having been built before the expansion of the city boundaries, the housing was without city water supply and city sewage connections, and extension of these utilities to this housing has not been very rapid. A house with a privy and an outside pump for water is a substandard dwelling unit in Helsinki, as in Boston, though such housing in Helsinki is more correctly compared to old-time rural housing than to urban slums. A properly constructed, sited, and tended privy, while inconvenient, is neither offensive nor a hazard to health, and while it is doubtful that any housewife prefers to carry in water, the water can be perfectly safe to drink. Lack of flush toilets and piped-in water in a crowded area, however, would be quite another thing.

Substandard housing is cheaper than housing without such defects, and this accounts, at least in part, for the predominance of blue-collar workers in the areas with large percentages of substandard housing. Some families were already living in these areas when they were included in the city and preferred to remain, and other families who could not afford better housing, or who wanted to live in these areas, have moved there. Higher income families on the whole prefer to live in the newer, better housing available elsewhere in the city.

New housing in Helsinki has obviously not included very much in the way of detached, one- or two-family dwellings, otherwise the picture would be different. Some detached homes have been built, but these are few and quite expensive. Nearly all recent housing construction in Helsinki has consisted of row houses and apartment buildings. Why is this so?

In answering this question, the first point to be made is that the prevalence of multiple units in recent housing construction in Helsinki is not unique to Finland, nor even to Scandinavia. In general, in European urban development, the practice is to construct multiple dwellings. Recent housing construction in Helsinki is in line with this practice.

The construction of multiple units rather than of detached housing in Finnish urban development is not strictly comparable to any very common American practices in city growth. In particular it is not equatable either to older housing projects in American cities, which so often consist of nothing but blocks of buildings set in a concrete desert, or to the rows of little boxes which are so often found in American suburban real-estate development. The Finnish practice is a complex affair, involving a cost factor and some distinctive norms about how to plan a residential area.

In regard to cost, it is cheaper to build row houses or apartment houses than detached housing. To construct the maximum number of good dwelling units, at a given cost, it is necessary to have multiple unit structures. This cost factor affects both housing planned by government and that planned by private developers. Government gets more housing for its money, and so does the private developer. A family can buy its own apartment or row house more cheaply than it can buy a detached house of equal quality. Public demand and public taste are such that there is no difficulty in filling the housing units in multiple unit structures.

Another cost factor has to do with transportation. Private autos are not so common in Finland as in America, and no city can afford good public transportation throughout dispersed residential areas. Multiple dwelling units mean that more people can live closer to bus and trolley lines.

The construction of new residential areas in Helsinki, as in many other European cities, is planned in a more comprehensive way than Americans are accustomed to. The public expects, and the government requires, that the construction of housing, whether by private developers or by the government, be coordinated with the expansion of public facilities such as transportation, schools, and parks.

For example, new residential areas in Helsinki are planned with a walking and bus-riding population, not a motoring population, in mind. Consequently, additional bus or trolley lines are included in the planning of the development.

Would Finns or other European urban dwellers live in American style suburbs if they could? Is the prevalence of multiple dwelling units in recent housing construction in Helsinki merely a matter of doing the best that can be done? The authors do not know what kind of housing Helsinki residents would choose if they had an unlimited choice, but housing construction in Helsinki is strongly influenced by public taste and demand, and if there were a larger market for detached housing, it surely would have been provided. Perhaps the point is that no population anywhere has an unlimited choice in housing, and whether by reasons of cost or by reasons of preference, or both, there is not much demand for detached housing in Helsinki.

Probably one reason, other than cost, for the lack of demand for detached housing in Helsinki is that the comfort and amenities provided for in housing developments which feature multiple unit construction are far better than what Americans are used to in apartment buildings or housing projects. The planning of a new residential area in Helsinki is not a matter only of how many dwelling units can be constructed. It also entrails planning for varied land uses: shops, schools, and public transportation.

The best-known residential development in Finland is the new town of Tapiola, just west of Helsinki, which was financed by a private, nonprofit corporation and which is famous around the world for its aesthetic and practical merits. But even in less notable housing developments in Helsinki there are a number of features which are strange to an American who has a typical American city, such as Boston, in mind.

For one thing, the apartments and row houses are constructed with some thought to soundproofing them. It is extraordinary what architects can do toward soundproofing an apartment, once they put their minds to it.

Second, the land has not been bulldozed over and then covered with buildings bordered by some feeble shrubs and straggling grass. The buildings are spaced so as to leave play areas for children and green walks for adults; the trees on the land and its natural contours are left as undisturbed as possible and are transformed into parks, for the gratification of the residents. Vehicular traffic is routed away from the park areas. Space is provided in the buildings to be leased for shops, for the convenience of the walking housewife, and arrangements are made for the construction of schools and the extension of bus and trolley service, so that these are available when people move in.

Thus far we have stressed normative and cost factors involved in the prevalence of multiple unit structures, and the characteristics of areas with much detached housing in Helsinki. There is another broader or more general point to be made, which we have only touched on so far. It is this: the amount of land devoted to detached housing is inextricably linked to how far the residents must travel to work and to shop, by what means they must travel, and how much park area they can have. Figuratively, the automobile and the bus or trolley are natural enemies, ecological competitors, and so are the supermarket and the neighborhood shop, and the private yard and the park and recreation area. Detached housing makes one flourish; multiple units encourage the other.

In the ecology of cities, as in many other aspects of societies, some ways of doing things are inseparable from ways of doing other things; if you accept one you must accept the others. Suburban dwellers are in the same kind of situation as the Great Plains Indians who took up the use of horses to hunt buffalo. They had formerly been farmers, but when they took up the use of horses and buffalo hunting, they let themselves in for a roving life. A roving life is not compatible with farming, so they gave up farming.

In American suburbs, low population density and single-family housing come in an expensive package together with superhighways, poor bus and passenger train service, and supermarkets. This kind of suburban housing is also linked with the deterioration of the urban core, where costly urban renewal programs and complex problems of traffic congestion and parking dominate the city planner's work. In Helsinki, on the other hand, where few families own cars compared to America, high density multiple unit housing, neighborhood shops for the wife, and commuting to work by bus for the husband form a logical combination.

A rapid increase in the number of private automobiles in Helsinki has been occurring in recent years, as a result of a general rise in the level of living. On a typical September day in 1959, 19,111 private autos were counted passing a major downtown intersection. Four years later, the figure had risen to 28,367, an increase of 48 per cent, and the number of cars continues to climb. Traffic requirements are already having effects on street and highway construction, on how open space in the downtown area is used, on the distribution of shops, and on plans for further construction of public transportation.

A crucial unknown factor in the future ecological development of Helsinki is the extent to which the public is willing to allow restrictions on commutation by auto. Continued uncontrolled increase in private automobile traffic in and out of the city will tip the future ecological development of Helsinki in the direction of the American pattern, with repercussions also on future housing construction.

Americans, provided their housing is not inferior, presumably like to live the way they do, and so do Finns. But what people like or do not like about their housing is only a small part of the determining forces at work. Underneath the available alternatives on which people can exercise a choice, whether it is a family choosing a place to live or a planner choosing a site for residential development, are massive and complex ecological processes, with a vast inertial force of their own.

References

FRANK L. SWEETSER, "Ecological Factors in Metropolitan Zones and Sectors," paper presented at the Symposium on Quantitative Ecological Analysis in the Social Sciences, Evian, France, September, 1966.

———, "Factorial Ecology: Helsinki, 1960." *Demography* 2: 372–386 (1965).

———, "Factor Structure as Ecological Structure in Helsinki and Boston." *Acta Sociologica* 8: 205–225 (1965).

———, *Patterns of Change in the Social Ecology of Metropolitan Boston: 1950–1960*. Massachusetts Department of Mental Health, Boston, 1962.

———, *The Social Ecology of Metropolitan Boston: 1960*. Massachusetts Department of Mental Health, Boston, 1962.

21 | Negroes in Cities

KARL E. TAEUBER and
ALMA F. TAEUBER

Residential segregation occupies a key position in patterns of race relations in the urban United States. It not only inhibits the development of informal, neighborly relations between whites and Negroes, but ensures the

SOURCE: Karl E. Taeuber and Alma F. Taeuber, *Negroes in Cities* (Chicago: Aldine Publishing Company, 1965), pp. 1–8. Copyright Karl E. Taeuber and Alma E. Taeuber, 1965. Reprinted by permission of the authors and publisher.

segregation of a variety of public and private facilities. The clientele of schools, hospitals, libraries, parks, and stores is determined in large part by the racial composition of the neighborhood in which they are located.

It is sometimes argued that personal contact between whites and Negroes is more common in the South than in the North, and that a mutually agreed-upon etiquette of race relations permits whites and Negroes to live side by side without overt conflict. In recent years, however, the rapid downfall of legal barriers to desegregation of schools and other public facilities has led whites in many Southern communities to a recognition that residential segregation can accomplish *de facto* what can no longer be accomplished *de jure*. In the North, too, residential segregation is a major focus of racial controversy and conflict. In both regions, residential segregation is not only a vital social issue in itself, but is closely intertwined with most of the problems confronting urban society.

In 1910, 73 per cent of the Negro population of the United States were rural; in 1960, 73 per cent were urban. Negroes have moved from farms and villages to cities within the South, and in even greater numbers to the large industrial cities of the North and West. In the course of this massive redistribution of Negro population, many Negro families moved from an isolated rural society to the heart of contemporary urban society. Like the European immigrants of earlier days, Negroes initially were fitted into the lowest status positions in the urban social structure, and were restricted in their housing opportunities. In sharp contrast to the immigrants, however, the social position of Negroes has remained at the bottom, and Negro ghettos are expanding rather than disappearing. Residential segregation persists as a major barrier to equality in race relations.

. . . . . .

Patterns of Residential Segregation

Negro protest groups often seek publicity with claims that their city is the most segregated in the nation, and Southerners often allege that residential segregation is greater in Northern than in Southern cities. However, systematic study of the block-by-block patterns of residential segregation reveals little difference among cities. A high degree of racial residential segregation is universal in American cities. Whether a city is a metropolitan center or a suburb; whether it is in the North or South; whether the Negro population is large or small—in every case, white and Negro households are highly segregated from each other. Negroes are more segregated residentially than are Orientals, Mexican Americans, Puerto Ricans, or any nationality group. In fact, Negroes are by far the most residentially segregated urban minority group in recent American history. This is evident in the virtually complete exclusion of Negro residents from most new suburban developments of the past fifty years as well as in the block-by-block expansion of Negro residential areas in the central portions of many large cities.

The poverty of urban Negroes is often regarded as contributory to their residential segregation. Because low-cost housing tends to be segregated from high-cost housing, any low-income group within the city will be residentially segregated to some extent from those with higher incomes. Economic factors, however, cannot account for more than a small portion of observed levels of racial residential segregation. Regardless of their economic status, Negroes rarely live in "white" residential areas, while whites, no matter how poor, rarely live in "Negro" residential areas. In recent decades, Negroes have been much more successful in securing improvements in economic status than in obtaining housing on a less segregated basis. Continued economic gains by Negroes are not likely to alter substantially the prevalent patterns of racial residential segregation.

For many Northern cities, the first rapid in-migration of Negroes occurred between 1910 and 1930, and this period witnessed the initial development of large, racially homogeneous areas of Negro residence. In Southern cities, residential segregation between Negroes and whites has been increasing ever since the Civil War, as less segregated residential patterns which originated during slavery have been gradually obliterated. Those cities whose principal growth has occurred since the Civil War probably began with a greater degree of residential segregation than older Southern cities, but differences diminished as time passed. For both Northern and Southern cities, therefore, levels of segregation have been increasing for many decades up to 1940. By then, a high degree of residential segregation typified every city with a sizable Negro population, although average levels of segregation were slightly lower in Southern than in Northern cities.

During the 1940's, wartime restrictions on new construction caused the housing supply to lag behind population growth. In a tight housing market, housing alternatives for both whites and Negroes were limited, and prevailing patterns of segregation narrowed the choice even more for Negroes. Under these circumstances, neither the pressures of rapidly growing Negro populations in many cities, nor improvement among Negroes in levels of occupational status and income had much effect on patterns of residential segregation. Because most of the new housing that was built between 1940 and 1950 was occupied on a segregated basis, small increases in levels of residential segregation were typical during the decade. Larger increases in segregation were most prevalent in the South, where many of the cities were new, small cities which still had vacant land within the city limits suitable for residential development.

During the period following World War II, the housing supply increased rapidly, and by the mid-1950's much of the "tightness" had gone out of the housing market. New residential developments were predominantly in the suburbs, and the rate of suburbanization increased rapidly, especially for whites. Many central cities lost white population, so that Negroes, as a result, had a much greater range of housing available within the city than during the previous decade. Substantial expansion in Negro residential areas occurred, in contrast to the crowding and congestion of the preceding decade. In this more permissive housing market situation, the pressure of a growing Negro population and the economic gains among Negroes were able to counteract some of the forces producing increases in segregation. In most Northern and Western cities, the historical trend toward increasing segregation was halted or reversed. Declines in segregation were common, although many decades of such declines would be necessary to reduce racial residential segregation to truly low levels. In Southern cities, by contrast, Negro economic gains and population growth were insufficient to overcome the long-term trend toward increasing segregation, and levels of residential segregation generally increased. By 1960, average levels of residential segregation were somewhat higher in Southern than in Northern cities.

Processes of Neighborhood Change

A high degree of residential segregation in a city is maintained by the creation of additional all-Negro and all-white neighborhoods. The typical process is assumed to be residential succession, in which a neighborhood "turns" from white to Negro as the dwellings left by white families moving out are occupied by incoming Negro families. Although an aura of inevitability is often attributed to this process, as in the popular notion of a "tipping point," processes of change in the racial composition of neighborhoods do not always follow such simple patterns.

Whether or not a city's neighborhoods increase in Negro proportion, as well as the rate at which such racial transition proceeds, is largely dependent on the rate of increase in Negro and white populations. The greater the rate of Negro population growth relative to white population growth in a city, the more likely an increase in proportion Negro in neighborhoods, and the faster the rate of racial change. A high growth rate of white population relative to Negro population, on the other hand, is accompanied by declines in the proportion Negro in many neighborhoods and a slow rate of racial change. Any "tipping point" would thus seem to have less to do with levels of racial tolerance among whites than with the levels of supply and demand for housing in areas that will accept Negro residents. In some Southern cities with low rates of Negro population growth, neighborhoods of both high and low proportions Negro have experienced little change in racial composition over several decades.

Most accounts of residential succession have been based on the experiences of Northern and border cities during periods of very rapid growth of Negro population coupled with a stable or declining white population. These cities have a substantial stock of older housing, much of which is difficult and expensive to rehabilitate and unattractive in comparison with newer housing. For cities in these circumstances, the conventional type of racial residential succession—Negroes taking up residence in homes formerly occupied by whites—has indeed been the prevalent pattern of

neighborhood change in racial composition. Racial homogeneity of neighborhoods may, however, be fostered by other processes, such as new
construction designed for occupancy on a segregated basis, or selective
demolition of dwellings in racially mixed areas. In many Southern cities,
new housing is built for both Negroes and whites, but in separate neighborhoods. An unusual example-of racial change is provided by Memphis
during the 1940's, a decade in which the rate of growth of the white population exceeded that of the Negro population. Most neighborhoods declined in proportion Negro, not as a result of white families taking over
housing previously occupied by Negroes, but primarily as a result of the
construction of additional housing to accommodate the growing population.

Because of the lesser volume of Negro in-migration and the alternative
offered by new construction, there appears to be less pressure for Negroes to
take over white-occupied housing in Southern cities than in Northern
cities. In Northern cities, on the other hand, vacant land is at a premium
and Negro residential areas are already densely built-up. A rapidly growing
Negro population must either crowd into existing Negro-occupied units or
move into white-occupied dwellings on the periphery of Negro areas. This,
then, represents a basic difference between Northern and Southern cities.
In most Southern cities, Negroes have continuously been housed in areas
set aside for them, whereas in the North, most areas now inhabited by
Negroes were formerly occupied by whites.

This regional difference in settlement pattern is reflected in the residential
locations of persons of differing social status. In Northern cities, Negroes
and whites respond in similar fashion to the social and economic forces producing a general differentiation of residential neighborhoods: whites and
Negroes living in racially mixed areas tend to be of rather similar socioeconomic status, and areas undergoing substantial changes in racial composition have nonetheless retained their general socioeconomic character.
High-status neighborhoods tend to remain high-status, and low-status
neighborhoods remain low-status.

In Southern cities, on the other hand, there is little relationship between
the characteristics of whites and Negroes living in the same neighborhoods—
high-status Negroes are as likely to live near low-status whites as near high-
status whites. Furthermore, there is a tendency for high-status Negroes to
live in predominantly Negro areas, whereas in the North high-status Negroes are more likely to live outside of the core of the ghetto, in recently
invaded neighborhoods or other neighborhoods of low proportion Negro.
The Northern Negro community was superimposed upon a pre-existing
pattern of urban residential differentiation, whereas in Southern cities the
initial pattern of residential differentiation already included an adaptation to
the presence of a large Negro population. Race is therefore an important
factor in the residential structure of Southern cities, but in Northern cities
residential structure is in large measure independent of the racial composition of the community's inhabitants.

Some of these patterns of neighborhood racial change may be altered in coming decades. Land suitable for residential use is becoming increasingly scarce in Southern cities, many of which are now experiencing the net losses of white population so common in Northern cities in recent decades. Continued growth of Southern cities is likely to result in a greater frequency of the patterns of residential succession typical in the North. At the same time, changes are occurring in processes of racial change in Northern cities. Urban renewal and rehabilitation programs, legal barriers to housing discrimination, rising socioeconomic levels among Negroes, and wider experience with successful examples of racially mixed neighborhoods portend gradual declines in levels of residential segregation.

Change is already evident in patterns of Negro migration. The picture of illiterate Negro peasants settling in congested slums is clearly inapplicable to the present scene. The high level of urbanization of the Negro population and the rising socioeconomic status of Negroes are reflected in changes in the characteristics of Negro migrants to cities and in the spatial distribution of migrants within cities. An increasing number of Negro migrants to cities are coming from other cities rather than farms; they are of higher average educational and occupational status than the resident Negro population in the cities to which they move. In-migrant Negroes seek housing corresponding to their socioeconomic status, and are distributed throughout the city much like the Negro non-migrant population. There is no evidence that the average Negro migrant faces housing problems any more severe than those faced by other Negroes.

Changing conditions within the Negro community reflect to a large extent changes occurring throughout the metropolitan area and the nation. With the decline in residential construction during World War II, the pace of suburbanization of the white population was retarded, and Negro population in many cities grew at a much faster rate than additional housing could be obtained. During the 1940's, therefore, Negro residential areas expanded only slowly, there was frequent conversion of existing dwellings into larger numbers of units, and pronounced increases occurred in the degree of congestion and overcrowding. In the 1950's, with the resumption of residential construction and a rapid rate of suburbanization among whites, there were substantial additions to Negro residential areas in many cities. The increase in the housing alternatives available to Negroes not only lessened overcrowding as many predominantly Negro areas lost population, but also provided Negroes greater opportunity to seek housing appropriate to their socioeconomic status. As compared with the previous decade, there were sharp increases in the degree of residential segregation within the Negro community of persons holding white-collar jobs from those holding blue-collar jobs.

It is virtually impossible to isolate neighborhood changes due to racial transition from those changes reflecting broader trends at work throughout the metropolitan area and the nation. As the position of the Negro in the national economy and the national social structure changes, accompanying alterations in processes of neighborhood change become inevitable. Traditional accounts of the process of racial residential succession, which stress the low socioeconomic status of the Negro population entering a new neighborhood, the overcrowding and deterioration of housing, the declines in property values, and the flight of whites from the neighborhood are outdated oversimplifications. Expansion of Negro residential areas in recent years has been led by Negroes of high socioeconomic status—not only higher than the rest of the Negro population, but often higher than the white residents of the "invaded" neighborhood. The invaded areas tend to be occupied by whites of moderately high socioeconomic status, and the housing is predominantly in good rather than substandard condition. To attribute the processes of racial transition primarily to racial attitudes—to whites fleeing incoming Negro population—is an exaggeration. Given the favorable conditions in the housing market since the late 1940's, and the prevalent tendency of high-status whites to seek newer housing on the periphery of the urbanized area, suburbanization has affected a disproportionate number of those whites in the central city who lived in higher-status neighborhoods. Similarly, higher-status Negroes have been seeking better housing, but within the segregated housing market they find their chief opportunities in those nearby neighborhoods being abandoned by whites. Among both Negroes and whites, the search for better housing is led by those who can best afford it. Patterns of racial transition reflect such general processes of urban change as well as the racial attitudes prevalent in the national society.

With the Civil Rights Act of 1964, steady progress in outlawing segregation in public places seems assured. Negroes have made rapid gains in economic welfare in recent decades, and although full equality is not in sight, further progress is likely. Patterns of residential segregation, however, have yet to show signs of significant weakening. Continuing conflict over residential segregation thus seems inevitable, not only because of Negro dissatisfactions over housing, but because residential segregation is a particularly tenacious barrier to the full participation of Negroes in the general society.

Part Three

━━━━━━━━━━

The Organization of Urban Life

For sociologists the major focus of interest in the city is social organization. In Part III we attempt to discover to what extent—and why—specific social behavior is associated with urban life by examining urban life in a variety of cultures and technological periods. Section A deals with some basic dimensions of social organization—institutions and forms of association—while Section B examines social stratification and mobility.

The growth of cities has gone through a particular historical sequence, in which the emergence of large cities and the penetration of urban influence to whole societies has been associated with industrialization and with a specific type of social organization. This social organization grew from Western sources and centers on a "pared-down" family and loose kinship ties; expansion and bureaucratization of non-family institutions; a corresponding multiplication of roles and increased participation in the related formal associations; rapid social mobility in a system fostering social change and basing stratification on competitive achievement. In the long run an industrial base is needed for large-scale urbanization. Preindustrial urbanization, which was based on commerce and administration, was on a small scale; only a small fraction of the total population could be supported in cities. The question is whether industrialization "requires" social organization on the Western order. We know that preindustrial urbanism was associated with institutional, associational, and stratification patterns that were different from those associated with industrial urbanism. All over the world such societies today, many of them former colonies, and some tribal and other nonurban societies, are reaching for industrialization. Vast social changes are under way. To predict and control their direction we must investigate the relationship between "modern" social organization and industrial-urban development.

"World Revolution and Family Patterns" by William J. Goode deals with what is generally regarded as the central social institution. His comprehensive survey of societies under the impact of various levels of "exposure" to industrialization suggests that "Their family systems are . . . approaching some variant of the conjugal system." As Goode makes clear, the dynamics are still obscure although it is already evident that there is no simple cause-and-effect relationship. In contemporary underdeveloped countries, ideological factors favoring the conjugal system may operate independently to produce it under conditions of minimal industrialization. Another indication that conjugal family systems are not produced by industrialization alone is that such systems may have *preceded* industrial development in Western nations. Goode also notes that the processes under study may be obscured because the terminology is empirically imprecise. Thus, the isolation of the conjugal family and the inclusiveness of the extended family may have been overstated. Neither should "industrialization" and "urbanization" be used as semantic umbrellas to hide the imperfections of data or logic. Bearing these cautions in mind, it is possible to suggest that a crucial linkage between industrialization and the conjugal family is that under industrialization control over jobs tends to pass from the kin group to non-kin groups. This tends to weaken familial control over behavior and social placement and loosens loyalty among family members at the further degrees of kinship, leaving those tied by close bonds of kinship and affection—the conjugal family.

Only one nation outside the mainstream of Western civilization has achieved a high level of industrialization—Japan. Therefore it is particularly instructive to examine the social context of the Japanese factory. In "Continuity and Change in Japanese Industry," James C. Abegglen reports on his study of nineteen large Japanese factories (2,000–8,000 employees) and thirty-four small ones (up to 200 employees). The Japanese factory, although it is highly productive, is not organized around norms of individualism, competition, and impersonality. The individual enters the factory as a blue-collar or white-collar worker directly from school, having been hired without special training, on the basis of academic record, family background, and the recommendations of teachers and professors who often have long-standing contacts, familial or of village origin, with given factories. Once he has entered the factory the commitment extends far beyond work—the individual will be retained and paid even when the firm is not prospering or if his work performance is not good; the employee's loyalty is also expected to be lifelong. Employees are seldom fired, but neither are they expected to seek other employment, even if dissatisfied. Thus, in Japanese factories job entry, job perquisites, and job mobility have many parallels to kinship relationships, and, in this, they differ sharply from factories in the Western world. In Japan industrialization seems to have taken root successfully while carrying over many features of preindustrial social organization. Abegglen suggests that ". . . although the preindustrial experience of the West may indeed have been the necessary cause of the development of industrialization, the introduction of industry to a society like that of Japan, which has not shared these earlier experiences and has a markedly different social system, makes necessary the fitting of the industrial mechanism to the earlier social system."

Japan is a revealing reverse confirmation of Goode's thesis that loss of job-control links industrialization with the decline of the extended family system. In Japan where the family has retained some control over job placement and where jobs entail many familial-type obligations on both firm and employee, the extended family has remained important as an organizing social force. Abegglen mentions several points of strain in the paternalistic Japanese factory system. Nevertheless the system has proved viable and the Japanese experience clearly indicates there are no easy generalizations in assessing the relationship between industrialization and society.

In "Urbanization, the Extended Family, and Kinship Ties in West Africa" by Joan Aldous we examine several aspects of social organization among peoples many of whose pre-urban social patterns were dominated by tribalism and colonialism. Joan Aldous reviews the published research relevant to Wirth's thesis that the extended family and kinship ties tend to disappear in the city. Her review covers both the industrial-urban cities of the West, especially the United States, and the contemporary, largely preindustrial, cities of West Africa. In both cases she concludes that Wirth's thesis is overdrawn, for some extended kin ties persist even in United States cities, while in West African cities they are quite important. Janet Abu-Lughod had suggested that the ecological effects of size, density, and heterogeneity as predicated by Wirth were modified by culture, technology, and social class. Joan Aldous' analysis suggests that the social effects of size, density, and heterogeneity require similar modification. In West African cities the extended family and kinship ties are important among migrants in providing housing, and in meeting economic, religious, legal, and recreational needs. This suggests that the extended family and kinship provide "cushions" enabling the migrant to adjust to the city. In that case they might be only transitory features of urban social organization. However, Aldous found that even among established urbanites the family and kinship remained strong. There are some signs that these attachments may be weakening but, on the other hand, they are "substitutes for a nonexistent public welfare program." The lack of such programs is pronounced in much of Africa, Asia, and Latin America where urban poverty is widespread, and this is probably an important explanation of the continued vitality of the extended family and kinship ties in these areas of the world.

Another aspect of Wirth's description of urban social organization is examined by William H. Key in "Rural-Urban Social Participation." Key's study is of special interest because it is one of the few subjecting Wirth's formulations to systematic empirical testing among a range of communities. Key focuses on the relationship between urbanization, as measured by city size, and participation in primary and secondary groups. Wirth maintained that with increased urbanization (increased city size) primary associations would decrease and secondary associations increase. Key developed scales to measure participation in six kinds of groups of presumably increasing impersonality—immediate family, extended family, neighborhood, informal groups, work groups, and formal groups—and applied them to people living in five community sizes ranging from rural to metropolitan. The results indicate that the relationship between social interaction and urbanization is more complex than Wirth's formulation of a progressive shift from primary to secondary groups as city size increases. Key's "profile" of contacts by community size indicates an increased frequency of primary group contacts in the largest urban areas. For the metropolite there are probably frequent secondary contacts in non-overlapping groups of shifting composition. For primary satisfaction he must seek the family—the one major primary group that is available to him. In the smaller urban areas, the secondary associations may themselves offer primary-type satisfaction, for the participants are drawn from a smaller population "pool" whose contacts are likely to overlap and be of long standing; hence the resident of smaller urban places is less likely to depend so wholly on the family for primary satisfaction. Key's data and their interpretation are suggestive rather than definitive. They imply that the dynamics of city size and interactive patterns may contain qualitative "breaks," rather than being a straight-line relationship. At a given point of large city size the very impersonality and transitoriness of contacts may exert a backlash effect; instead of producing isolated alienated individuals the extreme secondary contacts may lead him to seek more of the most primary contact—the family.

Kenneth Little's analysis of "The Migrant and the Urban Community" examines the associational structure through which the individual operates in the urban environment in a different range and setting than Key. Little focuses on only one relationship, voluntary associations (formal interaction in Key's terms), and presents his findings for the rural migrants in West African cities. In these rapidly growing cities the migrants are faced with new types of work and living conditions, the presence of individuals from many different tribal backgrounds, and the clash of Western and African cultures. For the rural migrant voluntary organizations in the city serve to bridge the gap between the traditional rural norms and those of urban life.

By inculcating "know-how" and exerting social control the urban voluntary associations are performing for the rural migrant some of the functions his family and kin performed in his native village. Voluntary associations in the city thus provide a buffer between the isolated individual and the specialized larger society. Aldous' analysis has already indicated that the extended family and kin retain considerable importance in West African cities as in others, partly because of their usefulness as "buffers" under difficult urban conditions. The family, voluntary organizations, and government are the three major sources which can ease the individual's entry into urban life. The kinds of "aid and comfort" which these three networks provide differ greatly from one another, but one can at least speculate that to some degree they are interchangeable and, under better urban conditions, reinforcing. Little's study is of a limited segment of new urbanites in a particular geographic area, and it would be unwise to generalize prematurely. However, his evidence indicates that the part played by voluntary organizations in facilitating psychological, material, and normative integration into urban life is considerable.

Section B deals with the hierarchical aspects of urban social organization rather than with the dimensions of complexity and differentiation dealt with in Section A. Two of the articles in Section B, those by Lipset and Bendix and by Martines, are concerned with social class, and the other two, by Wade and by Isaacs, are concerned with caste.

The highly urbanized industrialized societies of the Western world have developed in conjunction with a system of social class ranking which has permitted relatively large-scale movement among the ranks, particularly in fostering the upward mobility of those from the lower ranks. It has generally been thought that this fluid class structure made for a more efficient distribution of manpower suitable to the high production goals of an industrial society. Lipset and Bendix's "The Patterns of Opportunity in Large Cities" examines the dynamics of the association between city life and social mobility in urban-industrial society in one of the most specific ways possible. They study the factors which make for greater social mobility of lower-class *native* urbanites in large metropolitan cities than among lower-class *migrants* to the city from rural areas or smaller cities. This effectively focuses on the role of urbanization *per se* in social mobility. According to Lipset and Bendix, data from a variety of Western societies indicate that the important factors facilitating upward mobility in the metropolis are access to education, knowledge of a greater variety of occupational choices, and higher aspiration levels and motivation. For middle-class youth, wherever reared, social class training made up for the disadvantage of smaller communities, but for lower-class youth, the mobility-inducing features of the metropolis introduce factors lacking in social class training found in smaller communities. The process by which metropolitan life produces social mobility appears to lie not only in the complexity of the social organization which creates a greater variety of occupations and statuses, but in the kind of socialization experience the large city provides for those who otherwise would not have such experience.

Lauro Martines' "Social Place in Florence: Assumptions and Realities" presents the system of social stratification and mobility of a preindustrial city, Florence, in the period 1390–1460. The Florentine system emphasized ascription of social status and a limited elite widely separated in behavior and expectation from the lower classes, in marked contrast to the industrial cities described by Lipset and Bendix. The role of the city was crucial in social mobility in Lipset and Bendix's analysis because, in the main, status was based on achievement, and the city provided people, especially lower-class youth, with a broader form of preparation for achievement. However, in fifteenth-century Florence social class was based essentially on membership in an interlocking economic, political, and familial structure. Social mobility took place therefore at a slow pace.

The four criteria of high social class described by Martines include two directly linked with "inheritance" of social status—descent from established high-ranking families and marriage into such families. The remaining criteria, wealth and service in public office, also contained important non-acquired elements—wealth was preferably "old" or at least "honorably acquired," and public service was often on the basis of "connections" and family. As Martines indicates there were departures from this model, but the outline was clear. Florence at this period may be viewed as an example of the social stratification and mobility patterns attendant on the social organization of the preindustrial city described by Sjoberg ("The Preindustrial City," selection 9). This raises anew the question whether there is a *necessary* association between social organization and technology, a matter already discussed in the Introduction to Part I and in notes on earlier articles in Part III. Conflicting theories and evidence suggest that no definitive answer is yet available.

In this unresolved debate it becomes particularly important to examine as closely as possible the specific ways in which city residence *per se* sustains or undermines certain aspects of social organization, in this case social stratification and mobility. Lipset and Bendix's study was an example of such analysis. Richard C. Wade's "The Transformation of Slavery in the Cities" is another. He examines the role of city residence in weakening slavery, a status sometimes compared to a caste distinction. In any case, Wade examines a greater hierarchical division than Lipset and Bendix did, and examines it in southern cities before they were fully industrialized. Wade's analysis spells out how social distance between the races was profoundly altered under urban conditions. The change seemed to lie in the problem of maintaining social control over the slaves in the city. Significantly, Wade notes that "It was the total environment rather than industrial or commercial employment which eroded slavery in the cities." The chief ingredients of urban fermentation were geographic propinquity and urban complexity. The latter, whether expressed in the greater variety of Negroes' life styles in the city or in the advantage or convenience some whites—merchants, ministers, lawyers—might find in treating Negroes differently than custom demanded, resulted in loosening and blurring the simple distinction between master and slave. Geographic propinquity made it difficult to isolate urban slaves from these influences, particularly since free blacks concentrated in cities. There was a two-pronged attempt to protect the old slave order from the incursions of urban life. First, there was the simple expedient of removing slaves from the southern cities. Wade demonstrates that this was carried out on a significant scale in the decades immediately before the Civil War. Second, the southern cities devised a new means of social control in the city to compensate for the fact that the masters often could not directly supervise their slaves' behavior in the city. This was the far-reaching system of public racial observances and segregation in all phases of life that came to be called "Jim Crow."

Wade's analysis thus suggests countertendencies to the liberalizing effect of the city on social stratification, at least so far as slavery was concerned. Wade's discussion concluded at 1860. Since then slavery has not only been legally abolished but the decreasing demand for labor on southern farms and the increasing demand for labor in cities have brought a large Negro population into cities. By 1960 Negroes were more heavily urbanized than whites—72 per cent of the nonwhite population of the United States lived in cities but only 69 per cent of the white population. Interestingly, as legal status differences between whites and Negroes crumbled and Jim Crow practices have been abandoned, racial residential segregation has increased, a process analyzed in detail in Karl and Alma Taeuber's article, selection 21 in this volume. The cities' influence on racial status in the United States has been liberalizing, but as both Wade's analysis and events since 1860 indicate, the process is not so straightforward as the old saying, "*Stadt Luft macht frei.*"

Will urban life have the same liberalizing effect on deeply rooted status distinctions in other societies as they become urbanized? Will there be attempts to "salvage" the old system and adjust it to the conditions of city life? These questions are pertinent in theoretical terms but also in practical terms, for one of the major urbanizing countries is India, whose caste system, based on Hindu religion, is of long duration. Hinduism has four castes and one group, apart from and below all the castes, who were literally "untouchable" and were rigidly excluded from participation in education, intermarriage with the castes, and any but the most menial jobs. In 1949 the Indian Constitution abolished "untouchability" and the Indian government instituted special scholarships and job quotas to try to move the "ex-untouchables" along the road to social and economic mobility. There are 65 million ex-untouchables in India, about 15 per cent of the population according to the 1961 census. Although some changes are taking place, the vast majority of the "ex-untouchables," now often called members of the "scheduled castes," still live as before, regardless of legal changes in their status. Harold Isaacs interviewed a small number of ex-untouchables who had received higher degrees and moved into white-collar and professional occupations. One of his subjects, Mr. Ubale, an ex-untouchable who is a college official (at a school founded by an untouchable and largely attended by ex-untouchables), presents a vivid mixture of social mobility and restriction, change and tradition. Although he has a responsible position and a reasonable salary he lives in an abject slum. This may be partly voluntary because he is spending a considerable portion of his income to provide an appropriate traditional wedding for a sister. It is also true that known untouchables are often discriminated against in housing and also in other activities such as eating together, social contact, and intermarriage. Some ex-untouchables have used the cloak of urban anonymity to change their names to those not obviously "untouchable" or to convert to non-Hindu religions. Untouchables are often of darker skin color than caste Hindus but there are no clear guides or racial distinctions. Little systematic evidence is available on the current condition of the ex-untouchables. Whatever upward mobility they are experiencing is taking place in the cities. Whether the old distinctions will fade, or be replaced by nonlegal distinctions, remains an open question.

A | Industrialism, Urbanization, and Social Change

22 | World Revolution and Family Patterns

WILLIAM J. GOODE

It is clear . . . that at the present time a somewhat similar set of influences is affecting all world cultures. All of them are moving toward industrialization, although at varying speeds and from different points. Their family systems are also approaching some variant of the conjugal system. We have stated as an initial point of view, validated throughout by data, that the *direction of change* for each characteristic of the family might be very different from one culture to another even though the pattern of movement for the system as a whole is toward a variant of the conjugal type. For example, the divorce rate has dropped in Japan during the past half-century, whereas it has risen in the Western world; in both instances the move is toward a conjugal pattern. The illegitimacy rate has increased in urbanizing and industrializing Africa, but it has been dropping in the Western world.

Even though all systems are more or less under the impact of industrializing and urbanizing forces, we have not assumed that the amount of change is a simple function of one or the other, or even of combinations of both. On the contrary, we have asserted that we do not believe that the theoretical relations between a developing industrial system and the conjugal family system are entirely clear. On the empirical side we suggest that the changes that have taken place have been far more rapid than could be supposed or predicted from the degree of industrialization alone. We have

SOURCE: William J. Goode, *World Revolution and Family Patterns* (New York: The Macmillan Company, 1963), pp. 368–374. Reprinted with permission of The Macmillan Company. Copyright © 1963 by The Free Press of Glencoe, a Division of the Macmillan Company.

281

insisted, instead, on the independent power of ideological variables. Everywhere the ideology of the conjugal family is spreading, even though a majority does not accept it. It appeals to the disadvantaged, to the young, to women, and to the educated. It promises freedom and new alternatives as against the rigidities and controls of traditional systems. It is as effective as the appeal of freedom or land redistribution or an attack on the existing stratification system. It is radical, and is arousing support in many areas where the rate of industrialization is very slight. Yet, the ideology of the conjugal system would have only a minimal effect if each newly emerging system did not furnish some independent base for implementing the new choices implicit in the ideology. We believe that the crucial points of pressure from industrialization on the traditional family structure are the following:

1. It calls for physical movement from one locality to another, thus decreasing the frequency and intimacy of contact among members of a kin network—although at the stage of full industrialization this is partly counteracted by greater ease of contact at a distance (telephone, letter, etc.).

2. Industrialization creates class-differential mobility. That is, among siblings or kindred, one or more persons may move rapidly upward while the others do not, thus creating discrepancies in styles of life, taste, income, etc., and making contact somewhat less easy and pleasant.

3. Urban and industrial systems of agencies, facilities, procedures, and organizations have undermined large corporate kin groupings since they now handle the problems that were solved within the kin network before industrialization: political protection, pooling funds to educate bright youngsters, defending a locality, lending money, etc.

4. Industrialization creates a value structure that recognizes achievement more than birth; consequently, the kin have less to offer an individual in exchange for his submission. He has to make his *own* way; at best his kin can give him an opportunity to show his talent. Without rewards, control is not possible. The success of the Japanese family in keeping the kin group intact proves the rule more effectively, since some family control over jobs has been maintained. On the other hand, as industrialization has moved forward, the individual is more likely to be able to make his own way without his kin so that he need not consult them in important decisions. Note too that such a change brings new attitudes as well: Kin are less *willing* to call upon one another for such help because they would be embarrassed; they too accept the values of achievement.

5. Because of specialization, by which thousands of new jobs are created, it is statistically less likely that an individual can obtain a job for his kinsman. He may not be in a suitable sector of the occupational sphere, or at a level where his influence is useful.

We have noted the apparent theoretical harmony between the conjugal family system and the modern world and the modern industrial pattern, but have also pointed out some disharmonies. We stressed that though the conjugal system serves the needs of the industrial system, it is not at all clear that the latter serves the needs of the *family* pattern. The creation of a new family structure in China, which would further reduce the kinship ties that are part of the conjugal system, might well be more effective in industrialization; but it also has its costs.

To point to another theoretical and empirical obscurity, contemporary theory asserts that a society based on achievement is likely to have a conjugal system, but we suggest that various periods of the past—such as the twelfth and thirteenth centuries in Europe, or the beginnings of the four major Chinese dynasties prior to the 1911 Revolution—were to a considerable extent based on achievement, with no measurable trend toward a conjugal system.

Perhaps equally important, we have insisted that although some type of conjugal pattern and the ideology that often precedes it begins to emerge along with industrialization, we cannot suppose that only the industrializing elements are causally important. We must also entertain the hypothesis that the changes in the family itself may facilitate the process of industrialization. We have suggested, for example, that earlier changes in the Western family system, beginning perhaps with the seventeenth century, may have made that transition to industrialization easier than in other cultures. That is, the family variables are themselves independent and have an impact on the total social structure. The mere fact of their resistance suggests some independent power but we believe that in addition they may facilitate or retard the acceptance of industrialization. It is perhaps at this point that the ideology of the family plays an important role by opening the way to the new family behavior as well as to the industrial role pattern.

We have also emphasized that the conjugal family system is not equivalent to a "nuclear family" composed only of parents and children. We have shown on both empirical and theoretical grounds that the conjugal family has far more kinship ties and correlatively is under far more kinship control than is sometimes supposed by Western observers or non-Western analysts. It seems impossible to cut down the size of the effective conjugal family to its nuclear core only, either in the West or in any other society, without some type of political or coercive force. The additional kin who are included are there because of a direct emotional tie with some members of the nuclear core, a tie supported by the institutional structure: Siblings are necessarily involved with their siblings-in-law; husbands and wives are tied to their parents-in-law; grandparents are emotionally attached to their grandchildren and vice versa. The ties among these kin may be traced through some member of the nuclear core and it is impossible to eliminate these additional kin ties without disrupting the nuclear family itself. Thus, the corporate kindred or lineage may lose most of its functions under urbanization and industrialization, but these extensions of kin ties continue to remain alive and important in social control, through reciprocal gifts and exchanges, visits, and continual contacts.

But although we must not commit the error of *minimizing* the extension of kin in a conjugal family system, we must also avoid *exaggerating* the ties of the extended family which preceded the modern conjugal family. It seems empirically clear that prior to the modern era in the Western world, and in all of the cultures we have been examining, several generations of one family did not live under the same roof, and did not carry on all of their productive activities there. If only because of the brute facts of mortality and the necessity of gaining a living on small plots of land, this was true for both urban and rural strata. On the other hand, the extended kin played a substantial role in non-Western cultures even when they did not live together, and the *ideal* remained that of a common household. When an individual attained sufficient wealth and social standing, he succeeded in creating and maintaining a large assemblage of kin under his leadership.

Even when an extended family was created, as we suggested in India and the Arab world, this was often a *phase* in the development of a single family between the initial fission by which a man established a conjugal unit separated from his father's household and the next generation of fission when the man's grown married siblings began to break off from their father, or from the household after their father died. This was undoubtedly a common historical process in the past, and the present merely accentuates and intensifies it, since now there are more and earlier opportunities for the younger generation to break off and set up independent households.

With reference to the question of *how* the impact of industrialization occurs on the family, we have suggested that the primary process hinges on the control by elders of the new opportunities under industrialization. That is, do *they* create the new jobs and can *they* hand them out to the younger generation or to their women? A crucial difference between upper- and lower-class elders lies in the fact that the new opportunities are typically created and developed by upper-class elders, who can thus control their own sons or women and thus maintain their lines of authority long after these have begun to disintegrate among lower-strata families. Elders in lower-strata families cannot generate these opportunities. Consequently, they have little to offer the younger generation to counteract their normal tendency to independence. As a result, even in the modern Western world, upper-strata families maintain a far larger extension of kin and far greater control over their own young than do lower-strata families.

This central variable is qualified somewhat by the factor of ideology. Those who hold power cannot keep it unless they believe in the *rightness* of their authority. It is especially difficult to hold to that belief in the face-to-face relations of the family, because of the inherent love and affectional ties among its members. When that faith weakens under the impact of the new ideology, the normal push of the disadvantaged, the young, and women may become sufficiently strong to change family relations if new opportunities are available through which these younger people can obtain an independent social and economic base.

This same evidence of a role bargaining process may be found in the radically changing position of women in all of the cultures under examination. The fundamental transformation of woman's estate is sometimes overlooked, because in certain past epochs women had a considerable amount of *personal* freedom. The modern industrial world is the first cultural system, however, to permit women to occupy independent jobs. They have become independent of members of their family. They obtain their work by themselves, and also control the money they earn. This has meant an enormous increase in the economic productivity of populations that have made use of their women in this fashion. At the same time, it has changed the bargaining position of women within the family system. Needless to say, this is a reciprocal process. It is by virtue of a change in the general evaluation of women and their position in the large society that the permission is granted to work independently; but once women begin to take these positions in the large society, then they are better able to assert their own rights and wishes within the family. This process need not be, and probably rarely is, rational or even conscious.

Class differences remain, and so do their inherent paradoxes. Toward the lower strata, in all of these cultures, it is evident that the woman actually has had somewhat more authority. The sheer lack of funds and services at these levels has given the woman a key position within the family. This has been especially so in areas and places where she has held independent or semi-independent jobs: Japanese women divers in the coastal or forestry villages are an illustration of this pattern. Toward the upper strata, men have had less need of a particular wife, and could obtain almost any service a wife could perform by using alternative women as concubines, servants, housekeepers, and so on. The funds were available to seclude or protect the wife more, and the discrepancy between the man's economic and social power and her own was much greater.

Ideological *differences* in the modern world run in the opposite direction. Toward the upper strata, men who are better educated and more strongly affected by the new philosophy of the family are somewhat more willing on a philosophical level to concede rights, and women are somewhat more eager to demand them, although their behavior may in fact be less free than toward the lower strata. Men in the lower strata, by contrast, are much more traditional-minded than their counterparts in the upper strata, and are less willing to concede the new rights being demanded; but they have to do so because of the increased bargaining power of their women.

Thus, in the age-old war between the sexes and between generations, the entrance of a new ideology of the family plays a crucial role. It validates and speeds the emergence of some minority patterns into majority patterns; but it slows others down. It strengthens and gives bargaining power to some kinship positions, and weakens still others. It does this not only because of the demands on the part of those who seek new rights, or because of the values of those who resist the concession of the new rights, but also, and perhaps centrally, because the third parties, that is, other people involved in their role network, may support the recalcitrants or weaken the innovators.

However, we do not believe that any family system now in operation, or likely to emerge in the next generation, will grant full equality to women, although throughout the world the general position of women will improve greatly. The revolutionary philosophies which have accompanied the shifts in power in Communist countries or in the Israel *kibbutzim* have asserted equality, and a significant stream of philosophic thought in the West has asserted the right to equality, but no society has yet granted it. Nor does the movement in Western countries, including the Communist countries, suggest that the future will be greatly different. We believe that it is possible to develop a society in which this would happen, but not without a radical reorganization of the social structure. The family base upon which all societies rest at present requires that much of the daily work of the house and children be handed over to women. Doubtless, men can do this nearly as well, but they have shown no eagerness to assume these tasks, and families continue to rear their daughters to take only a modest degree of interest in full-time careers in which they would have equal responsibilities with men.

A subsidiary thesis in our analysis has been that different relations within the family, and between the family and the larger society, are under a differential tension even in the *traditional* system. Some relations are well-buttressed, while others contain great strains which are overborne by the dominant social patterns. When new elements enter, however, such as a new ideology, or differential opportunities, then the relations under greatest strain are likely to give way first. Still, many relations may continue with undiminished vigor. . . . For example, . . . in China the mother-in-law's domination over the daughter-in-law was a theme for literary and philosophical comment, and . . . the pattern continued although people deplored it. The new forces at work in China, from the 1911 Revolution on, had undermined the strength of this traditional relationship, and the Communists merely implemented the change further. In the new social system that has been emerging in China and Japan, the mother-in-law is less useful in the new household. Her husband, the father of her son, no longer has the same power over *his* son, and thus can no longer threaten the daughter-in-law to the same degree. The young man is more likely to have become emotionally attached to his wife even before marriage, so that he is less willing to support his mother in a dispute between the two. The young wife is more likely to be working, and thus making a real contribution to the prosperity of the household. At many points, then, the daughter-in-law can resist the mother-in-law more easily, and has been reared to believe that resistance is proper. The mother-in-law, on the other hand, does not feel the same certainty of success. Consequently, this relationship has changed substantially.

Yet, the intense mother-son relationship in the traditional Indian and Arab family systems was not under great strain, and has not been under any ideological attack. The newly emerging family patterns do not seem, therefore, to weaken it at any important point.

Since the world is becoming industrialized and urbanized simultaneously, it may not be possible to isolate these two processes as separate sets of causal factors. . . . A common theoretical error is to treat "urbanization" as *a single variable*, but to include in that variable almost all of the social changes that are now going on. Since these are the changes that are taking place, one cannot treat them as causal variables. Indeed, they are the phenomena to be explained. Or, alternatively, by including under this category almost every conceivable social change, one can say that "urbanization causes everything" simply because urbanization is so loosely defined as to include everything.

Similarly, industrialization cannot be defined as the *impact* upon the "social structure" of the factory system, rapid communication and transportation, a high level of scientific training, and so on. These are all part of the same complex. The former set of phenomena cannot come into being unless the social structure is being transformed somewhat. They are not, strictly speaking, to be viewed as a set of *causal* variables working on a static and passive set of social patterns. Rather, they *are* the changes to be explained. We cannot find cases in which suddenly there is a full industrial complex in interaction with a so-far unchanged social structure. Machines do not make social structures; people with specific social patterns make machines. At present, we see no great clarity emerging from these theoretical arguments, although we have tried to suggest various points at which industrialization may have an impact on the family, and have thereby selected from the total phenomena of industrialization a few of the key variables.

23 | Continuity and Change in Japanese Industry

JAMES C. ABEGGLEN

Thus far efforts to promote industrialization in non-Western societies have been devoted largely to problems of assistance and change in the areas of finance and technology. The results of these efforts have drawn attention to the importance of social organization and of patterns of social interaction

SOURCE: James C. Abegglen, *The Japanese Factory: Aspects of Its Social Organization* (New York: The Free Press, 1958), pp. 122, 127-141. Copyright © 1958, Massachusetts Institute of Technology. Reprinted with permission of the author and publisher.

to the process of economic change, and emphasize the need for a further understanding of the interaction between technology and human relations for effective economic development.

Japan's extraordinary history of industrialization remains a unique record of effective social change, compelling the attention of those concerned with problems of industrialization and economic development in non-Western societies. Japan strode from hard-held Asian insularity to a central role in world industry, world trade, and world power relations in a single, explosive burst of energy and remains the singular case of non-Western industrialization. The outlines of the story are familiar; its implications for present attempts effectively to bring about development in other countries are evident.

. . . . .

Of . . . fundamental importance . . . is . . . the degree of continuity or discontinuity in social structure and systems of social interaction from the preindustrial society to industrialization. The assumption is that industrial development on the Western model requires a social setting radically different in nature from preindustrial relationships, a system fundamentally akin to that which developed in the West. The problem is no less complex than it is important. It would be presumptuous, with the limited knowledge of Japan's social system now available, to state the answer for the Japanese case to the general proposition. Still the results of this study of the large Japanese factory bear on this issue.

It might be assumed that, more than any other institution, the large manufacturing plant would represent in its social organization the extreme accommodation of Japanese systems of organization to the demands of industrial technology. Differences in organization, retaining similarities to earlier forms, might persist in rural social groupings and not be directly relevant to this question of the connections between social change and economic change. However, such lags in adaptation would presumably be minimized in the large factory.

. . . It may . . . be possible . . . to make out differences between the usual American factory organization and that common in the large factories of Japan, and to make some general statement of the nature of the differences. Leaving aside exceptions and details, some general features of the Japanese organization might be summarized:

1. Membership in the Japanese productive group is a permanent and irrevocable membership. Workers at all levels of the factory customarily work in but one company. They spend their entire career in that single firm which is entered immediately on completing their education. The firm will continue to provide the worker's income at whatever disadvantage to itself, and the worker will continue in the company's employ despite possible advantage in moving to another firm.

2. Recruitment into the productive group is based on personal qualities without reference to a particular work task or set of skills. Selection is

based primarily on the individual's education, character, and general background. Inadequacy or incompetence shown subsequent to selection are not a basis for dismissal from the group.

3. Status in the group is a continuation and extension of status held in the society at the time of entrance to the group. The broad dichotomy of employees into *koin* and *shokuin** limits the movement of an individual in the factory system largely to the general category that his education entitled him to enter on recruitment.

4. Reward in the productive group is only partly in the form of money, and is based on broad social criteria rather than on production criteria. The recompense of workers is made up of such items as housing, food, and personal services, with the actual cash pay of the worker forming only part of the total. Pay is based primarily on age, education, length of service, and family size, with job rank or competence only a small part of the criteria for determining work reward.

5. The formal organization of the factory is elaborated in a wide range and considerable number of formal positions. Formal rank and title in the hierarchy are well defined, but authority and responsibility of ranks are not. Partly in consequence, the decision-making function is exercised by groups of persons, but responsibility for the decisions is not assigned to individuals.

6. The penetration of the company into the nonbusiness activities of the worker and the responsibility taken by the company for the worker are extensive. Management is involved in such diverse and intimate matters as the worker's personal finances, the education of his children, religious activities, and the training of the worker's wife. The company is responsible for the continued well-being of the worker and his family, and this responsibility is carried out both in formal personnel procedures and in the informal relations between the worker and supervisor.

If a single conclusion were to be drawn from this study it would be that the development of industrial Japan has taken place with much less change from the kinds of social organization and social relations of preindustrial or nonindustrial Japan than would be expected from the Western model of the growth of an industrial society. The rise and development of the industrial West is generally attributed in some considerable part to the development of an impersonalized and rationalized view of the world and of relations with others. Emphasis on individuality, the view of the workplace as a purely economic grouping clearly differentiated in goals and relationships from other areas of social interaction, the subordination of other values and interests of the economic goal in business activity, the use of money to discharge obligations for services in the business world—all these and related trends are seen as critical to the successful development of

---

* *Koin* are wage workers, apprentices, and foremen, who usually have only grammar school education. *Shokuin* are clerical supervisory employees who usually are high school or college graduates.—Ed.

large-scale industry. In sociological theory some of these tendencies have been set forth in polarities to indicate the nature of the differences. Thus, for example, "status" and "contract" have been contrasted as indicating the difference and direction of development with industrialization from a close, intimate personal group to the more rationalized and impersonalized relations of modern business. A more recent dichotomization is the differentiation of "particularism" and "universalism," or the move from a value emphasis on particular relationships and symbols, with stress on loyalty and intragroup harmony, to an emphasis on rationalized means-end relations, with stress on efficiency and performance.

These kinds of polarities are not altogether useful in discussing the Japanese case. Although it is possible to point to elements in the organization of the Japanese factory that fit the industrial and modern end of these polarities, a very considerable part of the organizational system remains more like the preindustrial pole. It does not seem warranted to hold that Japan is now at some mid-point in development. Such an argument is inconsistent with the view that contractual, universalistic relations are necessary to successful industrialization. Nor is it sufficient to say that since Japan's industrialization is relatively recent these divergencies from the pattern as seen and set forth in the West will in time mend themselves and fit harmoniously into one of these several categories without conflict or with few conflicting elements. In point of fact, as this report has attempted to indicate, the Japanese system is on the whole self-consistent. The recruitment methods and the incentive system fit together with the rules governing employment to make a unified whole. Change in one, as, for example, in employment rules, would drastically affect and require changes in other elements of the organization.

From this examination of the Japanese factory, the factory organization seems a consistent and logical outgrowth of the kinds of relations existing in Japan prior to its industrialization. The changes that took place in Japan during the last three decades of the nineteenth century are often termed a "revolution." That they represented in many respects drastic departures from the preceding period is clear enough. The manner of the "revolution," however, seems still open to question. At repeated points in the study of the factory, parallels to an essentially feudal system of organization may be seen—not, to be sure, a replication of the feudal loyalties, commitments, rewards, and methods of leadership but a rephrasing of them in the setting of modern industry.

It may well be that the kinds of experiences undergone by the West antecedent to the development of modern industry are indeed essential to an independent and *de novo* development of industry. The Japanese case suggests that these experiences and the organizational system used in the West are not necessary to the introduction of industry into another social system. From the observations of this study it would appear that, although the technology of modern industry was introduced into Japan, the factory organization at the same time developed consistent with the historical customs and attitudes of the Japanese and with the social system as it existed prior to the introduction of modern industry. Thus, looking beyond the modern equipment and the formal organization, the systems of relationships are more nearly similar to those which seem to have characterized an earlier Japan and which now characterize the nonindustrial areas of Japan than they are similar to the factory organization of the West.

Differences in the role of the individual in the Western and Japanese factory—the ways in which he is motivated, the extent to which responsibility and authority are assigned individuals, the kinds of rewards offered, and the behaviors that are rewarded—have a close relation to differences between the two cultural backgrounds. Japan's industry was superimposed in a matter of some few decades on a society that was profoundly and had for some centuries been feudal. The loyalty of the worker to the industrial organization, the paternal methods of motivating and rewarding the worker, the close involvement of the company in all manner of what seem to Western eyes to be personal and private affairs of the worker—all have parallels with Japan's preindustrial social organization.

This parallel does not underestimate the enormous changes that have taken place in Japan through the period of her industrialization. Japan has changed mightily; and changes continue. If the study of industrialization in Japan is to be relevant to the study of the developing economies of other Asian nations, however, the nature of the changes which have taken place must be clearly understood. What the results of this study of the social organization of the large Japanese factory suggest is that changes have taken place selectively—a point well remarked in other contexts—and, more important, that these changes have been such as to leave unchanged the underlying basis of social relationships. Rather than penetrating to the roots of the social system the changes have been built up from the kind of social relationships pre-existing in Japan.

A compact statement of the general nature of social relations in Japan has been provided by Stoetzel. He states: "In point of fact, as Ruth Benedict rightly guessed, the whole social structure of Japan is dictated by a concept of hierarchy deriving from the kinship of the clan." [1] Stoetzel then summarizes his conclusions:

To understand the Japanese social structure, three ideas must be brought into play, not separately, but together: (a) the idea of kinship, by blood, marriage, adoption, or service; (b) the idea of hierarchy, always conceived more or less on the *oyako* (father-son) model; (c) the idea of sharing in the protection offered by the tutelary deities, by a common cult or at least by a common burying ground. These three ideas are connected with each other,

---

[1] Jean Stoetzel, *Without the Chrysanthemum and the Sword: A Study of the Attitudes of Youth in Postwar Japan*, UNESCO publication (New York: Columbia University Press, 1955), p. 56.

particularly the first two: wherever there is kinship there is a hierarchical relationship, and the opposite as we have seen is also true; as for the common cult, it is the symbol of the family bond.[2]

Throughout this discussion of the large factory, parallels have been noted between the factory system and the clan or kinship organization. In terms of formal organization some of these have included both the manner of recruitment into the system and the kinds of reciprocal obligations thereby incurred by company and worker. Further, the formal system of motivation and reward has functional parallels to that of a kinship grouping.

In the informal organization as well the recurring relationship is modeled in the factory on the *oyako* relation, with hierarchical roles defined in terms of this pattern. This pattern is not . . . the formal *oyabun-kobun* structure, but is, rather, an informal father-son type of system.

Indeed, so pervasive are the parallels to a kinship-type organization in the large Japanese factory that it is not necessary for the observer to argue their presence from indirect evidences. For example, in a 1952 speech to his managerial employees, the president of a large steel company said, "Not only is there the fact that our life's work is our employment in our company, but I feel that as people in this situation we have two occasions that can be called a 'birth.' The first is when we are born into the world as mewling infants. The second is when we all receive our commissions of adoption into the company. This is an event that has the same importance as our crying birth." Here are both a direct statement of the kinship basis of company organization and an indication of the way in which the common bond is symbolized, by treating the company, its history, and present organization as an extended family with common values, common ancestors, and common beliefs. It is for this reason, for example, that elaborate histories and genealogies of the large firms are written and that common religious shrines and ceremonies may be found.

It might be added here parenthetically and as a further evidence of the nature of these underlying relationships that the *zaibatsu* groupings in Japan are seriously misunderstood when seen as cartels or monopolies on the Western model. These are in a very real sense clans, the furthest extension of kinship-type relations in the economic and industrial sector. To treat these, by the passing of anti-monopoly laws, as fundamentally economic and financial groupings was grotesque and doomed to failure from the first. It might be pertinent here to quote Lockwood . . . : "Too often in the case of Japan there is a tendency to apply easy labels, derived from Western experience. They may only obscure the complexities of the facts."[3] This statement does not say that the factory organization is

---

[2] *Ibid.*, p. 57.

[3] William W. Lockwood, *The Economic Development of Japan, Growth and Structural Change, 1868–1938* (Princeton: Princeton University Press, 1954), p. 200.

"caused" by Japanese family organization but that both family organization and factory organization are components of a common social structure; and as such the system of relationships within each grouping has a common structural base.

It would seem from this study, then, that the very success of the Japanese experience with industrialization may well have been a function of the fact that, far from undergoing a total revolution in social structure or social relationships, the hard core of Japan's system of social relationships remained intact, allowing an orderly transition to industrialization continuous with her earlier social forms. It would in fact be remarkable if social change of this magnitude and success could occur in any other way. Discontinuity will not lead to effective adaptation; rather, it will result in chaos. The exceptional durability of Japan's social system, often remarked upon and demonstrated anew in her response to total defeat in the Second World War, is not the result of a mystic ability of the Japanese to adapt but, rather, the consequence of the fact that through change a basis for social continuity has remained intact. It is of some interest to note in this connection that the same wondrous ability to selectively take on new elements in a society is now being attributed to Indian society. But selective adaptation should not be remarkable; it would be much more remarkable if any people were able in one fell swoop to put off their past, their training, and habits of mind and don successfully and permanently totally new social paraphernalia. Efforts to change the economy of other nations in the direction of industrialization might better then be concerned with an identification of basic elements of the preindustrial social system and with the introduction of new technologies and financial systems in the context of the older relationships than with making these nations over in the image derived from Western outcomes.

A partial explanation, therefore, of Japan's rapid industrialization might well be argued to lie in the amount and more especially in the kind of continuity throughout the transition rather than in an emphasis on change. In this connection one might note that there is reason to believe that the pressure of the family system in Japan toward social rigidity and inflexibility may be commonly overstated. Although an analysis of the family system is outside the limits of this study, in terms of the thesis of social continuity and its effects on industrial change, it should be emphasized that in two particulars at least there has been within the historical structure of the Japanese family a potentiality for flexibility and change.

The first of these is the practice of adoption, by which not only more distant relatives but also able and promising employees and servants have long been able to assume important roles in higher-status families and in family businesses. This practice, not far removed from the notion of employment as seen in the large factory, not only has made for continual social mobility and flexibility even under feudal regulations but also may well have provided a paradigm for methods of industrial recruitment.

The role of the younger son in Japan is also of some interest in this regard. Under rules of primogeniture in a country lacking sufficient land there are provided the conditions for the establishment of an urban work force. Further, there has been a tradition of continuity, despite such mobility by younger sons, through the establishment of "branch families" tied to the "main family" by bonds of obligation and duty. The main family, in, for example, a rural village, under industrialization also provided a buffer against economic hardship and depression—an advantage still in a country where social security measures are meager.

These and other elements of the Japanese family structure, aspects of family organization conducive to adaptation and change, may well have aided the transition to industrialization by making possible adjustment within the older family system rather than, as is sometimes suggested, industrialization and urbanization shattering the older family pattern. Finally, and most important from the point of view of factory organization, the principle of family loyalty and cohesion, when successfully symbolized and incorporated into military, industrial, and financial organizations, may have become an important source of energy and motivation for the transition to industrialization. It must again be emphasized that such structural elements as these would hold change within limits, order the great transition, and prevent the kind of social discontinuity which would be destructive of a society.

Turning now from such suggestions as this study of the large Japanese factory might provide for an understanding of Japan's past, we raise the question of possible future developments in the organization of Japanese industry. There is a perhaps inherent tendency in describing an on-going social organization to emphasize the integration and harmony of the several elements of the system at the expense of an analysis of stress or of present and future changes in the system. Yet in reviewing the Japanese factory the system appears to be stable in terms of the relationships between people in the organization. The organization is internally consistent and acceptable to its members so long as the membership is drawn from backgrounds in which the forms of relationships on which the factory is based are retained.

In terms of the people in the factory, two groups in particular seem to have some difficulty in adapting themselves to this kind of organization. Young Japanese who are urban reared, born in the large cities of laboring and white collar fathers, educated in urban schools beyond the legally prescribed minimum of middle school education, and steeped in the impersonality of modern cities do not fit well into these factory relationships. Here is a central problem of the large Japanese factory. Workers born into traditional extended and close-knit families in the farm villages of Japan, for example, have, in the words of the factory managers, "stable natures." Products of small family groups of the large cities, unfamiliar with the elaborate systems of obligations and duties spun by kinship and friendship ties in the stable villages, do not respond to the appeals and rationale of this factory system. Women, too, who by virtue of family training or education have been schooled in a newer pattern of relationships and role expectations and who have come to expect an occupational role different from that traditionally assigned Japanese women, protest their position in the factory.

Changes in the factory organization may proceed from two causes. The first is prior changes in the organization of and relationships in primary groups in the society. The second is the pressure of changes in technology and production methods that would lead to organizational change. . . . The pressure for change is great for example, to increase the flexibility of the work force to lead to greater adaptability to economic changes. The need for change has led, on occasion, to change in a limited sphere, as, for example, when a financial crisis and a subsequent "rationalization" movement led to the discharge of employees from a number of large factories. . . . However, it appears likely that makeshift and temporary adaptations which do not alter the general rules of employment and organization will be made. Real changes in factory organization will come about only when the point of view and the training of individuals in the system alter significantly. Thus the Japanese family system, under the pressure of urbanization, changes in religious thought and training, and under the constant impact of mass communication, may change the ways in which youths are trained and developed, thus changing the attitudes and expectations, motivation systems, and interaction patterns of youth. Although changes in primary group structures have not yet been carried to the point where the factory organization is in conflict with any major portion of the society's patterns of interaction, such a process of change, in large part the result of the growth of large industy, may in time alter the basis of factory organization.

It is easy here, as in looking at Japanese history, to mistake the nature of changes in cities and during the postwar period. The general formulas for the effects of urbanization have been developed out of Western experience. The almost total lack of close study of the nature of social interaction in the cities of Asia makes a prediction of the direction and kind of change induced by urbanization in Asia most hazardous. Further, it is far from clear at present as to how effective and lasting postwar experiments and adjustments may be in the Japanese case. It would be a daring observer indeed who would predict the outcome of the next two or three decades of Japanese events.

In summing up the results of this study, there appear to be two broad elements of difference between Japan and the West in relation to the nature of the social organization of the factory. First, the factory, or company, is relatively undifferentiated from other types of groups in the society. In terms of the commitment of members to the group, the nature of their recruitment and subsequent careers, and the extent of involvement of members with each other as part of the group, the Japanese factory grouping parallels other social groupings. Although the factory may be defined as an economic organization with its goals narrowly defined and relationships narrowly based on productivity and profit, the Japanese factory is not so defined. The Western view of life segments, each serving a special end with differentiated relationships in each—the family, the club or association, the workplace—makes possible a clear differentiation of activities and organization in each group. In Japan, the factory recruits involve and maintain their membership on a basis similar to that of the domestic and social groups of the society. Where the economic ends of the factory conflict with this broader definition of the group, as in the case of the incompetent employee who will not be discharged, the economic ends take a secondary position to the maintenance of group integrity.

This lack of differentiation between the large factory organization and other social groupings is not only an internal one. Status in the broader community, as reflected primarily in educational attainment, is the critical variable governing recruitment and is the dominating factor in rank and career progress in the factory. Moreover, the employee shares responsibility with the company for his family, his children, and his general well-being. The broader social activities are not set apart from his membership in the factory or company.

Closely related to this latter aspect of the lack of differentiation is the difference between the American and the Japanese organization in the extent to which there is an individualization or impersonalization of relationships in the factory. It is perhaps this lack of individualization that most sets off the day-to-day functioning of the Japanese production unit from its American counterpart. The apparatus of modern production in the West depends heavily on the assignment of individual responsibility, on individual incentive programs, on the job evaluation of the individual employee, and on a system of rewards in which individual competence and energy will be recompensed. In all of these respects the difference from Japan is marked. Individual responsibility is avoided, incentive systems have little relationship to individual output but, rather, depend on group success, and the motivating of energies appears to depend on the individual's loyalty and identification with the group and with his superior.

In short, it may be concluded from this study that, although the preindustrial experience of the West may indeed have been the necessary cause of the development of industrialization, the introduction of industry into a society like that of Japan, which has not shared these earlier experiences and has a markedly different social system, makes necessary the fitting of the industrial mechanism to the earlier social system. What must also be noted is the considerable industrial success that is possible under these circumstances. It may be true that the Western style of organization maximizes productivity, but substantial industrial progress can be made within quite a different style of organization. Rationalization and impersonalization are not, the Japanese experience seems to argue, necessary to the adoption from the West of an industrial economy.

24 | Urbanization, the Extended Family, and Kinship Ties in West Africa *

JOAN ALDOUS

The effect of urbanization upon extended family relations has been extensively investigated within the last 10 years. The starting point for many of these studies has been Wirth's analysis of urbanism as a way of life written in 1938. According to Wirth, the city is a social organization that substitutes secondary for primary group relationships. Though dependent on more people for the satisfactions of his wants, the urbanite, unlike his rural counterpart, is not dependent upon particular persons, and his dependence is limited to a "highly fractionalized" part of other persons' activities. Contacts are segmental and of secondary character; no group can claim the complete allegiance of the individual. The city's effect on the family, consequently, is to strip it to its bare essentials. The nuclear family of father, mother and children replaces the extended family. "The family as a unit of social life is emancipated from the larger kinship group characteristic of the country," so that relationships based on the extended family disintegrate in the city.[1]

Recent urban studies, however, have shown that kinship ties continue to exist. Using a sample representative of the Detroit area, Axelrod found interaction with relatives as manifested in friendship networks and mutual assistance to be important in all age and socioeconomic status groups.[2] Greer's sample of two middle-level census tracts in Los Angeles indicated that 73 percent of the high urban families and 76 percent of the low urban families were a part of family friendship networks.[3] The San Francisco study of Bell and Boat reported a similar finding. In their probability

* The preparation of this paper was carried out during the tenure of a predoctoral fellowship from the National Institute of Mental Health, United States Public Health Service. The author is indebted to Dr. Reuben Hill for his critical reading of a previous draft of the paper.

[1] Louis Wirth, "Urbanism as a Way of Life," *American Journal of Sociology*, 44 (July 1938), p. 21.

[2] Morris Axelrod, "Urban Structure and Social Participation," *American Sociological Review*, 21 (February 1956), p. 17.

[3] Scott Greer, "Urbanism Reconsidered," *American Sociological Review*, 21 (February 1956), p. 23.

SOURCE: *Social Forces*, XLI (October 1962), 6–12. Reprinted by permission of the publisher.

sample of adult males drawn from four census tracts representing different social types, six of ten men had a close friendship tie with at least one relative.[4] Seventy-six percent of the low income and 84 percent of the high income respondents, in addition, expected assistance from relatives even for prolonged illnesses.[5] Of the 195 parent-child relations Sussman studied in his New Haven research, 154 maintained mutual assistance patterns.[6] This was a white, Protestant middle-class sample, but Young and Willmott found much the same thing in London with their working class sample.[7] The same investigators' study of a middle-class London suburb showed that 25 percent of parents in their seventies lived with married children and the percent increased to 41 for those 80 and over.[8] Childless couples also turned to the extended family in old age; 53 percent of those of pensionable age lived with relatives.[9] In contrast to these results, Michel concluded that among the segment of the Parisian working class living in furnished hotels that she studied, kinship ties were disintegrating.[10] Data, therefore, collected from widely varying samples in such disparate cities as Detroit, London, San Francisco, Los Angeles and New Haven have not confirmed the disappearance of kinship ties in the urban milieu. Only in Paris did a study of a small part of the population appear to uphold the hypothesis.

Relevant African studies provide comparative data from different societies on the fate of the extended family in the city. Some variation of the extended family appears in all the basic culture areas of Africa—Mediterranean littoral, Sahara Desert area, western and eastern Sudan, the West Coast, Central-Southern and the East Horn, and the East African cattle area. In fact, the concept of the extended family itself developed from studies of African peoples. Life in the tribal villages follows a traditional pattern. The person is important only as he contributes to the extended family unit. In return he is given the security of not one but several fathers, mothers, brothers, sisters, uncles and grandparents. Such a social organization results in strong group solidarity with an attendant communal spirit. The purpose of this paper is to examine how this "powerful cementing framework" is affected by urbanization.[11]

---

[4] Wendell Bell and Marion D. Boat, "Urban Neighborhoods and Informal Social Relations," *American Journal of Sociology*, 62 (January 1957), pp. 394, 396.

[5] *Ibid.*, p. 396.

[6] Marvin B. Sussman, "The Help Pattern in the Middle Class Family," *American Sociological Review*, 18 (February 1953), p. 23.

[7] Michael Young and Peter Willmott, *Family and Kinship in East London* (Glencoe, Ill.: The Free Press, 1957).

[8] Michael Young and Peter Willmott, *Family and Class in a London Suburb* (London: Routledge and Kegan Paul Ltd., 1960), p. 40.

[9] *Ibid.*, p. 51.

[10] Andrée Michel, *Famille Industrialisation Logement* (Paris: Centre National de la Recherche Scientifique, 1959).

[11] Hugh H. Smythe, "Social Change in Africa," *American Journal of Economics and Sociology*, 19 (January 1960), p. 202.

The analysis will center on the Negro cities of West Africa.[12] Their social organization differs to a considerable extent from that of European and United States cities. Another advantage in using these cities for comparative purposes is that a number of urban studies have been done in this area. To obviate the problem of the varying completeness of the data upon which their conclusions are based, as complete a description as possible is given in this paper of the source of each study's data. The reader can decide for himself how much weight to give to each study's findings.

To test the hypothesis that extended family relations are absent in West African cities, it is necessary to set up some empirical referent for the concept of the extended family. There are several criteria that can be used to establish the existence of this kinship group. Among these is residence where two or more related nuclear family units live together or relatives share the nuclear family's quarters. A second criterion consists of the joint activities engaged in by the extended family members as an organized unit. These activities can be of various types ranging from economic and legal to welfare and leisure. Still another criterion is assistance between individual relatives based on normative expectations whether in the form of gifts or services. Friendship networks joining kinsmen constitute a fourth criterion. The presence of any of these criteria is taken as evidence of the existence of the extended family.

West African Cities

The fairest test of the hypothesis that the extended family structure will not be present in the African city would appear to lie in data from a long-settled, stable urban community. Otherwise, it could be argued that the extended family would occur in a city largely because its population is made up of recent migrants from villages who have not had time enough to be influenced by urbanization. Unfortunately for such a test, most of the cities of Africa are experiencing their greatest growth at the present time due to in-migration.[13]

The long-established city of Timbuctoo, however, is an exception.

---

[12] The Department of State classification system is used which includes the Congo and the Republic of the Congo in West Africa, as well as among others, Nigeria and the Mali Federation, consisting of Senegal and the Sudanese Republic. See G. Etzel Pearcy, *Africa: Names and Concepts* (Washington, D.C.: Department of State Publication 7129, January 1961), p. 9.

[13] Lagos, Nigeria, for example, with a population of 250,000 in 1952, had trebled in 25 years. In 1950 over one-half of its population was estimated to be immigrants. International African Institute, London, *Social Implications of Industrialization and Urbanization of Africa South of the Sahara* (Paris: UNESCO, 1956), p. 22. Population estimates as of 1959 for this and other cities mentioned in the paper are as follows: Brazzaville, Congo, 93,500; Dakar, Senegal, 185,820; Lagos, Nigeria, 364,000; Leopoldville, The Congo, 402,492; and Stanleyville, The Congo, 126,533. *UN Demographic Yearbook* (New York: United Nations Publications, 1960).

Miner, in his 1940 anthropological study, observed that though the fabled city's Arab, Taureg and Songhoi residents each possessed a distinctive culture, all three maintained extended family ties. Among the Songhoi the extended family's existence was manifested in joint activities, assistance patterns and friendship ties. Gathered in council, the extended family fulfilled a legal function meting out punishment or deciding upon reparations when a kinsman had engaged in robbery or murder or had himself been murdered.[14] Assistance took a number of forms. Wealthier relatives adopted the poor man's "surplus" children, thereby relieving him of the burden of their support. If this aid proved insufficient, relatives supplied food, clothing or shelter. Helping patterns were also present among the Tauregs, who followed the same adoption practice.[15] Like the Songhoi, they too participated in friendship networks with relatives, as did the Arabs. Arab men, for example, every morning after breakfast would go about the town exchanging greetings with parents, uncles, aunts and siblings. On Fridays they visited more distant relatives.[16] Thus in Timbuctoo the individual, far from being limited to the nuclear family, was involved in various forms of relations with the extended family.

Other examples of long-settled urban people exist among the Yoruba of Nigeria. Though living "long before colonial times" in cities of up to 100,000 residents, the Yoruba have maintained their traditional extended family patterns.[17] Individuals continue to feel strong obligations to give economic assistance to relatives while maintaining social ties, and the customary residential unit remains the lineage. For these reasons the anthropologist Bascom, although noting the weakening of kinship bonds, has declared "the city dweller need not feel lonely or insecure." [18]

In Lagos, a traditional city now subject to industrial influence, the kinship group remains important, though the anthropologist Comhaire described it as "teeming with political and business activities of the most modern kind." [19] This was demonstrated in the study Marris made in 1958–59 of a slum area in central Lagos in which he found the extended family existing according to all four criteria listed above. For his research he interviewed 372 men and women—110 households—intensively. There

---

[14] Horace Miner, *The Primitive City of Timbuctoo* (Philadelphia: American Philosophical Society, 1953), p. 140. Miner felt Timbuctoo readily fitted Wirth's definition of a city as a "relatively large, dense and permanent settlement of socially heterogeneous individuals" despite its rather small population of some 6000. *Ibid.*, p. 11, quoting Wirth, *op. cit.*, p. 8.

[15] *Ibid.*, p. 140.

[16] *Ibid.*, p. 147.

[17] Historical descriptions of the cities date from the sixteenth century. See William Bascom, "Urbanization Among the Yoruba," *American Journal of Sociology*, 60 (March 1955), p. 448.

[18] *Ibid.*, p. 451.

[19] Jean L. Comhaire, "Economic Changes and the Extended Family," *Annals*, 305 (May 1956), p. 48.

were still four properties on the four streets Marris surveyed in detail where the children of the founder of the family property followed the traditional custom and occupied it together with their families and descendants. Tenants, however, constituted 60 percent of the population of the area. Though they were less apt than owners to have relatives living with them, 38 percent had at least one brother or sister in the same residence, and among an additional 23 percent a half-brother or sister was present. Moreover, members of extended families when living apart were usually within a 10 to 15 minute walk from each other and showed a high degree of mutual affection. Friendship networks were maintained by daily meetings which served as opportunities to pass on family news and to discuss family problems.[20]

As for assistance patterns, the residents of central Lagos, like their rural counterparts, continued to regard the needs of their kinfolk as their first obligation. They supported aged aunts and cousins as well as parents, so it was customary to present their elderly kinsmen with gifts in cash or kind when visiting them. In addition, they often contributed to the marriage payments of younger brothers, reared nieces and nephews and helped married sisters. Such assistance coupled with open-handed hospitality and gifts to relatives still living in the country often proved a financial burden on the urban dwellers. Over one-half of the persons Marris interviewed, for example, spent at least one-tenth of their income assisting relatives. This aid, however, was not begrudged. The "sense of mutual obligation of the family group is the outstanding loyalty of Lagos social life," Marris concluded.[21] Its residents, therefore, rather than owing their primary loyalty to themselves or to their conjugal families, identified with the extended family.

In addition to the help given because of personal obligations ensuing from kinship ties, the extended family in Lagos as an organized unit engaged in welfare activities. Its members contributed funds which were distributed to relatives in need whether they were the orphaned, the elderly, the unemployed or the young eager for an education. Relatives and the extended family, therefore, substituted for the nonexistent public welfare program. The kinship group as a unit also held frequent celebrations. Funerals, naming ceremonies for the newborn and anniversaries served as such occasions, with each branch of the family paying for a part of the expenses. The extended family was "westernized" to the extent that as a group it often took on the formal character of a voluntary association. When this was the case, all the members met at regular monthly or weekly intervals instead of waiting for special occasions. At these meetings the kinsmen functioned as a legal body discussing family difficulties and settling dis-

---

[20] Peter Marris, "Slum Clearance and Family Life in Lagos," *Human Organization*, 19 (Fall 1960) p. 124.
[21] *Loc. cit.*

putes. At many such meetings the relatives contributed to a subscription fund to be used to repair the family house or to conduct corporate business in the name of the extended family's founder. Two-thirds of the men and women Marris interviewed belonged to families having such regular meetings.[22] Thus the extended family served as the basis for one of the new voluntary associations the residents of Lagos formed to forward their common economic interests.

Africans living in Leopoldville and Stanleyville, Republic of the Congo, have also been studied in some detail. Here too the extended family in various forms continues to remain important to the individual. In Leopoldville, the assistance patterns led to the doubling up of residential units. Comhaire declared, on the basis of his observations while an information officer in the Belgian Congo, that the unemployed or new arrivals to the city turned to relatives for shelter and sustenance.[23] A survey reported by UNESCO indirectly confirmed this observation when it showed that 16 percent of the average couple's food budget went to the support of adult dependents.[24] The extended family also manifested itself in joint religious activities which had an additional recreational function. The week-long funeral proceedings to whose expense even distant relatives contribute were the focus of urban social life, according to Comhaire. These family rites also served to strengthen the solidarity of the extended family as well as serving as an index of it. Even organizations based on professional or territorial interests were usually pseudo-kinship groups. Comhaire concluded on the basis of this evidence that the extended family institution would probably continue in Leopoldville for some time to come.[25]

In Stanleyville as in Lagos, Nigeria, permanent housing patterns attest to the strength of the extended family. A 1952 survey of a random sample of the population sponsored by the International African Institute showed that 34.9 percent of the tenants who were subletting property were closely related to the owner, while an additional 24.3 percent were more distant relatives. None of the close relatives and only a few of the more distantly related paid rent.[26]

Dakar, Senegal, in another new nation is yet another city whose inhabitants have been studied. The results show the continuing existence of the extended family. One survey described in a UNESCO report pointed to the increasing importance of the nuclear family as the household unit, a finding in line with the hypothesis that the extended family disappears in

[22] Loc. cit.

[23] Jean L. Comhaire, "Some Aspects of Urbanization in the Belgian Congo," American Journal of Sociology, 62 (July 1956), p. 11.

[24] UNESCO, op. cit., p. 33.

[25] Comhaire, "Some Aspects . . .," op. cit., p. 13.

[26] V. G. Pons, "The Changing Significance of Ethnic Affiliation and of Westernization in the African Settlement Patterns in Stanleyville," in International African Institute, op. cit., p. 644.

the urban environment.[27] The extended family continued, however, in assistance patterns, friendship networks and joint activities. Family unity, for example, served to stimulate help to relatives. The same UNESCO survey noted that the obligation to come to the aid of kinsmen was respected in all sections of the population.[28] Many immigrants were only able to subsist because they could take up residence with an already established single relative or family group, and this was also true of the jobless. As Dakar generally has a high unemployment rate—10 percent in 1955 —without the assistance its unemployed workers received from kinsmen, many of them would have to leave the city. By this help the extended family substituted for a nonexistent government unemployment compensation program. With only a few exceptions, family friendship ties were maintained through visits with relatives living in various parts of town. Joint celebrations served as occasions for the extended family as a whole to get together. The extended family also engaged in economic activities. The anthropologist Mercier observed that self-employment in such occupations as trading, gardening and fishing made possible the retention of the type of economic organization based on parental relationships almost unchanged from the form found in tribal villages.[29]

Brazzaville, the capital of what was formerly French Equatorial Africa, now Congo, has also been the subject of research. Here too the extended family was present. Mutual aid was prevalent, leading in some cases to persons sharing their residential quarters with relatives. The social anthropologist Balandier, in an intensive study of one African section of the city, found residents expected to take in relatives coming into town for seasonal work or education. They also contributed to the education costs of relatives.[30] If other work were unavailable students or other relatives could turn to trader kinsmen. These middlemen, as much as possible, gave available jobs to kinsmen rather than filling them according to merit, Balandier observed.[31]

So far the discussion has been largely limited to findings concerning specific cities. When one turns to descriptions of African cities in general, some of them are reminiscent of Wirth's analysis. McCall, from his experience in Ghana and Liberia, concluded that status in the city was achieved and not an ascribed status based on family membership. Kinsmen constituted only a small number of those with whom the African urbanite daily interacted. The extended family as a residential unit was breaking

---

[27] UNESCO, op. cit., p. 28.   [28] Ibid., p. 32.

[29] Comhaire, "Economic Changes . . .," op. cit., p. 48, quoting Paul Mercier, "Aspects de la société africaine dans l'agglomération dakaroise," Études sénégalaises, No. 5 (1954), pp. 11–40.

[30] Georges Balandier, "Sociological Survey of the African Town at Brazzaville," in International African Institute, op. cit., p. 108.

[31] Comhaire, "Economic Changes . . .," op. cit., p. 48, quoting Georges Balandier, Sociologie des Brazzavilles noires (Paris: Armand Colin, 1955).

down. Other relatives were rarely found in the nuclear family's town dwelling although in the country members of the extended family would live in the same compound.[32] Smythe, who had done field research in West Africa, wrote that emphasis on extended family loyalty, obedience to the tribal elders and devotion to clan and tribe were giving way to the Africans' desire for a big car, a good job having status, a nice home and especially money.[33] Even observers like these, however, who discount the importance of the extended family in the city describe its continued existence and influence. Thus McCall characterized the migrant to the city as pre-eminently an offshoot of the kinship group. As such he expected to assist through support and shelter other relatives who would follow,[34] a conclusion supported by the studies cited above.

The economist Okigbo, after noting that West African society was formerly based on family linkages, declared that it still retained some of its solidarity. But he added that the kinship structure had felt the weakening impact of growing individualism and new alignments based on similarity of outlook and education. With the rise in living standards, obligations to meet the needs of poor and nonproductive relatives had become an unpleasant duty. Evasions of such responsibilities, in his observations, were more common than formerly.[35] Another economist, Marcus, concluded from her interviews with "over 400" individuals in Tropical Africa that in some African areas the younger generation, "perhaps the third or fourth generation of city dwellers," was rebelling against the extended family system.[36]

Conclusions

Thus some observers see signs which indicate that individuals are less apt to honor assistance obligations to relatives than formerly. Trade union and other associations also cut across family lines to serve political, occupational and neighborhood interests. Yet, as detailed above, available research of West African cities shows the continued existence of the extended family. As Homans has written, kinship relations are not maintained unless they serve some purpose for those involved.[37] In the African cities

---

[32] Daniel McCall, "Dynamics of Urbanization in Africa," *Annals*, 298 (March 1955), p. 154.

[33] Smythe, *op. cit.*, p. 202.   [34] McCall, *op. cit.*, p. 159.

[35] Pius Okigbo, "Social Consequences of Economic Development in West Africa," *Annals*, 305 (May 1956), p. 130.

[36] Mildred R. Marcus, "Some Social Characteristics of Tropical African Peoples," *Sociology and Social Research*, 45 (October 1960), p. 42. If, however, rebellion against the responsibilities of family ties must wait for the third or fourth generation of urbanites, a widespread movement will be long in developing. The overwhelming majority of African urbanites are migrants.

[37] George C. Homans, *The Human Group* (New York: Harcourt, Brace and Company, 1950), p. 265.

of Brazzaville, Dakar, Lagos, Leopoldville and Stanleyville, the extended family is indeed functional. Besides filling recreational, religious, legal or economic needs of urbanites it substitutes for a nonexistent public social welfare program. Kinsmen provide for the elderly and support the sick, the jobless and the destitute. They give the new arrival from the country shelter and food and help him to get work or an education and to adjust to the bustling city. A corollary of this is that the individual urbanite, far from facing the complex urban milieu as a solitary individual, exists in a web of friendship relations in the extended family. It would, of course, be desirable if more information were available concerning urban life in these and other cities in this area. Since it is not, however, one can come to a tentative conclusion on the basis of the evidence at hand. On this basis, the hypothesis that the extended family will disappear would seem not to hold true. Rather, the existing data indicate not only the continued presence of the extended family, but the crucial functions it performs for the African in the urban milieu.

25 | Rural-Urban Social Participation

WILLIAM H. KEY

Numerous social scientists have made the point that there are fundamental differences between rural and urban social systems. Texts on the community typically cast their material in a rural vs. urban framework. Texts in both rural and urban sociology spend much of their time contrasting rural and urban communities. Finally, most of the material on the effects of industrialization couple industrialization with urbanization and assume certain characteristics of any society vary directly with the size of the population aggregate. Simmel,[1] Park,[2] Wirth,[3] and Sorokin and Zim-

---

[1] Nicholas J. Spykman, *The Social Theory of George Simmel.* Chicago: University of Chicago Press, 1925 (especially Ch. 2).

[2] Robert E. Park, *The City.* Chicago, Illinois: University of Chicago Press, 1925.

[3] Louis Wirth, "Urbanism as a Way of Life." *American Journal of Sociology,* 44:1–24 (July 1938).

SOURCE: This article has been especially prepared for this volume but represents a development of ideas expressed in two earlier articles by the author. They are "Rural-Urban Differences and the Family, "*Sociological Quarterly,* II (1961), 49–56; and "Urbanism and Neighboring," *Sociological Quarterly,* VI (1965), 379–385.

merman [4] wrote landmark theoretical statements about the difference between rural and urban areas; the published research on rural-urban differences has reached tremendous volume.

One specific area of interest in this general field has been the influence of place on the rural-urban continuum in relation to the existence and strength of primary groups. Wirth [5] and Redfield,[6] among others, advanced the arguments that urban areas are strongholds of secondary groups and inimical to primary groups. They argued that an increase in population size, heterogeneity, and density produces a decline in the importance of primary groups. Yet in recent years there has been an increasing body of research, most notably in connection with the family, which suggests that at least this primary group (the family) is still very important in meeting companionship, affection, and other psychological needs of its members.

Unfortunately, however well conceived and well executed the empirical studies in this area have been they do not provide a factual basis for the comparative statements given in most texts. Few direct comparisons have been made between samples of rural and urban dwellers to test the validity of the hypotheses. Most of the evidence adduced has been from secondary sources relying on historical works, census data, or on the evidence derived from studying individual communities at different points in time. This lack of direct comparison in a range of communities is a deficiency in our evidence. One of the major difficulties preventing direct testing of these hypotheses has been a methodological one. We lack valid scales to directly compare the participation patterns of rural and urban dwellers. It is the purpose of this paper to report work on a set of social participation scales with which such comparisons can be made. Social participation is only one of several approaches to the solution of the problem but we chose it because it seemed clear that our hypotheses assume that individuals in urban areas participate less in primary group activities and more in secondary group activities. The implication is that the shift in such participation is consistent as one goes from rural to urban.

The pioneer work in measurement of social participation was carried out by Queen [7] and by Bernard [8] and their scales formed the basis for the work reported here. Further development of the scales [9] was carried out through

---

[4] Pitirim Sorokin and Carle C. Zimmerman, *Principles of Rural-Urban Sociology*, New York: Henry Holt and Co., 1929.

[5] Wirth, *op. cit.*

[6] Robert Redfield, "The Folk Society." *American Journal of Sociology*, 52:293–308 (January 1947).

[7] Stuart A. Queen, "Social Participation in Relation to Social Disorganization." *American Sociological Review*, 13:251–57 (1948).

[8] Jessie Bernard, "An Instrument for the Measurement of Neighboring with Experimental Application" (unpublished doctoral dissertation, Washington University, 1935).

[9] Work on the scales was carried out cooperatively with Dr. Robert Schmidt, now with Lindenwood College, St. Charles, Mo. Dr. Schmidt subsequently used the scales in research conducted entirely within the St. Louis metropolitan area.

interviews in St. Louis and St. Louis County and the revised versions were later tested in Fayetteville, Arkansas.

Scales were developed to measure participation in six types of groups: immediate family, extended family, neighborhood, informal groups, work groups, and formal groups. Questions were chosen initially from the works of Queen and Bernard and other questions were added from suggestions of colleagues and from a review of the literature. Each sample of questions was tested for unidimensionality by the Guttman technique.[10] Each met the criteria for reproducibility and minimum marginal reproducibility and are hereinafter designated as scales. Questions, response patterns, and reproducibility information for the scales are available.[11] The familiar Chapin Scale was used to measure participation in formal groups and is not reproduced here.[12]

Operationally the definition of social participation is the frequency of group contacts where meaningful interaction may occur. It was after much trial and error that the decision was made to omit any question of "quality" of contacts from the definition and to focus on the frequency aspects of participation in groups. "Quality" poses a difficult problem of definition and measurement for both the researcher and his respondent. All aspects of interaction such as "Who originated the interaction?" "What type is the interaction?" and "How intense is the interaction?" have been omitted. All contacts have been assumed to be equal and the only variable tested was *frequency* of contact.

A similar decision (i.e., of what aspects of interaction to include in our definition of participation) had to be made with respect to urbanism. Some sociologists insist that size and density of population are not sufficient criteria for measuring the degree of urbanism. They usually include in their definitions, references to attitude, patterns of interaction, type of social organization, etc. It almost seems that they use urbanism as a synonym for a cosmopolitanism that is composed of many elements. Thus, Wirth,[13] Loomis and Beegle,[14] and others point to the many elements of urbanism and among others have popularized the phrase "Urbanism as a way of life." Beverly Duncan, in discussing my paper on "Urbanism and Family Social Participation" at the 1960 meetings of the Midwest Sociological Society, pointed out that Wirth and others had, in defining urbanism,

---

[10] Louis Guttman, "*The Cornell Technique of Scale and Intensity Analysis,*" *Educational and Psychological Measurement*, 7:247–79 (1947). Reproducibility for scales are as follows: Immediate Family .96; Extended Family .90; Informal Participation .95; Neighboring .97; Participation w/Work Groups .97.

[11] William H. Key, "Rural-Urban Social Participation" (unpublished doctoral dissertation, Washington University, 1953), Ch. 2 and Appendix #2.

[12] F. Stuart Chapin, *Social Participation Scale*. Minneapolis: University of Minnesota, 1938.

[13] Wirth, *op. cit.*

[14] Charles P. Loomis and J. Allan Beegle, *Rural Social Systems*. New York: Prentice-Hall, 1951.

contrasted it to Redfield's Folk Society and that the use of a rural-urban continuum perverted the meaning of Wirth's ideas.

Despite these objections a simple definition of urbanism based on size of population has much to recommend it. In the first place, it does not, as do the other definitions, prejudge the relationship between the demographic and behavioral elements as Wirth [15] did in his famous article. In the second place, it enables a clear specification of the independent variable. For these reasons, we chose a simple (i.e., demographic) definition of urbanism. It should be pointed out, however, that our choice of communities ranging from the Ozark Highlands to Indianapolis, Indiana, gives at least at the ends of the continuum, a probable identity of the two definitions.

The sample consisting of 357 individuals, on which this study is based, was chosen from the Midwestern states. The population was subdivided into rural dwellers (those living in unincorporated places), village dwellers (incorporated places of less than 2,500), residents of small towns (2,500–25,000), of medium-sized cities (25,000–100,000), and of metropolitan areas (more than 100,000). One locality was chosen from each of these five categories. Localities were chosen on the basis of accessibility. Dwelling units within the localities were listed and numbered. A probability sample of dwelling units was chosen using a table of random numbers. Since the number of interviews in each of the subsamples was small, we used rigorous controls and made return visits in the event a contact could not be made on the initial visit. Substitutions were allowed only in the event of a refusal on the part of the occupants or of a vacancy. Refusals were few, comprising in total 3 per cent of those approached. Substitutions were made from a list of alternate households chosen by random numbers. We decided beforehand to divide our sample into 50 per cent male and 50 per cent female and predesignated the sex of the respondent to be interviewed in a given household. All adults (i.e., those over twenty years of age or married individuals filling adult roles) of the predesignated sex were interviewed in a household. If the household contained no adults of the sex given, the adult head of the household was interviewed. For this reason we failed to achieve our balanced sex ratio.

Neighborhood was defined as the geographical area contiguous to the residence of the respondent and neighbor was anyone living within the neighborhood. Since the study included diverse settings it was difficult to rigorously define the size of the area included in neighborhood. As a compromise no arbitrary distances were used but the idea of contiguous locality was made clear at the outset of the interview and the area included in the definition of neighborhood was clearly stated. The author personally conducted 342 of the 357 interviews and there was little confusion in the actual interview.

The immediate family was defined as all individuals occupying a separate

---

[15] Wirth, op. cit.

household and related by marriage or by blood. Unattached individuals living in rooming houses were counted as constituting separate households. A relative was defined as any individual with whom a blood relationship was recognized or an individual who bore a recognized blood relationship to the informant's spouse if he or she was married. Informal groups were defined as consisting of people who were neither neighbors nor relatives. Activities carried out with friends and acquaintances in the framework of formal groups were expressly excluded from the informal group scale. The scale for measurement of interaction with fellow workers excluded conversations demanded by the job and was confined to interactions closely connected to the work setting to avoid insofar as possible overlap with interactions reported in other scales. The results of the research are presented in Table 1.

The results of this research confirm only partially the hypothesis of a straight line decrease in shifts of interaction from primary to secondary groups as one goes from rural to urban localities. There is the hypothesized "straight line" relationship between urbanism and neighboring and urbanism and work. The data though not always statistically significant on the

TABLE 1. Mean Scores on Social Participation Scales by Place of Residence

	Maximum Scale Score	Place of Residence				
		Rural	Village	Small Urban	Terre Haute	Indian- apolis
Immediate Family[a]	10	9.56	7.86	8.10	8.37	8.51
Extended Family[b]	10	6.22	5.19	5.50	5.92	5.87
Informal Groups[c]	6	3.00	3.60	4.50	4.00	4.00
Work Groups[d]	10	4.10	4.27	6.90	8.51	8.65
Formal Groups[e] (Chapin Scale)	unlimited	6.14	8.67	13.49	11.08	10.50
Neighboring[f]	10	6.26	5.67	5.40	5.30	4.50

[a] Rural-urban differences not significant for the total sample. Females differ significantly (p<.001). *Pattern* of distribution of scores is the same for all groups.
[b] Rural-urban differences not significant for any subsample.
[c] Rural-urban difference significant (p<.001).
[d] Males only included. Rural-urban differences significant (p<.001).
[e] Rural-urban differences are significant for total sample and males (p<.05). Not significant for females. Pattern of distribution of scores for all groups is the same.
[f] Rural-urban differences are significant for total sample and males and females separately (p<.001).

immediate family and the extended family forms a V with the low point coming in the village and small urban places rather than the hypothesized straight line relationship. The data on formal and informal groups form a weak inverted ∧ with the peak coming in the small urban places. This relationship is presented schematically in the diagrams below.

Consideration of all of this data presents a complex picture not in agreement with the general theory concerning the relationship between social participation in primary groups and urbanism. No general theory accounts for all of the results. Instead at least two separate types of explanation seem necessary. The results in neighboring and work seem to be related to the decreasing importance of one type of locality group, the neighborhood, and an increase in the importance of another type of locality group as one moves from rural to urban. This is probably related to the fact that urban neighborhoods are seldom collections of homogeneous population types who have a history of stable residence in one locality while place of employment brings together away from the neighborhood people of similar interests and values.

No such "simple" explanation accounts for the results on the remaining four scales. Except for the immediate family these are relationships which are chosen, not demanded, by the structure of the situation.

It has been commonly assumed that life in an urban area tended to pull families apart because of diverse contacts particularly those in secondary groups that *individuals* have. Wirth [16] gives the classic position when he says, "The family as a unit of social life is emancipated from the larger kinship group characteristic of the country, and the individual members pursue their own diverging interests in their vocational, educational, recreational, and political life." This view has not been substantiated for this sample and there is need for an altered explanation to account for the results.

It is probably in line with the theory of the relationship of primary

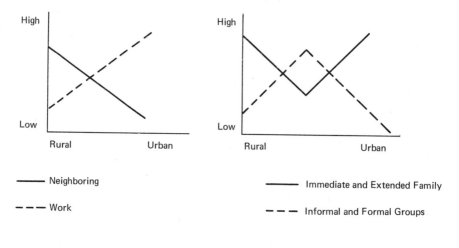

16 Wirth, *ibid.*

groups to personal satisfaction that any reduction in the number of satis-factory primary contacts makes those that remain more rather than less im-portant. It is the difficulty of making satisfactory primary contacts outside of the family that makes the immediate and extended family more impor-tant in rural *and* urban areas. In urban areas people have a large number of fleeting and specialized contacts which are seldom primary in nature. In the rural areas spatial isolation tends to force more frequent association with one's family. It is the absence of either spatial or social isolation which accounts for the low rate of family interaction and the high rate of extrafamilial interaction in village and small urban localities. In such a set-ting intrafamilial contacts may be replaced by contacts with friends of long standing and the whole village or small urban place takes on the char-acteristics of a primary group. Isolation, spatial or social, is at a minimum. From the standpoint of providing primary group support the family is less important in the village than in any other population grouping.

In the case of the extended family it is possible that there is a more special explanation for the emphasis upon its disintegration in urban so-ciology. It seems likely that the hypothesis of the disintegration of the extended family developed early in the history of urban sociology when at-tention was focused on recent immigrants to the city and before those in-dividuals had an opportunity to establish families. While there might have been a notable lack of contact with relatives during and immediately follow-ing the period of greatest migration to the city this seems to have been a temporary phenomenon. This condition was produced by migration, rather than by the city as such, and when possible (i.e., after time had elapsed and immigrants had attracted more of their kin or had produced and reared children on their own), isolation in the city increased pressure for associa-tion with such kin.

Two other aspects of these data which were not explained fully but should be noted briefly are:

(1) Participation scores of males were affected less by the transition from rural to urban. It appears that the lives of males are oriented around making a living in this society and that while there are differences, their lives seem to be much more similar with respect to amount of leisure time and outlook than is true of females, irrespective of the size of place of residence.

(2) The relationship between socioeconomic status and the measures of participation formed no regular pattern of change along the rural-urban con-tinuum. The larger the community, the greater the influence of socioeconomic status on the frequency of participation of females in informal and neighbor-hood groups. The trend of all other relationships between SES and measures of participation for females was toward zero. For males the relationship be-tween SES and participation in organized groups was increased in magnitude while the relationship of SES to all other measures diminished in magnitude at the urban end of the continuum.

One should not push the interpretation of this data too far. Questions of scale construction, such as item selection, and scale magnitude demand more attention. More sophisticated data analysis using additional variables might upset the interpretations presented. However, this research was intended to test the hypothesis of a straight line relationship between urbanism and participation in a variety of groups including both primary and secondary. The results indicate that for four of the groupings the hypotheses as they are usually presented were not supported.

26 | The Migrant and the Urban Community

KENNETH LITTLE

. . . African social change and transformation might be seen as an historical process of adaptation to new conditions of life and labour. These new conditions originate basically in something extraneous to West Africa itself, namely the industrial economy of the West. This market economy, along with other factors of Western contact, has extended the local scale of relationships and has brought indigenous societies into a wider social system than that of the tribe or even the nation. It also involves a greater specialization of institutions, thereby giving rise to a larger variety of new social groupings and networks than in the traditional system. At the same time, there is cultural and social continuity, because much of the older way of life persists despite migration and other factors.

In this context, therefore, adaptation proceeds through modification of the traditional institutions and their combination with Western cultural values, technology, and economic practices into a new social structure. The fresh functional relations involved are made possible by the restructuring of traditional roles and by the development of roles derived from the encompassing industrial system.

Voluntary associations assist this adaptive process by providing a new basis for social organization, which is all the more important because of the industrial town's lack of integration in comparison with the rural areas. Accra, for example, contains the representatives of more than sixty-five different tribes and peoples, and the populations of other large urban cen-

SOURCE: Kenneth Little, *West African Urbanization: A Study of Voluntary Associations in Social Change* (New York: Cambridge University Press, 1965), pp. 85–102. Reprinted by permission of the publisher.

tres are hardly less varied. Even in the smaller towns with less than 15,000 inhabitants there are frequently the elements of at least a dozen different tribes. The presence of educated Africans as well as Europeans and Asians adds further to the cultural mosaic and has to be taken into account, quite apart from age-old enmities and alliances between the tribes themselves. One of the most obvious in Ghana is the hostility of the Zabramas and the Gaos against the Hausas, and the friendship between the Moshies and the Zabramas; the Fulani are not popular with any group. These groups regard themselves as Molsems, but Islam is not strong enough on its own to override these differences and so the migrants have only one thing in common: they are foreigners. As such they are shunned by the indigenous inhabitants for whom any migrant is straight away assimilated with the natives of the Northern Territories: he is a 'bushman', a naked barbarian. The migrants retort in similar terms and refer to the people of the Coast as 'sons of slaves'.

Divided thus by traditional attitudes as well as by language, custom and religion the town can have no single system of social norms. Over inheritance, over marriage, and over many other institutions essential to community life notions of law and justice differ and there are no common bases for agreement. Nor can the town's own civic institutions give the lead when for most of the migrants the place in which they do their business is not a permanent home. They may own property, may make repeated visits, spend part of the year there, but without acquiring any feelings of attachment. Their social life remains in some other part of the country—among their lineage people in the place where they were born. Also, as we shall see later, owing to the clash of modern with traditional ideas of marriage, family institutions are under a special strain. And there is increased tension in relations between the sexes and between different generations.

In these terms the industrialized town presents a picture of conflicting as well as changing standards. It implies a social and psychological situation which might amount to Durkheim's notion of anomie were it not that voluntary associations provide a link between the traditional and the urban way of life. The new cults are an obvious example because in them indigenous beliefs are syncretized with supposedly more up-to-date forms of religion—Christianity and Islam. But ethnic unions and other such organizations similarly blend apparently divergent aims and interests. On the one hand, they emphasize tribal duties and obligations; on the other, they urge the adoption of a modern outlook and they establish new social practices. What is significant about this duality is that by continuing such familiar norms as kinship, the provision of proper burial rites, etc., the associations make the innovations seem less strange. They build for a migrant a cultural bridge and in so doing they convey him from one kind of social universe to another.

This is the case because, as their characteristic activities and objectives show, voluntary associations serve many of the same needs as the kin group and the lineage. Fraternity, for example, is particularly stressed; so much so that members are expected actively to regard each other as brothers and sisters, to sympathize with each other in time of difficulty, visiting each other when sick, and swelling the procession at a funeral. Sociability is also encouraged by the general practice of serving refreshments at every formal gathering of members—usually held at fortnightly or monthly intervals. Periodical outings, picnics and excursions, and more convivial gatherings such as dances, foster the same feeling. And social solidarity is further enhanced by emblems, mottoes and banners and by the custom of wearing a uniform style of dress. These regular meetings make for stability in the migrant's contacts because . . . a large proportion of the urban population is transient—people continuously come and go. Also, they help to restore to him the sense of identity he may have lost in moving so far away from his own community. Since one of the migrant's main needs is to be regarded as a person it is significant that many associations have a host of minor titles and offices available, thereby giving even the most humble member an opportunity to feel that he 'matters'.

Closely related to the latter problem is that of the migrant's general reorientation. This is obviously important because when the individual who is not content to remain in his rural village reaches the city, he learns that many of the traditional bonds are no longer available to him. He is no longer in a close-knit, tightly organized community and the sudden release from old ways and values leaves a vacuum which can be filled by new and different ones. In particular, having entered into an economic system founded on wages and profits, he needs versatility for dealing with the problems of getting a living, and he needs to adjust himself to an extended and unrestricted field of social relationships due to the multiplicity of contacts with 'foreigners'.

One of the ways in which associations aid the migrant's adaptation in these respects is by providing him with information about what is going on in the town. It will probably be some time before he adjusts to the idea of urban life being controlled not by individuals but by organizations, government departments, business firms, etc. An association keeps him in touch not only with its own people at home but with the town's institutions. It serves as a go-between if, for example, he needs an interpreter, and it introduces him to useful contacts, such as employers of labour, headmen of gangs, officials at the Employment Exchange, etc. The association also reduces the migrant's isolation by acting as a 'civilizing' agency on his behalf. It inculcates new standards of dress, social behaviour and personal hygiene; the advantage from the migrant's point of view being that he is regarded no longer as a 'country bumpkin' but is able to keep pace with his new neighbours. The association's own administration is a further means whereby he can achieve a more sophisticated status, because by taking on a particular duty, however minor, the migrant learns a fresh role. He is generally encouraged to branch out in this way and the fact that many of the officeholders concerned have Western titles, such as Doctor and Nurse, is not necessarily make-believe. It may signify the deliberate assumption of an already known and attractive pattern of conduct which the members concerned desire to follow.

What the migrant learns is also very helpful to him in practical terms. There are, for example, the association's rules, including fines for late attendance at meetings, which teach useful habits of punctuality. Thrift is encouraged by the demand for regular payment of dues, and its practice is taught by mutual benefit schemes as well as by savings clubs themselves. Presumably the lesson is well dinned home because the part played by these contribution clubs and similar practices in the acquisition of goods —produce for trading, a bicycle, etc.—and in bride-wealth is considerable. It is said that a man does not work in order to save money: he rather works in order to obtain his 'take-out' to pay for what he wants. Also, not only do these schemes help to supply the migrant with ready cash, but they take elaborate precautions—thumb-printing, countersigning, etc.—against fraud. They teach him, in fact, how to keep an account of cash and the safest way in which to conduct his own business dealings. More specifically, associations concerned with a particular trade accept initiates for training. A younger member has the opportunity of apprenticing himself in this way and of learning from watching or talking to the older and more experienced members. He may also acquire a smattering of literacy through the association's more formal efforts at education. Since many of the societies also teach modern hobbies and crafts, women have the same opportunities, including the earning of pocket-money for themselves. Crochet-work, in particular, seems to be a profitable side-line.

Finally, associations which have a tribally mixed membership enable the migrant to meet on friendly terms people of different origin. By assigning to him some common task in the society's activities they accustom him to the idea of co-operation with strangers. They help the migrant in this way to add to his stock of languages and to get better used to the kind of cosmopolitan atmosphere which he has to adapt himself to in the world outside. Nor do they necessarily circumscribe his choice of friends and acquaintances because quite often there is a system of affiliation offering reciprocal privileges of membership between different branches of the same group of associations.

In addition to moral and material support, voluntary associations also substitute for the kin group in providing for a good deal of the migrant's protection. This is the case because nowadays it is to the head of an association rather than to his lineage that a person in trouble turns for help or advice. He consults first the secretary or the president of, say, his tribal union. The latter refers the matter to the committee, and if it is a question of money the case is probably put before the entire association at its next meeting. Decisions involving the expenditure of cash are rarely taken without the consent of all the members and, in some cases, the society's money cannot be disbursed without a written order containing the principal officials' signatures. Alternatively, the person in difficulty may approach one of the society's patrons. The patrons are generally individuals of high social standing, such as a chief, a barrister, etc. They have been appointed on account of their local influence and in the expectation that they will use it on the society's behalf. If this appeal fails, it is quite common for the association itself to back a deserving member by paying for his legal expenses in the event of the case going to court. To be able to count on this assistance and the active support of fellow members is the more necessary because, unlike his situation at home, the migrant is frequently housed among strangers. In Accra, for example, Acquah found that more than four out of every five households shared dwellings with other families, and in Freetown families from four or five different tribes sometimes share the same house.

Voluntary associations also help to protect their members' occupational interests. Women traders, for example, boycott fellow-traders who undercut prices and among the new guilds described above wage rates are fixed according to the type of work done. This enables the craftsmen concerned to maintain a set level but no objection is raised to their charging friends and relatives less; nor does the guild mind if a rich customer can be persuaded to pay a higher rate. At the same time, the guild tries to maintain a reasonable standard of work in the craft and protects the customer against the craftsman who receives an advance payment for his work and then fails, without good reason, to complete the contract and is unable to refund the money. It also stops members from stealing work from each other. If a guild member is accused by some person outside the guild, and, in the opinion of the guild, the charges are unfounded, the guild will intercede on his behalf and the members' contribution will be used to fight the case in the King's Court. In judging cases between its own members the guild orders one or both parties to the dispute to pay a fine which will be used to buy beer for consumption at the meeting. There is a heavier fine if disrespect is shown to the guild head. The latter may be the eldest man practising the craft; or the first man to practise in that particular town; or he may be elected by the members and have neither of these qualifications.

Equally important—not only to the migrants, but to most of the urban population in general—is the question of supernatural protection. This kinship function, too, has been largely taken over by voluntary associations. The main reason is that individual and social problems in the urban environment are apparently beyond the scope of traditional ritual. There are, for example, acts of physical violence, robbery and petty larceny, drunkenness and prostitution. There are also various illnesses, such as veneral disease, which cause sterility and melancholia as well as physical discomfort. Three new malaises and disorders of society are very much more common in the town than in the countryside, and so the tendency, quite often, is to assume that they are the result of witchcraft and other evil influences.

Somewhat similarly, the competitive spirit evoked by new occupations is rationalized in terms of personal fortune or misfortune having a supernatural connection. A farmer growing cocoa for cash, for example, may lose his entire crop through blight, or a clerk may be dismissed from his post in an office. The explanation—malevolent forces are at work; jealous rivals possess a medicine more powerful than one's own.

For difficulties of the above kind the indigenous religion is too generalized in its methods to offer a solution. It has a remedy for everyday mishaps and it purports to ward off the calamities—failure of crops, depredations by wild animals, sudden storms and floodings—which ordinarily endanger the life and health of rural people. For the new worries and anxieties of the townsman it has no real answer. In contrast, the syncretist cults and sects give greater assurance and are more specific. Not only do they profess to cure both supernaturally and naturally caused disease and offer prophylactic protection against evil forces in general, they also claim the ability to detect and root out witches. They cater also for the special hazards and needs of urban life—accidents caused by motor transport, school, and professional examinations, interviews for a job, success in lovemaking, consolation in marriage, fame in outdoor sport, etc. By strictly forbidding their members to make use of sorcery and bad magic they alleviate mistrust and engender greater confidence in social relationships. . . .

Nor are the syncretist cults and messianic movements alone in performing these functions. Among the Moslem groups, too, there are many similar practices, including the provision of charms and the manufacture of talismans and other magical devices. Christianity, in addition, has a similar popular reputation—mainly through its association with the superior technology of Europeans. As a result, participation in Christian rituals is thought by many illiterate members of church associations to afford more effective forms of supernatural protection than they can obtain elsewhere. Women, in particular, believe that it will ward off or remove the curse of barrenness. This attitude is readily understandable when it is realized that, as among the Anang, infant mortality exceeds 40 per cent—miscarriages, stillbirths and deaths during infancy are usually attributed to attacks by malevolent forces. They believe that the power possessed by the Christian deity will afford them protection, allowing them to perform successfully this most important part of their role.

Catering as they do for urban needs, voluntary associations have also taken over traditional functions of social control. This includes supervising the private affairs of their own members. In Keta, for example, the pastor of a church is expected to settle the domestic problems of adherents, including matters relating to family dislocations or breaches of marital fidelity. An effort is made to reconcile the parties by arbitration in the lineage. However, if a satisfactory solution is not found, the pastor will certainly be the next resort. In more serious differences between non-kin members of the church, say, a member seducing another member's wife, it is considered un-Christian and therefore reprehensible for the aggrieved party to seek legal redress without first obtaining the advice of his pastor in the matter. Many other associations have the same attitude. Thus, a Nigerian club in Freetown not only decrees that no member shall take legal steps against any other member without first bringing the matter up to the hearing of the meeting, but claims the right to submit evidence in court if its own arbitration is ignored by the complainant. According to a report from Makurdi this kind of regulation was so effective among Ibo unions that Ibo people entirely deserted the courts except when drawn there by members of different tribes, or in the rare event of disloyalty on the part of a member of their own union.

That an association is able to arbitrate in this way—even when the matter is quite unconcerned with the life of that particular body—is due largely to factors which have already been stressed. Its members have been taught to regard themselves as belonging virtually to the same family, and this feeling is carried as far as sexual relations. A Freetown *compin*, for example, sternly decrees that 'no member shall fall in love with any female member of the society'. Other associations have their own rules about marriage that their members are expected to observe, and societies with members of both sexes which arrange entertainment take particular care to prevent unchaperoned women being seduced. Measures to prevent trouble of this kind are provided for and one such group rules that 'any male member found guilty of adultery is liable to a fine of £1.10s. od.; failing to pay this amount both man and woman will be expelled from the society entirely'.

Such precautions may be deemed necessary because otherwise husbands would not allow their wives to attend and some fathers would forbid their daughters. Unless an association has a good reputation, it may be unable to obtain sufficient female members to carry on its activities. These and other disciplinary rules form part of the constitution which a prospective member must agree to abide by before he is admitted. This constitution which is usually written or typed in a book is extensive enough, sometimes, to take up nearly two pages of small print. In addition to the motto of the society, appropriate greetings and responses, there are generally the formal aims, lists of officers and their duties, regulations about membership, election of officers, etc. . . . There may be more than two dozen separate by-laws.

Allowing for local differences in custom, the rules of most 'traditional' associations follow a common pattern. They prescribe a specific code of personal and moral conduct which is designed to regulate the public behaviour of members as well as their relations with each other. For example, a member who is reported for quarrelling in the town, for abusing elderly people, or for putting curses on others, may be suspended, fined or expelled. Similarly, in addition to adultery, where members are known to steal, or cause disorders at gatherings, they are warned to correct their behaviour. Very good care is taken that members are up to date with their dues and there are by-laws to regulate conduct in detail during the social as well as the business meetings of the association. Thus, in the dancing *compins,* a person may be fined if he or she refused to dance when called, or obstructs the officials. In other associations, members must not talk about their personal affairs or greet each other when business is in progress. They must regard what goes on in the society as strictly confidential. Members are also warned not to be unconventional or frivolous in the way they wear their dress.

Ordinarily, breaches of these regulations are dealt with by the committee. When there is doubt or difficulty over a case it will be referred to more senior members, such as the society's Patron or Founder, or the approval of a general meeting may be sought for disciplinary action. In the syncretist cults the situation is slightly different. There are priests who conduct the ritual, but other officials instruct the devotees in the laws and the general decorum of membership. One of them is virtually head of the cult, performing duties similar to those of a tribal chief or elder of a word. As well as acting as the cult representative in lay matters affecting the welfare of the cult in the wider community, he also settles intra-cult disputes. Like the other associations these groups also hold their own courts.

In addition, of course, to these formal tribunals, there are well-tried and salutary methods of a traditional kind for checking anti-social or improper conduct. Banton has described how some of the *compins'* songs can wield the weapon of ridicule and ensure conformity with the association's standards.

> The shame of it, Ai Kamara, the shame of it!
> Ai Kamara bore a child:
> He had no sooner grown up than she made him her husband.
> Ah friends, let us come together
> And consider if this is what is done in Temne-land?

An Achebe's description of a tribal union, although fictional, is relevant for the same reason. Obi Okonkwo has returned to Nigeria after qualifying in the United Kingdom where his studies were paid for by his fellow members. Being financially in low water he needs time to repay the loan. The Union is proud of Obi's achievement and is disposed to be generous, until it learns that he is moving around with a girl of 'doubtful' ancestry. She belongs to a special caste with whom Obi's people at home are strictly forbidden to marry or mate. This is pointed out to Obi at the Union's meeting in such certain terms that he has no alternative but to withdraw his request.

In fact, the association's practice of helping its own members with loans of money is probably one of the main sources of control. It enables the officials concerned to exert their authority more readily, particularly as recalcitrant members are sometimes the most needy. The ultimate sanction, however, lies in the fact that every reputable society is at pains to check applications for membership. They keep in touch with each other partly for this purpose. Since they will rarely admit a person who has earned a bad name for himself in another organization, this form of ostracism may be very effective, especially if the individual concerned has little hope of companionship outside his own tribe.

Finally, by setting social standards in ways of this kind, voluntary associations affect the wider community. This is the case because in terms of their total membership they contain a not unappreciable proportion of the total urban population—perhaps as many as two out of every three adult inhabitants of the town in some cases. They comprise literate and illiterate people alike, include men and women of all ages, sometimes children, and are not confined to any one class of individual. Very often their leaders are looked up to as 'progressive,' and among their patrons and supporters are many persons who are influential and of high social standing. There are tribal chiefs and elders as well as professional men and women, clergy and educators and well known politicians. In general, their membership is representative of most sections of the wider community. This means, therefore, that in substituting for the lineage and for other traditional institutions of kinship, voluntary associations perform a much wider function than the services rendered to their own members. They help to establish fresh social norms for society in general.

This is important because, particularly in respect of the urban family— the upbringing of children, marriage—there are few agreed patterns and moral standards are confused. According to which cultural values, for example, is an illiterate mother to prepare a daughter at school for marriage? Traditionally, a high degree of companionship is not regarded as essential and much greater emphasis is placed on the economic and procreative purposes of the institution. Western norms, on the other hand, stress a companionate relationship. Furthermore, after marriage has taken place, what is there to control the behaviour of man and wife? Formerly it was the responsibility of the relatives to see that they observed their marital obligations. Nowadays, marriage having become an individualistic affair, it is not rare that the kinsfolk of the one party are strangers to the kinsfolk of the other party. Formerly marital disputes were settled 'in the house'; both family groups had an interest in keeping the marriage intact. Now, it is no longer a union of two lineages or families and so there is no pressure on the couple to maintain the marriage. Ideological as well as economic factors conduce to make the small domestic group based upon the conjugal relationship of man and wife, rather than the kin group, the primary social unit.

In contrast to this ambiguity, voluntary associations have a clear policy of their own. They may, as in the case of the separatist churches, compromise with traditional attitudes to the extent of condoning polygamy. But they all strongly support marriage as an institution. They do their best to remove causes of marital friction, and they strengthen the relationship of man and wife in various ways. Some of the syncretist cults, for instance, go so far as to forbid their members to divorce. If a member does wish to end his or her marriage, this can only be done with the cult's consent after a full enquiry into the whole affair. Most of the associations specifically condemn adultery and some of them discourage other forms of promiscuity by debarring 'indecent sex-play', 'co-habitation out of doors', etc. Abortion is treated as a crime 'tantamount to murder', and special attention is given to matrimonial quarrels, including infidelity. Some of the women's groups not only upbraid members who create strife among other women but expel those who are constant trouble-makers in the home. Very often, these matters are dealt with by legislation, but there are the usual informal methods of social control. The following song of a Freetown *compin* was sung to a chief's wife when she was estranged from her husband:

'Oh Bom Posse, Oh Bom Posse, patience in marriage is a good thing,
Which God has given you,
When you grow old you will see how good is this thing,
Which God has given you'.

Other informal methods include a species of marriage guidance council. As mentioned above, church groups in this way try to get husbands and wives to talk their marital problems over together. They also give advice individually to their members. In addition, these church societies and many of the 'traditional' associations endeavour to influence the younger unmarried people, sometimes children, over family affairs. . . . One of the latter organizations—La Goumbé—appears to have taken the entire institution under its own wing. It restricts its female membership to nubile girls, supervises their marriages, and provides wedding presents and maternity benefits. More generally, . . . associations also obviate problems of courtship.

To sum up, then, urban life is characterized *inter alia* by a specialization of function. Instead of being carried on by the kin group and the tribe, activities of the town are divided among a larger number of institutions. There are mines, factories, shops and offices to organize economic production and conduct business, schools to undertake education and the training of the young; churches and mosques have charge of religion; law and order are the responsibility of magistrates and of the police; and with the new emphasis on individualism the trend is towards the small elementary family. The voluntary association serves as an adaptive mechanism in relation to these new institutions by facilitating role segmentation. In other words, it helps to adjust the rural migrant to his fresh status as a townsman, as a member of a multi-tribal community, as a breadwinner and as a partner in a monogamous marriage. Further, since they help to establish and validate fresh norms and exercise control over the personal conduct of their own members, voluntary associations are one of the means whereby an over-all system of relationships is integrated and law and order maintained among the town's heterogeneous population.

B | Social Class and Social Mobility

27 | The Patterns of Opportunity in Large Cities

SEYMOUR MARTIN LIPSET and REINHARD BENDIX

The cycle in which lower-class immigrants or migrants into large cities take over the lower-status positions while native urbanites from similar class backgrounds move up in the occupational structure has been one of the more important processes underlying social mobility ever since cities began to expand rapidly. It is this cycle which gives to cities their characteristic aspect of great mobility and ever-present change. Persons born and raised in cities seldom move to small towns or the country—although they often move to other cities—and consequently, if they are socially mobile, they are mobile in a city. On the other hand, persons from rural areas and small towns who rise above their parents' status are most likely to do so in a large city—while their less mobile neighbors remain in the small communities. Thus, more mobility takes place in the cities than in the country or small towns.[1] But this conclusion still leaves unexplained the factors which

---

[1][This] hypotheses . . . may seem to be challenged by the data given . . . . . . on the mobility of the farm population which migrates to the cities. In all countries except the United States for which comparable sample data were available, the sons of farmers engaged in nonfarm occupations had a better chance of obtaining nonmanual positions than did the sons of manual workers.

SOURCE: Seymour Martin Lipset and Reinhard Bendix, *Social Mobility in Industrial Society* (Berkeley and Los Angeles: University of California Press, 1966), pp. 216-217, 219-226. Copyright © 1959 by the Regents of the University of California. Reprinted by permission of the publisher.

facilitate the upward social mobility of lower-class native urbanites. Although little research has been done which bears directly on this problem, it is possible to suggest a number of factors which seem significant.

1. The greater social mobility in large urban centers is inherent in the simple fact that metropolitan areas are characterized by a greater degree of specialization and a more complex division of labor than smaller communities. The economies that flow from specialization of function are able to take effect primarily in metropolitan centers, so that increased size of community is related to the existence of a greater variety of positions. This means that there is a greater likelihood, on a chance or random basis alone, that people in large cities will move occupationally than there is that small community dwellers will do so.

2. In addition to greater specialization and a wider variety of positions in large cities, there is clear evidence that the larger the city, the greater the number of nonmanual positions in the labor force. . . . The larger the city, therefore, the greater the opportunity to move into a nonmanual position.

3. Since the beginning of the great trends toward urbanization and industrialization in the nineteenth century, cities have had tremendous

---

Several hypotheses may serve to explain these data: (1) The sons of farmers come from families of various socioeconomic levels; their occupational classification is not as closely correlated with socioeconomic status as is the occupational classification of the urban population. Consequently some of the sons of farmers who hold nonfarm positions come from high-status rural families. (2) The sons of farmers in nonfarm occupations are necessarily mobile geographically. As has been pointed out, there is a relatively strong relation between various types of mobility, those more geographically mobile being more mobile in number of jobs held and number of occupations. To some extent, we are comparing this mobile category of farmers' sons with all manual workers, including those who stayed in small communities, which have a low concentration of opportunities. (3) Those countries in which the urban sons of farmers have the least advantage, namely the United States, Sweden, and Russia, are also those which have the highest rate of movement off the farm into urban occupations. On the other hand, Switzerland and France, where urban sons of farmers have a definite advantage over urban sons of manual workers, have a much higher proportion of farmers' sons who remain in farming. This suggests that where the rate of rural-urban migration is slower, it is more selective, and that a greater proportion of the sons of high-status farmers move to the city than do the sons of poorer farmers. In the United States and Sweden, on the other hand, almost two-thirds of the sons of farmers are engaged in urban occupations, which means that migration cannot be highly selective. The samples that come from Germany give results which contradict each other. (4) In countries which do not have free public education, the class differences in education may be so great as to cancel out the geographical variation so important in the United States and Sweden. In other words, in the United States, the son of a manual worker in an urban area may get a better education than even a moderately well-to-do farmer's son. This may not be true where there are less "democratic" systems of education.

population and economic growth: they have far *more* than matched the growth of the countries in which they are found. This pattern of urban growth necessarily means there are more new (and higher level) positions to be filled in metropolitan centers than in smaller and demographically stable communities. In a small city like Newburyport (Yankee City), which has not increased in population for a century, the chances for a lower-class individual to rise must necessarily be less than in a large city in which new positions of higher status are constantly being created.

4. In spite of their rapid rate of growth, large cities have a lower birth rate than smaller communities and rural areas. Except for a brief period after World War II, cities over 100,000 did not reproduce their population. Thus, migration to metropolitan areas not only accounts for the expansion of urban population, but also fills in the gap created by low birth rates. Since it is also true that within urban society, the wealthier and higher-status socioeconomic strata have the lowest reproduction rates, it is clear that variations in fertility rates help account for the maximization of social mobility in the city.

The Advantages of Native Urbanites

The processes cited above clearly indicate why metropolitan areas have a higher rate of social mobility than small communities. They do not, however, suggest why native lower-class urbanites should be more successful than low-status migrants from smaller communities and rural areas. A few hypotheses may be suggested.

As was indicated earlier, lower-class individuals growing up in a large city are likely to secure more education than their counterparts in smaller communities. Almost every major city in the Western world has one or more universities, and natives of such communities can attend college or university while living at home. In addition, the simple fact that a child lives in a community which has a college or university within it should mean that he will be more aware of the possibilities and advantages of attending an institution of higher learning than will one who grows up some distance from a college. Metropolitan lower-class youth also benefit from the fact that the teaching staffs in their high schools are usually better paid and trained than those in smaller communities, and hence are likely to give their students greater incentive to attend college. Evidence that these assumptions are valid is contained in the Survey Research Center data,which show that 18 per cent of the sons of manual workers reared in big cities have some college education, compared with 12.5 per cent for those who grew up in small towns.

As well as having a better opportunity to obtain higher education, urban working-class youth are more likely to be acquainted with the occupational possibilities which exist in such communities than those who are raised in a less heterogeneous (occupationally) smaller community. In reanalyzing the occupational choices of school youth in a number of German and Austrian cities, Paul Lazarsfeld reported that "local variations in occupational choice are parallel to differences in the economic structure." Thus, the larger the proportion of persons working in a particular kind of job in a city, the greater the number of 14-year-old school youths who desired to go into that occupation. Lazarsfeld interpreted this finding as follows: "The nature of occupational choice is not determined primarily as an individual decision, but rather is a result of external infiuences. For the occupational impressions offered by daily life are proportional to the actual occupational distribution. The greater the number of metal workers, the more frequently will young people hear about that occupation, and the greater will they be stimulated to choose it."

Further evidence of the influence of social environment on an individual's perception and awareness of occupational careers is given by recent data from Belgium. Upwardly mobile sons of farmers tend to study agronomy and veterinary medicine; architectural students are likely to be sons of construction workers.

There are no corresponding American studies which attempt to relate the occupational structure of different communities to the frames of reference of school youth in making choices of occupation. Data collected by the National Opinion Research Center in 1947, however, do permit a partial test of the hypothesis that occupational goals are related to the occupational structure of the community. A national sample of youth between the ages of 14 and 20 were asked: "Exactly what occupation do you plan to go into?" By comparing the occupational choices of youth living in large cities with those of adolescents living in smaller communities, we can test the hypothesis that the more varied and bureaucratic occupational structure of large cities will result in higher aspirations among its youth, as compared with those in smaller communities. The data of the NORC study suggest that relative size of community is much more influential in affecting the occupational aspirations of the *children of manual workers* than those of children of men in nonmanual occupations. This finding, of course, is compatible with the assumption that aspirations are related to perceived opportunity. Middle-class youth, even those living in smaller communities, will receive the stimulus to obtain a high-status occupation from their families and from other aspects of their environment which are related to middle-class status. It is among the working-class youth that size of community makes a major difference. Those living in smaller communities will not be as stimulated by their environment to aspire to higher goals. Opportunity within the occupational structure is, in fact, more limited than it is in the large city, for there are fewer bureaucratic or professional jobs in these communities than in metropolitan centers; and consequently the frame of reference of such small-community working-class youth is different.

Because these youths derive lower levels of aspiration from their immediate class and community environment than do lower-class city youths, they will probably be less likely to try to obtain the education or skills which will permit them to be successfully upward mobile. These lower goals, plus the greater difficulty in securing training, mean that a lower-class youth not raised in a metropolitan center enters the labor market with greater handicaps than his big-city cousin. And, in the labor market of the metropolitan centers, we find that working-class youth who are native urbanites are, in fact, more successful than migrants with similar class backgrounds.

A recent study of California suburbanites does suggest that the advantage that the sons of urban workers have may occur among adults on the white-collar occupational level. Stephen Boggs found that white-collar workers of metropolitan origin had higher levels of aspiration for further occupational advance than those of nonmetropolitan origin. He postulates that men who grow up in cities have more experience in successful adjustments to the types of changes required for upward occupational mobility: changes in the job and its social relations, in primary group relations, and in residence. "Men from nonmetropolitan communities may lack such experience or have found it more disturbing."

The finding of the NORC study that there is relatively little difference in the level of aspiration of *middle-class youth* living in larger or smaller communities is comparable to the findings reported earlier from the Survey Research Center study, which indicated that being brought up in a large city was not a mobility asset for those whose fathers were in nonmanual occupations. These findings indicate, as was suggested above, that middle-class youth reared in small communities are motivated to retain their social position. It may even be posited that the lower rate of downward social mobility among them, suggested by the Survey Research Center data, reflects the fact that the status structure of smaller communities is more rigid and visible than that of larger cities. In a study which compares the intercorrelations of the status indicators which make up W. L. Warner's "Index of Status Characteristics" in a large city with their intercorrelations in a small one there is some empirical evidence for this. The authors found that the correlations among variables related to social-class position were much lower in the city of Minneapolis than in the smaller city of Jonesville. The more fluid status structure of large cities indicated by this study should mean that being in a nonmanual occupation, or possessing some other single attribute of higher status, will be less likely to mean that a given individual actually is part of a higher social class. Hence, it may be suggested that the sons of persons in nonmanual positions in smaller communities will be more likely to be exposed to more imperatives for middle-class behavior and motivation than will the sons of fathers in comparable occupations in larger cities. One bit of evidence that this is so may be found in the fact that sons of nonmanual parents who grew up in small towns are better educated than their class compeers reared in big cities. The Survey Research Center data indicate that 32 per cent of those from small towns completed college, as compared with 19 per cent of those who grew up in big cities, a fact which goes far to account for the lower rate of downward mobility among the sons of nonmanual workers who are reared in smaller communities.

Another factor which may help explain the greater motivation of the sons of nonmanual workers from small towns to retain their class status, and their apparent success in doing so, is the smaller absolute size of the middle class in smaller communities. The smaller the community, the greater the possibility that as a *social* class it will include all those who have some claim to middle-class status. This is particularly true for children who are members of age-sex groupings in the one high school of a small city. The number of middle-class children is small enough so that a tight peer-group control along class lines is possible. For example, if the 106 cliques found by Hollingshead in the "Elmtown" high school were equally distributed among the four age groups or school grades, two sex groups, and five "social class" groups that he used in his analysis of the stratification system, there would be an average of two and one-half cliques in each subclass. Not many school youth could escape being involved in such a close network, and hence being directly under primary-group controls within their social class. In a large city, on the other hand, many middle-class youth can and do escape the confines of continuous participation in social-class-linked primary groups.

The implication of these analyses of the situation of middle-class youth is that the motivational advantages and objective opportunities of those who grow up in a large city are counterbalanced by the motivational pressures induced by the rigidities of the status system of smaller communities. On the other hand, among working-class youth, the rigidities of small-town structures will probably operate to reinforce the liabilities flowing from the working-class status of their families.

Conclusions

[Here we have] focused primarily on the ways in which the relative size of the community of orientation affect an individual's training, opportunity, perception of the occupational structure, and aspiration, thus increasing or decreasing his chance to obtain a good position in the occupational structure. It should be recognized, however, that variation in the size of community of orientation is only a single example of the variables which determine the horizons and opportunities of individuals. The sociological and psychological mechanisms involved are little different from those set by socioeconomic origin, family patterns, education, or ethnic background. When documenting the effect of each variable on a given behavior pattern, the sociologist is calling attention to the way in which an individual's potential behavior is limited by, or responsive to, factors derivative from his loction in society.

28 | Social Place in Florence: Assumptions and Realities

LAURO MARTINES

1. Wealth

Florentine sources of the fifteenth century—chronicles, diaries, letters, domestic handbooks, and public documents—exhibit a striking degree of harmony in their assumptions about the factors that determined elevated social place. Broadly speaking, four factors were commonly taken to be important: honorably-acquired wealth, a substantial record of service in public office, descent from an old Florentine family, and bonds of marriage with another family of some political and economic consequence. Possessed in full, these were the attributes which best conferred superior social rank, and the more a man lacked them the more humble or lowly was his social position.

An account of the social importance of wealth in Florence seems a useful point of departure. For as wealth and poverty often influenced or determined the other factors associated with social place, the economic factor appears to merit a certain priority. Let us consider this factor in its relation first to marriage.

Promises of marriage were sealed by a financial arrangement: the father of the bride-to-be drew up a promise to pay a dowry, specifying its terms and sum. Other considerations also affected decisions about marriage, such as political reputation and antiquity of lineage, but these lacked the material precision of dowries. If a girl of the upper class wished to marry, she had to have a dowry. The more handsome it was the more likely was she to marry according to her family's ambitions. Normally, dowries involved government securities, cash, property, or a certain combination of these. A girl who could not lay claim to a dowry was unlikely to find a husband, unless she came from the poorest sector of the lower classes,

SOURCE: Lauro Martines, *The Social World of the Florentine Humanists* (Princeton: Princeton University Press, 1963), pp. 27-28, 30-32, 39, 50-51, 53-55, 57-58, 62.

and even then she was probably expected to have a marriage portion of some sort, such as linen or a few items of furniture.

A family of the "better sort" faced economic and social ruin if, being burdened with debts, it had also to provide for several unmarried daughters. Their distress exposed the head of the family to temptations: he might be persuaded to sell his vote or influence in the governing councils in return for a loan which covered the dowry of one of his daughters. Similarly, a man in search of a wealthy bride might offer his political influence to an intermediary who helped negotiate a marriage involving a substantial dowry.

. . . . .

In our account of the social importance of wealth, we must not fail to distinguish between its "honorable" and "dishonorable" forms. Honor in this connection refers to the acquisition of wealth. Clearly, some ways of earning money were more honorable or more socially dignified than others. It will be necessary to consider this theme in some detail.

Although Florence was a city of sharp commercial and finance practices, the "official" attitude of the business community (as expressed, for example, in manuals of conduct) included a severely critical view of disreputable or dishonest commercial activity. The moral assumptions behind this attitude were at once Christian, self-interested (i.e., protective of trade), and possibly even a bit chivalric. The object here, however, will be to bring out, so far as they were present, the *social* elements in the criticism against the amassing of riches in a certain way.

If a merchant proposed to acquire or maintain a place in the governing class, one of his foremost cares involved the question of his personal honor. To understand this, we have only to note the incidence and importance of the word *onore* in Alberti's *Della famiglia*. Or, looking into some of the other writings of the period, time and again we come upon the association of dishonor with sharp business practices, quick gain, or usury. Paolo da Certaldo, for instance, declared that "Usury is certainly destructive . . . just as it ruins the goods and honor of the world, so it corrupts the body and soul." Or again, "Profit made in a disreputable fashion ought rather to be called injury and loss." Giovanni Morelli warned the merchant to enter only into legal contracts, and neither to accept nor lend money at usurious rates, for nothing was more damaging to one's honor and good name. Lionardo Bruni stressed the fact that Palla Strozzi's riches "were well acquired," and singled this out as one of the things that made Palla the most fortunate man in Florence. Bruni's implied criticism of "ill-got" wealth was taken much further by Giovanni Cavalcanti, who denied that rapid gain could ever bear investigation. Paraphrasing one of his contemporaries, Cavalcanti remarked that "as no river ever swelled with clear water, so no fortune was ever made from licit and honest gain."

Florentine feeling against usury and swift gain was rooted in a strong medieval tradition, but one may also suppose that it formed part of the natural reaction of a society where trade and finance dominate economic life. Seen in this light, Florentine indignation against immoral business procedure seems to have been a form of coercion such as any society may require for its own survival. But the feeling against rapid gain was also inevitably turned into a resentment against new wealth, which in turn was associated with "shady" business practices, greed, and materialistic ruthlessness. And of course, in the mouths of men who represented the old Florentine families, these moral epithets were apt to take on a strong political and social flavor.

·   ·   ·   ·   ·

Moral censure, as we shall see, was not the only mode of social rejection. In some quarters, lowly trades and all forms of bodily labor were assumed to be socially degrading. This view seems to have been a permanent feature of the social code of upper-class Florence. The code was partly based on the city's hierarchy of occupational dignities, in which the grades more or less reflected the constitutional arrangement of the Florentine guild structure. There were seven major and fourteen minor guilds, and the various degrees of social rank which these enjoyed were roughly distributed according to what the twenty-one guilds represented in political, economic, and traditional terms. First in dignity was the custom-honored legal profession. Beside the lawyers were ranked the international bankers and merchants (wool and silk were the chief items of enterprise). Next were the furriers and wealthy merchants who imported spices, drugs, dyes, and specialties. Then came the tradesmen and artisans of the fourteen minor guilds; retailers, butchers, ironmongers, leathermakers, stationers, and so forth. Finally, at the base of the social pyramid stood the wood and silk workers: dyers, weavers, spinners, washers, combers, and beaters. They had no political representation and were at the juridical mercy of the *Seta* and *Lana* guild consulates.

·   ·   ·   ·   ·

But trade on an international scale was something else. Bernardo Castiglionchio, a Florentine nobleman and cleric, said to his father in the early 1370's: "It is true, I know, that some of your brothers and relatives were merchants; but they dealt in noble and honorable merchandise, not in humble goods. Traveling to France and England, they traded in cloth and wool, like all the best and most important men of Florence. This type of trade is considered very comely and grand, and those who practice it are liked and greatly respected in our country. This is why there is no one in our family who can be said to have demeaned himself because of having followed an inferior trade."

·   ·   ·   ·   ·

2. Public Life

Participation in the public life of Florence was, like wealth, one of the essential factors in high social rank. This was true of both the fourteenth and fifteenth centuries, the chief difference being that public life in the fifteenth century was more thoroughly institutionalized and more difficult to enter. Precisely how early the honors of civil office were courted in Florence is a mystery, but the custom must have gone back at least to the twelfth century.

. . . . .

[Various repressive measures and oligarchic tendencies] . . . transformed the ruling class into a ruling caste. That men of humble birth occasionally entered minor administrative and gubernatorial posts, even the Signoria and the *Diece di Balia*, was of no consequence for the distribution of power in Florence. On the whole, the ruling families retained the key offices, and increasingly valued them just because they were increasingly difficult to get. This trend extended the power of some offices (e.g., the *Octo Custodiae*), while others suffered a corresponding loss. The concentration of power in fewer hands enhanced the importance and social brilliance of the leading magistracies, and thus, in the period from 1390 to 1460, these offices became more and more essential to the achievement of high social rank.

3. Family: The Significance of a Tradition

The family in fifteenth-century Florence stands between the individual and society. It mediates and determines his relations with the world at large, for he confronts the social system conditioned by his family's position in society, and his place in public life is governed by the political place of his family.

This is the underlying theme of this section. On it we shall build our account of the nature and importance of family traditions.

In Florence, the man who distinguished himself reflected honor on his family; behaving disgracefully, he disgraced it. By the same token, he could not be born into an illustrious family without concretely sharing in its distinction. He also shared its dishonors and shame. The great fourteenth-century lawyer, Bartolus, is said to have observed that "In Florence and throughout Tuscany liability for a crime committed by one of their members was imposed upon members of the family group. Furthermore, each individual's party affiliation was presumed to be that of the family group or its head." Finding himself legally embroiled in Rome or Venice, the simple Florentine artisan could make no effective appeal to Florence, owing to his political and social obscurity. But men with names like

Soderini, Castellani, Peruzzi, Strozzi, or Guicciardini enjoyed the benefits of a family tradition, and traveled from one side of Italy to the other with the knowledge that their families would, if necessary, come to their aid through the diplomatic channels of the Florentine Republic.

The individual who stood out in public affairs bound his family to the state in a special and close relation. Often, indeed, family affairs and affairs of state were so closely bound that they tended to merge. Before Pisa surrendered to Florence in 1406, the Florentines had to guarantee that they would live up to their promises by turning a group of hostages over to Messer Giovanni Gambacorta. The hostages, twenty youths, were the scions of leading Florentine families, the sons in fact of the architects of Florentine foreign policy.

· · · · ·

Since the nature of the upper-class family was such that each of its members gave moral qualities to the whole, and the whole to the individual, no man in this order of society could easily free himself from what was commonly supposed about his family. Consequently, contrary to one of Jacob Burckhardt's themes, the prominent Florentine did not enter society, nor circulate in it, as a "free individual," hurt or elevated purely by his own vices or talents. He was too closely associated with and rooted in his family background. Did it follow, therefore, that the man who came from a family of no importance was freer? Certainly not. For generally he could make no social or political claims: he had no environmental resources. Hence he abided in his obscurity, free to move only in the politically impotent world to which he was born.

The first requirement of the family type which enjoyed distinguished social rank was that it be old and established. Two factors produced this trait: wealth and public office, or better, honorably-acquired wealth and a long record of participation in the political affairs of the city. At the beginning of the fifteenth century, most of the dominant families could lay claim to these qualifications. They had entered the Priorate for the first time during its earliest years—the 1280's, 1290's, and the first years of the fourteenth century; or else they were connected by marriage with houses which had figured in public affairs even before the establishment of the Priorate. Furthermore, the wealth of these families antedated their rise to political distinction and often went back to the middle years of the thirteenth century. . . .

· · · · ·

Neither wealth alone, nor civic eminence alone, normally sufficed to attain high social rank. The two, wealth and office, had to be combined; and being combined across a long enough period of time, they produced an entirely new factor—a family tradition. By dint of long association with the Republic's major offices, and by maintaining a solid position either as great landowners or in the area of banking and international trade, a family developed its specific reputation and authority in the city. This we call its tradition.

In the early fifteenth century, the Fortini (a branch of the Orlandini) were well-known as notaries, landowners, and merchants. Having a talent for dealing with administrative questions, they developed a powerful bureaucratic tradition. The Medici house, renowned in business circles, enjoyed the special allegiance of the lower classes. The Panciatichi, on the other hand, once scorned as usurers, were respected and feared because they combined vast landed wealth and finance capital with an illustrious feudal past. By contrast with the Medici, the Albizzi and Ricasoli were deemed to be intransigeant oligarchs, along with the Peruzzi and Castellani. A final example: the Pandolfini, a family of prominent spice and silk merchants and landowners, were associated with traditions of political caution, wise counsel, and skill in diplomacy.

. . . . .

4. Marriage

In fifteenth-century Florence the man of good family ("famiglia da bene") normally contracted marriage with a woman of his own class. This happened with enough frequency to warrant our viewing marriage as an aid in the social assessment of individual Florentines. Why marriage was class-bound (apart from the obvious reasons) it will not be difficult to see.

It has been shown that in the dominant orders of society young women were expected to have a substantial dowry. As a result, no one from this social sector was likely to give his daughter in marriage to a man who could not equal, complement, or otherwise surpass her own background. Similarly, if a wealthy young man married a girl with a small dowry, he was clearly seeking old family traditions or relatives with a distinguished record in public office. In such marriages, accordingly, although one social attribute had been used to procure another, the participants successfully remained within the dominant social strata.

The decisive factor in marriage, as practised among Florentines of the middle and upper classes, was their supposition that it was a political and social alliance between families, not merely a conjugal union between two persons. This alliance was assumed to bind the fortunes of the two families in such a way that if one suffered a political or economic reversal, the other also might be affected, or in any case called in to lend assistance. A few passages from Giovanni Morelli's memoirs will underline this supposition: "[When you decide to marry] Think of this first of all: don't demean yourself with a social inferior; try, instead, to improve your condition, though not to such an extent that she would want to be the husband and make you the wife. See that you marry into a family of prosperous merchants, a family composed of good citizens who do not abuse their standing by behaving arrogantly. Aside from being of old stock in the city, they should also be Guelfs who are honored by the Commune and who are free of all stains such as those associated with treason, robbery, murder, or illegitimacy. . . . Let them not be dogs about money, but rather people who use a tempered politeness. Be sure that your betrothed is well-born, that her mother comes from a family of substance and has honorable relatives."

. . . . .

5. Ideal and Reality

We have seen that rank or place in Florentine society depended on four attributes: honorable wealth, public office, a family tradition, and a well-connected marriage. The more a family was endowed with these the loftier was its place in society.

Yet we must not let ourselves be entirely deceived by the attractions of the ideal type. It is true that when a house had the four attributes it realized a social ideal, but while some families could lay claim to the four parts of our ideal, others—also prominent—could not. In the period from 1390 to 1460, dozens of important families could not meet the four qualifications. In many cases they attained their eminence by means of a special talent, or at any rate without being of old Florentine stock, wealthy, or even prominent in political affairs. Departures from the ideal sometimes involved the possession of critical skills, for example in law or in public speaking, and the omission of one or more of the basic attributes. . . .

29 | The Transformation of Slavery in the Cities

RICHARD C. WADE

By 1860 the institution of slavery was in great disarray in every Southern city. The number of Negroes had declined precipitously. Discipline over those remaining proved difficult to sustain. The network of restraint so essential to bondage no longer seemed to control the blacks nor wholly

SOURCE: Richard C. Wade, *Slavery in the Cities, The South 1820–1860* (New York: Oxford University Press, 1964), pp. 243-253, 256-259, 262-280. Copyright © 1964 by Oxford University Press, Inc. Reprinted by permission of the author and publisher.

govern the whites. The distance between the races as well as separation of free colored from slave could not be maintained in the kinetic world of the city. In the most dynamic towns the whites overwhelmed the Negro population; even places with a larger proportion of slaves and less impressive growth tended to slough off at least their male blacks. In any case an institution which had been an integral part of urban life in Dixie in 1820 was languishing everywhere in 1860.

The census figures outlined the story. Though the number of slaves rose throughout the South, the proportion living in cities declined. In addition, the Negroes lost their earlier share of the urban population. In 1820, 37 per cent of all town dwellers were blacks; by 1860 that portion had dropped below 17 per cent. Urban slaves fell from 22 per cent to 10. The most dramatic shifts came, of course, in the border area, but everywhere the same pattern appeared. . . .

This decline did not stem from any economic reasons. There was plenty of work which whites had traditionally considered appropriate to blacks and particularly suited to slaves. Industrial employment, moreover, had proved feasible in a variety of enterprises. Hiring rates continued to rise throughout the last ante-bellum decades. And, perhaps most conclusively, the price of urban slaves on the market more than matched the general increase. In short, the usual indices suggested the continuing profitability of slavery as an economic institution. . . .

Slavery's compelling problem in the city was not finding work for bondsmen, but controlling them when they were off the job. While busy, in the house or around the yard, on the docks or driving a dray, toiling in a factory or cotton press, they caused little trouble. When the task was finished or the supervision lifted, however, when the slaves became idle or contrived some free time, when dusk fell and the demand for service slackened, then the system weakened. And when the Negroes gathered by themselves, beyond the eye of masters and police, in homes, churches, or grog shops, the "peculiar institution" itself was jeopardized.

It was the total environment rather than industrial or commercial employment which eroded slavery in the cities. The problem was not what happened in the factory or shop but what happened in the back street, the church, the grocery store, the rented room, and the out-of-the-way house. It was not contact with machines or an industrial process which broke the discipline, it was contact with people of all kinds in numerous ways which generated the corrosive acids.

"The city, with its intelligence and enterprise, is a dangerous place for the slave," wrote a shrewd analyst. "He acquires knowledge of human rights, by working with others who receive wages when he receives none; who can come and go at their pleasure, when he from the cradle to the grave must obey a master's imperious will. . . . It is found expedient, almost necessary, to remove the slave from these influences, and send him back to the intellectual stagnation and gloom of the plantation." Bondage "does not thrive with master or slave when transplanted to cities," a Louisiana planter observed, adding that in such surroundings "the slaves become dissipated, acquire the worst habits," and were generally "corrupted."

.   .   .   .   .

Slaves, on the other hand, found urban life to their liking. "The negroes are the most social of all human beings," De Bow asserted, "and after having hired in town, refuse to live again in the country." Slavery's most famous refugee to attack the institution in all its aspects made the same point with eloquent simplicity: "Life in Baltimore, when most oppressive, was a paradise" compared to "plantation existence," Frederick Douglass wrote. When masters were forced to sell, their bondsmen pleaded to be kept in the city because—in the words of some Richmond blacks— "they had acquired town habits." And often those sent into the country headed back at the first opportunity to run away. In short, how could you keep them down on the plantation once they had seen Mobile?

.   .   .   .   .

II

The cause of slavery's difficulty in the city was the nature of urban society itself. In the countryside physical isolation comprised one dimension of a successful discipline. Another was the simple division between master and slave, with virtually no other important element. The distinction between field hand and house servant, while important to the Negroes involved, constituted no significant fracture in the system. Treatment and comforts might vary, privileges could be more extensive, and everyday tasks quite different, but no area of independence was thus created. Indeed, a house servant often fell more directly under the eye of his owner than the black in the field. Nor did the overseer create a new interest among the whites. Employed by the master, usually a short-term resident, living apart from the colored quarters, and only occasionally a confidant of the owner, the overseer had at most a marginal influence on the structure.

Between black and white the social distance was immense. Slaves were confined to primitive work at worst or acquired rudimentary skills at best. Their contacts with whites were few and seldom lasting. An occasional visitor sometimes broke the isolation; nearby white families were seen just often enough to be recognized; overseers came and went. Except for the infrequent trip to town or a neighboring farm, the possibilities of outside stimuli scarcely existed. Even on small plantations or farms, the contacts with the surrounding world were circumscribed. Indeed, without other slaves about he was deprived of even the most elementary association. Rural life had always involved some social remoteness; for the plantation slave, isolation, next to his servitude, was the most compelling fact of life.

The cities, on the other hand, developed more complex structures. Both white and Negro communities included many different parts, and in the larger places a highly sophisticated system evolved with almost endless groupings and distinctions. This fragmentation, which, of course, characterized urban life nearly everywhere, had a special significance for slavery. It meant that the great gap between owner and chattel would be filled with all kinds of diverse elements, inevitably disturbing the institution's ordinary relationships. The Louisiana planter who so feared town life saw this process clearly. "The distance is so vast between slave and master" under bondage, he argued, that in the city "the interval is filled up immediately by corrupting influences." And the slaveholder was helpless. He could perceive "the evil of his slave without being able to prevent it," since it sprang from the intractable nature of urban life itself.

III

The most obvious added ingredient in the urban scene was the free Negro. He was, to be sure, also a rural resident, but the distance and detachment of the countryside greatly diluted his influence on slavery. Often living in a remote spot, sometimes as a yeoman, more often a hired hand, he was bound to have a modest role. His opportunity there moreover was limited. Without resources he found it hard to buy land; without many others of his own kind his social life was sparse. Hence he gravitated toward the metropolis.

Freedmen constituted the most highly urbanized group in Dixie. By 1860 they outnumbered slaves ten to one in Baltimore and 9209 to 1774 in Washington. In the deep South, too, their numbers grew with each census. . . . Across the South nearly a third of the free blacks were found in the larger urban centers. The report of a visitor in 1836 that "the emancipated negroes generally leave the country, and congregate in the cities and larger towns" was a common observation.

The free Negro's position in Southern towns was always precarious, occupying, as one Southerner put it, "a sort of uncertain and undefined position in our midst." His color suggested servitude, but his status secured a portion of freedom. Hence he suffered many of the inhibitions of his slave brothers while enjoying some privileges denied them. His advantages over the slave were considerable. He could marry, have children, and enjoy something of a normal family life. He could own property, have the right to his earnings, and engage in a few trades forbidden the enslaved. Though the situation was never favorable to either domestic tranquillity or economic advancement, there was at least a measure of independence. And, most crucial of all, in the privacy of the home could be found a seclusion from the constant surveillance of the white world.

.   .   .   .   .

Despite . . . . obstacles, the free colored of every city struggled to establish a meaningful associational life. They formed congregations and erected churches, established schools and aid societies, and organized improvement projects aimed at bringing some of the better things of life to their members. Occasionally this activity became elaborate, the Negro equivalent of fashionable white life. The Bonneau Literary Society in Charleston, for example, met Wednesday evenings at nine "to further progress in Literary Improvement . . . and the Improvement of our Mental Faculties," while in New Orleans the famous masked balls were carefully planned to emulate the subtlest pretensions of the city's first citizens.

To a few Southerners the presence of free Negroes created no great problem. Indeed, a state legislator from New Orleans called "the better class of our free colored population . . . a powerful check on the turbulence of the more vicious of our slaves." . . .

But the common judgment went the other way. . . .

The central complaint . . . had less to do with the wretchedness of free Negro life, or even with their high crime rate, than with their influence on slaves. Living amongst bondsmen, yet without masters, carrying by color the stigma of servitude, yet without its most humiliating features, shut off from white society, yet released from the confinements of slavery, the free blacks were always a disturbing factor. "They are a plague and pest in the community," the New Orleans Daily Picayune asserted, because they brought "the elements of mischief to the slave population."

"The superior condition of the free persons of color," a memorial of Charleston citizens argued, "excites discontent among our slaves, who continually have before their eyes, persons of the same color, many of whom they have known in slavery, and with all of whom they associate on terms of equality." The slave saw these blacks "freed from the control of masters, working where they please, going whither they please, and spending money how they please." He thus became "dissatisfied" and "pants after liberty."

.   .   .   .   .

"The intercourse of free negroes with slaves," wrote a New Orleans paper, "is just as mischievous" as letting loose abolitionists among them. . . . If they do not render the slave insubordinate, they make him vicious." This "fact" was "so well understood that in the country" planters could only "with difficulty effect the emancipation of their slaves," and the law usually required that newly liberated slaves be removed from the state. "It is the saucy and insolent air of the *free* negroes," a St. Louis police report declared, "which is most dangerous to the slave population." Whatever the precise formulation of the argument, Southern town dwellers could agree that their free colored residents rendered control over their slaves increasingly difficult.

IV

They could also agree that there were some whites who were almost as unsettling to the system as freed blacks. These people had found a place at the edge of slavery where their economic life was enmeshed in the irregular relationships bred by the system in its urban environment. Some were grocers who sold to slaves; others ran shops which catered to a colored clientele; still others were ministers who organized Negro churches and sought to bring religion to the enslaved. Port merchants, too, could be included, since their trade brought ships with mixed crews into the harbor. Less easily identified, but also important, were whites sporadically connected with the informal life of town blacks. These interests were obviously quite different, but all developed a stake in the loose form of bondage which evolved in the cities.

The activity of some was illegal because it involved dealing with slaves who did not have the proper papers or permissions. Even ministers tended to allow bondsmen and free blacks to run the colored churches without the careful supervision required by law. And the association of whites in the demi-world of the Negro's night life violated both custom and law. Yet the interstices of slavery were so wide that these relations became a normal part of the functioning of the institution. Despite everything municipal officials could do, there were more whites in this position in the 1850's than ever before. Thus, there arose a white element whose influence, like the presence of free blacks, weakened the system of restraints and exclusions on which slavery rested.

The grocers and the grog-shop operators had the most obvious and deepest stake in the loose enforcement of police regulations. Nearly all dealt occasionally with slaves, and many depended on the trade. Though traffic in any goods was frowned upon, it was the sale of liquor that lay at the center of the controversy. Nearly all whites disliked this commerce; the master because it "led to the corruption of our servants and the loss of property," and others because it resulted in "the unrestrained intercourse and indulgence of familiarities between black and white." In short, the trade created conditions "destructive of the respect and subserviency which our laws recognize as due from the one to the other and which form an essential feature in our institutions."

· · · · ·

V

The role of the ministers proved more complicated. In stimulating the religious activity of Negroes, they felt they were discharging a public as well as a Christian duty. Believing that a pious slave was a well-behaved, docile, and obedient servant, most felt that the oftener he could be within earshot of the Word of God, the better for master and slave. Yet the elaborate regulations surrounding colored congregations tended to inhibit rather than encourage an enlarged spiritual life. Hence clergymen tended to bend if not break the law. Their control was formal rather than close; their attendance at meetings casual rather than constant.

. . . White ministers, believing in the necessity of religious instruction to the Negroes, tried to temper the enforcment of laws against colored congregations. Except in Charleston in the 1820's they proved uniformly successful.

A handful of lawyers in every city also discovered an interest in a lax system of slavery. They operated in the crucial intersection of slavery and freedom—the granting of emancipation papers. The complaint of a St. Louis man explained the practice and detailed the danger. The law permitted a Negro who claimed freedom to bring the case to court. "This is but right, rational and humane," "Topaz" admitted, "but the liberty has become abused, at least in St. Louis, by the ruthless encouragement of those who left-handedly profit by such suits." It worked like this: "Tom wants his freedom, and sallies in quest of legal advice; he states his case, and right or wrong, is flattered to proceed. Pleased with his prospects, he brags to Dick, who after a little scratching of the bump of his reminiscences, takes a notion he has a right to freedom too." Then the hope spreads through the black community. "Fired with untried hope, Dick flies to Ned . . . Ned catches flame and communicates it to Big Bill—Big Bill to little Jim, and little Jim to everything that wears wool." Soon discipline everywhere flags. The slave "grumbles at his master's commands—neglects his duties, and takes his chastisement with the sullen insolence of one who thinks he shall shortly be able to set the white man at defiance."

The lawyer's clients might be slaves whose manumission depended on the action of a municipal body when certain conditions and technicalities were under question. In New Orleans the number was so large that a committee of the city council asserted that everyone was "well aware" there were "persons who speculate and deal" in emancipation papers and made good money at it. Another transaction involved replacing lost documents or establishing the fact that a black was not a runaway. Everywhere a few lawyers discovered a stake in the untidy organization of urban slavery.

·   ·   ·   ·   ·

VI

In the metropolis the worlds of bondage and freedom overlapped. The line between free blacks and slaves became hopelessly blurred. Even whites and blacks found their lives entangled in some corners of the institution of slavery. No matter what the law said or the system required, this layer of life expanded. Though much of it was subterranean, at points it could be easily seen. The mixed balls, the numberless grog and grocery shops, the frequent religious gatherings, and the casual acquaintances in the streets were scarcely private. Physical proximity bred a certain familiarity that most residents came to expect. To be sure, when a Richmond officer saw "a white man, walking arm and arm with a black man," he demanded "to know the why and wherefore of such a cheek and jowel business." But occasional friendships that transcended the deference of slavery raised few eyebrows.

What did bother townspeople, however, was the evidence that beyond these visible contacts lay a world of greater conviviality and equality. In this nether world blacks and whites mingled freely, the conventions of slavery were discarded, and the worst fears of Southerners became realized. Not only did the men find fellowship without regard to color in the tippling shops, back rooms, and secluded sheds, but the women of both races joined in. Such mixing engaged a good deal of the private conversation of white people in cities, but its public manifestations were usually found in only police reports and the major's court.

. . . . .

New Orleans, with its large population of free and enslaved blacks, had the most famous demi-world in Dixie. The celebrated masked balls and the casual acceptance of colored mistresses seemed to reflect its Spanish and French roots. Yet that explanation is too facile. The rural areas of Louisiana, some of which reflected similar origins, did not develop the same mores; and, more persuasively, other cities with quite different beginnings did. Actually what visitors noticed about New Orleans was true of urban life throughout the South.

VII

Northern cities, too, had their disorganized elements who left a trail across police blotters, court records, and poor-house lists. There, too, community leaders, somewhat bewildered by the spread of undisciplined low life, sought some way to introduce system and stability. But, important as this was to civic leaders elsewhere, in the South the problem was greatly complicated by the existence of slavery. On the one hand, the institution required a high degree of order, the careful regulation of Negro affairs, and a fixed status for bondsmen. On the other hand, the city demanded fluidity, a constant re-allocation of human resources, and a large measure of social mobility. Initially, it appeared as though slavery could provide the discipline town life seemed to need. In the long run, however, the force of urbanization loosened the restraints of bondage, smudged the distinctions of status among Negroes, and at points pierced the racial walls of Dixie's cities.

This antithesis was early felt by some municipal leaders. Since slavery was presumed to be an established part of Southern town life for any foreseeable future, none talked about incompatibility. Instead, the dominant race sought to solve it with ordinances, the orderly development of a legal hiring-out system, and a plentiful police force in case of trouble. Yet the acids of urbanization continually eroded the discipline on which bondage rested. Though the disintegration was often hard to gauge, those close to the problem knew it was happening.

To arrest the attrition and handle its consequences, Southern cities moved along three lines. One involved the sale of young male blacks into the countryside. This removed one of the most disturbing elements from the urban scene while meeting a constant demand for field hands in the cotton and cane regions. A second was the tightening of emancipation procedures to stop the accumulation of free Negroes in towns. A third was to develop racial arrangements which took into account the new situation and which embodied most of the features later identified as segregation.

．．．．．

. . . The tendency to sell men into the country was pronounced. It was, in fact, the theme of John S. C. Abbott's diary of his Southern trip in 1859. "The slaves in the cities, working in the midst of the conversation of white men, listen eagerly, and gain some information," he noted. "This has alarmed their masters, and they are sending them off, as fast as possible, to the plantations where,. as in a tomb, no sight or sound of knowledge can reach them.". . .

While Dixie's towns sloughed off their male bondsmen, they also moved to reduce the number of free Negroes in their midst. . . .

The case of New Orleans was illustrative, because its policy encompassed both the widest leniency for most of the ante-bellum years and an absolute ban on the eve of war. Through most of the period, under Louisiana law, city councils could grant freedom on petition, and they did so on a substantial scale. In the four years between 1846 and 1850 the First Municipality alone emancipated 321 blacks, while the Second Municipality manumitted at a rate of about 75 annually. The grounds were usually "long important and faithful services" and most carried the notation, "without being compelled to leave the state." Masters wishing to let their slaves go generally got a sympathetic hearing from officials. . . .

New Orleans' liberal practice obscured somewhat the increasing hostility to emancipation of any kind in Louisiana. The 1830 law required the newly freed Negro to leave the state within thirty days; in 1852 the right to manumit was taken from city officials and given to the legislature. Flooded with petitions, worried about the influence of the unbonded on the slaves, and concerned about rumored insurrections, the state government in 1857 forbade manumission under any conditions. Two years before, a legislator had expressed the tighter attitude: "if slavery is not an evil . . . why should we emancipate under any circumstances in the State of Louisiana?" In 1859 provisions were made for free blacks to choose a master and return to bondage.

Other cities exercised less control over emancipation than New Orleans, but the tendency everywhere was the same. . . . By 1860 the percentage of free Negroes among the South's urban population had dropped considerably.

VIII

While Southern cities increasingly moved to reduce their colored population, both slave and free, they also developed a new system of racial deference more appropriate to urban life than slavery in its traditional form. As the institution of slavery encountered mounting difficulties and, as its control over the blacks weakened, another arrangement was devised which maintained great social distance within the physical proximity of town life. Increasingly public policy tried to separate the races whenever the surveillance of the master was likely to be missing. To do this, the distinction between slave and free Negro was erased; race became more important than legal status; and a pattern of segregation emerged inside the broader framework of the "peculiar institution."

In a sense this tendency was always present, though the reliance on traditional controls obscured its importance. The heart of the established system was, of course, the subordination of the slave to his owner. The wide discretion vested in the master made day-to-day discipline almost a private matter. But in the cities a public etiquette was needed to govern the relations of races when the blacks were beyond the supervision of their owners. Increasingly that etiquette required the separation of black and white without regard to legal status. Beginning in only a few areas, the arrangement spread to include the most important public aspects of life.

Taverns, restaurants, and hotels were always off-limits to the Negroes. The laws against trading with slaves, of course, covered all these areas, and their location in the business part of town prevented much laxity. Free blacks fell under the same ban, though by custom rather than by law. In public conveyances this discrimination appeared again. Richmond's ordinances, to cite but one case, prohibited Negroes from "driving, using or riding in any Hackney coach or other carriage for hire unless in the capacity of a servant." . . .

Public grounds, however, presented an even clearer case. Savannah's 1827 ordinances, for example, excluded "negroes, mullattoes, or other colored persons" from public promenade in South Broad street, or on that leading from thence to the Hospital." And the preamble said why: "for the purpose of protecting the Citizens while engaged in recreation upon the Public Walks, from molestation or intrusion of improper persons." A section of Richmond's Negro code was entitled "What place slaves not to Walk or be in.". . . The law relented if the slave accompanied his owner as employer, but the prohibition of free blacks was absolute.

Charleston's regulations kept colored people off the "enclosure of the Garden at White Point" and forbade them "to walk on the East or South Batteries." If attending white children, and if they had a ticket, slaves could enter. . . .

These measures simply excluded the blacks without providing alternative facilities. It was otherwise in the case of jails, hospitals, and cemeteries. Here the separation was careful and complete, if sometimes painfully contrived. Also, wherever Negroes shared public buildings with whites their quarters were set apart. The division was sometimes by room, at other times by floor. But in every case the segregation was clear and unmistakable.

Cultural and recreational enterprises were also segregated when they did not exclude Negroes entirely. Theaters provided special galleries for colored persons which were often approached through special entrances. Lyell found the upper tiers of boxes at the New Orleans Opera House assigned to Negroes. Another visitor reported, "some of them were pointed out to me as very wealthy; but no money can admit them to the pit, or to the boxes.". . .

On the stage, of course, no intrusion was permitted. When a Northern newspaper reported that a colored actress had performed in New Orleans, the *Bee* retorted indignantly: "We beg leave to contradict and unequivocally this remark. No negress ever has been, or ever will be permitted to appear on the stage of New Orleans. We are a slave-holding state, and whatever may be the pretended philanthropy of our Northern brethren in relation to our conduct, we possess too much self-respect to submit to any such degrading exhibition." The prohibition on reading and writing, of course, put libraries off-limits.

Negroes remained as segregated in death as in life. Funerals increasingly became wholly colored affairs. The law usually required a white minister at the service, and the master and the family sometimes attended, but a petition by Richmond's blacks to the state legislature indicated the reality. The Negroes noted that a new statute, passed in 1832, prohibited slaves and free Negroes from officiating at funerals. As a consequence, they lamented, "many coloured human beings are inter'd like brutes, their relatives and friends being unable to procure white ministers to perform the usual ceremony in the burial of the dead." Eleven clergymen joined in the memorial arguing that the "pressing engagements of white ministers left no time for this function."

The body was finally interred in a segregated cemetery. . . . The bulk of urban Negroes, slave and free, rested ultimately in places confined to their own race. Every city maintained at least one extensive "burial ground for negroes," and most churches kept separate cemeteries for black and white. . . .

IX

Religious organizations quickly developed segregated facilities without the help of municipal officials and the law. Nearly all Protestant denominations, especially those with large black contingents, either put their colored members in separate galleries during regular services or established special churches for them. This arrangement covered not only Sunday gatherings but prayer meetings during the week and Bible classes as well. The system, however, stemmed less from white design than Negro preference, for whenever the opportunity appeared colored worshippers patronized their own congregations. . . .

Colored churches, of course, reflected the tendency toward segregation even more clearly. Distrusted by whites, enthusiastically supported by Negroes, they represented the ambiguity of race relations under slavery. Whites developed elaborate devices to keep the races apart in public places and to seal off their own slaves from others in private life; but religious activity fell between these situations. Masters, often considering it a family affair, sought a compromise under one roof. Negroes, on the other hand, finding social as well as spiritual satisfaction by themselves, flocked to separate congregations. Except for some Catholic churches and a few Protestant ones, this combination made Sunday morning one of the most segregated moments of the week.

Slaves were excluded from schools by the legislation against teaching them to read and write, but the pattern of segregation applied to free blacks. Not only could they not attend white classes, but they had to make their own arrangements for education. Even these schools had uncertain careers, being subject to police interference and legal prohibitions as well as financial difficulties. . . . If some slaves managed to bootleg a little learning in a free colored school, no black was ever knowingly admitted to a white one.

. . . . .

X

Law and custom sanctioned the segregation of races in public places and accommodations as well as in churches and schools. To disentangle white and black in employment and housing was a different matter. Yet the significant fact is that such a separation took place increasingly often in the last few decades before the Civil War. Under the pressure of white craftsmen, Negroes were pushed out of one line of work after another. With the weakening of the reins of slavery, bondsmen found housing away from their owners and generally in areas of accumulating colored population. Both movements were far from complete, but the tendency was unmistakable.

In employment the clearest manifestation of segregation was the exclusion of blacks, slave and free, from the better jobs. . . . Charleston's ordinances prohibited teaching slaves "in any mechanic or handicraft trade," though the wording was vague and its enforcement almost impossible.

In Savannah the restrictions were more precise. No Negro could be apprenticed "to the trade of Carpenter, Mason, Bricklayer, Barber or any other Mechanical Art or Mystery." Later, cabinetmaker, painter, blacksmith, tailor, cooper, and butcher were added to the list. Georgia excluded blacks from "being mechanics or masons, from making contracts for the erection . . . or repair of buildings." Though no two cities had the same categories, all tried to keep colored workers out of the higher skills. The fact that practice often belied the law simply underlined the significance of the intent.

If slaves and blacks were still found in many of the better crafts in 1860, they had been pushed out of many of the lesser-skilled jobs. In Baltimore whites took the carting and draying business from them by 1830. A few years later, a visitor could report that "the Irish and other foreigners are, to a considerable extent, taking the place of colored laborers and of domestic servants." In 1823 the City Council of New Orleans directed the mayor "to hire white labor for the city works, in preference to negroes." Two decades later, some prominent citizens there described the extent of the attrition: "Ten years ago, say they, all the draymen of New Orleans, a numerous class, and the cabmen, were colored. Now they are nearly all white. The servants of the great hotels were formerly of the African, now they are of the European race.". . .

John S. C. Abbott, who toured the South in 1859, found this tendency pronounced everywhere. In Mobile, for instance, he was "surprised to see how effectually free labor seems to have driven slave labor from the wharves and streets." The Irish and Germans, he noted, did the outside work, while white girls moved into domestic service. . . .

Though the process varied in Dixie's cities and Negroes hung on in many skills, "job busting" became a normal tactic for the growing white labor force faced with traditional colored employment practices. As the black population dropped, white newcomers moved in and took over craft after craft. Occasionally accompanied by violence and usually with official sanction, slave and free colored workers were shunted into the most menial and routine chores. In 1830 Negroes, both slave and free, had been used in a wide variety of employments; by 1860 the number of possibilities had shrunk markedly. The movement toward segregation, so noticeable in other aspects of urban life, was rapidly invading employment.

In housing the same trend was perceptible, though less advanced. The spread of the "living out" system, both in its legal and irregular form, gave slaves some choice of residence. Since the urge to leave the enclosure reflected the freedom from surveillance it entailed, slaves sought spots as removed from whites as possible. For most this meant a retreat to the outer edges of the city or beyond the municipal line altogether. There was seldom any escape from all whites, but there were parts of town with clusters of colored inhabitants. By the 'forties and 'fifties it was apparent in most places that Negroes were settling on the periphery of the cities.

Savannah is a good illustration of this process. The central portion had always been the commercial heart of town. Immediately around it and stretching southward, the substantial and the wealthy built their houses. The best addresses bore the names of eight or ten squares directly away from the wharf toward Forsyth Park. The western and southern edges became the sites for the low-income whites and increasingly for the free colored as well. As slaves moved away from the master's yards, they headed for these areas.

The 1848 census, which listed slaves from their actual place of residence rather than from their master's addresses, revealed the concentrations. Old Oglethorpe Ward on the west had 1327 Negroes to 999 whites. In the same place there were only five brick houses to 451 wooden ones. To the east, Carpenter's Row, Trustees Gardens, and Gilmerville showed the same tendency with fewer numbers. There 300 blacks lived with 182 whites; none of the 127 houses was brick. Significantly enough, Currytown on the southeast edge of the city showed the same characteristics—Negro majorities and wooden dwellings. Elsewhere in Savannah, the figures ran the other way, with white preponderance and large numbers of brick homes.

The movement to the periphery was increasingly common, though in some towns colored concentrations grew up more haphazardly in small enclaves or strips in out-of-the-way places. And the centers of Negro life, formal and informal, followed the people. Colored churches, especially those established after 1840, sought locations in these neighborhoods. Grocery stores and dram shops, too, settled there. Even the cemeteries were put near the living. In Savannah's case, for example, four Negro churches, three Baptist, and one Methodist were on the west side, while another served the east side. The central city had none. Of 174 "grocers" 101 did business in the outer residential wards, West Broad alone accommodating 19. . . .

In no case did anything like full residential segregation emerge. Few streets, much less blocks, were solidly black. Everywhere some whites occupied nearby dwellings. Still the inclination to cluster here, to concentrate there, was more marked by 1860 than in 1820. The separation apparent in other areas of life was slowly insinuated into housing.

Thus, even before slavery had been abolished, a system of segregation had grown up in the cities. Indeed, the whites thought some such arrangement was necessary if they were to sustain their traditional supremacy over the Negroes. The countryside provided enough room to give meaning to racial separation. The master could be physically quite removed from his blacks, though sharing the same plantation or farm. And together both were isolated from others. In cities these spatial relationships were quite different. Both races were thrown together; they encountered each other at every corner, they rubbed elbows at every turn; they divided up, however inequitably, the limited space of the town site. Segregation sorted people out by race, established a public etiquette for their conduct, and created social distance where there was proximity. Urban circumstances produced this system long before the destruction of slavery itself.

Of course, the complete separation of races was impossible in the city, and the practice differed from place to place. In some towns, public conveyances remained mixed; in others Negroes were not excluded from all public grounds; in still others housing continued scrambled. Yet every city developed its own arrangement expressed in the contrived separation of colored and white in countless ways. Though never total, the segregation was so extensive that Negroes were never permitted to forget their inferior position.

XI

The rising incidence of segregation was another index of the increasing weakness of slavery in the cities. Rooted in the white's need for discipline and deference, it developed to take up the slack in the loosening system. It provided public control to replace dwindling private supervision of the master over his slave. To do this, the difference between free and enslaved Negroes had to be narrowed, depriving free blacks of part of their freedom even while permitting a wider latitude to bondsmen. To most whites, however, there seemed no alternative. The old system no longer really controlled; the walls no longer really confined; the chains no longer really held.

The decline of slavery in the cities was the central fact of race relations in the South's cities in the ante-bellum decades. It was also a fact that conditioned Negro life in subsequent generations, for it meant that, when emancipation finally did come, most of the colored population would be in the countryside rather than in cities. Accustomed only to routine tasks, imbruted by the severe limitations of plantation existence, and unused to managing their own affairs, they became free under the most difficult of circumstances.

If the Negro population in the cities had grown in the same proportion as the whites, there would have been present an invaluable pool of potential leadership, for there many blacks, even under slavery, had begun to develop the most important tools of citizenship. There they acquired some skills and learned the rudiments of reading and writing. There, too, many had commenced to manage their own affairs, and in churches they developed a capacity for organization. In short, the metropolis nourished the literacy and self-reliance needed in a free system.

Observers generally agreed on the other hand that rural blacks plainly bore the mark of their servitude. "The fieldhand negro is, on the average, a very poor and bad creature." Olmsted wrote sadly, "much worse than I supposed before I had seen him and grown familiar with his stupidity, indolence, duplicity, and sensuality. He seems to be but an imperfect man, incapable of taking care of himself in a civilized manner." House servants were presumably in a favored condition, but their contacts usually were only somewhat wider, their self-reliance seldom encouraged, and their horizons not appreciably better.

Olmsted found quite the opposite in the cities. "Slaves can never be brought together in denser communities but their intelligence will be increased to a degree dangerous to those who enjoy the benefit of their labor," he observed. "Hundreds of slaves in New Orleans must be constantly reflecting and saying to one another, 'I am as capable of taking care of myself as this Irish hod-carrier, or this German market-gardener; why can't I have the enjoyment of my labor as well as they? I am as capable of taking care of my own family as much as they of theirs; why should I be subject to have them taken from me by those other men who call themselves our owners?' " And the speculation no doubt extended to the next generation: " 'Our children have as much brains as the children of these white neighbors of ours, who not long ago were cooks and waiters at the hotel, why should they be spurned from the school rooms? I helped build the school house, and have not been paid for it. One thing I know, if I can't have my rights, I can have my pleasures; and if they won't give me wages I can take them.' "

Olmsted saw this distinction more clearly than most. But visitors from the North, travelers from abroad, in fact, masters and slaves, also understood the difference. It was an uncomfortable fact for the whites. To them it presaged a wider freedom for the Negro, with all the uncertainties and perhaps chaos that would follow. Hence the response of owners and officials was to tighten rather than adjust, to expel rather than emancipate, to segregate rather than liberate. At the end the "free air of the city" was being increasingly denied to a higher and higher proportion of blacks.

The full significance of the de-urbanization of the Negro under slavery was apparent only much later. Emancipation found him located primarily in the least dynamic area of American life. Capable of simple tasks, familiar only with rural routine, largely illiterate, and unused to managing his own affairs, he faced a long road to full freedom. Ultimately that road carried him to the city. Though confronted by both discrimination and segregation, he could find there the numbers and leadership which could one day spring him loose from the confinements of an earlier bondage.

30 ❚ India's Ex-Untouchables

HAROLD R. ISAACS

The Registrar of Siddarth College of Commerce, a heavy-set young man of twenty-seven whose name is Ubale and who holds M.A. and LL.B. degrees, insisted that we had to see for ourselves how educated ex-untouchables live in Bombay, so we fixed a time to visit him at his home. He came to our hotel to get us and we took a taxi for what proved to be a long ride across a good stretch of the city of Bombay. We pulled swiftly away from Marine Drive and the downtown neighborhoods where the new Indian middle class is filling comfortable-looking, even luxurious new apartment blocks, out through streets lined with their parked cars, out past quarter after quarter of more modest middle-class, working-class, and slum Bombay, through miles of suffocatingly crowded streets choked with traffic and people. Next to a vast block of low-cost government tenements, we came to the edge of a great open hollow, a huge shallow craterlike space every square foot of which was covered by what first looked like a mass of debris but was actually a mass of human dwellings. We left the taxi at the road's edge outside and went on by foot, sometimes across planks laid across mud, sometimes in the mud. We picked our way along the narrow lanes between the rows of houses put together out of every conceivable kind of junk, wooden boxes, pieces of corrugated tin, old doors and windows, pieces of wallboard, roofs of thatch or tin or wood, all the ingenious improvisations of the universal squatter shackville, with little rivulets of sewage running down each alley or street, naked or half-naked children running about, and people in the various postures of the utmost kind of squalid poverty. The masses of shacks were clustered in and around an occasional more substantial building, long, narrow, and high, with walls of brick and roofs of tin or tile. These were the original barrack buildings of Rawaly Camp, once an establishment for British troops at the

SOURCE: Harold R. Isaacs, *India's Ex-Untouchables* (New York: The John Day Company, Inc., 1956), pp. 85-89. Copyright © 1964 by Harold R. Isaacs. Copyright © 1965 by the Massachusetts Institute of Technology. Reprinted by permission of the publisher.

city's edge, and the place was still known by that name. These barrack buildings had been partitioned off into rooms of approximately 10 by 18 feet. In each of these a family lived. I have to confess that I thought Ubale had taken us into Rawaly Camp to show us how the lowest of the low live before taking us elsewhere to his own place, but he led us now into one of these ex-barracks rooms which turned out to be his own family's home.

Ubale's room was swept bright and clean. His young wife and two small children, a brother-in-law and his wife, waited there to greet us. Most of the people in Rawaly Camp got water from taps spaced at long intervals out in the lanes, but Ubale had piped water into his room and had brought an electric line over from the nearest building in the tenement block nearby. Several of the rooms in the barracks had these amenities, making theirs the best housing in the area. The Ubale room was divided by a semi-partition made up of a cabinet which held household supplies. On a shelf over the water tap a little row of brass pots and bowls gleamed in the half-dark at the end of the room. A low single kerosene burner on the floor provided heat for cooking. Near the front of the room was a low table and small benches. At night, Ubale explained, they pushed these aside, spread some mats, and slept on the floor. On a shelf near the door stood some of Ubale's books and some family pictures. The bare electric bulb hung from a cord over our heads. Smiling her bashful smile, Mrs. Ubale laid cups of tea and bowls of sweetened noodles before us while we talked and learned something about the economics of the Ubale household. For this room Ubale paid 23 rupees, or not quite $5 a month. Food cost 100 rupees ($21), clothing 10 rupees ($2.10) and medical costs were usually 15 rupees ($3.15.) His salary at Siddarth is R300 ($63) and he would just about be able to manage on this except that he is paying R100 a month on a loan of R2,000 ($420) he contracted for his sister's marriage the year before. His last sister was about to be married and he had borrowed another R2,000 to launch her properly. It would cost him R100 a month for the next four years to pay off these debts. It was impossible in any case to move now to some better locality because of the high cost of *pagdi*, the illegal premium that we would call "key money" which is needed to rent any space at all. For this room when he took it the year he married, in 1958, Ubale had paid R1,000 ($210) simply to move in. This has to be paid to the previous holder of the lease. "To move out of here now, I could not take less than R4,000 ($840)," he explained, "because in any better locality I would have to pay at least R5,000 ($1,050) to the occupants or to the landlord. I will have to borrow to make up any difference. If I find I cannot move to a better area, I will have to look for a larger place in another slum area." I ventured to wonder out loud why, in view of these facts and figures, it wasn't possible to spend something less than half a year's salary on a wedding, especially since the money had to be borrowed, and this young man, who was moving in a stream flowing against the ancient Law of Manu and 2,000 years of Hindu tradition, replied: "Oh, you can't go against custom, otherwise our own people would look down on us! We spend R2,000 on a wedding here and we wouldn't spend less than R1,000 even in the village. About 700 or 800 people will come. We hire a hall for the occasion. My sister," he added proudly, "appeared for the Secondary School Certificate and she is marrying a B.A."

Ubale waved at the squalid heaps and shacks outside and said there were 4 B.A.s and LL.B.s living in Rawaly, probably about 50 successful matriculates, and as many as 1,000 young men working toward the matric exam. They were living out in those shacks many of which, he said, were also so-called "black spots" or places where illegal liquor was made and sold, a major slum occupation. About 25,000 people live in Rawaly Camp, and other localities like it dot the city, many larger or smaller shackvilles occupying hollows or other low places in and around the slums of the city. There are between 500,000 and 700,000 ex-untouchables in Bombay—no one was sure of that figure either—and the bulk of them live in places like Rawaly Camp. We walked out back along the narrow lanes. The children, full of that particular vigor of the fittest who have survived, were racing around the place, only a few stopping to watch us go by. We reentered our cab and rode back through the great blocks of slums that now looked positively luxurious, back into the upper-class neighborhoods that seemed to be located on another planet, and out along the famous curving strand of Marine Drive where great crowds of people were, as always, slowly strolling along the sea's edge to feast their eyes on its open space and breathe in some of its clean air.

Part Four

▬▬▬▬▬▬▬▬▬

The Social
Psychology
of Urban Life

Of the three major foci for conceptualizing urban phenomena, two have already been presented in this volume. The ecological approach was examined in comparative perspective in Part II and the social organizational approach in Part III. The city may also be viewed as a psychological, personal phenomenon; Part IV examines this dimension of urban life. The most appropriate way for sociology to deal with psychology is at the point where society and the individual meet—a sub-field of both sociology and psychology called social psychology. For urban sociology the major social-psychological question is whether any features of personality are causes, correlates, or consequences of urban development. This question is the psychological counterpart of those questions raised in Part III on the relationship between social organization and urban development.

In Section A, "The Individual and the City," we deal directly with the personal implications of urbanization, first in the broad article by Alex Inkeles and then in the examples of individuals experiencing city life under various conditions, as presented in case studies of Turkey, Morocco, and London. Section A concludes with Joseph Zelan's empirical study of some alleged psychological effects of suburban life. Section B, "The City as Dream and Nightmare," presents the city as ideology. The articles by Carl E. Schorske, Elwin H. Powell, and Bennett M. Berger describe some ideological aspects of European urbanization, American industrial cities, and American suburbs, respectively. The articles by Hortense Powdermaker and Paul Charosh present homely examples of images of the city found in the mass media.

Alex Inkeles' "The Modernization of Man" rests on the assumption that some transformation of man's attitudes, values, and feelings is necessary if man is to live successfully in modern urban-industrial society. Inkeles sketches nine major personal attributes of modern man, ranging from his willingness to accept innovation and change to his belief in human ability to control the environment. In addition to these broad attitudinal states "modern man" also tends to differ from "traditional man" in his opinions on specific topics such as birth control, treatment of the aged, the role of women, religion, education, politics, consumer preferences, and the mass media. Inkeles points out that "modernity" and "traditionalism" are not all or none qualities. Neither is there a simple cause and effect relationship between a given social structure and psychological "modernity," although the factory system, national states, mass communication, and especially education are sources of modern attitudes.

The human meaning of the transformation from traditional to modern man is vividly depicted in Daniel Lerner's "The Grocer and the Chief: A Parable." Except for the unique features contributed by the Turkish cultural setting, the grocer with his receptivity to newness and change, his unorthodox opinions, his interest in money and material things, his concern with happenings beyond the village, his nonagricultural occupation, his belief in and search for improvement, even his wearing of Western style clothing and a tie, exemplifies the modern qualities sketched by Inkeles. The chief of Balgat with his emphasis on maintaining accepted practices, his confident enunciation of the basic virtues and concerns of life, his parochialism, his orientation toward agriculture and the land, is the epitome of the characterological aspects of traditionalism. The shepherd, the farmers, the chief's wife, sons, and daughters-in-law manifest the traditional attitudes, beliefs, and outlook appropriate to their particular statuses.

Lerner's presentation is especially valuable because of its "before" and "after" views of the same people. After modernization we find that the farmers whose main concerns had been family matters and agricultural problems and who had depended on the chief for advice now have their own opinions on a broad set of topics ranging from national politics to international oil agreements. Many of the farmers are indeed no longer farmers but have become workers in Ankara. Even the shepherd, who had had difficulty before even imagining himself living anywhere but his home village and said he would rather die than leave, now had left to work elsewhere. Following these lives enables us to search out the social dynamics of their personal transformation. Communication by bus transportation, radio, and movies helped break down the village isolation and put it in constant touch with other ways of thinking and doing. Other factors in Balgat's modernization were modern technology represented by tractors, electricity, mass-produced goods; a new economic nexus organized around nonagricultural jobs and cash; and a newly emergent national government. The "city" was "a factor" in that most of the items just noted related to Balgat's becoming more involved with the nearby city of Ankara. In effect we have specified some of the ways in which the "city" contributes to modernization. However, Lerner's major emphasis is on personal rather than social modernization. The "before" and "after" glimpses of individual Balgat residents provide a poignant picture of the personal adjustment to and costs of social modernization. The chief, whose position as chief will shortly be abolished in the administrative absorption of Balgat into the city of Ankara—and whose sons, despite their filial piety, are modern in outlook and occupation—emerges as a personal embodiment of the old order giving way to the new.

The case histories presented by Charhadi and by Mayhew are negative confirmations of Inkeles' description of "modern man." In both cases the city experience had limited impact in "modernizing" these urban residents of contemporary Morocco and Victorian London. The key obstacle appears to have been lack of education, the factor Inkeles indicated as the most important in leading to modernization of attitudes. The unschooled Victorian coster-lad (street peddler) and the illiterate Moroccan baker's helper have minimal learning and skills; without these the city is a place of all-encompassing poverty and disillusion. By preserving the coster-boy's words—grammar, accent, and all—Mayhew has given us a document which, despite its brevity, tells us a great deal about the boy's life. Although the story of the Moroccan baker's helper is called a novel, the fact that the author is an illiterate servant of limited experience (the narrative was tape-recorded) suggests it is safe to assume the story is based on autobiography and on observation of the urban life immediately around him. The main change wrought by the city on these young men is the development of an animal shrewdness for survival in the "urban jungle." It should be pointed out that although these young men are not "modern" neither are they "traditional." Their overriding poverty prevented them from being fully absorbed into and expressive of either rural-agricultural or urban-industrial attitudes and beliefs. The numbers of such people are legion in overpopulated, underdeveloped areas where many people in cities and on farms are marginally employed, and even in the affluent United States where discrimination and lack of skills debar many Negroes from full participation in the larger society. One cannot generalize on the basis of two case histories but these two young men serve to remind us that attitudinal modernization is not automatically associated with urban residence.

In the economically advanced parts of the world where metropolitan development is prominent the social-psychological question which has generated most discussion is whether there are distinctive suburban psychological characteristics. Joseph Zelan's "Does Suburbia Make a Difference: An Exercise in Secondary Analysis" investigates one aspect of this question: the assertion that suburban residence fosters anti-intellectual attitudes. Zelan's study is noteworthy because it is an empirical study in a field more marked by polemics and value judgments than by gathering of facts, and also because the empirical method chosen—secondary analysis—involves reanalyzing data gathered for other purposes. Zelan's data included questionnaire response from over 33,000 college seniors graduating in 1961 from 135 colleges in the United States. In evaluating and generalizing from Zelan's results it is necessary to keep in mind the group he studied and the questionnaire items by which anti-intellectualism was defined.

Zelan's initial comparisons showed no significant differences in intellectual attitudes between those college seniors who had been raised in cities and those who had been raised in suburbs. Zelan's further analysis showed that there *is* a relationship between suburban residence and anti-intellectualism but it is more complex than commonly supposed. When the items measuring anti-intellectualism (Culture Index) were cross-tabulated with the kind of communities students said they *wished* to live in (Community of Orientation) rather than by the communities the students had grown up in (Community of Origin) then the suburb-oriented students differed significantly from the urban-oriented students in anti-intellectualism. That is, those "who indicated a *desire* to live in the suburbs were less likely to be concerned with access to cultural activities and less likely to think of themselves as intellectuals."

The final analysis suggests that anti-intellectualism in suburbia is partly a result of family-cycle (more married students prefer suburbs and they are likely to have less time for intellectual activities), partly a result of selectivity (the students expressing a preference for suburban living are more anti-intellectual), and partly a result of the influence of community of origin (regardless of their marital status and intellectual attitudes, students who were brought up in suburbs more often expressed a desire to live in suburbs than those who had been raised in the city). Extrapolation from these student preferences indicates suburbia *is* different; but the extent and dynamics of the difference remain open for further study.

To this point we have been describing the city in terms of its psychological impact on the individual. In Section B we examine the city itself as a psychological product—that is, the city as the projection of man's beliefs, hopes, and fears. Some of this projective quality has already been evident in Zelan's description of the traits attributed to suburbia. The articles in this section introduce the organized body of projections on the city; that is, the ideology of the city. Ideology is not only a social-psychological product but has further social-psychological consequences; one of the truisms of sociology is that what we define as real has socially real consequences. Thus, if we believe the city has certain characteristics or effects we tend to act in terms of these beliefs. Obviously this complicates the analysis of the dynamics of urban ideology, for the ideology has the potential for validating itself.

According to Carl Schorske's "The Idea of the City in European Thought: Voltaire to Spengler," there have been three major ideological orientations toward the European city in the past two hundred years. The earliest of these, "the city as virtue," was associated with the Enlightenment philosophy of the eighteenth century. "The city as vice" was associated with the emerging industrialism of the early nineteenth century. Thereafter the city was viewed as a subjective phenomenon beyond good and evil. Schorske's presentation suggests that the ideological evaluation of the city reflected both broad philosophical and aesthetic trends and the misery and disruption attending the transition from agriculturalism to industrialism.

For the Enlightenment period Schorske documents his presentation with the views of the city expressed in the works of Voltaire, Adam Smith, and Fichte; to these men the city was the habitat of civilization. In the early nineteenth century the idea of the city as vice was reflected in various ways in the works of the French Physiocrats, the romantic poets, and many writers and intellectuals such as Fourier, Ruskin, Karl Marx, and Engels. Some, the archaists as Schorske calls them, wanted to abandon the wickedness and squalor of the city and return to the simple rural life. Others, the futurists, wanted to reform the ugly, evil city. But by 1850 the new current of subjectivism in European thought, which swept away hard-and-fast standards of morality, time, and aesthetics, again revalued the city. "As virtue and vice, progress and regression lost their clarity of meaning, the city was placed beyond Good and Evil." There were both positive and negative aspects in this view of the city. Baudelaire, Rilke, Le Gallienne, and other fatalists accepted the urban scene as given but "redeemed it daily by revealing the beauty in urban degradation itself." When a fatalist acceptance was merged with a negative view of the city, as in the theories of Oswald Spengler or the policies of the German National Socialists, they brought "the vices of the city to an undreamt-of fulfillment."

Elwin H. Powell's "The Evolution of the American City and the Emergence of Anomie" is concerned with ideology in a much different way than Schorske. Powell does not deal with ideological views of the city, but with the ideology represented in the physical and social organization of the city. Thus, Powell deals with the values reflected in the urban power structure, the division of wealth and class stratification, agencies of social control, and ecological patterns. Applying this approach to data for Buffalo from 1810 to 1910 Powell concludes that this nineteenth-century American city, probably representative of American cities of that era, was dominated by values of laissez-faire capitalism.

The significance of this conclusion lies not only in the delineation of the value base of these cities, but in Powell's linking it with the psychological effects on urbanites. According to Powell's data the city *per se* did not produce *anomie*, but unbridled capitalism did, for it left the workers isolated and unprotected. Personal disorganization then is not an inevitable result of urban life, but is produced in certain cultural contexts, in this instance those setting economic gain above other values.

In moving from nineteenth- to twentieth-century America the appropriate ideology to examine is that which has grown up around suburbia. Bennett M. Berger in "Suburbia and the American Dream" analyzes the "myth" of suburbia. The belief that the suburbs are homogeneous and hotbeds of conformity is a "myth," says Berger, for a number of studies have now demonstrated not only the variety of life styles in the suburbs but the tendency for these life styles to persist during suburban residence, or for the changes that do occur to result from factors other than suburban location. Berger's concern here is not so much to demolish the myth but to explain its relation to still deeper ideological currents. In so doing Berger is attempting a functional analysis of the suburban myth and thus his approach to ideology differs from Schorske's philosophical survey and from Powell's historical focus.

According to Berger the belief that suburbs are homogeneous operates to sustain a belief in the "American dream"—equals cooperating in a democratic society. The American dream is undermined by the realities of long-standing economic and ethnic differentiation and by our fundamental ambivalence toward melting-pot as opposed to pluralist courses. In view of the flaws in the American dream it becomes important to reaffirm it in the major new setting of American life—the suburbs. Thus, the myth of a homogeneous, classless suburbia persists.

The suburbs are not homogeneous or classless but the myth has real social consequences. Intellectuals are anti-suburbia because suburbs breed stifling uniformity and frantic togetherness. Knowledge is not necessarily an antidote against the myth. Berger admits that even he cannot rid himself of what he knows is an unreasonable antipathy against suburban living. His analysis of the myth of suburbia concludes that the root problem is our irresolution about the aims of the American dream and the values it exemplifies. He suggests that we squarely face the value conflict between the melting-pot and pluralist alternatives, particularly as they involve the physical planning and rebuilding of our cities.

The two final articles in Part IV provide us with some expressions of man-in-the-street views about the city. In "Listening to the Radio" Hortense Powdermaker presents some of the popular songs about the city, favorites among the native population of Copper Town in Rhodesia. Paul

Charosh presents the "home songs" of the United States, indicating there has been a less anti-urban attitude reflected in the more recent ones. By looking at the city in popular culture we feel the man-city relationship in a different way than through the poetry of Baudelaire or the systematic constructs of intellectuals.

The lyrics of the Rhodesian and American songs are clearly projective of attitudes—positive and negative—toward the city but they also help to shape the individual's attitudes and adjustment to the city. Thus, Powdermaker notes "The songs offered advice to urban young men faced with alternatives and gave them the comfort of knowing that their temptations and problems were not unique." Many of the lyrics Charosh presents were warnings about the dangers of the city. The personal costs of social change are vividly portrayed—as in the case of the rural Rhodesian girl who cannot meet the expectations of her urban husband:

> And after only six days,
> He said he did not want me any more
> Because I had shamed him
> In the presence of his people.

Poverty is often the reason for personal maladjustment in the city, as in the many songs Charosh cites detailing the plight of "fallen women":

> She sought for employment, but none could be found,
> She gave up at last in despair.
> She fell by the wayside, as others before her,
> Who came to the city where all is so bright.

These themes echo, on the common-man level, some of those discussed previously in Part IV.

The most important aspect of these articles, however, is that they deal with the symbolic character of the city as presented in the mass media. The potential for formation and dissemination of urban image-making enters a new era with the mass media. Listening to the radio was a recent experience to the Rhodesians and there is some difficulty in adjusting former personal, oral communication modes to this new method. Most significant, however, is that many of the urban symbols presented in the Rhodesian songs are incomplete or garbled versions of European or American views or practices. This is especially noticeable in the song "We are the smart men about town." What will be the character and effect of the urban ideology carried by the mass media as urbanization spreads throughout the world? Will it raise false hopes, provide a forum for demagoguery, or foster new ideals?

A | The Individual
and the City

31 | The Modernization of Man

ALEX INKELES

The main purpose of economic development is to permit the achievement of a decent level of living for all the people. But almost no one will
argue that the progress of a nation and a people should be measured solely
by reference to gross national product and per capita income. Development encompasses the idea of political maturation as well, as expressed in
stable and orderly processes of government resting on the expressed will of
the people. And it also includes the attainment of popular education, the
burgeoning of the arts, the efflorescence of architecture, the growth of
the means of communication, and the enrichment of leisure. Indeed, in
the end, the idea of development requires the very transformation of the
nature of man—a transformation that is both a *means* to the end of yet
greater growth and at the same time one of the great *ends* itself of the
development process.

But what is the modern man, and what makes him what he is? The
answer to this question is inevitably controversial, and almost no one enters
on a discussion of it without arousing a good deal of emotion. The reasons
are not hard to find. In the first place, the change from more traditional
to more modern qualities in man often means someone must give up
ways of thinking and feeling that go back decades, sometimes centuries;
and to abandon these ways often seems to be abandoning principle itself.
For another thing, the qualities that make a man modern often do not
appear to be neutral characteristics that any man might have, but instead
represent the distinctive traits of the European, the American, or the
Westerner that he is bent on imposing on other people so as to make them

SOURCE: Myron Weiner, ed., *Modernization* (New York: Basic Books, Inc.,
1966), pp. 138–150. Copyright © 1966 by Basic Books Inc., Publishers, New
York. Reprinted by permission of the publisher.

over in his own image. In the third place, many of the characteristics that are described as modern, and therefore automatically desirable, in fact are not very useful or suitable to the life and conditions of those on whom they are urged or even imposed. These are most serious issues, and we shall return to them briefly after sketching some details of what we mean by modern man.

The characteristic mark of the modern man has two parts: one internal, the other external; one dealing with his environment, the other with his attitudes, values, and feelings.

The change in the external condition of modern man is well known and widely documented, and it need not detain us long. It may be summarized by reference to a series of key terms: urbanization, education, mass communication, industrialization, politicalization. These terms signify that in contrast to his forebears living in the traditional order of his society, the modern man is less likely to work the land as a farmer and is more likely to be employed in a large and complex productive enterprise based on the intensive use of power and advanced technologies. The various economies yielded by the concentration of industry in certain sites and the further demands of those industrial concentrations make it likely that the contemporary man will live in a city or some other form of urban conglomeration. Here, he will experience not only crowding but access to all manner of resource and stimulation characteristic of urban life. Inevitably, one of these stimuli will be the media of mass communication: newspapers, radio, movies, and perhaps even television. His experience of new places and ideas will be augmented by the impact of schooling, if not directly for him, then for his children, who may carry the influence of the school into the home. He is much more likely to have some connection with politics, especially on the national scale, as he is more exposed to mass communication, more mobilized in the surge of urban life, more courted by the competing political movements that seek his support as he may enlist their aid to replace that of the chief, the patron, or the family head whose assistance he would ordinarily have sought in his native village. Indeed, another mark of the contemporary man is that he will no longer live enmeshed in a network of primary kin ties, perhaps supplemented by ties to a small number of fellow villagers, but rather will be drawn into a much more impersonal and bureaucratic milieu in which he is dependent for services and aid in times of distress on persons and agencies with which he has a much more formal and perhaps tenuous relationship.

These are all attributes of his life space that may impinge on the modern man, but in themselves they do not constitute modernity. The densest urban centers may still shelter the most traditional network of human relations; the media of mass communication may mainly disseminate folk ideas and traditional wisdom, factories may run on principles not far different from those of the estate or the hacienda, and politics may be conducted like an extension of the village council. Although his exposure to the modern setting may certainly contribute to the transformation of traditional man, and although that setting may in turn require new ways of him, it is only when man has undergone a change in spirit—has acquired certain new ways of thinking, feeling, and acting—that we come to consider him truly modern.

Although there is no single standard definition of the modern man that all accept and use, there is quite good agreement among students of the modernization process as to the characteristics that distinguish the more modern man from the more traditional. To convey my impression of his traits, I have chosen to describe him in terms of a series of attitudes and values that we are testing in a study of the modernization process among workers and peasants in six developing countries. This permits me not only to present the characteristic profile we define as modern but also to indicate some of the questions we are using to study its manifestation in concrete cases. The order in which these characteristics are presented here is not meant to suggest that this is the actual sequence in the process of individual modernization. So far, we are not aware that there is a clear-cut sequence, but rather have the impression that the process develops on a broad front with many changes occurring at once. Neither does the order in which the characteristics are given suggest the relative weight or importance of each characteristic in the total syndrome. Here, again, we have yet, through our scientific work, to assess the relative contribution of each characteristic to the larger complex of attitudes, values, and ways of acting that we consider modern. We do, however, assume that this complex of attitudes and values holds together: that in the statistical sense it constitutes a factor, and a relatively coherent factor. In time, our scientific evidence will show whether or not this is a reasonable assumption.

The first element in our definition of the modern man is his readiness for new experience and his openness to innovation and change. We consider the traditional man to be less disposed to accept new ideas, new ways of feeling and acting. We are speaking, therefore, of something that is itself a state of mind, a psychological disposition, an inner readiness, rather than of the specific techniques or skills a man or a group may possess because of the level of technology they have attained. Thus, in our sense, a man may be more modern in spirit, even though he works with a wooden plow, than someone in another part of the world who already drives a tractor. The readiness for new experience and ways of doing things, furthermore, may express itself in a variety of forms and contexts: in the willingness to adopt a new drug or sanitation method, to accept a new seed or try a different fertilizer, to ride on a new means of transportation or turn to a new source of news, to approve a new form of wedding or new type of schooling for young people. Individuals and groups may, of course, show more readiness for the new in one area of life than another, but we can also conceive of the readiness to accept innovation as a more pervasive, general characteristic that makes itself felt across a wide variety of human situations. And we consider those who have this readiness to be more modern.

The second in our complex of themes takes us into the realm of opinion. We define a man as more modern if he has a disposition to form or hold opinions over a large number of the problems and issues that arise not only in his immediate environment but also outside of it. Some pioneering work on this dimension has been done by Daniel Lerner,[1] of the Massachusetts Institute of Technology, who found that the individuals within any country, and the populations of different countries, in the Middle East varied greatly in their ability or readiness to imagine themselves in the position of prime minister or comparable government leader and thus to offer advice as to what should be done to resolve the problems facing the country. The more educated the individual and the more advanced the country, the greater was the readiness to offer opinions in response to this challenge. The more traditional man, we believe, takes an interest in fewer things, mainly those that touch him immediately and intimately; and even when he holds opinions on more distant matters, he is more circumspect in expressing them.

We also consider a man to be more modern if his orientation to the opinion realm is more democratic. We mean by this that he shows more awareness of the diversity of attitude and opinion around him, rather than closing himself off in the belief that everyone thinks alike and, indeed, just like him. The modern man is able to acknowledge differences of opinion without needing rigidly to deny differences out of fear that these will upset his own view of the world. He is also less likely to approach opinion in a strictly autocratic or hierarchical way. He does not automatically accept the ideas of those above him in the power hierarchy and reject the opinions of those whose status is markedly lower than his. We test these values by asking people whether it is proper to think differently from the village headman or other traditional leader and, at the other end, by inquiring as to whether the opinions of a man's wife or young son merit serious consideration when important public issues are being discussed. These questions prove to be a sensitive indicator in helping us to distinguish one man from another and, we believe, will be an important element in the final syndrome of modernity we shall delineate.

A third theme we deal with at some length is that of time. We view a man as more modern if he is oriented to the present or the future, rather than to the past. We consider him as more modern if he accepts fixed hours, that is to say, schedules of time, as something sensible and appropriate, or possibly even desirable, as against the man who thinks these fixed rules are something either bad or perhaps a necessity, but unfortunately also a pity. We also define a man as more modern if he is punctual, regular, and

---

[1]Daniel Lerner, *The Passing of Traditional Society* (Glencoe, Ill.: The Free Press, 1958).

orderly in organizing his affairs. These things can be very complicated, and this is a good opportunity to point out that it is a mistake to assume that our measures of modernity differentiate between traditional and non-traditional people as they would ordinarily be defined. For example, the Maya Indians had a better sense of time than their Spanish conquerors, and they preserve it to this day. The qualities we define as modern can, in fact, be manifested in a people who seem to be relatively unmodern when you consider the level of technology or the amount of power they have. We are talking about properties of the person, which in turn may be a reflection of the properties of a culture that could emerge in any time or place. Indeed, when I described this list to a friend of mine who is doing an extensive study of Greece, he said, "My goodness, you are talking about the ancient Greeks!" He said there were only two respects in which the Greeks did not fit our model of the modern man. And, of course, the Elizabethan Englishman would also fit the model. So, this concept is not limited to our time. "Modern" does not mean merely contemporary in our approach.

A fourth theme that we include in the definition is planning. The more modern man is oriented toward and involved in planning and organizing and believes in it as a way of handling life.

A fifth, and important, theme we call efficacy. The modern man is the one who believes that man can learn, in substantial degree, to dominate his environment in order to advance his own purposes and goals, rather than being dominated entirely by that environment. For example, a man who believes in efficacy is more likely to respond positively to the question, "Do you believe that some day men may be able to develop ways of controlling floods or preventing destructive storms?" The more efficacious man, even though in fact he has never seen a dam, would say, "Yes, I think that some day man could do that."

Sixth, an element we consider part of the modern complex and include in our set of themes is calculability. By our definition, the modern man is one who has more confidence that his world is calculable, that other people and institutions around him can be relied on to fulfill or meet their obligations and responsibilities. He does not agree that everything is determined either by fate or by the whims of particular qualities and characters of men. In other words, he believes in a reasonably lawful world under human control.

The seventh theme that we stress is dignity. The more modern man, we feel, is one who has more awareness of the dignity of others and more disposition to show respect for them. We feel this comes through very clearly in attitudes toward women and children.

The modern man has more faith in science and technology, even if in a fairly primitive way. This provides our eighth theme.

Ninth, we hold that modern man is a great believer in what we call, for this purpose, distributive justice. That is to say, he believes that rewards should be according to contribution, and not according to either whim or special properties of the person not related to his contribution.

You could easily extend this list; you could also divide some of these items into still others; but I think this will serve to give an idea of the complex of attitudes and values that we consider important in defining the modern man. We have chosen to emphasize these themes because we see them as intimately related to the individual's successful adjustment as a citizen of a modern industrial nation. They are qualities that we feel will contribute to making a man a more productive worker in his factory, a more effective citizen in his community, a more satisfied and satisfying husband and father in his home.

We must, of course, acknowledge that the nine themes just described are not the only way to approach the definition of modernity. Although we have stressed certain themes that cut across numerous concrete realms of behavior, some students of the problem prefer to emphasize attitudes and behavior relating mainly to certain important institutional realms, such as birth control or religion. Their position is certainly reasonable, and in the research we are conducting at the Harvard Center for International Affairs, we have therefore included questions on such themes as restrictions on family size; treatment of older people and obligations to one's parents and relatives; the importance of social change; the role of women, especially the rights of women; how to bring up a child; attitudes toward religion; attitudes toward the consumption of material and physical goods; social and political problems of the community, the nation, and the international realm; educational and social aspirations, including aspirations for social mobility; and contact with media of mass communication. For each of these realms, one can define a position that can be considered more modern and an attitude one can define as more traditional, although at times the process of definition becomes very complex.

There is, for example, a very widespread notion that people lose their religion merely because they leave the countryside and go to the city. As a matter of fact, exactly the contrary is very often the case. There are two forces that bring this about. In the first place, really to practice your religion well, you must be a reasonably well-composed, well-contained individual. The person who is emotionally disturbed neglects his social obligations and involvements. Despite the idyllic image that many people have of the countryside, the great majority of the world's peasants are in a state of culture shock produced not by modernity but by the hard conditions of rural life. When a man goes to the city, and especially if he secures a job in industry, he comes to have much more respect and become much more self-controlled. This makes it more feasible for him to practice his religion. He turns to things that he previously neglected in his effort just to hold himself together. He reintegrates himself, if you like, with the formal things around him, one of which is his religion.

The second factor that may contribute to facilitate religious practice in the city is economic. To practice your religion generally costs something. For example, you may have to buy candles. If there is a religious ceremony, usually the religious specialist who performs the ceremony must be given some kind of payment. Something is required of you. If you are living a sufficiently marginal existence as a peasant, this may be one of the costs you forgo. When you get to the city and earn a more stable and steady income, you may be more willing to underwrite these costs. So, on this issue we are actually taking a rather unorthodox position and predicting that our city workers are going to be more rather than less religious, if not in spirit at least in terms of performing their formal religious obligations.

So much for our conception of the qualities that make a man modern. What can we say about the forces that produce such a man, that most rapidly and effectively inculcate in a population those attitudes, values, needs, and ways of acting that better fit him for life in a modern society? Just as modernity seems to be defined not by any one characteristic, but by a complex of traits, so we find that no one social force, but rather a whole complex of influences, contributes to the transformation from traditional to modern man.

Within this complex of forces, however, one certainly assumes pre-eminence: namely, education. Almost all serious scientific investigations of the question have shown the individual's degree of modernity to rise with increases in the amount of education he has received. Some reservations must be introduced, of course, to qualify this statement. In many countries, the weakness of the nation's resources permits schooling to be only of very poor quality, and the pressures on the poorer people force the children to be quite irregular in their attendance. In a number of countries, it has been observed that if children can obtain only two or three years of schooling, and especially if they do so under conditions where their environment does not particularly reinforce or support the school, there the effects of education on modernization will be very modest indeed. Similarly, the degree of traditionalism of the school itself plays some role. Little or no change toward modernity is evident in the more traditional schools that devote themselves mainly to passing on religious practices or to inculcating and preserving traditional lore and skills. This is a characteristic of schools not only at the primary level; it may apply to those offering nominally advanced education. The "finishing" schools for young ladies from polite society in the United States may be taken as an example. Allowing for reservations of this sort, we may still say that education, especially in schools emphasizing the more modern type of curriculum, seems to be the most powerful factor in developing a population more modern in its attitudes and values. This effect depends in part on the direct instruction provided, but we assume as well that the school as a social organization serves as a model of rationality, of the importance of technical competence, of the rule of objective standards of performance, and of the principle of distributive justice reflected in the grading system. All these models can contribute to shaping young people in the image of the modern man as we have described him.

There is little agreement as to the rank order of influences other than education that we see affecting the degree of modernization of individuals. Many analysts of the problem propose the urban environment as the next most important input. The city is itself a powerful new experience. It encourages, and indeed to some degree obliges, the individual to adopt many new ways of life. By exposing men to a variety of ways of living, a wide range of opinions and ideas, increased mobility, more complex resources of all kinds, it accelerates the process of change. At the same time, in the city the prospect is greater that the individual will be relatively free from the obligations and constraints placed on him in the village by his extended kinship ties, the village elders, and the tight community of his neighbors. These structural differences free the individual to change; but, of course, they do not in themselves guarantee that he will change in ways that make him more modern. In many cities, there are powerful examples of rationality, of the use of technology to master the physical demands of life, of rewards adjusted to technical skill and competence, of the value of education, and of the guarantee of human dignity under law. But many great cities also provide powerful lessons that run counter to these modernizing influences on every score. If they breed a new type of man, they hardly make him in the image we have called modern. In addition, under conditions of very rapid growth, the city is often unable to absorb and integrate all the in-migrants, so that on the outer edges or in the older districts of the city, huge slum communities may develop in which people are in the city but not of it, cut off from many of its benefits and from the modernizing influence of urban life.

One source of modernization which generally accompanies urbanization but is also an independent influence is mass communication. Almost all studies of the growth of individual modernization show that those who are more exposed to the media of mass communication have more modern attitudes. Since such exposure, especially in the case of the newspaper, depends on literacy and education, it is important to stress that the modernization effects of the mass media can be shown to exert their influence within groups at almost any educational level. Of course, there remains the possibility that it is the man with modern attitudes who seeks out the mass media, rather than that the media make the man modern, but there seems little reason to doubt that the influence is at least mutual. These media greatly enlarge the range of human experience with which the individual can have contact, even if only vicarious. They constantly present and illustrate new tools, items of consumption, means of transportation, and a myriad of new ways of doing things. They show examples of efficacious behavior of the most powerful kind in the building of dams, the taming of floods, the irrigation of deserts, and even the conquest of space. They also provide models of new values and standards of behavior, some of which are far beyond the reach of most men, but many of which can be copied and do influence behavior directly. As in the case of urban influences, we must acknowledge that the media of communication can and often do carry messages that mainly reaffirm traditional values, beliefs, and ways of acting or disseminate a concept of the new that is nevertheless not congruent with the model of the modern man here described.

Another source of modernizing influence is the development of the national state and its associated apparatus of government bureaucracy, political parties and campaigns, military and paramilitary units, and the like. The more mobilized the society, the more dedicated the government to economic development and spreading the ideology of progress, the more rapidly and widely may we expect the attitudes and values of modernity to expand. Some of the agencies of the state—in particular, the army—may play an especially important role in introducing men to the modern world, both in the direct instruction they offer and indirectly in the model of routine, scheduling, technical skill, and efficacy that inheres in many of their operations. Here again, however, we must acknowledge that the power of the state may also be used to reinforce more traditional values: politics may be conducted in a way that hardly sets an example of modern behavior, and armies may be run so as scarcely to induce a man to exert himself, to practice initiative, or to respect the dignity of others.

One last source of modernizing influence that we may cite—one that holds a central place in the research we have been conducting at Harvard— is the factory or other modern productive and administrative enterprise. Certain features of the modern factory are relatively invariant, and they communicate the same message, no matter what the cultural setting in which they may be installed. In them there is always an intense concentration of physical and mechanical power brought to bear on the transformation of raw materials; orderly and routine procedures to govern the flow of work are essential; time is a powerful influence in guiding the work process; power and authority generally rest on technical competence; and, as a rule, rewards are in rough proportion to performance. In addition, a factory guided by modern management and personnel policies will set its workers an example of rational behavior, emotional balance, open communication, and respect for the opinions, the feelings, and the dignity of the worker which can be a powerful example of the principles and practice of modern living.

In modern times we are experiencing a process of change affecting everything, yet controlled by no one. It is, in a sense, strictly spontaneous; yet it is in some ways the most strictly determined process history has yet known. Since no one can escape it, no one may be unconcerned with it. Man himself is being transformed. Many evils are being erased, but no end of new forms of corruption and wickedness may be loosed in the world. Some people in backward countries are ready to believe that any change is for the good. Others feel that much they now have is superior to what is being offered, and they are deeply convinced that many of the changes the contemporary world is introducing into their lives are no improvement, while others are positively disastrous. I have pointed to a set of qualities of mind that I call modern, which I believe have much to recommend them. They are not compatible in all respects with qualities that are widespread in traditional cultures, but I believe they are qualities men can adopt without coming into conflict, in most cases, with what is best in their cultural tradition and spiritual heritage. I believe they represent some of the best things in the modernization process. But whether we view them as positive or negative, we must recognize these qualities that are fostered by modern institutions, qualities that in many ways are required of the citizens of modern societies. We must, therefore, come to recognize them, to understand them, and to evaluate them as important issues in contemporary life.

32 | The Grocer and The Chief: A Parable

DANIEL LERNER

The village of Balgat lies about eight kilometers out of Ankara, in the southerly direction. It does not show on the standard maps and it does not figure in the standard histories. I first heard of it in the autumn of 1950 and most Turks have not heard of it today. Yet the story of the Middle East today is encapsulated in the recent career of Balgat. Indeed the personal meaning of modernization in underdeveloped lands can be traced, in miniature, through the lives of two Balgati—The Grocer and The Chief.

My first exposure to Balgat came while leafing through several hundred interviews that had been recorded in Turkey during the spring of 1950. One group caught my eye because of the underlying tone of bitterness in the interviewer's summary of the village, his earnest sense of the hopelessness of place and people. These five interviews in Balgat were moving; even so, something in the perspective seemed awry. For one thing, the interviewer was more highly sensitized to what he saw than what he heard. The import of what had been said to him, and duly recorded in his reports, had somehow escaped his attention. I, having only the words to go by, was struck by the disjunction between the reported face and the recorded voice of Balgat.

SOURCE: Daniel Lerner, *The Passing of Traditional Society* (New York: The Macmillan Company, 1958), pp. 19-42. Reprinted with permission of The Macmillan Company. Copyright © The Free Press, a Corporation 1958.

For another thing, the interviews had been made in the early spring and I was reading them in the late fall of 1950. Between these dates there had been a national election in which, as a stunning surprise to everybody including themselves, practically all qualified Turks had voted and the party in power—Atatürk's own *Halk* Party—been turned out of office.

Nothing like this had ever happened before in Turkey, possibly because neither universal suffrage nor an opposition party had ever been tried before. The dazed experts could only say of this epochal deed that the Anatolian villagers had done it. Since it would be hard to imagine Anatolian villagers of more standard pattern than the Balgati whose collected opinions were spread before me, I had it on top authority that during the summer they had entered History. But it was not immediately obvious by what route.

What clues existed were in a few words spoken by the villagers. These words we collated with the words that had been spoken to the interviewers by hundreds of villagers and townspeople throughout the Middle East. As we tabulated and cross-tabulated, a hunch emerged of what in Balgat spoke for many men, many deeds. Comparing cases by class and country we gradually enlarged our miniature into a panorama. Our hypothesis, heavy now with vivid details and many meanings, took shape. Four years later an oversize manuscript on the modernizing Middle East was in hand. To see how close a fit to Middle East reality was given by our picture of it, I went out for a self-guided tour and final round of interviews in the spring of 1954. My odyssey terminated where my ideas originated: in Balgat, on the eve of a second national election. With Balgat, then, our account begins.

Balgat Perceived: 1950

The interviewer who recorded Balgat on the verge—his name was Tosun B.—had detected no gleam of the future during his sojourn there. "The village is a barren one," he wrote. "The main color is gray, so is the dust on the divan on which I am writing now." Tosun was a serious young scholar from Ankara and he loved the poor in his own fashion. He had sought out Balgat to find the deadening past rather than the brave new world. He found it:

I have seen quite a lot of villages in the barren mountainous East, but never such a colorless, shapeless dump. This was the reason I chose the village. It could have been half an hour to Ankara by car if it had a road, yet it is about two hours to the capital by car without almost any road and is just forgotten, forsaken, right under our noses.

Tosun also sought and found persons to match the place. Of the five villagers he interviewed, his heart went straight out to the village shepherd.

What Tosun was looking for in this interview is clear from his *obiter dicta:*

It was hard to explain to the village Chief that I wanted to interview the poorest soul in the village. He, after long discussions, consented me to interview the shepherd, but did not permit him to step into the guest-room. He said it would be an insult to me, so we did the interview in someone else's room, I did not quite understand whose. The Chief did not want to leave me alone with the respondent, but I succeeded at the end. This opened the respondent's sealed mouth, for he probably felt that I, the superior even to his chief, rather be alone with him.

When the shepherd's sealed mouth had been opened, little came out. But Tosun was deeply stirred:

The respondent was literally in rags and in this cold weather he had no shoe, but the mud and dirt on his feet were as thick as any boot. He was small, but looked rugged and sad, very sad. He was proud of being chosen by me and though limited tried his best to answer the questions. Was so bashful that his blush was often evident under the thick layer of dirt on his face. He at times threw loud screams of laughter when there was nothing to laugh about. These he expected to be accepted as answers, for when I said "Well?" he was shocked, as if he had already answered the question.

His frustration over the shepherd was not the only deprivation Tosun attributed to the Chief, who "imposed himself on me all the time I was in the village, even tried to dictate to me, which I refused in a polite way. I couldn't have followed his directions as I would have ended up only interviewing his family." Tosun did succeed in talking privately with two Balgat farmers, but throughout these interviews he was still haunted by the shepherd and bedeviled by the Chief. Not until he came to interview the village Grocer did Tosun find another Balgati who aroused in him a comparable antipathy. Tosun's equal hostility to these very different men made me curious. It was trying to explain this that got me obsessed, sleeping and waking over the next four years, with the notion that the parable of modern Turkey was the story of The Grocer and The Chief.

Aside from resenting the containment strategy which the Chief was operating against him, Tosun gave few details about the man. He reported only the impression that "the *Muhtar* is an unpleasant old man. Looks mean and clever. He is the absolute dictator of this little village." Nor did Tosun elaborate his disapproval of the *Muhtar*'s opinions beyond the comment that "years have left him some sort of useless, mystic wisdom." As a young man of empirical temper, Tosun might be expected to respond with some diffidence to the wisdom of the ancients. But the main source of Tosun's hostility, it appeared, was that the Chief made him nervous. His notes concluded: "He found what I do curious, even probably suspected it. I am sure he will report it to the first official who comes to the village."

Against the Grocer, however, Tosun reversed his neural field. He quickly perceived that he made the Grocer nervous; and for this Tosun disliked *him*. His notes read:

The respondent is comparatively the most city-like dressed man in the village. He even wore some sort of a necktie. He is the village's only grocer, but he is not really a grocer, but so he is called, originally the food-stuffs in his shop are much less than the things to be worn, like the cheapest of materials and shoes and slippers etc. His greatest stock is drinks and cigarettes which he sells most. He is a very unimpressive type, although physically he covers quite a space. He gives the impression of a fat shadow. Although he is on the same level with the other villagers, when there are a few of the villagers around, he seems to want to distinguish himself by keeping quiet, and as soon as they depart he starts to talk too much. This happened when we were about to start the interview. He most evidently wished to feel that he is closer to me than he is to them and was curiously careful with his accent all during the interview. In spite of his unique position, for he is the only unfarming person and the only merchant in the village, he does not seem to possess an important part of the village community. In spite of all his efforts, he is considered by the villagers even less than the least farmer. Although he presented to take the interview naturally, he was nervous and also was proud to be interviewed although he tried to hide it.

All of this pushed up a weighty question: Why did the Chief make Tosun nervous and why did Tosun make the Grocer nervous? These three men, representing such different thoughtways and lifeways, were a test for each other. Looking for answers, I turned to the responses each had made to the 57 varieties of opinions called for by the standard questionnaire used in Tosun's interviews.

The Chief was a man of few words on many subjects. He dismissed most of the items on Tosun's schedule with a shrug or its audible equivalent. But he was also a man of many words on a few subjects—those having to do with the primary modes of human deportment. Only when the issues involved first principles of conduct did he consider the occasion appropriate for pronouncing judgment. Of the Chief it might be said, as Henry James said of George Eliot's salon style, *"Elle n'aborde que les grandes thèmes."*

The Chief has so little trouble with first principles because he desires to be, and usually is, a vibrant soundbox through which echo the traditional Turkish virtues. His themes are obedience, courage, loyalty—the classic values of the Ottoman Imperium reincarnate in the Atatürk Republic. For the daily round of village life these are adequate doctrine; and as the Chief has been outside of his village only to fight in two wars he has never found his austere code wanting. This congruence of biography with ideology explains the Chief's confidence in his own moral judgment and his short definition of a man. When asked what he wished for his two grown sons, for example, the Chief replied promptly: "I hope they will fight as bravely as we fought and know how to die as my generation did."

From this parochial fund of traditional virtues, the Chief drew equally his opinions of great men, nations, issues. The larger dramas of international *politique* he judged solely in terms of the courage and loyalty of the actors, invoking, to acknowledge their magnitude, the traditional rhetoric of aphorism. Generations of Anatolian *Muhtars* resonated as he pronounced his opinion of the British:

I heard that they have turned friends with us. But always stick to the old wisdom: "A good enemy is better than a bad friend." You cannot *rely* on them. Who has heard of a son being friends with his father's murderers?

With his life in Balgat, as with the Orphic wisdom that supplies its rationale, the Chief is contented. At 63 his desires have been quieted and his ambitions achieved. To Tosun's question on contentment he replied with another question:

What could be asked more? God has brought me to this mature age without much pain, has given me sons and daughters, has put me at the head of my village, and has given me strength of brain and body at this age. Thanks be to Him.

The Grocer is a very different style of man. Though born and bred in Balgat, he lives in a different world, an expansive world, populated more actively with imaginings and fantasies—hungering for whatever is different and unfamiliar. Where the Chief is contented, the Grocer is restless. To Tosun's probe, the Grocer replied staccato: "I have told you I want better things. I would have liked to have a bigger grocery shop in the city, have a nice house there, dress nice civilian clothes."

Where the Chief audits his life placidly, makes no comparisons, thanks God, the Grocer evaluates his history in a more complicated and other-involved fashion. He perceives his story as a drama of Self *versus* Village. He compares his virtue with others and finds them lacking: "I am not like the others here. They don't know any better. And when I tell them, they are angry and they say that I am ungrateful for what Allah has given me." The Grocer's struggle with Balgat was, in his script, no mere conflict of personalities. His was the lonely struggle of a single man to open the village mind. Clearly, from the readiness and consistency of his responses to most questions, he had brooded much over his role. He had a keen sense of the limits imposed by reality: "I am born a grocer and probably die that way. I have not the possibility in myself to get the things I want. They only bother me." But desire, once stirred, is not easily stilled.

Late in the interview, after each respondent had named the greatest problem facing the Turkish people, Tosun asked what he would do about this problem if he were the president of Turkey. Most responded by stolid silence—the traditional way of handling "projective questions" which require people to imagine themselves or things to be different from what they "really are." Some were shocked by the impropriety of the very question. "My God! How can you say such a thing?" gasped the shepherd. "How can I . . . I cannot . . . a poor villager . . . master of the whole world."

The Chief, Balgat's virtuoso of the traditional style, made laconic reply to this question with another question: "I am hardly able to manage a village, how shall I manage Turkey?" When Tosun probed further ("What would you suggest for *your village* that you cannot handle yourself?"), the Chief said he would seek "help of money and seed for some of our farmers." When the Grocer's turn came, he did not wait for the question to be circumscribed in terms of local reference. As president of Turkey, he said: "I would make roads for the villagers to come to towns to see the world and would not let them stay in their holes all their life."

To get out of his hole the Grocer even declared himself ready—and in this he was quite alone in Balgat—to live outside of Turkey. This came out when Tosun asked another of his projective questions: "If you could not live in Turkey, where would you want to live?" The standard reply of the villagers was that they would not live, could not imagine living, anywhere else. The forced choice simply was ignored.

When Tosun persisted ("Suppose you *had* to leave Turkey?") he teased an extreme reaction out of some Balgati. The shepherd, like several other wholly routinized personalities, finally replied that he would rather kill himself. The constricted peasant can more easily imagine destroying the self than relocating it in an unknown, i.e. frightful, setting.

The Chief again responded with the clear and confident voice of traditional man. "Nowhere," he said. "I was born here, grew old here, and hope God will permit me to die here." To Tosun's probe, the Chief replied firmly: "I wouldn't move a foot from here." Only the Grocer found no trouble in imagining himself outside of Turkey, living in a strange land. Indeed he seemed fully prepared, as a man does when he has already posed a question to himself many times. "America," said the Grocer, and, without waiting for Tosun to ask him why, stated his reason: "because I have heard that it is a nice country, and with possibilities to be rich even for the simplest persons."

Such opinions clearly marked off the Grocer, in the eyes of the villagers around him, as heterodox and probably infidel. The vivid sense of cash displayed by the Grocer was a grievous offense against Balgat ideas of tabu talk. In the code regulating the flow of symbols among Anatolian villagers, blood and sex are permissible objects of passion but money is not. To talk much of money is an impropriety. To reveal excessive *desire* for money is —Allah defend us!—an impiety.

Balgati might forgive the Grocer his propensity to seek the strange rather than reverse the familiar, even his readiness to forsake Turkey for unknown places, had he decently clothed these impious desires in pious terms. But to abandon Balgat for the world's fleshpots, to forsake the ways of God to seek the ways of cash, this was insanity. The demented person who spoke thus was surely accursed and unclean.

The Grocer, with his "city-dressed" ways, his "eye at the higher places" and his visits to Ankara, provoked the Balgati to wrathful and indignant restatements of the old code. But occasional, and apparently trivial, items in the survey suggested that some Balgati were talking loud about the Grocer to keep their own inner voices from being overheard by the Chief— or even by themselves.

As we were interested in knowing who says what to whom in such a village as Balgat, Tosun had been instructed to ask each person whether others ever came to him for advice, and if so what they wanted advice about. Naturally, the Balgati whose advice was most sought was the chief, who reported: "Yes, that is my main duty, to give advice. (Tosun: *What about?*) About all that I or you could imagine, even about their wives and how to handle them, and how to cure their sick cow." This conjunction of wives and cows, to illustrate all the Chief could imagine, runs the gamut only from A to B. These are the species that the villager has most to do with in his daily round of life, the recurrent source of his pains and pleasures and puzzlements. The oral literature abounds in examples of *Muhtar* (or his theological counterpart, the *Hoca*) as wise man dispensing judgment equally about women and cows.

Rather more surprising was Tosun's discovery that some Balgati went for advice also to the disreputable Grocer. What did they ask *his* advice about? "What to do when they go to Ankara, where to go and what to buy, how much to sell their things." The cash nexus, this suggested, was somehow coming to Balgat and with it, possibly, a new role for the Grocer as cosmopolitan specialist in how to avoid wooden nickles in the big city. Also, how to spend the real nickels one got. For the Grocer was a man of clear convictions on which coffee-houses played the best radio programs and which were the best movies to see in Ankara. While his opinions on these matters were heterodox as compared, say, to the Chief's, they had an open field to work in. Most Balgati had never heard a radio or seen a movie and were not aware of what constituted orthodoxy with respect to them. Extremists had nonetheless decided that these things, being new, were obviously evil. Some of them considered the radio to be "the voice of The Devil coming from his deep hiding-place" and said they would smash any such "Devil's-box" on sight.

At the time of Tosun's visit, there was only one radio in Balgat, owned by no less a personage than the Chief. In the absence of any explicit orthodox prohibition on radio, the Chief, former soldier and great admirer of Atatürk, had followed his lead. Prosperous by village standards, being the large landowner of Balgat, he had bought a radio to please and instruct his sons. He had also devised an appropriate ceremonial for its use. Each evening a select group of Balgati foregathered in the Chief's guest room as he turned on the newscast from Ankara. They heard the newscast through in silence and, at its conclusion, the Chief turned the radio off and made his commentary. "We all listen very carefully," he told Tosun, "and I talk about it afterwards." Tosun, suspecting in this procedure a variant of the

Chief's containment tactics, wanted to know whether there was any disagreement over his explanations. "No, no arguments," replied the Chief,
"as I tell you I only talk and our opinions are the same more or less."
Here was a new twist in the ancient role of knowledge as power. Sensing the
potential challenge from radio, the Chief restricted the dangers of innovation by partial incorporation, thus retaining and strengthening his role as
Balgat's official opinion leader.

Tosun inquired of the Grocer, an occasional attendant in the Chief's
salon, how he liked this style of radio session. The grocer, a heretic perhaps but not a foolhardy one, made on this point the shortest statement
in his entire interview: "The Chief is clever and he explains the news."
Only obliquely, by asking what the Grocer liked best about radio, did
Tosun get an answer that had the true resonance. Without challenging the
Chief's preference for news of "wars and the danger of wars"—in fact an
exclusive interest in the Korean War, to which a Turkish brigade had just
been committed—the Grocer indicated that after all *he* had opportunities
to listen in the coffee-houses of Ankara, where the audiences exhibited a
more cosmopolitan range of interests. "It is nice to know what is happening in the other capitals of the world," said the Grocer. "We are stuck in
this hole, we have to know what is going on outside our village."

The Grocer had his own aesthetic of the movies as well. Whereas the
Chief had been to the movies several times, he viewed them mainly as a
moral prophylactic: "There are fights, shooting. The people are brave. My
sons are always impressed. Each time they see such a film they wish more
and more their time for military service would come so that they would
become soldiers too." For the Grocer, movies were more than a homily on
familiar themes. They were his avenue to the wider world of his dreams. It
was in a movie that he had first glimpsed what a *real* grocery store could be
like—"with walls made of iron sheets, top to floor and side to side, and on
them standing myriads of round boxes, clean and all the same dressed,
like soldiers in a great parade." This fleeting glimpse of what sounds like
the Campbell Soup section of an A & P supermarket had provided the
Grocer with an abiding image of how his fantasy world might look. It was
here, quite likely, that he had shaped the ambition earlier confided to Tosun
"to have a bigger grocery shop in the city." No pedantries intervened in
the Grocer's full sensory relationship to the movies. No eye had he, like
the Chief, for their value as filial moral rearmament and call to duty. The
Grocer's judgments were formed in unabashedly hedonist categories. "The
Turkish ones," he said, "are gloomy, ordinary. I can guess at the start of
the film how it will end. . . . The American ones are exciting. You know
it makes people ask what will happen next?"

Here, precisely, arose the local variant of the classic question. In Balgat,
the Chief carried the sword, but did the Grocer steer the pen? When
Balgati sought his advice on how to get around Ankara, would they then
go to movies that taught virtue or those that taught excitement? True, few

villagers had ever been to Ankara. But things were changing in Turkey and many more Balgati were sure to have a turn or two around the big city before they died. What would happen next in Balgat if more people discovered the tingle of wondering what will happen next? Would things continue along the way of the Chief or would they take the way of the Grocer?

Balgat Revisited: 1954

I reached Ankara in April after a circuitous route through the Middle East. The glories of Greece, Egypt, Lebanon, Syria, Persia touched me only lightly, for some part of me was already in Balgat. Even the Blue Mosque and St. Sophia seemed pallid, and I left Istanbul three days ahead of schedule for Ankara. I had saved this for last, and now here I was. I was half afraid to look.

I called a transportation service and explained that I wanted to go out the following day, a Sunday, to a village some eight kilometers south that might be hard to reach. As I wanted to spend the day, would the driver meet me at 8 A.M. and bring along his lunch?

While waiting for the car, next morning, my reverie wandered back through the several years since my first reading of the Balgat interviews. Was I chasing a phantom? Tahir S. appeared. With solitude vanished anxiety; confidently we began to plan the day. Tahir had been a member of the original interview team, working in the Izmir area. As Tosun had joined the Turkish foreign service and was stationed in North Africa, where he was conducting an inquiry among the Berbers, I had arranged in advance for Tahir to revisit Balgat with me in his place. Over a cup of syrupy coffee, we reviewed the questions that had been asked in 1950, noted the various responses and silences, decided the order in which we would repeat the old questions and interpolate the new ones.

As the plan took shape, Zilla K. arrived. She had no connection with the original survey, but I wanted a female interviewer who could add some Balgat women to our gallery. I had "ordered" her, through a colleague at Ankara University, "by the numbers": thirtyish, semi-trained, alert, compliant with instructions, not sexy enough to impede our relations with the men of Balgat but chic enough to provoke the women. A glance and a word showed that Zilla filled the requisition. We brought her into the plan of operations. The hall porter came in to say our car was waiting. We got in and settled back for a rough haul. Twenty minutes later, as we were still debating the niceties of question-wording and reporting procedure, the driver said briskly: "There's Balgat."

We looked puzzled at each other until Tosun's words of 1950 recurred to us: "It could have been half an hour to Ankara if it had a road." Now it did have a road. What was more, a *bus* was coming down the road, heading toward us from the place our driver had called Balgat. As it passed, jammed full, none of the passengers waved or even so much as stuck out a tongue at us. Without these unfailing signs of villagers out on a rare chartered bus, to celebrate a great occasion of some sort, we could only make the wild guess that Balgat had acquired a regular bus service. And indeed, as we entered the village, there it was—a "bus station," freshly painted benches under a handsome new canopy. We got out and looked at the printed schedule of trips. "The bus leaves every hour, on the hour, to Ulus Station. Fare: 20 Kurus." For about 4 cents, Balgati could now go, whenever they felt the whim, to Ulus in the heart of Ankara. The villagers were getting out of their holes at last. The Grocer, I thought, must be grinning over the fat canary he had swallowed.

We took a quick turn around the village, on our way to check in with the Chief. Things looked different from what Tosun's report had led us to expect. Overhead wires were stretched along the road, with branch lines extended over the houses of Balgat. The village had been electrified. Alongside the road deep ditches had been dug, in which the graceful curve of new water pipe was visible. Purified water was coming to Balgat. There were many more buildings than the 50-odd Tosun had counted, and most of them looked new. Two larger ones announced themselves as a school and a police station. An inscription on the latter revealed that Balgat was now under the jurisdiction of the Ankara district police. They had finally got rid of the *gendarmerie*, scavengers of the Anatolian village and historic blight on the peasant's existence. "These fellows are lucky," said Tahir drily. Feeling strange, we made our way along the erratic path through the old village, led and followed by a small horde of children, to the house of the Chief. Tahir knocked, an old woman with her head covered by a dark shawl appeared, the children scattered. We were led into the guest room.

The Chief looked as I had imagined. His cheeks a bit more sunken, perhaps, but the whole *présence* quite familiar. Tall, lean, hard, he walked erect and looked me straight in the eye. His own eyes were anatolian black and did not waver as he stretched out a handful of long, bony fingers. "*Gün aydin, Bey Efendim,*" he said. "Good day, sir, you are welcome to my house." I noted in turn the kindness which opens a door to strangers and the Chief responded that we honored his house by our presence. This completed the preliminary round of *formules de politesse* and steaming little cups of Turkish coffee were brought in by the Chief's elder son. The son was rather a surprise—short, pudgy, gentle-eyed and soft spoken. He bowed his head, reddening slightly as he stammered, "*Lütfen*" (Please!) and offered the tray of demitasses to me. I wondered whether he had learned to fight bravely and die properly.

As the Chief set down his second cup of coffee, signifying that we could now turn to the business of our visit, I explained that I had come from America, where I taught in a university, with the hope of meeting him. There, in my own country, I had read about Balgat in some writing by a young man from Ankara who, four years ago, had talked at length with the

Chief and other persons in his village. This writing had interested me very much and I had often wondered, as the years passed by, how things were going in the village of Balgat and among its people.When I had the opportunity to come to Turkey I immediately decided that I would visit Balgat and see the Chief if I could.

The Chief heard me through gravely, and when he spoke I knew I was in. He bypassed the set of formulas available to him—for rejecting or evading my implied request—and responded directly to the point. I was right to have come to see Balgat for myself. He remembered well the young man from Ankara (his description of Tosun in 1950 was concise and neutrally-toned). Much had changed in Balgat since that time. Indeed, Balgat was no longer a village. It had, only last month, been incorporated as a district of Greater Ankara. This was why they now had a new headquarters of Metropolitan police, and a bus service, and electricity, and a supply of pure water that would soon be in operation. Where there had been 50 houses there were now over 500, and even he, the Muhtar, did not know any more all the people living here.

Yes he had lived in Balgat all his life and never in all that time seen so much happen as had come to pass in these four years:

It all began with the election that year. The *Demokrat* men came to Balgat and asked us what was needed here and told us they would do it when they were elected. They were brave to go against the government party. We all voted for them, as the *Halk* men knew no more what to do about the prices then, and the new men did what they said. They brought us this road and moved out the *gendarmerie*. Times have been good with us here. We are all *Demokrat* party here in Balgat now.

The Chief spoke in a high, strong, calm voice, and the manner of his utterance was matter-of-fact. His black eyes remained clear as he gazed steadily at the airspace adjoining my left ear, and his features retained their shape. Only his hands were animated, though he invoked only the thumbs and the index fingers for punctuation. When he had completed his statement, he picked his nose thoughtfully for a moment and then laid the finger alongside the bridge. The tip of the long, bony finger reached into his eyesocket.

I explained then that the young lady had come with us to learn how such changes as the Chief mentioned were altering the daily round for village women. Might she talk with some of them while Tahir Bey and I were meeting the men? The Chief promptly suggested that Zilla could speak with the females of his household. (Tosun's resentful remark that, had he followed the Chief's suggestions, "I would have ended up only interviewing his family" came back to me later that evening, when Zilla reported on her interviews with the Chief's wife and daughters-in-law. All three had identified Balgat's biggest problem as the new fashion of young men to approach girls shamelessly on the village outskirts—precisely what the Chief had told me in answer to the same question. Tosun had been wise.) But if the Chief still used his containment tactics with the women, in other directions he had taken a decidedly permissive turn. Tahir and I, he said, could walk about Balgat entirely as we wished and speak with whomsoever it pleased us to honor—even, he added with a smile in response to my jest, some non-*Demokrat* Party men, if we could find any. We chatted a bit longer and then, having agreed to return to the Chief's house, we set out for a stroll around Balgat. Our next goal was to find the Grocer.

After a couple of bends and turns, we came to a coffee-house. Here was something new and worth a detour. We stopped at the door and bade the proprietor *"Gün aydin!"* He promptly rushed forward with two chairs, suggested that we sit outdoors to benefit of the pleasant sunshine, and asked us how we would like our coffee. (There are five ways of specifying the degree of sweetening one likes in Turkish coffee.) Obviously, this was to be on the house, following the paradoxical Turkish custom of giving gratis to those who can best afford to pay. In a matter of minutes, the male population of Balgat was assembled around our two chairs, squatting, sitting on the ground, looking us over with open and friendly curiosity, peppering Tahir with questions about me.

When our turn came, the hierarchy of respondents was already clear from the axis along which their questions to us had been aligned. Top man was one of the two farmers Tosun had interviewed in 1950. He too was tall, lean, hard. He wore store-clothes with no patches and a sturdy pair of store-shoes. His eyes were Anatolian black and his facial set was much like the Chief's. But his body was more relaxed and his manner more cocky. He sat with his chair tilted back and kept his hands calmly dangling alongside. This seemed to exercise punctuation from his discourse and he ambled along, in response to any question, with no apparent terminus in view. Interrupting him, even long enough to steer his flow of words in another direction, was—the obvious deference of the whole group toward him constrained us—not easy. His voice was deep and harsh, with the curious suggestion of strangling in the throat that Anatolian talk sometimes has. The content was elusive and little of his discourse made concrete contact with my notebook.

As I review my notes on that tour of monologue-with-choral-murmurs, he appears to have certified the general impression that many changes had occurred in Balgat. His inventory included, at unwholesome length, all the by-now familiar items: road, bus, electricity, water. In his recital these great events did not acquire a negative charge, but they lost some of their luster. The tough old farmer did not look shining at new styles of architecture, nor did he look scowling, but simply looked. Under his gaze the new roofs in Balgat were simply new roofs. The wonder that these new roofs were *in Balgat* shone in other eyes and cadenced other voices.

These other voices were finally raised. Either the orator had exhausted the prerogative of his position (he had certainly exhausted Tahir S., whose eyes were glazed and vacant) or the issue was grave enough to sanction discourtesy toward a village elder. The outburst came when the quondam farmer undertook to explain why he was no longer a farmer. He had retired, over a year ago, because there was none left in Balgat to do an honest day's work for an honest day's lira. Or rather two lira (about 36 cents)—the absurd rate, he said, to which the daily wage of farm laborers had been driven by the competition of the voracious Ankara labor market. Now, all the so-called able-bodied men of Balgat had forsaken the natural work praised by Allah and swarmed off to the Ankara factories where, for eight hours of so-called work, they could get five lira a day. As for himself, he would have none of this. Rather than pay men over two lira a day to do the work of men, he had rented out his land to others and retired. He was rich, his family would eat, and others might do as they wished.

The protests that rose did not aim to deny these facts, but simply to justify them. Surprised, we asked whether it was indeed true that there were no farm laborers left in Balgat any more. "How many of you," we quickly rephrased the question, "work on farms now?" Four hands were raised among the 29 present, and all of these turned out to be small holders working their own land. (These four were sitting together and, it later turned out, were the only four members of the *Halk* Party among the group, the rest being vigorous *Demokrat* men.)

Galvanized by the intelligence now suddenly put before us (even Tahir S. had reawakened promptly upon discovering that there were hardly any farmers left in Balgat), we started to fire a battery of questions on our own. As this created a din of responding voices, Tahir S.—once again the American-trained interviewer—restored order by asking each man around the circle to tell us, in turn, what he was now working at and how long he had been at it. This impromptu occupational census, begun on a leisurely Sunday, was never quite completed. As it became clear that most of the male population of Balgat was now in fact working in the factories and construction gangs of Ankara—*for cash*—our own impatience to move on to our next questions got the better of us.

How did they spend the cash they earned? Well, there were now over 100 radio receivers in Balgat as compared to the lone receiver Tosun had found four years earlier. There were also seven refrigerators, four tractors, three trucks, and one Dodge sedan. Most houses now had electric lights and that had to be paid for. Also, since there was so little farming in Balgat now, much of the food came from the outside (even milk!) and had to be bought in the grocery stores, of which there were now seven in Balgat. Why milk? Well, most of the animals had been sold off during the last few years. What about the shepherd? Well, he had moved to a village in the east a year or so ago, as there were no longer any flocks for him to tend. How was the Grocer doing? "Which one?" The original one, the great fat one that was here four years ago? "O, that one, he's dead!"

Tahir S. later told me that my expression did not change when the news came (always the American-trained interviewer!). I asked a few more questions in a normal way—"What did he die of?", "How long ago?" —and then let the questioning pass to Tahir. I don't recall what answers came to my questions or to his. I do recall suddenly feeling very weary and, as the talk went on, slightly sick. The feeling got over to Tahir S. and soon we were saying goodbye to the group, feeling relieved that the ritual for leavetaking is less elaborate than for arriving. We promised to return and said our thanks. *"Güle, güle,"* answered those who remained. ("Smile, smile," signifying farewell.)

"What a lousy break," growled Tahir in a tone of reasonable indignation as we started back toward the house of the Chief. He was speaking of the Grocer. I didn't know what to say by way of assent. I felt only a sense of large and diffuse regret, of which indignation was not a distinct component. "Tough," I agreed. As we came up to the Chief's house, I told Tahir we might as well return to Ankara. We had gathered quite a lot of information already and might better spend the afternoon putting it together. We could come back the next day to interview the Chief. The Chief agreed to this plan and invited me to be his guest for lunch next day. We collected Zilla K. and our driver and drove back to the city. Zilla did most of the talking, while Tahir and I listened passively. The driver said only, as I paid him, "I didn't need to bring along my lunch after all."

The Passing of Balgat

While dressing slowly, the next morning, I planned my strategy for lunch with the Chief. Had he learned anything from the Grocer? Clearly his larger clues to the shape of the future had come from Atatürk, whose use of strong measures for humane new goals had impressed him deeply as a young man. But surely he had also responded to the constant stimuli supplied by the Grocer, whose psychic antennae were endlessly *seeking* the new future here and now. The Chief, rather consciously reshaping his ways in the Atatürk image, had to be reckoned a major figure in the Anatolian transformation. But the restless sensibility of the Grocer also had its large, inadequately defined, place. Whereas the masterful Chief had been able to incorporate change mainly by rearranging the environment, the nervous Grocer had been obliged to operate through the more painful process of rearranging himself. Most villagers were closer to his situation than to the Chief's. The Grocer then was my problem and, as symbol of the characterological shift, my man. It was he who dramatized most poignantly the personal meaning of the big change now under way throughout the Middle East.

I recalled Tosun's unflattering sketch of him as an anxiety-ridden pusher, an "unfarming person" who "even wore some sort of necktie." What had located these details, what had made the Grocer a man I recognized, was Tosun's acid remark: "He most evidently wished to feel that he is closer to me than he is to [other villagers] and was curiously careful with his accent all during the interview." Tosun had seen this as vulgar social climbing, but there was something in this sentence that sounded to me like History. Maybe it was the 18th century field-hand of England who had left the manor to find a better life in London or Manchester. Maybe it was the 19th century French farm lad, wearied by his father's burdens of *taille* and *tithe*, who had gone off to San Francisco to hunt gold and, finding none, had then tried his hand as mason, mechanic, printer's devil; though none of these brought him fortune, he wrote home cheerfully (in a letter noted by the perspicacious Karl Marx) about this exciting new city where the chance to try his hand at anything made him feel "less of a mollusk and more of a man." Maybe it was the 20th century Polish peasant crossing continent and ocean to Detroit, looking for a "better 'ole" in the new land.

The Grocer of Balgat stood for some part of all these figures as he nervously edged his psyche toward Tosun, the young man from the big city. I'm like you, the Grocer might have been feeling, or I'd like to be like you and wish I could get the chance. It was harsh of Tosun, or perhaps only the anti-bourgeois impatience of an austere young scholar looking for the suffering poor in a dreary village, to cold-shoulder this fat and middle-aged man yearning to be comfortably rich in an interesting city. But the Grocer had his own sort of toughness. He had, after all, stood up to the other villagers and had insisted, even when they labeled him infidel, that they ought to get out of their holes. Though dead, he had won an important victory. For the others, despite their outraged virtues, *had* started to come around, once they began to get the feel of Ankara cash, for advice on *how* to get out of their holes. Had they also acquired, along with their new sense of cash, some feel for the style of life the Grocer had desired? That was what I wanted to find out in Balgat today.

I walked out of the hotel toward Ulus station, just around the corner. This time I was going to Balgat by bus, to see how the villagers traveled. We crowded into a shiny big bus from Germany that held three times as many passengers as there were seats. The bus was so new that the signs warning the passengers not to smoke or spit or talk to the driver (while the bus is moving) in German, French, and English had not yet been converted into Turkish. There was, in fact, a great deal of smoking and several animated conversations between the driver and various passengers occurred, in the intervals between which the driver chatted with a crony whom he had brought along for just this purpose.

In Balgat I reported directly to the Chief. He appeared, after a few minutes, steaming and mopping his large forehead. He had been pruning some trees and, in this warm weather, such work brought the sweat to his brow. This was about the only work he did any more, he explained, as he had sold or rented most of his land in the last few years, keeping for himself only the ground in which he had planted a small grove of trees that would be his memorial on earth. Islamic peoples regard a growing and "eternal" thing of nature, preferably a tree, as a fitting monument, and a comfortable Muslim of even diffident piety will usually be scrupulous in observing this tradition—a sensible one for a religion of the desert, where vegetation is rare and any that casts a shade is especially prized. The Chief agreed to show me his trees and as we strolled away from the house he resumed his discourse of yesterday.

Things had changed, he repeated, and a sign of the gravity of these changes was that he—of a lineage that had always been *Muhtars* and land-owners—was no longer a farmer. Nor was he long to be *Muhtar*. After the coming election, next month, the incorporation of Balgat into Greater Ankara was to be completed and thereafter it would be administered under the general municipal system. "I am the last *Muhtar* of Balgat, and I am happy that I have seen Balgat end its history in this way that we are going." The new ways, then, were not bringing evil with them?

No, people will have to get used to different ways and then some of the excesses, particularly among the young, will disappear. The young people are in some ways a serious disappointment; they think more of clothes and good times than they do of duty and family and country. But it is to be hoped that as the *Demokrat* men complete the work they have begun, the good Turkish ways will again come forward to steady the people. Meanwhile, it is well that people can have to eat and to buy shoes they always needed but could not have.

And as his two sons were no longer to be farmers, what of them? The Chief's voice did not change, nor did his eyes cloud over, as he replied:

They are as the others. They think first to serve themselves and not the nation. They had no wish to go to the battle in Korea, where Turkey fights before the eyes of all the world. They are my sons and I speak no ill of them, but I say that they are as all the others.

I felt at this moment a warmth toward the Chief which I had not sup-posed he would permit himself to evoke. His sons had not, after all, learned to fight bravely and die properly. His aspiration—which had led him, four years earlier, to buy a radio so his sons would hear the Korean war news and to see movies that would make them "wish more and more their time for military service would come"—had not been fulfilled. Yet the old Chief bore stoically what must have been a crushing disappointment. These two sons through whom he had hoped to relive his own bright dreams of glory had instead become *shopkeepers*. The elder son owned a grocery store and the younger one owned Balgat's first clothing store. With this news, curiosity overcame sympathy. I rattled off questions on this subject which, clearly, the Chief would rather have changed. As we turned back to the house, he said we would visit the shops after lunch and his sons would answer all my questions.

Lunch consisted of a huge bowl of yogurt, alongside of which was stacked a foot-high pile of village-style bread, freshly baked by the Chief's wife and served by his younger daughter-in-law. Village bread fresh from the oven is one of the superior tastes that greets a visitor. As I went to work with obvious relish, the Chief suggested that I eat only the "corner" of each sheet. Village bread is baked in huge round double sheets, each about the diameter of a manhole cover and the thickness of a dime. A large glob of shortening is spread loosely around the center between the sheets, which are baked together around the circumference. These sheets are then folded over four times, making the soft buttery center into a "corner." The corner is the prerogative of the male head of the household, who may choose to share it with a favored child. To invite a guest to eat *only* the corners is, in the frugal Anatolian village, a sign of special cordiality that cannot be ignored.

As I chewed my way happily through a half-dozen corners, I wondered who was going to be stuck with my stack of cornerless circumferences. Mama and the daughters-in-law? I asked about the children and learned that, as befits the traditional extended family, the Chief now had nine descendants living under his roof. Moreover, while some were taking to new ways, *his* grandchildren had been and were being swaddled in the traditional Anatolian fashion—for three months a solid mudpack on the body under the swaddling clothes, thereafter for three months a mudless swaddle. (Geoffrey Gorer's association of Russian swaddling with *ochi chornya* seemed due for an Anatolian confirmation, since Turkish eyes are every bit as lustrous black as Slavic eyes.) I glanced up at the large clock on the wall, which had stood firmly at 11:09 since I first entered the room at 9:16 the preceding day. It was clearly intended only as an emblem of social standing. In the very household where swaddling continued, possibly the first clock in Balgat (as once the first radio) had won a place. And though the clock was only decorative rather than useful, yet the hourglass was no longer visible. Times had changed. The Chief noticed my glance and suggested that we could now go out to see the shops of his sons.

We went first to the elder son's grocery store, just across the road and alongside the village "fountain," where Balgat women did the family wash as in ages past (though this would pass when the new municipal water supply became available at reasonable rates). The central floor space was set out with merchandise in the immemorial manner—heavy, rough, anonymous hemp sacks each laden with a commodity requiring no identity card, groats in one and barley in another, here lentils and there chicory. But beyond the sacks was a distinctive innovation, a counter. What is more, the counter turned a corner and ran parallel to two sides of the square hut. Built into it was a cash drawer and above each surface a hygienic white porcelain fixture for fluorescent lighting. Along the walls was the crowning glory—rows of shelves running from "top to floor and side to side, and on them standing myriads of round boxes, clean and all the same, dressed like soldiers in a great parade." The Grocer's words of aspiration came leaping back as I looked admiringly around the store. His dream-house had been built in Balgat—in less time than even he might have forecast—and by none other than the Chief!

The irony of the route by which Balgat had entered history accompanied us as we walked in quartet, the Chief and I ahead, the sons behind, to the clothing store of the younger son. This was in the newer part of the village, just across the new road from the "bus station." The entrance to the store was freshly painted dark blue, a color imbued by Muslim lore with power to ward off the evil eye. The stock inside consisted mainly of dungarees, levis, coveralls (looking rather like U.S. Army surplus stocks). There was a continuous and growing demand for these goods, the Chief stated solumnly, as more and more Balgati went into the labor market of Ankara, first discarding their *sholvars* (the billowing knickers of traditional garb in which Western cartoons always still portray the "sultan" in a harem scene). In a corner of the store there was also a small stock of "gentleman's haberdashery"—ready-made suits, shirts, even a rack of neck-ties.

The younger son, who maintained under his smile of proprietary pleasure a steady silence in the presence of the Chief, replied to a direct question from me that he had as yet sold very few items from this department of the store. One suit had gone to a prospective bridegroom, but the Balgat males by and large were still reticent about wearing store-bought clothes. A few, indeed, had purchased in a *sub rosa* sort of way neckties which re-mained to be exhibited in public. But wearing them would come, now that several owned them, as soon as an older man was bold enough to wear his first. The owners of the neckties had only to get used to them in private, looking at them now and then, showing them to their wives and elder sons, and some one of them had to show the way. I remembered Tosun's rather nasty comment about the Grocer: *"He even wore some sort of a necktie."* As one saw it now, the Grocer *had* shown the way, and it was now only a hop, skip and jump through history to the point where most men of Balgat would be wearing neckties.

The Grocer's memory stayed with me all that afternoon, after I had ex-pressed intense satisfaction with the shops, wished the sons good fortune, thanked the Chief again and, with his permission, started out to walk among the alleys and houses of Balgat. On the way, I absently counted 69 radio antennas on the roofs and decided that yesterday's estimate of "over 100" was probably reliable. And only four years ago, I counterpointed to myself, there was but a single battery set in this village. The same theme ran through my recollection of the numbers of tractors, refrigerators, and "unfarming persons." Several of these newly unfarming persons, recogniz-ing their interlocutor of yesterday's coffee-house session, greeted me as I strolled along. One stopped me long enough to deliver his opinion of the Turkish-Pakistani pact (strong affirmation) and to solicit mine of the proposed law to give Americans prospecting rights on Turkish oil (qualified affirmative).

Weary of walking, I turned back to the coffee-house. The ceremony of welcome was warm and the coffee was again on the house. But the conversational group was smaller, this being a workday. Only eleven Balgati appeared to praise the weather and hear my questions. The group got off on politics, with some attention to the general theory of power but more intense interest in hearing each other's predictions of the margin by which the *Demokrat* party would win the elections next month. There was also general agreement, at least among the older men, that it would be better to have a small margin between the major parties. When the parties are competing and need our votes, then they heed our voices—thus ran the underlying proposition of the colloquy. "The villagers have learned the basic lesson of democratic politics," I wrote in my notebook.

The afternoon was about over before I got an appropriate occasion to ask about the Grocer. It came when the talk returned to the villagers' favorite topic of how much better life had become during the past four years of *Demokrat* rule. Again they illustrated the matter by enumerating the new shops in Balgat and the things they had to sell that many people could buy. There was even a new barber shop, opened last month by the son of the late Altemur after going for some time to Ankara as apprentice. "How are these new grocery shops better than the old grocery shop of years ago owned by the fat grocer who is now dead?" I asked. The line of response was obvious in advance, but the question served to lead to another: What sort of man had the Grocer been?

The answers were perfunctory, consisting mainly of *pro forma* expressions of goodwill toward the departed. I tried to get back of these ritual references by indirection. How had the Grocer dressed? Why had he been so interested in the life of Ankara? The light finally shone in one of the wiser heads and he spoke the words I was seeking:

Ah, he was the cleverest of us all. We did not know it then, but he saw better than all what lay in the path ahead. We have none like this among us now. He was a prophet.

As I look back on it now, my revisit to Balgat ended then. I went back several times, once with gifts for the Chief's grandchildren, another time with my camera (as he had coyly suggested) to take his picture. On these visits I felt less tense, asked fewer questions, than during the earlier visits. The last time I went out with the publisher of a prominent Istanbul newspaper ("The New York Times of Turkey"), a dedicated *Demokrat* man, who was eager to see the transformed village I had described to him. He was enchanted with the Chief, the stores, the bus service and electricity and other symbols of the history into which his party had ushered Balgat. He decided to write a feature story about it and asked permission to call it

"Professor Lerner's Village." I declined, less from modesty than a sense of anachronism. The Balgat his party needed was the suburb inhabited by the sons of the Chief, with their swaddled children and their proud new clock, their male "corners" and their retail stores, their filiopietistic silence and their movies that teach excitement. The ancient village I had known for what now seemed only four short years was passing, had passed. The Grocer was dead. The Chief—"the last *Muhtar* of Balgat"—had reincarnated the Grocer in the flesh of his sons. Tosun was in North Africa studying the Berbers.

33 | A Life Full of Holes

DRISS BEN HAMED CHARHADI

Two years later I was still a shepherd, but I was working for my mother's husband, and sleeping in his house.

There was a boy named Rhanrha who worked with me, watching the cows and sheep and goats. One day Rhanrha told me: My friend, I'm going into the city and look for work. This is no work.

Where are you going to work? I asked him.

I'm going to try and find some man with an oven who'll let me carry the bread for him.

I said to Rhanrha: Good. Do what you can. If you want to go and be a terrah, go.

Tomorrow I won't be here with you watching the animals.

You know what you're doing, I told him. I did not believe he meant what he said.

All that day we stayed in the valley watching the animals. Evening came, and we drove them ahead of us and took them back home. He went with his goats and I went with my cows and sheep. The next day I took them out again. I went to the valley, and there I met another shepherd.

Hasn't Rhanrha come yet? I asked him.

No, he said. I haven't seen him. I wonder where he's taken his goats. I don't know.

Six or seven days went by, and I did not see Rhanrha. I had not seen him since the day he had told me he was going to look for an oven. One day I went into the city, and I met him.

Ahilan, Rhanrha! Is everything all right? Where are you these days?

SOURCE: Driss Ben Hamed Charhadi, *A Life Full of Holes*, a novel tape-recorded in Moghrebi and translated into English by Paul Bowles (New York: Grove Press, Inc., 1964), pp. 71-88. Copyright © 1964 by Grove Press, Inc. Reprinted by permission of the publisher.

I'm working, he said.

Where?

At an oven near here. That oven by the steps of Ibn Batuta.

Near the cinema?

Yes, that one, he said.

Is it good? Look and see if you can't get work for me there too, with you, or at some other oven.

Yes, he said. There's a maallem who's looking for a terrah now. If you want I'll take you to him.

Where is the maallem?

His oven is in Djenane el Kaptan.

Ouakha, I said. I'll go home and talk with my mother, and tomorrow I'll come and find you at the oven.

I went home. Mother, I said.

Yes?

I'm not going to be a shepherd any more. I'm going to work in the city at an oven.

Do as you like, she said. Go if you want.

Tomorrow morning I'm going to go and see Rhanrha, I told her. He's the one who's going to take me to the maallem.

The next day I got up, put a basket on my arm, and went to the oven at the foot of the steps. Let's go, I told Rhanrha.

We went into the Medina. I did not know any of the streets. We climbed up to Djenane el Kaptan, and Rhanrha took me to a man named Maallem Mohammed.

Maallem Mohammed, here's the terrah I told you I was going to bring you.

Come in, my son, come in, he said. Hang your basket up on that nail.

There was already a terrah named Abdeslam working there, but the maallem needed an extra one because so many people brought him bread to bake for them.

I hung up my basket. The maallem told Rhanrha: Go now. If Ahmed doesn't know the way, you can come by for him this evening after work.

Rhanrha went back to his work, and I stayed sitting in the oven. Soon a woman came by and stuck her head inside. My bread is ready to be baked, she said. I need a boy to come and get it.

Go with her, the maallem told me. I went with the woman to her house, got the bread, and carried it to the oven on my head. When it was baked, I took it back to her, and she gave me a quarter of a loaf. Each woman gives something when the terrah takes her back the bread. Some give a quarter of a loaf and some give a half. The first day I did not get very much. Three pieces of bread, no more. I put them into my basket, and at sunset Rhanrha came to get me. We went home.

Ah, aoulidi! So this is the work you're doing! said my mother. No money. Only a few little pieces of bread.

Just let me learn, I told her. When I'm bigger I'll know all about how to bake bread, and I'll have my own oven. I'll be a maallem and everything.

Whatever you like, said my mother.

I went to sleep. In the morning I got up and went to Rhanrha's house, and we walked together to the Medina. I went up to my oven in Djenane el Kaptan, and he went to his oven by the steps of Ibn Batuta. And a woman who made bread to sell in the street came to the oven and said to the maallem: I need a boy to bring my bread from the house. When it's baked he must carry it down to the bread market in the Saqqaya.

I thought the maallem would tell Abdeslam to go. But he asked me: Can you do it?

Yes, I told him. I thought it would be like carrying any other bread.

Good, he said. Take these three boards and go with her.

I took the boards and put them on my head. Each one was as big as a door, and could hold thirty-five loaves of bread before it was baked. And I went to the woman's house. I put the boards down outside the door and stood there. She came and got them one by one, and put the loaves of bread on them. I went in and carried out the first board covered with loaves of bread, and took it to the oven. Then I went and got the second, and then the third. When the bread was baked, I piled it all on a different board, still bigger, and started down the steps to go to the Saqqaya. The woman was walking behind me. There were a hundred loaves of bread, and they were very heavy for me. My legs would not stand up under them. I tried to put the board down on the steps, and it slipped. All the loaves of bread were rolling down the steps, and many people were picking them up. And the woman was screaming: Allah! Allah! The terrah has ruined all my bread! A man who was coming up the steps said to her: A small boy like that can't carry so much bread all at once. The woman went back up to the oven and got Abdeslam. He wiped the bread off and carried it to the Saqqaya for her. When Abdeslam came back I asked him why the maallem had not told him to carry the woman's bread for her in the first place.

He knows I don't like to work for her. She's stingy, he said. She sells bread, and so she wants to keep all she can.

The next day I went by the oven where Rhanrha worked. I said to him: Look. This work I'm doing up there is hard. I had to carry a hundred loaves down the steps from Djenane el Kaptan to the Saqqaya. Can't you look around for some other work for me?

I'll see, he said.

I went on working at the same oven for a month or so, and one day Rhanrha came to see me there. Do you want to come and work at my oven? he asked me. The maallem says if you want to you can.

Ouakha, I said. I spent that day working for the Maallem Mohammed, and the next day I went with Rhanrha to his oven.

Rhanrha said to the owner of the oven: Si Larbi, here's the terrah I said I'd bring you.

Well, my son. Do you want to work?

Yes, I said. I came to work.

You've been working in Djenane el Kaptan with the Maallem Mohammed? Sit down.

And I sat down. There were several terrahs working there, and they knew all the houses in the quarter. I did not know any. I went with them to learn, but I did not carry any bread that day, and I went home with nothing in the basket.

Not even one piece of bread today, aoulidi? my mother said. Yesterday you brought bread.

I'm working now at a different oven, I told her. This one is better than the other. I'll get bread later.

For a few days I went with the other terrahs to learn about the houses in the quarter. When one of them went to a house I went with him. I got to know the houses, and when somebody came to the oven asking for a terrah I would start to run, and try to get to the house before any of the others. The first one who got to the door took the bread and carried it up to the oven. I needed the bread for my mother, and more than that, I did not want to be beaten by the maallem. Each terrah had to have at least ten pieces of bread by the time the maallem went home at night. If he had fewer the maallem would beat him. Every maallem knows each loaf of bread he bakes, so we could not buy pieces of some other bread and say it was his.

Today and tomorrow I worked at the oven by the steps of Ibn Batuta, and two years went by that way. And I was earning money. I got money from the Jews. On Fridays I would carry their pots of skhina, with meat and eggs and vegetables in it, to the oven, and take them back when they were ready, and they would give me money. Sometimes I slept at the oven for two or three nights at a time, until I had enough money or bread to take home. Friday night nobody could sleep at the oven, because the Jews sent their hazzan to lock it up. That night all the ovens are full of pots of skhina. The Jews think that if a Moslem sleeps in the oven he may open one of the pots and eat some of the skhina. If he does that, all the pots will have to be thrown away, and they will have no skhina to eat on Saturday.

One day a Jewish woman came to the oven and asked the maallem: Do you want to buy some firewood?

The maallem said he would look at it. There was a Riffian boy named Gordo working there with me. He was about five years older than I was. The maallem said to him: Go with her, Gordo. And he told me: You go too. Both of you go with her. Look at the wood, Gordo, and come and tell me if it's good. You can bring it back in the handcart.

We went through the streets with that Jewish woman. When we got to her house we climbed up with her to the roof, and Gordo began to talk with her about how much the wood was worth. After a while they made a price, and we went back to the oven and told the maallem. He gave Gordo the money, and we pushed the cart to the Jewish woman's house. After Gordo paid her, we began to carry the wood down from the roof to the street. We filled the cart and took it to the oven, and we went back for the second load.

The wood on top of the pile was very old, and at the bottom it was still older. When Gordo lifted up one of the logs, there was a bundle there, covered with a rag.

What's that? I asked him.

Shut up, he said. It's an old bundle.

Open it up. Let's see what's in it, I told him.

He undid the knot in the rag. It was full of Spanish banknotes. The rats had bitten pieces out of them.

It's money, he said.

Half of it's mine, I told him.

Shut up! Do you want me to kick you off the roof? He says I've got to give him half! The maallem sends me to buy wood from the Yehoudía, and I'm supposed to give you half! And now keep your mouth shut and I'll give you five rials. But keep quiet.

He was much bigger than I was. All right, I said.

And we carried all the wood to the oven on the second trip. When it was piled next to where the maallem sat, Gordo took me out and gave me five rials from the inside of the bundle where the notes had no holes in them. Then he said: This money. Where am I going to change it?

I don't know, I said. They might take it at some bacal.

And if the maallem finds out about it?

Don't worry about the maallem, I told him. He won't do anything. He's not going to see you.

I left him standing in the doorway of the oven and began to walk down the street. I was thinking. Then I went back to the door. Give me one of the hundred peseta notes, I told him. I'll see if I can change it for you. He took out a bill and gave it to me. Here, he said. It was one of the old banknotes that the rats had been chewing.

I went into a bacal in the Calle de Italia and asked for a pack of cigarettes. The man looked at the bill. This bill has no numbers on it, he said. You'll have to take it to the bank.

I went back to Gordo and told him: It's no use. They won't take it. How much will you give me if I change it all for you?

Where?

Don't worry about that. I can change it. Tomorrow, incha'Allah, I'll give it to somebody I know. He'll change it for me.

You will? Is that the truth?

I swear!

So he said: Ouakha. Here it is. He took the bundle out of his pocket. How much is there? I asked him.

Count it, he said. There's five hundred rials in there.

I don't know, I told him. There may be five hundred or three hundred.

I did not know how to count the money. I said: I'll get it changed for you. You give me another five rials and it's finished.

Take it, he said.

I took the bundle. That night I slept at the oven. In the morning about ten o'clock I climbed up to the Boulevard. There I asked a man where the Banco de España was. Over there, he said. The one with two doors. Go in there.

I went across to the bank and walked in. There were people waiting in line. One of the Moslem guards saw me. He kept looking. Then he came over and said to me: What do you want here, boy?

Nothing, I said. I have some money, and I want to change it.

Go over there, he said.

And I went up to a Nazarene who stood behind a counter, and gave him the money. He began to count it, and he counted and counted. Then he gave me new bills. I looked at what he had handed me. It was only a little, and I had given him a big handful.

I gave you a lot, I told him. Look how little you gave me back.

That's the right amount, he said. Count it. Don't you know how to count?

Yes, I said. I put the money in my pocket and went out. That day I did not go back to the oven. I stayed in the street drinking gaseosas and playing ruleta in front of the cinema. I bought a pair of sandals, because I was barefoot. And I walked through the second-hand stalls in Bou Araqia and bought a shirt and a jacket. I slept at home that night. The next morning at half past ten I went back to the oven.

When I went in the maallem said: Where have you been?

Maallem, I said, yesterday they took me to the police station. And I stayed there all night.

What for?

Nothing. I was fighting with somebody, that's all.

You always go into things that aren't your business, he told me. You see what happens? You sleep in the comisaría. Why do you get into fights?

It's all over now, I said.

I went out and called Gordo. You know what happened? Because of you I had to sleep last night in the comisaría. And this afternoon at three o'clock I've got to go back there. All because of your money. And the money's at the comisaría too. What they're going to do to me at three o'clock I don't know. But I've got to go, and if they ask me about the money I'll have to tell them it's yours.

No, no! he said. By your mother, don't tell them that! The money's not mine. We just happened to find it together. If they want to keep it, let them keep it. But don't tell them it's mine! If the maallem hears we found it with his wood and didn't give it to him, he'll say we're thieves. We'll have no work.

I told him: If you want me to say that to the police you'll have to give me ten rials.

All right, he said. I'll give you the money. We went to the street where the oven was, and he said to me: Wait here for me. Don't come to the oven with me.

He went into the oven. Each terrah had his own money-box inside. In a minute he came out with the money.

I took the ten rials and put them into my pocket. Allah ihennik, I told him. If I come back tonight, you'll see me. If I don't, you'll know they kept me there again.

That afternoon I walked all around the city. After a while I got tired, and I said to myself: This is the time to look for a woman. Everybody says it's good. Now I've got the money I can try it. I can take one and see what it's like. I was in the Derb el Oued. There were houses in that quarter, with Spanish women. I went into the alleys and began to look. In front of some of the houses there were girls standing. I saw one Spanish girl and I thought: That one is good. I'm going up with her. I said to her: Shall we go up?

All right, she said.

How much? I asked her.

Five rials.

Ouakha, I told her.

When I came down from the room and went out into the street, I was thinking: It's true! Women are good! I'll come back and do it again.

It was almost dark. I went by the oven. The maallem had gone home but the oven was open. At night the owner, Si Larbi, always stood in the doorway selling pastries. If one of the terrahs wanted to go in and sleep, he could. Gordo was sitting inside in the dark.

What happened, Ahmed?

Thanks to Allah! I said. We're out of it. The police kept the money. They beat me again. All on account of you. Anyway, it's finished. This isn't the time to complain.

You're right, he said. Let the money go. We can't do anything about it.

You see? I told him. I asked you to give me half, and you wouldn't do it. That's what happens. Neither one of us got anything out of it.

The money's gone, he said. It's all the same.

Every day I went to the Spanish girl until all the money was spent. And I went on working at the oven. One house would give me skhina, another sweets, and that was the way I lived. Two or three rials a day and the basket full of bread. And my mother was much happier.

One day Si Larbi, the owner, came by the oven. He began to talk with the maallem. I'm going to rebuild my house, he told him. The next day he took workmen and materials to his house. Then he came again to the oven and started to talk to me.

Ahmed, you've been working a long time here. Why don't you come and help the workmen at my house?

I said: Si Larbi, if I go and work on your house I won't be getting any money or any bread either. And who'll keep me alive?

Work here at the oven in the morning, and come to my house in the afternoon. When the Aïd el Kebir comes. I'll buy you some new clothes.

Ouakha, I said.

And I began to work that way. We tore down two rooms, and we built up walls and put in two doors, one on each floor. Every afternoon for two months or so I worked there for him. We had to finish the house in time for the Aïd el Kebir.

Two or three days before the festival, Si Larbi came to the oven. The other terrahs were there. I said: Si Larbi, now the day is almost here. It's time to buy what you promised me. We've finished the house, and now I need the clothes. If you will.

Have you got any money? he asked me.

No, I told him. But you said you were going to buy them.

If you have the money, he said, I'll buy you the clothes. If you haven't, I won't. I'm not going to pay for your clothes.

I see, I said. You know best. And I was thinking of what my mother had always told me: If you see a Molsem who has been lucky, you'll know he didn't have another Moslem with him.

I went outside. There's a rich man who has everything he wants, with houses and an oven and everything, and he does that to me! Let him have his money. Allah will arrange it when the day comes.

I heard Gordo behind me. You know, he said, I've been giving Si Ahmed a few pesetas each day because he told me he'd buy me a pair of trousers for the Aïd el Kebir. And now he's got twenty rials of mine, and he says I never gave him any money.

Then Hamadi, another terrah, came out of the oven. He had been working six or seven years there. Do you see this broken tooth? he asked me. I said: Yes.

I had a fight, he said. And when Si Larbi saw the tooth he told me: Give me a little money every day. I'll save it up for you, and when there's enough, I'll have a gold tooth made for you. You have to have a hundred rials. A hundred Spanish rials to get a gold tooth! So when I'd given him a hundred rials, I said to him: Si Larbi, will you have the tooth made now? And he said: I've got no money to spend on teeth for you.

Yes, I said. A man who has his own and wants everybody else's too. But that's all right. Let him have it. He cheated me, but I'll get it back.

So I kept on working there. After that, every time I had the chance, I stole from Si Larbi. If he sent me to buy something, I would buy half and keep the rest of the money, and when he said: Is that all? I would say: That's all, Si Larbi.

Today and tomorrow, today and tomorrow, I went on working. One day a boy who sold pastries at the door of the oven said to me: Ahmed, the Nazarenes' big holiday will be here soon. The festival when they get drunk in the street and put trees inside their houses. My father knows a Spaniard who'll buy an arar tree from you. Why don't you and Pitchi go and get one and sell it to him?

How much will he pay? I asked him.

Maybe a hundred or a hundred and fifty pesetas.

I called Pitchi. Tomorrow is Sunday. Let's go to Boubana and cut down an arar tree and see if we can get something for it.

Yes? said Pitchi. You believe that? A dead tree?

I turned to the boy who was selling pastries. Is it true, Mohammed? That Nazarene your father knows will buy a tree if we bring it down to him?

I swear he will, he said. I know he will. Just get it and bring it.

So we went. We slept that night at the oven, and the next morning we walked out into the country to Boubana. There is a forest of arar trees on the mountain above the place where the Nazarenes play golf. We were standing there, and in a little while a Nazarene came by in his car. He stopped and got out, and began to cut down a young tree. He went on cutting trees until he had six or seven small ones.

We said to the Nazarene: Can we have one of your trees?

Cut one, he said. You can cut all you want.

Are they yours? I asked him.

Yes, they're mine. Don't you see how many I'm taking with me? He got into his car and went away. I began to cut one of the young arar trees with a saw. When I had four trees I told Pitchi: That's enough. We'll sell one to the friend of Mohammed's father, and the others we'll take to the market.

Let's go, he said.

You take two and I'll take two.

They were heavy. We carried them, one over each shoulder, until we got to the Souq el Bqar. We rested a while. Then we carried them on down to the market, and I waited there with three of them while Pitchi took one up to the oven. He came back and sat down with me. In a little while a Moslem walked up and said: Do you want to sell those trees?

Yes, we told him. Do you want to buy them?

I'll give you ten rials for the three.

More. They're worth more than that, we told him. One of them costs twenty rials, and you want three for ten?

Ten rials, if you want to sell them.

No, we said.

We were sitting there, and a policeman came up. Those trees, he said. Where did you get them?

They're ours, we told him.

Who gave them to you?

We were in a forest near Boubana and a Nazarene came and was cutting trees, and he said we could cut some too. We asked him for a tree, and he said to cut them ourselves. We asked him if they were his, and he said yes.

Pick up those trees. Come with me.

We picked up the trees and went with the policeman down to the comisaría in the Souq Ndakhel.

Ahah! they said to us. So you steal trees! Sit down.

They took the belts out of our trousers, and the laces out of our shoes, and they took away our cigarettes, and then they said: All right. Go on in, you two. And we stayed in there in the dark until the next day.

In the morning they came and said: Where are the ones who stole the trees?

Here we are, I said. They took us out into the corridor. The three trees were there. Pick up those trees, they told us. We picked them up and carried them outside, and went on carrying them through the street. Two policemen were walking with us. At the bottom of the steps by the Cinema Americano there was a police jeep waiting. We got into it and they drove us to the comisaría at Oued el Ihud.

Inside there was a very fat Belgian. I used to watch him get into a jeep. It leaned to one side when he got in. He looked at us and began to shout: Ha! So you're the thieves we've been looking for! You're the ones who've been cutting down all the trees!

Then he looked at me and yelled: Say something!

I told him how we did it.

What's that Christian's name?

He had a green station-wagon, I told him.

Lies! Sit down! There!

And we sat down and waited while they sent a jeep to the forest at Boubana. They came back with a shepherd. The Belgian asked the shepherd: Did you see those boys cutting the trees?

Yes, said the shepherd. There was a Nazarene there cutting trees too.

I said to the Belgian: You see? I wasn't lying. He said they were his.

So you stole them! The Belgian began to slap my head back and forth with his hand.

You aren't supposed to hit me, I said. You make out the papers here and send us to the Mendoubía.

Shut up, you son of a whore! Lie down there!

I lay on the floor and he stepped on my belly. You're going to kill me! I cried. Then he sat down on top of me. I couldn't move or shout or do anything, he was so heavy. He was like a truck on top of me.

When he got up he hit me some more, and then he put us into the cellar. The next day they wrote out the papers and took us to the Mendoubía to Monsieur Bompain's office. He said to us: Now where did you take those trees from? We told him the story.

Nothing but lies. I'm going to send you to jail.

So they put us in jail. That was the first time I had ever been sentenced to jail. They walked with us through Djenane el Kaptan, and Pitchi was hand-cuffed to me. We went by the oven, but the maallem was not there. Mohammed was standing in the doorway selling pastries.

And there was hunger there in the Casbah jail. At mealtime they gave out the bread first. By the time they served the soup everybody had finished eating the bread. The bread had worms in it. They were dead. The oven had killed them.

When I did not go home for several nights, my mother went to the oven. The maallem told her I was in the Casbah jail. Then every day she brought me food.

I was talking to Pitchi. You know, I said, my mother's bringing me food now. If you want to eat it with me, you'll have to pay me a rial a day.

But I haven't got any money here, he said.

When we get out you can give it to me.

Ouakha. And we began to eat the food together.

We stayed on there. And each day my mother was running up and down, talking to the khalifa, trying to help me get out, but it did no good. One day Si Larbi went to the Mendoubía. Those two boys work for me, he said, and I'll be responsible for them.

They let us out. We worked four or five days there at the oven. Then they called us to the Mendoubía. There they said: You stole those trees?

We started to tell them about it, but they only told us: Get out of here! Don't do it again. You should have ten days in jail. But this time you can go.

So we went back to the oven. Now that I had been in prison, the maallem did not like me. He shouted at me and blamed me for everything. And each time I could, I would steal two or three pesetas from him. One day he took a broom and began to beat me with it.

I said to him: Look! If you don't want me to work for you, say so, and I'll go and work somewhere else.

No! You'll stay and work here whether you like it or not, he said. You're not going to work anywhere else. You think I want to teach a new terrah how to work?

If I stay with you, keep away from me.

I stayed working for him, but he went on beating me every day and shouting at me, until it was very bad. One day he took the bread shovel out of the oven and tried to hit me with it. I pulled it out of his hand and threw it on the floor.

That's enough of you and your oven! I said.

The terrah says that to the maallem? He picked up the shovel and pushed it hard into my belly. I grabbed it away from him. I let it come down on his shoulder. Then I ran out of the oven.

I was walking around in the Calle de Italia in front of the cinema, and one of the terrahs came by. Allah, Ahmed! he said.

What's the matter?

The maallem's gone to get Si Larbi. You'd better not go back to the oven again.

Why shouldn't I go back? I said. I'm going back now. I want my things.

I went up to the oven. Si Larbi was there. So the terrah wants to be the master? Have you gone crazy? Don't you know what you're doing any longer?

The maallem took the bread shovel and tried to break my belly with it, I said.

Pack up your things, he told me.

I took everything and went home. My mother was there.

What's the matter? Why don't you want to work there any more? What's the matter with you?

They're no good! Si Larbi cheated me. Every day the maallem hits me. And I'm going to carry their bread?

34 | The Life of a Coster-Lad

HENRY MAYHEW

One lad that I spoke to gave me as much of his history as he could remember. He was a tall stout boy, about sixteen years old, with a face utterly vacant. His two heavy lead-coloured eyes stared unmeaningly at me, and, beyond a constant anxiety to keep his front lock curled on his cheek, he did not exhibit the slightest trace of feeling. He sank into his seat heavily and of a heap, and when once settled down he remained motionless, with his mouth open and his hands on his knees—almost as if paralyzed. He was dressed in all the slang beauty of his class, with a bright red handkerchief and unexceptionable boots.

'My father,' he told me in a thick unimpassioned voice, 'was a waggoner, and worked the country roads. There was two on us at home with mother, and we used to play along with the boys of our court, in Golding-lane, at buttons and marbles. I recollects nothing more than this—only the big boys used to cheat like bricks and thump us if we grumbled—that's all

SOURCE: Henry Mayhew: *London Labour and the London Poor*, Vol. I (London: Griffin, Bohn, and Company, 1861), pp. 39–40.

I recollects of my infancy, as you calls it. Father I've heard tell died when I was three and brother only a year old. It was worse luck for us!—Mother was so easy with us. I once went to school for a couple of weeks, but the cove used to fetch me a wipe over the knuckles with his stick, and as I wasn't going to stand that there, why you see I ain't no great schollard. We did as we liked with mother, she was so precious easy, and I never learned anything but playing buttons and making leaden "bonces," that's all,' (here the youth laughed slightly). 'Mother used to be up and out very early washing in families—anything for a living. She was a good mother to us. We was left at home with the key of the room and some bread and butter for dinner. Afore she got into work—and it was a goodish long time—we was shocking hard up, and she pawned nigh everything. Sometimes, when we hadn't no grub at all, the other lads, perhaps, would give us some of their bread and butter, but often our stomachs used to ache with the hunger, and we would cry when we was werry far gone. She used to be at work from six in the morning till ten o'clock at night, which was a long time for a child's belly to hold out again, and when it was dark we would go and lie down on the bed and try and sleep until she came home with the food. I was eight year old then.

'A man as know'd mother, said to her, "Your boy's got nothing to do, let him come along with me and yarn a few ha'pence," and so I became a coster. He gave me 4d. a morning and my breakfast. I worked with him about three year, until I learnt the markets, and then I and brother got baskets of our own, and used to keep mother. One day with another, the two on us together could make 2s. 6d. by selling greens of a morning, and going round to the publics with nuts of a evening, till about ten o'clock at night. Mother used to have a bit of fried meat or a stew ready for us when we got home, and by using up the stock as we couldn't sell, we used to manage pretty tidy. When I was fourteen I took up with a girl. She lived in the same house as we did, and I used to walk out of a night with her and give her half-pints of beer at the publics. She were about thirteen, and used to dress werry nice, though she weren't above middling pretty. Now I'm working for another man as gives me a shilling a week, victuals, washing, and lodging, just as if I was one of the family.

'On a Sunday I goes out selling, and all I yarns I keeps. As for going to church, why, I can't afford it,—besides, to tell the truth, I don't like it well enough. Plays, too, ain't in my line much; I'd sooner go to a dance—it's more livelier. The "penny gaffs" is rather more in my style; the songs are out and out, and makes our gals laugh. The smuttier the better, I thinks; bless you! the gals likes it as much as we do. If we lads ever has a quarrel, why, we fights for it. If I was to let a cove off once, he'd do it again; but I never give a lad a chance, so long as I can get anigh him. I never heard about Christianity; but if a cove was to fetch me a lick of the head, I'd give it him again, whether he was a big 'un or a little 'un. I'd precious soon see a henemy of mine shot afore I'd forgive him,—where's the use? Do I understand what behaving to your neighbour is?—In coorse I do. If a feller as lives next me wanted a basket of mine as I wasn't using, why, he might have it; if I was working it though, I'd see him further! I can understand that all as lives in a court is neighbours; but as for policemen, they're nothing to me, and I should like to pay 'em all off well. No; I never heerd about this here creation you speaks about. In coorse God Almighty made the world, and the poor bricklayers' labourers built the houses arterwards— that's *my* opinion; but I can't say, for I've never been in no schools, only always hard at work, and knows nothing about it. I have heered a little about our Saviour,—they seem to say he were a goodish kind of man; but if he says as how a cove's to forgive a feller as hits you, I should say he know'd nothing about it. In coorse the gals and lads goes and lives with thinks our walloping 'em wery cruel of us, but we don't. Why don't we?—why, because we don't. Before father died, I used sometimes to say my prayers, but after that mother was too busy getting a living to mind about my praying. Yes, I knows!—in the Lord's prayer they says, "Forgive us our trespasses, as we forgive them as trespasses agin us." It's a very good thing, in coorse, but no costers can't do it.'

35 | Does Suburbia Make a Difference: An Exercise in Secondary Analysis*

JOSEPH ZELAN

The Problem of Secondary Analysis

It is an unfortunate consequence of the current fashionable status of large scale social research that investigators are encouraged, directly and indirectly, to embark on new and ambitious data-gathering adventures rather

*The bulk of the research reported here was performed while the author was on the staff of the National Opinion Research Center. The data are taken from two NORC studies. The college senior study was supported by the U.S. Office of Education, The National Institutes of Health, and the National Science Foundation. The graduate student study was sponsored by the National Academy of Sciences–National Research Council, the Social Science Research Council, and the American Council of Learned Societies, under a grant from the Fund for the Advancement of Education.

SOURCE: This article is published for the first time in this volume.

than to utilize fully the vast amount of data already at their disposal. In the storage rooms of our major survey research centers, for example, there lie, neglected and often forgotten, quantities of social data which have never been analyzed. Every survey researcher finds it relatively easy to add one more item to a questionnaire, and rare is the investigator who is not tempted to add several more, especially when he is uncertain which will turn out to be the important items in his analysis. But the exigencies of sponsors' schedules, and the time and energy required of data analysis as compared with data gathering, often consigns the major portion of the data to oblivion.

When a social researcher is faced with the decision whether to use existing data to answer a question of interest to him, called secondary analysis, or to collect new data, the latter usually appears as the more enlightened choice. The reasons are numerous, but they include the ease with which funds for new research are now obtained, the emphasis on real or imagined "originality," and the very real and serious failure of social scientists to communicate to one another what they are doing and to facilitate the systematic progress of their science by coordinating their efforts in some way.

The Question of Suburban Differences

A scholarly tradition that granted legitimacy to secondary analysis probably could have shortened the long and by now tedious discussion about the distinctive structural and social-psychological phenomena supposedly engendered by the dramatic move of population to the suburban fringes of our metropolitan areas during the last two decades. The discussion began with an era which saw "suburbia" treated as an undifferentiated entity, suitable for vehement denunciation or rhapsodic panegyrics, but apparently not for detached analysis. This was ultimately followed by the work of rather more systematic behavioral scientists who saw a need to differentiate among types of suburbs in order to distinguish the characteristics of suburbs which could be attributed to their ecological position as distinct from the characteristics attributable to the class position of their inhabitants.[1]

However, in the transition from an era of gross generalization to one of empirical differentiation, researchers seem to have neglected a possibly important intermediate step. Nowhere have I been able to find an empirical study based on a national or other sizable sample which attempts to discover if suburban dwellers, taken in the aggregate, do manifest any discernible characteristics of a social-psychological nature, as opposed to the

---

[1] Bennett M. Berger, *Working Class Suburb*, Berkeley and Los Angeles: University of California Press, 1960; William M. Dobriner, *Class in Suburbia*, Englewood Cliffs; Prentice-Hall, 1963.

ecological and demographic, which set them off from city dwellers. It is obvious why few researchers would be anxious to investigate this question once it had been demonstrated that suburbs do vary in many of the characteristics which previously had been claimed to be uniquely suburban. Nevertheless, this omission leaves a gap in our knowledge of a phenomenon about which assertions continue to be made on the basis of pure speculation—assertions which can never be confirmed or refuted until we have troubled ourselves to acquire evidence.

It was an admittedly speculative assertion which sparked my present inquiry. In a statement which will sound familiar to those conversant with the early writings on suburbia, Kingsley Davis has said that suburban life styles appear to have negative consequences for the intellectual development of young people. Davis feels that "the main interest of the youngster is in conforming to the group's expectations." These expectations are alleged to include "a kind of anti-learning or anti-effort bias . . . Intellectual effort is identified with the alien and inimical adult world." [2]

My own adventure in secondary analysis began when I realized that these assertions could perhaps be tested without embarking on a new data-gathering operation. I was, at the time, engaged in research at the National Opinion Research Center, among whose vast data collections, old and new, were several studies of American students, in which the researchers had collected information about the places where these young people had grown up.

The first block of data at which I looked was taken from NORC's national study of the June 1961 graduating class in American colleges and universities. One hundred and thirty-five institutions were represented, with 33,982 respondents. [3] The respondents were classified as coming from central cities or from suburbs in metropolitan areas of 100,000 or more population or from cities and towns of less than 100,000 population, on the basis of their answers on a self-administered questionnaire to the question "Which of the following best describes the community which you think of as your home town during high school days?"

As in much secondary analysis, we can arrive at our goal only indirectly. In this case the data could tell me nothing about the presence of a group of

---

[2] Kingsley Davis, "Urbanization—Changing Patterns of Living," in Hoke S. Simpson, editor, *The Changing American Population*, New York: Graduate School of Business, Columbia University, and Institute of Life Insurance, 1962, pp. 66–67. Since the data used to test this assertion pertain to persons who grew up and attended high school in the pre-sputnik era, it will not be necessary to deal with the possibility that the situation has since changed.

[3] Most of this analysis is based on a representative subsample of 3,397 cases. The contextual analysis, however, utilized the entire sample. Details of the sample as well as an extensive report on the survey will be found in James A. Davis, *Great Aspirations*, Chicago: Aldine Publishing Co., 1964.

attitudes in high school, but only about their persistence through college. Yet if it be argued that such attitudes do not persist through college, I must reply that they are then of little interest.

An attempt to glean from the voluminous data a single group of items tapping a unidimensional entity we could call "intellectualism" was unsuccessful, and I settled for two pairs of items which exhibit moderately high intercorrelations among members of a pair, and lower but positive correlations between pairs. They consist of the endorsement of two items from a list of self-descriptive adjectives ("intellectual" and "cultured") and of two items from a list of values which would be important in picking a job or career ("opportunities to be original and creative" and "living and working in the world of ideas").

When students from cities, suburbs, and small towns were compared on endorsement of these four items, the differences between city and suburb were negligible and inconsistent in direction, while students from small towns were consistently less likely to endorse the items.[4] A similar pattern appeared when the three residence groups were compared on actual intellectual performance in college.[5]

Thus, there appears to be no simple relationship between intellectual attitudes and suburban versus city residence. Proponents of the view that such a relationship does exist might argue, however, that our data fail to give sufficient weight to the argument, which Kingsley Davis makes, that anti-intellectualism among suburbanites reflects conformity to the expectations of the peer-group. Those students, the argument might continue, who interact in college with their suburban compeers will reflect the suburban values most accurately, while those who choose their associates from more diverse backgrounds will be more likely to endorse the intellectual items.

The original study contained no sociometric items, so I was unable to test the foregoing propositions using data on actual interactions. As a substitute for actual interactions I used the *probability* that a suburbanite will interact with other suburbanites: the greater the proportion of suburbanites in a college, the greater is the probability that an individual will be subjected to "suburban" values. If peer-group influence is decisive in eliciting non-intellectual responses among suburbanites, such responses should be given by a greater proportion of suburbanites where suburbanites represent

---

[4] The largest difference between city and suburb is 2 per cent. The smallest cell in the table contains 711 cases.

[5] The cross-tabulation of college performance and community of origin revealed higher performance among suburbanites than among city youth, but this difference disappeared when SES was controlled. The lower performance of small town students remained, however. The measure of performance is an index consisting of college grade-point-average corrected for quality of college, in order to make performances comparable across colleges. See James A. Davis, *op. cit.*, Appendix III, "Notes on the Validity of the Academic Performance Index."

a greater proportion of the college population. Such a "contextual" analysis yielded four graphs, one for each of the intellectualism items.[6]

For none of the four items did the anti-intellectual response increase with an increasing proportion of suburbanites in the college. For three of the four items, the lines on the graph representing city dwellers is identical with that for suburban dwellers. (The exception is self-definition as an intellectual, where the lines diverge.) Again, I had to conclude that data from a national sample of graduating college seniors provided no evidence for differences in intellectual attitudes between city bred and suburb bred youth.

Selection in Suburb Migration

A different approach to the problem of suburban differences is that which seeks evidence of differential *selection* among potential migrants to suburbia. As contrasted with seeking the effects of suburban living, this approach has produced some convincing empirical findings.[7]

My ability to proceed with the selectivity question was due to the foresight of the persons who designed NORC's 1958 study of American arts and science graduate students. In addition to inquiring about community of origin the researchers also asked the respondent what type of community he would prefer to live in.[8] The question I asked of these data was whether those graduate students who prefer to live in the suburbs are less

---

[6] The technique for contextual analysis employed here is explained at length in James A. Davis, Joe L. Spaeth, and Carolyn Huson, "A Technique for Analyzing the Effects of Group Composition," *American Sociological Review*, 26, April 1961, pp. 215–229. Copies of the original graphs from the present analysis are available from the author on request.

[7] For example, Fava's findings about greater neighboring among suburban dwellers, even when demographic and economic factors are controlled. Sylvia Fleis Fava, "Contrasts in Neighboring: New York City and a Suburban County," in William Dobriner, editor, *The Suburban Community*, New York: G. P. Putnam's Sons, 1958, pp. 122–131. See also Herbert J. Gans, "Urbanism and Suburbanism as Ways of Life: A Re-evaluation of Definitions," in Arnold Rose, editor, *Human Behavior and Social Processes*, Boston: Houghton Mifflin, 1962, p. 635; Herbert J. Gans, "Effects of the Move from City to Suburb," in Leonard J. Duhl, editor, *The Urban Condition*, New York: Basic Books, 1963, pp. 184–198.

[8] If one grants that there is some positive association between the attractiveness of a goal and efforts to attain it, we can dispense with the question whether these respondents did, in fact, end up in the kind of community they said they preferred. The "origins" question in the graduate student study unlike the college senior study, permitted multiple responses. This analysis therefore includes only those who gave a single response—either "suburb of a large metropolis," or "large metropolis." The "orientation" question was: "All other things equal, in which type of community would you most like to live? (Circle one): A large metropolis, A suburb, A medium sized city, A small town." This analysis includes only the first two responses.

intellectually oriented than those who prefer to live in the city. The measures of intellectual orientation are self-definition as an intellectual [9] and an index of the perceived importance of access to various cultural activities.[10]

When the proportion of graduate students endorsing these items was tabulated simultaneously by community of origin and community of orientation, there was very little difference by origins, but those students oriented toward the suburbs consistently came out at the less intellectual end of the dependent variable, and these differences were sizable and statistically significant.[11] Thus, graduate students who indicated a *desire* to live in the suburbs were less likely to be concerned with access to cultural activities and less likely to think of themselves as intellectuals.

In seeking an explanation for this result I discovered that preference for living in the suburbs was associated with marital status, married students being more likely to express a preference for the suburbs than single students. I began to suspect that I had merely stumbled upon a common demographic phenomenon. When viewed this way, the explanation is simply that married persons tend to value cultural and intellectual activities less than the amenities of family living to be found in the residential suburbs. If this be true, the intellectual differences should disappear when marital status is controlled.

In Table 1 we see the proportion oriented toward living in the suburbs, by community of origin, marital status, and the culture index. In each of the four possible comparisons of married students with single students, we see that the married students are more likely to be oriented toward the suburbs (the pairs of percentages are: 41–49, 62–77, 57–61, 75–84). Similarly, students with low culture index scores are more likely to be oriented toward the suburbs than those with high culture index scores (comparing vertically, the pairs of percentages are: 41–57, 49–61, 62–75, 77–84). But the most striking comparison is that between students with different community origins. Those who come from the suburbs are more likely to prefer the suburbs in all four comparisons (the pairs of percentages are: 41–62, 49–77, 57–75, 61–84). The relative weight of community of origin can be

---

[9] The question was, "Do you think of yourself as an 'intellectual'? (Definitely, in many ways, in some ways, definitely not)."

[10] The Culture Index is a Guttman type scale, constructed from answers to the question: "If you did not have an opportunity to have ready access to the activities or resources listed below, how dissatisfied would you be with your place of work? (Extremely dissatisfied, quite dissatisfied, somewhat dissatisfied, wouldn't bother me):

Opportunities to hear live performances of serious music;
Opportunities to see serious drama;
A theater which shows foreign and art films."

[11] The zero-order N's, community of origin—community of orientation are: city-city, 274; city-suburb, 120; suburb-city, 60; suburb-suburb, 160.

exemplified by remembering that married students and low culture index students are more oriented toward the suburbs and single students and high culture index students are less oriented toward the suburbs, but introduction of the single item, community of origin, results in single, high culture index students from the suburbs (the third entry in the top line) having an equally high orientation toward the suburbs (62 per cent) as married, low culture index students from the city (the second entry in the bottom line; 61 per cent).[12]

While these data continue to support the notion that life cycle stage and familistic values are important concomitants of spatial mobility,[13] they also indicate the viability of the notion of selectivity of suburban migrants according to value systems, independent of demographic characteristics. From this point of view, the non-representativeness of the sample, vis a vis the U.S. population, makes the finding even more striking. The fact that among a group as highly selected on intellectual characteristics as arts and science graduate students one can predict preference for suburban living on the basis of intellectual attributes is strong, though not conclusive, evidence for their importance in suburban selection. The importance of intellectual attitudes, however, is overshadowed by community of origin.[14]

TABLE 1. Community of Orientation by Community of Origin, Marital Status, and Culture Index (Per cent Oriented toward Suburb)

Culture Index	Community of Origin			
	City		Suburb	
	Marital Status		Marital Status	
	Single	Married	Single	Married
High	41 (159)	49 (143)	62 (60)	77 (35)
Low	57 (127)	61 (130)	75 (71)	84 (51)

---

12 Essentially the same pattern appears when intellectual self-conception is substituted for the culture index.

13 Peter H. Rossi, Why Families Move, Glencoe, Illinois: The Free Press, 1955; Wendell Bell, "Social Choice, Life Styles, and Suburban Residence," in William Dobriner, editor, The Suburban Community, pp. 225–247.

14 Statements about the relative strengths of the relationships of several variables to a dependent variable cannot generally be made with assurance on the basis of percentage differences alone, especially when one deals with complex multi-variate tables. In the present instance, calculation of measures of association for partials in Table 1 confirmed the impressions derived from the percentage differences.

Summary

Secondary analysis of data from a national sample of graduating college seniors provided no evidence for the notion that persons who grew up in the suburbs differ in intellectual attitudes from those who grew up in the city, although those who were raised in smaller cities and towns tend to show small differences. Data from a national sample of arts and science graduate students indicate that for this group intellectual differences and marital status are both predictive of *preference* for living in the suburbs—married persons and persons who find access to cultural activities less important are more likely to evince a preference for suburban living. But the greatest predictive power is shown by community of origin—those who have lived in the suburbs are most likely to be oriented toward suburbs.

B | The City as Dream and Nightmare

36 | The Idea of the City in European Thought: Voltaire to Spengler

CARL E. SCHORSKE

During two hectic centuries of social transformation, the problem of the city pressed relentlessly upon the consciousness of Europe's thinkers and artists. The response of the intellectuals to this pressure was infinitely varied; for social change brought in its train transformations in ideas and values more protean than the alterations in society itself. No man thinks of the city in hermetic isolation. He forms his image of it through a perceptual screen derived from inherited culture and transformed by personal experience. Hence the investigation of the intellectuals' idea of the city inevitably carries us outside its own frame into a myriad of concepts and values about the nature of man, society, and culture. To chart in its proper context the changing idea of the city since the eighteenth century far transcends the bounds of the possible in a brief paper. I can do no more than present a few major strands of thought on the city, in the hope that the resulting pattern may suggest further lines of investigation.

One may, I believe, discern three broad evaluations of the city in the past two hundred years: the city as virtue, the city as vice, and the city beyond good and evil. These attitudes appear among thinkers and artists in temporal succession. The eighteenth century developed out of its philosophy of

SOURCE: Oscar Handlin and John Burchard, eds., *The Historian and the City* (Cambridge: The M.I.T. Press, 1963), pp. 95–114. Copyright © 1963 by the Massachusetts Institute of Technology and the President and Fellows of Harvard College. Published under the auspices of the Joint Center for Urban Studies.

Enlightenment the view of the city as virtue. Industrialism in the early nineteenth century brought to ascendancy an antithetical conception: the city as vice. Finally there emerged, in the context of a new subjectivist culture born in the mid-nineteenth century, an intellectual attitude which placed the city beyond good and evil. No new phase destroyed its predecessor. Each lived on into the phases which succeeded it, but with its vitality sapped, its glitter tarnished. Differences in national development, both social and intellectual, blur the clarity of the themes. Moreover, as the decades pass, strands of thought once seen as antithetical merge to form new points of departure for thought about the city. In the history of the idea of the city, as in other branches of history, the novel fructifies the old more often than destroys it.

Surely it was the unspoken assumption of the great middle class in the nineteenth century that the city was the productive center of man's most valued activities: industry and higher culture. This assumption was an inheritance from the preceding century, an inheritance so powerful that we must devote some attention to its character. Three influential children of the Enlightenment—Voltaire, Adam Smith, and Fichte—had formulated the view of the city as civilized virtue in terms congenial to their respective national cultures.

Voltaire sang his first lauds of the city not to Paris, but to London. London was the Athens of modern Europe; its virtues were freedom, commerce, and art. These three values—political, economic, and cultural—spring from a single source: the respect of the city for talent.

> Rival of Athens, London, blest indeed
> That with thy tyrants had the wit to chase
> The prejudices civil factions breed.
> Men speak their thoughts and worth can win its place.
> In London, who has talent, he is great.[1]

London was for Voltaire the fostering mother of social mobility against the fixed hierarchical society.

The virtues he found in London, Voltaire soon generalized to the modern city as such. His views of the city form a belated chapter in the Battle of the Books, of Ancients versus Moderns. Voltaire wielded his rapier smartly against the defenders of a vanished past, of the golden age of Greece and the Christian garden of Eden. Why should mankind exalt the poverty-stricken Greeks?—or Adam and Eve with their matted hair and broken fingernails? "They lacked industry and pleasure: Is this virtue? No, pure ignorance." [2]

---

[1] Verses on the Death of Adrienne Lecouvreur, as translated by H. N. Brailsford in his *Voltaire* (Oxford, 1947), 54.

[2] Voltaire, "Le Mondain" (1736), *Oeuvres complètes* (Paris, 1877), X, 84.

Industry and pleasure: these two pursuits distinguished urban life for Voltaire; together they produced "civilization." The urban contrast between rich and poor, far from holding terrors for the *philosophe*, provided the very basis of progress. Voltaire modelled his rich man not on the captain of industry, but on the spendthrift aristocrat pursuing a life of ease in the city, a true child of the pleasure principle. Voltaire described his *mondain's* luxurious rococo *hôtel*, with its exterior "ornamented by the striking industry of a thousand hands." [3] He savoured the rich man's daily rounds, his life of refined sensuality: the *mondain* rides in a handsome gilded carriage across imposing city squares to an assignation with an actress, then to the opera and a lavish meal. Through his sybaritic mode of existence, this squandering *bonvivant* creates work for countless artisans. He not only provides employment for the poor, but becomes a model to emulate. Aspiring to the life of civilized ease led by their betters, the poor are encouraged to industry and parsimony, and thus improve their state. Thanks to this happy symbiosis of rich and poor, elegant ease and thrifty industry, the city stimulates progress in reason and taste and thus perfects the arts of civilization. [4]

Despite his rather bourgeois stress on the city as a force for social mobility, Voltaire regarded the aristocracy as the crucial agency in the progress of manners. The removal of the nobles to the city, especially in the reign of Louis XIV, brought a "sweeter life" to the uncouth townsman. The gracious wives of noblemen formed "schools of *pôlitesse*," which drew the urban young people away from the life of the pothouse, and introduced good conversation and reading. [5] Voltaire thus viewed the culture of the new city somewhat as, in our day, Lewis Mumford and others have seen the planning concepts which inspired it: as an extension of the palace. But where Mumford found baroque despotism—a strange combination of "power and pleasure, a dry abstract order and an effulgent sensuality," coupled with a deterioration of life for the masses—Voltaire saw social progress. [6] Not the destruction of community, but the diffusion of reason

---

[3] *Ibid.*, 83.

[4] *Ibid.*, 83–86. Voltaire here secularizes the traditional medieval view of the division of function between rich and poor in the social economy of salvation. In the medieval view, the rich or "noble" were saved by their generosity, the poor by their sufferings. Each was necessary to activate the virtues of the other. Voltaire introduced into this static symbiosis the dynamic of social mobility. (Cf., for a Baroque statement of the traditional view, the ideas of Abraham a Santa Clara analyzed by Robert A. Kann, *A Study in Austrian Intellectual History* [New York, 1960], esp. 70–73.)

[5] Voltaire, *Le siècle de Louis XIV* (2 vols., Paris, 1934), ch. III, 43–44.

[6] Lewis Mumford, *The Culture of Cities* (New York, 1938), 108–113, 129–135. For a more differentiated analysis of the development of the modern city, see Martin Leinert, *Die Sozialgeschichte der Grossstadt* (Hamburg, 1925), III, *passim*.

and taste to individuals of all classes: such was the function of the city for Voltaire.

Like Voltaire, Adam Smith attributed the origin of the city to the work of monarchs. In a wild and barbarous feudal age, the cities, needed by the kings, were established as centers of freedom and order. The city thus laid the foundations for progress in both industry and culture: ". . . When [men] are secure of enjoying the fruits of their industry," Smith wrote, "they naturally exert it to better their condition and to acquire not only the necessaries, but the conveniences and elegancies of life." [7] For Voltaire, the advent of the nobility civilized the towns; for Smith, the town civilized the rural nobility and at the same time destroyed feudal lordship. The nobles, "having sold their birthright not like Esau for a mess of pottage in time of hunger and necessity, but in the wantonness of plenty for trinkets and baubles . . . , became as insignificant as any substantial burgher or tradesman in the city." [8] The city levelled nobles down and burghers up, to produce a nation orderly, prosperous, and free.

The dynamic of civilization thus lay in the city for Smith no less than for Voltaire. Yet both as economist and as moralist, Smith committed himself less fully to urbanism than Voltaire did. He defended the city only in its relationship to the country. The exchange between raw material and manufacture, between country and town, formed for him the backbone of prosperity. "The gains of both are mutual and reciprocal." But Smith regarded mobile capital as essentially unstable and, from the point of view of any given society, untrustworthy. ". . . [A] very trifling disgust," wrote Smith, "will make [the merchant or manufacturer] remove his capital and . . . all the industry which it supports from one country to another. No part of it can be said to belong to any particular country, till it has been spread over the face of that country, either in buildings, or in the lasting improvements of lands." [9] The urban capitalist is thus a rather unpatriotic nomad. Although the city improves the countryside by providing a market and manufactured goods, although it enriches mankind by making possible the transcendence of animal needs, its enterprising denizens are socially unreliable, labile.

Other vices of a subtler sort accompany the urban virtues: "unnaturalness and dependence." Smith maintained that "to cultivate the ground was the natural destination of man." Both by interest and by sentiment, man tended to return to the land. Labor and capital gravitated naturally to the relatively risk-free countryside. But above all, the psychic satisfactions of the planter surpassed those of the urban merchant or manufacturer. Here Adam Smith showed himself an English preromantic: "The beauty of the country, . . . the pleasures of the country life, the tranquility of mind which it promises and, wherever the injustice of human laws does not dis-

---

[7] Adam Smith, *The Wealth of Nations* (New York, 1937), 379.
[8] *Ibid.*, 390–391.   [9] *Ibid.*, 395.

turb it, the independency which it really affords, have charms that more or less attract everybody. . . ." [10] The city stimulated, the country fulfilled.

Smith pressed his psychological prejudices even at the expense of his economic logic when he argued that the farmer considered himself an independent man, a master, while the urban artificer felt always dependent on his customer, and thus unfree.[11] If the virtue of the city was that of the stimulus to economic and cultural progress, it did not afford the sense of security and personal freedom of the farmer's life. Adam Smith's model for the "natural" return of men and capital to the land was North America, where primogeniture restricted neither personal freedom nor economic progress.[12] Here alone city and country stood in their proper relationship. The city stimulated thrift, wealth, and craft; it thus provided the artificer with the wherewithal to return to the land and to fulfill himself ultimately as an independent planter. Thus even this great champion of *laissez faire* and of the city's historic role, expressed that nostalgia for the rural life which was to characterize so much of England's thought on the city during the nineteenth century.

The intellectuals of Germany took little interest in the city until the early nineteenth century. Their indifference was understandable. Germany had no dominant capital in the eighteenth century to correspond to London or Paris. Her cities fell into two basic classes: on the one hand, there were surviving medieval towns, such as Lübeck or Frankfurt, still centers of economic life but with a rather sleepy traditional bourgeois culture; on the other hand, there were new baroque political centers, the so-called *Residenzstäde*, such as Berlin or Karlsruhe. Paris and London had concentrated political, economic, and cultural power in their hands, reducing the other cities of France and England to provincial status. In divided Germany, the many political capitals coincided only infrequently with the many economic or cultural centers. German urban life was at the same time more sluggish and more variegated than that of England and France.

The generation of great intellectuals which arose at the end of the eighteenth century in Germany elaborated its ideas of freedom against the arbitrary power of the princes and the stultifying conventionality of the old burgher class. In neither dimension was the role of the city as an active element of progress of central concern to them. Against the atomizing and dehumanizing impact of despotic state power, the radical German humanists exalted the communitarian ideal of the Greek city-state.

During the Napoleonic Wars, Johann Gottlieb Fichte broke with the retrospective classical ideal to formulate a view of the city which governed

---

[10] *Ibid.*, 358.

[11] *Ibid.*, 359. The farmer likewise depends, in Smith's theory, on his customer, for only the sale of his surplus enables him to purchase city-made necessities. In a free market economy all are interdependent.

[12] *Ibid.*, 392–393.

much of German thought in the nineteenth century. Fichte adopted from western thinkers the notion of the city as the culture-forming agent *par excellence*. But where both Voltaire and Smith attributed the development of the city to the freedom and protection granted it by the prince, Fichte interpreted the German city as a pure creation of the *Volk*. The Germanic tribes which fell under the sway of Rome became victims of western *raison d'état*. Those which remained untouched in Germany perfected their primitive virtues—"loyalty, uprightness (*Biederkeit*), honor and simplicity"—in medieval cities. "In these [cities]," Fichte wrote, "every branch of cultural life quickly developed into the fairest bloom." [13] To the branches of culture recorded positively by Voltaire and Smith—commerce, art and free institutions—, Fichte added yet another: communitarian morality. Precisely in the last, the German folk soul expressed itself. The burghers, in Fichte's eyes, produced "everything which is still worthy of honor among the Germans." They were neither made civilized by aristocrats and enlightened monarchs as in the view of Voltaire, nor motivated by self-interest as in the view of Smith. Inspired by piety, modesty, honor and, above all, by a sense of community, they were "alike in sacrifice for the common weal." The German burghers had shown for centuries that, alone among the European nations, Germany was "capable of enduring a republican constitution." Fichte called the age of the German medieval city "the nation's youthful dream of its future deeds, . . . the prophecy of what it would be once it had perfected its strength." [14]

In his glorification of the city as civilizing agent, Fichte thus added several new dimensions. The city in his vision became both democratic and communitarian in spirit. The medieval city took on the sociocultural characteristics assigned by other German thinkers—Schiller, Hölderlin, and the young Hegel—to the Greek polis. Fichte thus fortified the self-consciousness of the German bourgeoisie in its struggle for nationalism and democracy with a concrete model from its own history, a lost paradise of its own creation to regain. And with it, enemies to combat: the princes and the immoral state. The bloom of the city had been "destroyed by the tyranny and avarice of the princes, . . . its freedom trodden under foot" until Germany had sunk to its lowest ebb in Fichte's age, when the nation suffered the imposition of the Napoleonic yoke.[15] While he did not devaluate the role of the city in commerce, he rejected Smith's "swindling theories about . . . manufacturing for the world market" as an instrument of foreign power and corruption.[16] Fichte had neither Voltaire's appreciation of the role of aristocratic luxury in urban culture-building, nor Smith's fear of the city entrepreneur's rootlessness. By extolling the burgher-city as a model ethical community, Fichte introduced ideal stan-

[13] J. G. Fichte, *Reden an die deutsche Nation* (Berlin, 1912 [?]), 125–126.
[14] *Ibid.*, 127, 128.   [15] *Ibid.*, 126.   [16] *Ibid.*, 251.

dards for the later critique of the nineteenth-century city as a center of capitalist individualism.

The stronger medieval survivals in German society permitted Fichte to develop notions which transcended in their historical import the ideas of the city held by his French and English predecessors. For Voltaire and Smith, the city possessed virtues making for social progress; for Fichte, the city as community incarnated virtue in a social form.

Even while the idea of the city as virtue was being elaborated during the eighteenth century, a counter current began to make itself felt: the idea of the city as vice. The city as seat of iniquity had, to be sure, been fair game for religious prophets and moralists since Sodom and Gomorrah. But in the eighteenth century, secular intellectuals began to raise new kinds of criticisms. Oliver Goldsmith deplored the destruction of England's peasantry as mobile capital extended its sway over the countryside. Unlike Adam Smith, he saw accumulating wealth produce decaying men. The French Physiocrats, whose notions of economic well-being centered upon maximizing agricultural production, eyed the city with suspicion. One of their leaders, Mercier de la Rivière, presented what seems like a deliberate transformation of Voltaire's urban gentleman riding gaily to his assignation: "The threatening wheels of the overbearing rich drive as rapidly as ever over stones stained with the blood of their unhappy victims." [17] Social concern for the prosperity of the peasant freeholder brought anti-urbanism in its wake, no less surely in Mercier's Europe than in Jefferson's America. Other intellectual currents only reenforced developing doubts about the city as "civilizing" agent: the preromantic cult of nature as a substitute for a personal God, and the sense of alienation which spread among the intellectuals as traditional social loyalties atrophied.

By the end of the eighteenth century, the spendthrift rich and the industrious artisans of Voltaire and Smith became transformed into Wordsworth's getters and spenders, equally wasting their powers, equally alienated from nature.[18] The rationality of the planned city, so prized by Voltaire, could appear to William Blake to impose "mind-forged manacles" on both nature and man. How different is Blake's poem, London, from Voltaire's earlier paean of praise:

> I wander thro' each charter'd street,
> Near where the charter'd Thames does flow,
> And mark in every face I meet
> Marks of weakness, marks of woe.[19]

---

[17] Quoted from Mercier de la Rivière's Tableau de Paris in Lewis Mumford, The Culture of Cities (New York, 1938), 97.

[18] William Wordsworth, "The World," in Oxford Book of English Verse (Oxford, 1931), 609.

[19] William Blake, "London," in The Portable Blake (ed. Alfred Kazin, New York, 1946), 112.

Before the full consequences of industrialization were made manifest in the city, the intellectuals had already begun that revaluation of the urban environment which has not yet run its course. The reputation of the city had become entangled with concern over the transformation of agrarian society, with the fear of "mammonism," the cult of nature, and the revolt against mechanistic rationalism.

To this emergent view of the city as vice, the spread of industrialism in the first decades of the nineteenth century gave a powerful new impetus. As the promise of the beneficient operations of natural law in economic life became transformed into the findings of the "dismal science," so the hopeful mutual identity of interest of rich and poor, town and country turned into the warfare between Disraeli's "two nations," between the insouciant wealthy and the depraved slum dwellers.

What the romantic poets had discovered, the prose writers of the English social realist school in the 1840's described in its specific urban setting. The city symbolized in brick and grime and squalor the social crime of the age, the crime which more than any other preoccupied the intelligentsia of Europe. The *cri de cœur* first raised in Britain spread eastward with industrialism until, a hundred years after Blake, it found voice in the Russia of Maxim Gorki.

Were poverty, squalor, and upper class hardheartedness *novae* in the urban universe? Assuredly not. Two developments account for the fact that the city in the early nineteenth century became the stigmatic symbol of these social vices. First, the dramatic increase in the rate of urbanization and the establishment of the jerry-built industrial town dramatized urban conditions which had hitherto passed unnoticed. Second, this negative transformation of the social landscape came against the background of Enlightenment expectations, of optimistic thinking about the progress of wealth and civilization through the city such as we have seen in Voltaire, Smith and Fichte. The city as symbol was caught in the psychological trammels of disappointed hopes. Without the dazzling picture of the city as virtue, inherited from the Enlightenment, the image of the city as vice could hardly have achieved so firm a grip on the European mind.

The critical responses to the industrial urban scene may be loosely distinguished between archaistic and futuristic. The archaists would abandon the city; the futurists, reform it. The archaists, such as Coleridge, Ruskin, the Pre-Raphaelites, Gustav Freytag in Germany, Dostoievsky and Tolstoy, firmly rejected the machine age and its modern megalopolis. In their respective ways, all sought a return to agrarian or small-town society. The utopian socialists in France, such as Fourier with his phalansteries, and even the syndicalists showed similar antiurban traits. For the archaists, the good life simply could not be lived in the modern city. They revived the communitarian past to criticize the grinding competitive present. Their vision of the future involved, to a greater or lesser degree, the recapture of a preurban past.

It is my impression that the failure of nineteenth-century urban architecture to develop an autonomous style reflected the strength of the archaistic current even among the urban bourgeoisie. Why, if railway bridges and factories could be built in a new utilitarian style, were both domestic and representational buildings conceived exclusively in architectural idioms antedating the eighteenth century? In London even the railway stations struck archaic poses: Euston Station sought in its façade escape to ancient Greece, St. Pancras to the Middle Ages, and Paddington to the Renaissance. This Victorian historicism expressed the incapacity of city dwellers either to accept the present or to conceive the future except as a resurrection of the past. The new city builders, fearing to face the reality of their own creation, found no aesthetic forms to state it. This was almost as true for Napoleon III's Paris, with its strong tradition of controlled architectural continuity, as for Wilhelmian Berlin and Victorian London with their more flamboyant historical eclecticism. Mammon sought to redeem himself by donning the mask of a preindustrial past that was not his own.

Ironically, the true archaistic rebels against the city, whether esthetic or ethical, found the medieval styles they advocated caricatured in the façades of the metropolis. Both John Ruskin and William Morris bore this cross. Both turned from an archaistic estheticism to socialism, from the classes to the masses, in the search for a more promising solution to the problems of industrial urban man. As they did so, they became somewhat more reconciled to modern industrialism and to the city. They passed from archaistic estheticism to socialism, from the classes to the masses, in the dustrialism and to the city. They passed from archaism to futurism.

The futuristic critics of the city were largely social reformers or socialists. Children of the Enlightenment, they found their faith in the city as civilizing agent severely strained by the spectacle of urban misery, but their melioristic thrust carried them over the chasm of doubt. The thought of Marx and Engels shows in its most complex form the intellectual adaptation of the progressive outlook to the era of industrial urbanization. Both revealed in their early writings a Fichtean nostalgia for the medieval artisan, owner of his means of production and creator of his entire product. The young Engels, in his *Condition of the Working Classes in England* (1845), described the plight of the urban poor in terms little different from those employed by the English middle-class urban reformers, social novelists and parliamentary commissioners of the 1840's. Engels described the industrial city realistically and indicated it ethically, yet offered no serious solution to its problems. Neither he nor Marx, however, suggested that the clock be turned back; nor did either support the "model community" solutions so favored by the nineteenth-century utopians.

After nearly three decades of silence on the urban problem, Engels once again turned his attention to it in 1872, treating it now in the context of matured Marxian theory.[20] While still rejecting the industrial city existen-

---

[20] "The Housing Question," in Karl Marx and Friedrich Engels, *Selected Works* (2 vols., Moscow, 1958), I, 546–635.

tially, he now affirmed it historically. Where the domestic worker who owned his home was chained to a given spot as victim of his exploiters, Engels argued, the urban industrial worker was free—even though his freedom was that of a "free outlaw." Engels scored the "tearful Proudhonist's" looking backward to rural small-scale industry, "which produced only servile souls. . . . The English proletarian of 1872 is on an infinitely higher level than the rural weaver of 1772 with his 'hearth and home.'" The driving of the workers from "hearth and home" by capitalist industry and agriculture was not, in Engels' view, retrogression, but rather "the very first condition of their intellectual emancipation." "Only the proletariat . . . herded together in the big cities is in a position to accomplish the great social transformation which will put an end to all class exploitation and all class rule." [21]

Engels' attitude toward the modern city paralleled exactly Marx's attitude toward capitalism; both were equally dialectic. Marx rejected capitalism ethically for its exploitation of the worker and affirmed it historically for socializing the modes of production. Similarly, Engels excoriated the industrial city as the scene of labor's oppression, yet affirmed it historically as the theater *par excellence* of proletarian liberation. As in the struggle between big capital and small entrepreneurship Marx espoused the former as the "necessary" and "progressive" force, so in the struggle between urban and rural production, Engels favored the industrial city as the purgatory of the fallen peasant or small-town artisan, where both were to be cleansed of servility and both were to develop their proletarian consciousness.

What place would the city occupy in the socialist future? Engels shied away from concrete blueprints. Yet he was convinced that a start must be made toward "abolishing the contrast between town and country, which has been brought to its extreme point by present-day capitalist society." [22] Late in life, Engels resurrected in his discussion of the city of the future the antimegalopolitan outlook of the utopian socialists. He saw in the model communities of Owen and Fourier the synthesis of town and country—and lauded this synthesis as suggesting the social essence, though not the form, of the living-unit of the future. Engels' anti-megalopolitan stance was clear: "To want to solve the housing question while at the same time desiring to maintain the modern big cities is an absurdity. The modern big cities, however, will be abolished only by the abolition of the capitalist mode of production." [23] Under socialism, the "intimate connection between industrial and agricultural production," and "as uniform distribution as possible of the population over the whole country . . . will . . . deliver the rural population from isolation and stupor" and bring the blessings of nature into city life.[24] Engels refused to specify his ideas of population-centers more precisely, but his whole argument suggested a strong affinity to the small-city ideal common to urban reformers since the close of the nineteenth century.

[21] *Ibid.*, 563–564.   [22] *Ibid.*, 588.   [23] *Ibid.*, 589.   [24] *Ibid.*, 627–628.

Where Adam Smith, on the basis of a theory of reciprocal urban and rural development, had seen the city man's fulfillment in a return to the land as an individual, Engels envisaged socialism as uniting the blessings of town and country by bringing the city to the country as a social entity; and conversely, nature to the city. In the course of three decades, his thought had passed from ethical rejection of the modern city, through historical affirmation of its liberating function, to a transcendence of the urban-rural debate in a utopian perspective: the synthesis of urban *Kultur* and rural *Natur* in the town of the socialist future. Though bitterly critical of the contemporary city, Engels rescued the idea of the city by integrating its very vices into his economy of social salvation.

A new generation of continental writers in the 1890's expressed views not far removed from Engels'. Unlike the English social novelists of the 1840's, they thought neither of pre-industrial life as bliss nor of Christian-ethical solutions to modern urbanism as viable. Emile Zola, in his trilogy *Trois villes*, painted Paris as a sink of iniquity. The Christian message was too weak and corrupted to regenerate modern society; neither Lourdes nor Rome could help. The cures must be found where the disease centered: in the modern metropolis. Here, out of degradation itself, would arise the humanistic moral and scientific spirit to build a new society. Emile Verhaeren, an active socialist as well as an avant-grade poet, showed the modern *Villes tentaculaires* sucking the life's blood out of the countryside. Verhaeren shared with the archaists a strong feeling for earlier village and town life, but the horrendous vitality of the city had turned the archaistic dream into the modern nightmare-actuality of bigotry and emptiness which ruled in rural life. The last cycle in his poetic tetralogy, entitled *Dawn*, showed that the industrial energies which, for a hundred years, had dragged man into oppression and ugliness, were also the key to redemption. The red light of the industrial mills betokened the dawn of the regenerated man. The red revolution of the masses would work the transformation.[25]

Were the archaists then dead by the end of the century? No. But they flowered in more fateful blooms, the *fleurs du mal* of totalitarian nationalism: Léon Daudet and Maurice Barrès in France, the proto-Nazi litterateurs in Germany. Condemners of the city all, they assaulted not the city as vice, but its people as vicious. The liberal urban rich were at best the allies of the Jew; the urban poor were the depraved and rootless masses, supporters of Jewish materialistic socialism. Back to the provinces, the true France, cried the neo-rightist French! Back to the soil where blood runs clear, cried the racist Germans! The German proto-Nazis—Langbehn, Lagarde, Lange—joined to their cult of peasant virtue the idealization of Fichte's medieval burg. But where Fichte used his archaic model to democratize German political life, his successors employed it for a revolution of rancor against liberalism, democracy and socialism. Fichte spoke for a

---

[25] Cf. Eugenia W. Herbert, *The Artist and Social Reform* (New Haven, 1961), 136–139.

middle class on the way up; his proto-Nazi successors, for a petty bourgeoisie which felt itself on the way down, crushed between big capital and big labor. Fichte exalted the communitarian city against the despotic *Residenzstadt*; his successors, against the modern metropolis. In short, where Fichte wrote in hope as a communitarian rationalist, the proto-Nazis wrote in frustration as blood-and-soil irrationalists.

The second wave of archaism may be most easily distinguished from the first by its lack of sympathy for the city man as victim. The sympathetic attitude had passed by 1900 largely to the futurists, the social reformers or revolutionaries who accepted the city as a social challenge and hoped to capitalize its energies. The remaining archaists viewed the city and its people not with tears of pity but with bitter hatred.

How does the idea of the city as vice in 1900 compare with that of the city as virtue a century before? For the futurists of 1900, the city possessed vices, as for Voltaire and Smith it had possessed virtues. But those vices, the futurists believed, could be overcome by the social energies born of the city itself. The neo-archaists, in contrast, had fully inverted Fichte's values: for him the city had incarnated virtue in a social form to be emulated; for them it incarnated vice, and was to be destroyed.

Somewhere about 1850, there emerged in France a new mode of thought and feeling which has slowly but forcefully extended its sway over the consciousness of the West. No agreement yet exists on the nature of the great sea-change in our culture ushered in by Baudelaire and the French Impressionists, and given philosophical formulation by Nietzsche. We know only that the pioneers of this change explicitly challenged the validity of traditional morality, social thought, and art. The primacy of reason in man, the rational structure of nature and the meaningfulness of history, were all brought before the bar of personal psychological experience for judgment. This great revaluation inevitably drew the idea of the city into its train. As virtue and vice, progress and regression lost their clarity of meaning, the city was placed beyond Good and Evil.

"What is modern?" The intellectual transvaluators gave a new centrality to the question. They asked not, "What is good and bad about modern life?" but, "What *is* it? What true, what false?" Among the truths they found was the city, with all its glories and horrors, its beauties and its ugliness, as the essential ground of modern existence. Not to judge it ethically, but to experience it fully in one's own person became the aim of the *novi homines* of modern culture.

Perhaps we can most readily distinguish the new attitude from older ones by examining the city's place in relation to the ordinance of time. Earlier urban thinking had placed the modern city in phased history: between a benighted past and a rosy future (the Enlightenment view) or as a betrayal of a golden past (the anti-industrial view). For the new culture, by contrast, the city had no structured temporal locus between past and future, but rather a temporal quality. The modern city offered an eternal *hic et nunc*, whose content was transience, but whose transience was permanent. The city presented a succession of variegated, fleeting moments, each to be savoured in its passage from nonexistence to oblivion. To this view the experience of the crowd was basic: all its individuals uprooted, each unique, all conjoined for a moment before the parting of the ways.

Baudelaire, by affirming his own deracination, pressed the city into the service of a poetic of this modern life-attitude. He opened vistas to the city dweller which neither lamenting archaist nor reforming futurist had yet disclosed. "Multitude and solitude: [these are] terms that an active and fertile poet can make equal and interchangeable," he wrote.[26] He did so. Baudelaire lost his identity, as the city-man does, but he gained a world of vastly enlarged experience. He developed the special art he called "bathing himself in the crowd." [27] The city provided a "drunken spree of vitality," "feverish joys that will always be barred to the egoist." Baudelaire regarded the poetic city dweller as cousin to the prostitute—no longer an object of moralistic scorn. The poet, like the prostitute, identified himself with "all the professions, rejoicings, miseries that circumstances bring before him." "What men call love is a very small, restricted and weak thing compared with this ineffable orgy, this holy prostitution of a soul that gives itself utterly, with all its poetry and charity, to be the unexpectedly emergent, to the passing unknown." [28]

For Baudelaire and the *fin de siècle* esthetes and decadents who followed him, the city made possible what Walter Pater called "the quickened, multiplied consciousness." This enrichment of personal sensibility, however, was bought at a terrible price: detachment from the psychological comforts of tradition and from any sense of participation in an integrated social whole. The modern city had, in the view of the new urbanite artists, destroyed the validity of all inherited integrating creeds. Such creeds had been preserved only hypocritically as masks of bourgeois reality. To the artist fell the duty of striking off the masks in order to show modern man his true face. The esthetic, sensuous—and sensual—appreciation of modern life became in this context only a kind of compensation for the lack of anchorage, of social or credal integration. Baudelaire expressed this tragically compensatory quality of the esthetic acceptance of urban life in desparate words: ". . . The intoxication of Art is the best thing of all for veiling the terrors of the Pit; . . . genius can play a part at the edge of the tomb with a joy that prevents it from seeing the tomb." [29]

To live for the fleeting moments of which modern urban life was composed, to jettison both the archaistic and the futuristic illusions, could pro-

---

[26] Baudelaire, "Short Poems in Prose," *The Essence of Laughter* (ed. by Peter Quennell, New York, 1956), 139.

[27] Cf. Martin Turnell, *Baudelaire, a Study of his Poetry* (London, 1953), 193.

[28] Baudelaire, *Essence of Laughter*, 139, 140.

[29] *Ibid.*, 147–148.

duce not only reconciliation but also the wracking pain of loneliness and anxiety. The affirmation of the city by most of the decadents had the character not of an evaluation, but of an *amor fati*. Rainer Maria Rilke represented a variant of this attitude; for while he conceded the city's fatality, he evaluated the city negatively. His *Book of Hours* showed that, if art could veil the terrors of the pit, it could disclose them too. Rilke felt imprisoned in "the cities' guilt," whose psychological horrors he described with all the passion of a frustrated reformer:

> But cities seek their own, not others' good;
> they drag all with them in their headlong haste.
> They smash up animals like hollow wood
> and countless nations they burn up for waste.

He felt himself pinioned in the stone grip of the city, and the result was anguish, "the anguish deep of cities monstrous grown." The city here, though surely not beyond good and evil, was a collective fatality which could know only personal solutions, not social ones. Rilke sought his salvation in a poetic neo-Franciscanism, which negated in spirit the empty fate —the "spirally gyration"—which urban man called progress.[30] Despite his clear social protest, Rilke belonged rather to the new fatalists than to the archaists or futurists; for his solution was psychological and meta-historical, not socially redemptive.

Let us not fall into the error of some critics of the modern city by ignoring the genuine *joie de vivre* which the esthetic acceptance of the metropolis could generate. In reading the sophisticated urbanites of the *fin de siècle* one cannot but sense a certain affinity to Voltaire. For example, take Richard Le Gallienne's "London":

> London, London, our delight,
> Great flower that opens but at night,
> Great city of the midnight sun,
> Whose day begins when day is done.
>
> Lamp after lamp against the sky
> Opens a sudden beaming eye,
> Leaping a light on either hand,
> The iron lilies of the Strand.[31]

Le Gallienne expressed the same delight in the vital gleaming city as Voltaire. To be sure, the source of radiance was different: sunlight bathed Voltaire's Paris; nature glorified the work of man. Le Gallienne's city, in contrast, defied nature with mock-bucolic iron lilies and gaslit midnight

---

[30] Rainer Maria Rilke, *The Book of Hours* (trans. by A. L. Peck, London, 1961), 117–135.

[31] Quoted in Holbrook Jackson, *The Eighteen Nineties* (London, 1950), 105.

suns. Not art but artificiality was celebrated here. Pleasure-seeking noc-
turnal London blotted out its grimy day. The Blakean meter of Le Gallienne's poem—was it intentional?—recalled Blake's workaday London, the
gray historical transition from Voltaire's brilliant daylight to Le Gallienne's
garish night-light. The night-bloom of London—as Le Gallienne showed he
knew in other poems—was a flower of evil. But in an urban world become
fatality, a flower's still a flower. Why should a man not pluck it? Voltaire's
pleasure principle still had life in the *fin de siècle*, though its moral force
was spent.

However marked their differences in personal response, the subjectivist
transvaluators were at one in accepting megalopolis with its terrors and its
joys as the given, the undeniable ground of modern existence. They banished both memory and hope, both the past and the future. To endow
their feelings with esthetic form became the substitute for social values.
Although social criticism sometimes remained strong, as it did in Rilke, all
sense of social mastery atrophied. The esthetic power of the individual replaced social vision as the source of succor in the face of fate. Where the
social futurists looked to the redemption of the city through historical action, the fatalists redeemed it daily by revealing the beauty in urban
degradation itself. What they saw as unalterable, they made endurable in a
stance strangely compounded of stoicism, hedonism and despair.

Baudelaire and his successors unquestionably contributed to a new appreciation of the city as a scene of human life. Their esthetic revelation has
converged with the social thought of the futurists to issue in richer and
more constructive thinking about the city in our century. Since this form
of thought is generally familiar, I shall close instead on another more som-
ber intellectual synthesis, one which drove to its ultimate extreme the idea
I have been discussing: the city beyond good and evil. This idea—with its
historistic equivalent, the city as fatality—achieved its fullest theoretical
formulation in the thought of Oswald Spengler, and its practical realization
at the hands of the German National Socialists.

In his conspectus of civilization, Spengler brought together in the most
spohisticated way many of the ideas of the city we have traced here. The
city was for him the central civilizing agency. Like Fichte, he viewed it as
an original creation of the folk. Like Voltaire, he called it the perfector of
rational civilization. Like Verhaeren, he observed it suck the life out of the
countryside. Accepting the psychological analyses of Baudelaire, Rilke, and
Le Gallienne, he regarded modern urban humanity as neo-nomadic, dependent upon the spectacle of the ever-changing urban scene to fill the void
of a desocialized consciousness. With all these affinities to his predecessors,
Spengler differed from them in the most crucial area: he transformed all
their affirmations into negations. This most brillant of all historians of the
city hated his subject with the bitter passion of the *fin de siècle* neo-
archaists, the frustrated anti-democratic rightists of the lower middle class.
Though he presented the city as fatality, he clearly welcomed its demise.

The German National Socialists shared the attitudes of Spengler—though surely not his richness of learning. The example of their urban policies illuminates the consequences of the fusion of two of the strands we have discussed: neo-archaist values with the notion of the city as a fatality beyond good and evil.

Translating neo-archaist notions into public policy, the Nazis began their rule with an active policy of returning the urban population to the holy German soil. They tried both permanent resettlement of urban workers on the land, and the education of urban youth in rural labor service.[32] Their antiurbanism did not, however, extend to Fichte's cherished medieval cities. Although the Nazi movement originated in a *Residenzstadt*, Munich, it chose medieval Nuremberg as the appropriate site for its annual party congress. The demands of the modern industrial state, however, could only be fulfilled in an urban setting. The Nazis, while excoriating the "pavement literature" of the 1920's, and branding urban art as decadent, brought out in their city-building all the elements which the urban critics had almost strongly condemned. Was the city responsible for the mechanization of life? The Nazis slashed down the trees of Berlin's Tiergarten to build the widest, most monotonously mechanical street in the world: the *Achse*, where rurally regenerated youth could ride their roaring motorcycles in black-uniformed formation. Was the city the scene of the lonely crowd? The Nazis built huge squares in which the crowd could intoxicate itself. Had the city-man become deracinated and atomized? The Nazis made him a cog in a huge machine. The hyper-rationality which the neo-archaists deplored reappeared in the Nazi parade, the Nazi demonstration, the organization of every aspect of life. Thus the whole cult of rural virtue and the medieval, communitarian city revealed itself as ideological veneer, while the reality of antiurban prejudice brought the vices of the city to an undreamt-of fulfillment: mechanization, deracination, spectacle and—untouched behind the great squares of men on the march one knew not where—the still-festering slums. Truly the city had here become a fatality for man, beyond good and evil. The antiurbanites had brought to fruition the very features of the city they had most condemned. For they were themselves children of the unreformed city of the nineteenth century, victims of an Enlightenment dream gone wrong.

---

[32] Frieda Wunderlich, *Farm Labor in Germany, 1810–1945* (Princeton, 1961), 159–202, *passim*.

37 | The Evolution of the American City and the Emergence of Anomie: A Culture Case Study of Buffalo, New York: 1810–1910*

ELWIN H. POWELL

Sociologists have often postulated a relationship between urbanism and anomie. The city is pictured as a 'motley of social worlds which touch but do not interpenetrate' (Park), as a 'society of strangers' (Meyer). More a population aggregate than a community the city is functionally integrated through the cash nexus, but there is 'no communication and no consensus . . . [and] human relations are symbiotic rather than social' (Park). Men are isolated from one another and alienated from the larger society; anomie is reflected in social pathologies as well as in the decay of public life (de Grazia). Lewis Mumford describes the modern megalopolis in four words: 'external regularity; internal disruption'.

Seeking an explanation for the character of urban life sociologists first turned to demography and ecology. For R. E. Park human society consisted of an ecological base and a cultural superstructure, and the former determined the latter. Following Simmel and Durkheim, Louis Wirth reasoned that 'as the number of people interacting [dynamic density] increase, social relations become superficial and segmentalized, producing the "schizoid character of the urban personality"'. The anonymity and transience of urban life engenders a sophisticated and calculating self-centredness. 'No single group has the undivided allegiance of the individual . . . and there is little opportunity for the individual to obtain a conception of the city as a whole or to survey his place in the total scheme of things.' Or, as Park put

* Revision of a paper read before the Western New York Sociological Society, Fall, 1959. For criticism I am indebted to Dr. Sidney Willhelm of San Francisco State College.

SOURCE: *British Journal of Sociology*, XIII (June 1962), 156–166. Copyright © 1962 by Routledge and Kegan Paul, Ltd. Reprinted by permission of the publisher.

it, 'man gains his freedom but loses his direction'. The demographic-ecological thesis can be represented schematically as follows:

$$\text{Dynamic Density} \rightarrow \left[\begin{array}{l} \text{Heterogeneity} \\ \text{Division of Labour} \rightarrow \text{Anonymity} \rightarrow \text{Anomie} \\ \text{Mobility} \end{array} \right.$$

Kingsley Davis follows a similar argument: population density gives rise to heterogeneity, anonymity, and finally 'an atomization of the constituent individuals'. Following the dissolution of communal solidarity there is a competitive struggle for existence, and competition is the foundation of the laws of urban ecology.

Yet the demographic-ecological framework has never proved completely satisfactory as an explanation of the urban way of life. First, it may be culturally limited; not all cities correspond to the American pattern. Secondly, there are serious logical contradictions in the conceptual scheme itself. And finally, as Walter Firey has shown, the 'laws' of ecology are not 'natural' but cultural phenomena. Firey demonstrated that the ecological configuration was partially the product of social institutions. Similarly in a chapter on 'localized anomie' Firey maintains that the deterioration of communal and kinship solidarity, so characteristic of the American city, is a function of the economic system rather than urbanism as such. Furthermore the economic order is ultimately the creation of cultural values.

The present paper is an attempt to delineate some of the historical and institutional sources of the anomie of urban life.

Method: Historical

Sociologists have not availed themselves of the relative abundance of historical material on the American city. Reference is occasionally made to Adna Weber and Arthur Schlesinger, senr., but the raw data from the archives are rarely used. Several people have written on the pre-industrial city, and the late Howard Becker was working on a typology of the Greek city. Yet the twenty-five page bibliography of the 1957 edition of the Hatt and Reiss *Reader in Urban Sociology* contains hardly a reference to the nineteenth-century American city. This is especially unfortunate because the tansition from a rural to an urban society began immediately after the Civil War and reached fruition in the decisive period between 1890 and 1910 when the 'core culture' which has more or less prevailed since then came into being. To fully understand the urban present it is necessary to know at least the broad contours of the past.

Data: Buffalo, New York: 1810–1910

Demographically Buffalo's development typifies the American city. Almost a small town until the 1850's, it was a full-grown metropolis by the turn of the century, afterwards spreading out into a megalopolis. Between 1810 and 1850 the population doubled each decade, growing from a village of 1,508 to a city of 42,261 at mid-century. . . . The first settlers were New Englanders moving west. In 1830 some 10 per cent of the population was foreign-born, mainly German and Irish stock. By 1860 the population was nearly half German—30,000. Polish immigration began in the 1880's and 1890's; Italians came in large numbers around the turn of the century. By the time of the First World War the foreign-born (one-third of the city) population was 26 per cent Polish, 17 per cent German, 13 per cent Italian, with the remainder of Irish, English and Eastern European descent. While Buffalo was once called a Polish city there is today little to distinguish it from other heavy-industry centres of the north-east.

(1) *Buffalo as Community: 1810–1860*

Although Buffalo was primarily a commercial centre there was still a strong sense of social solidarity in the 1830's and 1840's. One writer speaks of the community as 'a band of brothers and sisters'—doubtless an exaggeration. Nevertheless, both necessity and common values created a kind of mutual dependence which is seldom found in the modern city. Eight months of the year, from April to December, were devoted to business but the other four months of ice-bound winter were 'quite generally given up to social enjoyment. . . . One never expected to be without several friends on any evening where there was not an important social affair taking place. . . . It was not uncommon . . . to write three hundred or four hundred invitations to a party.' The society is described as 'full of ceremony and courtly usage, at the same time quaintly provincial. . . .' The public lecture —on subjects ranging from animal magnetism to 'The Progress of Literature in the 13th and 14th Centuries'—was a popular entertainment, and many activities revolved around the church. Of course there were outsiders, e.g. an anomic waterfront element, who did not participate fully in the cultural life of the community, but the open frontier siphoned off many of the misfits and 'riff-raff'. The resident population thought of themselves as simple, democratic folk possessed of that sense of equality which de Tocqueville made the key to American character.

The extremes of wealth and poverty were less pronounced than in subsequent decades. Few people lived off the unearned increment of capital; the owners of property were usually the managers of their holdings. Most establishments employed no more than twenty or so workers; manufacturing (ship building, iron working) was still a handicraft. Like the merchant the artisan served a small personally-known clientele, and there is no record of serious and sustained labour trouble (though there were occasional riots). The workers, as Professor Horton comments, 'were not aiming at working class solidarity but tried rather through individual exertions to rise above their class and enter business or the professions'. Classes were not segregated ecologically; of the four residential wards of the city the assessed value of real estate was approximately the same in each—$2,500,000. A businessman's 'word was as good as his bond' and merchants freely borrowed money from one another when low on cash. As late as 1840 the city council had no fixed time to meet; members simply gathered in a local tavern or hotel when there was business to be discussed. Buffalo had only one policeman until the mid-'forties and did not have a uniformed police force until 1866. Seemingly informal (primary group) control was sufficient to maintain order and carry on the business of the community (although it is also possible that more disorder could be tolerated in this early period, when the social structure still had a certain looseness about it). But by the late 'forties as Mrs. Poole reflects, 'changes were foreshadowed. . . . The introduction of the railway brought strangers of every condition and kind to our doors. That exclusiveness which the locality, surroundings, climate and conditions of the times forced upon us was now at an end, never to return.' Both the sources and the profundity of the 'change' eluded most of the observers of the time. There was an imperceptible hardening of class lines, a gradual closing of the avenues of social ascent, a solidification of the power of the ruling élite.

(2) Buffalo as Class Society: 1860–1910

While the nature of the city did not change overnight, by the late 1860's the outlines of a new society were clearly visible. At the top of the social pyramid were men of great wealth; at the bottom was an industrial proletariat, a detached and indigent population. Arrests for both major and minor crimes increased sharply in the 1860's . . . . By the 1870's around 5 per cent of the population was receiving poor relief from the city. Of the 7,696 people on relief in 1879, 17 per cent were native-born Americans, 36 per cent were Irish, 30 per cent German and the remainder of miscellaneous European stocks. Vagrants were sent to the 'poor farm' for 30 days; petty thieves received as much as 60 days in the workhouse for such crimes as stealing a coat or a pair of boots. This was the age of the vagabond when tramps roamed the country as 'pitiful caricatures of the pioneer'.

Some sense of the time can be gained from a review of the chronic labour trouble of the period. Railroading was the primary industry of Buffalo, and when in 1877 wages were reduced from $1.50 to $1.38 a day (12 hours) a major strike was precipitated. The local press insisted that the 'strikers' rebellion' must be put down, and for that purpose the state militia was finally called to the scene. After the return to normalcy the press seemed puzzled that neither the railroad nor the employees 'consider that they owe any sort of allegiance to each other'. Of course the workers 'had a right to decline to work at the reduced pay, but there their rights ceased'. However just their complaint 'there can be no toleration of the strikers' course. For the right of a person to employ labourers to work at any price they may agree upon without interference is one without which society cannot exist.' Although the press assumed the 1877 strike would 'make the corporation more solicitous to avoid giving occasion for strikes in the future', the same scene on a larger scale was re-enacted in 1892. After the local police proved unable to subdue 700 striking railroad switchmen, 8,000 troops were dispatched to Buffalo. The switchmen finally capitulated, saying they could not fight the U.S. Army and a half-dozen corporations too, but for several days martial law reigned; the saloons were closed (often at bayonet point) and the streets of the city were deserted. The railway workers were the first to unionize and later the crafts followed suit, saying simply: 'We organize because we must.' Concentrated capital created conditions where it was no longer possible to bargain on an individual basis.

The decade of the 1890's was the high noon of Buffalo capitalism. The city boasted 60 millionaires, twice the number in all the United States in 1850. Congruent with the prevailing myth men were said to have acquired their fortunes through hard work, thrift and individual genius—the virtues of the Protestant Ethic. One writer contends that none of the Buffalo millionaires inherited great wealth, and the assertion contains a kind of literal truth: there was no great wealth to inherit in 1850. But inherited position had a decisive effect on individual destiny. The ten richest families had been well established in the city since 1840. Between 1860 and 1890 when the fortunes were made the population of the city trebled—from 81,000 to 244,000—and the businessman or landowner already established in the community was bound to prosper. Without question the rich got richer, and there is some evidence that the poor became poorer; during the period the per capita personal wealth appears to have declined . . . . A more intangible change also occurred; men came to look differently on wealth and poverty. Increasingly business and labour inhabited different social worlds. Writing in a Buffalo union publication Samuel Gompers stated the case clearly, 'Modern society is based on one simple fact, the practical separation of the capitalist class from the great mass of workers. It is not so much a difference in industrial rank as social status . . . a distinction scarcely noticeable in the United States before the previous generation'.

In the 1890's the separation acquired even a physical or ecological dimension. Upper-class families of enormous wealth, Anglo-Saxon origin and Protestant religion built three- and four-storey palaces along Delaware Avenue.

"This fashionable section was only a small part of the city [writes Mable Dodge Luhan], but it seemed to us the only real Buffalo. . . . On Delaware Avenue you knew everyone you met on the street, but people never talked to each other except of outward things. There was hardly any real intimacy between friends and people had no confidence in each other . . . they neither showed their feelings nor talked about them. . . . In those days only the outermost rim of life was given any conscious attention."

The life of the upper class was sombre and humourless, bearing almost no resemblance to the musical comedy conception of a 'gay nineties', and a mood of alienation permeated the reflective writing of the time.

A small and literate patrician element looked with longing to the past, a spirit embodied in Buffalo's most accomplished poet, David Gray. Independently wealthy and a Buffalo newspaper editor for forty years Gray could speak with equal force to the intellectual and the business community. With a pessimism faintly suggestive of Henry Adams, Gray's last years were spent in bewildered revolt against progress, industrialism and the city. But the 'new rich' greeted the future with brassy optimism. Progress meant money, and money was the sacred value around which all else revolved. As Mrs. Luhan says of her grandfather: 'He had a sense not only of the importance but the holiness of money.'

Money was the cornerstone of the polity as well as the economy. Thrift was the highest civic virtue, and at the dedication of the new city and county hall in the 1870's the noblest words the orator could find are these, 'The people . . . have secured a building at less cost than has been expended for any similar structure in this country.' The theme is reiterated on every ceremonial occasion, even down to the present. Thus from the 1870's on, the annual message of the mayor to the city council begins with a *ritual of frugality*. In 1875 Mayor Dayton told the council, 'For the first time in years the questions of government—municipal, state and national—are now considered as ones of finance and political economy. Men everywhere are . . . governing their actions by business principles.' Even Grover Cleveland, whose rapid rise to national fame began as a reform mayor of Buffalo, climaxed his first address to the council in this vein: 'We are . . . trustees and agents of our fellow citizens, holding their funds in sacred trust.' The philosophy of politics as business reaches something of a high point in 1895 when Mayor Jewett told the council, 'Enterprizes are attracted by a wise, conservative and business-like government. . . . To me the city of Buffalo appears to be, not a political hive, but a vast business corporation.' Except for the abortive effort at reform between 1898 and 1910 when plans for municipal socialism (city ownership of utilities) were seriously promoted by even the local business class, there has scarcely been a departure from the credo of laissez-faire capitalism.

Around the turn of the century the economic base of the city was changing. Ownership and control of key industries were passing to outside interests. The formation of the Lackawanna Steel Company in 1901 was the prototype of subsequent industrial development. The company was founded with a capital investment of $30,000,000, 17 per cent of which was local. Ten years later local ownership had dwindled to 7 per cent. Only two of the twenty-man board of directors were Buffalonians, but the company was handed a *carte blanche* by the city. No building restrictions were imposed and there was no protest against health and safety conditions even though there were as many as 4,000 injuries a year and one fatality a day in a work force of 6,000. By 1906 the steel works covered 1,500 acres and had an authorized capital stock of $60,000,000 (doubled since 1901) and in that year alone sold over $28,000,000 in products. Yet the employees, mainly Polish and Slavic immigrants, worked twelve hours a day, seven days a week, at wages ranging from ten to twenty cents an hour.

Worse than wage slavery was the threat of unemployment. From the 1870's on unemployment rates were abnormally high and the census of 1900—a prosperous time—records the [high unemployment] figures . . . .

With heavy industry came the slums, where in Hobbesian style the life of man was 'bitter, brutish and brief'. The Buffalo of 1910 was a replica of Upton Sinclair's *Jungle*. Fifty to sixty people crowded into ten-room houses in the steel districts, and sometimes boarders could not rent rooms but only spaces on beds for a night or day turn. Ninety-four per cent of the Poles in Buffalo had an income of less than $635, the estimated living wage for the time, and the Hungarian settlement held 'the astonishing record of 10,000 human beings without a single bathtub'. One observer notes that

at night gangs roam the streets and come toward each other . . . roaring at the top of their voices. When they meet they start fighting simply for the sake of fighting which has become a sport for these people. They use clubs, knives and revolvers. . . . Police are called but refuse to come to the area. . . . Children have no place to play except with the pigs and goats who wallow about in the slime and swamps.

This latter observation is verified by photographs published in the local press.

While the lot of the craftsman had improved, the unskilled factory worker, isolated from the larger community and unprotected by union power, was hardly more than a piece of machinery. The personnel policy of Lackawanna Steel was both a cause and a symbol of this new way of life.

Of the five or six thousand employees [writes the *Buffalo Times*], everyone is so recorded that not a man can loaf or beat his time a minute without the heads of different departments being cognizant of the fact and his wage cut accordingly. When a man is hired, a card record is taken . . . and he is given a number. . . . After assuming this number the laborer loses his name and thereafter is known only by the figures on his coat.

While material conditions have improved since 1910, with the further regimentation of the work force still others have 'lost their name' and become a cipher in a ledger.

Interpretation: Anomie as a Product of Capitalism

Outwardly placid, the nineteenth century closed on a note of foreboding. Metaphorically speaking the century ended at the Pan American Exposition in Buffalo where a Polish 'anarchist' assinated President William McKinley. The act seemed to materialize the secret fears which the wealthy had harboured for 20 years. Earlier Buffalo Congressman James O. Putnam had warned: 'We are rapidly becoming a nation of great cities. In them gather the dangerous elements of society. In them anarchy hatches its plots of murder and lights its revolutionary fires. . . .' The prophesy was more a projection of guilt than a rational assessment of the radical movement; nevertheless, the Buffalo of 1900 was anything but confident. 'The Gilded Age', as Professor Horton remarks, 'was an age of innocence only for sheltered dowagers and debutantes; it was an age of apprehension.'

In the 1840's the young men of Buffalo were advised that success came only through a wise self-reliance and was 'incompatible with all presumption upon Destiny and excluded all dependence on Adventious Circumstances'. By the turn of the century the advice seemed all but irrelevant; the lives of most people were shaped by circumstances quite beyond their own control. For the working-class unemployment came like a natural disaster, unrelated to the actions of men. Even the merchant class, supposedly the incarnation of individual initiative, owed its affluence as much to the mysterious dynamics of population growth and industrial expansion as to its own efforts. Success was largely the consequence of being at the right place at the right time with the right connections. In addition, there was the fortuitous gyration of the business cycle, which, defined as beyond rational control, actually became so. More than ever chance seemed to rule the affairs of men. With the separation of the social classes it became increasingly difficult for either class to gain a rational comprehension of the actions of the other. With the emergence of the trans-local corporation remote authorities could make decisions affecting the lives of thousands who had no alternative but acquiescence. A people who a century earlier had conquered nature was now unable to master its own creation—the social environment. Both individually and collectively, men seemed impotent in the face of the urban problem, and there was a general retreat into the sphere of private life.

In the progressive period in Buffalo (1900–10) there was an heroic effort at municipal reform, which in the end accomplished little. Once the labour movement was co-opted into the corporate structure, the energy for social transformation was dissipated. In the 1890's labour was explicitly socialistic, calling for collective ownership of all means of production and distribution as well as higher pay and an eight-hour day. In Buffalo by 1910 the wages of craftsmen had been raised substantially, but the proposals for collective ownership were abandoned. Henceforth, the A.F. of L. asked for its members nothing more than 'the right to sell their labor to the best advantage of themselves'; far from revolutionary ,'the principle upon which organized labour is founded . . . is the best bulwark of society against the threat of socialism'. The demand for radical reform subsided as the principle of self-interest, the spirit of capitalism, prevailed.

Since its foundation the American city has been dominated by the economic institution—first the market, then the corporation. Neither local political nor religious institutions were able to regulate economic activity; indeed, both merely reinforced the existing system. The key to the city is the economic institution:

First, the business idology was clearly embodied in municipal organization. From the 1870's onward the objective of local government was the creation of a climate favourable to business enterprise, which means minimal taxation and control. If the purpose of the city was to stimulate investment what better incentive than a compliant administration. Given this definition of the situation it was inevitable that the 'spirit of graft and lawlessness', as Lincoln Steffens called it, should assert itself. Under laissez-faire capitalism the city could play at best *only a regulative not a productive* role in economic life. As early as 1873 the socialists had proposed public works programmes to solve the unemployment problem, but the most Buffalo offered the indigent was the county poor farm. Private charities were left to cope with all the problems created by starvation wages, immigration and unemployment.

Secondly, the industrial corporation as the main employer of men determined their style of life in countless ways. First it created an 'employee mentality', a submissiveness quite at odds with the ideal of self-reliance. Occupying a role of passive subordination eight or twelve hours a day did not condition men to take an active part in a democratic community. There was an active and anarchic rebellion, an aggression bred of frustration and expressed in crime, but no interest in social reconstruction. The insecurity of wage-labour and unemployment also contributed materially to the high crime rates of the urban slums. The slum was the product of industrial capitalism; it was created *in* not *by* the city. As we have seen, it was corporate policy (of the railroads in the nineteenth century and the steel mills in the twentieth) which precipitated the bitterest labour trouble in Buffalo. Given the premise of profit-making it was inevitable that wages should be cut to the subsistence level. For the middle class, status in the corporation was beginning to replace status in the territorial community as the primary bond upon which one's fate depended. Since its ownership was translocal, the corporation had only a nominal and pecuniary interest in the city of Buffalo. In the nineteenth century the local capitalist élite, while amassing wealth, still took pride in the city, and established organizations of enduring benefit to the community: a remarkable park system, a museum of natural history, art galleries, libraries and the historical society. But as the power and autonomy of the local élite declined, the city lost much of its colour and high culture.

Finally, the ecology of the city is a product of economic institutions rather than sub-social, biotic competition. A 'cultural institution'—the railroads—blocked the development of a 'natural' harbour for seventy-five years. The spatial order of the American city is rational only in serving the ends of profit for the property holders. In the context of the needs of the community land use may be quite irrational. For instance, the city of Buffalo has been desperately deficient in park space for forty years; yet more and more public land is being sold to private interests. This is not an expression of the natural law of ecology but the cultural law of profit.

Conclusion

Urban sociology links the nature of the city to its demographic-ecological composition. The size and heterogeneity of the modern city creates an anonymous milieu which 'individuates the person and secularizes society' (Park). The city dissolves the primary group; the result is isolation and finally disorientation or anomie. Yet in the evolution of Buffalo from a cohesive community to an atomized society it is not the process of urbanization but the development of the economic institution which is the decisive factor. The social character of the American city—the anomie of the urban way of life—is a product of the spirit of capitalism.

38 | Suburbia and the American Dream

BENNETT M. BERGER

Americans have never been other than ambivalent in their commitment to cultural variety, as against their longing for cultural uniformity. Today, this ambivalence is becoming a central concern of public policy. For, as urban planning becomes an increasingly visible and legitimate part of the activity of the public sector, its power will grow to support or to undermine cultural diversity in the traditional seat of that diversity—the cities. Like the myth of a homogeneous "suburbia," which for a long time obscured, and to some extent still obscures, the actual variety of suburban life, complacence about the cultural diversity of cities may blind us to the conditions which sustain it. My aim in this essay is to take what I and others have learned about the variety of suburban styles of life, and to relate this knowledge, first to some of the more pervasive pluralisms of American culture, and then to a few of the problems of planning for urban diversity.

SOURCE: Reprinted from *Planning for a Nation of Cities* by Sam Bass Warner, Jr., by permission of The M.I.T. Press, Cambridge, Massachusetts. Copyright 1966 by the Massachusetts Institute of Technology. This appeared as "Suburbia and the American Dream" in *The Public Interest*, 2 (Winter, 1966).

The Persistence of the Myth of Suburbia

Some years back, I undertook a study (reported in *Working-Class Suburb*, Univ. of Calif. Press, 1960) in order to observe the transformation of a group of automobile assembly line workers into the "suburbanites" who had become stock figures in American popular culture in the 1950's through the satirical and other efforts of a variety of popular magazines. It seemed to me that, having found a working class population more than two years settled in a new suburb, I was provided with an almost natural experimental setting in which to document the processes through which "suburbia" exercised its profound and diffuse influence in transforming a group of poorly educated factory workers into those model middle-class Americans obsessed with the problems of crab-grass and "conformity."

Well, it is now a matter of public record that my basic assumption was wrong. As the interview evidence piled up, it became clearer and clearer that the lives of the suburbanites I was studying had not been profoundly affected in any statistically identifiable or sociologically interesting way. They were still overwhelmingly Democrats they attended church as infrequently as they ever did; like most working class people, their informal contacts were limited largely to kin; they neither gave nor went to parties; on the whole they had no great hopes of getting ahead in their jobs; and instead of a transient psychology, most of them harbored a view of their new suburban homes as paradise permanently gained.

But (appropriately enough for a Ph.D. candidate) I was cautious in the general inferences I drew from that study. It was, after all, based only on a small sample, of one suburb, of one metropolitan area, in one region, and it suffered from all of the methodological limitations inherent in small case studies. None of my findings gave me any reason to doubt the truth of what William H. Whyte, for example, had said of his organization men; but it also seemed to me that there was little reason *not* to believe that my findings in San Jose would be repeatedly confirmed in many of the less expensive suburbs around the country whose houses were priced well within the means of unionized workers in heavy industry, and of lower white collar employees as well. I did, in short, question the right of others to generalize freely about suburbia on the basis of very few studies of selected suburbs which happened to be homogeneously middle or upper middle class in character—especially when it seemed apparent that suburban housing was increasingly available to all but the lowest income levels and status groups.

The considerable bulk of research that has been done on suburbs in the years since I did my work has given me no reason to alter the conclusions I drew then. Indeed, none of this research can be expected to give much comfort to those who find it convenient to believe that a suburb exercises some mysterious power over its residents, transforming them into replicas of Whyte's practitioners of "The Outgoing Life." There seems to be increasing consensus among students of suburbia that suburban development is simply the latest phase of a process of urban growth that has been going on for a long time, that the cultural character of suburbs varies widely in terms of the social make-up of its residents, and of the personal and group dispositions that led them to move to suburbs in the first place; that the variety of physical and demographic differences between cities and suburbs (and there *are* some) bears little significance for the way of life of their inhabitants, and that some of these differences, although statistically accurate, are sociologically spurious, since the appropriate comparisons are not between residential suburbs and cities as wholes, but between suburbs and urban residential neighborhoods. In general, the reported changes in the lives of suburbanites were not *caused* by the move to suburbia, but were reasons for moving there in the first place. In suburbs, as in city apartments, social class, the age-composition of residents, the age of the neighborhood, etc., are much more profound predictors of the style of life than is residential location with respect to the city limits. Analysis of national samples has provided confirmation neither of a trend to Republicanism in politics nor a return to religion. Suburbs, in short, seem—as Reissman and Ktsanes have characterized them—to be "new homes for old values."

It appears, then, that there are no grounds for believing that suburbia has created a distinctive style of life or a new social character for Americans. Yet the myth of suburbia persists, as is evident from the fact that it is still eminently discussable over the whole range of our cultural media, from comic books to learned journals. One should not be surprised at this, for myths are seldom dispelled by research; they have going for them something considerably more powerful than mere evidence. And though nothing I say here can change this fact, it may give us some comfort to understand the sources of the myth, the functions it performs for the groups by whom it is sustained, and the nature of its appeal to America's image of itself.

In my book, and then, again, later in an article, I undertook a functional explanation of the myth of suburbia. I pointed first to the fact that suburbs were rich with ready made visible symbols: patios and barbecues, lawn-mowers and tricycles, shopping centers, station wagons, and so on, and that such symbols were readily organizable into an image of a way of life that could be marketed to the non-suburban public. I also pointed out that this marketing was facilitated by the odd fact that the myth of suburbia conveniently suited the ideological purposes of several influential groups who market social and political opinion—odd because these groups could usually be found disagreeing with each other, not only about matters of opinion, but about matters of fact as well. Realtor-chamber-of-commerce interests and the range of opinion represented by the Luce magazines could use the myth of suburbia to affirm the American Way of Life; city planners, architects, urban design people and so on could use the myth of suburbia to warn that those agglomerations of standardized, vulgarized, mass-produced cheerfulness which masqueraded as homes would be the slums of tomorrow. Liberal and left-wing culture-critics could (and did) use the myth of suburbia to launch an attack on complacency, conformity, and mass culture, and found in this myth an up-to-date polemical vocabulary with which to rebuke the whole slick tenor of American life: what used to be disdained as "bourgeois" was now simply designated as "suburban." In short, the *descriptive* accuracy of the myth of suburbia went largely unchallenged because it suited the *prescriptive* desires of such a wide variety of opinion, from the yea-sayers of the right to the agonizers of the center to the nay-sayers of the left.

But though I still think this analysis of the myth makes good sense, I think too that there is something more—something, if I may be permitted to say so, deeper, profounder, and which I was only dimly aware of then. I think now that the myth can be understood also as our society's most recent attempt to come to terms with the melting pot problem, a problem that goes straight to the heart of American ambivalence about cultural pluralism.

Cultural Pluralism and the Melting Pot

America has never really come to terms with the legend of the melting pot. That legend, if I may quote the windy text of its original source, saw America as the place where "Celt and Latin, Slav and Teuton, Greek and Syrian, Black and Yellow, Jew and Gentile, the palm and the pine, the pole and the equator, the crescent and the cross" would together build "the Republic of Man and the Kingdom of God." Despite the hope that a unified American culture might emerge from the seething cauldron, it didn't happen; instead, the formation of ethnically homogeneous communities—ghettoes—helped the immigrants preserve large segments of their cultures, and the tendency to endogamy helped them preserve it beyond the first generation. But in spite of the evident facts of our cultural pluralism (by which I mean the persisting correlation of significant differences in values and behavior with ethnic, regional, and social class differences), attempts are continually made to create an image of *the* typical or representative or genuine American and his community. These attempts have usually succeeded only in creating stereotypes—most familiarly, perhaps, a caricature of one or another variety of Our Town: white, Anglo-Saxon, Protestant, and middle class. *Saturday Evening Post* covers, white picket fences, colonial houses, maple hutches and the like have historically played an important role in such attempts. *The myth of suburbia is the latest attempt to render America in this homogeneous manner,* to see in the highly visible and proliferating suburban developments a new melting pot which would receive the diverse elements of a new generation from a society fragmented by class, region, religion, and ethnicity, and from them create *the* American style of life. Suburbia as America is no more false a picture, probably, than Babbitt or Our Town as America; but it fails as a melting pot for the same reason that the original melting pot idea failed: like many other urban neighborhoods, specific suburbs developed a tendency to homogeneity, almost always in terms of social class and very often in terms of ethnicity.

The myth of American cultural homogeneity and the stubborn fact of heterogeneity reflect a persistent ambivalence in American society regarding cultural unity and diversity, between the melting pot idea and the pluralist idea. During and after the period of rapid immigration into the "teeming cities," for example, free public education expressed the need for some minimum "Americanization," whereas the ghetto expressed the impulse to cultural self-preservation (both by the natives who excluded and the immigrants who segregated themselves). In the rest of the country, 4th of July style patriotic rhetoric expressed the gropings toward an elementary national identity, whereas provincial arrogance—and hostility to "the government" and to centers of cosmopolitan influence—expressed the affirmation of narrow local autonomies. The ambivalence was really a double ambivalence; each polar position was itself unstable: to be truly tenable, a pluralist ideology must accord intrinsic honor and value to a diversity of life styles, and this it has never completely done. The salient features of minority subcultural styles have more often than not been regarded as stigmata by dominant groups, tolerable so long as they were temporary, that is, *transitional* to something approaching the dominant cultural style. On the other hand, the attempts of provincial, nativist ("WASP") groups to secure their own style as *the* American style stopped short of supporting the emergence of broadly inclusive *national* institutions which would have facilitated that transition. The most enthusiastic celebrators of "Americanism' 'were precisely the groups who were most wary of integrating the varieties of the national life into a unified culture.

Indeed, a unified national culture has until quite recently been a most improbable prospect, since the United States has traditionally been a society without very powerful national institutions with which to promote that unity and pass it on down the generations. Without an established church or a powerful federal government, without national political parties or a standardized educational system, enormous distances and poor communications enabled local economies to breed a highly differentiated system of *native* subcultures—in addition to those created by the immigrants. Even today, there are probably dozens of distinctive American types, to some extent stereotypes, perhaps, but which nevertheless call attention to the wide variety of *native* styles: Vermont farmers and Boston Brahmins, Southern Bourbons and Tennessee hillbillies, beatniks and organization men, Plainvillers, Middletowners, and cosmopolitan intellectuals, to say nothing of teenagers, the jet set, and many, many more, all American, all different, and none probably very eager to be integrated into an idea of "*the* American" at a level of complexity suitable for a *Time* cover story or a patriotic war movie.

It is not surprising, then, that when one tries to abstract from American life a system of values which can be called distinctively or representatively American, the task is immensely difficult. The most systematic attempt by a sociologist, that of Robin Williams in his book *American Society*, is foiled by the fact that important groups in American society do not share the 15 or 16 values which he offers as basically American. There is no question that values such as "achievement," "work," "efficiency," "equality," and the rest have played a significant role in creating the quality of American life, but important parts of the lower and working classes (important because of their numbers) do not share them, and important parts of the upper class (important because of their influence) do not share them—although they may affirm them when a journalist is nearby.

Myths and Styles of Life

The persistent attempts to find some transcendent principles or values which define the unity of American culture have been defeated by the persistence of important class and ethnic differences. Even under natural or "organic" conditions, then, "American" patterns of culture are enormously difficult to describe with any accuracy. This difficulty is exacerbated when a society becomes sophisticated enough to be self-conscious about its culture and rich enough to do something about it. The maturity and the luxury of our civilization constrain its elites to define an "American" style, and the miracle of our technology arms us to manufacture it. Our society is wealthy enough to support a substantial class of intellectuals devoted to staying on top of contemporary events to "spot the trend," "see the pattern," "find the meaning," "discover the style." And our media are such that these spottings and seeings are more or less instantaneously communicated to audiences of millions, whose demand upon the marketers of opinions and interpretations for sensible and coherent syntheses is greater than the available supply.

Under such conditions, we do not get serious historical interpretation of contemporary events; we do not even get responsible journalism; we get myths, which themselves become part of the forces shaping what is happening, and which hence function ideologically. The myth of suburbia fosters an image of a homogeneous and classless America without a trace of ethnicity but fully equipped for happiness by the marvelous productivity of American industry: the ranch house with the occupied two-car garage, the refrigerator and freezer, the washer and dryer, the garbage disposal and the built-in range and dishwasher, the color TV and the hi-fi stereo. Suburbia: its lawns trim, its driveways clean, its children happy on its curving streets and in its pastel schools. Suburbia, California style, is America.

Most American intellectuals have sustained this myth in order to hate it; but the bases of their antipathy have never really been made clear. Somehow associated with these physical symbols of suburbia in the minds of most intellectuals are complacency, smugness, conformity, status anxiety, and all the rest of the by now familiar and dreary catalogue of suburban culture. But the causal connection between the physical character and the alleged cultural style of suburbia has never been clearly established. It is almost as if American intellectuals felt, like some severe old Calvinist prophet, that physical comfort necessarily meant intellectual sloth. Perhaps it is because we have been too well trained to believe that there is somehow a direct relationship between the physical structure or the esthetic shape of a residential environment and the sort of values and culture it can possibly engender—so that the esthetic monotony of suburbia could house nothing but a generation of dull, monotonous people, and its cheerful poverty of architectural design could breed nothing but a race of happy robots. The only trouble with this view is that there is little evidence and less logic to support it. Most of the adult suburbanites were *urban* bred, and hence presumably already shaped by the time they became suburbanites. And although it is still a little too early to tell what kind of culture will be produced by the generation bred in the manufactured environment of suburbia, we might remember that the generation bred in the endless and prison-like New York tenements did not do badly.

But becoming aware of the myth of suburbia, and pointing to the disparities between it and what we actually know of suburbs we have closely studied, should not be confused with a *defense* of suburbia. Nor should anything I have said about the critics of suburbia be interpreted as an expression of my personal bias in favor of suburbia. As I suggested earlier, myths are potent enough to survive evidence; they are not disarmed by understanding. Quite the contrary. Once myths gain currency, once they go, as we say, "into the cultural air", they *become real*, and function frequently as self-fulfilling prophecies. Life copies literature; fact is affected by fiction; history is constrained by myth. "If a situation is defined as real," said William I. Thomas, "it is real in its consequences," and I have no doubt (though I have no data) that family decisions regarding whether to move to the suburbs have been affected (both pro and con) by the myth of suburbia. And despite everything reasonable I have said about suburbs, I *know* that the fact that I unreasonably dislike them has been conditioned, *beyond the possibility of redemption by mere research* by the very myth of suburbia I have helped explode.

In the sense in which I have been speaking of them, myths are more or less noble fictions; fictions in that they are *made*, and noble depending on the art with which they are made, the extent to which one is in favor of the consequences they foster, and, most particularly, the forms of solidarity they promote. In the context of the debate over "suburbia," what is usually at stake is whose version of America shall become "American."

Pluralism and Planning

Whose shall? I want to suggest that the question is relevant to the way in which the future quality of urban life is planned. Like Emile Durkheim, who suggested that the punishment of crime was significant less as a deterrent or as simple revenge than as a collective reaffirmation of cultural values, I want to suggest that we look more closely at the images of solidarity which inform the proposals for dealing with social problems in general, and with urban problems in particular. For social problems, of course, have no objective existence—although the facts to which they refer may. It is objectively true that some people have always lived in dilapidated, unsafe, unheated, vermin-infested residences, but "slums" have not always been a social problem. Slums become a social problem when a large enough group of important people decide that poor people ought not to live in such places.

Americans have a propensity to find social problems. By defining them as real and hence setting ameliorative forces into action, we affirm our liberal heritage. To find problems, to mobilize opinion about them, to shake our social structure by its metaphorical shoulders and force it to *pay attention* to these matters, nourishes our beliefs in progress and perfectibility. America is a country dedicated to the propositions that no evils are ineradicable, no problems insoluble, no recalcitrance beyond conciliation, no ending need be unhappy; we are a most un-Greek democracy. Finding and dealing with problems, then, are necessary conditions for the verification of these propositions; the very existence of social problems to ameliorate reffirms our principles more than any imaginable utopia could. But not just any problems at any time. Because at any given moment there is an indefinitely large number of social problems which are theoretically identifiable, public concern with some (to the exclusion of others) can be understood not only in terms of the salience of the difficulties of those who *have* the problems but also in terms of the relevance of proposed solutions to the dominant forms and rhetoric of solidarity.

When we set out to improve the quality of urban life, what we are most likely to be doing is altering the conditions under which weak and vulnerable sections of the population live. The wealthy, who also have problems, are protected from the welfare impulses of others. The strong and the autonomous grant no one the right to alter the conditions of their lives— that is what strength and autonomy are about. Public concern over, and desire to plan for, "the problem of" the increasing proportions of aged persons in our society, for example, do not extend to Dwight Eisenhower, Harry Truman, or H. L. Hunt, all of whom qualify for the statistical category "aged," but not for our image of those who need help—although, if consulted, I might have several suggestions as to how they might spend their declining years more wholesomely. The people who have the problems which are defined as "real" are those who are vulnerable to public action, and thus to the implicit images of solidarity which underlie that action. I think it is essential that we be very clear about these images, for to plan for the *quality* of urban life is to be concerned with the *culture* of urban life, and hence with the forms of human solidarity which planning is likely both to foster and discourage.

I see three broad alternatives for those who are confronted with the problem of planning the quality of urban life. First of all, planners can simply abdicate from any concern for the cultural consequences of what they do, and instead interpret their mandate narrowly—for example, the improvement of the physical environment for the poorly housed. To the extent that they have been planned at all, most new, inexpensive suburbs have been developed in this way—with occasional exceptions, as in the gestures by the Levittowns toward the provision of some institutional facilities. More centrally located urban residential development for the poor and the less-than-affluent has also been dominated by considerations such as square footage, hygiene, and domestic technology. Now to provide room, cleanliness, comfort, and convenience to people who have previously been without them is an important achievement; but it is not planning for the quality of urban life. Quite the contrary; the *quality* of urban life is precisely what is usually left out of consideration—perhaps as a luxury rendered expendable by the need to bring large numbers of people up to some minimum physical standard. Under these conditions of planning, images of human solidarity seem limited exclusively to *households* within which *family* solidarity may be symbolized by culinary and recreational technology (refrigerators, freezers, barbecues, TVs, etc.), whereas solidarities beyond that of the family and household seem irrelevant, alien, or distant. There is a sense in which this alternative is evasive because such planning *does* engender a quality in urban life, but it is the quality that most cultivated foreign observers complain about in most American cities.

Planning's second alternative, it seems to me, is to make a conscious effort to alter the environments of certain groups, with the overt intention of bringing their culture closer to some monolithic or homogeneous ideal. Presumably, this would be some more advanced version of the melting pot idea, in which either a bureaucratic or entrepreneurial version of a middle class life-style would be given as an ideal toward which the poor should be encouraged to reach. Here the aim would be to make the society more monolithically what it already dominantly is. This alternative founders on its utopianism, on its assumption that a cultural consensus can be engineered or induced in a society in which conflict is endemic and which will remain so as long as the interests of groups and classes remain opposed. In the absence of any ability by planners to wipe out class differences, we must expect, in any multi-class community, controversy not only over the appropriate means to reach agreed-upon goals but over the goals themselves and the priorities to be assigned to them. This is the stuff of politics and culture, and where interests and norms are rooted in a class-based style of life, the attempt by one group to elicit the commitment of the entire community to a specific goal will very likely threaten another group and elicit its opposition. Moreover, these political and cultural diversities have a right to exist and persist. We can be reasonably sure that the vulnerable and dependent groups most readily affected by planning would gladly be rid of their slums, their poverty, and the discrimination against them. Beyond this it is difficult to assume anything with great assurance except, perhaps, that groups develop an attachment to those aspects of their culture which have not been imposed by necessity, an attachment made evident by their tendency to take the culture with them when they move from one environment to another, and to preserve whatever of it that circumstances permit. On the other hand, utopian planning dominated by visions of profound cultural changes is always interesting, and such planners might well devote more energy to making these visionary ideals manifest and rhetorically vivid, if only in order to help others to know whether to be for or against the form of solidarity they envision.

The Pluralist Alternative

Finally, there is the pluralist alternative, an alternative perhaps best expressed in the recent work of Herbert Gans, and, to a lesser extent, of Jane Jacobs. Whatever reservations one may have about the work of either, each of them projects an unambiguous image of the kind of human solidarity they would like to see fostered by urban planning. This solidarity is loose and heterogeneous, composed of more or less autonomous groups and neighborhoods formed on the basis of ethnicity and social class; communities attached, perhaps, to the notion that good fences make good neighbors, but necessarily related to one another through those political and economic accommodations long characteristic of urban life. If they are open to criticism as "romanticists" (although it is not clear to me why a preference for dense street life, or an insistence that an ethnic working-class neighborhood is not necessarily a slum, renders one vulnerable to such criticism), it should at least be said in their defense that they obviously care enough about the *quality* of urban life to evoke a strong and clear image of it (something their critics do not always do)—strong enough in Mrs. Jacobs' case and clear enough in Professor Gans' case to make it easy for a reader to be for or against them.

I am mostly for them, since planning for pluralism seems to me not only the most sensible way of responding to the fact of persisting cultural diversities but the most honorable way as well. In making their assumptions, planners might first of all assume (it is the most reasonable assumption) that most groups which are displaced by planning *will take their culture with them* if they can. Planners would do well to anticipate this, and to modify their plans accordingly, to facilitate the preservation of those parts of their culture that the groups want preserved. This means that planning would have to be done *for specific types of people with distinctive cultural styles*, that is, for a variety of specific, known tastes rather than for faceless densities with a given amount of disposable income for housing. A working class group with a durable pattern of sexual segregation (husbands and wives living largely separate extra-familial lives) requires for its sustenance residential and community facilities different from those required by a middle class group with a culture pattern emphasizing companionable family togetherness.

If the strain put upon the middle class biases of professional planners by such considerations seems excessive, I ask only that you think of the problem of the Negro ghetto and the potential controversy about whether *its* subculture ought to be preserved. People as different as a sociologist like Lee Rainwater and a Negro leader like James Baldwin have remarked (without clearly deploring it) upon the Dyonisianism prevalent in the Negro ghetto. Now, this is a culture pattern which clearly is both at once an adaptation to the trapped character of ghetto life, and a means of providing compensatory satisfactions for that blocked access to middle class life. If the satisfactions are not only compensatory but real, planners might think about providing facilities for the nourishment of this psycho-cultural pattern—even as they think about eliminating the enforced segregation and demoralization which make it more attractive.

Even after discrimination on the basis of race disappears, however, we have no evidence to suggest that segregation will ever disappear. If the experience of other ethnic groups is any guide (and I know of no better guide), many Negroes will choose to live among their own "kind" even after they have formally free choice of housing. However "kind" may be defined in the future, there is no reason *not* to expect social class and ethnicity to continue to play an important role—although it is quite conceivable that color may eventually not have much to do with ethnicity. We know little enough about the nature of ethnicity—and even less, perhaps, about which members of an ethnic group *prefer* to live in ghettoes, or why, even after they can live almost wherever they please. But the *fact* that many of them do is beyond question. We have no reason *not* to expect this to be true of Negroes also, particularly of those whose views are represented by the most militant Negro leaders, insistent upon the acceptance of Negroes into American society; *as Negroes*—with all that this historically implies.

I hope it is clear that these remarks are not the elaborate rationalizations of a conservative searching for an acceptable rhetoric to defend the *status quo*. Quite the contrary; they are the remarks of a sociologist who, being for the extension of the widest possible range of choice to all segments of the population, nevertheless knows that choices are hardly ever random, and that no man is so free that he is not constrained by the norms of the groups to which he belongs or would like to belong. This is as it should be; but the sense of choice rests on the existence of real alternatives. Cultural diversity has somehow been maintained in the suburbs without much help from planners. We may not be so lucky in the cities unless planners begin to understand the conditions of cultural distinctiveness and to design for it.

39 | Listening to the Radio

HORTENSE POWDERMAKER

Broadcasting to Africans started in 1941, when a small government station was set up in Lusaka to keep the Africans informed, through community receivers, of the progress of the war, to stimulate their war effort, and to convey orders in case of serious emergency. Harry Franklin, the Director of Information, ran the station in his spare time. After the war he proposed that a central African station be set up in Lusaka to broadcast exclusively to Africans in Northern Rhodesia, Southern Rhodesia, and Nyasaland and that it be used as a medium for mass education, entertainment, and to "play a great part in the sensible enlightenment of the masses." Financial help for buying transmitters and a studio was obtained from the British government in London; and, after three years of searching, Franklin found a company willing to manufacture a dry-battery receiving set cheap enough for Africans to buy. The first sets, known as "The Saucepan Special" because the metal case which protected the set resembled a saucepan, were introduced in October 1949. It was estimated that twelve hundred sets were sold to Africans in Northern Rhodesia during the first four months. Since then the battery sets have been improved, and a number of models were available at the time of the survey, ranging in price from about the equivalent of $16 to $25. Africans living in houses wired for electricity usually had electric radios.

Radio-listening was available to everyone in the township through radios at the welfare centers. Twenty per cent owned their own radios; each home-owned radio reached at least one listener other than the members of the household. Fifty per cent of the adults on the mine township listened to radio, 57 per cent of them at welfare centers. The remainder listened at home or at a friend's home, with naturally more women in this group. Sixty-four per cent of the listeners were men and 35 per cent were women. The majority, 60 per cent, were under thirty and 70 per cent had some European education. But a significant minority, 41 per cent of those between thirty and forty years of age and 36 per cent of those over forty—many with no school education—were also among the radio audience.

For the listeners, radio meant a change in sensory perceptions. In the past Africans heard voices and music only directly from human beings. Now

SOURCE: Hortense Powdermaker, *Coppertown: Changing Africa* (New York: Harper and Row, 1962), pp. 231–232, 235, 238–241. Copyright © 1962 by Hortense Powdermaker. Reprinted by permission of Harper and Row, Publishers.

they can also hear them from a "box." This new experience seemed to be both a miracle and a new form of reality. For some who did not listen, it seemed "childish to listen to something which is in a box, without seeing the person talking." Some of the same non-listeners also did not want to see "the shadows and unreal things which move as human beings in the cinema." Radio and movies, as forms of indirect and secondary communication, involve an extension of sensory perceptions and the capacity to accept and enjoy new forms of indirect participation. Modern man has been trained to recognize and accept the differences between primary and secondary communication, although many of us still prefer the "live" music of the concert hall to the "canned" music of the record or radio.

. . . . .

Music and Songs

It is not surprising in view of the traditional enjoyment of music that all the radio audience listened to and enjoyed the musical programs and that approximately half of the listeners preferred them. These programs were somewhat more popular among women and the uneducated, but the difference was not significant. Songs were diverse: modern, traditional, cowboy, "jive" songs, Christian hymns. Modern songs were concerned with love, sex, town and rural wives, "good-time" girls, the loneliness of men away from home, joys and dangers of town life and other choices open to townsmen. Although only a few of the songs expressed the feelings of women, they too enjoyed them. Listeners said the songs helped them; in most songs the listeners were hearing about themselves.

The majority of radio listeners in the mine township said they preferred modern songs and music. But this did not mean European music. The music was often traditional or an altered traditional form, although the singer was accompanied by a modern guitar. The words were in a vernacular language. . . .

. . . . .

Many . . . popular songs were concerned with town and rural wives, love and sex.

1. Goodbye my love, I am going away
   From where I came.
   I am tired of waiting for you to change your habits.
   You will die alone.
   Do not forget your responsibility over children.
   Although I am going away, I will give you help
   In all your difficulties.
   You have wronged me by asking for a lot of money
   Which I, the unfortunate, cannot afford.

A typical comment:

I like this song because it teaches us that if you marry a town girl, even if you stay with her for two years, you will still divorce each other, because most of them are only after money and not real marriage. If a man is not careful, he is left bankrupt.

2. Some young men are not wise.
   When they see a Kapenta
   They put all their attention to her.
   They forget their houses.
   That is very saddening.
   They start speaking in English,
   "Hulla, Mama, the Beautiful One,
   Come live with me in town.
   You will be very fat, you girl
   If you live with me.
   You're gonna get bread and butter.
   I have everything.
   There are plenty new looks.
   You'll have so many dresses,
   You'll be changing clothes all day.
   In the morning you will eat
   Coffee, toshta, and butter.
   When we two appear in public
   Young men will be shaking
   Because of your beautiful clothes."

Kapenta is the name given to a woman who paints her lips red like a European. She is one of the town good-time girls. This song was regarded as a warning to men not to spend all their money on good-time girls.

3. If you want to choose a girl for a wife
   You better wait for the month of June*
   This is the time you will choose a clean girl
   Because some bathe in hot season only,
   But when it is cold in June, they stop!

4. What a world!
   I was surprised when a young townsman married me.
   And after only six days,
   He said he did not want me any more
   Because I had shamed him
   In the presence of his people.
   Then I begged, "No, no, my love
   I'm new to married life
   Give me a chance to remain with you

---

* June is in the Northern Rhodesian winter.

Only another six months."
"No," said the man,
"I asked you to make tea,
But—surprise!
You cooked the leaves like vegetables
And poured on ground-nuts like gravy.
I did not know village women were so ignorant.
You must go back to your house.
Here, take this ticket. It is ready.
The bus is waiting for you there!"

This song, by Nkhata, indicates that all is not necessarily well if a man goes home to the village for a rural bride. The village girl may be awkward in her new surroundings and shame her husband.

5. Let me tell you about the town wives.
   Even though I give mine plenty of fish,
   Even though there is a bag full of salt—enough to sit in,
   Yet she'll complain, "There is not meat."
   All day long she is never satisfied.
   She threatens, "I'll not stay with you."
   Yet . . . she remains, for I satisfy her at night.
   At night I fondle her.
   Her body becomes our playground.

6. We are the smart men about town. We eat from tables.
   We are the smart men about town. We've got the girls.
   We are the smart men about town. We put on shoes.
   We are the smart men about town. We look like teachers.
   We are the smart men about town. Wonderful wires stretch
       into our houses.
   We are the smart men about town. We have electric lights
       and tin roofs.
   Now come and see what-hell-of-a-fellows we are!

Songs 5 and 6 were among the lusty, boasting ones about town life.
   Songs with traditional themes were much less popular in this township than those with modern themes and were remembered only infrequently. One of the few was:

When Maiwaso catches the locusts
She does not give some to her friends.
Hm . . . hm . . . hm . . .
The locusts will mourn for you!

Comment:
It is true that if a person is very stingy he cannot be popular to his friends, and the time will come when he will fall ill, and not many will feel sad with

him. That also happens if he dies; there will not be many people at his funeral, and that is not good at all. Even if you have little, you should share some with your friends.

Traditional hospitality was still a much prized value among these Copperbelt Africans.

The songs express well the ambivalences felt by the men in their new situation. Men want the new town wives who ape the looks and clothes of the European women, and who are supposedly "champions" in a strong sex life. Men boast that they have these women. Yet they complain that the same women leave them bankrupt. They also yearn for the supposedly unspoiled rural women, now somewhat romanticized. Yet they are shamed by her awkwardness in the ways of town life. The romantic yearning for one woman exists side by side with the desire for good-time girls, the champions.

A major problem for tribal peoples becoming modern is that for the first time they are faced with many choices. Traditional-minded elders who disapprove of new town customs could not give guidance. The songs offered advice to urban young men faced with alternatives and gave them the comfort of knowing that their temptations and problems were not unique.

40 | The Home Song

PAUL CHAROSH

A song called "I Left My Heart in San Francisco" achieved wide popularity during 1962, circulating successfully through mass media which more frequently carry tales of unhappy adolescents. Essentially, 'I Left My Heart in San Francisco" is an old-fashioned "home song," expressing sentiments which may be found in popular music nearly one hundred and fifty years old. How unlike modern San Francisco was the "Home Sweet Home" (1823) of John Howard Payne:

> 'Mid pleasures and palaces, though we may roam,
> Be it ever so humble, there's no place like home . . .

> An exile from home, splendour dazzles in vain!
> Oh! Give me my lowly thatch'd cottage again!
> The birds singing gaily that came at my call,
> Give me them with the peace of mind dearer than all . . .

SOURCE: This article was especially prepared for this volume.

Song lyrics are documents which reflect the cultural milieu in which they were created, and through them we may watch Home move from rural-agrarian to urban-industrial settings. Also, we may learn something of the problems which accompanied this move, and observe contrasting reactions to these problems.

A mid-nineteenth-century lyric notes that " 'Tis home where the heart is, where e'er its loved ones dwell / In cities or in cottages, throng'd haunts or mossy dell." Nevertheless, during the nineteenth and well into the twentieth century, "home songs" generally remained in rural settings. Ultimately an elaborate stereotype evolved, congenial to the presence of traditionally organized kinship and religious institutions, social relationships in general, and pleasant natural phenomena. This stereotype is employed in "My Home of Long Ago" (1898), "Childhood Days" (1896), "Back to the Old Homestead" (1897), "The Old Home is Good Enough For Me" (1893), and in at least one song which is still sung today, "On the Banks of the Wabash, Far Away" (1899). "Where the Sunset Turns the Ocean's Blue to Gold" (1902) is a typical "home song" of this period:

> When the busy day is o'er, and the sun is sinking lower,
> Then I seem to see a dear old southern home.
> And the long years roll away, just a child again I play,
> With my playmates in the woods we used to roam.
> And at eve my mother there listens to me say my prayers,
> And I feel her kiss as in the days of old.
> But now mother's old and gray, waiting for me far away,
> Where the sunset turns the ocean's blue to gold.
>
> Oh, the old church bells are ringing,
> And the mocking birds are singing,
> As they sang around the place in days of old.
> And though I am far away,
> All my heart has been today,
> Where the sunset turns the ocean's blue to gold.

Songs of this type appear so frequently during this time that a deliberate effort to be different is made in "A Large Front Room on Broadway" (1899):

> All the songs you hear it seems this year are of some country home,
> The meadows and the fields of new-mown hay.
> There's a babbling brook, the shady nook thro' which
>   they once did roam,
> And they're always situated far away.
> There's the sweetheart in the churchyard, how we miss her, darling Sue.
> She's sleeping there from eating home made bread.
> Oh, they sing of hills in the old Catskills, and the place where
>   grass is blue.

But here's the truest thing they ever said:
You can have your New Hampshire and your wildwood ever dear,
Your old Kentucky Home and Oyster Bay;
You can live down in the dell, but give me some good hotel,
With a large front room that faces on Broadway.

Life in the city may indeed be pleasant at times, as "On a Sunday Afternoon" (1902) suggests:

There's a day we feel gay, if the weather is fine,
Ev'ry lad feels so glad, if the sun does shine.
In his best, he is dressed, and with smiling face,
He goes with his Pearlie, his own little girlie, to some nice place.

On a Sunday afternoon, in the merry month of June,
Take a trip up the Hudson or down the bay,
Take a trolley to Coney or Rockaway.
On a Sunday afternoon, you can see the lovers spoon.
They work hard on Monday, but one day that's fun day is
Sunday afternoon.

The simple pleasures of working-class people are idealized in "Maggie Murphy's Home" (1890):

Behind a grammar school-house, in a double tenement,
I live with my old mother, and always pay the rent.
A bedroom and a parlor is all we call our own,
And you're welcome every evening at Maggie Murphy's home.

On Sunday night it's my delight and pleasure, don't you see,
Meeting all the girls and all the boys that work downtown with me.
There's an organ in the parlor to give the house a tone,
And you're welcome every evening at Maggie Murphy's home.

And "Down in Poverty Row" (1896):

Within a crowded tenement where poorest folks abound,
There lives a pretty working girl, the best that can be found.
She helps to keep her mother and her little brother Joe.
She's as sweet as can be and they all say she is the belle
     of poverty row.

However, these people maintain their good character and cheerful dispositions in spite of their environment, not because of it. Perhaps the best remembered song of this type is "The Sidewalks of New York" (1894), which inspired the following parody:

East side, west side, you'll find it is the same.
Every one is on the make, of course they're not to blame.

A lady meets a sailor, and into McGuirk's they stalk.
And in the morning he's dead broke on the sidewalks of New York.

Uptown, downtown, you'll hear the same old cry.
"Will you come into my parlor," says the spider to the fly.
Two ladies meet a farmer who's made up like a gawk.
They both yell out, "I saw him first" on the sidewalks of New York.

In general, city life is customarily portrayed as inimical to the presence of phenomena which are assigned positive value in the rural "home song." "Chicago in Slices" (c. 1890) tells us:

. . . If you never have altered your name in your life,
Or never did up to a bar go,
Or never run away with another man's wife,
They won't let you live in Chicago.

Some folks send by Adams express,
And others put faith in Old Fargo,
But if you want to go to the devil direct,
Just enter yourself for Chicago.
The city with fast gals and gay gamboliers
Is as full as a ship with a cargo.
And it is truthfully said that the very best men
Fight chickens and dogs in Chicago.

The infants they feed on whiskey direct,
And for liquor they to their Ma go,
And the muly cows give, as some might expect,
Whiskey punch in the town of Chicago.
They won't let the ministers live in the town,
For on him they will put an embargo—
Unless he drinks wine with all his young friends,
And then he may stay in Chicago.

"Upstairs in My Bedroom" (1895):

The air is quite salubrious in the attic near the skies,
Cockroaches have a picnic with a thousand million flies.
They make Dutch cheese in the cellar, which sends up a tough perfume.
The cats on the roof play opera bouffe at night, over my bedroom.

In a "Row of Tenement Houses" (c. 1895), "Each day, each day, each day, some family would move away/For that row of tenement houses never seemed to please or pay."
"The Streets of the Crowded City" (1895) tells of a "sweet little maid" who goes to the city, certain that she will find "something to do."

But little she thought of the sorrow she'd know,
Or of danger awaiting her there.
She sought for employment, but none could be found,
She gave up at last in despair.
She fell by the wayside, as others before her,
Who came to the city where all is so bright.
She has broken the heart of her darling old mother,
There's one more lost soul in the city tonight.

A similar picture of urban life is drawn in "While the City Sleeps" (1895):

When nightfall settles o'er the town and lights begin to glow,
The weary workers of the day seek rest and homeward go.
But in the gilded haunts of crime, the sound of revel leaps.
And vice and virtue struggle on, while the city sleeps.

While the city sleeps, the mighty pulse throbs slow,
Still the strife of life goes on among the high and low.
Many eyes with tears are dimmed, 'ere the gray dawn peeps.
Hearts are broken, homes are wrecked, while the city sleeps.

Up in a dingy attic room, a starving woman weeps,
Beside a cradle where her babe in endless slumber sleeps.
Alone, uncared for, cast aside by him she loved, betrayed,
While the guilty one goes free, to boast of conquests made.

Along the river front a man is seen to wend his way,
Until he pauses on a dock, just at the break of day.
He's pale and worn, ambition gone, his ruin seeks to hide.
A plunge, a splash, next morn they'll find an unknown suicide!

As midnight chimes upon the air, a murderer runs by.
Police pursue him, bid him halt, yet he heeds not their cry.
He dashes on, a pistol shot, a scream of wild despair,
He falls, they'll find him there stone dead, beneath the lamp-light's glare.

During this period, it would seem that rural-agrarian and urban-industrial life are symbolically antithetical. The city cannot readily be home because requirements for the emotional allegiance implied in the word are met primarily within the small-town or rural milieu in which these requirements were established.

During the second decade of the twentieth century, in addition to "Happy Little Country Girl" (1913) and other songs depicting rural bliss, songwriters offer the public a number of violently anti-urban songs which achieve wide popularity. "In the Heart of the City That Has No Heart" is listed in the Edison record supplement for July 1914 with the comment:

"A song with a moral! How seldom it is in these days that we find such a one! More and more, people are awakening to the fact that knowledge of city conditions is needed. Of course Thomas S. Allen primarily desired to write a ballad that would give enjoyment to those hearing it, but his story is true to life, nevertheless, and points out a forceful moral. It tells of a girl who left the country, and what became of her in the city." She falls victim to an unspecified vice and drifts along, with no one to care if she lives or dies, laughs or cries—she is a lost sister who finds that nobody's missed her. When she left home, her father declared that he would rather see her dead than a source of shame and disgrace to the family, and she has no place to turn for help. The song leaves her in the heart of the city that has no pity.

New York is particularly susceptible to attack in songs of this type, with Broadway depicted as a haven for the morally bankrupt. "There's a Broken Heart for Every Light on Broadway" (1915) is typical. The individual is usually portrayed as incapable of resisting the lure of the city, and meeting with subsequent ruin. Even in "How 'Ya Gonna Keep 'Em Down on the Farm? (After They've Seen Paree)" (1919), which is essentially comic, we are advised that "wine and women play the mischief with a boy who's loose with change." The title "While the City Sleeps" is used again in 1916, and the printed music observes that a "splendid effect . . . may be obtained by stopping singing" at an appropriate line, "and reciting the following Poem accompanied by slow chords pp. on the piano:

> Stand in your window and scan the sights,
> On Broadway with its bright white lights.
> Its dashing cabs and cabarets,
> Its painted women and fast cafés.
> That's when you really see New York.
> Vulgar of manner, overfed,
> Overdressed and underbred.
> Heartless and Godless, Hell's delight,
> Rude by day and lewd by night.
> Bedwarfed the man, enlarged the brute,
> Ruled by crook and rum to boot.
> Purple robed and pauper clad,
> Raving, rioting, money mad.
> A squirming herd in Mammon's mesh,
> A wilderness of human flesh.

During the early 1920s, women go astray in "Broadway Rose" and "I Found a Rose in the Devil's Garden," while the subject of Irving Berlin's "Homesick" fondly recalls a cozy little shack, a little red school, the sight of his father riding a mule, and the motto "God Bless Our Home" on the wall. After the last echo of this group of songs fades from vaudeville houses, pianos, and phonograph horns, the battle between Good and Evil symbolized in rural and urban settings is not fought frequently in popular song lyrics. Certain aspects of city life are still depicted as unpleasant, although the urban dweller may not know how to alter the situation. One may have "Big City Blues" (1929) and passively acknowledge that one does not know what to do:

> Each evening at six p.m.,
> Lights light and I look at them.
> I'm hoping that some nice person will meet me, greet me.
> Before I know it it's twelve o'clock,
> I feel like jumping right off a dock,
> Because I haven't found a person to cheer me, dear me,
> No one ever comes near me.[1]

Twenty-five years later, the subject of "I Left My Heart in San Francisco"[2] reports similar feelings of isolation. He feels very much alone and forgotten in Manhattan, and has left his heart in San Francisco, "where little cable cars climb halfway to the stars." He does not long to desert New York for a country cottage, but for another city, and this may reflect waning sensitivity to desirable aspects of life which are traditionally found in a rural or small town milieu.

For several generations, the "Swanee" River, in abstract, was the residence of everyone's "Old Folks at Home" (1852). However, if one is willing to grant positive value to conditions found in an urban setting, even life on the "Swanee" may be deemed objectionable. A parody on the song appears on a 1902 phonograph record, and includes the terms "darkey," "coon," and "nigger," which were then commonly used in song lyrics. The text has not been altered:

> You've all heard the song about the Swanee River,
> They tell you it's a pretty little spot.
> For the benefit of people knowing nothing at all about the place,
> A lot of information I have got.
> Why the darkey in the city ever wanted to return,
> Is something really more than I can say.
> But I'm willing to admit the nigger showed alot of sense,
> When he made up his mind to come away.
>
> Way down on the Swanee River,
> That's the place to give you inflammation of the liver.
> That's where the old folks love to stay,
> They've got to stay because they cannot get away.

---

[1] From "Big City Blues." Copyright © 1929 by DeSylva, Brown & Henderson, Inc. Copyright Renewed. Used by permission.

[2] By Douglass Cross and George Cory. Extract reproduced with permission of the copyright owner, General Music Publishing Company, Inc.

Way down on the Swanee River,
No more I wish to roam.
Oh the coons, they say, are glad to get away,
Far from the old folks at home.

An analysis of "home songs" popular during the last generation would probably reveal that elements of the rural stereotype have not been completely abandoned by lyricists. In general, however, rural and urban images ultimately become less clearly antithetical, and neither "throng'd haunt" nor "mossy dell" may be assumed to be all Evil or all Good; these concepts coexist, no longer within a single value system, but within a number of value systems. Without the concept of absolute value, the requirements for emotional allegiance are less readily defined. Home is still where the heart is—even in San Francisco.

Part Five

Urban Housing and Redevelopment

In this final part of the book we turn to some of the problems of cities around the world and the plans and philosophies which attempt to deal with them.

Section A is concerned with two major problems—housing and transportation. The opening selections, describing the housing of *favela* dwellers in São Paulo, Brazil, and of poor Chinese households in Singapore, make it clear that the slums of economically underdeveloped areas do not conform to ideas of slums derived from observation of slums in the United States and other industrial nations.

"Oh, São Paulo! A queen that vainly shows her skyscrapers that are her crown of gold. All dressed up in velvet and silk but with cheap stockings underneath—the *favela*." So wrote Carolina Maria de Jesus in her diary, which a journalist ultimately heard of and had published. It is a searing account of life in a desolate physical and social environment, as the author struggled to support herself and her three children by collecting and selling old paper, tin cans, and bottles. She arrived in São Paulo penniless and constructed her shack in the *favela* with her own hands out of scrap materials. Such makeshift "homes," with no sanitary facilities or urban amenities such as sidewalks, street lighting, or garbage collection, are typical of the squatter shantytowns which are a major feature of cities in Latin America, Asia, and Africa. The diary of Carolina Maria de Jesus, who had only two years of school, became a best seller in Brazil and the proceeds enabled her to move her family out of the *favela*, but recent circumstances may force her return.[1]

"Some Residents of Upper Nankin Street, Singapore" presents a picture of very high residential density in a Chinese section of Singapore. The average population density for "Chinatown" was 230,000 per square mile and in one section it was 450,000 per square mile. Average density in New York City is 25,000 per square mile. Families often have a room—sometimes only a cubicle—rather than an apartment. Wong Ah Sam, her husband, and two children share a windowless attic cubicle 12 feet by 10 1/2 feet; the Lees, two adults and five children, live in a room 7 feet by 10 feet. These are not short-term arrangements, as many of the families have lived in their quarters for long periods; Yip Sam Mui has rented her bunk-space for twenty-four years, while the family of Leong Chee Chiew has occupied their cubicle for fourteen years. Overcrowding, lack of privacy, and health hazards seem obvious, despite any possible cultural variation in acceptable levels. Indeed the Singapore Improvement Trust has accorded the Upper Nankin Street area a high priority for demolition. The rates of demolition of such housing are low in Singapore as in many other rapidly growing cities. Poor as the housing is, it is at least housing. Tens of thousands of residents of Singapore, Calcutta, and other cities literally have no roofs over their heads—they live on a patch of sidewalk or perhaps a section of rooftop.

Housing in the industrial West has, in the past, been as crowded and unwholesome on a large scale as that in the underdeveloped countries. The lodging houses described by Henry Mayhew are indeed "low," in terms of both physical and moral amenities. Mayhew describes two types of lodging houses, those of the "patterers" (street-sellers of stationery, literature, papers, or pictures who promote the sale of their wares by ornate speeches) and those of the dock laborers. Another variety of cramped, rubbish-strewn quarters is described in "The Street Where the Boy-Sweepers Lodged." Mayhew, a journalist, is now chiefly remembered for his documentary accounts of the life of the poor in Victorian London. He gathered his material through interviews and observation. Reading Mayhew at the distance of over a century raises the obvious question of whether the wretched living conditions of the underdeveloped countries will improve as did those of London's poor. As will become clear in the section on "Programs and Theories" the answer is, unfortunately, not obvious.

What are the housing problems in the richest nation in the world? Alvin Schorr examines one important aspect in "How the Poor Are Housed in the United States." He finds that at the lowest levels of poverty (annual income of $2,500 or less for a family of four) the housing problems are acute. When families in this category rely on their own resources, the vast ma-

---

[1] "Better to be Poor," *Ebony* (December, 1966).

jority are found living in substandard housing, for the private unsubsidized market falls far short of serving them adequately. When such families are served by various public housing programs, major shortcomings are evident. Programs directed at stimulating housing construction in general on the theory that some of the older housing will "filter down" to the poor have not operated to substantially improve the housing of the very poor under current conditions of heavy demand for housing. Public subsidized housing programs serve disproportionately few of the lowest income groups among the urban poor, partly because of a change in the characteristics of the low-income population (proportionately more are now dependent Negro families). In response public housing policy seems to be moving slowly and reluctantly toward "a rehabilitative program for the seriously dependent and troubled poor." The housing of the poor is also affected in the public sector by welfare payments to those on public assistance. Surveys show the housing of welfare recipients is bad. Schorr notes there are many reasons but indicates the major reason is the insufficiency of the funds allotted to welfare budgets. In effect, the richest nation in the world has not yet decided to "afford" decent housing for all its citizens.

Automobile traffic may be regarded as an urban problem peculiar to affluent societies. Jack Long's "Europe's Traffic Jam" deals with this problem in the capitals of three European nations whose traffic snarls are compounded by street patterns lingering from preindustrial and even medieval eras and by a multiplicity of historic, centrally located buildings. London, Paris, and Rome each have adopted roughly comparable principles for long-range solutions of their central city traffic congestion, including "belt" highways on the outskirts of the city, promotion of satellite cities and decentralization of homes and industries, and separation of through and local traffic in the city center. The plans are large-scale, long-term, and expensive. The traffic problems of contemporary London and Paris are illuminated by other articles in this reader. The ecological patterns of London and Paris are detailed in Hauser's "The Ecological Patterns of European Cities" (selection 15) while their metropolitan growth and government structure are discussed in Bollens and Schmandt's "The Metropolitan Trend in London, Ibadan, Tokyo, and São Paulo" (selection 48).

Is the automobile a "villain"? In his article "Growth and Change in Metropolitan Areas and Their Relation to Metropolitan Transportation: A Research Summary," Mark Reinsberg summarizes the research results of several studies, conducted mainly in Chicago, on the relationship between automobile transit, mass urban transportation, and the decline of the central city. Clearly the automobile and the truck have enabled population, industry, and commerce to move to suburban areas and the increase in auto transportation has been directly related to the decline of urban mass transit. Reinsberg points up, however, the superficiality of labeling the car the "cause" of urban decay and mass transit deficits. Private choice is involved in transportation and suburban location and, as Reinsberg notes later in his discussion, so are public policies such as the federal government's decision to subsidize highway construction. Reinsberg reviews the major propositions advanced by those advocating the economic advantages of public investment in mass urban transit and concludes that the propositions "rest on sentiment not fact," and that the public underwriting of mass urban transit cannot therefore be defended on economic grounds. Reinsberg argues that the question then becomes whether "social considerations" favoring mass transit should take precedence over economic factors. The Watts riots in which inadequate public transportation was one underlying source of frustration in a low-income area come to mind as an example. Reinsberg's survey suggests not only the need for continuing research on the facts of automobile and other urban transit, but the basic value decisions which transportation policies pose for the individual and the nation.

In Section B we are concerned with the policies and programs designed to improve the urban environment. The role of government is central in this process. In the underdeveloped areas urban problems are so vast that only government could hope to handle them. In the developed nations, government assistance is needed to fill the gaps left by private enterprise (for example, as Schorr showed, the housing needs of the poor are not met by the private market even in the United States) and to plan on a broad basis for metropolitan communities. Four articles in this section deal with various aspects of the role of government in the planning process; another selection presents the influential views of Lewis Mumford.

The evolution of housing and land use policy in Europe and North America is presented by Charles Abrams in "The Growth of Government Power and Policy," and contrasted to that in the underdeveloped countries. According to Abrams, in the developed nations the government's power has expanded to ameliorate urban problems, but is balanced by a strong private sector, so that shortcomings in urban housing and amenities have been corrected while preserving individual rights. Abrams traces this development through major "revolutions" in political, land, and industrial, and welfare spheres which were spread over a long period in the developed nations. However, the underdeveloped nations are "having all their revolutions simultaneously." Furthermore, the changes are taking place in the context of an ideological world struggle between capitalism and communism. One may reasonably conclude from Abrams' analysis that there is no guarantee or even a high probability that the future course of governmental powers in cities in the underdeveloped nations will parallel that in the developed nations.

Government structure and policy are key issues in relation to the problems of metropolitan areas in developed and underdeveloped areas. Bollens and Schmandt focus on this aspect of the role of government in their analysis, "The Metropolitan Trend in London, Ibadan, Tokyo, and São Paulo." In London there has long been major implementation of plans to control the metropolis's growth. Under a 1963 bill the Greater London

Council was given even greater powers, but Bollens and Schmandt suggest these powers were probably insufficient to direct growth at the rapidly expanding outer edge of greater London. Ibadan, Nigeria, is an example of one type of metropolis in a newly independent nation. In the case of Ibadan, the city was large, even by Western standards, long before colonalization by Europeans, since the Yoruba have traditionally been an urban people (see Bascom, selection 6). One consequence has been that many new institutions brought in by the colonials—such as banks, department stores, industries, and Western-style residences—have been located on the outskirts of the metropolis since the central area was already densely settled. Modern Ibadan must therefore cope with an outlying "central business district." Traditional tribal loyalties also impede solution of metropolitan problems, a situation which has become more serious with the secession in 1967 of Eastern Nigeria (Biafra) from Nigeria. Ibadan is located in Western Nigeria. Tokyo is the first non-Western country to move toward both high levels of urbanization and high levels of industrialization. Tokyo, like London, has developed plans for decongesting its urban core and has allotted considerable public funds to this goal. However, it appears that some of the problems are beyond the scope of a metropolitan authority and require national powers. São Paulo, although it is in an underdeveloped country, has escaped some of the financial problems of that status, because of the large-scale commercial and industrial expansion in the metropolis. The financial status of metropolitan areas in Brazil is usually poor because the basic unit of government, the *municipio*, comparable to the United States county, has broad powers but scant financial resources. Thus, while the governmental powers for metropolitan planning exist at the local level the funds do not. Most taxing powers reside at the state and national level. In the diversity presented by these four great metropolitan areas Bollens and Schmandt see a trend toward centralization as a way of meeting metropolitan needs—through metropolitan-wide agencies and authorities or through nonlocal governmental units such as states and the nation. By implication one may contrast the approaches of these four metropolitan areas to those of United States metropolises. Both London and Tokyo, in the drawing of long-range plans and the commitment of public funds and power to them, are more advanced in their attempts to provide a viable metropolis than such cities as New York, Los Angeles, or Chicago.

How is the American metropolis planned? How does the process differ from that in the U.S.S.R.? The articles by Bernard Weissbourd, "Segregation, Subsidies, and Megalopolis," and by Robert J. Osborn, "How the Russians Plan Their Cities," provide at least some answers to these questions. Weissbourd presents a picture of government policies in the United States whose long-range influence has vitally affected the spread of metropolis and the composition of its central city and suburban population. The role of the United States government in determining the metropolitan environment is large, although the effects are not always planned or in-

tended. Osborn's report on planning in Russian cities indicates that the
U.S.S.R. has moved toward a less total Communist approach to planning.
Thus, in practice, neither the United States nor the Soviet Union conforms
completely to the planning norms of its ideology. However, their planning
practices are very different and there is no indication that in the future their
practices will converge midway between ideological poles.

Weissbourd contends that federal policies have subsidized the movement of middle-income white population to the suburbs, thus contributing
to the segregation of Negroes in the central city. The subsidies have taken
such forms as federal highway grants and government-insured mortgages on
private housing. On the other hand, Weissbourd contends the federal
government's policies have shortchanged the central city—for example in
the location and quality of public housing and in disregard for the plight of
mass urban transit. Weissbourd makes various recommendations for government action which would decrease racial segregation by the encouragement of middle-income neighborhoods in the central city, the revitalization
of the central business district, recasting the premises of public housing,
and industrially and racially balanced "new towns" in the outer metropolis.
"If America is not prepared to accept interracial communities, there is little
hope of arresting the decline of the city."

Osborn's discussion of Soviet urban planning describes its major characteristics and explodes some myths. The basic urban planning unit is the
"microdistrict," a self-contained neighborhood, which bears no resemblance to the notions of "communes." Plain architectural forms are now
preferred to ornate styles. There is much debate and relatively little ideology in Russian planning circles. Optimum city size is a matter of particularly heavy current debate.

In the planning process, as elsewhere, ideas are powerful tools. One of
the most influential thinkers in this field is Lewis Mumford, whose views on
the city have been discussed for almost half a century. Mumford continues to write and his ideas are complex. No definitive appraisal of his work is
now possible but the broad outlines are clear. As presented in Marvin D.
Koenigsberg's "Urban Development: An Introduction to the Theories of
Lewis Mumford," Mumford's central value orientation emphasizes harmony, balance, and unity. This is evident in Mumford's contentions that
the city must serve the needs of both private man and of public man, that
urbanites should experience country living as well, that urban residents
should identify with their communities, and that organic growth and urban
scale should characterize the physical city. Mumford's concern with balance,
harmony, and unity seems justified in the light of the disorganization and
upheaval attendant on the rapid, uncontrolled growth of large industrial
cities in the past century. Mumford's contribution to urban theory is
unique but some sources for his viewpoint may be pointed out. Mumford
himself acknowledges his intellectual debt to Peter Kropotkin, Patrick Geddes, and Ebenezer Howard whose concepts of deconcentration, regional-

ism, and garden cities he incorporated into his thinking. Whether Mumford's guidelines for urban form can or should be universal is a matter for discussion. There are some blind spots in his work. He is very favorably inclined toward the medieval city, but leaves aside the ignorance and cruelty of many aspects of medieval life. On the other hand, he displays a bias against industrial cities, especially the modern metropolis and leaves aside the many positive aspects of that life. The basic dilemma posed by Mumford's views is, however, the dilemma growing out of contemporary Western industrial democracies—the potential conflict between individual choice and the "public interest." Mumford gives one view of what constitutes the best over-all plan for urban development. If it were decided on as a working plan, what about those who oppose its impact on their own lives?

It is appropriate that this volume end on the note of conflict, values, and choice for they are central to the building and rebuilding of our cities. Throughout this volume there have been references to the importance of culture and social organization in shaping urban life. It is one of the basic reasons for a comparative approach to urban sociology. Many readings on the planning process have also indicated the importance of value orientation and social context. Planning, it turns out, is not just technology, but sociology, and not just sociology, but a matter of individual choices and national goals.

A | Problems

41 | The Diary of Carolina Maria De Jesus, Favela Resident

July 15, 1955 The birthday of my daughter Vera Eunice. I wanted to buy a pair of shoes for her, but the price of food keeps us from realizing our desires. Actually we are slaves to the cost of living. I found a pair of shoes in the garbage, washed them, and patched them for her to wear.

I didn't have one cent to buy bread. So I washed three bottles and traded them to Arnaldo. He kept the bottles and gave me bread. Then I went to sell my paper. I received 65 cruzeiros. I spent 20 cruzeiros for meat. I got one kilo of ham and one kilo of sugar and spent six cruzeiros on cheese. And the money was gone.

I was ill all day. I thought I had a cold. At night my chest pained me. I started to cough. I decided not to go out at night to look for paper. I searched for my son João. He was at Felisberto de Carvalho Street near the market. A bus had knocked a boy into the sidewalk and a crowd gathered. João was in the middle of it all. I poked him a couple of times and within five minutes he was home.

I washed the children, put them to bed, then washed myself and went to bed. I waited until 11:00 for a certain someone. He didn't come. I took an aspirin and laid down again. When I awoke the sun was sliding in space. My daughter Vera Eunice said: "Go get some water, Mother!"

July 16 I got up and obeyed Vera Eunice. I went to get the water. I made coffee. I told the children that I didn't have any bread, that they would have to drink their coffee plain and eat meat with *farinha*.[1] I was feeling ill and decided to cure myself. I stuck my finger down my throat twice, vomited, and knew I was under the evil eye. The upset feeling left and I

---

[1] *Farinha:* a coarse wheat flour.

SOURCE: David St. Clair, trans., *Child of the Dark: The Diary of Carolina Maria De Jesus* (New York: E. P. Dutton & Co., Inc., 1962), pp. 17–19, 38–44. Copyright © 1962 by E. P. Dutton & Co., Inc. and Souvenir Press, Ltd. Reprinted by permission of the publishers.

went to Senhor Manuel, carrying some cans to sell. Everything that I find in the garbage I sell. He gave me 13 cruzeiros. I kept thinking that I had to buy bread, soap, and milk for Vera Eunice. The 13 cruzeiros wouldn't make it. I returned home, or rather to my shack, nervous and exhausted. I thought of the worrisome life that I led. Carrying paper, washing clothes for the children, staying in the street all day long. Yet I'm always lacking things, Vera doesn't have shoes and she doesn't like to go barefoot. For at least two years I've wanted to buy a meat grinder. And a sewing machine.

I came home and made lunch for the two boys. Rice, beans, and meat, and I'm going out to look for paper. I left the children, told them to play in the yard and not go into the street, because the terrible neighbors I have won't leave my children alone. I was feeling ill and wished I could lie down. But the poor don't rest nor are they permitted the pleasure of relaxation. I was nervous inside, cursing my luck. I collected two sacks full of paper. Afterward I went back and gathered up some scrap metal, some cans, and some kindling wood. As I walked I thought—when I return to the favela there is going to be something new. Maybe Dona Rosa or the insolent Angel Mary fought with my children. I found Vera Eunice sleeping and the boys playing in the street. I thought: it's 2:00. Maybe I'm going to get through this day without anything happening. João told me that the truck that gives out money was here to give out food. I took a sack and hurried out. It was the leader of the Spiritist Center at 103 Vergueiro Street. I got two kilos of rice, two of beans, and two kilos of macaroni. I was happy. The truck went away. The nervousness that I had inside left me. I took advantage of my calmness to read. I picked up a magazine and sat on the grass, letting the rays of the sun warm me as I read a story. I wrote a note and gave it to my boy João to take to Senhor Arnaldo to buy soap, two aspirins, and some bread. Then I put water on the stove to make coffee. João came back saying he had lost the aspirins. I went back with him to look. We didn't find them.

When I came home there was a crowd at my door. Children and women claiming José Carlos had thrown stones at their houses. They wanted me to punish him.

July 17 Sunday A marvelous day. The sky was blue without one cloud. The sun was warm. I got out of bed at 6:30 and went to get water. I only had one piece of bread and three cruzeiros. I gave a small piece to each child and put the beans, that I got yesterday from the Spiritist Center, on the fire. Then I went to wash clothes. When I returned from the river the beans were cooked. The children asked for bread. I gave the three cruzeiros to João to go and buy some. Today it was Nair Mathias who started an argument with my children. Silvia and her husband have begun an open-air spectacle. He is hitting her and I'm disgusted because the children are present. They heard words of the lowest kind. Oh, if I could move from here to a more decent neighborhood!

. . . . . .

[1958] At 8:30 that night I was in the favela breathing the smell of excrement mixed with the rotten earth. When I am in the city I have the impression that I am in a living room with crystal chandeliers, rugs of velvet, and satin cushions. And when I'm in the favela I have the impression that I'm a useless object, destined to be forever in a garbage dump.

May 20   Day was breaking when I got out of bed. Vera woke up and sang and asked me to sing with her. We sang. Then José Carlos and João joined in.

The morning was damp and foggy. The sun was rising but its heat didn't chase away the cold. I stayed thinking: there are seasons when the sun dominates. There's a season for the rain. There's a season for the wind. Now is the time for the cold. Among them there are no rivalries. Each one has a time.

I opened the window and watched the women passing by with their coats discolored and worn by time. It won't be long until these coats which they got from others, and which should be in a museum, will be replaced by others. The politicians must give us things. That includes me too, because I'm also a *favelado*. I'm one of the discarded. I'm in the garbage dump and those in the garbage dump either burn themselves or throw themselves into ruin.

The women that I see passing are going to church begging for bread for their children. Brother Luiz gives it to them while their husbands remain home under the blankets. Some because they can't find jobs. Others because they are sick. Others because they are drunk.

I don't bother myself about their men. If they give a ball and I don't show up, it's because I don't like to dance. I only get involved in fights when I think I can prevent a crime. I don't know what started this unfriendliness of mine. I have a hard cold look for both men and women. My smile and my soft smooth words I save for children.

There is a teen-ager named Julião who beats his father at times. When he hits his father it is with such sadism and pleasure. He thinks he is unconquerable. He beats the old man as if he were beating a drum. The father wants him to study law. When Julião was arrested the father went with him with his eyes filled with tears. As if he was accompanying a saint in a procession. Julião is a rebel, but without a cause. They don't need to live in a favela; they have a home on Villa Maria hill.

Sometimes families move into the favela with children. In the beginning they are educated, friendly. Days later they use foul language, are mean and quarrelsome. They are diamonds turned to lead. They are transformed from objects that were in the living room to objects banished to the garbage dump.

For me the world instead of evolving is turning primitive. Those who don't know hunger will say: "Whoever wrote this is crazy." But who has gone hungry can say:

"Well, Dona Carolina. The basic necessities must be within reach of everyone."

How horrible it is to see a child eat and ask: "Is there more?" This word "more" keeps ringing in the mother's head as she looks in the pot and doesn't have any more.

When a politician tells us in his speeches that he is on the side of the people, that he is only in politics in order to improve our living conditions, asking for our votes, promising to freeze prices, he is well aware that by touching on these grave problems he will win at the polls. Afterward he divorces himself from the people. He looks at them with half-closed eyes, and with a pride that hurts us.

When I arrived from the Palace that is the city, my children ran to tell me that they had found some macaroni in the garbage. As the food supply was low I cooked some of the macaroni with beans. And my son João said to me:

"Uh, huh. You told me we weren't going to eat any more things from the garbage."

It was the first time I had failed to keep my word. I said:

"I had faith in President Kubitschek."

"You had faith, and now you don't have it any more?"

"No, my son, democracy is losing its followers. In our country everything is weakening. The money is weak. Democracy is weak and the politicians are very weak. Everything that is weak dies one day."

The politicians know that I am a poetess. And that a poet will even face death when he sees his people oppressed.

May 21   I spent a horrible night. I dreamt I lived in a decent house that had a bathroom, kitchen, pantry, and even a maid's room. I was going to celebrate the birthday of my daughter Vera Eunice. I went and bought some small pots that I had wanted for a long time. Because I was able to buy. I sat at the table to eat. The tablecloth was white as a lily. I ate a steak, bread and butter, fried potatoes, and a salad. When I reached for another steak I woke up. What bitter reality! I don't live in the city. I live in the favela. In the mud on the banks of the Tieté River. And with only nine cruzeiros. I don't even have sugar, because yesterday after I went out the children ate what little I had.

Who must be a leader is he who has the ability. He who has pity and friendship for the people. Those who govern our country are those who have money, who don't know what hunger is, or pain or poverty. If the majority revolt, what can the minority do? I am on the side of the poor, who are an arm. An undernourished arm. We must free the country of the profiteering politicians.

Yesterday I ate that macaroni from the garbage with fear of death, because in 1953 I sold scrap over there in Zinho. There was a pretty little black boy. He also went to sell scrap in Zinho. He was young and said that those who should look for paper were the old. One day I was collecting scrap when I stopped at Bom Jardim Avenue. Someone had thrown meat into the garbage, and he was picking out the pieces. He told me:

"Take some, Carolina. It's still fit to eat."

He gave me some, and so as not to hurt his feelings, I accepted. I tried to convince him not to eat that meat, or the hard bread gnawed by the rats. He told me no, because it was two days since he had eaten. He made a fire and roasted the meat. His hunger was so great that he couldn't wait for the meat to cook. He heated it and ate. So as not to remember that scene, I left thinking: I'm going to pretend I wasn't there. This can't be real in a rich country like mine. I was disgusted with that Social Service that had been created to readjust the maladjusted, but took no notice of we marginal people. I sold the scrap at Zinho and returned to São Paulo's back yard, the favela.

The next day I found that little black boy dead. His toes were spread apart. The space must have been eight inches between them. He had blown up as if made out of rubber. His toes looked like a fan. He had no documents. He was buried like any other "Joe." Nobody tried to find out his name. The marginal people don't have names.

Once every four years the politicians change without solving the problem of hunger that has its headquarters in the favela and its branch offices in the workers' homes.

When I went to get water I saw a poor woman collapse near the pump because last night she slept without dinner. She was undernourished. The doctors that we have in politics know this.

Now I'm going to Dona Julita's house to work for her. I went looking for paper. Senhor Samuel weighed it. I got 12 cruzeiros. I went up Tiradentes Avenue looking for paper. I came to Brother Antonio Santana de Galvão Street, number 17, to work for Dona Julita. She told me not to fool with men because I might have another baby and that afterward men won't give anything to take care of the child. I smiled and thought: In relations with men, I've had some bitter experiences. Now I'm mature, reached a stage of life where my judgment has grown roots.

I found a sweet potato and a carrot in the garbage. When I got back to the favela my boys were gnawing on a piece of hard bread. I thought: for them to eat this bread, they need electric teeth.

I don't have any lard. I put meat on the fire with some tomatoes that I found at the Peixe canning factory. I put in the carrot and the sweet potato and water. As soon as it was boiling, I put in the macaroni that the boys found in the garbage. The *favelados* are the few who are convinced that in order to live, they must imitate the vultures. I don't see any help from the Social Service regarding the *favelados*. Tomorrow I'm not going to have bread. I'm going to cook a sweet potato.

May 22   Today I'm sad. I'm nervous. I don't know if I should start crying or start running until I fall unconscious. At dawn it was raining. I couldn't go out to get any money. I spent the day writing. I cooked the macaroni and I'll warm it up again for the children. I cooked the potatoes and they ate them. I have a few tin cans and a little scrap that I'm going to sell to Senhor Manuel. When João came home from school I sent him to sell the scrap. He got 13 cruzeiros. He bought a glass of mineral water: two cruzeiros. I was furious with him. Where had he seen a *favelado* with such highborn tastes?

The children eat a lot of bread. They like soft bread but when they don't have it, they eat hard bread.

Hard is the bread that we eat. Hard is the bed on which we sleep. Hard is the life of the *favelado*.

Oh, São Paulo! A queen that vainly shows her skyscrapers that are her crown of gold. All dressed up in velvet and silk but with cheap stockings underneath—the favela.

The money didn't stretch far enough to buy meat, so I cooked macaroni with a carrot. I didn't have any grease, it was horrible. Vera was the only one who complained yet asked for more.

"Mama, sell me to Dona Julita, because she has delicious food."

I know that there exist Brazilians here inside São Paulo who suffer more than I do. In June of '57 I felt rich and passed through the offices of the Social Service. I had carried a lot of scrap iron and got pains in my kidneys. So as not to see my children hungry I asked for help from the famous Social Service. It was there that I saw the tears slipping from the eyes of the poor. How painful it is to see the dramas that are played out there. The coldness in which they treat the poor. The only things they want to know about them is their name and address.

I went to the Governor's Palace.[2] The Palace sent me to an office at Brigadeiro Luis Antonio Avenue. They in turn sent me to the Social Service at the Santa Casa charity hospital. There I talked with Dona Maria Aparecida, who listened to me, said many things yet said nothing. I decided to go back to the Palace. I talked with Senhor Alcides. He is not Japanese yet is as yellow as rotten butter. I said to Senhor Alcides:

"I came here to ask for help because I'm ill. You sent me to Brigadeiro Luis Antonio Avenue, and I went. There they sent me to the Santa Casa. And I spent all the money I have on transportation."

"Take her!"

They wouldn't let me leave. A soldier put his bayonet at my chest. I looked the soldier in the eyes and saw that he had pity on me. I told him:

"I am poor. That's why I came here."

Dr. Osvaldo de Barros entered, a false philanthropist in São Paulo who is masquerading as St. Vincent de Paul. He said:

"Call a squad car!"

---

[2] Like most Brazilians, Carolina believes in going straight to the top to make her complaints.

The policeman took me back to the favela and warned me that the next time I made a scene at the welfare agency I would be locked up.

Welfare agency! Welfare for whom?

May 23   I got up feeling sad this morning because it was raining. The shack is in terrible disorder. And I don't have soap to wash the dishes. I say "dishes" from force of habit. But they are really tin cans. If I had soap I would wash the clothes. I'm really not negligent. If I walk around dirty it's because I'm trapped in the life of a *favelado*. I've come to the conclusion that for those who aren't going to Heaven, it doesn't help to look up. It's the same with us who don't like the favela, but are obliged to live in one. . . . It doesn't help to look up.

I made a meal. The grease frying in the pan was beautiful. What a dazzling display! The children smile watching the food cooking in the pans. Still more when it is rice and beans—it's a holiday for them.

In the old days macaroni was the most expensive dish. Now it's rice and beans that have replaced the macaroni. They've crossed over to the side of the nobility. Even you, rice and beans, have deserted us! You who were the friends of the marginal ones, the *favelados*, the needy. Just look. They are not within reach of the unhappy ones of the Garbage Dump. Who has not flown off is senhor cornmeal. But the children don't like cornmeal.

When I put the food on the table João smiled. He ate and didn't mention the black color of the beans.[3] Because black is our life. Everything is black around us.

In the streets and shops I see the posters with the names of candidates for deputy. Some names are already known. They are the repeaters who have already failed once at the ballot boxes. But the people are not interested in elections. Our elections are just a Trojan Horse that appears once every four years.

The sky is beautiful, worthy of contemplation because the drifting clouds are forming dazzling landscapes. Soft breezes pass by carrying the perfume of flowers. And the sun is always punctual at rising and setting. The birds travel in space, showing off in their happiness. The night brings up the sparkling stars to adorn the blue sky. There are so many beautiful things in the world that are impossible to describe. Only one thing saddens us: the prices when we go shopping. They overshadow all the beauty that exists.

---

[3] Black beans in almost every part of Brazil, except Rio, are looked down upon as the lowest thing that can be eaten. In the northeast poor families shut their windows out of shame that neighbors will see them eating black beans rather than brown ones.

42 | Some Residents of Upper Nankin Street, Singapore

BARRINGTON KAYE

Wong Kwok Tong

. . . Wong Kwok Tong lives with his two unmarried sons. He is 66 years old; his sons are 26 and 24. He has occupied the cubicle for about 20 years; he left his previous residence because it was too small. He was born in Kwangtung Province, and came to Singapore at the age of 22.

. . . . .

He occupies a back room on the first floor, lit by two windows, one of which looks on to the backs of houses, the other into an air well. The partitions of the room go right up to the ceiling. The room measures 9 ft. × 7 ft., and is furnished with a double bed, sideboard, and table. Wong Kwok Tong and one of his sons sleep on the bed; the other son sleeps on the floor. There is no electric light, and the room is lit by oil lamps at night.

. . . . .

Wong Ah Sam

. . . Wong Ah Sam lives in an attic cubicle with her husband and two children; a daughter aged 5 years, and a son aged 4 years. She herself is 37 years old: her husband is 38.

Her husband, a Cantonese, was born in Indonesia, where he went to Chinese Middle School. He came to Singapore in 1936 at the age of 19, and took a job under a building contractor, fitting drainpipes into houses under construction. He has done the same kind of job ever since, taking casual employment where he can. He is not able to find enough work to keep him fully occupied.

She herself is a Cantonese, born in Singapore, and did not go to school. They were married 12 years ago in a Registry Office, and they arranged their own marriage without the help of relatives.

SOURCE: Barrington Kaye, *Upper Nankin Street, Singapore: A Sociological Study of Chinese Households Living in a Densely Populated Area* (Singapore: University of Malaya Press, 1960), pp. 227–230, 233–236, 238, 243. Reprinted by permission of the publisher.

The cubicle which they inhabit is approached by a ladder at an angle of almost 90 degrees. The room measures 12 ft. × 10½ ft., and is windowless. As it is an attic-cubicle, there is only room to stand in the centre of the floor; at the sides the rafters come down to within 4 feet of the floor. Apart from boxes and chairs, the cubicle is furnished with a double-bed (5 ft. × 6 ft.) and a sideboard. Her husband sleeps on the bed; she herself sleeps on the floor with the children.

. . . . .

Leow Ah Thai

. . . Leow Ah Thai, an old lady of 66, lives by herself in a second-floor cubicle. The cubicle, which she has occupied for 12 years, is windowless, and measures 7½ ft. x 7 ft. It is furnished with a single bed and a shelf. There is no electric light, but enough light trickles over the top of the partition from the window at the end of the corridor to enable her to move about. At night she uses oil lamps.

. . . . .

Chung Lai Cheng

. . . Chung Lai Cheng (39 years old) lives with her husband (65 years) and her two children (a daughter aged 16 and a son nearly 2) in a front cubicle on the second floor.

Her husband was born in Kwangtung Province, China, and came to Singapore at the age of 13. Before then he attended the village school for 7 years, where he received an old-type education in the classics. He works as an accounts clerk in a wholesale provision shop; he has done the same kind of work since he first came to Singapore.

The Chung household occupy a cubicle measuring 10 ft. x 7 ft., which is lit by a window overlooking Upper Nankin Street. The cubicle is furnished with a double bed, which occupies hearly half the floor space, a sideboard, and a sewing-machine. The parents and the baby sleep in the bed; their daughter sleeps on the floor.

. . . . .

Lee Ah Mok

. . . Lee Ah Mok is 26 years old. She lives with her husband (31 years), and her five children aged 6, 5, and 4 years, 18 months, and 2 months respectively.

Her husband was born in Kwangtung Province, China, and first came to Singapore at the age of 15. He attended the village school for 4 years beforehand. He is a tinker, and specializes in repairing leaking oil-drums. He travels round the oil-factories in Singapore, taking on odd jobs of this kind. He has done this type of work for 7 years.

The Lee family occupy a front room on the first floor, with a window on to Upper Nankin Street. The room, of which the partitions reach right up to the ceiling, measures 7 ft. x 10 ft., and is furnished with a double bed and two sideboards. This leaves an area of footspace about 6 ft. x 5 ft., on which all five children have to play. The parents and baby sleep on the bed; the remaining four children sleep on the floor. There is no electric main, and the room is lit by battery.

. . . . .

Lam Ah Thai

. . . Lam Ah Thai is 43 years old. She lives with her husband, aged 47, and their seven sons, whose ages range from 16 years to 18 months.

Her husband was born in Kwangtung Province, where he went to the village school. He came to Singapore at the age of 17, and has not since returned. He is a bricklayer, a trade he has followed since he first arrived.

The three eldest sons go to a Chinese primary school; two of them have part-time employment, one as a building labourer, the other doing odd jobs in a printer's shop.

The Lam family occupy a cubicle without windows on the second floor. The internal measurements are 8 ft. × 7 ft., and it is furnished with a double bed and a sideboard. The mother and the two youngest children sleep on the bed; the father and the remaining five sons on the floor. (At the House Condition Survey interview, one of the sons complained that it was very hot at night, being forced to sleep so close together.) There is no electricity, and oil lamps are used.

. . . . .

Yip Sam Mui

. . . Yip Sam Mui, an old woman of 62, lives with her 32-year-old son, who works as a smelter in an engineering shop. They have no cubicle, but occupy two bunk-spaces in a first-floor corridor. She has occupied her bunk-space for 24 years.

. . . . .

Leong Chee Chiew

. . . Leong Chee Chiew, a man of 49, lives with his wife and their three children in a front cubicle on the first floor. Their daughter is 14 years old; their two sons are 8 and 4.

Leong Chee Chiew's wife was born in Saam Shui district of Kwangtung Province, and first came to Singapore at the age of 23.

The cubicle, which they have occupied for 14 years, has a window on to Upper Nankin Street. It measures 9 ft. x 8 ft., and is furnished with a double bed, a sideboard, and a shelf. Attached to the end of the bed is a board, supported by chains to the ceiling. Leong Chee Chiew, who suffers from tuberculosis, sleeps on this board; his wife and two of the children sleep on the bed. His daughter sleeps on the floor.

43 ▮ Housing in London, 1851

HENRY MAYHEW

Of the Low Lodging-Houses of London

The patterers, as a class, usually frequent the low lodging-houses. I shall therefore now proceed to give some further information touching the abodes of these people—reminding the reader that I am treating of patterers in general, and not of any particular order, as the 'paper workers.'

In applying the epithet 'low' to these places, I do but adopt the word commonly applied, either in consequence of the small charge for lodging, or from the character of their frequenters.

· · · · ·

The proprietors of these lodging-houses mostly have been, I am assured, vagrants, or, to use the civiller and commoner word, 'travellers' themselves, and therefore sojourners, on all necessary occasions, in such places. In four cases out of five I believe this to be the case. The proprietors have raised capital sufficient to start with, sometimes by gambling at races, sometimes by what I have often, and very vaguely, heard described as a 'run of luck'; and sometimes, I am assured, by the proceeds of direct robbery. A few of the proprietors may be classed as capitalists. One of them, who has a country house in Hampstead, has six lodging-houses in or about Thrawl-street, Whitechapel. He looks in at each house every Saturday, and calls his deputies—for he has a deputy in each house—to account; he often institutes a stringent check. He gives a poor fellow money to go and lodge in one of his houses, and report the number present. Sometimes the person so sent meets with the laconic repulse—'Full'; and woe to the deputy if his

SOURCE: Henry Mayhew: *London Labour and the London Poor* (London: Griffin, Bohn, and Company, 1861), I, 251–257; II, 503–505; III, 312–315.

return do not evince this fulness. Perhaps one in every fifteen of the low lodging-houses in town is also a beer-shop. Very commonly so in the country.

To 'start' a low lodging-house is not a very costly matter. Furniture which will not be saleable in the ordinary course of auction, or of any traffic, is brought by a lodging-house 'starter.' A man possessed of some money, who took an interest in a bricklayer, purchased for 20*l.*, when the Small Pox Hospital, by King's-cross, was pulled down, a sufficiency of furniture for *four* lodging-houses, in which he 'started' the man in question. None others would buy the furniture, from a dread of infection.

. . . . .

Some of the lodging-houses present no appearance differing from that of ordinary houses; except, perhaps, that their exterior is dirtier. Some of the older house have long flat windows on the ground-floor, in which there is rather more paper, or other substitutes, than glass. 'The windows there, sir,' remarked one man, 'are not to let the light in, but to keep the cold out.'

In the abodes in question there seems to have become tacitly established an arrangement as to what character of lodgers shall resort thither; the thieves, the prostitutes, and the better class of street-sellers or traders, usually resorting to the houses where they will meet the same class of persons. The patterers reside chiefly in Westminster and Whitechapel.

Some of the lodging-houses are of the worst class of low brothels, and some may even be described as brothels for children. . . .

The beds are of flock, and as regards the mere washing of the rug, sheet, and blanket, which constitute the bed-furniture, are in better order than they were a few years back; for the visitations of the cholera alarmed even the reckless class of vagrants, and those whose avocations relate to vagrants. In perhaps a tenth of the low lodging-houses of London, a family may have a room to themselves, with the use of the kitchen, at so much a week— generally 2*s*. 6*d*. for a couple without family, and 3*s*. 6*d*. where there are children. To let out 'beds' by the night is however the general rule.

. . . . .

Of the Filth, Dishonesty, and Immorality of Low Lodging-Houses

In my former and my present inquiries, I received many statements on this subject. Some details, given by coarse men and boys in the grossest language, are too gross to be more than alluded to, but the full truth must be manifested, if not detailed. . . .

And first, as to the want of cleanliness, comfort, and decency: 'Why, sir,' said one man, who had filled a commercial situation of no little importance, but had, through intemperance, been reduced to utter want, 'I myself have slept in the top room of a house not far from Drury-lane, and you could study the stars, if you were so minded, through the holes left by the slates having been blown off the roof.' . . .

The same man told me (and I received abundant corroboration of his statement, besides that incidental mention of the subject occurs elsewhere), that he had scraped together a handful of bugs from the bedclothes, and crushed them under a candlestick, and had done that many a time, when he could only resort to the lowest places. He had slept in rooms so crammed with sleepers—he believed there were 30 where 12 would have been a proper number—that their breaths in the dead of night and in the unventilated chamber, rose (I use his own words) 'in one foul, choking steam of stench.' This was the case most frequently a day or two prior to Greenwich Fair or Epsom Races, when the congregation of the wandering classes, who are the supporters of the low lodging-houses, was the thickest. It was not only that two or even three persons jammed themselves into a bed not too large for one full-sized man; but between the beds—and their partition one from another admitted little more than the passage of a lodger—were placed shake-downs, or temporary accommodation for nightly slumber. In the better lodging-houses the shake-downs are small palliasses or mattresses; in the worst, they are bundles of rags of any kind; but loose straw is used only in the country for shake-downs. . . .

At some of the busiest periods, numbers sleep on the kitchen floor, all huddled together, men and women (when indecencies are common enough), and without bedding or anything but their scanty clothes to soften the hardness of the stone or brick floor. A penny is saved to the lodger by this means. More than 200 have been accommodated in this way in a large house. The Irish, at harvest-time, very often resort to this mode of passing the night. . . .

Another man who had moved in good society, said, when asked about his resorting to a low lodging-house: 'When a man's lost caste in society, he may as well go the whole hog, bristles and all, and a low lodging-house is the entire pig.'

Notwithstanding many abominations, I am assured that the lodgers, in even the worst of these habitations, for the most part sleep soundly. But they have, in all probability, been out in the open air the whole of the day, and all of them may go to their couches, after having walked, perhaps, many miles, exceedingly fatigued, and some of them half-drunk. 'Why, in course, sir,' said a 'traveller,' whom I spoke to on this subject, 'if you is in a country town or village, where there's only one lodging-house, perhaps, and that a bad one—an old hand can always suit his-self in London—you *must* get half-drunk, or your money for your bed is wasted. There's so much rest owing to you, after a hard day; and bugs and bad air'll prevent its being paid, if you don't lay in some stock of beer, or liquor of some sort, to sleep on. It's a duty you owes yourself; but, if you haven't the browns, why, then, in course, you can't pay it.' . . .

I have now to speak of the habitual violation of all the injunctions of law, of all the obligations of morality, and of all the restraints of decency, seen continually in the vilest of the lodging-houses. . . .

Some of the 'fences' board, lodge, and clothe, two or three boys or girls, and send them out regularly to thieve, the fence usually taking all the proceeds, and if it be the young thief has been successful, he is rewarded with a trifle of pocket-money, and is allowed plenty of beer and tobacco.

. . . . .

The licentiousness of the frequenters, and more especially of the juvenile frequenters, of the low lodging-houses, must be even more briefly alluded to. In some of these establishments, men and women, boys and girls,—but perhaps in no case, or in very rare cases, unless they are themselves consenting parties, herd together promiscuously. The information which I have been given from a reverend informant indicates the nature of the proceedings, when the sexes are herded indiscriminately, and it is impossible to present to the reader, in full particularity, the records of the vice practised.

Boys have boastfully carried on loud conversations, and from distant parts of the room, of their triumphs over the virtue of girls, and girls have laughed at and encouraged the recital. Three, four, five, six, and even more boys and girls have been packed, head and feet, into one small bed; some of them perhaps never met before. On such occasions any clothing seems often enough to be regarded as merely an incumbrance. Sometimes there are loud quarrels and revilings from the jealousy of boys and girls, and more especially of girls whose 'chaps' have deserted or been inveigled from them. At others, there is an amicable interchange of partners, and next day a resumption of their former companionship. . . . The younger lodgers in such places live by thieving and pocket-picking, or by prostitution. The charge for a night's lodging is generally 2d., but smaller children have often been admitted for 1d. If a boy or girl resort to one of these dens at night without the means of defraying the charge for accommodation, the 'mot of the ken' (mistress of the house) will pack them off, telling them plainly that it will be no use their returning until they have stolen something worth 2d. . . .

The indiscriminate admixture of the sexes among adults, in many of these places, is another evil. Even in some houses considered of the better sort, men and women, husbands and wives, old and young, strangers and acquaintances, sleep in the same apartment, and if they choose, in the same bed. Any remonstrance at some act of gross depravity or impropriety, on the part of a woman not so utterly hardened as the others, is met with abuse and derision. One man who described these scenes to me, and had long witnessed them, said that almost the only women who ever hid their faces or manifested dislike of the proceedings they could not but notice (as far as he saw) were poor Irishwomen, generally those who live by begging: 'But for all that,' the man added, 'an Irishman or Irishwoman of that sort will sleep anywhere, in any mess, to save a halfpenny, though they may have often a few shillings, or a good many, hidden about them.' . . .

There are now fewer of such filthy receptacles than there were. Some have been pulled down—especially for the building of Commercial-street, in Whitechapel, and of New Oxford-street—and some have fallen into fresh and improved management. Of those of the worst class, however, there may now be at least thirty in London; while the low lodgings of all descriptions, good or bad, are more frequented than they were a few years back. . . .

.   .   .   .   .

The Street Where the Boy-Sweepers Lodged

I was anxious to see the room in which the gang of boy crossing-sweepers lived, so that I might judge of their peculiar style of house-keeping, and form some notion of their principles of domestic economy.

I asked young Harry and 'the Goose' to conduct me to their lodgings, and they at once consented, 'the Goose' prefacing his compliance with the remark, that 'it wern't such as genilmen had been accustomed to, but then I must take 'em as they was.'

The boys led me in the direction of Drury-lane; and before entering one of the narrow streets which branch off like the side-bones of a fish's spine from that long thoroughfare, they thought fit to caution me that I was not to be frightened, as nobody would touch me, for all was very civil.

The locality consisted of one of those narrow streets which, were it not for the paved cartway in the centre, would be called a court. Seated on the pavement at each side of the entrance was a costerwoman with her basket before her, and her legs tucked up mysteriously under her gown into a round ball, so that her figure resembled in shape the plaster tumblers sold by the Italians. These women remained as inanimate as if they had been carved images, and it was only when a passenger went by they gave signs of life, by calling out in a low voice, like talking to themselves, 'Two for three haarpence—herrens,'—'Fine hinguns.'

The street itself is like the description given of thoroughfares in the East. Opposite neighbours could not exactly shake hands out of window, but they could talk together very comfortably; and indeed, as I passed along, I observed several women with their arms folded like a cat's paws on the sill, and chatting with their friends over the way.

Nearly all the inhabitants were costermongers, and, indeed, the narrow cartway seemed to have been made just wide enough for a truck to wheel down it. A beershop and a general store, together with a couple of sweeps, —whose residences were distinguished by a broom over the door,—formed the only exceptions to the street-selling class of inhabitants.

As I entered the place, it gave me the notion that it belonged to a district coster colony, and formed one large hawkers' home; for everybody seemed to be doing just as he liked, and I was stared at as if considered an intruder. Women were seated on the pavement, knitting, and repairing their linen; the doorways were filled up with bonnetless girls, who wore their shawls over their head, as the Spanish women do their mantillas; and the youths in corduroy and brass buttons, who were chatting with them, leant against the walls as they smoked their pipes, and blocked up the pavement, as if they were the proprietors of the place. Little children formed a convenient bench out of the kerbstone; and a party of four men were seated on the footway, playing with cards which had turned to the colour of brown paper from long usage, and marking the points with chalk upon the flags.

The parlour-windows of the houses had all of them wooden shutters, as thick and clumsy-looking as a kitchen flap-table, the paint of which had turned to the dull dirt-colour of an old slate. Some of these shutters were evidently never used as a security for the dwelling, but served only as tables on which to chalk the accounts of the day's sales.

Before most of the doors were costermongers' trucks—some standing ready to be wheeled off, and others stained and muddy with the day's work. A few of the costers were dressing up their barrows, arranging the sieves of waxy-looking potatoes—and others taking the stiff herrings, browned like a meerschaum with the smoke they had been dried in, from the barrels beside them, and spacing them out in pennyworths on their trays.

You might guess what each costermonger had taken out that day by the heap of refuse swept into the street before the doors. One house had a blue mound of mussel-shells in front of it—another, a pile of the outside leaves of broccoli and cabbages, turning yellow and slimy with bruises and moisture.

Hanging up beside some of the doors were bundles of old strawberry pottles, stained red with the fruit. Over the trap-doors to the cellars were piles of market-gardeners' sieves, ruddled like a sheep's back with big red letters. In fact, everything that met the eye seemed to be in some way connected with the coster's trade.

From the windows poles stretched out, on which blankets, petticoats, and linen were drying; and so numerous were they, that they reminded me of the flags hung out at a Paris fête. Some of the sheets had patches as big as trap-doors let into their centres; and the blankets were—many of them —as full of holes as a pigeon-house.

As I entered the court, a 'row' was going on; and from a first-floor window a lady, whose hair sadly wanted brushing, was haranguing a crowd beneath, throwing her arms about like a drowning man, and in her excitement thrusting her body half out of her temporary rostrum as energetically as I have seen Punch lean over his theatre.

'The willin dragged her,' she shouted, 'by the hair of her head, at least three yards into the court—the willin! and then he kicked her, and the blood was on his boot.'

It was a sweep who had been behaving in this cowardly manner; but still he had his defenders in the women around him. One with very shiny hair, and an Indian kerchief round her neck, answered the lady in the window, by calling her a 'd————d old cat;' whilst the sweep's wife rushed about clapping her hands together as quickly as if she was applauding at a theatre, and styled somebody or other 'an old wagabones as she wouldn't dirty her hands to fight with.'

This 'row' had the effect of drawing all the lodgers to the windows— their heads popping out as suddenly as dogs from their kennels in a fancier's yard.

The Boy-Sweepers' Room

The room where the boys lodged was scarcely bigger than a coach-house; and so low was the ceiling, that a fly-paper suspended from a clothes-line was on a level with my head, and had to be carefully avoided when I moved about.

One corner of the apartment was completely filled up by a big four-post bedstead, which fitted into a kind of recess as perfectly as if it had been built to order.

The old woman who kept this lodging had endeavoured to give it a homely look of comfort, by hanging little black-framed pictures scarcely bigger than pocket-books, on the walls. Most of these were sacred subjects, with large yellow glories round the heads; though between the drawing representing the bleeding heart of Christ, and the Saviour bearing the Cross, was an illustration of a red-waistcoated sailor smoking his pipe. The Adoration of the Shepherds, again, was matched on the other side of the fireplace by a portrait of Daniel O'Connell.

A chest of drawers was covered over with a green baize cloth, on which books, shelves, and clean glasses were tidily set out.

Where so many persons (for there were about eight of them, including the landlady, her daughter, and grandson) could all sleep, puzzled me extremely.

The landlady wore a frilled nightcap, which fitted so closely to the skull, that it was evident she had lost her hair. One of her eyes was slowly recovering from a blow, which, to use her own words, 'a blackgeyard gave her.' Her lip, too, had suffered in the encounter, for it was swollen and cut.

'I've a nice flock-bid for the boys,' she said, when I inquired into the accommodation of her lodging-house, 'where three of them can slape aisy and comfortable.'

'It's a large bed, sir,' said one of the boys, 'and a warm covering over us; and you see it's better than a regular lodging-house; for, if you want a knife or a cup, you don't have to leave something on it till it's returned.'

The old woman spoke up for her lodgers, telling me that they were good boys, and very honest; 'for,' she added, 'they pays me rig-lar ivery night, which is threepence.'

The only youth as to whose morals she seemed to be at all doubtful was 'the Goose,' 'for he kept late hours, and sometimes came home without a penny in his pocket.'

.   .   .   .   .

Cheap Lodging-Houses

I now come to the class of cheap lodging-houses usually frequented by the casual labourers at the docks. . . .

On my first visit, the want and misery that I saw were such, that, in consulting with the gentleman who led me to the spot, it was arranged that a dinner should be given on the following Sunday to all those who were present on the evening of my first interview; and, accordingly, enough beef, potatoes, and materials for a suet-pudding, were sent in from the neighbouring market to feed them every one. I parted with my guide, arranging to be with him the next Sunday at half-past one. We met at the time appointed, and set out on our way to the cheap lodging-house. The streets were alive with sailors, and bonnetless and capless women. The Jews' shops and public-houses were all open, and parties of 'jolly tars' reeled past us, singing and bawling on their way. Had it not been that here and there a stray shop was closed, it would have been impossible to have guessed it was Sunday. We dived down a narrow court, at the entrance of which lolled Irish labourers smoking short pipes. Across the court hung lines, from which dangled dirty-white clothes to dry; and as we walked on, ragged, unwashed, shoeless children scampered past us, chasing one another. At length we reached a large open yard. In the centre of it stood several empty costermongers' trucks and turned-up carts, with their shafts high in the air. At the bottom of these lay two young girls huddled together, asleep. Their bare heads told their mode of life, while it was evident, from their muddy Adelaide boots, that they had walked the streets all night. My companion tried to see if he knew them, but they slept too soundly to be roused by gentle means. We passed on, and a few places further on there sat grouped on a door-step four women, of the same character as the last two. One had her head covered up in an old brown shawl, and was sleeping in the lap of the one next to her. The other two were eating walnuts; and a coarse-featured man in knee-breeches and 'ankle-jacks' was stretched on the ground close beside them.

At length we reached the lodging-house. It was night when I had first visited the place, and all now was new to me. The entrance was through a pair of large green gates, which gave it somewhat the appearance of a stable-yard. Over the kitchen door there hung a clothes-line, on which were a wet shirt and a pair of ragged canvas trousers, brown with tar. Entering the kitchen, we found it so full of smoke that the sun's rays, which shot slanting down through a broken tile in the roof, looked like a shaft of light cut through the fog. The flue of the chimney stood out from the bare brick wall like a buttress, and was black all way up with the smoke; the beams, which hung down from the roof, and ran from wall to wall, were of the same colour; and in the centre, to light the room, was a rude iron gas-pipe, such as are used at night when the streets are turned up. The floor was unboarded, and a wooden seat projected from the wall all round the room. In front of this was ranged a series of tables, on which lolled dozing men. A number of the inmates were grouped around the fire; some kneeling, toasting herrings, of which the place smelt strongly; others, without shirts, seated on the ground close beside it for warmth; and others drying the ends of cigars they had picked up in the streets. As we entered the men rose, and never was so motley and so ragged an assemblage seen. Their hair was matted like flocks of wool, and their chins were grimy with their unshorn beards. Some were in dirty smock-frocks; others in old red plush waistcoats, with long sleeves. One was dressed in an old shooting jacket, with large wooden buttons; a second in a blue flannel sailor's shirt; and a third, a mere boy, wore a long camlet coat reaching to his heels, and with the ends of the sleeves hanging over his hands. The features of the lodgers wore every kind of expression: one lad was positively handsome, and there was a frankness in his face and a straight-forward look in his eyes that strongly impressed me with a sense of his honesty, even although I was assured he was a confirmed pickpocket. The young thief who had brought back the 11½d. change out of the shilling that had been entrusted to him on the preceding evening was far from prepossessing, now that I could see him better. His cheek-bones were high, while his hair, cut close on the top, with a valance of locks, as it were, left hanging in front, made me look upon him with no slight suspicion. On the form at the end of the kitchen was one whose squalor and wretchedness produced a feeling approaching to awe. His eyes were sunk deep in his head, his cheeks were drawn in, and his nostrils pinched with evident want, while his dark stubbly beard gave a grimness to his appearance that was almost demoniac; and yet there was a patience in his look that was almost pitiable. His clothes were black and shiny at every fold with grease, and his coarse shirt was so brown with long wearing, that it was only with close inspection you could see that it had once been a checked one: on his feet he had a pair of lady's side-laced boots, the toes of which had been cut off so that he might get them on. I never beheld so gaunt a picture of famine. To this day the figure of the man haunts me.

· · · · ·

The lodging-house to which I more particularly allude makes up as many as 84 'bunks,' or beds, for which 2d per night is charged. For this sum the parties lodging there for the night are entitled to the use of the kitchen for the following day. In this a fire is kept all day long, at which they are allowed to cook their food. The kitchen opens at 5 in the morning, and closes at about 11 at night, after which hour no fresh lodger is taken in, and all those who slept in the house the night before, but who have not sufficient money to pay for their bed at that time, are turned out. Strangers who arrive in the course of the day must procure a tin ticket, by paying 2d. at the wicket in the office, previously to being allowed to enter the kitchen. The kitchen is about 40 feet long by about 40 wide. The 'bunks' are each about 7 feet long, and 1 foot 10 inches wide, and the grating on which the straw mattress is placed is about 12 inches from the ground. The wooden partitions between the 'bunks' are about 4 feet high. The coverings are a leather or a rug, but leathers are generally preferred. Of these 'bunks' there are five rows, of about 24 deep; two rows being placed head to head, with a gangway between each of such two rows, and the other row against the wall. The average number of persons sleeping in this house of a night is 60. Of these there are generally about 30 pickpockets, 10 street-beggars, a few infirm old people who subsist occasionally upon parish relief and occasionally upon charity, 10 or 15 dock-labourers, about the same number of low and precarious callings, such as the neighbourhood affords, and a few persons who have been in good circumstances, but who have been reduced from a variety of causes. At one time there were as many as 9 persons lodging in this house who subsisted by picking up dogs' dung out of the streets, getting about 5s. for every basketful. The earnings of one of these men were known to average 9s. per week. There are generally lodging in the house a few bone-grubbers, who pick up bones, rags, iron, &c., out of the streets. Their average earnings are about 1s. per day. There are several mud-larks, or youths who go down to the water-side when the tide is out, to see whether any article of value has been left upon the bank of the river. The person supplying this information to me, who was for some time resident in the house, has seen brought home by these persons a drum of figs at one time, and a Dutch cheese at another. These were sold in small lots or slices to the other lodgers.

The pickpockets generally lodging in the house consist of handkerchief-stealers, shop-lifters—including those who rob the till as well as steal articles from the doors of shops. Legs and breasts of mutton are frequently brought in by this class of persons. There are seldom any housebreakers lodging in such places, because they require a room of their own, and mostly live with prostitutes. Besides pickpockets, there are also lodging in the house speculators in stolen goods. These may be dock-labourers or Billingsgate porters, having a few shillings in their pockets. With these they purchase the booty of the juvenile thieves. 'I have known,' says my informant, 'the speculators wait in the kitchen, walking about with their hands in their pockets, till a little fellow would come in with such a thing as a cap, a piece of bacon, or a piece of mutton. They would purchase it, and then either retail it amongst the other lodgers in the kitchen or take it to some "fence," where they would receive a profit upon it.' The general feeling of the kitchen—excepting with four or five individuals—is to encourage theft. The encouragement to the 'gonaff' (a Hebrew word signifying a young thief, probably learnt from the Jew 'fences' in the neighbourhood) consists in laughing at and applauding his dexterity in thieving; and whenever anything is brought in, the 'gonaff' is greeted for his good luck, and a general rush is made towards him to see the produce of his thievery. The 'gonaffs' are generally young boys; about 20 out of 30 of these lads are under 21 years of age. They almost all of them love idleness, and will only work one or two days together, but then they will work very hard. It is a singular fact that as a body, the pickpockets are generally very sparing of drink. They are mostly libidinous, indeed universally so, and spend whatever money they can spare upon the low prostitutes round about the neighbourhood. Burglars and smashers generally rank above this class of thieves. A burglar would not condescend to sit among pickpockets. My informant has known a housebreaker to say with a sneer, when requested to sit down with the 'gonaffs,' 'No, no! I may be a thief, sir; but, thank God, at least I'm a respectable one.' The beggars who frequent these houses go about different markets and streets asking charity of the people that pass by. They generally go out in couples; the business of one of the two being to look out and give warning when the policeman is approaching, and of the other to stand 'shallow;' that is to say, to stand with very little clothing on, shivering and shaking, sometimes with bandages round his legs, and sometimes with his arm in a sling. Others beg 'scran' (broken victuals) of the servants at respectable houses, and bring it home to the lodging-house, where they sell it. You may see, I am told, the men who lodge in the place, and obtain an honest living, watch for these beggars coming in, as if they were the best victuals in the City. My informant knew an instance of a lad who seemed to be a very fine little fellow, and promised to have been possessed of excellent mental capabilities if properly directed, who came to the lodging-house when out of a situation as an errand-boy. He stayed there a month or six weeks, during which time he was tampered with by the others, and ultimately became a confirmed 'gonaff.' The conversation among the lodgers relates chiefly to thieving and the best manner of stealing. By way of practice, a boy will often pick the pocket of one of the lodgers walking about the room, and if detected declare he did not mean it.

44 | How the Poor Are Housed in the United States

ALVIN L. SCHORR

In arguments about the adequacy of public relief, occasionally someone is heard to say: "But where are these people who are in such difficulty? After all, no one starves in the United States." It is approximately as ambiguous to say that everyone in the United States is, after all, under a roof. Some are malnourished, as some are malhoused. In order to examine the question how families get under a roof, it will be useful to visualize the income that they require.

Analysis by Warren Jay Vinton of income and new housing in the years 1947 to 1958 shows that it was, on the whole, those families with over $6,000 a year [1] who were served. Families with less than $6,000 account for 88 percent of the substandard housing in the country, suggesting that they are not served very well by existing housing either. Many have adequate housing, especially if they are close to $6,000 income or if the income supports one or two people rather than four or five. But it seems clear that income of at least $6,000 is required to assure adequate family housing. . . . It is evident that the family to which we are addressing our attention, with income equivalent to $2,500 or less for a family of four, will have to make adjustments of some kind in their housing expenditures.

How do poor families pay for housing? The question has dimensions that are private and public. As a private matter, the question is answerable in terms of budget management and family arrangements. As a public matter, one answers in terms of specific public programs or of the concept that housing filters down to the poor as those who are better off move on to better housing. . . . Two national programs, public assistance and public housing, incorporate a means test and intervene directly in the housing of the poor. They will merit special attention when we come to the public dimension of the provision of housing to the poor.

．　．　．　．　．

[1] Dollar figures used in this paragraph are for years from 1956 to 1959. They are not adjusted here, as they are being used to establish the magnitude of income that is necessary rather than a precise amount.

SOURCE: Alvin Schorr, *Slums and Social Insecurity*, Research Report Number 1, Social Security Administration, Division of Research and Statistics (Washington, D. C.: U. S. Department of Health, Education and Welfare, 1963), pp. 98–99, 107–110, 112–116, 118–124, 134–137.

The Private Dimension

As a private matter, . . . poor families get and apply money wherever they can. They use a variety of strategies, some because they come to hand and some in which there is a measure of choice. An aged widow will make different adjustments from a young father, for example. But few of the deliberate choices that are open seem attractive. Families can go without standard housing. They can borrow from food to pay housing. Few who are poor will have saved money; those who have, can use it. They can struggle to buy on credit or to borrow. They can try to buy instead of rent. Those who manage to bring this off may make out better in the end. Others will face additional difficulty because they are borrowing from other budget items and are leaving themselves less room to maneuver in the next emergency. They can extend the size of their households, trading crowdedness and tension for shelter and a measure of financial flexibility. Families can break up or at least give up children. Throughout, they can seek ways to improve their income. Some poor families try all of these. For some but not for others, purchasing a house and sending additional members to work, when they are possible, are constructive steps. For the rest of it, the avenues that are open go around in a tight little circle, enmeshing families deeper and deeper in deprivation.

The Public Dimension

Broadly speaking, the first line of action in providing housing to those who are poor lies in the normal operation of the economy, stimulated and secured by the Federal insurance programs. Clearly, there have been gains in housing poor families that result from the operation of economic forces not directly concerned with them. The number of substandard units in the country has declined steadily in the past two decades, though the total housing inventory has increased by over 50 percent.[2] On the other hand, substandard housing or crowding is still the common and not the exceptional fate of 32 million Americans who live in modern poverty. The normal operation of the economy is not dealing adequately with the housing of the poor while it deals with them incidentally.

We have already observed that new housing does not flow to families with less than $5,000 or $6,000 income, much less to those with half that income. But it is held by some that if the total housing supply increases, some units will be released to "filter down" to poor families. Why has filtration not worked to more substantial effect? Three kinds of factors appear

---

[2] Standards of housing do not remain static over 20 years, any more than other consumption standards. Whether the housing of those who are poor has improved at the same rate as general standards of housing is not evaluated here.

to interfere with filtration as a method of providing housing to poor families.

First, filtration requires that the real estate market operate in a situation of stable demand and continuing supply, without impediment. We face a situation, however, in which the total population surges upward and inwards to our cities. To add to the pressure, the postwar babies should, by 1965 to 1975, be marrying and establishing new households at a high rate. . . .

Second, though housing may become less desirable over time, compared to what is currently available, it does not necessarily become cheaper. The price of housing that is released depends upon competiton; where even substandard housing is in short supply the price will not drop. For example, the median rent (in real dollars) in the lower East Side of New York City actually rose over a long period of time. Yet the housing had clearly declined in a scale of values relating it to other housing. Thus, though filtering down may occur in some senses of the term and though one may see housing obviously undergoing transition in quality and tenancy, the process does not necessarily serve the family whose real income remains below the $2,500 level.

Third and finally, . . . housing that is sold, converted, and put to uses for which it was not initially designed exacts a nonmonetary price from the families who live in it. If housing is substandard, families pay the cost of design that does not lend itself to their purposes and of dilapidation and crowding. Even standard housing may be ill-designed for families who occupy it because they must, rather than because it is suitable. Moreover, filtration means that the poor must live where the middle class lived under different circumstances; that is, before the development of travel by auto, when unskilled jobs were all in the center of the city, and when services of good quality were available in the neighborhood. Thus, for some, filtration may provide shelter, but it does not provide what we seek—housing that affords the optimum opportunity for escaping from poverty.

Public housing and public assistance, in different ways, address themselves directly to the housing needs of poor families. How do they serve?

Public Housing

Public housing is not a single program, historically; it is a single vessel that has been used for diverse public purposes. In the 1930's, public housing was intended for families who voluntarily sought to improve their housing but could not afford private rentals. This group was not regarded as dependent. Indeed, some housing authorities limited the number of public assistance recipients they would accept and others would not admit any. In the 1940's, the program was redirected to provide housing for war workers. Following the Housing Act of 1949, public housing was oriented

again to poor families—with a difference. Partly because postwar amend-
ments gave priority to families having the most urgent housing need, to the
aged and to those displaced by urban renewal, this third generation in
public housing contains a high concentration of depressed, untutored, and
dependent families.

.   .   .   .   .

The alteration in its population also leads to a financial problem for public housing. Tenants' income (in constant dollars) has remained level in
the past decade, but each year the tenants' income falls further below the
median for the country. That is, in 1955 the median net income of families
admitted to public housing was 46.5 percent of the median income of all
families in the United States. In 1961, it was less than 40 percent. Consequently, the rents that may be collected from tenants do not rise as
rapidly as maintenance costs. Between 1950 and 1958 monthly receipts
from rent increased by 25 percent (from $28.93 to $36.50 per unit per
month), but expenditures increased by 52 percent (from $21.32 to $32.50).
Not unexpectedly, then, the Federal contribution to local housing authorities has been moving steadily toward its permissible maximum. With the
overall Federal contribution reaching 87 percent of the maximum in fiscal
year 1961, some local housing authorities find themselves still with substantial leeway and others with rather little.

Public housing is faced with grave problems which go to the heart of its
ability to remain solvent and shape the kind of housing, in the sense of
total social and physical environment, that it is able to provide.[3] What are
the consequences for tenants? The first and perhaps the most serious consequence is that public housing is not available to more than a small proportion of the low-income families. Though the Housing Act of 1949 authorized 810,000 units, that authorization is as yet far from exhausted.
There are in all something over half a million units—roughly 1 percent of
the housing supply. If public housing were limited to the lowest incomes,
with current resources it could house 2 million of the 32 million we have
defined as poor. As it reaches above the very lowest incomes, it houses
even a smaller percentage of the poor than these figures indicate. Consequently there are waiting lists of people eligible for public housing. In the
District of Columbia, the number of families awaiting admission has at
times exceeded the total number of housing units.

---

[3] Not all of the problems have been touched on here. For a careful description of policy and financial developments, see Warren Jay Vinton, "Working
Paper," in *Interim Report on Housing the Economically and Socially Disadvantaged Groups in the Population.* Prepared for the Conference of Housing
the Economically and Socially Disadvantaged Groups in the Population, New
York, February 26–27, 1960. For a development of the meaning of the change
in tenant population, see Elizabeth Wood, "Public Housing and Mrs. McGee,"
Journal of Housing, XIII, 11 (December 1956), 424–427.

Since public housing must look to its receipts, it tends to exclude families with the lowest incomes who cannot pay minimum rents. . . . That is, the bulk of families entering public housing have incomes under $4,000 a year. Among the families having less than $4,000, in the total population roughly one in four has under $1,500 income. But only one in eight of those who move into public housing has less than $1,500.[4] Families may be excluded as undesirable, too. Though such exclusions would doubtless diminish if there were more public housing, they represent an effort to maintain a degree of acceptability among tenants. On the other hand, when careful study was made of 82 families excluded as undesirables in New York City, the decision was reversed for 33 of the families. Other reviews have produced higher percentages of reversal. In addition to the limited capacity of the program, . . . many presumably eligible families are not willing to live in public housing. Their reluctance must arise, to some degree, from the program's current difficulties, but it also represents a feeling about living in a managed—particularly, in a Government-managed—community. As early as 1946, a local study reported that only a third of those eligible were willing to live in public housing. In sum, public housing is limited by its quantity, its fixity upon the middle range of low incomes, and by management and tenant views of acceptability.

Americans are often more attentive to the tempo and direction of a trend than to the underlying facts. Because we are preoccupied with the problems and movement of public housing, we may conceivably overlook the function it is performing. When they are asked, the majority of families who live in public housing say that they like it. They appreciate its facilities; their general morale is higher than it was in substandard housing. One must of course, take into account that those who would object most to public housing never enter it, or they leave.[5] Nevertheless, for those who take up tenancy, public housing represents a considerable improvement in physical surroundings. Moreover, the aspects of the environment which are offensive to some families may be secondary or even functional for others. Kurt W. Back finds that two types of people move into public housing, those who seek to use it as a vehicle for change and those who see it as an end in itself. Of the latter, he writes:

In general, the tenants form the weaker and more vulnerable part of the [public housing] population. They have less income, less secure income, and are more likely to represent broken homes. In a very real way they need the protection afforded by government action, and many of them received some

---

[4] Perhaps half of the families with less than $1,500 income who move into public housing are public assistance recipients. The nonrecipient with very low income is therefore represented in a very small proportion indeed.

[5] The rate of moveouts, though it signals difficulty in some places, is not strikingly high compared with general population mobility. It is lower overall than the movement rate for rental housing insured by FHA.

government aid. These people apparently look on government housing as a type of institutional support, which they need.

Thus, public housing performs at least acceptably for those poor families who see it as an improved, somewhat protected environment. Presumably, it offers their children a better start than they might otherwise have had. Analysis of turnover statistics suggests that others use public housing as a way station to improved housing. In this sense, too, public housing serves the prevention of poverty.

Thus, strictly managed housing may suit one family—or at least not trouble it—and trouble others very much. Public housing is pressed, if it is going to serve families with any precision, to define its objectives and to alter policies to further these objectives. At least three choices are open: (1) A real estate operation for the respectable poor—the purely poor. (2) A rehabilitative program for the seriously dependent and troubled-poor. (3) A greatly enlarged and altered program, at least in part deinstitutionalized, with a variety of kinds of housing opportunities. In the absence of a settled decision to seek the third course and of the legislation that would make it possible, local housing authorities are moving slowly, in most cases with pronounced reluctance, toward rehabilitative programs. Under present circumstances the families who are entering public housing make such a course inevitable. Not only are the families isolated and segregated; increasing numbers are aged, many receive public assistance, and many are in broken families. They cannot be abandoned to their problems; they must be served. Moreover, when they are not served, buildings deteriorate, delinquencies occur, and deprived youngsters grow into disabled adults. It becomes plain that neglect is expensive.

Ambivalence about what course to take is reflected in the development of practices concerning the provision of health and social services. During most of its postwar third stage, public housing has been a real estate operation in theory if not in fact. Health and social services, except as they contributed directly to management, have been regarded by the Public Housing Administration as an inappropriate cost. At most, housing authorities might provide space to community agencies and employ staff members to direct tenants to appropriate community services. . . .

The provision of direct services by public housing would, necessarily, raise the question whether the Federal subsidy is adequate to the current task of public housing. Generally speaking, the subsidy covers capital costs and debt service; operating cost must be met out of income. In effect, additional costs mean tenants must pay higher rent. Other considerations than providing health and social services suggest that the subsidy requires reexamination. We have noted, first, that management costs have risen more sharply than the income of tenants. Second, the lowest of the low-income families are finding it doubly hard to get into public housing. Third, almost half the families in public housing are paying 20 percent or more of their income for rent. Some are paying over 30 percent. We have suggested that this is too much. Recent legislation provides a special additional subsidy for housing very low-income, aged persons. Thus, the problem has been recognized, but the problem is by no means limited to the aged.

Health and social services are a significant element of a rehabilitative program, but they are undermined if the structure of the program is, in other significant respects, antirehabilitative. (Services are undermined too, to be sure, if larger community forces are antirehabilitative—if, for example, there are no jobs for the public housing tenant who has been retrained.) A number of policy and legislative changes that are required for a rehabilitative program have been the subject of public discussion and are fairly well understood.

There have been attempts to develop "vest pocket" or "scattered" sites for public housing—that is, small units wherever opportunity and cost permit. Vest pocket housing may be built new or existing housing rehabilitated. On a reasonably large scale, such a development would help to dissolve tenants' feelings of isolation. It would allow housing to be assigned because it is particularly suited to a family's size or housekeeping competence. Scattered sites might also be a solution to the increasingly serious problem of finding space for public housing. On the other hand, many neighborhoods show considerable resistance to public housing of any sort or size. Similar in purposes is another proposal to establish statewide housing authorities which would be able to distribute public housing more widely and rationally than municipal authorities can.

Various devices are offered to secure a more representative cross section of tenants in public housing. Special efforts may be made to provide housing developments with a sufficiently high proportion of white occupants to assure continuing integrated tenancy. In at least some places, a percentage of apartments is reserved for white tenancy. (The proposition that a "benign quota" is constructive or is discriminatory provides the basis for a highly sophisticated controversy in race relations.) A legislative change might permit over-income tenants to remain, perhaps with some limitation as to their maximum numbers. In addition to diversifying tenancy, this would meet the problem that, at a particular income level, additional earnings may mean having to move out. Apart from the intrinsic merits of the proposal, it may be difficult to visualize taking such a step while eligible low-income families await admission.

It may conceivably be possible to work out a method for tenants to purchase their living units as their income rises. The idea is not entirely novel; war housing was disposed of to tenant cooperatives. Vest pocket public housing might readily be sold to occupants, and the money turned over into new rental dwellings. The caution has been offered that, in individual ownership of public housing, "there is a danger of crystallizing minimum standards." That is, once people purchase, they may tend to stay even though they are able to afford improved housing. As a practical matter, it is probably a more serious difficulty that, on however small a scale, the Government would be building for eventual low-income ownership. On the other hand, the possibility of ownership offers an attractive method of combating feelings of isolation and encouraging families to strive for higher income.

Such proposals may be viewed discretely, taking each one on its merits and balancing its cost against its contribution to a rehabilitative program. Providing a thoroughly constructive environment for a group of seriously dependent and troubled poor families is not a mean task. If the proposals are taken together, however, it is possible to make out the shape of a program that meets a larger objective. It would provide standard housing to all who are too poor to buy it in the private market; provide housing in a fashion that is open ended, tends to move families up the income scale, and leaves them in time able to pay for private housing; and would be sufficiently flexible and diversified to have room for those who are both poor and require protection or rehabilitation. Within this context, one sees proposals in a somewhat different light.

The magnitude of the larger objective provides, by contrast with the present program, part of the answer to the question—How does public housing serve the poor? It serves some of them, a small minority of them. Those it serves, does it serve them well? Some of them, only some of them.

Public Assistance

People who do not have enough money for decent living may be helped by public assistance. Major assistance programs, representing a partnership of Federal and State Governments, are addressed to children in family homes, to the aged, the blind, and the disabled. Some States and localities also provide general assistance for needy people not eligible under the categorical programs. In accordance with the Social Security Act, assistance in the Federal-State programs is given to recipients in money, without stipulating how it must be spent.[6] As this practice suggests, the intent of the legislation was to provide funds for subsistence, without public intrusion into the choices that must be made in family management. Public assistance agencies have, therefore, tended to refrain from dealing directly with landlords. But assistance provides the means for securing housing. When recipients have difficulty in securing adequate housing, assistance agencies are perforce involved in their clients' problems. At the beginning of 1962, over

---

[6] However, payments may be made on behalf of a recipient to a person or organization providing medical or other remedial care. In aid to families with dependent children, in a limited number of cases where it is in the children's interest, the entire payment may be turned over to a third party to spend on behalf of the recipient family.

7 million people were receiving assistance. Though less directly than public housing, to be sure, public assistance is the largest national program concerned with the housing needs of the poor. It is important, therefore, to ask about the quality of housing that assistance recipients secure and about the welfare department's influence upon it.

Although information about the quality of recipients' housing has not been systematically collected, it is clear that the quality is poor. . . . Measures of crowding suggest that over [long periods of] time assistance recipients are not improving their housing at the same rate as the general population. In the decade from 1950 to 1960, the median number of persons per room in the AFDC [Aid to Families with Dependent Children] household declined from 1.0 to 0.94. In the same period, the national median declined from 0.75 to 0.59. That the median number of persons per room in the AFDC household is now 0.94 means that almost half the families are crowded. One in five of the AFDC families are "critically overcrowded," living in households in which there are 1.5 persons or more per room.

Special State and city studies provide a more intimate appraisal of the housing of public assistance recipients. Florida reviewed 13,000 cases of aid to families with dependent children to determine whether the homes were suitable for children. The study noted "excessively high rents for unspeakably inadequate slum homes." A survey of recipient families with dependent children in the State of Maine found that four out of five did not have central heating. . . .

. . . . .

The repetition of percentages about crowding and sanitary facilities may fail to convey what caseworkers see and recipients experience. The Commissioner of Welfare in New York City quotes a caseworker as follows:

In this six-story building, converted into furnished rooms, filth prevails throughout—filled garbage cans without covers line the hallways with the surplus refuse spilling over; roaches and rats abound; broken flooring, plumbing, windows, lighting fixtures and plaster are observable throughout. The average room size [occupied by a family] is 13 x 15 with two beds, a dresser, two chairs, a table, a refrigerator and a closet, as the standard equipment supplied by the landlord. One community kitchen is used by seven families. Twelve toilets are intermittently in service on six floors. There is no lock on the door from the street and vagrants, including drug addicts and alcoholics, often wander in to sleep in the unlocked kitchens and bathrooms. This is the abode of thirty families and 105 children. . . .

One has to ask how such conditions occur for so many people in programs intended to maintain health and decency and to strengthen family life. It goes without saying that, by the nature of the problem that makes recipients of them, some families are handicapped in finding and maintaining decent housing. Old age, physical disability, and a broken marriage or no marriage may each, in its own way, make a family poor tenants. But there are simpler, more powerful causes of the problem.

Fundamentally, the amount of money paid to recipients of public assistance in most places is not enough to pay for proper housing and the other elements of a healthful and decent budget. . . .

. . . . .

How does public assistance serve in providing housing for poor people? It leaves many in poor housing and some in desperately poor housing. Basically, its failure is a failure to provide recipients with enough money to pay for decent housing. Because of this failure, public assistance is pressed to offer special aids and protection for its clients. These help, to some degree, but to larger degree are frustrated by limitations of available housing and inability to force legal maintenance of housing. Because public assistance has not historically regarded itself as a provider of housing, agencies may also fail to invest their fullest energies in the securing of housing.

Two old studies suggest the direction and pace with which public assistance has moved in relation to housing. A U.S. Children's Bureau study of Mother's Aid (a predecessor to AFDC) in 10 representative communities in 1928 reports: In 1940, the U.S. Housing Authority and the Social Security Board reviewed common areas of their programs. Among their conclusions:

Except in one large city, where housing conditions left much to be desired, the families were for the most part in decent, sanitary dwellings or flats in respectable neighborhoods; many were in comfortable one-family houses, and a considerable number had flower gardens. If families were found living in too congested quarters, under insanitary conditions, or in neighborhoods where morality was questionable, the courts required them—or the agencies persuaded them—to move to better locations.

In 1940, the U.S. Housing Authority and the Social Security Board reviewed common areas of their programs. Among their conclusions:

. . . it is apparent that relief and public assistance families are inadequately housed. . . . It is estimated that 50 to 90 percent of such families occupy the *worst* kind of shelter.

. . . . Inadequate housing is related to inadequate income with but few exceptions.

. . . . There are no *generally accepted* basic standards of the quantity and quality of housing considered a minimum essential for every family.

So far as the housing of public assistance recipients is concerned, the direction between 1928 and 1940 was downward. The recommendations that followed from the findings of the 1940 study are obvious: adequate payments, applying objective standards to recipients' housing, regular reporting of the quality of recipients' housing, more public housing to use for assistance recipients. Prescriptions that were plain when the Social Security Act was new have yet to be acted upon.

Can Poor Families Be Housed?

If one reflects upon the ways in which poor families pay for housing in their private lives and upon the ways in which public policies assist them, it is possible to perceive a discrepancy. The private and the public dimensions are out of balance. Poor people pay for housing as a total effort, out of their food and out of the fabric of their lives together. The effects of the struggle are experienced without Sabbath and without holiday. But public efforts to assist them are directed only to a minority. Out of those who are reached, many are helped meagerly, subject to conditions that may be relevant, irrelevant, or even self-defeating.

In public efforts to provide housing we have so far relied chiefly upon stimulation and subsidy of private industry. The results, for those with incomes over $5,000 or $6,000, have been respectable. Recent legislation attempts to extend the impact of such activity to lower incomes. The problem has so far appeared to be one of interesting builders and developers in such a market. It appears likely that some gains will be made. But it must be evident that the problem of the poor will not be met in this manner. We have referred to the reasons; they require only to be brought together.

First, though special incentives for low-income building and contraction of demand in the middle-income market may lead to more builder interest in low-cost housing than heretofore, it is unlikely that interest will reach down to the families with $2,500 incomes. High risks, limited profits, and other difficulties that have discouraged business from building for families with $5,000 incomes will seem insuperable at half those incomes.

Second, it is not unreasonable that builders and banks should take pause. A family of four with less than $2,500 income is not able to buy a house or pay a rent that provides a profit on it, no matter how low the interest rate on the mortgage. The family's income is not adequate to its need for food, clothing, and other items—even if it were paying no rent at all.

Third, inducing low-income families to pay 25 or 30 percent of their incomes carries a heavy risk of its own and is not sound public policy. The housing that is bought at the expense of food or medical care is dearly bought.

This is not to say that we are unable to provide decent housing for all American families. Public housing and public assistance provide avenues for decent housing, providing that the serious limitations of these programs are corrected. Small-scale experiments of other sorts are being tried. A number involve public subsidy to those who provide housing for low-income families, with purchasers or tenants making such payments as they can afford. There has been recurrent consideration of the possibility of providing a direct subsidy to low-income families to be used for purchasing or renting standard housing. Such a proposal was considered by the Senate Subcommittee on Housing and Urban Redevelopment headed by Senator Robert A. Taft. Reporting in 1945, the subcommittee rejected direct subsidies, mainly because they might flow to substandard housing. There was also objection to channeling such funds through public assistance agencies. After more than a decade of experience with urban renewal, attention has been turning again to the possibility of providing a direct subsidy to poor families. A number of schemes have been put forward that provide protections against misuse; nor would subsidies necessarily be furnished through public assistance agencies.

We can indeed shape a program that will provide "a decent home and a suitable living environment for every American family." Such a program need not appear to be favoritism. On the contrary, aids that have so far been devised (income tax advantages, mortgage insurance) reach middle- and upper-income families with special effect. Resources and techniques are available to right the balance.

45 | Europe's Traffic Jam

JACK LONG

"If we are to have any chance of living at peace with the motorcar, we shall need a different sort of city." This blunt warning comes from a group of British planners who took a hard look at the situation in their country and recently published a study called *Traffic in Towns*, widely known as the Buchanan Report. Experts elsewhere in Europe have come to similar conclusions and so has the ordinary man stalled in the streets.

The traffic problem is serious in most large European cities but worst of all in London, Paris, and Rome. Nowhere is it quite the same as in America. Europe's capitals grew from medieval fortresses, and their centers are spiderwebs of narrow streets and close-packed buildings that once huddled within circling walls. It took the power of emperors to cut a few broad avenues through for triumphal parades. But no one has such means at his disposal today. Ingenuity, imagination, and persuasion are used instead.

There is one principle on which authorities in London, Paris, and Rome agree. It is the need for replacing stopgap solutions with comprehensive city plans that will not be outmoded by the time the work is finished. Computers have been digesting figures on vehicle movements and project-

SOURCE: *The Lamp*, XLVII, 1 (1965), 11–14. Reprinted from *The Lamp* by permission of the Standard Oil Company of New Jersey.

ing future trends. Travel times have been measured and decible counts made. Economic and population forecasts have been assembled and analyzed. Now the time to act has arrived, and long-awaited building programs are getting under way.

London's case is considered in a chapter of the Buchanan Report. To illustrate the "different sort of city" they have in mind, the authors chose a congested 148 acres in the central part of the city and prepared a complete redevelopment plan. They treat the section as an "environmental area" that would be linked to the rest of the city by several "primary distributor" express roads built twenty feet below ground level. At ground level they propose a grid of one-way streets for local traffic, with access roads leading to garages and service entrances of buildings. Up above, pedestrians would have undisturbed use of a third level of broad elevated walkways between buildings containing shopping arcades, gardens, and cafés. Elevators, ramps, and escalators would lead to lower level garages and to bus and underground railway stations. The result would be a vertical separation of through traffic, local traffic, and foot traffic, each moving without interference from the others.

The drafters of the report recognize that rebuilding London along these lines would be a gigantic and costly undertaking. As alternatives they suggest partial redevelopment that would still achieve the basic aim of traffic separation.

Before proceeding further, the British Ministry of Transport and the London County Council went in search of more facts. They hired the American engineering firm of Wilbur Smith and Associates to make a traffic survey that is one of the largest ever undertaken. Its purpose is to determine exactly how, why, and where people move in and through London; by what kind of vehicles, public and private; and how well present facilities meet their needs. The first volume of the survey was published in July, 1964. It confirms what every Londoner suspected—that traffic is terrible and will get worse unless something is done about it.

The survey covers Greater London—940 square miles populated by more than nine million people. About 38 per cent of the households in the area own cars (the figure is 75 per cent in most urban areas in the United States), and the number is growing rapidly. To drive from Charing Cross, the city's center, to the boundary of the survey area—a distance of roughly fifteen miles—was found to take from fifty-five to sixty-five minutes during the five to seven p.m. peak hours. Great congestion was found on the Thames bridges and very heavy traffic on main radial trunk roads to the north and west of London. Only one route, the North Circular Road, which forms a great arc north of the city, offers a way for traffic to avoid the heart of the city while moving in the heavily traveled east-west direction.

This diagnosis of the city's difficulties will be followed soon by Volume II of the London Traffic Survey, with proposed solutions. It is possible to guess what some of these will be from a careful study of Volume I and from talking to the men who made it. It is likely that the main radial roads leading into the city, and the North Circular Road around it, will be improved to the status of high-capacity four- and six-lane urban motorways. There will undoubtedly be more bottleneck-breaking structures such as the new, partly elevated freeway on the road to London Airport and the underpass opened in 1962 at Hyde Park Corner, one of the city's busiest intersections. Improved bridge approaches will almost certainly be recommended. While capacity may be increased to some extent by improvements on the most heavily burdened east-west traffic corridors through the city center, new bypass routes to draw vehicles away from these choked avenues will probably be advised. The survey makes it clear that London's fast, comfortable public transport system, especially the Underground Railways, is one of the city's greatest assets. Although there is still some reserve capacity on the Underground, a major extension is being built, and suburban railway facilities are also being improved.

Overall solutions to the city's problems await a final plan. Meanwhile the London County Council is spending some ten million pounds a year ($28 million) for road improvements. Controversy continues. One group proposes a pay-as-you-drive system that would charge motorists varying fees for the use of streets in congested areas. Others advocate doing away with the railroads and turning their tracks into expressways. Many planners agree that decentralization is the best way to reduce pressure on the central area. An example is the six-acre development being built at Highgate Hill, on one of the main routes to the north, which will have 200,000 square feet of office space plus shopping centers, flats, and car parks.

Across the Channel in Paris a monumental master plan for regional development was adopted in 1964. Huge projects are called for to bridge the gap of a century since Napolean III's brilliant city planner, Baron Haussmann, carved out the broad boulevards and many of the squares and parks of today's Paris. In Haussmann's day the vehicular traffic of the city and its suburbs consisted of some 30,000 horse carriages. Today there are more than 1.5 million automobiles. A French magazine describes the city as caught in "the inferno of its traffic," with motorists condemned to perpetual motion in search of parking space. No visiting tourist soon forgets the awesome sight of massed motorcars immobilized on some of the world's widest boulevards, their horns silenced by law and their drivers beating in frustration on the sides of their vehicles.

Relief of the parking shortage may be in sight. For some time a central area of the city, called the "blue zone," has had strict controls that forbid truck deliveries between one and eight p.m.—and limit car parking to an hour on week days. Business has been helped and traffic circulation improved by ending day-long "garaging" in the streets. Under the Esplanade des Invalides, between Napoleon's tomb and the Seine, a two-level parking garage for 1,320 cars was recently completed. Space for 1,200 more cars is being excavated beneath Avenue George V. Plans call for more parking

spaces in the central part of the city in underground and elevated mul-
tistory garages. An additional 40,000 to 60,000 spaces will be provided on
the city's outskirts near subway and bus stations, and a somewhat smaller
number are planned at outlying suburban railway stations.

Like the Buchanan group, Paris authorities are making efforts to separate
pedestrian and local traffic from through traffic moving on urban expressways. The vertical separation principle will be applied in a number of huge
building developments now under way. The first of these is the partly completed Maine-Montparnasse complex that will occupy a twenty-acre site
over the old Montparnasse railroad station on the Left Bank. There will be
a 600-foot-high hotel and office building, two mammoth eighteen-story
office and apartment buildings with nearly four million square feet of floor
space, and basement parking for 4,500 cars. The railroad tracks coming in
from the south and west will occupy one underground level; major roadways will sweep over the tracks and around the periphery; and pedestrians
will walk between the buildings on covered promenades. Along the Left
Bank beyond the Eiffel Tower, in an area of decayed housing, factories, and
warehouses, demolition is under way for eighteen thirty-story apartment
buildings to be widely spaced over seventy-five acres. This Front de Seine
riverside project will house 14,000 people, carry motor traffic on the ground
level, provide parking on a mezzanine, and give pedestrians garden walks on
various upper levels.

To break the traffic jams on the city's streets, the Paris regional plan calls
for a network of expressways to be superimposed on the present street
plan. These roads will connect new suburban developments with one
another and with the city. They will form concentric rings at increasing
distances from the city center, crossed by radial highways. The main ring
road, or Boulevard Périphérique, will carry four lanes of traffic each way
for most of its twenty-two-mile length, following the line of the old city
fortifications. This great urban expressway, with interchanges every half
mile, is under construction and will be completed by 1970 at a cost of
about $14.5 million per mile. East-west mid-city *autoroutes* are being built
along the Seine. A south *autoroute* already exists, with a spur leading to
Orly Airport, eight miles from the city center. A northwest expressway is planned as well as a southwest route along the Montparnasse
railroad tracks. The north *autoroute* is under way, part of it being built
over a filled-in barge canal to avoid unnecessary demolition.

Despite careful planning and sophisticated design, there are protests
from traditionalists who would preserve the old at all cost. Progressive
leaders reply that today's greater Paris population of 8.5 million—which
may reach 12 to 15 million by the end of the century—cannot continue to
live by simply expanding the Paris of Napoleon III. They say that more
satellite cities, connected by improved rail transportation, must be built to
relieve the pressure on the central area. Historic quarters can then be rescued
from decrepitude and preserved as part of the world's cultural heritage.

As in Paris, the traffic problem in Rome has reached the stage where it threatens the viability of the city. Through its millenniums of history the commercial, cultural, and governmental affairs of Rome have been carried on within an area of a few square miles bounded by the irregular semicircle of the ancient city walls on one side and the Tiber River on the other. Here the jumbled treasures of antiquity—the Colosseum, the Forum, the Pantheon, and innumerable other temples, arches, columns, monuments, fragments—sit serene and immovable among the churches, squares, fountains, and imposing piazzas of the Renaissance and the hotels, office buildings, and shopping streets in which modern men struggle to conduct their daily business. The city has grown to a population of more than two million, and the past threatens to strangle the present. The Colosseum itself is the center of a congested traffic circle.

The scale of the problem is seen in a pair of figures: the number of private automobiles in Rome has grown from 100,000 to 500,000 in ten years. Public transportation consists of a single subway line, modernized trolleys, and buses that must often squeeze through medieval streets with a foot or two of clearance beyond each rearview mirror. At rush hours the main radial avenues leading from the city center are so jammed that drivers sometimes surface through the sun roofs of their cars to stretch and read a paper while a roadblock clears.

The municipal authorities are meeting the challenge with a combination of emergency first-aid measures and long-range plans to control the city's growth pattern. Many new traffic signals have been installed, zebra stripes have been painted to mark pedestrian crossings, and a one-way street system has been imposed where possible on the haphazard central street pattern. Parking has been limited to an hour in the entire area inside the ancient walls, and the immediate construction of a dozen parking garages is planned. A number of important avenues such as the Corso d'Italia, circling just outside the city wall, and a small section of the Via Nomentana, a radial to the northeast, have been made into divided roadways with underpasses, despite complaints over the removal of trees for this purpose.

The best hope for Rome's future lies, however, with the general town plan adopted by the municipal council in December, 1962. Some citizens call this the first serious attempt to solve the city's problems since Nero is supposed to have set Rome afire in order to undertake his own redevelopment program.

The plan calls for relief of pressure on the central city area by the creation of several new residential, business, manufacturing, and shopping centers east and south of the historic section. The first of these is well advanced. It is on the site of the former E.U.R. exposition grounds five miles south of the Colosseum on the expressway Cristoforo Colombo. Around a broad plaza in a setting of trees and parkland are grouped handsome new buildings housing government bureaus recently moved from downtown Rome. Nearby are new headquarters, some occupied and some under construction, for companies that could no longer find adequate facilities in the city center. High-rise apartments with plenty of parking space have been built along the avenue, which may eventually become a 300-foot-wide roadway carrying ten lanes of traffic.

The city plan calls for similar centers at Pietralata, northeast of central Rome, and at Tuscolana, to the southeast. These will be linked by a future expressway that will circle to the east of the mid-city area. It will connect the north and south terminals of the Highway of the Sun leading to Florence and Naples. Along the way it will intersect the main streets fanning out from the city center, carrying through-traffic around the busiest sections.

To give the city an adequate public transport system, a new subway map has been drawn with the present north-south line, running from the central railroad station to E.U.R., as a main axis to be extended to the northeast. A second line will cross it and run southeast beneath the Appian Way and the Via Tuscolana to the outer limit of development. This line is under construction and may be ready for use in 1968. Others will follow.

Most Romans agree that their new city plan is a document of hope, although many wonder, in view of the city's financial problems, where the necessary money will come from. Yet growth will continue, with or without the plan, and authorities point out that the unregulated spread of the city can benefit only speculators and profiteers. The new plan offers a way to transform Rome into a more open, decentralized city in which twice the present population will be able to live.

Like London and Paris, Rome is dealing with the problems of urban growth and congestion in a way that suits its particular needs. Yet the three cities have a great deal in common from an urban planner's point of view despite their vastly different heritages. Each is built on a river. Each contains a central core filled with buildings and monuments that will be preserved at all cost, even though they limit land use and block traffic movement. Each has developed over the years a radial road pattern that funnels too many vehicles through these congested areas.

Like the common problems, the proposed solutions are similar. In each city the maps of the future show great circular highways beyond the fringes of dense population. New satellite cities are being planted around these circles to relieve congestion in the center. New expressways will cut across the great circles—either through the center or tangentially—to remove traffic from meandering streets and clogged boulevards.

When these plans are transformed into steel, asphalt, and concrete, men may indeed live at peace with the motorcar. Most British, French, and Italian planners see motor transportation as a social and economic force that offers tremendous benefits when fitted into a rational pattern of development—which must include the parallel improvement of public transportation. In order to end Europe's traffic jams, all factors are being considered, including population growth, changes in industry, shifts in jobs, and housing. Already the new expressways, plazas, office towers, and shopping arcades are giving new form and style to the three great capitals, pleasing many of their citizens and distressing others. As the work continues, London, Paris, and Rome may well become the most modern and at the same time the most history-laden cities in Europe.

46 ▌ Growth and Change in Metropolitan Areas and Their Relation to Metropolitan Transportation: A Research Summary

MARK REINSBERG

The transportation problems of our major cities, we should remind ourselves at the outset, are the fruits of progress, prosperity and personal freedom. In a regimented society where jobs and housing are assigned, urban mass transit does not lose customers. In a land where the private citizen cannot buy an automobile, highways remain uncongested and parking presents no difficulty. Civic groups in such a society set up no clamor over the decline of a central business district.

But in a nation that builds ten million privately owned one-family non-farm dwellings between 1950–60, selecting sites for the majority outside of the central cities; in a nation that buys sixty million private passenger cars in the same decade, while spending some $80 billion on highways and streets; in a land where the location or relocation of business has not yet become the prerogative of state planners, there are bound to be certain changes. Our problems, to repeat, are the result of choices we have always been free to make as a people, but relatively more so since World War II.

By their business fortunes or misfortunes, the various modes of transportation often reflect profound developments in community life, some of an intangible nature. In attempting to understand the plight of urban transit—withering away almost universally amid pleas for increased subsidy

SOURCE: Mark Reinsberg, *Growth and Change in Metropolitan Areas and Their Relation to Metropolitan Transportation: A Research Summary* (Evanston, Illinois: The Transportation Center at Northwestern University, 1961), pp. 7–23. Copyright © 1961 by Northwestern University. Reprinted by permission of the publisher.

—we must appreciate the high value Americans have placed on personal mobility. It is an attitude, Stanley L. Warner found, that offsets measurable disadvantages in commuting time and cost. As an illustration, nearly everyone in a Cook County, Illinois, sample believed that it was more expensive to travel to work by car than by transit. Yet a very high percentage of these people, faced by the two alternatives, still chose to drive to work. A study by Walter Y. Oi, covering the cities of Atlanta, Chicago, Omaha, Portland and Providence, showed that increases in family income meant a decreased share of the budget for transit and a greater-than-proportionate increase in expenditures for auto travel. While income provided no clue as to which passengers would choose to drive, or ride transit, to work, it had an unmistakable influence on the choice of transportation for nonwork trips, which are by far the most numerous. Mobility is valued. The consequences for the urban transit industry have been disastrous.

From a peacetime peak of 17.2 billion passengers in 1926, transit patronage has ebbed to a record low of 9.3 billion passengers in 1960—this, despite a 57 per cent growth in urban population in the same period. The automobile has indeed undermined the transit industry, but we mistake the effect for the cause when we make villains out of cars and thoroughfares. These are the choices the people in metropolitan areas have made.

Declining Central Cities

The appeal for help of a dwindling nationwide industry supplying nine billion units per year of almost any useful commodity would merit the most serious consideration. Unfortunately, the problem is not solely, perhaps not even most importantly, that of urban transit. As Donald S. Berry states, "Transit service is predicated on the mass movement of people along principle corridors of travel. Transit primarily serves central business district trips, particularly worker trips destined thereto." The fates of bus lines, subways and elevateds, trolleys and suburban railroads are inextricably wound up in the destiny of the commercial core.

The difficulties of the central city are familiar and perplexing. The business district becomes more congested with automobiles; traffic facilities expand but rarely catch up, as parking lots and expressways "consume" the civic center. Higher income families move out to the suburbs. Low-income families move in. As a result, the city carries an increased burden of welfare costs on a reduced tax base. Meanwhile, industry is steadily lost through relocation beyond municipal limits, further reducing the tax base. As a final aggravation, the central city continues to provide many services to suburban residents, such as cultural and recreational facilities, out of its own budget, without adequate compensation.

Thus, urban transportation has become the sharp focus of a larger disturbance, the tug-and-pull between central cities and their suburban areas for population and industry. It resembles a problem of gravity and escape velocity. The core attracts powerfully, even in its decline, with jobs and shops. Individuals do break away, sometimes taking with them a chunk of industry, torn from the city's vitals. Rarely escaping completely from the core's gravitational field, they go into the near and far suburban orbits we comprehend on our maps as the Metropolitan Area.

Here again, at a superficial level, the difficulties of the central city can be attributed to the private automobile and the truck. While cars have helped populations to "escape," trucking has had a profoundly loosening effect on the locational patterns of industry and commerce.

Even casual observation would show that truck terminals react on a city in a different way than terminals for railroads and waterways. In the past, Johannes F. Schwar notes, "The terminal of a transport mode or a break in the transport network have been strong poles of attraction for economic activity." Railroads and waterways were in that sense the making of cities. The truck, in its versatility, freed industry from some of the rigidities of transportation, among them the need to cluster at the railheads and harbors which formed the original nucleus of most cities. Trucks have therefore accelerated the development of metropolitan areas.

Dispersal of manufacturing activity from the inner zones of the central city was the dominant trend in plant location throughout the United States in 1950–60. In Chicago, typically, the greatest gains in activity took place in an arc ten to fifteen miles from the central business district. The greatest losses occurred within five miles of the core. Warehouses, in particular, moved from inner zones to the periphery, situating themselves close to areas of population growth and expanded manufacturing activity. To call this process suburbanization may be too much of a simplification.

Leon N. Moses observed a marked tendency for business growth to take place at the fringe of the city as well as in adjacent suburbs. This could be regarded as an example of the "gravitational" effect, the restraining and holding influences of ties with other firms, convenient labor supply, established banking relationships, even reluctance on the part of management to commute or shift residence. In any case, firms moving into the metropolitan area from elsewhere built at greater distances from the Loop than did Chicago firms which relocated.

If any point is clear amid the general dispersion, it is the fact that public transportation routes and schedules were never designed to meet the needs of reverse commuting to peripheral employment centers. A sample drawn from firms located on the edge of Chicago disclosed that 80 per cent of the employees came to work by auto—two and a half times the percentage of workers driving to and from jobs in the central business district. Women, generally, have been placed at a transportation disadvantage by the dispersal of industry, as have those peripheral firms which need relatively unskilled female clerical help. Edward J. Taaffe found that although car pools were relatively unimportant in travel to peripheral employment, with an average number of auto commuters per car even lower than the city average (1.39 vs. 1.5), female employees were rather dependent on car pool arrangements. Women were considerably more likely to be a passenger in the automobile than to be its driver; three times more women than men commuted to peripheral plants by bus.

Investment in Transit

Concerned over the lack of public transportation in new location areas, a number of peripheral plants in Boston instituted charter bus services, only to abandon the effort upon finding how little use employees actually made of the service. Clearly, an investment in public transportation could not have been justified in these instances, and the transit-authority was spared from undertaking one more losing proposition.

Purely from an investor's outlook, the position of urban mass transit across the nation is unattractive. Almost all of the indicators point downward now, as they have for many years past. To look only at the last ten years, between 1950 and 1960, the transit industry owned 24 per cent fewer vehicles, drove 25 per cent less vehicle miles, lost 45 per cent of its passengers, and suffered a 25 per cent decline in net revenue. In the same period, operating expenses (as a per cent of revenue) rose about 2 per cent, and taxes increased from 57 to 74 per cent of net revenue. About the only improvement recorded was a meager 2 per cent growth in total route mileage. This was caused by a steady expansion in motor bus route miles which was substantial enough to offset shrinkage in railway and trolley coach service, but hardly commensurate with the population growth of our nation's metropolitan areas.

On what basis, then, ought we to consider putting money into this declining industry? Proponents seek to show the economic desirability of public investment in urban transit by means of three related propositions:

1) the 'harm' that automobiles inflict on the central business district;
2) the superior 'efficiency' of mass transit;
3) the 'benefits' to motorists.

One conclusion growing out of a composite study of the problem by the Transportation Center is that these particular arguments rest on sentiment rather than fact.

Autos and Productive Land Use

The first proposition is concerned with the amount of real estate withdrawn from commercial use.

Under the influence of private transportation, the amount of downtown land devoted to such unproductive uses as streets and parking lots has increased to the detriment of commerce and industry.

The weakness of this argument, says Moses, is the narrow restriction of territory along with the ambiguity of the term "unproductive." Testing the proposition on a city possessed of a classic downtown area, Chicago, we find that the proportion of that city's total developed land devoted to streets, alleys and parking lots *fell* in the fifteen years between 1941 and 1956. There were undoubtedly more parking lots in the central business district, relatively and absolutely. But at the same time this concentration was taking place, the proportion of land devoted to commercial and residential purposes in the city as a whole increased. While the total stock of Chicago land in manufacturing use dropped slightly, percentage-wise, it grew in absolute terms because the total amount of developed land in the city increased 15 per cent from 1941 to 1956. Growth in transportation uses of land in the central businesss district reflected an increased use of land for residential, commercial and manufacturing purposes elsewhere. More precisely, there was a decentralization of population in which numerous families selected residences dependent on the private automobile; meanwhile, in the central business district, the rate of job decentralization lagged behind the rate of population decentralization.

Turning to the meaning of the term "unproductive," it is clear that this is a value judgment. Highways have immensely increased the total stock of land in active use over the entire city and metropolitan area. In dollars and cents, parking facilities have proved more "productive" than many a vacant movie house or outmoded office building. It is unlikely that an owner of real estate would tear down a profitable edifice to make way for a less profitable parking lot.

When we look at the prosperous outlying shopping centers created since World War II we find enclosed areas that are as much as 75 per cent parking lot. Conservators of the central business district, one assumes, would not altogether ban the private automobile, hence would relegate a certain proportion of real estate, however minor, to automotive use. What proportion?

Efficiency and Transit

The second proposition supporting urban transit subsidy contains, implicity, a mechanistic view of society.

Public transportation must be improved and expanded because, as compared with the automobile, it requires less land per passenger carried.

Let us begin by acknowledging the capacity of transit. A bus, subway, or commuter train may theoretically carry as many passengers per day on its right of way as a ten-, twenty- or thirty-lane boulevard. Various studies suggest that some forms of transit can move more bodies in an hour than cars driving on city streets of equivalent size could transport in an entire day. Where comparisons of capacity begin to deceive is where planners use them as the basis of their expectations.

Chicago's recently completed eight-lane Congress Street Expressway features a rail-rapid transit line on its median strip. In theory the expressway can accommodate up to 8,000 motor vehicles per hour in one direction (four lanes), carrying a total of 40,000 passengers, assuming five people sat in each car. In theory a single-track transit line could also carry 40,000 passengers per hour in one direction. Practically speaking, both figures are improbable. In sad reality, transit carries about one-fourth of its peak-load capacity, and then only during the rush hours on weekdays, over a limited portion of its route near downtown. By the same token, though automobile volume on the parallel expressway does in fact approach theoretical limits during rush hours, the average load is about 1.5 passengers per car. From current observation, it appears that about the same numbers of passengers are being carried by each mode during the peak hours.

Capacity, then, is not a reliable argument for transit subsidy. At least, not as long as passengers can exercise a choice. Even if we assume that the potential could be used as an indicator of the actual, the superior "efficiency" of urban transit cannot be shown solely on the basis of how much land it uses. It is impossible to ignore matters of time, convenience, consumer preference, and items of cost other than land, in transportation as in other areas of family expenditures.

In a free society consumer choice is a complex matter. One considers, in transportation decisions, the time and cost of riding transit vs. the cost and time of driving an automobile, not only to and from work each day. One considers transportation to and from schools, business clients, shopping centers, doctors, restaurants, civic groups, theaters, recreation and the like—in variable combinations, frequencies, and distances, alone or accompanied, with or without impedimenta. Add weather to this formula plus multiple-car families, plus car pools, and it is apparent that "efficiency" is an equation each individual had best solve for himself.

Efficiency, in the meaning most commonly encountered in discussions of urban transportation, is one man's opinion about what would be logical for someone else to do. Nutritionists may find that dried navy beans contain everything needed to sustain life, and in that sense represent the most "efficient" of all foods. Who would choose to live solely on navy beans except under compulsion? And why, ask Herbert D. Mohring and Constance Schnabel, if we concede people the privilege of eating steak and French fries, do we advocate Spartan concepts in transportation? The most efficient means of transportation is, for all practical purposes, the choice an individual makes of various transportation alternatives (including walking and bike riding) in the day-to-day circumstances of his own life.

Benefits to Motorists

The third proposition entertains the benefits that metropolitan area motorists should receive from the subsidy of urban mass transit.

Lowered fares and improved service will encourage many motorists to use transit in place of the automobile, thus reducing congestion on the highways and benefiting the remaining motorists who, for that reason, should be happy to pay part of the cost of public transportation.

That is, adamant car users ought to be willing to subsidize—to induce—people to shift from auto trips to subway or bus trips.

Here the important question is not "Would the car users be willing?" The key question is "Would such inducement work?" As with the non-productive land-use propositions, this argument cannot hold up under a widening of its application. There are more parties interested in this matter than subsidy enthusiasts at first recognize.

Here, they say, is a natural community of interest between transit users, transit firms, the central business district, and metropolitan area motorists. Everyone benefits!

They ignore other possible communities of interest which might embrace both motorists and transit users: configurations of oil companies, tire and automobile manufacturers, parking lot and filling station operators, not to omit suburban shopping centers. If it is fair game for one interest group to encourage use of transit, it is equally fair for a second interest group to promote use of the automobile. An original inducement of lower transit fares might be cancelled out by the counter-inducement of price reductions in gasoline, parking, or cars.

There is yet another reaction which might neutralize the effect of a subsidy to transit. Let us call this the "passenger feedback." If some motorists are induced to leave their cars at home and ride transit to work, then highways will indeed become less congested. Under the best of planning, some transit vehicles may become more crowded. In these circumstances some transit users might be motivated to return to the use of the automobiles. This feedback principle would continue until a new equilibrium had been established, in which the comparative disadvantages of transit vs. automobile travel had been weighed and decided upon by all passengers able to make the choice. As between counter-inducement and feedback, the net gain for subsidized travel could be zero.

Another "benefit-to-motorist" proposition which has not been explicitly treated in this study is the argument on behalf of standby capacity. It is reasoned as follows: when emergencies arise, such as severe weather conditions or motor trouble, many drivers turn gratefully to mass transit. Perhaps motorists are indifferent to the fact that on some occasions they swamp transit facilities, causing inconvenience to regular transit users. But the knowledge that there is an alternative gives most motorists a feeling of security, a peace of mind they might not enjoy if the automobile were their only resource. Transit, therefore, is important to urban area motorists whether they use it or not. If only as a safety measure (comparable to the fire escape, kerosene lamp, savings account, Armed Forces, or any other reserve provision in life) motorists should be happy to pay a certain amount of money just to keep transit in business.

This is a serious consideration, but it is possible there may be ways of meeting this argument other than by subsidy. A conventional means would be the pricing mechanism of differential rates, single as against multiple rides.

Overruling the Marketplace

Economists recognize three conditions of the free enterprise system under which the subsidy treatment may be economically justified: economies of scale, indivisibility, and second-best considerations.*

All three of these conditions apply in one or another respect to the urban transit industry. They also apply to the construction of highways. Mohring and Schnabel say the evidence to date is not sufficiently reliable to support a claim that the mass transit component of urban transportation is either more or less deserving of subsidy than the auto transportation component.

There is a fourth condition which economists acknowledge as a basis for subsidy, though it is outside the sphere of economics. This comes under the heading "social considerations" and has to do with the values of a community rather than its rational organization.

Even though a man may be "worthless," that is to say, completely unemployable, our society does not believe he should be allowed to starve. By giving him funds to survive—by subsidizing him—we are overruling the market-determined optimum organization of economic activity.

Thus it may be that public transportation is desirable for aesthetic, national defense, health or political reasons entirely unrelated to its economic value. It may well be deemed socially desirable to provide

---

* Some inputs can be readily increased up to a certain point, resulting in lower average-costs—*economies of scale*. Thus, a factory can use more raw materials or hire more employees; a commuter railroad can load an engine with more cars or schedule more roundtrips per day, until a practical limit is reached. Beyond that point you must build a larger factory or buy another engine. *Indivisibilities* arise when further inputs can only be applied through relatively large investments. A more theoretical state is described by the term "*second-best considerations*," applying to circumstances in which it is necessary to set prices below actual cost.

public transportation for people who need to travel to and from their jobs but cannot afford or are unable to drive automobiles.

Whether these non-market virtues of urban mass transit justify subsidy is a matter for the citizenry as a whole, not economists, to decide. About all economists can do in that event is provide some notion of the costs involved. The noneconomic aspects of this problem, it should be emphasized, lie beyond the scope of Transportation Center studies at the present time. It might be appropriate, however, to examine a few commercial and industrial trends suggestive of future roles for the compact urban area intensely served by mass transit.

Outlook for the Central City

The shift of economic activity from central cities, particularly their core areas, to fringe and suburban areas, has led to considerable speculation as to the future of the central city. Some people have tended to write off the manufacturing function of the central city and to search for those service industries that might expand in and near core areas. Moses questions this sentiment; he observes that the supply of low-wage, low-skilled labor is still increasing in areas near the core. Certain industries draw heavily upon this labor pool which is not to be found in the suburbs. Thus, in Chicago, a number of manufacturing industries show closer attachment to the central business district than do some of the service sectors. Three industries which decentralized the least were ones requiring relatively heavy inputs of relatively low-wage labor: Textiles and Apparel, Lumber and Furniture, Food Products.

To put the matter more precisely, between 1957 and 1960 employment in every form of industry shifted away from the core. But the relative decline was less for these three manufacturing activities than for all of the service industries. The central city's manufacturing function could even expand if long distance inter-urban freight transportation became less costly.

Another misconception is that only firms in the core city are relocating. We find that in all areas of the city, proportionately, departures of industry took place at a roughly uniform rate. These uprootings generally increased the distance of the firms from the core of the city.

On the other hand, there is evidence of a very distinct tendency among new small firms to establish themselves near the central business district. Almost 25 per cent of all new small firms took locations within two miles of the core area; only 3.6 per cent of new large plants settled in this zone. Within an enlarged radius of four miles, locations were chosen by 54 per cent of the new small plants, as compared to 14 per cent of new large plants. The portions of the city encompassed by both zones are (excepting the lakefront) largely slum area. To account for this set of circumstances economists have formulated a "seedbed hypothesis."

New small firms usually lack capital to build their own facilities and must depend on lease space. Considering the metropolitan area as a whole, such space is most readily available in the inner portions of the central city, especially in the decaying "grey" area. It is advantageous in other ways for small firms to be located near the central business district, for there are to be found the auxiliary services which small firms are less likely to be able to provide for themselves. There, too, they have ready access to the low-wage labor pool.

Here is a paradox of interest to city planners and others concerned with urban renewal. The grey area, the slum that appears to be so badly in need of cleaning up, is precisely the area that permits the central city to perform and benefit from its function of encouraging the growth of new enterprises. New buildings arising in the wake of slum clearance would probably allow the city to perform this function more effectively, but it is likely that new buildings would entail higher rents unless subsidized.

Crisis of Urban Transit

The survival of urban mass transit in its present form seems rather improbable. Most users of public transportation assign it only a narrow role in their lives today, principally to get to and from work. Here it is possible to make an exception of suburban rail, which has remained a somewhat less neglected alternative to the automobile for nonwork trips, with noticeable appeal to female passengers, and advantages growing out of speed and distance. But, in general, transit continues to be patronized heavily during week day rush hours, less and less at other times. The peaks remain almost as high; the valleys grow deeper.

In contrast, the automobile is used increasingly during non-rush hours as well as to and from work. As the time profile of daily use grows more jagged for transit, it becomes smoother for automobile travel. This is the crux of the problem. Transit remains profitable during the rush hours, but insufficiently so to carry the losses of all other hours.

A certain number of people are "forced" by the circumstances of their lives to use transit. It is conceivable that transit systems could continue to increase fares for years to come, losing some passengers at each increase but retaining a sufficient number to boost net revenue. But the time would come when virtually all such fares would be during rush hours; it might then prove impossible to increase non-rush-hour transit patronage even by offering rides free of charge. The survival of urban mass transit may depend on the understanding it brings to these and other consumer preferences, and on the intelligence of its adaptation to special local circumstances.

Cities, obviously, are not alike. Different social, economic, historical and geographical factors operate in each metropolitan area. One of the most important of all, Berry believes, is density of population. Metropolitan areas with low densities of population—that is, below 10,000 persons per square mile in the central city—would probably be unable to sustain rail-rapid transit systems. Technologically, bus-rapid transit systems are better suited for such communities (Los Angeles provides an example). Low density metropolitan areas of the future can be expected to lean toward auto-dominant urban transportation systems, emphasizing freeway development. Inescapably, central business districts would need more off-street parking as well as improved means of pedestrian circulation. Effective bus transit systems would probably require some roadways and terminals; for despite the high orientation of Los Angeles to the private automobile, 31 per cent of all passengers entering its central business district in 1956 did so by means of mass transit.

A high density metropolitan area such as Chicago (17,500 persons per square mile in the central city) has already focused its rapid transit and commuter rail lines on the central business district. Two-thirds of all passengers entering the core area are traveling on one or another mode of public transportation. If transit's share of peak-hour travel in the Chicago Loop were reduced from the present 87 per cent to 60 per cent, and total trips remained constant, the number of peak-hour automobile trips destined to the Loop would *triple*. "Destined" is used here advisedly because with present facilities, many motorists would have to settle for parking places one to two miles away from the downtown area, after possibly an hour's delay in traffic. In Philadelphia, where 64 per cent of all passengers arrive in the core area by means of mass transit, the problem would be no less serious. In New York City (83 per cent) it might assume calamitous proportions.

The growth of employment opportunities on the periphery of the city could relieve some of the rush-hour strain on the city's transportation facilities. However, continued decentralization of industry may give rise to a new set of problems for the central city. Taaffe believes there is a possibility that if employment mobility greatly exceeds residential mobility (if people relocate their jobs but not their homes) the city will suffer further congestion from a mounting volume of crisscross traffic, flowing in all directions at once during rush hour. To avoid this, industry may wish to plan its moves with more careful reference to the capacity and contiguity of laborsheds at the new site; and less carefree reliance on the omnimeant qualities of the automobile.

Conclusion

The central city, bereft of its population, has named the automobile co-respondent in an alienation of affections suit. It could with equal justice be described as a failure on the part of the city to adapt political forms in the face of changed conditions. By the middle of the twentieth century, in America, the advantage of urban life vs. rural life had declined for many city-dwellers. Rather it had become possible to extend those advantages to semi-rural areas. The reality facing the central city is simply this: the auto, the truck and the highway offer consumers and producers a broader set of alternatives in location of homes, jobs, store sites and factories than can be encompassed by present concepts of city government.

We are led ultimately, as in so many attempts to understand and control forces at work on the local scene, to consider the responsibility of federal government. In what way, if any, have national policies and programs, such as federally financed road building, contributed to the city's embarrassment? By what means, if desired, can the vast, inchoate forces shaping entire metropolitan regions be controlled?

Assuredly, one of the most effective ways of holding down the continued expansion of large, mature metropolitan areas is to halt expansion on freeways, arterials, circumferentials, interchanges and other features of urban highway development. Had there, in fact, been no improvements in intra-metropolitan roadways, in Moses' opinion, we would have seen a much smaller expansion of population in the established large metropolitan areas and a much greater expansion in the number and size of secondary metropolitan areas. Future investments in transportation may well bear an added burden of responsibility, considering, along with the flow of goods and people, the direction and goals of our society.

Research Studies Cited

"Technology of Urban Transportation," by Donald S. Berry, Professor, Department of Civil Engineering; George W. Blomme, Port of New York Authority; John Hugh Jones, Assistant Professor, Department of Civil Engineering; and Paul W. Schuldiner, Assistant Professor, Department of Civil Engineering, Northwestern University

"The Economics of Urban Transportation Subsidies," by Herbert D. Mohring, Associate Professor, Department of Economics, University of Minnesota; and Constance Schnabel, Instructor, Department of Economics, Iowa State University.

"Transportation and the Spatial Distribution of Economic Activity Within Metropolitan Areas," by Leon N. Moses, Director of Research, The Transportation Center, and Associate Professor, Department of Economics, Northwestern University

"The Economics of Urban Travel," by Walter Y. Oi, Research Economist, The Transportation Center, Northwestern University

"The Changing Pattern of Truck Terminals and Truck Traffic Within the Metropolitan Region of Chicago," by Johannes F. Schwar, Assistant Professor, Department of Civil Engineering, Ohio State University

"A Geographic Consideration of the Journey to Work to Peripheral Employment Centers," by Edward J. Taaffe, Associate Professor, Department of Geography; and Barry J. Garner, Graduate Student, Department of Geography, Northwestern University

"Stochastic Choice of Mode in Urban Travel," by Stanley L. Warner, Research Economist, The Transportation Center, and Assistant Professor, School of Business, Northwestern University

B | Programs and Theories

47 | The Growth of Government Power and Policy

CHARLES ABRAMS

Political systems of countries may be altered through assimilation, adoption of another society's ideas, or through revolution. Revolution, however, has been violent only in a few cases, but even where the revolution was peaceful, it effected major shifts in the relationships between social classes. These shifts are still not completed, but there is nevertheless a well-defined and almost universal trend in almost all countries toward using public processes to rectify some of the social and economic inequalities of the unregulated economic process.

When social and economic inequalities first gained notoriety during European industrialization, they were cited as the inevitable results of capitalism's shortcomings. More moderate reformers in Europe and the United States thought the state could rectify some of the injustices within the existing political framework. In Russia the less moderate view was adopted. Since many developing countries are grappling with the problem of urbanization and are in the course of weighing the values of the alternate systems, the historical development of legal processes affecting shelter and urban land policy in Europe and in North America becomes relevant.

The Contrast Between the More and Less Developed Countries

The more developed and the less developed nations, though they are worlds apart in wealth and technology, are both experiencing the impacts

SOURCE: Charles Abrams, *Man's Struggle for Shelter in an Urbanizing World* Cambridge: The M. I. T. Press, 1964, pp. 40–50. Copyright © 1964 by the Massachusetts Institute of Technology and the President and Fellows of Harvard College. Reprinted by permission of the publisher.

of population inundations that have created city slums, overcrowding, and urban land problems. Both suffer from the stubborn disparity between income and shelter cost, the competition for urban land, the chaotic urban development, and the many other distortions caused by rapid urbanization, population swell, and slum living.

Yet, though the symptoms are similar, the nature of the malady and its prognosis are of a different color. The more developed nations have acquired greater political stability and can better afford to make mistakes; experiments that fail are not fatal. Their people have skills and higher incomes. They can boast of a middle class and a better opportunity for the lower class to reach a higher estate. The supply of used housing allows for a turnover of dwellings among residents as their circumstances change. Though housing cost is usually beyond the average worker's means, a construction industry functions for those who can pay the price, while the government can better afford to bridge the gap for lower-income families.

There is generally also an established legal framework in Europe and the United States within which the problems of urbanization can be tackled. Landownership is respected or restricted according to certain norms and is usually subject to compulsory purchase for the public interest. There are more likely to be well-established private mortgage mechanisms for investors and for buyers who can pay the going costs. Contracts are enforceable by courts, and if rights and duties are not always crystal-clear, they can at least be roughly approximated. Though government has intervened with sterner measures when the private mechanism has faltered, the line between governmental and private action is more or less plainly drawn; property rights are not sacrificed as the public sector is gradually enlarged. These refinements of power have taken place over a long period marked by crisis and debate, trial and error, experimentation and amelioration.

Revolutions in the More Developed Nations

The current pattern has evolved in Europe and the United States through what might be identified as four revolutions: political, land, industrial, and welfare. They were partly sequential, partly concurrent, producing in the end a mixed but reasonably well-articulated order which has succeeded in raising the standard of living without sacrificing individualism or its freedoms.

Out of these four revolutions has emerged a rough rule of reason defining the limitations and prerogatives of states in relation to property, as well as a reconciliation of public rights and duties with respect to the welfare of those deprived of life's essentials. The revolutions which gave rise to these reconciliations were:

1. A political revolution, in which the individual's rights within the state were defined and protected against its arbitrary or capricious actions. The rise of merchant cities in centuries past and the traders' demands for greater freedom of action had aided the birth of individual freedoms. These freedoms have essentially survived. They include such advances as the safeguarding of property rights against unreasonable regulation, security of the home against search and seizure, and guarantee of compensation and due process in the expropriation of property.

In securing the rights of property generally, the state had been loath at first to put too great a restriction upon property of any kind, with the result that for a long period real estate (including slum property) benefited from the protection given to all property. "Police power," the fountainhead of property regulation, was an unknown term, which in fact did not receive its full christening until 1827.

The imposition of building regulations as a function of police power was of course hardly novel. Such regulations had existed in Babylonia earlier than 2000 B.C., had appeared among the Chinese before 1000 B.C., and may be found in the archives of the Roman Empire. But they were always conditioned by the principal motivating forces of a particular era, and drastic restrictions on building were felt to be inconsonant with the age in which the businessman and the middle-class were coming into their own.

Except for some quaint ordinances and some rare evidences of private benevolence in the nature of almsgiving, it was not until 1838 that concern for the housing of the poor began to manifest itself in England, and it was only after 1851 that the first constructive regulations against slums were adopted. But even then, and for more than a half century thereafter, many people were still holding stubbornly to the view that the slum was the fault of the slum dweller and the haven of the irresponsible, the inebriate, and the criminal. It was not until the twentieth century that a broader web of regulatory laws was spun, becoming more and more embracing as the execrations of reformers continued to chip away at the esteem of slum owners and slum builders.

Regulation required more and more of owners until hope for further reform through regulation crashed on the rock of reality. The rock was the hard fact that the more drastic the regulation, the higher the rent; the higher the rent, the fewer who could pay it. More practical devices were needed, and soon the tax power was brought to the fore as a possible alternative.

The tax power ran a course somewhat similar to the police power. Taxation was the state's special hunting ground, but at best it proved to be a limited preserve. Taxation had been viewed by Blackstone as only a supplement to other sources of revenue such as crown lands, mines, penalties— what the great commentator termed "ordinary" revenue. Taxes he classed as "extraordinary." In this hidebound context, aiding the underprivileged through taxation of the rich would be looked upon as expropriation of wealth. While the laissez-faire attitude achieved for property an unprecedented freedom from state interference, it left the alleviation of poverty to the poor and to those whose sympathy would pry open their purses. The poor in fact had long been elevated to the rank of "God's poor" and placed in the church's charge. It was unthinkable that the state would ever be allowed to become God's delegate in this respect. As recently as 1892, Charles Booth had identified the three greatest causes of poverty as old age, sickness, and drink. Manifestly good housing provided by the state would not stay old age, and while it might allay some distempers, it could not be expected to appease a poor man's thirst. The indigent, said Booth, should be taught to build their own dwellings. In the United States up to the time of the New Deal, slums were thought to be the fault of the slum dweller and the product of his filthy habits. That he would put coal in a bathtub, if given one, was considered gospel, at least until central heating made the tub unnecessary as a coal bin.

The compulsory purchase of property had been early recognized as a government prerogative and was in fact implicit in the government formula, though Blackstone in 1765 referred to it as "an exertion of power, which the legislature indulges with caution." In the United States and England, even private parties such as railroads (and in America drainage companies as well) could use the expropriatory privilege so long as the "purpose" was public and the compensation just. But whether eminent domain was exercised privately or publicly, the scope of "public purpose" in the United States up to the 1940's continued narrow, particularly where the federal government was concerned. It was a "limited sovereignty," which meant that its power to act in such matters as war was unlimited but for "general welfare" it did not exist at all. Acquiring slum property for housing as part of the war effort was lawful, but it was unauthorized for welfare. As for the states, they might use their welfare power to regulate private investments so as to prevent slums, but they could neither spend the taxpayers' money to build housing for the poor nor take land for any purpose or project that would not be "used by the public." Taking land on the grounds that it would "benefit the public" was viewed as going too far. Until the 1930's, in most state jurisdictions in the United States, *all* the people had to have access to a project to authorize condemnation, and the poor were not all the people.

The political revolution up to 1936 failed to solve the slum problem in the United States. But it did attack the problem in the only way that the reformers of the period had proposed and with the only tool that the era would countenance, i.e., regulation under the police power. Further, the very failure of the police power to eliminate slums served to high-light the futility of the approach and speeded the advent of more comprehensive devices.

2. The land revolution had been going on fitfully for several hundred years. The revolution had been impelled by the individual's urge for a piece

of ground. This generally entailed the division or sale of large estates irrespective of whether they were in the public or private domain. In the United States, denationalization of land had been the public policy almost from the beginning, so that small individualized holdings soon found their way into the hands of the many. Even the larger land grants made to railroads were segmented into smaller parcels and sold in order to speed settlement along their lines. In France and Belgium, the Napoleonic code had caused the breakup of larger holdings into smaller parcels—frequently too small for efficiency. In the United Kingdom at the turn of the century, some 600 peers held a fifth of the nation's domain, and about 7400 other individuals still owned half of its land. Tenure has been so stubborn there that some of the 999-year leases made at the time of William the Conqueror have survived and are today being negotiated for renewal. But even this stronghold of property rights has more recently been witnessing a breakup of holdings as owners have sought cash to pay death duties. Simultaneously, as England's cities expanded, suburban land was subdivided and sold to individuals for homes, further increasing the number of landowners.

Though industrialization and increased housing demands moved considerable urban and suburban land within reach of the steam shovel, it was not until after the 1940's that governments became impelled to speed the process of land deconcentration or, where oversegmentation existed, reassemblage.

Whether by economic pressures, the lure of industrial profits, taxation, contract, statute, or appropriation by the squatter on the frontier lands, the general effect of the land revolution has been not only to split up larger holdings and increase the number of owners but also to move government toward bringing land within reach of the many.

3. The industrial revolution (or revolutions) altered the uses of land from the beginning, so that many rural plots became the sites of factories, shops, public utilities, and urban houses. The whole character of the housebuilding operation was changed. The house was no longer a homemade product, whose materials were obtained and put together by the owner himself. Building entrepreneurs now took over the operation, and home building became a powerful stimulus to economic activity. With the rise of intangible personalty (in the form of stocks, bonds, patents, claims, debt, and credit), real property remained a major form of investment but lost its primacy in the new play of economic and political power.

But though industrialization brought hardship, it also expanded the individual's challenges and his opportunities; it increased the yield of the world's food-producing lands and the number of mouths to receive their product. As industrialization helped to swell the world's population, the excess was drawn to the cities, where not only man's destiny but his hopes became centered.

4. The welfare revolution, the most recent of the revolutions, was

marked by the assumption by governments of new functions, in an effort to remedy some of the worst deficiencies of the industrial and urbanizing processes. Greater government intervention was justified by repeated periods of depression; by the inability of private enterprise to ease the hardships of poverty, insecurity, illness, and old age; and by the failure of private enterprise to alleviate housing shortage and slums. Progress and growth, not simply continuity, became the new aim. Government took over many of the responsibilities formerly left to private charity and investment. It augmented its tax, spending, police, and compulsory-purchase powers in an effort to stimulate economic activity and remove social disparities. In addition, government entered upon new activities such as housing for the underprivileged, and it increased public works to broaden employment during depressions. Besides building dams, power plants, roads, and a wide variety of other job-making operations, it expanded public educational facilities, financed private building, and insured investment risks. It subsidized a diverse group of public and private enterprises and levied heavier taxes upon the haves to finance its operations for the have-nots. Finally government moved to control the sporadic growth of cities and improve their environments. In the process, its powers were widened so that it was in a position to manipulate the emerging scene and mold many of its prominent features.

One of the more perplexing and unsettled questions of the welfare revolution was the precise role of the private and public sectors. Hitherto, private enterprise had occupied the main field, while government operated only where "the profit could never repay the expense to any individual." Schools, roads, and the post office were viewed as public operations, while housing, industry, and other profit-making ventures were considered strictly private. When the welfare function expanded, the question arose as to whether government should act directly or merely subsidize private ventures to achieve the new welfare aims. The general tendency was to do both, as the occasion demanded or the pressures forced a particular action. England subsidized the private entrepreneur at first, then built public housing itself. The United States did both, ultimately channeling the bulk of its aid by underwriting the risks of private investment. Mortgages were insured, deposits in savings and loan associations were guaranteed to encourage deposits, and aid was given to private builders who put up homes for moderate-income families and war veterans. Other aid was given to colleges and nursing homes and for building homes for the elderly. Land subsidies were given by federal and city governments for "urban renewal," and slum sites were compulsorily acquired by cities to enable private entrepreneurs to redevelop them for more profitable and more becoming uses.

The powers of police, taxation, and eminent domain have not spread without some dissent. But there is no turning back. With the accelerated trend toward greater urbanization, there is every indication that the public power plant in developed countries will never revert to its narrower limits. Neither Russia's managers nor America's entrepreneurs have come up with a magic formula for solving the trilemma of urbanism, mass migration, and housing. A modern computer might pour forth the calculus of housing need, but the solution eludes electronics. Housing programs still require identification of objectives, long periods of time, relocation of families, large capital outlays, expansion of materials production, innovation in financing mechanisms, mobilization of skills, and expert direction under cohesive, well-formulated policies.

The more developed areas in Europe and North America have taken the progressive growth of power and function in stride. The gains made 150 years ago or more in guaranteeing the individual's privacy, his protection against outright confiscation, and his rights under contract have not been drastically affected. They have simply moved into a new social context, which has been accepted as part of a new just norm. The shift to industrialization was accomplished with little or no violence. The democratic state was able to take steps—imperfect as they may be—to correct some of the inequities of industrialization. While the urban land problem continued to be stubbornly troublesome, there were few efforts by the land-needy to take law into their own hands.

Though the welfare revolution has not yet produced all the answers to the social problems of urbanization, powers for confronting them have been released and the first steps taken to wield these powers more effectively. What is referred to as "social balance" now employs economic policy to stimulate private activity and generate improved purchasing power while simultaneously trying to compensate for its shortcomings through policy such as social security, public housing, and other social programs. If world tensions are eased and the enormous expenditures for defense and war can be used for more of the social exigencies, the day may not be distant when urban blight can be eliminated and when the beleagured urban family may well be able to afford a decent home—provided, of course, that social motivation continues to have a place in political calculations.

The Position of the Less Developed Areas

In contrast with the series of revolutions in the more developed countries, the underdeveloped countries are having all their revolutions simultaneously. There have been few existing patterns to build on, no firm old threads of precedent to which the new policies could be tied. Industrialization, urbanization, and the land and political revolutions have all arrived concurrently and almost precipitously.

Often a political coup by an ambitious military junta adds another complication to the problems of the developing nations. In Latin America, the military controls not only the arms but also the course of political events. Rivalries within the military establishments make for internal plotting and counterplotting, and even constitutionally elected regimes may depend on the sufferance of the generals. In the eighteen months preceding October 1963, for example, the five elected governments of Argentina, Peru, Guatemala, Ecuador, and the Dominican Republic were overthrown; in each case a military junta was the controlling element.

In Africa, new contrasts and conflicts have arisen: between barter or trade-in-kind and money; between human cooperation in meeting life's challenges and the specialization of function that accompanies industrialization; between animism and the missionary's crucifix; between the old established ethics and those imported from the more acquisitive societies; between sharing and individual savings; between the British or other prevailing system and tribal conventions; between the political demands of the rising central state and the village, the chief, the elders, the tribe, and the individual; between the representatives of the people and the determinations of the new man who heads the state. The old system of gift that once carried its own dignity confronts the interdictions against bribery in the new order. Furthermore, the task of setting up an independent civil service confronts the nepotistic inclinations which derive naturally from tribal fealty. The old reverence toward the chief is converted by some into a faith in the omniscience of a new prime minister. What would be looked upon as the loyal opposition in British politics is sometimes confused with a hostile tribe.

The shift from village to city or from tribe to family as the basic social unit has effected a mutation in ways of life that had stood fast for more than a millennium. Changes in political patterns have been sudden and revolutionary as well. Often the new state would be trestled on a constitution glowing with lofty language but with no precedents for applying it to a specific set of facts. "Freedom," "social security," dedication to the "public welfare" are all promised before there is the experience, tradition, purchasing power, or industry to bring them into bud.

Policies in the developing countries have often been inconsistent and convulsive, kind to one type of investment and harsh to another, with the prospective investor never knowing when, where, or whether the winds might shift. Raw materials lie in abundance in Bolivia's altiplano, but few entrepreneurs will gamble a dollar to dig them out. Uranium in the Congo and water power in Africa beckon for exploitation, but venturers think twice before taking the risk. Elsewhere, at the first sign of industrial activity, the human surplus disgorged by agricultural inadequacy heads for the cities, almost always in numbers far greater than the economies can absorb.

These changes are taking place in a great arena in which each of the two great ideologies is proclaiming its preeminence. Both ideologies lean on the word "democracy" as a term with strong ethical connotations and alluring overtones, but the two are worlds apart in the measure of essential freedoms granted to the individual.

One ideology is postulated on the theory that private enterprise is essential for a country's development and should be encouraged by appropriate laws, inducements, and guarantees. Where this fails to function, as in housing, government will assume the responsibility. In any event, private ownership of farms and homes is widely recognized as a paramount right.

The other ideology, based on summary revolution, at first asserted that all land belongs to the state and that neither private enterprise nor private ownership has a place in society. Private ownership, even of peasant holdings, was liquidated; farm dwellings and implements were seized; agriculture was collectivized; and urban land was confiscated. The confiscated urban land was to be publicly owned or dedicated primarily to the use of collectivized industries.

Yet it was not long before this proscription of private homeownership in the U.S.S.R. had to be modified in the face of the realities. Though all land, urban and rural, has remained in the state and private landownership was banned, the right to build one's own home has had to be conceded to some extent. The state has even granted some credits to the individual home builders. Plots have been allotted for building, the right to use them has been granted "in perpetuity," and the new dwellings have been declared "the personal property of the builders." In addition to giving protection against confiscation by making adequate compensation after appraisal, the state has provided alternative land and dwelling accommodation for those displaced. Sales of residences were permitted, provided the seller did not sell more than one house within three years of purchase.

Poland, which nationalized its larger industries, passed a statute in 1947 that assisted private builders by means of land grants and priorities in obtaining building materials. It freed all new buildings from rent controls, exempted new buildings from taxation for five years, and provided that if a new building was sold at a profit during the period of tax exemption, the profit would not be taxed as income. Even more advantageous measures were granted to attract "new capital in private hands" which was being "kept under cover." A black marketeer who invested his secreted gains in building would thus be guaranteed against investigation into the source of his funds.

More recently, however, a new policy has gained ground behind the Iron Curtain. It is probably impelled partly by the seeming inability of the system to cope with the housing problem. Building of individual housing is being curtailed. Most new Soviet housing . . . will be in multiple units. Some of the amenities (kitchens, private bookshelves, etc.) may give way to more communal facilities. Partly because of the need for female labor and partly because of the lack of individual space, there may be less opportunity for the raising and care of the children by the family. A greater emphasis is being put upon more "public upbringing."

Thus while the countries with Western traditions continue their respect for ownership of homes in which family controls can operate, the bulk of U.S.S.R. families will continue to be tenants of the state, with the child shaped more in accord with the concept of the "Soviet man."

Between these two worlds, the underdeveloped countries are seeking to carve out their own values, which are by no means clear or simple. Those countries which have inherited shreds of the British system are trying to maintain them, at least in form, but are superimposing their own innovations. In others, drastic limitations on rights are not infrequent. In still others, there is respect for some types of property but not for all.

Legal processes in these less developed countries are in the incubation period, and the earliest important exercises of power are apt to occur in housing and planning. In these areas, political patterns are being set for the sensitive relationships between government and the individual, between government and property, between public and private spheres of interest, and between central and local controls.

The postwar constitutions of many of the newer governments, which proclaimed respect for the individual and for his property rights, have shown little consistency in their application. Private ownership of rural as well as urban land was usually assured. The general trend has been to break up large holdings, but sometimes, particularly in rural areas, large estates have been not only tolerated but even encouraged by freedom from tax levies. In urban and suburban areas, speculation has often been completely unrestrained. Frequently land is withheld from the market to await the inevitable upward spiral. Drastic control of real estate operations is often vexing to foreign investors in industrial enterprises, who demand guarantees from their home countries as insurance against confiscation or inflation, insist on free factory sites and minimal capital outlays as a condition for investment, or demand generous subsidies. Meanwhile, squatters extend their trespasses, and as they grow in numbers, they create their own laws and conventions.

The transition from a rural to an urban economy called for the creation of sound tenure in the cities. Homeownership programs providing a minimum of decent standards for the structures and secure tenure for the urban as well as the small-farm family might have captured the imagination of the rank and file as the concept of free land did after the American Revolution. By 1964, however, there was no evidence that the older democracies had even sensed the dangers in the leap from agricultural to urban life in the newly independent countries or the potentials for rescuing democratic norms out of the gathering chaos.

48 | The Metropolitan Trend in London, Ibadan, Tokyo, and São Paulo

JOHN C. BOLLENS and
HENRY J. SCHMANDT

In 1959 the International Urban Research Center at the University of California published a study entitled *The World's Metropolitan Areas*. Departing from the usual practice of gathering and presenting demographic data by "cities" when urban communities are considered on a worldwide basis, the study attempted to delimit metropolitan areas in each country by criteria similar to that employed by the U.S. Bureau of the Budget in defining American SMSA's [Standard Metropolitan Statistical Areas]. Some 1064 such areas were identified as in existence at the middle of this century. The largest number outside the United States was found in the Soviet Union (129) with Communist China (103) and India (70) following next in order.

. . . . .

International comparative studies of urban problems and metropolitan political systems are still in their infancy. The endless variety of local customs and institutions—both among nations and even within the same country—presents formidable obstacles to such inquiries and makes generalization exceedingly hazardous if not impossible. What we shall do here is to give a sample or broad overview of local government and its responses to urban growth in various regions of the world. For this purpose we have chosen four widely scattered urban centers: the venerable metropolis of London, the indigenous African town of Ibadan, the oriental city of Tokyo, and the Brazilian metropolis of São Paulo. Although representing different cultures, each of them faces the same relentless pressures of urbanization.

London

Known as a nation of townspeople, England has been highly urbanized for many decades. Its present density of 790 persons per square mile is exceeded by only one other major European country, the Netherlands. The

SOURCE: John C. Bollens and Henry J. Schmandt, *The Metropolis* (New York: Harper and Row, 1965), pp. 552–557, 559–563, 565–576. Copyright © 1965 by John C. Bollens and Henry J. Schmandt. Reprinted by permission of publisher.

urban population first surpassed that in the rural areas around 1850. By the end of the nineteenth century, three-fourths of the people lived in cities and towns. Since 1939, when the number of urbanites reached 80 percent of the total population, there has been little change in the proportion. However, the long prevalent pattern of migration from farm to town has given way to the movement from one urban area to another, particularly from the older industrial centers of the north to London and other cities in the southeast. Today, over 40 percent of the population is concentrated in London and five other smaller metropolitan areas.

Physical and Demographic Characteristics

The metropolis of London dominates British life. As the political and cultural capital of the nation, the center of its commerce, and the head-quarters of its major financial institutions, London exercises an enormous gravitational pull on the rest of the country. Someone once remarked that to create an approximate American equivalent we would have to merge New York, Washington, and Chicago into one overwhelmingly dominant metropolis, compared with which all other urban centers in the United States would appear provincial.

In speaking of London, it is necessary to recognize that there are several Londons. There is the ancient city at the center, "a small island of obstinate medieval structure," which contains but one square mile of territory and a population of less than 7000. There is the former county of London with 117 square miles and slightly over three million people. There is the Greater London conurbation, which is composed of the former county and the adjacent ring of suburbs and encompasses a total area of 723 square miles and a population of 8.2 million, over 60 percent of whom live in the suburban belt. Finally, there is the London region which, in addition to the conurbation, includes an outer ring extending to about a fifty-mile radius from the center. (As its boundaries are defined by the Ministry of Housing and Local Government, the London region contained a total of approximately 12.5 million people in 1961.) Separating this outer regional ring from the Greater London conurbation is a metropolitan greenbelt varying in width from five to fifteen miles.

The London Region is growing substantially in population but the accretion is taking place in the outer ring beyond the greenbelt. During the inter-censal period, 1952–1961, the number of inhabitants in this area increased by 891,000 in contrast to a decrease of 183,000 in the county of London and 29,000 in the remainder of the conurbation. This pattern is a continuation of the trend which started late in the last century as the British government began a planned program to reduce density and congestion in the center. The city of London, for example, had a population of 130,000 in 1850; today it has less than 7000. Since 1921, the county of London has lost steadily in the number of residents while the suburban ring has recorded substantial gains.

Planning for urban growth began early in Great Britain. Before the concept was discussed in other than a few American municipalities, Parliament passed a town planning act in 1909, the same year that the University of Liverpool inaugurated the first formal program in city planning offered by an academic institution. British planning has been strongly influenced by the "garden-city" movement as it found expression in the work of Ebenezer Howard and his followers. They proposed that the large urban centers, such as London, be decentralized by establishing and developing small satellite towns in the outlying reaches of the region. London planners have followed this general concept. Even before World War I, the London County Council had taken steps to effect a redistribution of the population by a program of slum clearance and the construction of new housing outside the central area. The program was accelerated in the 1940s as a result of the war damage which necessitated reconstruction of large sections of the core. It was also aided by the wartime evacuation which reduced the population of the county of London from four million in 1939 to 2.5 million at the end of 1944.

Starting in the 1900s, various "advisory" plans were drafted for the London area, some commissioned by the national government, others by local authorities and private organizations. Probably the most influential has been the Greater London Plan of 1944, which was prepared under an appointment from the Minister of Works and Planning. The plan called for a continuation of decentralization by moving out large numbers of people and their related employment from central London to new towns in the outer ring. It also proposed a metropolitan greenbelt encircling the built-up urbanized area of the conurbation. Drafters of the plan regarded the greenbelt as a strategic device for halting the continued spread of suburban growth. As they conceived it, such a belt, aided by the creation of self-sufficient new towns in the outer region and the barring of new industrial development in the interior, would serve as a barrier to the further enlargement of the London commuting zone.[1]

Many of the provisions of the Greater London Plan have been followed in principle, including redistribution of population, creation of the greenbelt, and the channeling of new industry into the outer zone. But the forces of growth and change have proved too strong to permit the degree of decentralization envisaged by the planners. Like the borough of Manhattan in New York City, the heart of postwar London has served as a powerful attraction for the location of new office sites, an attraction too great to be overcome by the public planners. As a result, the central area gained approximately 260,000 jobs, mostly of white-collar or clerical nature, during the

---

[1] See Daniel R. Mandelker, *Green Belts and Urban Growth* (Madison: University of Wisconsin Press, 1962).

1952–1961 census period. Thus while a drastic reduction in the area's resident population was accomplished by the redistribution plans, the problem of traffic and congestion in central London has increased as more than 1.3 million persons commute to the core each week day. As one scholar has observed, the Greater London planning experience provides an object lesson in the relentless forces of growth. It demonstrates that containment is extremely difficult even when implemented by controls far more powerful than those available to public authorities in the United States.[2]

A measure of coordinated planning has been achieved in Greater London despite the unusual fragmentation of local units. Until the reorganization of the governmental structure in 1963, . . . the planning function was shared by the six counties and three county boroughs in the metropolis. Each was charged by law with the responsibility of preparing a redevelopment plan and administering planning controls for the area within its jurisdiction. In formulating their plans, local authorities were required to follow the broad policies laid down by the national Ministry of Housing and Local Government. This latter agency also reviewed and approved the local development plans and oversaw the administration of planning controls. These centralized checks tended to promote a higher degree of coordinated planning among the local units than would otherwise have been possible. They also enabled area-wide advisory plans, such as the Greater London Plan, to have more impact than similar documents prepared by regional planning agencies in the United States.

Governmental Pattern

. . . . .

The bill [recommended in 1960 by the Royal Commission on Local Government in Greater London and] enacted by Parliament in late 1963, specifically charges the new metropolitan council with carrying out a survey of Greater London and the preparation of a general development plan, including policy with respect to land use. Each borough is required to formulate a redevelopment plan for its own area embodying the relevant features of the metropolitan plan. The metropolitan council is also vested with responsibility for traffic management throughout the area, main roads, trunk line sewers and sewage disposal facilities, major cultural and recreational facilities, refuse disposal, fire protection, and civil defense. All remaining local governmental functions including education (except in central London where the school system is to be administered by a special committee of the metropolitan council) are borough responsibilities.

---

[2] Donald L. Foley, *Controlling London's Growth, Planning the Great Wen* (Berkeley and Los Angeles: University of California Press, 1963), p. 157.

The London experience poses the dilemma that the architects of metropolitan reorganization face. Although the plan is far-reaching and its territorial coverage large, it still falls short of constituting an answer to the problem of governmental structure *vis-à-vis* urban growth. That the adopted arrangements will bring more efficient and effective local government and greater control over land use and physical development within the territorial boundaries of the new council can scarcely be denied. That they will provide a solution to the more crucial problem of guiding and controlling the continued outward expansion of the metropolis is another matter. For even though the areal jurisdiction of the Greater London Council will be very extensive, it will still lack control over the outer ring where much of the new development is taking place.

There is obviously a limit in territorial size to which a unit can expand and yet retain its essential characteristics as a local government. On the other hand, planning for the limited area may be impaired or nullified by independent action on the periphery. The plan for lowering population density in central London, for example, can be effective only if provision is made for accommodating the displaced families in the outer zone. Here the London reorganization plan is deficient since it gives the new government control only over the already built-up area; it provides no assurance that the independent local units outside the territorial jurisdiction of the Greater London Council will be willing to accommodate the overspill, particularly if lower-income families are involved. Superimposing national controls on the outer zone authorities can at least partially substitute for centralized local direction. Such action, as we have seen, is possible in Great Britain; it would not be at the present time in the United States.

Ibadan

The tendency toward urbanization, as an UNESCO study shows, is one of the outstanding characteristics of present-day life in Africa.[3] Virtually the entire continent is in a state of rapid transition. Colonialism has been brought to a speedy and often abrupt termination, new nations are coming into being, industrial expansion is taking place at an accelerated pace, and migration from the rural areas to the cities and towns is a common phenomenon. As in the more advanced countries, the urbanizing trends in Africa have brought with them overcrowding and slum conditions in the population centers, the emergence of a labor class, important social and cultural changes, the formation of new types of associations connected with occupations, cults, and recreational activities, and the progressive disintegration of wider kinship groups and family stability.

---

[3] *Social Implications of Industrialization and Urbanization in Africa South of the Sahara* (Paris: United Nations Educational, Scientific, and Cultural Organization, 1956).

The problems of governmental reconstruction facing the new and under-developed nations are monumental. Sweeping away the foundations of a colonial structure and adapting traditional political institutions to the changing needs of an emerging urban society have everywhere produced difficulties. At the local level, it has required the transfer of authority from tribal councils to new elective assemblies and the creation of native administrative systems to replace the body of professional civil servants utilized by colonial powers. The shortage of educated and skilled personnel among the native population contributes to the difficulty of building up an efficient local bureaucracy. In addition, the influx of migrants into the towns often overstrains the labor market and the local economy, not to mention public facilities, and thus helps to create restlessness and insecurity.

Although no individual city can be said to be typical of African municipalities, we have chosen Ibadan, Nigeria, the famous center of the Yoruba tribe, as an example of a major community and its travails of urban growth and adjustment. . . . Ibadan . . . is a "Negro" city, the largest, in fact, on the African continent. As a unit of a country which only recently achieved statehood (1960), it is in the throes of adapting its governmental structure and institutions to the needs of independence. Its industry, although expanding, is still predominantly oriented toward the processing of agricultural crops from the surrounding countryside. These are characteristics common to many African towns.

Physical and Demographic Features

Nigeria, a federal parliamentary state and an independent member of the British Commonwealth, is divided into four regions: North, East, West, and Mid-West, the last being carved out of the western section in 1962. Ibadan, the capital of the western region, is located inland, seventy miles northeast of Lagos, the national capital, and had an estimated population in 1960 of 600,000, an increase of almost 100,000 in less than five years. The urban populace in Nigeria is increasing more rapidly than the rural. As in most of Africa, the percentage of its people now living in towns of 5000 or more varies from region to region. In the East it is approximately 14 percent; in the North around 10 percent; and in the West, one of the most highly concentrated areas on the continent, it is nearly 50 percent.

Although the majority of African towns owe their origin in large measure to foreign initiative, Ibadan is an outstanding example of a town founded by the indigenous peoples. It originated as a small forest settlement or war encampment of the Yoruba tribe around 1821, and by the time formal British control was established over western Nigeria in the late nineteenth century, the population of the town was well over 100,000. Under colonial administration the influx of newcomers was accelerated as wider trade relations and better communications (including the construction of a railroad from the coastal city of Lagos) were developed. The successful cultivation of cocoa, which began early in the present century, converted the Ibadan area into a rich agricultural district and increased the city's importance as a service and trading center. In 1948 the University of Ibadan was established by the national government and more recently large-scale industries of a European type have been introduced into the city.[4]

The core or oldest part of the city extends out for about a half mile on all sides of the town hall. Density is remarkably high (as many as thirty houses to the acre in some sections), open space is negligible, roads are few, and access to many of the houses is by means of footpaths. More than a third of Ibadan's inhabitants, generally the poorer families, are concentrated in these congested districts, many of them living in what were once compounds surrounded by mud walls. The walls have since disappeared but a few to several hundred inhabitants are still found congregated together in the same small space. Ibadan has a town planning authority that could effect a population redistribution as was done in the Greater London area, but the problems that would result from displacing so many people have caused officials to shy away from such efforts including slum clearance.[5]

The inner core with its large market and town hall was at one time the economic heart of the city. However, with the arrival of the railway at the turn of the present century, the town began to attract numerous European economic institutions such as department stores, banks, trading firms, specialized shops, and motor garages, as well as the colonial administrative agencies. Since land for these various activities could not be found in the congested core of the city, they located at the periphery, thus creating a large commercial section, the equivalent of the American downtown or central business district. This development caused the economic center of gravity to shift from the core to the suburban ring. It also made further expansion of the old town impractical and lessened economic incentive to redevelop the now obsolescent areas in the inner city.[6] One might speculate what the fate of American CBD's and their surrounding areas would have been had the commercial center of the metropolis been shifted to an outer location early in the twentieth century.

The suburban areas surrounding the inner city house the more affluent members of the community, including the Europeans and other "wealthy" immigrants who began to enter Ibadan after the British assumed control. Here the housing is better, the lots more spacious, and the density far lower. Today, the newcomers who are flocking into the city settle where their means permit. The poor and uneducated Africans must seek homes in the crowded districts of the core, while the educated Africans, or those with

---

[4] For a description of Ibadan, see N. C. Mitchel, "Yoruba Towns," in K. M. Barbour and R. M. Prothero (eds.), *Essays on African Population* (London: Routledge and Kegan Paul, 1961), pp. 279–301.

[5] Akin Mabogunje, "The Growth of Residential Districts in Ibadan," *Geographical Review*, LII (January, 1962), pp. 56–77.

[6] See A. L. Mabogunje, *Yoruba Towns* (Ibadan, Nigeria: Ibadan University Press, 1962), p. 13.

some means, settle in the suburbs. (The growing number of non-Africans also turn to the lower-density residential neighborhoods of suburbia.) A surprisingly large proportion of recent African migrants are young men and women who have had some education or training and are therefore better equipped than many of the indigenous population to compete in the rapidly changing society. Spatial patterns, not unexpectedly of course, have become almost a measure of social and economic status as migrants from different cultures and with different skills and competencies tend to congregate together in different sections of the community.

Governmental Pattern

· · · · ·

The problems of local governmental organization in Ibadan and other African urban areas are not greatly different from those in Western nations. If anything, the difference is a matter of degree rather than kind. The observations of Ronald Wraith, formerly of the University of Ibadan, are pertinent in this regard. He notes that the difficulty in developing countries like Nigeria is that the mass of people are not sufficiently informed to be able to think of local government in terms of areas suitable for efficient administration. (For that matter, neither are they in developed nations such as the United States, although the difficulty may not stand out as sharply.) The ordinary citizen in these countries tends to see local government in terms of traditional rivalries and distrust of neighboring towns or townspeople with whom he is unwilling to share his own resources and whom he suspects of getting more than their fair share of benefits. The solution, as Wraith sees it, and the one toward which Western Nigeria has been slowly working is to "leave the 'neutral areas,' in which peoples' local loyalties reside, untouched; to give them as much to do as possible; but not to give them powers and duties in connection with the major services on which the progress of Nigeria as a nation depends." [7] The philosophy underlying much of the current thinking on metropolitan reorganization in the United States is closely akin to this approach.

Tokyo

Asia, the largest of the five continents, has almost three-fifths of the world's population and more than a third of its land surface. The sharp reduction in mortality in recent decades (due largely to antibiotics and other products of the laboratory) has combined with continuing high fertility to produce rates of population growth unparalleled in human history.[8] The

---

[7] *Local Government in West Africa* (New York: Praeger, 1964), pp. 87–88.
[8] See Irene B. Taeuber, "Asia's Increasing Population," *Annals of the American Academy of Political and Social Science*, 318 (July, 1958), pp. 1–8.

people of Asia are predominantly village-dwelling agrarians, but the degree of urbanization is showing gains as both old and new nations seek to step up their industrial output. The number of cities with populations of one million or over, for example, increased from thirteen in 1935 to thirty-four in the mid-1950s. Not unexpectedly, the problems resulting from this massive growth have been intense for the local as well as national governments.

Of the Asian countries, Japan is the first to reach western levels of urbanization and the first to approach western standards of living. The world's fourth ranking industrial power, Japan is already in an advanced stage of urbanization. More than three-fifths of its 95 million people live in cities, and the proportion is steadily increasing. In 1950, the farming population accounted for 45 percent of the total; by 1960 this figure had dropped to 37 percent. Density is also high, 660 persons to the square mile, with concentrations as large as 50,000 in some of the Tokyo wards.

Administratively, Japan consists of two tiers below the central government: provinces (called prefectures) and municipalities. Each of the forty-six provinces into which the country is divided is governed by a popularly elected council and an elected chief executive. Before World War II, local government was rigidly controlled by national authorities; in 1947, the governmental system was decentralized and local units given a large measure of autonomy. Since the end of the United States military occupation in 1952, the trend has again been toward greater centralization, especially at the provincial level. During the 1950s a program of urban amalgamation was undertaken to increase municipal efficiency, with the national government offering financial inducements to communities that would agree to merge. Under the program, the number of cities and towns was reduced from 9622 to 3475.

Physical and Demographic Characteristics

Tokyo, the capital of Japan, is the largest urban concentration in Asia and one of the most intensely crowded cities of the world. Like Egypt's legendary bird, the Phoenix, Tokyo has risen from its ashes twice in the space of two generations. It was destroyed by an earthquake followed by a tidal wave and fires in 1923; and in World War II large portions of it were leveled by Allied fire bombs. Today it is a teeming, congested, and expanding metropolis, the political, cultural, financial, and industrial center of Japanese life. In 1950 the population of the ward area (the equivalent of a central city) was 5.4 million and that of the metropolitan area 8.0 million; in 1963 these populations were estimated to be 8.6 million and 10.2 million, respectively.

As is the case with the typical large American metropolis, Tokyo is experiencing severe growing pains. Schools are overcrowded, the street system is wholly inadequate, housing shortages exist, public facilities and services are badly overburdened, and the suburban development continues to move further out. Each year approximately a quarter of a million people are added to the area's population, 70 to 80 percent of whom are migrants from rural areas seeking better employment and other opportunities. Since most of the newcomers are unskilled laborers of little means, this influx places a heavy burden on the city's welfare and service resources.

In 1962 the Tokyo Metropolitan Government, to be discussed later, announced a ten-year program to attack such problems as over-concentration of population, urban sprawl, and inadequacy of public facilities. The program is designed primarily to carry out the Metropolitan Government's responsibility of enforcing plans made by the National Capital Regional Development Commission, a body appointed by the central government. According to national law, local authorities are required to cooperate in the development of the capital region, an area within a radius of approximately 65 miles from the center of Tokyo.

Plans prepared by the Commission provide for a greenbelt six miles wide around the presently built-up area. Hospitals, universities, and other institutions, and airports and cemeteries will be located in this setting of forests and farmlands. Beyond the greenbelt, a necklace of satellite towns is to be developed. These are not to be bedroom suburbs but communities with industry and other sources of employment. To facilitate this development, the central government assures local authorities of necessary funds to build home sites and public facilities. It also makes funds available to private entrepreneurs for constructing railways and factories in these areas.[9] The major objective of these plans is to restrict further industrial growth in the highly built-up sections of Metropolitan Tokyo and to redistribute or channel a portion of the population to the new towns on the periphery. The similarities to the Greater London plan can be seen in these developments. So also can the contrast between the Japanese and American approaches to urban growth be observed. Not only are greater governmental controls exercised over expansion in Japan, but public funds are also used far more extensively there to encourage and direct development in accordance with comprehensive plans.

Governmental Pattern

. . . . .

. . . Local government in the Tokyo area is basically a two-level system with some services handled exclusively by the upper tier or Metropolitan Government, some relegated to the lower or municipalities and wards, and others jointly administered. What distinguishes this system from the American practice of local federalism is the high degree of control exercised by

---

[9] For a more extended description of these developments, see *An Administrative Perspective of Tokyo* (Tokyo: The Tokyo Metropolitan Government, 1963).

the upper tier over the local units and their activities. The Tokyo structure, in other words, unlike the typical American pattern, provides a means of minimizing the debilitating effects of governmental fragmentation on metropolitan development and functioning.

The Tokyo experience, however, indicates that even where these controls exist, the problem of government in rapidly expanding metropolitan areas is far from solved. A consultative body to the governor of Tokyo pointed this out in a report submitted in 1962. It noted, among other things, that (1) the task of providing public facilities and other services for a city growing as rapidly as the Japanese capital is so voluminous as to overtax the administrative structure badly; (2) no effective system of coordinating the activities of the many local units has yet been devised; and (3) with population spillover into adjacent provinces, it has become difficult for the Tokyo Metropolitan Government to deal with its administrative affairs effectively without some institutionalized system of cooperation with neighboring prefectures.

These difficulties have led some Japanese scholars and statesmen to propose a larger role for the national government in metropolitan affairs. It has been suggested, for example, that a new agency under national control be established to take over responsibility for certain metropolitan functions, particularly the construction of public facilities and the formulation of development plans. As the following quotation shows, the Tokyo government reacted strongly to this suggestion:

> Even if it is an admitted fact that the administration of the metropolitan area now carried on by the Tokyo Metropolitan Government is still far from perfect, its cause may be attributed to a lack of a centrally and locally coordinated plan and to the central government's various financial restrictions upon metropolitan administration. It is no wonder that the central government should make studies in the metropolitan system, but such ideas from some authoritative sources as tramping upon home rule are reckless and unconstitutional.[10]

São Paulo

Contrary to popular impression, the fastest growing population in the world today is found not in India or Communist China but in tropical South America, a 5.3 million square mile area encompassing nine nations: Bolivia, Brazil, Colombia, Ecuador, Peru, Venezuela, and the three Guianas. This area, with a population in 1963 of approximately 121 million, is growing at an average rate of 3.2 percent annually compared to about 2 percent for India and China. As elsewhere around the globe, most of this increase is occurring in urban areas.

Brazil, by far the largest of the South American nations in both population (estimated at 78 million in 1963) and territorial size (3.2 million square

---

[10] *An Administrative Perspective of Tokyo,* p. 8.

miles, an area almost equal to that of the United States), is a federal republic composed of twenty-one states, five federal territories, and the federal
district containing the new capital, Brasilia. The country is still basically
agricultural with approximately 60 percent of its labor force engaged in farming and related employments. However, the increased emphasis on industrial
development during the last several decades is rapidly altering this picture.
Production of crude steel, to cite one indication of the trend, increased almost eighteen times between 1940 and 1960. During this same span of
time, the percentage of the population classified as urban also increased significantly: from less than one-third in 1940 to almost one-half by 1960.

Physical and Demographic Characteristics

São Paulo, 200 miles southwest of Rio de Janeiro, is Brazil's largest urban
area and the most industrialized center south of the Rio Grande River. Referred to by some as the "Chicago" of South America, it is one of the fastest
growing metropolises in the world. It celebrated the 400th anniversary of its
founding in 1954, but until the latter part of the nineteenth century it was a
quiet town of 25,000. Today, it is a center of great industrial and commercial
activity, shining skyscrapers, and congestion. Its population, approximately
4 million in 1963, is growing at the rate of 150,000 a year, largely the result
of internal migration from the rural areas.

The city is laid out in the shape of an irregular polygon. At the core is
the historic "triangle," the community's economic and bureaucratic center,
where the department stores, banks, private and governmental office buildings, and hotels are located. The residential neighborhoods near the core,
formerly the quarters of the aristocrats, have become favorite points for
middle-class penetration. Only the construction of centrally located luxury
apartments has prevented the total flight of the élite to the gardened sites
of suburbia. Growth outward from the core has been concentric and has
occurred at immense speed without zoning regulations or comprehensive
land use plans. This development has been under way for some time. For
example, in the period from 1934 to 1940 the population increase within
a two-mile radius of the city center was less than 10 percent; between 2 and
4.5 miles, it was 50 percent; and beyond this circumference it was over
85 percent.[11]

Outside the city proper but within the metropolitan area are a host of
suburban nuclei of various types that range from modern industrial aggregations to rural settlements lacking electricity and piped water. In one
section are industrial suburbs that include the plants of such well-known
American companies as General Motors and Firestone. In another are

---

[11] Richard M. Morse, *From Community to Metropolis* (Gainesville: University of Florida Press, 1958), p. 272.

residential sub-communities of middle- or lower-class families. And in still another are the attractively laid out residential enclaves of the well-to-do that stand in stark contrast to the crowded slums of the industrial areas. Beyond the urbanized portions of the municipality's 700 square miles of territory are the rural villages and agricultural areas.

People and goods in São Paulo are moved over a road network dominated by a loop-and-spoke system of broad radial and circumferential avenues. As in the typical metropolis in the United States, people converge on the core or central business district from all directions. The city has a good public transit system but the demands placed on it are too great to handle this volume of traffic with facility. Moreover, the street and parking system is wholly inadequate to accommodate the area's growing automobile population. The result is intense congestion in and around the core.

Despite gestures by local authorities to encourage decentralization of central business district activities, the core of the metropolis retains a strong pull on commercial and civic functions and on office building use. Some large department stores are invading the suburbs and a few radial streets offer retail shops and service establishments at a distance from the "triangle," but these developments have in no way detracted from the prominence of the city center. Tall skyscrapers continue to rise within its confines and large luxury apartments continue to be constructed on its periphery. Fortunately, the industrial suburbs provide a degree of decentralization for the area that helps to spread peak-hour traffic loads and affords some relief, however small, to the problem of congestion.

Governmental Pattern

The basic, in fact the only, unit of local government in Brazil is the municipality (*municipio*). Since each of the twenty-one states is completely subdivided into municipalities and no other units such as counties, townships, or special districts exist, Brazilian local government has an apparent simplicity that contrasts strongly to the pattern in the United States. The municipality is more comparable to the American county than to a city or town since it includes suburban settlements and rural villages in addition to the urban center or city. Unlike the American county, however, the Brazilian municipality does not share governmental responsibility with any other local entity. Instead, it enjoys jurisdiction over the entire area with no separately incorporated towns and villages or other autonomous units to challenge its authority.

.   .   .   .   .

Despite the fact that the municipalities are granted substantial powers by the national and state constitutions, local self-government has developed far less in Brazil than in the Anglo-Saxon world. A major reason for this difference is the heavy financial dependence of the local units on higher levels of government. With the exception of São Paulo and possibly a few other major communities, municipalities seldom collect over 10 percent of their total revenue from local levies. For the remainder they must rely on state and federal grants and shared revenues and on the direct financing and administration of certain local services by these higher levels. State-operated primary schools, for example, outnumber those administered locally by more than a two-to-one margin. This reliance has encouraged the political subservience of municipalities to the upper-governmental echelons. Evidence of this subserviency is found in the considerable importance that municipal officials place on maintaining favorable political relations with state and national authorities.[12]

A second, although lesser, reason for the inability of local units to exercise their full panoply of powers is territorial instability. In many municipalities there has been a tendency to elevate the subunits or districts to municipal status, thus introducing an element of governmental fragmentation into what is otherwise a simplistic pattern of organization. The tendency has been particularly strong in the outlying suburban and rural sections where residents feel their needs are given short shrift by the city-dominated administration. This development is interesting to American observers of metropolitan political institutions because of its implications for governmental consolidation. Most importantly, it suggests that there are limits to the territorial size of a local unit for responsible and equitable policy-making and administration. Making the units larger still leaves the problem of how to provide government which is both effective and convenient for those who live in the villages and peripheral communities.

São Paulo occupies a more favored position than most municipalities in the Brazilian local governmental system, due largely to its economic status. Because of its degree of industrialization, its resources are substantial and its standard of living high compared to other communities in the country. The median per capita income of its residents is about three times that of the entire nation. These factors make the city less dependent financially on the state and national governments and enable it to exercise a greater degree of control over its local affairs.

Public services and facilities in São Paulo are among the best in Latin America. Utilities, recreation areas, transportation arteries, hospital and social welfare services, sanitation, and the primary and secondary school system are well developed despite persistent material and administrative deficiencies. There are, of course, chronic problems, a common feature of metropolitan areas everywhere. Water distribution, for example, has not kept pace with population growth; inadequate land use planning and control have permitted the indiscriminate intermingling of commercial, in-

---

[12] See L. Donald Carr, "Brazilian Local Self-Government: Myth or Reality?" *Western Political Quarterly*, 13 (December, 1960), pp. 1043–1055.

dustrial, and residential zones; and park and playground facilities are inadequate. Many of São Paulo's difficulties are, of course, attributable to its rapid growth, and no amount of governmental resources or foresight could have coped fully with this development.

Metropolitan Communities in a World Setting

No thorough consideration of the metropolis in time and space can overlook either its social and economic facets or its governmental institutions. The informal means of social control which once regulated the communal affairs of primitive settlements have given way to the more formal methods of modern society. As the populations of cities and metropolitan areas have grown in size and heterogeneity, larger and more complex governmental organizations have evolved as instruments of control and direction. Historically, it has been the emergence of local government that has weakened the bonds of familial or tribal social organization and marked the transference of local loyalties to the broader community.

The patterns of local government that have emerged and are still evolving show great diversity, not only between countries but within individual nations as well. To a large extent these patterns and the manner in which their formal and informal structures function are conditioned by the culture of the country and its subparts. We have had occasion to note this relationship in the case of Nigeria where British institutions and practices have been modified under the pressures of local tradition. The same phenomenon is observable elsewhere where the governmental forms imposed by colonial powers have been reshaped or modified in the crucible of local culture.

The basic tasks of urban government are everywhere the same, whether in the cities of Nigeria and Brazil or those in Great Britain and the United States. Throughout the world, metropolitan communities and their governmental systems are being subjected to heavy strains and incessant demands. The responses to these forces have varied from nation to nation. At one extreme, local units have tended to abdicate their responsibilities and become mere administrative arms of the state or national governments. At the other extreme, too great an emphasis on local autonomy has hindered the development of effective public mechanisms for meeting the problems and needs of an increasingly technological society.

Despite the great variations, however, the overall trend has been toward greater centralization, and this has been so even in cases where the fragmentation of local units continues unabated. Key functions are assumed by or transferred to area-wide agencies, provincial and national governments exercise greater control over local operations either by direct fiat or by means of financial inducements, and the power to make and execute many decisions affecting the small units is increasingly passing upward to higher echelons of public and private authorities. The phenomenon is universal;

it differs only in degree and particulars. Metropolises in all sections of the world have a common kinship and a common set of problems. All of them are striving to work out their destiny in a world that is daily becoming more urbanized and more complex.

49 | Segregation, Subsidies, and Megalopolis

BERNARD WEISSBOURD

From 55,000,000 to 60,000,000 *more* people will be living in metropolitan areas in 1980 than were living there in 1960. How will we manage? Already our cities are decaying faster than they can be rebuilt. Parking is a universal problem. The tax base of the city is eroding as industry moves to the suburbs. A significant part of the white population is also moving to the suburbs, while the cores of our cities are filing with Negroes as the migration from the South steadily rises. The cost to the cities of trying to adjust the migrants to a new kind of existence imposes additional burdens upon the city's tax base.

Taxes are also rising in the suburbs to pay for the high cost of municipal services spread out over areas of low population density. Open space is being consumed at a terrifying rate, so that suburbs once in open country are now surrounded. Travel time to the city has multiplied as the expressways get clogged during rush hours.

Some experts do not find these problems of city decay and suburban sprawl unduly alarming. They maintain that the continuing dispersal that present trends indicate for the future is inevitable, and not necessarily undesirable. I believe the opposite.

Suburban sprawl and urban decay have *not* come about solely because people have made a free choice in a free enterprise market. That choice has been influenced by federal housing subsidies, which, purporting to be neutral, have in fact subsidized low-density middle-income living in the suburbs and have thereby financed the flight of white population from the city. Another factor affecting this dispersal has been our segregation practices within the city.

The lack of public discussion about the influence of housing segregation and federal housing subsidies upon urban growth patterns has been a bar-

SOURCE: *Occasional Paper No. 1 on the City* (Santa Barbara, Calif.: Center for the Study of Democratic Institutions, 1964), pp. 2–12. Reprinted by permission of the publisher.

rier to understanding the problems of the city and suburbs and has created a feeling of hopelessness about the future of America's cities. It is my purpose here to show that it is possible to deal constructively with the problems of the metropolitan region if these important factors are not ignored.

The Low-Density Urban Region

Compared to the time span of Western civilization the modern urban complex, sometimes called megalopolis, is a new, young phenomenon. Some people are confident that a new technology of communication and transportation will solve many of the most intractable problems of the metropolitan region and that, in time, the region of the future will emerge.[1] "The spatial patterns of American settlements," it is now believed, will "be considerably more dispersed, varied and space consuming than they ever were in the past . . ."[2] One author envisions "continuous low density urban belts stretching from Maine to Virginia, from Toronto and Pittsburgh to Milwaukee, and from Amsterdam to Frankfort and Mannheim . . . However, there seems to be no reason why, properly organized and interlaced with greenbelts, freeways, natural reservations and sites of historic interest, and accented vertically by occasional high-rise elements, these low-density urban regions of tomorrow should not be more livable and effective in satisfying the totality of human values than the tansitional urban forms of today."[3]

Acceptance of low-density regional development as the pattern for the future is encouraged by the lack of genuine popular support for a massive attack on the problems of the city and the region. To most suburban residents their experience "seems not one of personal retrogression but of continuous improvement. By moving out of the slag heaps of the worked-out city they have improved their surroundings sufficient for a generation."[4]

While no businessman whose offices must be located in the central business district, and no dweller in the city slums, can accept the decline of the city with equanimity, it is quite likely that if we do nothing to alter present trends the low-density urban region will be the pattern of the future. The New York metropolitan region, for example, has grown outward along major transportation arteries. The axis of growth extended five miles in 1900, twenty-five miles in 1960, and may become fifty miles by 1985.

---

[1] Webber, "Order in Diversity: Community Without Propinquity," in L. Wingo (ed.): *Cities and Space, The Future Use of Urban Land*. Baltimore: Johns Hopkins Press, 1963, 43.

[2] Ibid., 23

[3] Christopher Tunnard and Boris Pushkarev, *Man-Made America: Chaos or Control*, 1963, 443.

[4] Raymond Vernon, *The Myth and Reality of Our Urban Problems*. Joint Center for Urban Studies of the Massachusetts Institute of Technology and Harvard University, 1961, 30–31.

Under existing zoning patterns of low-density development twice the amount of land will be developed in the next twenty-five years as in the entire history of the New York region.[5] A similar pattern emerges for every metropolitan region in the United States as a projected 45,000,000 to 50,-000,000 *more* people are added to suburbia by 1980.

Acceptance of low-density regional growth also implies a curtailment of mass transportation, for mass transportation works well only in highly concentrated areas where trip origins and destinations are clustered and not where they are widely dispersed. Conversely, the automobile, which functions so efficiently for decentralized traffic, becomes highly inefficient under conditions of intense demand. Suburban sprawl will thus bring about a further decline in mass transportation, as increasing reliance on the automobile brings more congestion to the central districts.

The Decline of the City

Each new expressway not only undercuts the market for mass transportation but accelerates the movement of industry away from the central cities. The truck and the car have given the manufacturer new opportunities to select sites in outlying areas. The movement of industry from central city locations to outlying suburban locations has created a new phenomenon—out-commuting. "The movement each morning of people from homes in the center portions of the urban areas to jobs on the periphery is growing fast. The spectacle of groups of blue-collar workers traveling outward by car pool against the flow of incoming traffic is now a common sight on the roads of many large cities. In fact the spotty and fragmentary information on this phenomenon suggests that it may be one of the fastest-growing streams of traffic among the complex currents of our urban areas." [6]

Nor have the results of the federal programs for slum clearance, urban renewal, and public housing so far given any reason to expect that the trend toward city decline and low-density regional settlement will be reversed. Slums in the cities are growing faster than we can clear them. Even in New York City, which has had the largest slum clearance and rebuilding program of any city in the United States, the rate of deterioration of housing units has been as great as the rate at which new housing has been constructed. We should not expect urban renewal to work so long as there is no place for persons evacuated from the slums to live. People displaced by urban renewal and by the new expressways have created new slums.

The new luxury apartment buildings constructed since the end of World

---

[5] Stanley Tankel, "Importance of Open Space in the Urban Patterns," in *Cities and Space, The Future Use of Urban Land*, 1963, 53.

[6] Raymond Vernon, *The Myth and Reality of Our Urban Problems*. Joint Center for Urban Studies of the Massachusetts Institute of Technology and Harvard University, 1961, 6.

War II have not prevented the exodus of middle-income white families to the suburbs. It was thought that upper-income families would move into these expensive apartments and people in the next income level would move into the apartments thus vacated. Instead, the vacated apartments were converted for occupancy by lower-income people. Middle-income families who could not afford private schools for their children moved to the suburbs, leaving behind in the cities people without children, upper-income families, and low-income families who had no choice. The problem was compounded by the impact of segregation practices. Apartment buildings vacated by those who moved into new luxury accommodations were converted into slums overnight. The "trickle-down" approach failed as the trickle became a torrent.

Moreover, no one is satisfied with public housing. By rejecting all those whose incomes exceeded the prescribed limits public housing has developed a concentration of those members of society who are not able to support themselves. Coupled with the fact that most cities have followed a deliberate program of segregation in public housing, the result has been to create in many places an environment lacking in all of the positive attributes of urban life. The second generation of many public housing occupants is now coming to maturity and it is already clear that many of them will never become viable members of society.

Urban renewal programs aimed at aiding the central business district show greater promise of long-range success, probably because there is considerable strength in the central business district to begin with. New office buildings in the central areas of each of the metropolitan regions demonstrate that financial and commercial institutions, public utilities, newspapers and magazines, and government, together with the lawyers, accountants, stock brokers, and others involved in serving these institutions, require a centralized location.[7] Most cities in the United States have only one business district. The fact that Los Angeles now has several scattered clusters of office buildings does not indicate a decentralization of office activities. The diffusion may make doing business in Los Angeles a little more difficult than in Chicago or Baltimore, for example, but the clusters of office buildings in the California city are still reasonably close together in relation to the region as a whole. It is certainly not possible for the office activities of Manhattan Island to be spread out over suburbia. Even most of the retail stores in the central business districts, which declined for a while because of the competition of suburban shopping centers, have begun to revive.

Thus, although a sizable number of people and industries has moved out of the central city, there has been far less movement of office activities to outlying areas than some reports would lead us to believe.

---

[7] Ibid., 42. Also see Edwards, "Central Business Districts," 4 *Journal of Housing*, 186.

The Exploding Population

The movement of white population to suburban areas and the concentration of Negro population in the central city will be intensified during the next fifteen years if present trends continue.

In 1960 about 63 per cent of the total population of the United States or about 112,000,000 persons lived in what are known statistically as "standard metropolitan areas." [8] Between 1970 and 1980 as much as 73 per cent of the total population will reside within the urban complex. If the post-war birth rate continues, the total population will have increased between 1950 and 1980 from 150,000,000 to 260,000,000, an increase of 110,000,000 people in thirty years (a single human generation).[9] More than two-thirds of these 110,000,000 people will have settled in megalopolis, if events do not alter present trends.

Population projections beyond the year 2000 begin to reach astronomical numbers. It is not necessary, however, to look that far ahead. The children are already born who will be forming households in 1980, only sixteen years from now. It is becoming clear that the new dwellings, transportation, offices, and factories that these people will require will either contribute further to city decay and suburban sprawl or provide the opportunity for creating a new regional environment.

Since the end of World War II the Negro population has been increasing even faster than the white population. Philip Hauser points out that the decline of the non-white death rate together with the increase in their birth rate has resulted in a rate of growth for non-whites 60 per cent higher than for whites.[10] This great national rise is dwarfed by an even more explosive increase of non-whites in metropolitan areas.[11] By 1990 about 2,500,000 Negroes are expected to be living in the Chicago metropolitan area, about 1,500,000 more than in 1960. "At that time there would still be a slight majority of whites in the city of Chicago and one-fourth of the entire consolidated area population would be non-white." [12] These projections assume accelerated suburbanization of non-whites in the future. However, "if the exact trends of the 1950 to 1960 decade were to be extrapolated into the future they would show a majority of non-whites in the city of Chicago by 1975 and a substantially higher proportion of non-whites for the total consolidated areas." [13]

---

[8] Philip Hauser, *Population Perspectives*. New Brunswick, N. J.: Rutgers University Press, 1960, 72.

[9] Ibid., 35.   [10] Ibid., 58.   [11] Ibid., 59.

[12] Donald Bogue and Dandekar, *Population Trends and Prospects for the Chicago-Northeastern Indiana Consolidated Metropolitan Area: 1960–1990*, 1952, 28.

[13] Ibid., 28.

The migration to the cities of rural Negroes and Southern whites and Puerto Ricans has already imposed heavy tax burdens on the city. In 1959, for example, New York City spent $50,000,000 for remedial programs for its Puerto Rican newcomers, more than it spent on all its parks, libraries, zoos, and museums in that year.[14] In its 1959–60 budget New York City assigned 23 per cent to public hospitalization, health, and welfare and 20 per cent to education.[15] The great growth rate of the Negro population in New York, through continued migration as well as natural increase during the next fifteen years, will tend to increase even further the city's costs for welfare, health, and education.

The picture that emerges from these forecasts is far from salutary. Low-density regional settlements in which industry and the white population spread out over the countryside without adequate mass transportation contrasts with the concentrated Negro occupancy of the center city, whose tax base has diminished by the flight of industry and whose expenses have increased for the care of its immigrants. Moreover, a growing number of the center-city population will be commuting to jobs in the suburbs while many of the suburban whites will continue to travel to jobs in a still strong central business district.

The waste of human resources and money in this increased commuting, the inability of the automobile and the expressways to handle the traffic, the changing character of the city largely occupied by a financial and business community and a segregated Negro population, the financing of public services for a migrant population in the face of disappearing industry and lost taxes, the interdependence of the financial and commercial life of the suburbs and the city—these are all reasons for not allowing present trends to continue.

But are there alternatives? As we have noted, there are many who doubt whether the trends are reversible. I believe the pattern can be changed, but first it is necessary to say something about the federal housing subsidies, because they are both one of the causes of suburban growth and one of the possible tools for creating a different picture for the future.

The Influence of Federal Subsidies

It is important to understand that dispersal of the urban population in the United States has not come about solely as a result of a free and open market. Government inducements to buy in the suburbs have been substantial and have brought about a remarkable increase in home ownership since the war. In 1957, of the total mortgage debt of $107,000,000,000 on one- to four-family non-farm homes, $47,200,000,000 were FHA-insured or

---

[14] Edward Higby, *The Squeeze*. New York: William Morrow, 1960, 38.
[15] Ibid., 42.

VA-guaranteed.[16] Of the balance, so-called conventional loans, a substantial portion was held by savings and loan associations.[17] The funds involved in the federal encouragement of home ownership is thus enormous compared to the amounts involved for rental housing in the city. Inducements for home ownership, of course, have been of little or no value to the city, since land has not been available in most of America's major cities for single-family homes.

The success of the federal housing program in suburbia results from the availability of mortgage funds that have not had to measure up to the usual free-market considerations of risk and competitive yield of other investments. Guarantees and insurance by the United States provide money for suburban home ownership at interest rates lower than the market over longer periods of time.

A subsidy is also involved in the activities of federal and state savings and loan associations. Because law restricts the investments of these associations largely to home mortgages,[18] the flow of capital has been directed artificially to suburbia, and money has been made available for houses at rates lower than those which would have been available if the home owner had had to compete for the funds with other sources of investments of comparable risk. To the extent that deposits in savings and loan associations are insured by the federal government under the Federal Home Loan Bank System, capital is attracted that *must* be invested in home mortgages. The federal insurance, then, constitutes an indirect subsidy.[19]

Another heavily subsidized federal housing program—public housing— has also contributed to the condition of our cities. Public housing has been the prisoner of its opponents, who have largely determined its character. Locating public housing projects in the inner city has contributed to keeping lower-income people in the city and has strengthened the patterns of segregation, except in a few cases where careful planning has been able to achieve successfully integrated projects.[20] One arm of the federal housing program has financed housing for middle-income families in the suburbs. The question may well be asked: Why should not the opposite program have been adopted?

---

[16] Charles Haar, *Federal Credit and Private Housing*, 1960, 132. Mr. Haar deliberately excluded the role of the savings and loan associations from an otherwise excellent book.

[17] Ibid., 138.

[18] 12 USCA Sec. 1464(c). See also Ch. 32 Ill. Rev. Stat. 791.

[19] The special tax treatment under the Internal Revenue Code for state and federal savings and loan associations also requires that a certain portion of their funds be invested in "residential real property containing 4 or fewer family units." 1954 Internal Revenue Code, Subtitle F, Ch. 79, Sec. 7701(a) 19. See, also, Internal Revenue Code, Subtitle A, Ch. 1H, Part II, Secs. 591–593.

[20] Harold Mayer and C. Stein, "Public Housing as Community," *Architectural Record*, April 1964, 169.

Other federal subsidies have also had their influence. The disproportionate amount of the federal budget allotted to agriculture [21] has helped
bring about the mechanization of the farm and speeded up the migration
of both Negro and white farm labor to the city. Similarly, the federal defense highway program has represented an enormous subsidy to the automobile at the expense of mass transportation. Whether these subsidies
have been beneficial or detrimental is not pertinent here; what they indicate is that the condition of our metropolitan regions is not the result of
"natural" forces alone. The federal government has played a major role in
contributing to the shape and character of urban America.

The goals of the federal housing program originated in the New Deal
attempt to house the one-third of the nation that was ill-housed. Attention
was focused on home ownership for the middle class and public housing
for the needy. The impact of these programs on the physical and economic
aspects of the city and region was not considered. Moreover, the acute
housing shortage of the post-World War II period obscured the need for a
national long-term housing program. In more recent years social goals have
been subordinated to the desire to stimulate the construction industry in
order to minimize unemployment. It is impossible to predict what the
shape and character of city and region might have been if the United States
had had a national long-range program designed to provide housing for
middle-income workers in the city and sites for industry and lower-income
industrial workers in outlying areas. Surely, if the country had decided in
1948 that it wanted to subsidize higher-density apartment development in
the suburbs rather than lower-density home ownership, and mass transportation rather than expressways, it is unlikely that all of the forecasts
would point to suburban sprawl as the pattern of the future.

Catherine Bauer, in noting "the general past trend, however imperfectly
realized, toward Everyone in His Place, in a standardized one-class, one-
age-group, and one-color district, devoted wholly to residence," has pointed
out that "this was not, however, the result of any conscious over-all plan or
public decision to encourage maximum social segregation. It came about
more or less by accident, as a side result of forces and policies employed
for quite different and often distinctly progressive or idealistic ends, and
because we were reluctant to assume any conscious collective responsibility
whatsoever for the social pattern. . . . What we failed to recognize was
that the powerful tools employed for civic development and home production *also* predetermine social structure to such an extent that there is little
room left for free personal choice or flexible adjustment. The big social decisions are all made in advance, inherent in the planning and building
process. And if these decisions are not made responsibly and democrat-
ically, then they are made irresponsibly by the accidents of technology, the

---

[21] Statement by Senator Harrison A. Williams, Jr. is particularly pertinent.
11 *Journal of Housing* 609.

myths of property interest, or the blindness and prejudice of a reactionary minority." [22]

Toward Renewal and New Development

To avoid the implications of present trends America will have to assume some responsibility for its over-all social patterns and use the "powerful tools employed for civic development and home production" to reshape the areas of "free personal choice."

The forces at work in the city and region are cumulative. They all move together toward making the city a more desirable or less desirable place to live. The federal subsidies that have encouraged highway construction instead of mass commuter transportation and thus drawn industry out of the city have reduced the city's tax base. A lower tax base means less money for education and for the adjustment of rural migrants to urban life. Poor schools and changing neighborhoods encourage middle-class white families to move to the suburbs. Higher welfare costs increase the tax rate and thus encourage industry to relocate in outlying areas. All these factors are interrelated. If they can be altered, it might be possible to reverse the cycle of urban decay and deterioration and move the forces of the market-place toward renewal and reconstruction.

A total program is needed that recognizes the interdependence of city and suburbs. The creation of new communities on the outskirts of suburbia is a necessary element in the restoration of the inner city. The vitality of the city is, in turn, important for all of the inhabitants of the region. A total program must be able to differentiate between which of the forces must be shaped by government action in a private enterprise system and which may not.

We cannot, for example, prevent those industries which do not require a central location from moving to less expensive land in outlying areas. However, through a regional open-space plan, we can limit the areas in which these industries may choose to locate. We cannot prevent middle-class white families from leaving the cities because their children are not being educated in accordance with middle-class standards. But we can induce middle-class families to live within the city if we can create areas large enough to establish a genuine community with good schools. We can find the land for these communities by clearing industrial as well as residential slum property, provided that we undertake to relieve the city of part of its tax burden or change the methods by which it collects taxes.

"New towns" are already being created in areas beyond suburbia to ac-

---

[22] Catherine Bauer, "Social Questions in Housing and Community Planning," 7 *Journal of Social Issues* 21–3. Cf. Miss Bauer's "The Form and Structure of the Future Urban Complex," in *Cities and Space, The Future Use of Urban Land,* 1963, 73.

commodate an exploding population, but these "new towns" may become exclusive suburbs, which in time will be engulfed by suburban sprawl.

I am suggesting a different kind of "new town" program. We should attempt to create "new towns" pursuant to regional open space and transportation plans. These towns will also accommodate industrial workers and industries displaced by an intensified residential and industrial slum clearance program in the core areas of our major cities. At the same time, on the land within the cities made available by slum clearance, new communities can be established for middle-income families.

This program would make both the central city and the "new towns" more heterogeneous in social composition, reduce travel distances to work and thus diminish the transportation problem, and, finally, bring suburban sprawl under control by regional planning of open spaces and mass transportation.

Segregation

Present segregation practices are a serious obstacle to this kind of program; at the same time they provide an additional reason why a program designed to create heterogeneous communities both within the city and beyond the suburbs has become imperative. If there were no racial problem in the United States, we might have begun long ago to shape our policies toward moving industry and industrial workers to outlying locations and restoring the city to city workers.

Not only is the Negro population of our cities increasing in numbers but housing for Negroes is becoming increasingly segregated. The question of segregation is always present when the character and location of public housing and urban renewal projects are being determined. An unwillingness to face up to it has paralyzed city planning. It is necessary to deal with the question not only for the sake of civil rights for Negroes but in order to free city planning from some unspoken assumptions that underlie almost everything that happens about housing in our cities.

Juvenile delinquency and adult crime, school drop-outs and unemployment, the spread of slums and the cost of welfare, are all related to segregation in the cores of our cities. The social and economic costs of these problem areas both to the Negro and to the community as a whole are enormous.

Some sociologists compare the urbanization of the migrant Negro from the rural South to the Americanization of the earlier waves of immigrants from Europe.[23] It is true that each new immigrant group settled at the center of our cities, often in slums, becoming part of the labor pool. Each

---

[23] Oscar Handlin, *The Newcomers*. Cambridge, Mass.: Harvard University Press, 1959. Cf. Charles Silberman, *Crisis in Black and White*. New York: Random House, 1964, 36–58.

worked its way up toward social and economic success despite the discrimination practiced by older and more established members of the community. It is true that the same cycle is also going on in the Negro community. But the process is slow, the numbers involved are large, and the rising discontent of the Negro people will not permit patterns of segregation to continue without increasingly severe upheaval.

Migrants from the rural South, whether they are Negro or white, come from a culture very different from that of urban America. The problems of educating their children so that they will be equipped to work in the modern world of science and automation are enormously compounded by cultural segregation. And because the ghetto has become so large, the problem has changed in character. Some of the students in Chicago high schools located in the midst of Negro neighborhoods have never been "downtown." Some have never seen a suburb. Their contact with the urban culture of the metropolis is limited to school and to television. Their culture is that of the rural Negro living in the city, a culture that cannot interact with the urban culture unless the two can come in contact. Under these circumstances education for Negro children is of primary importance. Yet the segregated school pattern will be very difficult to change wherever there is a substantial segregated Negro population within the boundaries of the city.[24] In Chicago, just as one example, more than 50 per cent of the children in the public grade schools are non-white.

The Negro ghettos will not dissolve of themselves. The middle-class Negro family has had great difficulty in finding suitable housing outside of the segregated lower-income neghborhoods; only very recently has housing for these and higher-income Negroes begun to open up. A policy of non-discrimination in rentals or sales can help, but the ghettos are still so large that only a major plan to induce a substantial part of the Negro working population to live in outlying "new towns" can bring about a more uniform and just distribution of these people among the population as a whole.

We should not underestimate the difficulties of creating interracial communities. Experience shows, however, that it is possible to create interracial housing in stable communities where the housing is sufficiently subsidized. New York's state-subsidized housing program has produced a number of interracial projects. Prairie Shores in Chicago, a successfully integrated housing project, demonstrates that racial antagonism recedes if the accommodations are "a bargain." It is easier to establish integrated housing in new developments than in areas that are already either all-white or all-Negro, but it is not necessary for every neighborhood in a "new town" to be interracial. If there is no policy of segregation, neighborhoods can develop by choice, as has happened in ethnic communities created by second-generation European immigrants.

The existence of heterogeneous communities in outlying areas will make

---

[24] See Philip Hauser, in *Chicago Perspective*, June 1964, 36.

it more possible for the Negro to relate to the urban culture. Schools in a smaller community, for example, can be so located that even if there are neighborhoods within the community that are predominantly white or predominantly Negro all of the children can attend the same schools. So many industrial workers are Negro that any program for creating outlying "new towns" for industry and industrial workers must aim for heterogeneity. As for the cities, where Negroes are already established, a program to bring back middle-income white families must encompass the creation of interracial middle-income neighborhoods. If America is not prepared to accept interracial communities, there is little hope of arresting the decline of the city.

The Value of City Land

There has been a tendency to assume that the flight to the suburbs means that people prefer a suburban home to a city home. But the ability to make a choice has not been possible since the 1920's when most of the land within the borders of every American city was built upon; the choice ever since has been between apartment living in the city and a house in the suburbs.

Land values are perhaps the best measure of what people prefer. The fact that residential land values in the city are everywhere substantially higher than in the suburbs shows how desirable central location is to most people. The amount of new construction of high-rise apartment buildings in the city indicates that some people with means are willing to pay more for apartments built at higher cost on more expensive land in the city than for houses built at lower cost on less expensive land in outlying areas, even if their choice means sending their children to private schools. Moreover, the current boom in suburban garden apartment developments suggests that when close-in suburban land for homes is scarce many people choose close-in suburban apartments rather than outlying homesites despite the subsidies available for the latter.

Central location still retains great economic value, and this is the best evidence that the city can be restored. Land value, in the end, is the measure of economic potential. Favorable economic forces do exist in the city, and therefore the restoration of middle-income communities in the city becomes a possibility. The task of restoring the city also becomes easier because large areas of relatively inexpensive industrial land are available in virtually every American city.[25] Most of these areas are centrally located, having been the sites of the early industries around which the city clustered. They are now often used for very low economic purposes, such as coal and lumber storage and no-longer-functional railroad yards. Many of the buildings in these industrial slums are dilapidated; some are aban-

---

[25] Vernon, *The Myth and Reality of Our Urban Problems*, 1961, 45–46.

doned. Several square miles of this type of land exist in Chicago along the south branch of the Chicago River and in the railroad yards south of the Loop. In Baltimore, the Baltimore & Ohio Railroad owns more than 150 acres of such land south of the Camden Station within a stone's throw of downtown. If new outlying communities are created, thereby increasing the total housing supply for people now living in city slums, the values of both residential and industrial slum property will decline and thus reduce the cost of acquiring this ill-used land for urban renewal.

Federal Subsidies Redirected

Only a slight extension of the tools already in hand is needed to foster the development of middle-income communities within the city and of "new towns" on the outskirts of suburbia. The Housing Community Development Act of 1964 (which was not enacted into law) proposed for the first time that the Federal Housing Administration insure mortgages for the purchase of land leading to the development of new communities. The Administration thus proposed to finance "new town" developments, although the result may well have been that under such a program the "new towns" would have become exclusive suburbs like many "new towns" now being built with private financing.

Assume, however, that FHA and VA financing were abandoned except in urban renewal areas in the city and in "new town" developments. In addition, assume that a regional open space and transportation plan were required before this financing is made available. Assume, further, that the regulations governing savings and loan associations were amended to allow them to allocate a substantial portion of their funds to financing mortgages for multiple dwellings, and to limit financing of either homes or multiple dwellings to established suburban areas, to the cities, or to "new towns," in regions where an open space and transportation plan exists. Moreover, suppose that the VA and FHA regulations prohibiting discrimination because of race were also applied to savings and loan associations. Suppose, in addition, that the FHA programs for middle-income housing (Section 221d3) were made available in the "new towns," so that the goal of an economically heterogeneous community would be vigorously pursued. Suppose, finally, that each "new town" were required to provide some minimum of public housing and housing for the elderly in order to be eligible for federal financing.

These federal tools, almost all of them readily adaptable, would be powerful inducements for the creation of heterogeneous "new towns" in which individuals and industry displaced from the city, together with some of the 80,000,000 new people to be housed between now and 1980, could be accommodated. Moreover, federal incentives could be geared to the creation of "new towns" of higher density so that effective mass transportation between them and the center city could be developed.

Assume that the federal urban renewal programs for clearing residential slums and renewing central business districts were extended to permit the clearance of industrial slums. And assume that the federal government were prepared to finance the construction of industrial facilities in "new town" industrial parks. Can there be any doubt that such a program would have enormous impact in hastening the creation of "new town" developments and in clearing land within the city for the construction of middle-income communities?

The large subsidies involved in public housing might also be used to encourage these developments. From the beginning public housing in the United States has always been intimately associated with welfare, but more than thirty years have now passed without any examination of this underlying premise. The question today might well be: Why should public housing subsidies be associated with welfare at all?

The defects of the public housing program result largely from the segregation practices of most cities and from the income limitations on the occupants. The result in most large cities has been to concentrate the lowest-income Negroes in these central city projects. As soon as a family exceeds the income limits, it is evicted. But if the income is still inadequate for a middle-class dwelling, the family often has to move into a slum dwelling. As long as our cities are not free from slums, the question may properly be asked whether the slums should be occupied by employed lower-income families or by people on public welfare.

This is not the place for a full exposition of the problems associated with public housing. The questions are raised, however, to show that if we were to make welfare payments for rent to persons needing shelter, and use the public housing program to build housing for industrial workers in "new town" developments, the resulting housing would be more in keeping with the needs of the city and the region.

London's "New Towns"

An approach similar to the one proposed here has been undertaken in England. The enormous urban population growth that is now occurring in the United States was anticipated in England some thirty years ago. London was the capital of an empire and its population crossed the million mark about 1800. The trend to the suburbs was already well under way in the 1920's; in the two decades before World War II the smaller ring around London gained 1,700,000 residents and the regional ring gained 5,900,000, while the county of London lost population.[26]

London's answer was the creation of "new towns." They were built beyond the greenbelt that had been established outside the suburban ring.

---

[26] Donald Foley, *Controlling London's Growth*. Berkeley: University of California Press, 1964, 9–10.

Occupants of the East End and industry resettled there. The program has been the subject of controversy, but it is now generally conceded that, on the whole, it has been successful; current criticism centers about errors in planning, lack of culture in the new towns, and other faults not directly pertinent here.[27] Although conditions in the United States are very different from those in England, and London's program cannot be imitated here, the establishment of "new towns" to accommodate economic expansion, population growth, and what the English call "over-spill" from the areas being cleared inside the city is a sound idea.

Regional Planning

It should be clear by now that I am proposing regional planning only in a most restricted sense. It is not necessary for public agencies to provide comprehensive master plans for each region, leaving no room for diversity created by private choices. Some planning, however, is necessary, particularly by the agencies responsible for water, sewer, and transportation because they must be able to project the future needs for public services of an ever-expanding population. In many places these agencies plan independently of each other, and the federal agencies that subsidize housing do no planning at all. What each region now needs is a plan covering all of the agencies already involved in the expenditure of public funds, which states where and when the public will spend its money for water systems, sanitary and storm sewers, highways and rapid mass transportation, and in what areas subsidies will be available for housing. Regional growth can thus be controlled, with private enterprise left to develop variety within the over-all framework of the plan.

The agencies that decide on the location of public buildings, such as federal office buildings and state college campuses, should also be involved in this planning, because where these buildings are placed greatly influences the direction of regional growth. The General Services Administration of the federal government, for example, has been seeking a site for a new United States Patent Office, to be built on the outskirts of Baltimore. The Urban Renewal Administration, on the other hand, has spent a great deal of federal money in renewing the central business district of Baltimore. It apparently had not occurred to anyone that building the Patent Office in downtown Baltimore might substantially help the downtown renewal process and that land might be available there. Fortunately, the situation may yet be rectified since the Baltimore & Ohio Railroad has offered a free site for the Patent Office on the undeveloped industrial land that it owns within a stone's throw of downtown Baltimore and of the commuter station between Baltimore and Washington. The location would have many advantages both for the Patent Office and for Baltimore's renewal process.

---

[27] John Madge, "The New Towns Program in Britain," *Journal of the American Institute of Planners*, Vol. XXVIII, No. 4, Nov. 1962, 208.

Real Estate Taxes

An essential part of this program is the clearance of industrial slums at the cores of most of America's cities. One of the major obstacles to this has been the reluctance of cities to lose industry for fear of further jeopardizing their real estate tax base. But industry is moving to the suburbs anyway, and the real estate tax structure of the city will have to be revised in any event. Real estate taxes in most places have already reached the limits of economic feasibility, representing 18 to 25 per cent of the gross rentals of residential properties. Assessments against property are still the major means by which cities collect taxes, and they have fallen behind in their share of the total tax dollar. In 1932 all cities collected $2,600,000,000 in taxes, all states collected $2,300,000,000, and the federal government collected only $2,000,000,000. By 1959 the cities had become poor relatives and collected only $11,000,000,000 compared to $20,000,000,000 by the states and $73,000,000,000 by the federal government.[28]

A case can be made that the wealth produced by the cities has been drained out by federal taxes and re-distributed first to agriculture, second to suburbia, and third to the cities. At the same time the welfare costs of the cities have increased their tax rates, so that what the federal government has contributed in the form of urban renewal has been taken away by the costs of municipal services. The cities must revise the methods by which they raise revenues, and a greater share of the cost to health, welfare, and education must be allocated to the federal government. The migration to the cities of rural Negroes, Southern whites, and Puerto Ricans is a national problem; the federal government should bear the tax burdens this has created.

Before state as well as federal power becomes available to solve the problems of real estate tax revision and regional planning, the now rural-dominated state legislatures must develop greater sympathy than they have exhibited for the problems of the city and region. The recent decisions of the United States Supreme Court on reapportionment give some hope that city and suburb may soon have more influence upon state legislatures in their dealings with urban problems.

Conclusion

Obviously, each city or each region has unique problems that require more specific solutions than a generalized paper like this can provide. Nevertheless, these proposals are not offered just as a panacea. We should bring suburban sprawl under control so that we can get better transportation, water and sewer control, and more open space, but a regional plan will

---

[28] Higby, *The Squeeze*, 1960, 31.

not necessarily produce a beautiful region. There is still much to learn about "new town" development, about the creation of communities in which the citizens can govern themselves and in which life is pleasant and interesting. Similarly, the restoration of middle-income families to the city does not automatically solve the financial problems of the city, nor will troubles in race relations disappear even if all communities are racially heterogeneous. We should not try to control too much. At best, we can give direction to economic and social forces already at work and seek to provide better communities in which people can create a variety of environments appropriate to their way of life.

It is possible to shape the character of our urban environment. The population explosion provides the opportunity and existing federal subsidies provide a means. If we deal realistically with segregation and with the sources of city revenues, we can create a more livable community. Public thinking and discussion can clarify what we value about urban life. If we know what kind of urban environment we want, the power and the tools to create it are at our disposal.

50 | How the Russians Plan Their Cities

ROBERT J. OSBORN

The Communist Manifesto of 1848, which called for a revolution of the proletariat, had very little to say about the way people would live after the revolution. Among the few fairly concrete recommendations made by Marx and Engels was that of "the gradual abolition of the distinction between town and country, by a more equitable distribution of the population over the countryside." This utopian counsel is the Manifesto's only mention of urban planning. If all Russians were as rigidly ideological in their thinking as some Americans suppose, surely their city planners would have made some effort to implement Marx's mandate. By now they could have had houses built all over the Siberian steppes. But instead they very sensibly reinterpreted the proposal, in the 1930's, to mean that country people should be given all possible urban conveniences, and also that there should be more new medium-sized cities and less growth of large cities.

This down-to-earth type of behavior on the part of Soviet planners is

SOURCE: *Trans-Action*, III (September–October, 1966), 25–30. Reprinted by permission from *Trans-Action* magazine, Washington University, St. Louis, Missouri.

misunderstood by some Western observers. In the capitalist democracies we are fond of a parlor game which can be called "Open versus Closed Societies." It consists of finding ideological rather than practical reasons for every Soviet action. The Russians are supposed to behave the way they do either because they are Communists, or, hopefully, because they are veering away from communism—never, by any chance, out of plain common sense.

Urban planning offers recent examples of both types of misconception. Since 1958 an officially approved unit of Soviet city organization has been called the "microdistrict." It is a self-contained residential neighborhood, in which anywhere between 5,000 and 20,000 people live in apartments grouped around shops, parks, and other common facilities. Microdistricts are designed for the convenience of their residents, and not for any kind of political control. But the impression still can be found in the West that they are a revival of the old "commune"—an attempt to break up family life and substitute for it communal existence and loyalties.

An opposite impression has arisen also. One interesting fact is that since the dismissal of Khrushchev there have been more favorable conditions for privately built housing, which has done something to relieve the acute shortage. Another fact is that Soviet architects have not hesitated to express admiration for American-type shopping centers. On evidence such as this, wishful thinkers foresee an increasing "privatization" of Soviet living circumstances.

To add to the confusion in the Western mind, the Russians play the ideological game too, by their own rules. Soviet theoretical writers dig around for ideological reasons to explain away anything which was once in favor but is now rejected. This includes most of the building done under Stalin. The heavy, ornate architecture of the Stalin period catered, no doubt, to nationalist pride as well as to the dictator's personal taste. There was never anything particularly Marxist about it, either correct or deviant, and its wedding-cake style has been called "Stalinist Gothic." The best known example is the 15-year-old building of Moscow State University. Another is the Soviet Army Theatre, constructed in the shape of the Red Army's five pointed star.

In 1955, largely for economic reasons, the Party opened a campaign against "architectural excesses" and in favor of plainer, cheaper building styles. Since that time a few Soviet architects, such as the late Vladimir Kucherenko, have felt obliged to explain the past sins of their colleagues in terms of a politically deviant "cult of the personality."

While there is doubtless truth in this accusation it is a mistake, both for the Russians and ourselves, to try to explain pre-1953 Russian architecture entirely in terms of Marxist ideology and distortions thereof. If there was a "Stalinist ideology" in this area it was mixed with Russian nationalism, which, at this time, favored grandiose architectural projects for the sake of domestic morale and also for display to the outside world. The

forces which produced these cannot be called "ideological" in any specifically Marxist sense any more than the philosophy underlying the Burnham
plan for Chicago at the turn of the century can be called an ideology. It
makes equally little sense to describe post-Stalin building in terms of a
trend "away from Marxist ideology" and "towards a more pragmatic approach." The most that can be said is that there have been changes in
some of the factors, social and economic as well as philosophical, underlying Soviet architecture and planning.

Practical vs. Classical

Most ideological interpretation and comparisons such as the above,
whether they come from Communist or capitalist sources, obscure the real
problems and trends in Soviet city development. These are similar in many
ways to problems in America, or any other industrialized country. Urban
planning in the Soviet Union has been left in the hands of professionals,
who are not rigidly bound by political theory or unduly subject to party
interference.

While studying Soviet city development at first hand, in 1963 and 1964,
I found the atmosphere in the planning field free and creative (whatever
may have been the case under Stalin). Russian planners and architects are
well informed about experimental work in different parts of the world and
willing to use ideas they find practical, irrespective of their source. Graduates of architecture schools have a good idea of what has been done, for
example, in the "new towns" around London and in the various Levittowns in this country.

Within the planning profession there is a wide variety of opinion and
taste. It is true that national economic priorities, in which civil construction must often give way to industrial production, place a premium on
plain, inexpensive designs, mass production techniques, and the use of pre-
fabricated panels and stereotyped layouts. This and nothing more sinister
is the reason why so much new city building in the Soviet Union is
monotonous. Less utilitarian designs are by no means taboo, though they
may draw criticism. Old-fashioned architects still prefer the ornate "Stalin-
ist-traditional" style, while others favor the "international-modern" trend.

Old and new ideas in planning are debated as hotly in Soviet circles as
anywhere else in the world. This is particularly so in experimental areas
such as new city design. Recently the Arctic city of Norilsk, built from
scratch on the 69th parallel, was visited by Canadian planners. The visitors
praised the technical skill shown in handling new problems, for example
in implanting nine-story structures in permanently frozen soil. But controversy erupted in the Soviet press. While no one criticized the enormous
engineering skill of the city's chief architect, he was taken to task by his
junior colleagues for his conventional "little Leningrad" layouts. He should,
they claimed, have exploited the city's freedom from planning traditions

by adapting style and technique to the arctic surroundings. According to the critics the "little Leningrad" concept, in this case, meant not only a traditional classical layout for the main thoroughfares and squares, but conventional residential districts instead of designs especially adapted to the extreme cold.

Marxism stresses the decisive impact of the environment on man. But city planners in Russia seem at present to be less ideological, in the sense of pursuing a social ideal through planning, than their Western counterparts. It was expected that the master plan for Moscow, the first of its kind to be designed by a Communist country, would be laden with Socialist theory. But the plan, when it finally came out in 1935, turned out to be merely a sensible compromise between the opposing ideas which planners call "urbanism" and "disurbanism." Both were in essence rejected, in favor of the preservation of historical Moscow, restriction of population and industrial growth, and decongestion of residential areas. The reconstruction plans for Moscow made by Frank Lloyd Wright and Le Corbusier were much more "ideological" than was the Communist version in the sense of an unswerving pursuit of a social philosophy.

There are signs that the planning profession is becoming uneasy about its lack of philosophical guidance. To quote from a recent statement by the director of the Institute for the Theory, History and Long Range Problems of Soviet Architecture:

It must be said, unfortunately, that we still have no rounded concept of the Communist city. There is a glaring deficiency in this branch of science. We should look at the Socialist city in its organic social, cultural and architectural unity. If we fail to do this it may be difficult for us, in the future to attain urban social unity.

There are two "ideological" but still very practical principles on which Soviet planners agree. They cannot see how successful urban growth is possible without, first, state ownership of land, and, secondly, centralized planning for its use. In the USSR both exist. But this does not prevent planners from having troubles similar, in many ways, to those in any industrialized economy. Americans who worry about trends toward centralized land use planning in the United States should take heart from the difficulties which surround both twenty-five-year "master plans" and seven-year "priority construction plans" in the Soviet Union. Often both have to be scrapped as soon as they are made.

Gosstroi, the Soviet central urban planning agency, is a powerful organization, responsible for a wide range of research and administrative functions. It has branches in all the fifteen republics, which enforce building norms as well as setting them. There is one Gosstroi division for civil construction and one for industry.

But its powers over industry are less than adequate. There are many other centralized agencies, as strong and stronger than Gosstroi, which decide the location of factories and other industrial facilities. Here is where the shoe pinches. The problems of enforcing city planning directives are not the fault of local government agencies, which can usually be brought into line. It is the central industrial ministries that can play havoc with harmonious city development. The American parallel is that of large corporations operating out of New York.

The main reason why Gosstroi is upstaged is that national economic priorities place industrial development ahead of residential building. Housing, in turn, comes before shops and other urban amenities. City planners must do the best they can to keep the situation in balance.

Here are a few examples of Gosstroi's problems. In the USSR, as elsewhere, industry is mainly interested in getting new factories into production as fast and cheaply as possible. City planning policy calls for the industrial development of small towns. One hundred of these are supposed to be built up industrially during the next few years. But agencies which control the location of new factories would far rather place them in large industrial cities, where railroad spurs and other utilities do not have to be specially built. At the moment this problem is being handled through a campaign to group new factories in complexes, where they can share utilities.

It is tempting to think that under a Communist system industries can be forced to consider community welfare, as well as their own long term needs. But this is not necessarily so. Soviet factories are often placed on river banks in the middle of cities, for convenient transportation and waste disposal. There they pollute the air and water and may find themselves boxed in when they want to expand. These same factories are supposed to use part of their "enterprise funds"—which are derived from planned enterprise profits—to build and maintain streets and other community facilities. But they often prefer to build "company towns" for their workers only.

Another planning headache is the unbalanced growth of residential areas. The building of shops and other necessary conveniences often lags behind new housing. There are various reasons for this. The main one is the priority for housing construction to relieve the housing shortage. Another cause is that most new building, so far, has been in large open areas on the edge of cities, where stereotyped layouts can be used over and over again. Since, in these locations, no schools or other facilities were being torn down there was no particular pressure to supply them at the same rate as housing. The situation is bound to change as Russian cities press up to the limits of their "green belts." An ever-larger proportion of construction will take place inside built up areas. Consequently there will be an even stronger demand for the preservation of existing urban values and conveniences. We may even see something similar to the zoning fights so common in American cities. Another hopeful sign is the popularity of the micodistrict idea, with its careful balance of housing with services and amenities.

How Big Is Too Big?

These are some of the difficulties Soviet city planners meet in trying to put over their ideas of sound urban development. Just what are these ideas, and how do they relate to the economy of the country, on the one hand, and the welfare of the city dweller, on the other?

City size is discussed a good deal. Opinion in the profession favors a moderate size, of somewhere between 100,000 and 300,000 in population. The reason is not dislike and disapproval of large cities such as we feel in America; a Harvard study (during the postwar period) of displaced persons from the USSR indicated that Soviet citizens identify readily with large groups. It is just that the planners have a general notion, which is now being questioned, that medium-sized towns are cleaner, more convenient, and cheaper to build and operate.

The "optimum size" concept may not be justified by economic realities. In the Soviet Union there are over 500 cities with less than 50,000 inhabitants. These are no bigger because there is no particular economic reason for them to grow. On the other hand there are larger industrial cities which refuse to stop growing, in spite of directives to the contrary. Several years ago the city of Kharkov passed the one million mark it was not supposed to reach until 1980. One of its understandably frustrated planners recently demanded the setting up of a special demographic institute to help local planning officials by making more accurate predictions of city growth.

Present efforts to control, or at least, predict city growth center around a concept called, in Soviet terminology, the "city forming factors." The population of a given city is supposed to be roughly three times as big as the work force of those employed in "city forming" occupations. These include all industry, commerce, research, and education of more than local importance. According to the formula, population growth will be in a three-to-one ratio to the number of such new jobs created over a given period. The proportion of workers to non-workers seems rather high, even allowing for all the working Soviet wives. But even if the figure used is dependable (it has been questioned), the behavior of industrial planners is not. New factories are placed by the concerns of central industrial agencies, not according to city planning directives. On the local level, many party and government officials add to the problem by lobbying for new factories as avidly as any American Chamber of Commerce.

The city planning profession may soon give up the whole idea of an "optimum size" for cities as unfruitful and impossible to enforce. One

Soviet geographer recently challenged the idea that large cities are in any way inferior to medium-sized and smaller ones. He pointed out that in territory with a large urban component, cities of all sizes are economically interdependent. None can be planned for and developed in isolation from each other or the surrounding territory. The future, he stated, does not lie with individual cities at all. It lies with the "urbanized region" in which industrial, recreational, and agricultural land uses will be mixed. He sees these regions developing as large cities leapfrog over their present green belts and invade, in a less dense form, the open countryside.

"Commune" or Community?

The above prediction sounds as if Marx's proposal for spreading out the population may yet come true. In the meantime, what do Soviet urban planners have in mind for those who still live in conventional cities? So far, among Soviet city planners, the microdistrict idea for internal city organization leads the field. Primitive misunderstandings about it persist in the West. It is thought that these self-contained residential neighborhoods are devices either for the administrative control of the residents or for compulsory communal living. The latter misconception dies hardest. Somewhere in our thinking there still lurks the notion that what the Old Bolsheviks really wanted was barracks living and common kitchens for everyone. But if the Old Bolsheviks wanted this, the New Bolsheviks certainly do not. The urban "commune," in the form of shared living, died once and for all over forty years ago. No one influential person, with the possible exception of the eminent economist Strumilin, has shown any desire to revive it.

Recently publicity was given in the Soviet press to the building of "hotel like" apartments without kitchens—no space for anything bigger than a hot plate. Immediately some Western observers jumped to the conclusion that Strumilin's ideas for communal dining were actually being tried. As it turned out there was no threat to family solidarity. The accommodations were for single people, a more comfortable version of the dormitories for young, single factory workers found in every Soviet city.

The other idea, that microdistricts have some king of police function, is equally wrong. Early last year I visited a microdistrict in Yaroslav which had been written up in the press as well run, thanks to the work of a committee of pensioners. I found it well run indeed, but as a neighborhood enjoying good committee work, not as an administrative unit. Microdistricts are meant to provide the framework for a large array of community services. However, these are strictly voluntary. Volunteers staff kindergartens and libraries and help the police keep order. But neither the microdistricts nor the larger residential districts into which they fit have any official function. Their boundaries do not coincide with administrative divisions, which are much bigger.

Families and the Urban Plan

Misunderstanding of the microdistrict (as well as of other Soviet institutions, such as boarding schools) is based, I believe, on confusion about the relationship between the Russian family and the state. There is no doubt that Soviet policy makers, as well as city planners, intend more meals to be eaten outside the home than is customary in the West. There is no doubt, likewise, that they intend more Soviet children to go to boarding school. Soviet mass media are always urging the citizen to give time to neighborhood organizations and be community conscious in general. But none of these facts necessarily mean that the state is trying to break up family life and substitute loyalty to state and community. In my own experience I have found almost nothing which smacks of state institutions snatching children from the hands of unwilling parents. The present picture is rather of parents trying, not always successfully, to find day care centers and other institutions which will help look after their children.

It is important to look at the whole picture in the light not only of present social conditions but of history, particularly the history of family life over the last fifty years. My impression of the Soviet family is not that of a once-stable institution presently being encroached on by the state. It began its existence during the social upheavals of the Revolution and Civil War. Later it suffered from the rapid industrialization of the 1930's, and still more from World War II. Conditions for decent family living have improved considerably since these hard years. But housing is still unbelievably crowded. A universal norm of nine square meters of floor space per person is still some years in the future. Urban families, for this and other reasons, are small—one or two children, as a rule, except in some predominantly non-Russian cities. To me it is not surprising that Soviet parents, especially the millions of working mothers, are more than willing to take advantage of the services offered in some microdistricts and planned for others. Soviet city planners should be commended for helping them to provide a better way of life for their families.

In the Soviet Union urban planners are conscientious professional architects, pragmatic in their social outlook, and occupied, as in other countries, with building design, land use patterns, city growth and urban amenities. In many of these areas their problems can realistically be compared with those of American city planners. Their aims and accomplishments deserve serious attention abroad. In this field, at least, there is no room for narrow judgments based on any "open versus closed society" dichotomy.

51 | Urban Development: An Introduction to the Theories of Lewis Mumford

MARVIN D. KOENIGSBERG

For over forty-five years Lewis Mumford has been writing on cities. He is America's foremost thinker on the history and dynamics of urban development, and in more than twenty books and hundreds of articles has dealt with the character of modern Western civilization as it is reflected through the urban form. This article attempts to assess briefly some of his major ideas through a discussion of his values, the men who have influenced him, and the limitations that his orientation have imposed upon his view of urban dynamics. He is a wide-ranging, complex thinker whose full intellectual dimensions can only be understood by a reading of his major works—*The Culture of Cities, Technics and Civilization,* and most importantly, *The City in History.*

The following pages may serve, however, as an introduction to his work.

Mumford's Value Orientation

Clearly Mumford's values play a great part in his attempts to assess the role of the city. These values are the cornerstones of his approach, not only to the contemporary scene, but to his interpretation of history. In effect, he has held up these values as his criteria for the *good* city. We can distinguish at least four major values that underlie his work.

1. *Private and Public Man:* Mumford asserts that the dimensions of life embrace contrasting states of experience; that just as man spends his life alternately awake and asleep, so is there a need for a round of activities that take in the requirements for rest and action, privacy and communion, withdrawal and return. These activities take diverse forms. Thus we have privacy in bed, privacy at home, an enclosed occupational life in the city, and their respective opposites—the public hall, the public street, the involvement in the public media of recreation and communications. The private and public spheres are both necessary to a full and creative life. For Mumford the greatness of the city is unrealized if conditions unduly favor one type of experience over another.

SOURCE: This article has been especially prepared for this volume.

2. *City and Country:* Allied to the first point is Mumford's estimate of the relative value of the city and country. He believes that all citizens should have in their earliest years an intimate contact with farm life, perhaps a "compulsory service," which would allow all individuals to extend their awareness of the world beyond the urban setting. Beyond this, the countryside refreshes the mind and body, though Mumford does not consider the rural way of life in any sense more desirable or more noble than city dwelling. For Mumford city and country are part of an ecological unity, which can be ignored only at the expense of one's physical and mental health.

3. *Community:* Mumford believes the city should be the place where the populace holds certain values in common, starting with a shared sense of the neighborhood in which they live. According to Mumford this sense of communality rarely has been found in large cities since the middle ages, when land was held in stewardship and trust for the entire population. Mumford holds that a community is formed when moral law takes precedence over private desires or individual whims. The high incidence of vandalism and public unconcern with the aesthetics of public property, safety and cleanliness indicate this absence of the communal spirit. It is the sense of community that gives full expression to what Mumford calls the *dialogue,* the open public involvement in the community for the good of all. It was the dialogue which originally made the city attractive, for in earliest times the sense of communion was established through religious meetings and trade centers. The church and the marketplace were the sites within which men held "dialogues" with their gods and with other men. When the city loses these functions, then there is a loss in fraternalization that is especially acute when property is no longer felt to be collectively held. For Mumford, cities operate most effectively when controlled publicly and where there is a high degree of public ownership. The "laissez-faire" economy is destructive to harmonious social organization and urban development.

4. *Organic Growth:* Fundamental to his concept of the good city is his belief that the city is in some way an organism. For Mumford, all organisms have limits of growth and expansion beyond which they cannot maintain themselves effectively. If these organic units go beyond their limits, they do so at the expense of their surroundings. By losing those aspects of their neighbor's activities that contributed to their own well-being, they adversely affect themselves. Thus, Mumford refers to Aristotle's notion of "controlled growth," which is also taken from an analogy in the organic world:

In every biological species, [Mumford writes] there is a limit to size . . . if a town is too small, no matter what its architectural pretensions or its legal status, it is still a village. If it overpasses the bounds of growth, absorbing more people than it can properly house, feed, govern, or educate, then it is no longer a city; for its ensuing disorganizations keeps it from carrying on a city's functions.[1]

Mumford seeks to extend the idea that there is a balance for each particular environment, including the cultural sphere. The concept is further expanded in his use of the term "organicism," by which he means:

. . . a whole complex of ideas and allusions, apart from the vertebral one, that of partaking of the nature of an organism, as distinct from a lifeless object, a system, a machine, or an abstraction. Among these ideas [are] those of vitality, rootedness, indigenousness; being part of a larger whole; adhesion to a place, a period, a culture; and finally—not least—traveling freely back and forth between the inner and the outer world, . . .[2]

Mumford does reject false biological analogies, such as those of Herbert Spencer, who pushed the comparison between societies and organisms to a point of defective conceptualization. The analogy is useful only when it points to parallel processes, reactions, and conditions without being a literal equation. Mumford is trying to specify an abstract concept, Culture, by referral to the concrete phenomenon, the city.

If the principles of organic growth and natural limits go unheeded then the city becomes oppressively overburdened according to Mumford. This happens in two types of city building which ignore space and size limitations. The first type is best exemplified by Baron Haussmann's design for Paris in the nineteenth century, where abstract patterns are forced upon natural forms; the second type is produced by architects, such as Le Corbusier, who impose their own ego-expressions as primary over human desires. Thus Mumford writes:

In designing Unity House, Le Corbusier betrayed the human contents to produce a monumental aesthetic effect. The result is an egocentric extravagance, as imposing as an Egyptian pyramid, which was meant to give immortality to a corpse, and—humanly speaking—as desolate.[3]

Closely related to the concept of organic growth (which concerns itself with population size) is that of urban scale, which concerns the physical size of the city and its individual structures.

For Mumford the size of an institution or a structure should be determined by the uses of the facility. Thus a city's size and makeup cannot be rigidly prescribed, as its functions and purposes can indicate a rather wide

---

[1] Mumford, *The City in History* (New York: Harcourt, Brace & Co., 1961).

[2] Mumford, "On the Dial," *The New York Review Of Books*, Vol. II, No. 1 (February 20, 1964), p. 4.

[3] Mumford, *The Highway and the City* (New York: Harcourt, Brace & Co., 1963), pp. 65–66.

range. Therefore, large, monumental planning is acceptable to Mumford if it is in accord with the primary human needs to which all urban building should be connected. Grandeur in and of itself is not to be rejected. Thus, as an example, Baroque planning, which is often thought of as ugly and decadent, was usually effective according to Mumford, "when it had most to contend with, in crowded neighboring buildings or irregular topography," but became overblown and vacuous when the city designer had "limitless resources and no human obstacles to overcome." [4]

For Mumford, the Greek city was a great example of the urban scale:

. . . being neither too small nor too big, neither too rich nor too poor, it kept the human personality from being dwarfed by its own collective products, whilst fully utilizing all the urban agents of cooperation and command.[5]

Sources of Influence

Industrialism was introduced to Europe at such a tempo that it was not possible, in such a brief and frenzied time, to design and construct livable communities. The technology of the nineteenth century, based as it was on coal, steam, and rail transportation, had the effect of encouraging the centralization of the factory. This resulted in urban centers growing faster and to a larger size than at any previous period in history. In Mumford's words:

If the history of the nineteenth century is . . . the history of an illness, that of the twentieth century might be called the story of a strange kind of medical care and treatment which sought to allay the symptoms, while sedulously maintaining all the agonizing conditions that caused the disease—and actually produced side reactions that were as bad as the disease.[6]

At the end of the nineteenth century the metropolitan area began to expand outward from the core city. Provisions for transportation, water, and traffic were seldom adequate. Politics became even more complicated as the overlapping metropolitan governmental units were overwhelmed with educational, social, and housing problems so difficult that they remain largely unresolved to the present day. It is against this background that Mumford has been writing and thinking about urban conditions. His scholarly investigations into the cities of the past are undertaken primarily as a key to his understanding of the present. The meaning of Mumford's work may also be examined by noting the men whose ideas influenced him most. With the exception of Aristotle, they were men who lived and

---

[4] *City in History*, Text Plate 27.

[5] *Ibid.*, p. 148.

[6] *Ibid.*, p. 469.

worked at the turn of the century. In 1961, in his book *The City in History*, which stands as the culmination of forty years' work, he was able to name just a handful of men who were able to grasp the total situation of urban phenomena as he understands it: "With a few exceptions, like Patrick Geddes, Peter Kropotkin, Ebenezer Howard, and Max Weber, one still looks in vain for fullness of understanding of the normal processes that the city furthers." [7]

Of these four men, Mumford has been critical generally only of Weber, whose outstanding work in the area of urban studies, *The City*, Mumford has evaluated as ". . . excellent for its day (1921) but no longer adequate as a general theory of the city." [8] Consequently, Weber is mentioned very occasionally by Mumford, and when he is it is as liable to be in criticism as in support.

The other three men, Kropotkin, Geddes, and Howard, have each contributed central themes to Mumford's ideas on urban development. In Kropotkin's emphasis on deconcentration, Geddes' over-all concern for regional planning, and Howard's advocacy of the Garden City, we can draw the main outlines of Mumford's position on city planning. These themes overlap to some extent; moreover other men contributed minor but important additions to Mumford's orientation. Indeed Mumford's own talent is not as an original thinker but as a superb synthesizer and developer of this essentially European tradition in urban studies. Mumford, as its leading proponent, has championed this tradition almost alone in America. Thus, in the following discussion, we touch upon not only Mumford's progenitors but in substance his own position as well.

Deconcentration

The utopian geographer and socialist Peter Kropotkin (1842–1921) has been singled out by Mumford for his sensitivity to the need of man to find expression and meaning in his work life and leisure time lest he be depersonalized and fragmented. This idea was shared by such Kropotkin contemporaries as Proudhon, Owen, and Marx. Mumford has emphasized two of Kropotkin's ideas based on this "full expression" theme: (1) the value of the small workshop (deconcentration) and (2) the need to break down the great division that has existed between country and city life.

Deconcentration was a central idea of Mumford and his associates in the Regional Planning Association of America, an organization that became active in the 1920's. One of the members of this association, Catherine Bauer, called the group the "Decentrists," in that the end result of the city planning idea that they were advocating would result in the decentraliza-

---

[7] *Ibid.*, p. 532.   [8] *Ibid.*, p. 631.

tion of cities and the dispersal of business enterprises and populations into smaller units.[9]

Kropotkin foresaw that with the advent of electric power, industry would be no longer tied to the coal mine or the railroad; thus it was no longer a matter of efficiency or economy to have centralized industrial production. Beyond the value of efficiency, he believed that the rapid transit system combined with mass communication would put the small community on a par with the overpopulated city, at least in its essential technical and social facilities. The once isolated small town communities, with their unskilled population and generally low cultural and economic levels, could benefit by the city's scientific knowledge, artistic enterprises, and cohesive formal organizations. Thus the distance, both physical and social, between the urban worker and the farmhand would be minimized. Mumford agrees: "With the small unit as a basis, he [Kropotkin] saw the opportunity for a more responsible and responsive local life, with greater scope for the human agents who were neglected and frustrated by mass organizations."[10]

Kropotkin was well known for his distrust of government, and he believed that its intervention in social affairs invariably spelled repression. His belief in self-government on an exclusively local level of administration was championed on the basis of his suspicion of existing order in all its forms. Kropotkin's anarchy was in reality a belief not in the absence of government but in a hostility towards the domination of the state. Mumford shares this distrust. When the late President Kennedy recommended setting up a new cabinet post, Secretary for Urban affairs, Mumford was against it, feeling that it would federalize decision-making about city planning and thus lead to conformity and standardization. For Mumford the region should be the unit of political action.

Regionalism

Mumford's ideas on regionalism stem from several sources. Lubove, in his study of the Regional Planning Association, credits Mumford with bringing the French regionalist movement of 1850–1860 to the attention of the association.[11] This movement stressed cultural and administrative decentralization. These "felibres," as they called themselves, devoted their attention to a revival of provincial medieval culture; they were in revolt against the French government, which since the revolution had tended to

---

[9] Cited in Jane Jacobs, *The Death and Life of Great American Cities* (New York: Random House, 1961), p. 20.

[10] *City in History*, p. 515.

[11] Roy Lubove, *Community Planning in the 1920's: The Contribution of the Regional Planning Association of America* (Pittsburgh: University of Pittsburgh Press, 1963), pp. 83–84.

become overwhelmingly centralized in administration and culture. This group started, Mumford notes, "the conscious beginning of a regionalist movement that has grown slowly but steadily ever since." [12] Mumford approves of this emphasis on the primacy of an autonomous regional life, as he approves of the principle of cultural autonomy.

Patrick Geddes emphasized the biological and sociological dimensions of regionalism rather than the cultural aspects, and Mumford has continuously acknowledged the great intellectual debt that he owes him. He has compared Geddes' knowledge of demography, civics, and government to Aristotle's; he believes that "no one in his generation probably knew more about urban development, as both historian and sociologist, than Geddes did . . . ." [13] In America, Mumford has been pretty much alone in carrying the torch for Geddesian principles, and is probably the only scholar who has extended his ideas. Mumford has been strongly affected by Geddes' reformist views and style of thought, though he tends to be more dogmatic and forceful in his statements and more attentive to the aesthetics of the city's environment.

Geddes was one of the most outstanding influences in applied sociology during the first quarter of the twentieth century. His impact in America was through his writings on community studies and his exhaustive survey of Edinburgh in 1886, which focused attention on slum problems. Geddes ". . . was one of the pioneers who sold to social workers and social reformers the idea of the need for a careful survey of a situation before proceeding with a reform effort." [14]

Perhaps the essence of Geddes' thinking can be summed up in his concept of *synthesis*, just as the core of his methods can be seen to be based on his belief in learning how to "look at" cities and how to evaluate their development. Geddes, like many city planners, was fascinated by the possibility of achieving a coordination of many fields of knowledge and their application to community living. One English architect said of him twenty-one years after his death in 1932:

[Geddes] . . . was always at war against the narrowing specialism of the scientists. He took all knowledge for his province, one of his chief aims being to promote a continous interchange between the isolated fields of thought. He was especially anxious to lay a sound basis for the social sciences, as well as to correlate sociological investigation with immediate social ends. Perhaps his greatest merit was that he transcended the merely scientific approach. He was passionately concerned with religion, with art, with history.[15]

---

[12] Mumford, *The Culture of Cities* (New York: Harcourt, Brace & Co., 1938), p. 350.

[13] Mumford, *The Human Prospect*, edited by Harry T. Moore and Karl W. Deutsch (Boston: Beacon Press, 1955), p. 113.

[14] M. C. Elmer, *Contemporary Social Thought* (Pittsburgh: University of Pittsburgh Press, 1956), p. 89.

[15] J. B. Coates, "Inspiration Is Not Enough," *The Fortnightly*, 179 (February 1953), p. 112.

These comments can be applied to Mumford. Not a word need be changed.

Central to Mumford's thinking is the concept of the Regional Survey, which Geddes has set forth as the culminating point of his work. In his various writings on the regional concept,[16] Mumford, building on Geddes, emphasizes two major features that a survey should involve. First, the observation of the activities of man and nature should be extensive and detailed. Knowledge is gained through direct experience. Second, is the historical dimension. The environment is not only seen in its spatial relationships but also in time relationships. Mumford considers the historical element as a much needed corrective to "unilateral and unitemporal thinking"; it is the feature distinguished from most other surveys that analyze specialized areas for city planning ends. The Geddes–Mumford survey concerns itself with all the details of man's life. Thus, "the knowledge of where people live, what they do, how they feel and express themselves, what types of association they form, in what realm their fantasies play . . ." [17]—all this constitutes the regional survey.

From the Regional Survey, and still following Geddes, Mumford discusses the *regional complex* as being composed of three distinctive qualities:

1. Its distinctive character, including its climate, soil, agriculture, and vegetation.

2. It's "balance," which is a condition of dynamic equilibrium of its various parts. "When any large alteration is made in one section of the environment," writes Mumford, "corresponding or compensating changes must be made, as a rule, in every other part." [18]

3. The absence of any definite physical boundaries. Mumford conceives of regions not as political units, e.g. Texas, but in terms of the communities that are found there. All boundaries are arbitrary. He defines a region not in terms of its periphery but of its centralizing nucleus. His explanation of this point sums up rather well his attitude toward the importance of cities in civilization:

. . . in human culture generally, the urban spheres of attraction become geographic facts of utmost importance: for the urban center tends to focus the flow of energies, men and goods that passes through a region, concentrating them, dispersing them, diverting them, re-routing them, in short, exerting a close and controlling influence over the development of region as a dynamic reality.[19]

Mumford's concept of regionalism leads to centralization as well as decentralization. The region is to be used as a planning unit which could

---

[16] *Culture of Cities*, pp. 307–355; "Regionalism and Irregionalism," *Sociological Review*, XIX (October 1927), pp. 277–288.

[17] Mumford, *Values for Survival* (New York: Harcourt, Brace & Co., 1946), p. 53.

[18] *Culture of Cities*, p. 312.   [19] *Ibid.*, p. 315.

build up old centers, break up overpopulated areas, and found new centers for social, commercial, and industrial purposes. The regional city is to be thought of as a process rather than as a fixed form. It is Mumford's intention that a symbiotic rather than a parasitic relationship will exist between the country and the city, with a balanced regional distribution of population, facilities, and social institutions. But as to specific dimensions or size he remains flexible, believing that no one particular size or type of city is to dominate a region. The place of work and the type of work decide the amount of concentration desired, from the village settled in the farming community to the regional center, which is "an area large enough to embrace a sufficient range of interests and small enough to keep these interests in focus and to make them a subject of direct collective concern." [20]

No region can dominate a nation either economically or culturally, according to Mumford, for there is no region rich enough or varied enough to supply all requirements of modern civilization. "What regionalism does aim at is a more even development of local resources: a development that does not gauge success purely by the limited financial profits obtained through a one-sided specialization." [21] Men misuse the resources of a region due to their bent for exploitation for profit. Economic planning should be undertaken completely. When the means of determining "for a given region and period, the norms of consumption in terms of food, clothing, recreation, education, and culture" [22] in addition to industrial and service needs are met, only then can the several functions reach maximum efficiency.

The alternative to regionalism is "conurbation," a term first coined by Geddes to describe the sprawl of factory, slum, suburb, and mill, which threatened to eat up all land and lead to the disappearance of the city itself. The modern city can scarcely serve the needs of its people, Mumford believes, for too much capital is spent on complicated, expensive facilities such as transportation, water supply, etc., which in turn encourages congestion by raising the value of land. The suburb destroyed the environs of the city and produced fragmented communities having neither the physical nor the social completeness of town life. So the suburb with its low density and incomplete cultural and economic life and the city with its overintense centralization are rejected by Mumford as suitable areas, for they both lack the essential economic and geographic balances.

Mumford's regional planning ideas are essentially those of Geddes; any regional plan should include a careful use of all land, widespread conservation programs, and attention to such pressing issues as water and air pollution and the avoidance of waste; it should include attention to "folk, work and place"; it should include *genuine* planning. The usual plan is undertaken by an institution, area, or civic entity, under its local jurisdiction, for its own internal activities. This is a contrivance, Mumford em-

[20] *Ibid.*, p. 314.   [21] *Ibid.*, p. 345.   [22] *Ibid.*, p. 347.

phasizes, to evade realities and avoid the responsibilities of action. Piecemeal planning has two disadvantages:

. . . a lack of understanding of the social meaning of the plan, and a failure to achieve co-ordination with other organizations, by dove-tailing, under a common authority, into a broader scheme for regional and inter-regional planning.[23]

Genuine planning is based on four stages: (1) Taking a survey of the land, (2) assessing the needs and activities of the people—both in terms of what purpose is to be served and what ideal is to be striven for, (3) a phase of "imaginative reconstruction and projection" in which dispersed and separate projects are seen in terms of their spatial and temporal interrelationships, and (4) a last stage in which the public is informed, involved, and absorbed by the plan, and the various economic and political agencies translate the proposals into action.

In discussing this fourth stage Mumford makes three specific organization suggestions, that is, ways in which to implement planning within a community:

First, the setting up of a special educational body, in an advisory capacity, which would be called the City Planning Council. This council would be made up of the major professional and occupational groups of the region.

Second, the establishment of a "Plan Director" who would be in charge of all issues regarding the survey, including architectural, economic, and engineering problems. The director would be the regional head, an appointed official, who would hold his post for at least ten years; this would give him time to show his ability without having pressures brought to bear that would induce him to try for premature effects. This would be the key position, because in Mumford's experience American cities have suffered from a lack of power on the part of those commissioned to expand the city's activities.

Third, he would set up a collaborating "Board of Public Works," consisting of the elected officials who would administer the various city departments. Their interest and sympathy are crucial.[24]

The regional plan requires all four stages for its development. In such a way the plan subsumes agricultural, industrial, and city planning under its aegis. Otherwise there is piecemeal or metropolitan planning, which tends to be mechanical and "inorganic" in its approach. The regionalism to which Mumford aspires to would satisfy Geddes' idea of synthesis and would result in the "conscious direction and collective integration of all those activities which rest upon the use of earth as site." [25]

---

[23] *Ibid.,* p. 375.
[24] Mumford, "Report on Honolulu," *City Development; Studies in Disintegration and Renewal* (New York: Harcourt, Brace and World, 1945).
[25] *Culture of Cities,* p. 374.

Garden Cities

Since the time of his earliest writings Mumford has been a partisan of the work of Sir Ebenezer Howard (1850–1928), the English stenographer turned city planner. In 1898 Howard published a book which set forth plans to arrest the further congestion of the English cities and particularly to set up "Garden Cities" around the periphery of London, thereby relieving the terrible slums that engulfed the working classes.[26] Each "city" would have agricultural and recreational space and a green belt circling the residential areas. But his ideas and actions went beyond a concern for open spaces and gardens. Howard sought to find, through his own experiments, the right size and form for efficient and pleasant living. He acquired some land, received the backing of a few wealthy and devoted disciples, and built his first city, Letchworth, in 1903. There was enough enthusiasm for the town for him to create another Garden City, Welwyn, in 1920.

For his efforts he was knighted, and at his death he was a much admired leader of an international movement devoted to his ideas. After the second world war England turned to his followers and instituted the New Towns Act, which was empowered to build cities along the Garden City model. As of 1966 there were at least nineteen New Towns in England as well as a scattering of them in the Scandinavian countries and the United States. They have been described by one commentator as ". . . comprehensively planned, self-sufficient new communities which offer their residents employment as well as pleasant dormitories in which to raise children." [27]

Mumford has championed two of Howard's ideas for more than forty years—the natural limits of growth and those physical features of city living which incorporate the best of the rural and urban environment.

Howard, who was dealing with the London slums primarily, placed his limit for a Garden City at 32,000 people; enough, he felt, to provide a variety of occupations and a fully developed social life. Mumford, though in basic agreement, felt the figure to be no more than a "shot in the dark."

Mumford wants the city large enough to provide "a stage upon which the drama of social life may be enacted, with the actors taking their turns as spectators and the spectators as actors." [28] Mumford advocates "in-between" densities. Specifically this means that he is against urban areas that have a density higher than two hundred to five hundred people per

---

[26] Ebenezer Howard, *Garden Cities of Tomorrow*, revised edition, (London: Faber and Faber, 1945).

[27] Wolf von Eckardt, "New Towns in America," *New Republic*, 149 No. 17 (October 26, 1963), p. 16.

[28] Mumford, quoted in Jane Jacobs' *Life and Death of Great American Cities* (New York: Random House, 1961), p. 211.

acre. Rather he wants to see housing ". . . that will permit parks and gardens as an integral part of the design, at densities not higher . . . at most . . . of 125 persons per acre." [29] That is his suggestion. But he is not rigid about the figures for it is still difficult to determine what an absolute size limit should be. Speaking about the New Towns being built in England he said in 1961:

No city is self-contained; . . . our problem is that of organizing the smaller units into larger units which will have all the resources of the city of 5,000,000 population. I believe that there are certain things in our civilization that need a basic population of 5,000,000 or 10,000,000 people. You cannot have a university unless you have a base of, at least, one million people . . . But they do not all have to live within the same contiguous built-up area.[30]

In 1928 two associates of Mumford, Henry Wright and Clarence Stein, built Radburn, New Jersey, as an example of the ideas that they wanted realized as a result of their activity in the Regional Planning Association of America and the influence of Ebenezer Howard. It was their belief, shared by Mumford, that the most effective way of dealing with population increase and city congestion would be to build new cities which would form "town clusters" that could carry on the traditional functions of the metropolis without destroying the recreational spaces and the rural flavor of the adjoining countryside. Mumford considers the building of Radburn as a serious innovation in city planning in the United States.

The Radburn plan (which had been preceded by Stein and Wright's Sunnyside Gardens in Long Island) introduced, according to Mumford, three important qualities at once—the superblock, the continous park belt, and a distinct separation of the domestic neighborhood from vehicular traffic.

The basic unit of Radburn is not the street but the superblock, which is a series of dead-end streets that end in a public park, surrounded by avenues for wheeled traffic. The commercial establishments are also segregated from domestic residence and the green areas. Implied in this plan is the belief that the street is an unnecessary feature of city structure and gives advantages only to the real estate interests that value land by the amount of front footage that is available. Mumford has always been critical of the street as being used for commercial exploitation. "The rectangular street and block system, projectable indefinitely toward the horizon, [is] the universal expression of capitalistic fantasies." [31]

Another principle that Radburn illustrated was that of the organization of the domestic neighborhood around a community center. Mumford would like to see community centers embodying the settlement house tradition established in every neighborhood. This was done in Radburn.

---

[29] *Ibid.*,
[30] Mumford, "The City as Both Heaven and Hell," *The Listener*, (September 28, 1961), p. 465.
[31] *Culture of Cities*, p. 188.

As a place for debate, social action, education, and cultural occasions—not unlike the Hull House of Jane Addams in Chicago—the community center, Mumford feels, could restore with modern concepts and facilities one of the oldest features of the city, the *quarter*. The community center in Radburn restores self-direction and initiative to the local group. It is capable of being:

. . . a challenge to partisan loyalties, one-sided decisions and remote control. Once established, the community center might launch out in many directions . . . forming a center for the spiritual and cultural life of the neighborhood, as the church had once done.[32]

Mumford strongly advocates easy accessibility to schools and playgrounds, commercial areas and work centers. He particularly likes Radburn because it makes all community needs (except for places of work) easily available within walking distance. "Distance has an effect similar to density in breaking down associated life," so that there is, Mumford believes, a basic need for "spatial nearness for all primary forms of intercourse." [33]

The third principle that Radburn displays is in its separation of the highway from the local roads and streets. The pedestrian paths and the vehicular roads form two independent systems separated by a neighborhood park where a "ribbon of green" unites the superblocks. Thus Radburn has two features that are designed to deal with leisure activities and transportation—the neighborhood park and the separation of modes of traffic. In reconciling safety and traffic with pleasant living conditions Mumford considers this town to be a unique and important experiment in applied sociology.

Radburn differs from the English New Towns in one important matter. Neither industry nor local business took root in Radburn, and the economic base is located in nearby New York City. It has also appealed to an essentially middle-class group, and since its founding in 1929 the class basis has remained the same. Though it failed to materialize as a New Town and was an economic disaster in its early years (largely due to the depression), it became, especially after the second world war, a popular place to live. A present-day estimate of the town was written by sociologist Alvin Boskoff:

[Radburn demonstrated] that suitable, orderly neighborhoods could be achieved without the drab uniformity of "packaged" suburbs, and yet with adequate provision for future growth. It is no surprise, then, that the essentials of Radburn are already "classic" and that several European cities have adopted these features in constructing extensive additions to established communities.[34]

Mumford believes that his ideas on regionalism have not become popular whereas the Garden City idea has, as is seen in the work of Stein

---

[32] *City in History*, p. 501.
[33] *Ibid.*, p. 251.
[34] Alvin Boskoff, *The Sociology of Urban Regions* (New York: Appleton-Century-Crofts, 1962), p. 355.

and Wright in the United States and the New Towns program in England. . . . As he said in 1961:

Regional rehabilitation really demands a more fundamental change in our whole culture . . . And one does not expect such a change to be effected within a single generation. After all, the garden city idea has been in existence for over fifty years and is only just coming to the beginnings of a fruition.[35]

The Garden City movement has been growing, to the point where nineteen New Towns have already been built in England and many more are in the planning stages. And they have been generally well received. They were built as a magnet—to draw people and business away from London and the other heavily congested cities of England. London is an area that covers 17 per cent of Britain's land mass while it contains one third of the nation's population. As the population continues to grow, Mumford believes, many more towns will have to be built. It is also his hope that the older small towns could be enlarged gradually "until it becomes a balanced community of a larger area and a larger population which in turn will have to be related to other such communities in a new kind of regional pattern." [36]

Basically he is satisfied with the New Town development. In speaking of the towns that were built in England after the second world war he found them "strikingly successful":

In many of their factory precincts, and in some of their new town centers, they vie with Coventry, Rotterdam . . . in delineating the beginning of a fresh urban form. Already nearly 500,000 people live in these salubrious towns planned to contain from 15,000 to 19,000 people each.[37]

Radburn, Sunnyside, the Greenbelt towns and similar programs of Mumford's have had much less influence in the United States. Isolated elements, such as the superblock, have been incorporated in much recent building but the total complex of open space and public facilities Mumford envisioned has rarely been attempted. A major reason is that, unlike Great Britain, Holland, or Sweden, American building is carried out and managed by a combination of private corporations and, to a much lesser extent, the federal government and numerous local and state governments. Under these conditions it is very difficult to form and implement an overall plan, such as the New Towns program.

Mumford's Critics

In Mumford's writings it is clear how much of a moralist he is, for he editorializes historical events and personalities in terms of his own values. Mumford defends the value-laden approach as proper to his analysis:

---

[35] "The City as Both Heaven and Hell," *op. cit.*, p. 470.
[36] *Ibid.*, p. 471.
[37] Mumford, "The Future of the City," *Architectural Record*, Vol. 133, No. 2 (February 1963), p. 119.

Since value is integral to all human experience, a theory that eliminates value as a primary ingredient inevitably smuggles it back again by making sensations or impulses, as such, the seat of value; whereas value comes into existence through man's primordial need to distinguish between life-maintaining and life destroying processes, and to distribute his interests and his energies accordingly.[38]

This statement in itself would probably be acceptable to most historians. The great question would be what the particular values were for each age. Mumford is unconcerned with this issue, for he uses his values as a yardstick. He attributes the decline of past civilizations to the failures of their societies to uphold a set of values that are his.

Two areas can be singled out where Mumford shows apparent bias. First, he tends to favor certain epochs over others on the basis of his predilection for the type of cities they had. A well-knit, aesthetically pleasing urban environment tends to produce a more defensible way of life, for Mumford, in the economic, religious, and political areas. This has prompted Wayne Andrews, the author of an outstanding volume on American architecture, to feel that there is a "moral fallacy" in Mumford's historical evaluation.

Even though there is no evidence that the most beautiful building in the world . . . has improved anyone's morals, this has not stopped certain modern critics from suggesting that more than one problem could be solved on the drafting board. Lewis Mumford for instance, refers to the modern American kitchen as "the moral flower of that long discipline of the spirit which Western man has undertaken during the last millennium under the forms of monasticism, militarism and mechanism." [39]

Thus Mumford tends to minimize the favorable developments in Baroque times while he attacks the corruptive influence of the power state and mercantile capitalism. The urban sociologist Gideon Sjoberg feels that Mumford's tendency to "invoke the past to evaluate the present, and to dream about the future, is ineffective." [40] Sjoberg is suspicious about Mumford's almost idyllic medieval city, as is Paul Goodman, who is more forgiving about the "amiable" bias Mumford displays:

In his enthusiasm for their integral planning, he overlooks the cruelty and superstition of medieval towns; and he attacks the forcefully imposed rationalism of the Baroque as if it were not the age of Spinoza and Galileo; but in such cases he is obviously righting unbalanced judgments current in his youth.[41]

---

[38] Mumford, *The Condition of Man* (New York: Harcourt, Brace & Co., 1944), p. 270.

[39] Wayne Andrews, *Architecture, Ambition and Americans* (New York: Harper and Brothers, 1947), p. 253.

[40] Book review of *The City in History*, *Annals of the American Academy*, (September 1961), p. 214.

[41] Paul Goodman, "The Pragmatism of His Boyhood," *The Hudson Review*, XIV, No. 3 (Autumn, 1961), p. 445.

Another serious charge against Mumford is that he has a strong anti-urban bias that blinds him to the virtues of the metropolis. That he has lived most of his adult life in Amenia, a small town in upstate New York, only serves to confirm that impression. Thus Herbert Muller and Stanley Tankel feel that his view is valuable because it represents the opinion of an essentially nonurban temperament. Tankel feels that Mumford has gone so far in this bias that

Positive statements very much to the point are often contradicted by a growing undercurrent of resentment toward cities. This culminates in the invoking of elements of Ebenezer Howard and the Garden City movement which are out of scale with contemporary needs and even with the spirit of urbanization in Mumford's own terms.[42]

Mumford believes cities are influenced decisively by a small but differently composed group in each historical epoch. This group—be they priests, kings, financiers, dictators, or industrialists—is responsible for the evils of city life, for they have been manipulators interested in selfish ends. The people suffer from their abusive policies. Yet Mumford is aware that the "insensate industrial town" is not entirely the work of the capitalists, for the gas stations, hot dog stands, and the rest of the blight that lines the highways are there to serve the people's needs. If the people did not want them they would not be there. Crane Brinton feels that Mumford looks for "a series of personal devils, the designing, wicked few who . . . rule the earth" as a reason for the evils of mankind rather than to the general population itself, for Mumford's humanistic credo binds him to certain solutions. Thus Brinton writes:

He cannot explain [ugliness, cruelty, suffering and other evil] . . . by any Christian answer to the problem of evil, nor can he, as an egalitarian and lover of his fellow men, explain it by anything deeply rooted in ordinary human beings . . . as he looks back at history he sees a long line of villains insuring that Wrong shall be forever on the throne, that Right shall occupy its somewhat uncomfortable permanent post on the scaffold.[43]

Mumford acknowledges that he has approached the present-day city in an extremely negative manner. But he feels that there is a good reason why he has harped on the disintegration of urban life today:

. . . only those who are aware of [the disintegrations] will be capable of directing our collective energies into more constructive processes . . . No small part of the urban reform and correction that has gone on these last hundred years, and not least this last generation . . . has only continued in super-

---

[42] Stanley Tankel, book review of *The City in History*, *Architectural Forum*, 114 No. 6 (June 1961), p. 173.

[43] Crane Brinton, "Urban Jungles," *The Saturday Review*, XVII, No. 25 (April 16, 1938), p. 6.

ficially new forms the same purposeless concentration and organic de-building that prompted the remedy.[44]

Thus Mumford finds fault with much, if not most, of the urban "solutions" of slum clearance, suburban expansion, urban renewal, model housing, and civic building splendor (such as a Lincoln Center in New York). A piecemeal approach to the city will result in futility. Only a large-scale searching attack will awaken people to the serious condition of the urban situation.

Conclusion

Lewis Mumford's career, though fluctuating in emphasis and mood, has revealed a fundamental attachment to certain basic values. He has been primarily the moralist, and his interest in the development, structure, and process of urban forms has been subordinated to his concern for the ethical values involved in modern city life. Thus his concern about the importance of the individual within the community has underlain his rejection of political and social absolution, his distrust of concentrated power, and his disapproval of an unchecked and laissez-faire economic system. His goals, stated in his earliest writings and up to the present, have remained constant, and he has scarcely changed their rationale in the intervening years. These values emerged from nineteenth-century pragmatic Utopianism and from romantic and transcendental sources.

Mumford's own values are sometimes in conflict. For example, he believes strongly in the democratic community and has been forthright in his denunciation of modern totalitarian regimes. Yet many of the cities that he most admires as being built for maximum beauty and usefulness were constructed under the direction of great authoritarian leaders or by elitist interests. Greek cities were ruled by less than one-eighth of the population, while medieval cities were dominated by the Church and the nobility, and the Dutch and Italian cities of the Renaissance were the products of powerful and small commercial groups. Even the New Towns in England, which represent the best expression of most of Mumford's ideas on city planning, are directed by autonomous public authorities; that is, ". . . public bodies of experts, irrevocably given a good deal of power, and largely immunized from the intense pressures of community opinion . . ." [45] Is there not in Mumford a profound conflict between the democratic expression of a society and the enlightened planners and humanists whose values do in fact collide with the popular will?

---

[44] *City in History*, p. 560.

[45] Eugene and Edna Rostow, "Law, City Planning, and Social Action," *The Urban Condition*, Leonard Duhl, editor (New York: Basic Books, 1963), p. 368.

Selected Bibliography

This bibliography is intended for students who wish further information on comparative urban development and is divided into five parts corresponding to the parts of the reader. It is limited to works in English, most of which will be found in college libraries. It does not include books and articles from which materials have been reprinted in this reader. Generally a work is listed only once in the bibliography. Since many works cover several topics, students are urged to consult the citations under other sections of the bibliography, especially checking for citations to collections of articles, special issues of journals, etc. Students are also advised to consult the chapter bibliographies in Gist and Fava, *Urban Society*, which are organized under the same major headings as this bibliography and which contain many relevant items for comparative study. The bibliographies were designed for a minimum of overlap.

Urban Theory in Comparative View

ABU-LUGHOD, JANET, "Urban-Rural Differences as a Function of the Demographic Transition: Egyptian Data." *American Journal of Sociology*, LXIX (March, 1964), 476–90.

AMERICAN SOCIETY FOR PUBLIC ADMINISTRATION, Comparative Administration Group. *Comparative Urban Development: An Annotated Bibliography*. Compiled by William Bicker, David Brown, Herbert Malakoff, William J. Gore. Papers in Comparative Public Administration, Special Series no. 5, Washington, D.C., 1965.

ANDRESKI, STANISLAV, *The Uses of Comparative Sociology*. Berkeley: University of California Press, 1965.

ARENSBERG, CONRAD, "A Comparative Analysis of Culture and Community," in Arensberg and S. T. Kimball (eds.), *Culture and Community*. New York: Harcourt, Brace and World, 1965.

BLACK, C. E., *The Dynamics of Modernization: A Study in Comparative History*. New York: Harper and Row, 1966.

BRAIDWOOD, ROBERT, and GORDON WILLEY (eds.), *Courses Toward Urban Life*. Chicago: Aldine, 1962.

BREESE, GERALD, *Urbanization in Newly Developing Countries*. Englewood Cliffs, N.J.: Prentice-Hall, 1966.

CAHNMAN, WERNER J., "The Historical Sociology of Cities: A Critical Review," *Social Forces*, XLV (December, 1966), 155–62.

COE, MICHAEL D., "A Model of Ancient Community Structure in the Maya Lowlands," *Southwestern Journal of Anthropology*, XXI (Summer, 1965), 97–114.

COX, OLIVER C., "The Preindustrial City Reconsidered," *The Sociological Quarterly*, V (Spring, 1964), 133–44.

DURAND, JOHN, and C. PELAEZ, "Patterns of Urbanization in Latin America," *Milbank Memorial Fund Quarterly*, XLIII (October, 1965), pt. 2, 166–96.

ELDREDGE, H. WENTWORTH (ed.), *Taming Megalopolis*. 2 vols. New York: Doubleday, 1967.

FAVA, SYLVIA F., "Suburbanism as a Way of Life," *American Sociological Review*, XXI (February, 1956), 34–37.

———, "Recent Books in the Urban Field—An Essay Review," *Social Problems*, XIV (Summer, 1966), 93–104.

FRANK, ANDREW G., "Urban Poverty in Latin America," *Studies in Comparative International Development*, II, 5, Social Science Institute, Washington University, St. Louis, 1966.

FREEDMAN, RONALD (ed.), *Population: The Vital Revolution*. New York: Doubleday Anchor Books, 1964.

GADD, C. J., "The Cities of Babylonia," *Cambridge Ancient History*, vol. I, chap. 13, (fasc. no. 9), 1962.

GOTTMANN, JEAN, *Megalopolis: The Urbanized Northeastern Seaboard of the United States*. New York: Twentieth Century Fund, 1961.

GREER, SCOTT, *New Urbanization*. New York: St. Martin's Press, 1968.

GUSFIELD, JOSEPH R., "Tradition and Modernity: Misplaced Polarities in the Study of Social Change" (India), *American Journal of Sociology*, LXXII (January, 1967), 351–62.

GUTMAN, ROBERT, and DAVID POPENOE (eds.), "Urban Studies: Present Trends and Future Prospects in an Emerging Academic Field," *American Behavioral Scientist*, VI (February, 1963), 4–62.

HANSSEN, B., "Urban Activity, Urban People and Urban Environment in Scandinavian History," *International Journal of Comparative Sociology*, IV (September, 1963).

HARRIS, DAVID R., "New Light on Plant Domestication and the Origins of Agriculture: A Review," *The Geographical Review*, LVII (January, 1967), 90–107.

HAUSER, PHILIP M., *Population Perspectives*. New Brunswick, N. J.: Rutgers University Press, 1960.

——— (ed.), *Urbanization in Asia and the Far East*. UNESCO Tensions and Society Series, 1958.

——— (ed.), *Urbanization in Latin America*. UNESCO Tensions and Society Series, 1961.

HOYT, HOMER, "The Growth of Cities from 1800 to 1960 and Forecasts to Year 2000," *Land Economics*, XXXIX (May, 1963), 167–73.

INTERNATIONAL AFRICAN INSTITUTE (London), *Social Implications of Industrialization and Urbanization in Africa South of the Sahara*. UNESCO Tensions and Society Series, 1956.

INTERNATIONAL URBAN RESEARCH, *The World's Metropolitan Areas*. Berkeley: University of California Press, 1959.

KUPER, HILDA, *Urbanization and Migration in West Africa*. Berkeley: University of California Press, 1965.

LIPSET, S. M., *The First New Nation: The United States in Comparative Perspective*. New York: Doubleday Anchor Books, 1967.

LORENZ, ROBERT, PAUL MEADOWS, and W. BLOOMBERG, A *World of Cities: A Cross-Cultural Urban Bibliography*. Publication no. 12. Prepared for the Cross-Cultural Project. Syracuse, N. Y.: Center for Overseas Research, Maxwell Graduate School, Syracuse University, 1964.

LUBOVE, ROY, "The Urbanization Process: An Approach to Historical Research," *Journal of the American Institute of Planners*, XXXIII (January, 1967), 33–38.

MC KELVEY, BLAKE, *The Urbanization of America, 1860–1915*. New Brunswick, N. J.: Rutgers University Press, 1963.

MANN, PETER H., *An Approach to Urban Sociology*. London: Routledge and Kegan Paul, 1965.

MARSH, ROBERT M., *Comparative Sociology*. New York: Harcourt, Brace and World, 1968.

MERRITT, RICHARD C., and STEIN ROKKAN, *Comparing Nations: The Use of Quantitative Data in Cross-National Research*. New Haven, Conn.: Yale University Press, 1966.

MINER, HORACE (ed.), *The City in Modern Africa*. New York: Praeger, 1967.

MURVAR, V., "Some Tentative Modifications of Weber's Typology: Occidental versus Oriental City," *Social Forces*, XLIV (March, 1966), 381–89.

OPPENHEIM, A. LEO, *Ancient Mesopotamia: Portrait of a Dead Civilization*. Chicago: University of Chicago Press, 1964.

PICKARD, J., "Future Growth of Major United States Urban Regions," *Urban Land*, XXVI (February, 1967).

SIMMS, RUTH P., *Urbanization in West Africa: A Review of Current Literature*. Evanston, Ill.: Northwestern University Press, 1965.

SJOBERG, GIDEON, "Comparative Urban Sociology," in R. K. Merton, L. Broom, and L. S. Cottrell (eds.), *Sociology Today*. New York: Basic Books, 1959.

———, "The Rural-Urban Dimension in Preindustrial, Transitional and Industrial Society," in R. E. L. Faris (ed.), *Handbook of Sociology*, Chicago: Rand McNally, 1964.

———, " 'Folk' and 'Feudal' Societies," *American Journal of Sociology,* LVIII (November, 1952), 231–40.

———, *The Preindustrial City.* New York: The Free Press of Glencoe, 1960.

SMITH, ROBERT J., "Preindustrial Urbanism in Japan: A Consideration of Multiple Traditions in a Feudal Society," *Economic Development and Cultural Change,* IX (October, 1960), pt. II, 241–57.

SMITH, T. LYNN, "Urbanization in Latin America," *International Journal of Comparative Sociology,* IV (September, 1963), 227–42.

STEWARD, J., "Cultural Causality and Law: A Trial Formulation of the Development of Early Civilizations," *American Anthropologist,* LI (January-March, 1949), 1–27.

TAEUBER, IRENE, "Urbanization and Population Change in the Development of Modern Japan," *Economic Development and Cultural Change,* IX (October, 1960), pt. II, 1–28.

TURNER, ROY (ed.), *India's Urban Future.* Berkeley: University of California Press, 1962.

UNITED NATIONS DEPARTMENT OF ECONOMIC AND SOCIAL AFFAIRS, *Migration, Urbanization, Economic Development.* Volume IV of the Proceedings of the World Population Conference, 1965. New York: UNESCO Publications Center, 1967.

"Urbanism and Urbanization," *International Journal of Comparative Sociology,* XIV (September, 1963), 99–273.

WEBER, MAX, *The City.* Trans. Don Martindale and Gertrud Neuwirth. New York: The Free Press of Glencoe, 1958.

WESTERGAARD, JOHN H., "Scandinavian Urbanism: A Survey of Trends and Themes in Urban Social Research in Sweden, Norway, and Denmark," *Acta Sociologica,* VIII (1965), 304–23.

WILKINSON, T. O., "A Functional Classification of Japanese Cities: 1920–1955," *Demography,* I no. 1 (1964), 177–86.

WIRTH, LOUIS, *On Cities and Social Life: Selected Papers.* Ed. and with an introduction by Albert J. Reiss, Jr. Chicago: University of Chicago Press, 1964.

———, *Community Life and Social Policy: Selected Papers by Louis Wirth.* ed. Elizabeth Wirth Marvick and Albert J. Reiss, Jr. Chicago: University of Chicago Press, 1956.

YOUNG, FRANK, and RUTH YOUNG, "The Sequence and Direction of Community Growth: A Cross-Cultural Generalization," *Rural Sociology,* XXVII (December, 1962), 374–87.

Urban Ecological Patterns Reviewed

ABU-LUGHOD, JANET, "Tale of Two Cities: The Origins of Modern Cairo," *Comparative Studies in Society and History,* VII (July, 1965), 429–57.

BERGEL, EGON, "The Patterns of Two World Cities: Manhattan, New York and Paris, France," *Urban Sociology*. New York: McGraw-Hill, 1955.

BERGER, MORROE (ed.), *The New Metropolis in the Arab World*. Sponsored by Congress for Cultural Freedom. New Delhi and New York: Allied Publishers, 1963.

BOGUE, DONALD J., *Skid Row in American Cities*. Chicago: University of Chicago Press, 1963.

BURGESS, ERNEST W., and DONALD BOGUE (eds.), *Contributions to Urban Sociology*. Chicago: University of Chicago Press, 1963.

CAPLOW, THEODORE, SHELDON STRYKER, and SAMUEL E. WALLACE, *The Urban Ambiance: A Study of San Juan, Puerto Rico*. Totowa, N. J.: Bedminster Press, 1964.

CHANG, SEN-DOU, "Peking: The Growing Metropolis of Communist China," *Geographical Review*, LV (July, 1965), 313–27.

DARLING, F. FRASER, and JOHN P. MILTON (eds.), *Future Environments of North America*. Garden City, N. Y.: The Natural History Press, 1966.

DEAKIN, NICHOLAS, "Residential Segregation in Britain: A Comparative Note," *Race*, VI (July, 1964), 18–26.

EDWARDS, G. FRANKLIN, "Community and Class Realities: The Ordeal of Change," in Talcott Parsons and Kenneth Clark (eds.), *The Negro American*. Boston: Houghton Mifflin, 1966.

EBERHARD, W., "Data on the Structure of the Chinese City in the Preindustrial Period," *Economic Development and Cultural Change*, IV (1955–1956).

EWALD, WILLIAM R. (ed.), *Environment for Man: The Next Fifty Years*. Bloomington, Ind.: Indiana University Press, 1967.

FARIS, ROBERT E. L., *Chicago Sociology 1920–1932*. San Francisco: Chandler, 1967.

GREY, ARTHUR L., JR., "Los Angeles: Urban Prototype," *Land Economics*, XXXV (August, 1959), 232–42.

GRIER, EUNICE, and GEORGE GRIER, "Equality and Beyond: Housing Segregation in the Great Society," in Talcott Parsons and Kenneth Clark (eds.), *The Negro American*. Boston: Houghton Mifflin, 1966.

GRIFFIN, DONALD, and R. PRESTON, "A Restatement of the 'Transition Zone' Concept," *Annals of the Association of American Geographers*, LVI (June, 1966), 339–50.

HALL, PETER, *The World Cities*. New York: World University Library, McGraw-Hill, 1966.

HANDLIN, OSCAR, *The Newcomers: Negroes and Puerto Ricans in a Changing Metropolis*. Cambridge, Mass.: Harvard University Press, 1959.

HERBERT, D. T., "Social Area Analysis: A British Study," *Urban Studies*, IV (February, 1967), 41–60.

HOYT, HOMER, *According to Hoyt 1916–1966*. Fifty Years of Homer Hoyt: Articles on Law, Real Estate Cycle, Economic Base, Sector Theory, Shopping Centers, Urban Growth. Distributed by Homer Hoyt, Washington, D. C., 1967.

JONES, EMRYS, "Preindustrial Cities," *Towns and Cities*. Opus 13, Oxford University Series, New York: Oxford University Press, 1966.

KATES, R. W., and J. F. WOHLWILL (eds.), "Man's Response to the Physical Environment," *Journal of Social Issues*, XXII (October, 1966).

KEYFITZ, NATHAN, "The Ecology of Indonesian Cities," *American Journal of Sociology*, LXVI (January, 1961), 348–54.

LIEBERSON, STANLEY, *Ethnic Patterns in American Cities*. New York: The Free Press of Glencoe, 1963.

MABOGUNJE, AKIN, "The Growth of Residential Districts in Ibadan," *Geographical Review*, LII (January, 1961), 56–77.

MAYER, HAROLD, and CLYDE KOHN (eds.), *Readings in Urban Geography*. Chicago: University of Chicago Press, 1959.

MC ELRATH, DENNIS, "The Social Areas of Rome," *American Sociological Review*, XXVII (June, 1962), 376–90.

MC ENTIRE, DAVIS, *Residence and Race*. Berkeley: University of California Press, 1960.

MOSES, LEON, and HAROLD WILLIAMSON, JR., "The Location of Economic Activity in Cities," *American Economic Review*, LVII (May, 1967), 211–23.

ORLEANS, PETER, "Robert Park and Social Area Analysis," *Urban Affairs Quarterly*, I (June, 1966), 5–19.

PARK, ROBERT E., ERNEST W. BURGESS, and RODERICK D. McKENZIE, *The City*. Introduction by Morris Janowitz. Chicago: University of Chicago Press, 1967 (reissue of 1925 volume).

PRED, ALLAN R., *The Spatial Dynamics of United States Urban-Industrial Growth, 1800–1914: Interpretive and Theoretical Essays*. Cambridge, Mass.: MIT Press, 1966.

RAND, CHRISTOPHER, "The Ultimate City" (Los Angeles), *New Yorker Magazine* (October 1, October 8, October 15, 1966).

RODWIN, LLOYD, "Residential Growth and Structure: Hypotheses and Generalization," *Housing and Economic Progress*. Cambridge, Mass.: MIT Press, 1961.

SCHNORE, LEO F., "On the Spatial Structure of Cities in the Two Americas," Philip M. Hauser and Leo F. Schnore (eds.), *The Study of Urbanization*. New York: John Wiley and Sons, 1965.

————, *The Urban Scene: Human Ecology and Demography*. New York: The Free Press of Glencoe, 1965.

SCHNORE, LEO F., and P. EVENSON, "Segregation in Southern Cities," *American Journal of Sociology*, LXXII (July, 1966), 58–68.

SJOBERG, GIDEON, "Spatial Arrangements," *The Preindustrial City*. New York: The Free Press of Glencoe, 1960.

TAEUBER, KARL and ALMA TAEUBER, "The Negro as an Immigrant Group: Recent Trends in Racial and Ethnic Segregation in Chicago," *American Journal of Sociology*, LXIX (January, 1964), 374–83.

THEODORSON, GEORGE (ed.), *Studies in Human Ecology*. New York: Harper and Row, 1961.

ULLMAN, EDWARD, "Presidential Address: The Nature of Cities Reconsidered," *Regional Science Association: Papers and Proceedings*, IX (1962), 7–23.

WARNER, SAM, *Streetcar Suburbs: The Process of Growth in Boston, 1870–1900*. Cambridge, Mass.: Harvard University Press, 1962.

WEBBER, MELVIN, (ed.), *Explorations into Urban Structure*. Philadelphia: University of Pennsylvania Press (City Planning Series), 1964.

WOODS, ROBERT A., and ALBERT J. KENNEDY, *The Zone of Emergence*. Ab. and ed. with a preface by Sam Warner. Cambridge, Mass.: Harvard University Press, 1962.

YAZAKI, TAKEO, *The Japanese City*. Rutland, Vt.: Japan Publications Trading Co., 1963.

The Organization of Urban Life

ABU-LUGHOD, JANET, "Migrant Adjustment to City Life: The Egyptian Case," *American Journal of Sociology*, LXVII (July, 1961), 22–32.

BEIJER, C., *Rural Migrants in Urban Setting* (Europe). The Hague: M. Nijhoff, 1963.

BENDIX, REINHARD, and SEYMOUR LIPSET (eds.), *Class, Status, and Power: Social Stratification in Comparative Perspective*, 2nd ed., New York: The Free Press of Glencoe, 1966.

BLUMER, HERBERT, "Industrialization and the Traditional Order," *Sociology and Social Research*, XLVIII (January, 1964), 129–38.

BRACEY, H., *Neighbours: Subdivision Life in England and the United States*. Baton Rouge: Louisiana State University Press, 1964.

BRUNER, E., "Urbanization and Ethnic Identity in Northern Sumatra," *American Anthropologist*, LXIII (June, 1961), 508–21.

BURKS, A. W., "The City, Political Change, and Modernization in Japan," *International Journal of Comparative Sociology*, VII (March, 1966), 29–51.

CLARK, S. D., *The Suburban Society*. Toronto: University of Toronto Press, 1966.

COULT, ALAN, and ROBERT HAMENSTEIN, "The Study of Extended Kinship in Urban Society," *Sociological Quarterly*, III (April, 1962).

EISENSTADT, S. N., "Transformation of Social, Political, and Cultural Orders in Modernization," *American Sociological Review*, XXX (October, 1965), 659–74.

———, *Comparative Perspective on Social Change*. Boston: Little, Brown, 1968.

EVERS, H. D., "The Formation of a Social Class Structure: Urbanization, Bureaucratization, and Social Mobility in Thailand," *American Sociological Review*, XXXI (August, 1966), 480–89.

FOSTER, GEORGE, *Traditional Cultures and the Impact of Technological Change*. New York: Harper and Row, 1962.

FREEDMAN, M., "Immigrants and Associations: Chinese in Nineteenth Century Singapore," *Comparative Studies in Society and History*, III (October, 1961) 25–48.

GANS, HERBERT J., *The Levittowners: Ways of Life and Politics in a New Suburban Community*. New York: Pantheon, 1967.

———, *The Urban Villagers*. New York: The Free Press of Glencoe, 1962.

GEERTZ, CLIFFORD, *The Social History of an Indonesian Town*. Cambridge, Mass.: MIT Press, 1965.

GIST, NOEL P., "Caste Differentials in South India," *American Sociological Review*, XIX (April, 1954), 126–37.

GLASS, Y., "Industrialization and Urbanization in South Africa," in J. F. Holleman, Joan Knox, J. W. Mann, and K. Heard (eds.), *Problems of Transition*. Pietermartizburg, Natal: Natal University Press, 1964.

GOTTLIEB, DAVID, et al., *The Emergence of Youth Society: A Cross-Cultural Approach*. New York: The Free Press of Glencoe, 1966.

GREENFIELD, SIDNEY M., "Industrialization and the Family in Sociological Theory," *American Journal of Sociology*, LXVII (November, 1961), 312–22.

GULICK, JOHN, *Tripoli: A Modern Arab City*. Cambridge, Mass.: Harvard University Press, 1967.

HERRICK, BRUCE, *Urban Migration and Economic Development in Chile*. Cambridge, Mass.: MIT Press, 1965.

HOSELITZ, BERT F., "Role of Urbanization in Economic Development: Some International Comparisons," in Roy Turner (ed.), *India's Urban Future*. Berkeley: University of California Press, 1962.

HOSELITZ, BERT F., and WILBERT MOORE (eds.), *Industrialization and Society*. UNESCO. Paris: Mouton, 1963.

HUMPHREYS, ALEXANDER J., *New Dubliners: Urbanization and the Irish Family*. New York: Fordham University Press, 1966.

KUPER, HILDA (ed.), *Urbanization and Migration in West Africa*. Berkeley: University of California Press, 1965.

KUPER, LEO, *An African Bougeosie: Race, Class and Politics in South Africa*. New Haven: Yale University Press, 1964.

LAMBERT, RICHARD D., *Workers, Factories and Social Change in India*. Princeton, N. J.: Princeton University Press, 1963.

LEWIS, D., and A. HALLER, "Rural-Urban Differences in Preindustrial and Industrial Evaluations of Occupations by Japanese Adolescent Boys," *Rural Sociology*, XXIX (September, 1964), 324–30.

LIPSET, S. M., and S. SOLARI, *Elites in Latin America*. New York: Oxford University Press, 1967.

LLOYD, PETER, and DARYLL FORDE, *The New Elites of Tropical Africa*. New York: Oxford University Press, 1966.

MACDONALD, JOHN, and LEATRICE MACDONALD, "Urbanization, Ethnic Groups and Social Segmentation," *Social Research*, XXIX (Winter, 1962), 433–48.

MILLER, ELIZABETH (comp.), *The Negro in America: A Bibliography*. Cambridge, Mass.: Harvard University Press, 1966.

MILLER, DELBERT, "Industry and Community Power Structure: A Comparative Study of an American and an English City," *American Sociological Review*, XXIII (February, 1958), 9–15.

MOGEY, JOHN, "Family and Community in Urban-Industrial Societies," in Harold T. Christensen (ed.), *Handbook of Marriage and the Family*. Chicago: Rand McNally, 1964.

MOORE, WILBERT, "Social Change and Comparative Studies," *International Social Science Journal*, XV (1963), 519–27.

MORRILL, W. T., "Immigrants and Associations: The Ibo in Twentieth Century Calabar," *Comparative Studies in Society and History*, V (1963), 424–48.

MORRIS, MORRIS DAVID, *The Emergence of an Industrial Labor Force in India: A Study of the Bombay Cotton Mills, 1854–1947*. Berkeley: University of California Press, 1965.

PAUW, B. A., *The Second Generation: A Study of the Family Among Urbanized Bantu in East London* (South Africa). Cape Town, South Africa: Oxford University Press, 1963.

REISSMAN, LEONARD, and T. KTSANES (eds.), "Urbanization and Social Change in the South," *Journal of Social Issues*, XXII (January, 1966), 1–116.

RICHARDS, CARA, "City Taverns," *Human Organization*, XXII (Winter, 1963–64), 260–68.

ROBINSON, WARREN, "Urbanization and Fertility: The Non-Western Experience," *Milbank Memorial Fund Quarterly*, XLI (July, 1963), 291–307.

ROSS, AILEEN D., *The Hindu Family in its Urban Setting*. Toronto: University of Toronto Press, 1961.

SHANAS, ETHEL, PETER TOWNSEND, DOROTHY WEDDERBURN, HENNING FRIIS, POUL MILHØJ, and JAN STEHOUWER, *Old People in Three Industrial Societies*. London: Routledge and Kegan Paul, 1967.

SMELSER, N., and S. M. LIPSET (eds.), *Social Structure and Mobility in Economic Development*. Chicago: Aldine, 1966.

SMITH, ROBERT J., "Aspects of Mobility in Preindustrial Japanese Cities," *Comparative Studies in Society and History*, V (July, 1963), 416–23.

SOUTHALL, A. (ed.), *Social Change in Modern Africa*. London: Oxford University Press, 1961.

SRINIVAS, N., and A. BETEILLE, "The 'Untouchables' of India," *Scientific American*, CCXIII (December, 1965), 13–17.

SUZUKI, PETER, "Peasants Without Plows: Some Anatolians in Istanbul," *Rural Sociology*, XXXI (December, 1966), 428–38.

SWANSON, BERT, *Current Trends in Comparative Studies* (political behavior). Kansas City, Mo.: Community Studies, Inc., 1962.

THRUPP, SYLVIA L., *The Merchant Class of Medieval London*. Ann Arbor, Mich.: University of Michigan Press, 1948.

VAN DEN BERGHE, PIERRE L., *Caneville: The Social Structure of a South African Town*. Middletown, Conn.: Wesleyan University Press, 1963.

——— (ed.), *Africa: Social Problems of Change and Conflict*. San Francisco: Chandler, 1965.

VOGEL, EZRA F., *Japan's New Middle Class*. Berkeley: University of California Press, 1963.

WILKINSON, T. O., "Family Structure and Industrialization in Japan," *American Sociological Review*, XXVII (October, 1962), 678–82.

———, *The Urbanization of Japanese Labor, 1868–1955*. Amherst, Mass.: University of Massachusetts Press, 1965.

WILSON, MONICA, *Langa: A Study of Social Groups in an African Township*. Cape Town, South Africa: Oxford University Press, 1963.

The Social Psychology of Urban Life

ARDEN, EUGENE, "The Evil City in American Fiction," *New York History*, XXXV (July, 1954), 259–79.

BENET, F., ."The Ideology of Islamic Urbanization," *International Journal of Comparative Sociology*, IV (September, 1963), 211–27.

BIESHEUVEL, S., "Work and Its Effect on Personality Development in Africans," in J. F. Holleman, Joan Knox, J. S. Mann, and K. Heard, (eds.), *Problems of Transition*. Natal: Natal University Press, 1964.

BLOOM, L., "Some Psychological Concepts of Urban Africans," *Ethnology*, III (January, 1964), 66–95.

CLINARD, MARSHALL, "Cross-Cultural Replication of the Relation of Urbanism to Criminal Behavior," *American Sociological Review*, XXV (April, 1960), 253–57.

DE RIDDER, J. C., *The Personality of the Urban African in South Africa*. London: Routledge and Kegan Paul, 1961.

DUNLAP, GEORGE ARTHUR, *The City in the American Novel 1789–1900*. New York: Russell and Russell, 1965 (reissue).

GLASS, RUTH, *London's Newcomers: The West Indian Migrants*. Cambridge, Mass.: Harvard University Press, 1961.

GOWANS, ALAN, *Rural Myth and Urban Fact in the American Heritage*. Wilmington, Del.: Wemyss Foundation, 1965.

GULICK, JOHN, "Old Values and New Institutions in a Lebanese Arab City," *Human Organization*, XXIV (Spring, 1965), 49–52.

GULICK, LUTHER, *The Metropolitan Problem and American Ideas*. New York: Knopf, 1962.

JACOBS, NORMAN, "The Phantom Slasher of Taipei: Mass Hysteria in a Non-Western Society," *Social Problems*, XII (Winter, 1965), 318–28.

JAHODA, G., "Aspects of Westernization: A Study of Adult Class Students in Ghana," *British Journal of Sociology*, XII (December, 1961), 375–88.

KILLIAN, LEWIS M., and CHARLES M. GRIGG, "Urbanism, Race, and Anomia," *American Journal of Sociology*, LXVII (May, 1962), 661–66.

LEIGHTON, H. ALEXANDER, T. A. CAMBO, CHARLES C. HUGHES, DOROTHEA LEIGHTON, JANE M. MURPHY, and DAVID B. MACKLIN, *Psychiatric Disorder Among the Yoruba*. Ithaca, N. Y.: Cornell University, 1963.

LEVINE, ROBERT A., *Dreams and Deeds: Achievement Motivation in Nigeria*. Chicago: University of Chicago Press, 1966.

LOWENSTEIN, SUSAN F., "Urban Images of Roman Authors," *Comparative Studies in Society and History*, VIII (October, 1965), 110–23.

MANNHEIM, HERMANN, *Comparative Criminology*. Boston: Houghton Mifflin, 1966.

MAYER, PHILIP, *Townsmen or Tribesmen: Urbanization in a Divided Society*. Capetown, South Africa: Oxford University Press, 1961.

MC CLELLAND, DAVID C., *The Achieving Society*. Princeton, N. J.: Van Nostrand, 1961.

MEADOWS, PAUL, "Industrial Man: Urban Ideologist," in Paul Meadows (ed.), *Industrial Man: Profiles of Developmental Society*. Publication no. 14. Syracuse, N. Y.: Center for Overseas Research, Maxwell Graduate School, Syracuse University, 1965.

MINER, H., and A. DE VOS, *Oases and Casbah: Algerian Culture and Personality in Change*. Anthropological Papers, Museum of Anthropology, no. 15. Ann Arbor, Mich.: University of Michigan Press, 1960.

NADER, LAURA, "Communication between Village and City in the Modern Middle East," *Human Organization*, XXIV (Spring, 1965), 53–58.

PARKER, SEYMOUR, *Mental Illness in the Urban Negro Community*. New York: The Free Press of Glencoe, 1966.

PARR, A. E., "Psychological Aspects of Urbanology," *Journal of Social Issues*, XXII (October, 1966), 39–45.

PETERSEN, WILLIAM, "The Protestant Ethos and the Anti-Urban Animus," in Robert Lee (ed.), *The Church and the Exploding Metropolis*. Richmond, Va.: John Knox Press, 1965.

ROTONDO, H., "Psychological and Mental Health Problems of Urbanization based on Case Studies in Peru," in P. Hauser (ed.), *Urbanization in Latin America*. UNESCO Tensions and Society Series, 1961.

SHOHAM, S., N. SHOHAM, and A. RAZEK, "Immigration, Ethnicity and Ecology as Related to Juvenile Delinquency in Israel," *British Journal of Criminology*, VI (October, 1966), 391–409.

SKLARE, MARSHALL, and JOSEPH GREENBLUM, *Jewish Identity on the Suburban Frontier*. New York: Basic Books, 1967.

SMITH, PAGE, *As a City Upon a Hill: The Town in American History*. New York: Knopf, 1966.

STRAUSS, ANSELM (ed.), *The American City: A Source Book of Urban Imagery*. Chicago: Aldine, 1968.

THOMAS, W. I., and F. ZNANIECKI, *The Polish Peasant in Europe and the United States*. New York: Dover Books, 1958 (2 vols., reissue of 2nd ed.).

VERNON, RAYMOND, *The Myth and Reality of Our Urban Problems*. Cambridge, Mass.: Joint Center for Urban Studies of MIT and Harvard University, 1962.

WHITE, MORTON, and LUCIA WHITE, *The Intellectual Versus the City*. Cambridge, Mass.: Harvard University Press, 1962.

WHYTE, WILLIAM H., "The Anti-City," in E. Geen (ed.), *Man and the Modern City*. Pittsburgh: University of Pittsburgh Press, 1963.

WOOD, ROBERT, *Suburbia—Its People and Their Politics*. Boston: Houghton Mifflin, 1958.

YOUNG, F., and R. YOUNG, "Individual Commitment to Industrialization in Rural Mexico," *American Journal of Sociology*, LXXI (January, 1966), 374–89.

Urban Housing and Redevelopment

ABRAMS, CHARLES, *Squatter Settlements: The Problem and the Opportunity*. Prepared for Agency for International Development by the Department of Housing and Urban Development, Division of International Affairs, Washington, D. C., 1966.

ALONSO, WILLIAM, "The Historic and Structural Theories of Urban Form: Their Implications for Urban Renewal," *Land Economics*, XL (May, 1964), 227–31.

BELLUSH, JEWEL, and M. HAUSKNECHT (eds.), *Urban Renewal: People, Politics and Planning*. New York: Doubleday Anchor Books, 1967.

BRIGGS, MARTIN S., "Town Planning from the Ancient World to the Renaissance," in Charles Singer, E. J. Holmyard, A. R. Hall, and T. I.

Williams (eds.), *A History of Technology*, vol. III. New York: Oxford University Press, 1957.

CLINARD, MARSHALL, *Slums and Community Development: Experiments in Self-Help* (India). New York: The Free Press of Glencoe, 1966.

Community Development Abstracts. Prepared for the Agency for International Development by Sociological Abstracts, Inc., New York, 1965.

FISHER, JACK, "Planning the City of Socialist Man," *Journal of the American Institute of Planners*, XXVIII (November, 1962); "Comments," by Zygmunt Pioro and Milos Savic, XXXI (February, 1965), 31–42.

FOLEY, DONALD, *Controlling London's Growth: Planning the Great Wen 1940–60*. Berkeley: University of California Press, 1967.

FRANKFORT, H., "Town Planning in Ancient Mesopotamia," *Town Planning Review*, XXI (July, 1950), 108–15.

FRIED, MARC, "Functions of the Working-Class Community in Modern Urban Society: Implications for Forced Relocation," *Journal of the American Institute of Planners*, XXXIII (March, 1967), 90–103.

FROLIC, B. MICHAEL, "The Soviet City," *Town Planning Review*, XXXIV (January, 1964), 285–306.

GANS, HERBERT J., "Urban Poverty and Social Planning," in P. Lazarsfeld, W. H. Sewell, and H. Wilensky (eds.), *The Uses of Sociology*. New York: Basic Books, 1967.

GREBLER, LEO, *Urban Renewal in European Countries: Its Emergence and Potentials*. Philadelphia: University of Pennsylvania Press, 1964.

GREER, SCOTT, *Urban Renewal and American Cities*. Indianapolis: Bobbs-Merrill, 1965.

GUTKIND, E. A., *International History of City Development*. Vol. 1, *Urban Development in Central Europe*. Vol. 2, *Urban Development in the Alpine and Scandinavian Countries*. Vol. 3, *Urban Development in Southern Europe, Spain and Portugal*. New York: The Free Press of Glencoe, 1967.

GUTKIND, P. C. W., "Urban Conditions in Africa," *Town Planning Review*, XXXII (April, 1961), 20–31.

HUNTER, DAVID R., *The Slums: Challenge and Response*. New York: The Free Press of Glencoe, 1964.

HUTCHINSON, R. W., "Prehistoric Town Planning in and around the Aegean Sea," *Town Planning Review*, XXIV (January, 1953), 261–79 and XXV (April, 1953), 5–22.

JACOBS, JANE, *The Death and Life of Great American Cities*. New York: Random House, 1961.

LEWIS, OSCAR, "Even the Saints Cry," *Trans-Action*, IV (November, 1966), 18–24.

LOWE, JEANNE R., *Cities in a Race with Time: Progress and Poverty in America's Renewing Cities*. New York: Random House, 1967.

LUBOVE, ROY, *The Urban Community: Housing and Planning in the Progressive Era.* Englewood Cliffs, N. J.: Prentice-Hall, 1967.

MANGIN, WILLIAM, "Squatter Settlements," *Scientific American,* CCXVII (October, 1967).

MARRIS, PETER, *Family and Social Change in an African City: A Study of Rehousing in Lagos.* Evanston, Ill.: Northwestern University Press, 1962.

MEZIROW, JACK D. (comp.), *The Literature of Community Development.* Washington, D.C.: Agency for International Development and the Peace Corps, 1963.

MITCHELL, ROBERT (ed.), "Urban Revival: Goals and Standards," *Annals of the American Academy of Political and Social Science,* CCCLII (March, 1964), 1–151.

MOYNIHAN, DANIEL P., "Urban Conditions: General," in *Social Goals and Indicators for American Society.* Special issue of *Annals of the American Academy of Political and Social Science,* CCCLXXI (May, 1967), 159–67.

MUMFORD, LEWIS, "The Skyline: Mother Jacobs' Home Remedies," *New Yorker Magazine* (December 1, 1962).

OSBORN, FREDERIC J., *The New Towns.* New York: McGraw-Hill, 1963.

OWEN, WILFRED, *The Metropolitan Transportation Problem.* Garden City, N. Y.: Doubleday Anchor Books, 1966.

PETERSEN, WILLIAM, "Urban Policies in Africa and Asia," *Population Review* (Madras), X (January, 1966).

A Reference Guide to Metropolitan Transportation. An annotated bibliography prepared by the Library of the Transportation Center, Northwestern University. Evanston, Ill., 1964.

ROSOW, IRVING, "The Social Effects of the Physical Environment," *Journal of the American Institute of Planners,* XXVII (May, 1961), 127–33.

SCHNORE, LEO F., and HENRY FAGIN (eds.), *Urban Research and Policy Planning.* Vol. 1, Urban Affairs Annual Reviews. Beverly Hills, Cal.: Sage Publications, 1967.

SEELEY, JOHN, "The Slum, Its Nature, Use and Users," *Journal of the American Institute of Planners,* XXV (February, 1959), 7–14.

SHILLABER, C., "A Review of Planning Bibliographies," *Journal of the American Institute of Planners,* XXXI (November, 1965), 352–60.

SMALLWOOD, FRANK, *Greater London: The Politics of Metropolitan Reform.* Indianapolis: Bobbs-Merrill, 1965.

SPIEGEL, ERIKA, *New Towns in Israel: Urban and Regional Planning and Development.* New York: Praeger, 1967.

STOKES, CHARLES, "A Theory of Slums," *Land Economics,* XXXVIII (August, 1962), 187–97.

TURNER, JOHN, "Barriers and Channels for Housing Development in Modernizing Countries," *Journal of the American Institute of Planners*, XXXIII (May, 1967), 167–81.

UNITED STATES SENATE, Subcommittee on Housing, Committee on Banking and Currency. *Study of International Housing*. Washington, D.C.: United States Government Printing Office, 1963.

WARNER, SAM B., JR. (ed.), *Planning for a Nation of Cities*. Cambridge, Mass.: MIT Press, 1966.

WHEATON, WILLIAM, GRACE MILGRAM, and MARGY ELLIN MEYERSON (eds.), *Urban Housing*. New York: The Free Press of Glencoe, 1966.

WHYTE, WILLIAM H., *Cluster Development*. New York: American Conservation Association, 1964.

WILSON, JAMES Q. (ed.), *Urban Renewal: The Record and the Controversy*. Cambridge, Mass.: MIT Press, 1966.

Index

Index